IDEAS

A VOLUME OF IDEAS,

LIVING, DYING, DEAD & FOSSIL,

WHICH WE ARE MOVED BY

OR WERE MOVED BY

LONDON

THE WAVERLEY BOOK COMPANY LIMITED

THE FIRST THREE VOLUMES of this series, PEOPLE, PLACES and THINGS, dealt with the definite, more or less, whether it was the creeper-grown walls of Zimbabwe or the history of the zip-fastener, or the peculiarities of Peter the Great, of Li Po the Chinese poet or of Madame de Pompadour. This fourth volume deals with some of the ideas, living, dying, dead and fossil, which we are moved by or were moved by at one time.

'Idea' may not be strictly used. A mixed bag of notions and emotions are described. Some are easy to explain, some difficult. Some have a clear, some a confused story. Some need just their story and their common sense explanation – the 'idea' of Mrs Grundy, for example, the idea of Atlantis, the idea of the land of Cokaygne or the idea of the Great Chain of Being, which was once so powerful.

Others, from the Elixir of Life or the Philosopher's Stone to the notion or idea of the Gentleman, are infinitely more complex and more curious than we might guess them to be. Others, again, from that Absolute which Hegel described as a night on which even the cows are black, to the 'Angst' of our time or to the idea of a First Cause, involve the philosopher.

No less than the earlier volumes, we hope this one, designed not to be too solemn or too academic, not to be an encyclopaedia nor yet to be trivial, will give its readers entertainment as well as information. Not only from philosophy,

PEOPLE, PLACES AND THINGS

VOLUME FOUR

IDEAS

People, Places and Things

General Editors

GEOFFREY GRIGSON & CHARLES HARVARD GIBBS-SMITH

A series of books epitomizing the tastes, achievements
and aspirations of mankind. All volumes have 16 colour
plates, 160 pages of illustrations in black and white, and
upwards of 200,000 words of text

VOL. 1 **PEOPLE** VOL. 2 **PLACES**

VOL. 3 **THINGS** VOL. 4 **IDEAS**

PEOPLE, PLACES AND THINGS

Designed and produced for The Grosvenor Press Ltd
28–30 Grosvenor Gardens, London SW1
by Rainbird, McLean Ltd, 8 Wyndham Place, London W1

Printed in Great Britain
by Richard Clay & Company Ltd, Bungay, Suffolk
Colour plates printed by Tillotsons (Bolton) Ltd
Endpapers printed by Van Leer of Amsterdam
First published 1954

MADE AND PRINTED IN GREAT BRITAIN

but from theology, from sciences and semi-sciences, from psycho-analysis, economics and politics, from art and letters, ideas – or catchphrases to which ideas are attached – become part of our currency; meanings are often obscured or perverted.

Do we all know what we mean when we put some trait down to Original Sin? Or when we describe some object as belonging (see the idea of the Three Ages System) to the Bronze Age? Are we sure of the meaning of Trotskyism? Or Nihilism? Or the Superman? Who was the Noble Savage? What were considered to be the Rights of Man? What was implied by Religion as the Opiate of the People? How did Germany adopt ideas of a Herrenvolk, of Blut und Boden or Anti-Semitism? From Marx, and from Moscow, what is Dialectical Materialism? From the East, what is Yoga, and what is the Transmigration of Souls?

All of us are ruled more by words than we realize; and words label and embody our ideas and the forces which impel us. Here are 183 ideas.

Colour Plates

The endpapers are of *The School of Athens* by Raphael.
A key to this appears on pages 462 & 463.

Black and White Plates

CONTRIBUTORS TO THIS VOLUME INCLUDE

IDEAS

A

The **ABSOLUTE,** found in the writings of many philosophers, is the name for whatever is considered to be the ultimate ground of all reality.

It is impossible to arrive at a clear understanding of the meaning of the term – not because there is something peculiarly baffling or elusive about the Absolute, but simply because no two philosophers have meant the same thing by it. This is not as strange as it may seem at first sight, since it is the function of the idea of the Absolute to stand in contrast to, and be somehow the explanation of, the relative, the dependent, the temporal, the changing – whatever, in fact, is thought or felt to be in need of further and deeper explanation. The term is often used as a synonym for God, since one of the functions of the idea of God (q.v.) is to explain the otherwise apparently inexplicable – for example, the fact that the world exists at all.

A. N. Whitehead writes: 'What are enduring things, as distinguished from 'appearances' such as colour and shape? How are they possible? What is their status and meaning in the universe? It comes to this: What is the status of the enduring stability of the order of nature? There is the summary answer, which refers nature to some greater reality standing behind it. This reality occurs in the history of thought under many names: The Absolute, Brahma, The Order of Heaven, God.' (*Science and the Modern World.*)

The exploration of this reality has been the self-appointed task of both mystics and philosophers, the former claiming to speak of the nature of the Absolute from direct personal experience. 'This overcoming of all the usual barriers between the individual and the Absolute', writes William James in *Varieties of Religious Experience* (1902), 'is the great mystic achievement. In mystic states we become one with the Absolute and we become aware of our oneness. This is the everlasting and triumphant mystical tradition, hardly altered by differences of clime or creed. In Hinduism, in Neoplatonism, in Sufism, in Christian mysticism. in Whitmanism, we find the same recurring note, so that there is about mystical utterances an eternal unanimity which ought to make a critic stop and think ...'

Here the identification of the Absolute with the Divine is complete. However, the writings of the mystics are often, as James remarks, 'little more than musical compositions': and that branch of philosophy which is properly called Metaphysics consists in the use of reason to arrive at conclusions concerning ultimate reality – in other words, by thinking out in detail the problems raised by what to many philosophers has seemed the fragmentary and unsatisfactory nature of our experience.

The metaphysicians thus differ from the mystics in their methods; but their motives, as Bertrand Russell points out, have often been the same: 'Parmenides is the source of a peculiarly interesting strain of mysticism which pervades Plato's thoughts – the mysticism which may be called "logical" because it is embodied in theories on logic. This form of mysticism, which appears, so far as the West is concerned, to have originated with Parmenides, dominates the reasonings of all the great mystical metaphysicians from his day to that of Hegel and his modern disciples.'

It is the mystical strain in this class of philosophers which accounts for their preoccupation with the illusory nature of what for them are 'appearances', with the unreality of time and with the twin 'illusions' of plurality and of evil. These topics predominate in the works of Plato, and have been handled again and again by philosophers after him. Fundamentally, the whole Platonic tradition in philosophy consists in the attempt to elucidate the Absolute by means of logic.

The Absolute derives its imposing capital letter from the fact that the term was imported into English philosophy from the writings of the German school of Idealist philosophers, where, of course, as a noun (*das Absolute*), it bears a capital letter simply as a matter of grammar – though no doubt this was retained in English in order to distinguish the substantival use of the word from its traditional use as an adjective.

German Idealism came into existence as a result of the work of Kant (1724–1804). Kant himself subjected the traditional metaphysical arguments to a searing criticism, and came to the conclusion that they were worthless, on the ground that, our minds being so constructed that we can only apply them validly to what comes to us through our senses, all speculation as to what is *behind* appearances (and so inaccessible to the senses) is necessarily invalid. He calls the unknown something which stands behind appearances, the Thing-in-itself. This, though inaccessible to our reason no less than to our senses, can in some rather mysterious way be experienced in ourselves, since, according to Kant, each of us has a 'phenomenal' self – our self as an inhabitant of the world of appearances – and a 'noumenal self', which is a Thing-in-itself and which stands behind and is the source of the effects we produce in the world of appearances. This noumenal self operates when we act in accordance with the moral law, and may be thought of as a sort of moral core of ultimate reality at the centre of our being.

The first step in the development from this rather negative view was taken by Kant's follower, Fichte (1762–1814): if the only Thing-in-itself of which we can have any inkling is our noumenal self, then why not say boldly that all appearances proceed from a self of this sort? Fichte takes this step, and arrives at the idea of a *single* self – which he calls the Absolute Self – that is both the source of everything which I experience and is equally my own self, and so the source of my own being. His train of thought may

be simply illustrated as follows. If there is an unknown x behind each set of appearances, and a similar unknown x in each of us which is somehow identical with the true self, then it will be much neater and more satisfying to assimilate all these miscellaneous xs and assume a single all-pervading X in the nature of an Absolute Self. And so we get the picture of the Absolute Self as a kind of metaphysical person who, growing bored with existing all alone, splits himself up for the pleasure of being able to peer at a bit of himself through the mind of another bit of himself.

There could be no better example of a piece of metaphysics which, beginning from a *logical* development of Kant's closely reasoned conclusions, ends in a kind of creation-myth commonly found in Eastern religious thought. In Germany, Schelling (1775–1854), in England, Hamilton (1788–1856) and Mansel (1820–1871), took up the idea of the Absolute, but held that the limitations of our powers exclude the possibility of any knowledge of it; it became virtually synonymous with *The Unknowable*, under which title it occupies the opening chapters of Herbert Spencer's *First Principles* (1862).

An Absolute of this sort was described by Hegel (1770–1831) as 'a night in which all cows are black'; and accordingly he set himself to throw as much light as possible on the nature of the Absolute. Hegel's thought is extremely hard to follow, since, although he claims all the time to be proceeding with rigorous logic, his arguments often proceed by arbitrary steps which are not made less arbitrary by being dressed in an elaborate logical terminology.

His Absolute is an *active* principle which manifests its nature in the twin realms of mind and of nature, but is not something *apart* from them. In other words, the Absolute is Hegel's name for the totality of things; and its nature is, for him, mental. To be real is to be intelligible – hence the famous dictum that what is real is rational and what is rational is real – and to be self-contradictory is to be less than real. Hegel sees nature as the realm in which the Absolute works out its logical schemes in terms of space and time, though space and time are ultimately unreal: 'History too shows the Absolute on the march', and 'the State is the Idea of Spirit in the external manifestation of human Will and Freedom'. The finger of Hegel's Absolute can be traced in every pie.

These philosophies of the Absolute were the dominant influence among English philosophers during the second half of the nineteenth century; but with the rise of the school of thought which goes by the name of Logical Positivism they have become almost entirely neglected. This is not surprising when one considers that the basic tenets of the new movement were a demand for strict verifiability by scientific methods and an insistence that any statement not so verifiable is without meaning. Thus in 1936 A.J.Ayer in his important *Language, Truth and Logic* wrote: 'Such a metaphysical pseudo-proposition as *the Absolute enters into, but is itself incapable of, evolution and progress* (a 'remark taken at random' from *Appearance and Reality*, by the greatest of the English Idealists, F.H.Bradley (1846–1924)) is not even in principle verifiable. For one cannot conceive of an observation which would enable one to determine whether the 'Absolute did or did not enter into evolution and progress ... Until [the author of such a remark] makes us understand how the proposition that he wishes to express would be verified, he fails to communicate anything to us.'

This somewhat cavalier dismissal of metaphysics is less prevalent than it was; and today perhaps the most rewarding way of studying the theories of the philosophers of the Absolute is to read them with sympathetic attention in the effort to understand exactly what features of experience, of logic and of language, led their authors to speak in such unfamiliar ways.

ILLUSTRATION: Pages 26 and 27.

Ananias or the false artist

ACADEMIC ART is now, on most occasions, a term of abuse which would surprise those who nourished the academic ideal in earlier centuries.

The first academies, in the middle of the fifteenth century, were informal gatherings of learned men for the discussion of philosophy and literature. They borrowed the name from the *Akademeia*, the garden in which Plato taught in Athens, which in turn was named after the hero Akademos. These academies stood for the intellectual freedom of the humanists; and in the same way the first Academies of Art proclaimed the independence of the artist. This they tried to demonstrate by giving the artist an education based on intellectual learning rather than on technique. Alberti in 1435 was the first to lay down this ideal. The earliest painter to become the centre of an academy was probably Leonardo da Vinci about 1500, though we know nothing of this academy. An engraving of 1531 shows the Academy of Bandinelli, a Florentine sculptor. It is an informal meeting of artists who draw and talk after the hours of serious work.

The first formal Academy of Art was the Accademia del Disegno, founded in 1562 by the efforts of Vasari (1511–1574), painter, architect and first systematic historian of art. It soon became moribund, but in 1593 one of its members, Zuccari, founded the Roman Accademia di San Luca, which prospered and had an elaborate teaching system, including the progression from copying drawings to drawing plaster casts and live models. Finally, the student learned composition, which is the mark of academic teaching.

The art of these early academies is not recognizably 'academic' in our sense. It was grandiose, it was suitable for the decoration of palaces and public buildings. The qualities especially valued were invention, grace, ingenuity, and rapidity of execution. But at the end of the sixteenth century the Carracci and their followers came to Rome from Bologna and attempted a return to the classical spirit of Raphael. Their work is the earliest which is recognizably 'academic', largely because the later academicians admired and imitated it. Nicolas Poussin (1594–1665) also lived in Rome for much of his working life and was a member of the Academy. He was able to push reason in art to a very high pitch, to the point at which drawing, colour, composition and expression are each perfectly distinct and readable.

In 1648 the French Academy of Fine Art was founded and soon after obtained a grant from the King and, most important, the protection of the Minister Colbert. The Academy, in fact, was intended by these patrons to glorify the King and to provide for the production of luxury goods within the country so that they need not be imported. But the artists saw it as a vindication of their own status as educated men rather than craftsmen. Drawing, outline, were exalted because they corresponded to Aristotelian substance and were felt to be definite, while colour was imprecise and accidental, a view which is essential to the academic ideal. Prestige was attached to systematic thought. Charles Le Brun (1619–1690), chief of the Academicians, published a book of facial expressions appropriate for every emotion. Artists were to be given a wide education, including geometry, 'the perfect science'.

The needs of the patrons prevailed over those of the artists. The work that was actually produced was Baroque, of the rhetorical style that came from Rome and Flanders which suited the grand manner of Louis XIV's court. By the end of the century the energetic flourish of the Baroque was being replaced by the decorative twirls of the Rococo. The Academy suffered a decline and its exhibition, the Salon, was discontinued for most of the first thirty-five years of the eighteenth century. Nevertheless nearly all artists of any quality continued to be Academicians, so that there was no distinct 'academic' art.

The enormous prestige of the court of Louis XIV caused Academies to spring up all over Europe. The academic ideal of art also spread, slowly acquiring a life of its own. Its intention was moral: to elevate the mind of man. Johann Joachim Winckelmann (1717–1768), the greatest academic theorist of the eighteenth century, did not depart from the academic ideal, except to insist on what had been implicit before: that although there was beauty in nature, this was difficult to find without the help of some artist who had knowledge of it. For Winckelmann, Greek sculptors had this knowledge just as, for Le Brun, Raphael possessed it. The driving force of the academic ideal still lay in the conception of art as noble. For this reason it involved the doctrine that the subject-matter of a picture ought at best to be historical. Portraiture, landscape, still-life occupied successively lower places.

The Royal Academy in London was founded in 1768 with Reynolds (1723–1792) as President. The Royal Academy was founded expressly to raise the status of the artist and 'the art', indeed to make gentlemen of painters; and for a while it was a by no means unrespectable or unworthy body of artists.

None the less its most important feature was not its school, and not its official or semi-official standing; but its annual exhibition, where painters hung their more striking wares in the hope of attracting commissions. Reynolds, in his *Discourses*, had botched together a noble ideal, based on French academic thought of the seventeenth century. Academicians soon followed an art trader's ideal, exhibiting few large-scale histories, and mainly portraits in the grand tradition of Van Dyck. William Blake, journeyman, craftsman, painter and poet, who remained outside the Academy, was contemptuous of Reynolds, contemptuous of the Academy and aloof from all and everything which seemed to him 'hired by the devil to depress art'. Yet till the eighteen-forties most of the livelier artists were brought, if not always readily or with grace, into the academic fold – including painters so little classical or academic as John Constable (1776–1837), who had much that was bitter to say about the Academy and his Academic colleagues, and their sycophancy, and J. M. Turner (1775–1851).

Academic art in France and in England in the nineteenth century fell to the lure of success. Within a limited ambience of feeling attuned to the limited outlook of their new mercantile and industrial patrons, nineteenth-century academy artists took to an extraordinary variety of subject-matter and treatment. They were able to describe with archaeological accuracy every historical nation and period of man. They assimilated every historical style, and made themselves distinct only by a pretence of high-mindedness, a preference for painting 'elevating' and often prurient nudes and scenes of trivial pathos.

'We demand', wrote a protagonist of 'high art' in the later Victorian era, 'that a painter should choose for his theme beautifully-shaped objects, such as human figures, male or female, in graceful attitudes, nude and exquisitely formed, with rounded limbs, or clothed in flowing drapery, Greek or Roman, Oriental or Florentine; animals like the fawn, the panther, the Arab charger, the swan, the butterfly; the cataract leaping in an arch from the crag; Naples, Vesuvius, Tivoli and

Niagara, the curved horizon of ocean, the thous-
and inlets of a highland loch; graceful pottery,
elegantly-moulded goblets, flagons and vases,
slender beakers, shapely chalices; the domes and
minarets of Stamboul, the sweeping arches of
Tintern and Poitiers, the columns of Paestum, the
rounded tiers and galleries of the amphitheatre.'
(Grant Allen, *Physiological Aesthetics*, 1877.)

The heyday of the Academicians who supplied
this demand, with no certainty of aim except the
bank balance, the carriage and pair, and public
adulation, and no principles except a set of rules
for drawing and composition, ossified from the
older academic dictates, has well been called the
heyday of Ananias or the false artist. J.A.M.
Whistler (1834–1903), the Anglo-American painter who was the most notable of the contemners
of the debased academic ideal in the nineteenth
century, made fun of a passage in the autobiography of the popular painter of pathetic subjects,
W.P. Frith, R.A., Frith having rashly and brashly
admitted that in his youth it was a toss up
whether he became 'an artist or an auctioneer'.

The academic rule was in part a slavish naturalism; to which Whistler replied, 'To say to the
painter that Nature is to be taken as she is, is to
say to the player that he may sit on the piano.' In
part it was the mannerism of art reflected from
previous art (thus the properties in Grant Allen's
'demand' all belonged to already existing art) to
this one of the cleverest critics of the century,
R.A.M. Stevenson (1847–1900) replied, 'A picture cannot be the efficient, the first cause of a
picture; all true art originates in the personal predilections of an individual mind, and in personal
sensitiveness to external nature. The rest is disguised copying, artistic or inartistic mannerism.'
That defines academic art by its opposite.

The depth of bathos to which the inartistic
mannerism of academic art in the nineteenth century could descend is well seen in the canvases of
such distinguished Academicians as Frederick,
Lord Leighton, Sir Lawrence Alma-Tadema
and Marcus Stone, dimly reflecting the art of
Boucher or Fragonard. Yet one may add that
two academic arts now exist side by side, one of
them rampant in the endless bathos of imitating
yesterday's abstractions.

ILLUSTRATION: Pages 24 and 25.

Appealing to the senses

AESTHETICS as a word was invented by the
eighteenth-century German philosopher Baumgarten, who defined it: 'Aesthetics is the science
of sensuous knowledge ... the end of Aesthetics is
the perfection of sensuous knowledge as such;
this is beauty. The defect of sensuous knowledge
is ugliness.'

He contrasts things known by the senses with
things known by the 'higher faculty'; and he calls
them respectively confused and distinct knowledge, a classification which comes from Leibniz (1646–1716) (who also identified art with the
confused knowledge – *Je ne sais quoi* – 'I don't
know what'), and ultimately from Plato. Plato
himself condemns pictorial art as an imitation of
what is known through the senses, but postulates
a higher art which would deal with forms that
can be distinctly known. He says: 'I mean straight
lines and curves and the surfaces or solid forms
produced out of these by lathes and rulers and
squares'.

Aristotle believed that both rhythm (formal and
distinct knowledge) and imitation (sensuous and
confused knowledge) together make up the arts,
but that the former is weak in painting and
strong in music, and vice versa; the value of both
is to purge man of passion. The unknown author
of the *On the Sublime* (c. first century A.D.),
usually known as Longinus, extended the idea
and created a higher category than beauty,
namely, the 'sublime', which transcends correctness and appeals to the ability of man's mind
'to overstep the bounds of space'.

Plotinus (third century A.D.), the expounder of
Neoplatonism, a synthesis of mysticism with
Platonic thought, saw in symmetry and proportion, unity and perfection, the expression of the
'One' (*i.e.* God). Neoplatonism was revived in the
fifteenth century in the circle of Lorenzo de'
Medici. Pico della Mirandola tried to synthesize
the whole of philosophy and revealed religion
into degrees of perfection ranging from matter
to God. The contemplation of the beauty of a
Venus was a means of obtaining an idea of heavenly beauty, and so climbing a degree higher. Proportion became again a sign of divine unity. But
later in the sixteenth century Lomazzo, like

Plotinus, thought that the artist has a direct knowledge of truth. He felt free, therefore, to dispense partly with naturalism, proportion and symmetry, which had been so important since the early renaissance.

Francis Bacon, at the beginning of the seventeenth century, found that 'There is no excellent beauty that hath not a strangeness in the proportion'. After Leibniz, Gravina held that the lively images of art could do for ordinary people what pure knowledge could not do. By 1701 Dennis, following Milton and Dryden and reviving Longinus, said that passion was more necessary than harmony to sublime poetry and that genius and passion were all one. Young maintained the same of art, and Burke found that the sentiment of the sublime was provoked by 'the obscure, the terrible, the eternal, the infinite, the empty', and so on, but he gives very common-sense reasons: darkness, for example, is terrifying because it causes the pupils of the eyes to dilate too wide.

Meanwhile, the idea had been communicated to Germany where it produced the movement 'Sturm und Drang' (q.v.), and was fed by the discontent of a new educated class which had no power. Sturm und Drang led both to bohemianism and to an exaltation of art above morals, religion or state.

This was not yet quite the case with Kant (1724–1804) who, contradicting the normal utilitarian views of eighteenth-century philosophers on beauty, extended Aquinas's argument that beauty is essential to the nature of seeing. He believed that the way we know the world is determined by our nature as knowers, and that beautiful things are those that are in forms which make them easy to know. The idea, on a less philosophic plane, has been elaborated by the Gestalt psychologists, who have shown that the mind tends to sum up perceptions into simple patterns. Kant's idea expressly separates beauty from any criterion of judgment, whether of utility or of the good, in fact from all desire and purpose.

Schopenhauer (1788–1860) conceived the whole world as will (desire), including reason, and held that the only way out was to sink oneself in perception, to achieve a higher state of freedom from will in contemplation of the beautiful. The peak was reached by Nietzsche, who claimed that 'the existence of the world is only justified as an aesthetic experience' (1871).

Hegel in 1835 modified Kant's view and said: 'Natural beauty manifests itself as only a reflection of the beauty which properly belongs to the mind.' Croce at the beginning of this century refined on this with his doctrine of intuition, in which art is not the actual painting, but a vision in the mind of the artist which, when the picture which expresses it is seen, lives in the mind of the one who sees it.

Most German philosophers distinguish between music and the other arts, following Aristotle, but each in his own way. They find that its rhythm and harmony directly express the motions or will. Painters have often attempted to take into their art something of music in this sense. In the sixteenth century, the architect Palladio used the proportions which make the twelve-note scale to set out the rooms in the villas he designed. Kant believed that colours worked directly on the emotions. Herbart (1808) wanted to create an aesthetic on the pattern of musical harmony. Fechner, the psychologist, tried in 1857 to show that simple shapes can affect us in a musical way. The academic French theorist Charles Blanc agreed to this, and also to the view that rising lines express happiness, descending lines sorrow, etc.

The next generation of painters took this seriously. Seurat and Signac from the eighties embodied it in their pictures. Sérusier and other young artists went to the abbey of Beuron in Germany, where the use of the Golden Section was being revived in an almost mystic sense (the Golden Section is a way of cutting a line so that the proportion of the smaller to the larger part is equal to that of the larger to the whole line). The Golden Section has now become very popular. Recent experiments, however, have shown that it is not more pleasing than a wide range of other proportions, except to a highly and specially trained viewer.

Another aesthetic which has a psychological basis has not proved so arid. This is Lipps's theory of Empathy (1903), according to which the mind feels itself inhabiting a work of art – i.e. one feels in the work, and not about it. This has been shown to happen most intensely in looking at a picture for a mere fraction of a second.

Aesthetics is the science of beauty in itself, though Marx saw it as the expression of the economic state of society, and Freud saw it as the expression of subconscious desires. John Ruskin (1819–1900) believed that good art was the product of craftsmen who worked with a love of their materials, and so he came to the view that art must be true to its materials, just as Michelangelo had done for a quite different reason. Viollet le Duc, Ruskin's contemporary, held the same belief about structure, and on them most twentieth-century theories of architecture have been founded.

The systematic study of perception, personality, and art as language and as history has somewhat reduced the field of aesthetics and has modified what is left. A man's aesthetics nowadays is just the sum of those things he likes to see and calls art. Some objects he likes because they remind him of things in frames (works of art), and some works of art he likes because they look like objects. This way of thinking is not new; it is very near to common sense. Marcus Aurelius (A.D. 121–180) said, 'There are cracks and little breaks in the surface of a loaf which though never intended by the baker have a sort of agreeableness in them.' In eighteenth-century England, Reynolds loved the Belvedere Torso as much for its battered surface as for its forms; and gardens were made to look like the popular landscape paintings of Claude, Rosa, Wilson and others, and so reduced from geometry to disorder. This led to the cult of the Picturesque, of which Sir Uvedale Price said (1794) that the most efficient causes were roughness, sudden variation and irregularity. But the Picturesque is merely an inversion of the centuries-old aesthetic of the imitation of the antique.

Nowadays instead of Claude or Praxiteles, painters use statistical diagrams, the electron-microscope and Victorian photographs.

The desire not to die

AFTER-LIFE, the continued personal existence of a man after his physical death, essentially involves the notion of *personal* survival, since absorption with loss of identity into the World Spirit in the manner of the Stoics and others is practically speaking the same as complete extinction: it *is* complete extinction of the person.

Belief in personal survival has been almost universal among uncivilized peoples of all times and all parts of the world. Some races, such as the American Indians, set little store by it, and the forms of survival vary enormously; but only among civilized peoples, and then seldom, has there been any general disbelief in immortality of some sort.

There are many possible reasons, more or less sound, for believing in a life after death. Of the more important there is, in the first place, the sheer difficulty of imagining that a personality well known to one has finally and irrevocably ceased to exist, when all the material concomitants of his existence, children, house and personal possessions, live on. Primitive people are specially prone to this, but we all know the feeling.

Dreams provide primitive man with two reasons for belief in a life after death. They are for him the chief evidence that his soul is separate from his body and can at suitable times wander freely through the world. And secondly they are occasions when the dead can reappear.

These first two reasons may not weigh much with us today. But the third reason is still with us. Apparitions suggest to many a continuing existence for the dead, whether they are visible ghosts, voices which whisper and twitter, or unseen hands which move or alter things. In fact, the evidence for these phenomena, confusing though it may be, is for many people today the only rational reason for the belief.

In more advanced communities, which have the conception of a judgement after death, the desire for reward or revenge is an extraordinarily powerful motive for belief. Many look forward avidly to a Heaven where the first shall be last and the last shall be first, and where the rich and the unjust shall burn in Hell in compensation for their evident triumphs in this world.

The ways in which the dead can live on are innumerable. Among primitive people they usually remain on earth, haunting their relations or their enemies, their graves or where they died. In the

Philippines it was thought that they inhabited trees. In the Gilbert Islands they hovered unseen about the eaves and in the trees and would at times re-enter the skeletons or skulls of birds, which were carefully preserved for this purpose. These souls remaining near at hand had power to help or harm, and could be usefully consulted if they were invoked in the right way.

Often these spirits themselves were thought to die. In the Philippines they died when their tree died. The Manus of the Admiralty Islands 'survive a little as strong ghosts immediately after death and then dribble away into lower and lower levels of sea-slugs and slime'. They are like the ghosts in *Hassan*, deriving substance only from a passionate interest in life, and steadily waning as this fades.

Among more civilized peoples only the religions which favour metempsychosis allow souls to remain in this world after death. In these the soul may spend ages spiralling up or down through the different orders of being. In a sense, however, they do not recognize a true life after death at all, but rather a succession of lives until the final achievement of Nirvana.

The belief that after death one has to face a judgement on one's former life is very ancient. In the Egyptian *Book of the Dead*, forty-two sins have to be denied by the dead soul before forty-two judges, and not until they have acquitted it is the soul allowed to join Osiris and taste the joys of paradise. In Greece, Minos and Rhadamanthus judge the dead in similar fashion. In both cases, however, there is also the feeling that if the correct rites have been performed over the dead or dying man this is itself enough to secure his happiness in the next life. Among Christians, the Roman Catholics share this belief in the extreme importance of the last rites, but the other branches of Christianity hold that ceremonies are not essential to the belief that salvation follows judgement, which is granted on the basis of right conduct and right belief alone.

The conflict in Christian tenets between the belief in a judgement and assignment to Heaven or Hell immediately after death, and the belief in a Last Judgement, has not been satisfactorily resolved. But there have been very clear ideas about the condition of the three possible lives after death.

The Greeks thought of Elysium in terms of meadows, yet could not help feeling it a shadowy and unsubstantial place. The Mohammedans are more precise: in Heaven physical desires will be satisfied and there is spiritual felicity as well. The popular Christian idea of Heaven, derived from the *Book of Revelation*, is of a great bejewelled crystalline city, where those who are saved go about in white robes and are probably winged. But there is apparently no activity save perhaps choral singing. The official Christian idea of Heaven is much less concrete. It is still a place, but now its appearance is vague, though undoubtedly radiant, and its heavenliness is spiritual. It is everlasting bliss through nearness to God, and it is endless praise and worship of God in return.

All through the ages it has never been entirely clear how many souls arrived in Heaven. The Greek Elysium is a somewhat aristocratic place, and it is unlikely to have been open to slaves. On the other hand, all, whatever their status, who had been ritually cleansed in the Eleusinian and other Mysteries considered themselves 'saved'. Christianity made its first great gains by offering salvation to the poor and miserable, by picturing a God who was not only All-Powerful but also All-Loving, and through whom all could hope for everlasting happiness. Yet Fr Godts has written: 'It is vain to seek even a single saint [among the medieval theologians] who has taught that the number of the elect forms a majority'; medieval preachers habitually put the proportion of the saved at one in a thousand, or even in ten thousand.

Similarly there are fairly precise views on Purgatory and Hell; the Roman Catholic doctrine is perhaps the simplest. The souls who have been forgiven their sins by God nevertheless have to be punished for sinning. They therefore spend a certain time in Purgatory, where they are tortured, first by desiring God and yet being shut off from Him, secondly by actual 'physical' torture. St Thomas Aquinas holds that the flames of Purgatory are a real fire, and St Francis de Sales 'that the greatest sufferings on earth cannot challenge comparison with the torments of Purgatory'. Yet its inhabitants have the consolation of knowing that in the long run they will graduate to Heaven.

Those souls who are condemned by God (and perhaps the great majority) go after judgement to Hell. There they will be tortured for ever, both by knowing that God is merciless and has set his face against them eternally, and, as in Purgatory, by suffering actual 'physical' torture, world without end. The popular picture is of furnaces and devils to stoke them.

The Protestant churches have abolished Purgatory, but have retained Hell as a place of eternal damnation. The Christian must therefore accept its existence, and reconcile it as best he may with the belief that God is Love.

ILLUSTRATION: Pages 30 and 31.

'Freedom and not servitude is the cure of anarchy; as religion, and not atheism, is the true remedy for superstition'

ANARCHISM postulates that society can and should exist without a government. Anarchists regard the State as evil, and their aim is to abolish it.

While 'anarchy' has always been used to describe the lack of an effective government, Proudhon (1809–1865) in his *Qu'est-ce que la Propriété?* (1840) was the first man to use it of a system in which the authority of the government has been deliberately destroyed. While many countries have passed through periods of anarchy in the more general sense, no nation has yet become an anarchy in Proudhon's specialized meaning of the term.

Ever since political theory first began there have been two main tendencies in thought about the relations between State and Society. One is towards the conviction that it is best for the State to control every branch of human activity, while the other tends to the belief that the State's authority must be as severely limited as possible.

At one extreme stands the German philosopher Hegel's view that the State is the necessary means to the moral good of mankind, from which he deduces that the State is an end in itself. At the opposite pole there is the anarchists' opinion that the State is an unnecessary evil which hinders man's moral development. Their theory is not an intellectual freak: it is the liberal's desire to limit the power of the State carried to an extreme conclusion.

Anarchists use the word 'State' in the specialized sense of the organs of government. It is these alone which should be abolished; the whole hierarchy of institutions and organizations into which society is voluntarily organized will remain. In fact, it is these organizations which will extend their activities to include those beneficial duties of the State that anarchists recognize as essential. Voluntary associations will, for example, take over responsibility for education, sanitation and traffic control in an anarchist society. Order and harmony in such a society will be achieved by free agreement between these hundreds of voluntary groups.

The reason for the anarchists' wish to transfer these activities is their belief that the State misuses its power. The State controls force, and can coerce its subjects into acting against their will. The citizen can have complete freedom of choice in matters of will only when there is no fear of punishment; only then will the full development of his individuality be possible.

Behind these arguments, however, lies a deeper hatred of the State. The majority of anarchists believe that the State uses its power to maintain the capitalist system, and for many this is the real reason why they want to do away with it. Looking at the State historically, they regard it as the instrument for establishing monopolies in favour of the ruling minorities. As long as it has the coercive authority of the State to maintain it, capitalism will continue to defraud the masses of the just rewards of their labour.

Anarchists are thus akin to communists in their hatred of the capitalist system, but they disagree fundamentally over their proposals for a remedy. Communists believe that the State should take over the means of production, but anarchists argue that to hand over land and industry to the State merely gives it new means of tyranny.

Anarchists believe that the control of production should be in the hands of the producers; in this they are similar to the syndicalists.

Anarchism in this modern sense is a doctrine of the last hundred years, but one finds hatred of the State in political, as opposed to economic, affairs as far back as Ancient Greece.

Zeno, the founder of Stoic philosophy (335–263 B.C.), believed in a free community without a government. He thought that every individual should act according to his own moral judgement, and not be coerced into obeying laws of which he disapproves. This moral aspect of anarchism has had many supporters, from medieval churchmen to the eighteenth-century Encyclopaedists. Whenever a State makes and upholds laws which are considered wrong, this attitude is liable to have a resurgence.

William Godwin, the English political thinker, put forward a theory of decentralization similar to later anarchism in his *An Enquiry Concerning Political Justice*, in 1793. He proposed that society should consist of small, free communities, managing all their affairs by consent. While this might not be realized immediately, mankind was quickly progressing towards a level of perfection at which coercive government would be unnecessary.

Proudhon was the first to link dislike of the State with hatred of capitalism, and recent anarchism owes far more to him than to Godwin. Strangely enough, the great attacker of capitalism, Marx, also prophesied eventual anarchism. After the establishment of true equality the need for coercion will cease, and the State 'will wither away'.

After Proudhon's death it was the Russian Bakunin who championed anarchism. Like Proudhon, he believed that the State was an evil thing that must be destroyed; and to this end he founded an intimate circle – a secret society in fact – of able persons from various countries. This group created an uproar in the First International of 1864. Marx and Bakunin were the leading figures at this concourse of international revolutionaries, but it was soon clear that their mutual hatred of capitalism could not prevent their disagreement. Marx believed that the State was the necessary instrument for the abolition of capitalism and the establishment of communism. Bakunin wanted to overthrow both State and capitalism simultaneously, and replace them by a free, locally organized society without a government.

There was a unique and abortive attempt to establish such a system in 1871, when the Paris Commune revolted against the French Government after the Franco-Prussian War. It was hoped that other cities of France would rise and pro-

claim their independence, but the Government was too strong and the Communards were beaten.

This failure did not lessen support for anarchism; instead it continued to win members on both sides of the Atlantic. By this time the anarchists had broken completely with the First International and formed their own International Social-Democratic Alliance. They called themselves communist anarchists, and appealed to many socialists who disliked Marx's highly authoritarian doctrines.

When Bakunin died in 1876, another Russian, Kropotkin, became the leading exponent of anarchism and put forward a well-reasoned case for it in articles, books and pamphlets among the first of which was *An Appeal to Youth* in 1880. He saw the international possibilities of anarchism; freely constituted local groups will come together to form free nations, and eventually free international organizations. There will be free federation from the outside to the centre, instead of the present compulsory centralization.

Kropotkin died in 1921, but anarchism had been rapidly declining since the Russian Revolution. Communism no longer had any room for such unorthodox views, and the necessity for a powerful State to maintain the communist system became increasingly obvious in Russia under Lenin and Stalin. In addition, anarchists had acquired a reputation for violence, both through non-anarchist books such as Sorel's *Reflections on Violence* and through actual outbreaks of terrorism.

Anarchists today form a very minute group, and their views are generally in disfavour. Their theories seem unrealistic and Utopian, though many people share their dislike of the increasing encroachments of State power. Their proposals are based on an over-optimistic view of human nature. It is obvious to most people that without laws, and punishments for their infringement, there could be no orderly and civilized community life. Nor do the majority of citizens find themselves forced by the State into making decisions against their better moral judgement. Attempts at co-operative production by small groups of workers have usually ended in failure.

Yet anarchism will always have a strong appeal in certain circumstances, and its recession may well be only temporary. Whenever optimism about human behaviour overcomes the lessons of experience, there will be people to advocate the abolition of that evil necessity, the State. It will also always have an attraction for those who are badly governed, and where a ruling clique maintains a tyranny for its own benefit.

Anarchism is a useful reminder that the State should exist only as long as it serves the needs of its citizens, and that it is an organization for limited purposes only. With anarchist theory before us, there is no danger of thinking that the State is the master and not the servant of its members.

ILLUSTRATION: Page 23.

The link between life and death

ANCESTOR WORSHIP, one of the great branches of the religions of mankind, is found in the civilizations of the East, among the Hindus, the Parsees, the Chinese and the Japanese, and in the less advanced races, including the Polynesians, the Melanesians, the Ashanti and Dahomey races of Africa, and American Indians.

The fundamental ideas underlying Ancestor Worship can best be studied in primitive societies where the different currents of thought about death and what lies beyond it can be disentangled. In savage and barbarian, as well as in civilized, belief, death does not sever a person from his social unit, his family, clan, tribe or community. The social relations of the living world are maintained in the next. One can say, broadly speaking, that the worldly estimation of a person accompanies him into the shadowy land of spirits. This leads to a variety of ways in which the dead are treated. If a person is of little account in the life of his community, he is not as a rule a source of much anxiety after death. If he played an important part in life, as a medicine man, a sorcerer, a witch doctor, for instance, his magical powers go with him and are sometimes magnified. If he has acted as a repository of wisdom, as the head of a family in a patriarchal system, or as one of the elders of the tribe, he carries with him that respect and wisdom and is sought out to guide the living. Among savages, then, the dead may be treated with contempt, with fear, or with respect,

but these attitudes are complicated by further considerations.

Death is thought of as a terrible and contagious disease, especially when caused by violence and sickness, and measures must be taken against it. The dead are helpless. They cannot fend for themselves and must be provided for in the same way as a sick or feeble medicine-man or tribal counsellor. Chiefs and sorcerers become more powerful in death and must be propitiated. The dead may return and be re-born into the family or tribe. Those who have been dead for some time tend to fade from memory or are idealized into 'great spirits', and the survivors seek to rid themselves of the ghost, to drive him out of his earthly habitation.

Consequently it is not surprising that the dead are rarely neglected and that measures are taken to help them or propitiate their spirits, that they are duly accompanied into the spirit world with weapons, with food and drink, with prayers and magic exhortations, and that attempts are made to communicate with them through sacrifice and invocation. The general attitude of the savage is one of awe and fear towards the dead, with or without affection. The conceptions of death as a terrible disease, of death conferring power on men who have already wielded it in life, and the curious alchemy of time which transforms and idealizes those long dead into superior beings, all tend towards some form of ancestor worship.

The provision for the needs of the dead is so widespread a custom that it has given rise to the fallacious theory that 'provision' or 'tendance' is synonymous with worship. Though there are few peoples who do not provide a death cult in some form for the placation of the spirit, and their gratification, *it is only when prayers, sacrifices and a belief in their superior powers co-exist that it amounts to ancestor worship.*

Those who have been powerful, efficient or valued by the tribe in life are solicited to return; unsatisfactory members are not. Those expected to return are worshipped in the hope of their bringing material benefits with them.

'Anything which transcends the ordinary,' says Spencer in his *Principles of Sociology* (1876–96), 'the savage thinks of as supernatural or divine; the remarkable man among the rest. This remarkable man may be simply the remotest ancestor remembered as the founder of the tribe; he may be a chief famed for strength or bravery; he may be a medicine man of great repute; he may be the inventor of something new. And then, instead of being a member of the tribe, he may be a superior being bringing arts or knowledge, or he may be one of a superior race predominating by conquest. Being one or other of these, regarded with awe during his life, he is regarded with increased awe after his death, and the propitiation of his ghost, being greater than the propitiation of ghosts less feared, develops into an established worship.'

Spencer, who was a passionate evolutionist, proceeded from this account to a wider generalization. He says, 'Using the phrase Ancestor Worship in its broadest sense as comprehending all worship of the dead, be they of the same blood or not, we conclude that Ancestor Worship is the root of every religion.' This is going too far, because it leaves out of account the other great source of religions, animism, which often exists side by side with ancestor worship. Indeed, when religion has reached as high a state of development as Brahmanism, for instance, three elements are found to exist within it, animism (the worship of nature spirits), ancestor worship, and worship of a single divine essence or supreme being.

However, it is perhaps true to say that this singling out of a particular person for worship, the founder of the tribe, or the ancestor of the tribal leader, has played a very great role in uniting larger social communities, and is originally the source of public as opposed to private (family) worship. Side by side with the rites due to the individual dead, the tribe as a whole addresses itself to a Great Chief. Thus, the spirit of a Samoan chief is consulted on all serious occasions, and is supposed to be *nearer* than that of common people.

In this way, by public devotions or sacrifices to the most powerful spirit, it is hoped to secure benefits for the good of all – for instance, in prayers and rites for crops or hunting, and in time, as among the people of Ashanti and Dahomey in Africa, worship of the tribal forebears becomes the State cult. (In its most elaborate form it is developed into a complete national religion based on Ancestor Worship, as, for example, in Japanese Shinto.)

The best known example of private worship of the ancestors is the Cult of the Manes, the 'good people', as they were euphemistically called by the early Romans. This cult did not adhere to particular people, but to the existence of the Life Force transmitted from each family head or house-father to the next generation. The Genius of the family, the begetter, was held to reside in the person of the head of the family; those who had died, the life force having gone out of them, were provided with food, with wine and garlands, and during special festivals, such as the *dies parentales* in February, these were laid in potsherds in the middle of the road for the Manes who inhabited the earth. Ovid (43 B.C.–A.D. 17) tells a story in the *Fasti*, an uncompleted chronicle of the Roman Year, that when the rites of the Parentalia were neglected a plague fell on the city which lasted until the rites were restored.

This festival was followed by the Caristia, a family reunion. At the festival of the Lemuria in May, which is a far more profane celebration, the householder rose in the night, and dropping beans from his mouth said, 'With these beans I ransom me and mine.' Cymbals were beaten, and the householder cried out: 'Go forth, ye divine shades of my fathers.'

This seems like the survival of the very primitive exorcisms for driving out the ghosts from their homes which are often found among savages. Both these festivals took place significantly at the spring time of the year, and were undoubtedly designed to seek the benign influence of the spirits on the crops. The Manes were also worshipped at the 'mundus', a trench opening out of the other world which was usually situated in the heart of the city, where offerings and sacrifices were made, and oracular help was sought.

The Roman Manes were thought of as being deprived of their vital force. This idea that the soul was weak once it was deprived of its body goes back to primitive beliefs, but it is shown very clearly in Homer's description of Odysseus's journey to Hades, where he was sent by Circe to consult the spirit of Tiresias. He gives a picture of the dark world of the shades, and of the suffering of the spirit who is deprived of proper burial – that is to say Odysseus's companion, Elpenor. Odysseus is speaking:

The sun dipped into the sea. A steady wind drove our ship to the end of the world, to the land of the Cimmerians, which is wrapt in eternal mists and never lit by the rays of the sun. And there was Oceanus the river which bounds the earth. We came to the rock and the streams which join their waters, and there we made offerings just as Circe had told us. The moment the blood from the throats of the sheep flowed into the pit we had dug for the sacrifice, the souls of the dead emerged from the cleft.

Odysseus is movingly begged by the shade of Elpenor for a proper burial. His mother is there, but cannot recognize him until she has drunk of the blood of sacrifice. With his sword Odysseus keeps off the innumerable shades thirsting for the blood, until Tiresias, who is to prophesy his home-coming, steps forward, drinks, and tells him his fate. Here most clearly seen is the idea of the sacrificial blood providing the link between the two worlds.

Perhaps the Chinese family patriarchal life typifies the most harmonious aspect of Ancestor Worship. The continuity of family life is here its most important feature, each member of the Chinese family securing his Ancestor rights in the next world by producing an heir to perform the devotions in this. The Chinese regard the Ancestors as mediators between themselves and God, occupying the rank of spirits next to the Supreme Being approached by invocation and sacrifice.

ILLUSTRATION: Page 71.

In the Age of Anxiety

ANGST – in German 'dread' – is regarded philosophically by Martin Heidegger (e.g. in his *Existence and Being*, 1927, English translation, 1949) as one of the basic realities of existence.

In effect, this 'Angst' is well depicted in a cartoon by Max Beerbohm in which the nineteenth-century man and the twentieth-century man stand contrasted. Nineteenth-century man is shown imagining complacently a future that consists of a larger and larger version of himself; twentieth-century man sees a future in which he becomes all the time more wraith-like, until finally he dwindles into a question mark. Twentieth-century man in the cartoon, and in reality, is suffering from Angst – an all-pervading sense of anxiety with its background of guilt, sin and humiliation.

An age may be known by the catchwords it bandies about. Our concern is with 'the human predicament', and signs of this are the frequency with which we talk about frustration, maladjustment and disintegration, and our intense awareness of cruelty, violence and sadism. Faith, hope and charity are held to belong to empty churches. Charity (q.v.), the greatest of the Christian virtues, is thought of, if at all, as being nothing more than 'almsgiving'.

These are symptoms of a spiritual malady which is not confined to neurotic or unhappy people; in one form or another it is escaped by almost no one. It is a collective world malady which may be said to have begun with the undermining of modern man's confidence in himself. On the threshold of this 'Age of Anxiety', Darwin taught that man evolved from the humblest form of life by a process of natural selection that was quite automatic. Freud taught that religion is the result of the sense of guilt that arises from the Oedipus Complex, and that almost all human activities spring from sexuality.

Jung in *Modern Man in Search of a Soul* says that as a result in particular of such teachings the platform of man's beliefs has collapsed. The teachings of scientists have made him doubt whether he is the glorious summit of God's creation. Man, according to Jung, is at present suffering from an unappeasable hunger for God. He has lost faith in God the Father, and has not learned to do without some 'father figure' at whose feet he still unconsciously longs to grovel. He suffers a sense of miserable insecurity in relation to a universe whose awful and indifferent vastness is making an impact upon his imagination through the popularization of the findings of scientists. Martin Buber has written of man feeling no longer *at home* in his world.

The almost infinitely various manifestations of Angst are reflected in the art of the time, and perhaps most comprehensively in its literature. Thomas Hardy's novels dealt with mankind's predicament in the universe. His reflective mind was overcast by clouds of doubt. As a young man he was influenced by the higher criticism of the Bible and the Darwinian theory of evolution. If this universe, as seemed possible, was only a mechanical process, what was the significance of those moral and spiritual values which man had learned to regard as the most precious things in life? Hardy saw mankind 'swept from darkness to darkness, like a straw on a torrent, by a ruthless, mysterious and ignoble force'. When his favourite character, Tess of the D'Urbervilles, is hanged, Hardy comments in a famous passage: ' "Justice" was done, and the President of the Immortals ... had ended his sport with Tess.' Instead of a loving God, Hardy envisaged at best an indifferent blind force, at worst a malignant being who sported with mankind, enjoying the torment it caused.

In modern literature – and modern art – is to be found the record of the breakdown of a settled and established order. One chosen symbol to represent the period is that of seediness, which extends from the novels of Franz Kafka (1883–1924) to the cruder novels of Graham Greene. 'Seedy' and 'shabby' are among Greene's favourite adjectives in his evocation of contemporary atmospheres. Thus *The Power and the Glory* begins: 'Mr Tench went out to look for his ether cylinder, into the blazing Mexican sun and the bleaching dust. A few vultures looked down from the roof with shabby indifference: he wasn't carrion yet.'

Guilt and anxiety have been steadily mounting with each betrayal, each wilful blindness and each crime against humanity that 'slaves the ordnances of Heaven' and that implicates everyone. There has been the guilt about Munich, the guilt of Belsen and Dachau, Buchenwald and Auschwitz, the gas chambers, the concentration camps and the mass graves; the lampshades made of human skin and the soap made of human fat; the guilt of the atom bomb, the guilt and terror aroused by the hydrogen bomb. The 'Age of Anxiety' is being succeeded by the 'Age of Terror', and of a new 'scientific fiction', dealing with the super-explosives, bacteriological warfare, space ships and devil men from Mars.

In Graham Greene's film *The Third Man*, Harry Lime the racketeer says: 'In these days nobody thinks in terms of human beings. Governments don't, so why should we? They talk of the people and the proletariat, and I talk of the mugs. It's the same thing. They have their five-year plan and so have I.'

In his long poem, the *Age of Anxiety* W.H. Auden (whose first master was Thomas Hardy) gives this account of modern man:

> ... crazed we come and coarsened we go
> Our wobbling way: there's a white silence
> Of antiseptics and instruments
> At both ends, but a babble between
> And a shame surely.

*'When Good King Arthur ruled this land
He was a goodly king'*

ANTIQUITY is the remote past. The idea of antiquity is the conception of the past as held by different societies. These conceptions vary between the reverent devotion of the Chinese for their forebears and the reputed opinion of the American motor magnate, Henry Ford, that 'History is Bunk'. 'Antiquity' is therefore a coloured word. The pendulum has always swung, and in any generation rebels have applauded or deplored 'the Past' against the current intellectual tide.

Primitive tribes today, like the cultures of prehistory, do not formulate ideas of Antiquity. They reverence the past, in myth and saga. But they have no theoretical ideas about it. It was the theorists of the Ancient World of the Greeks and Romans who first related their society to history, and felt that they were living in something less than the Golden Age (q.v.) which they believed had existed in the past. They shared this belief in a current decline from a happier period with the then obscure Israelites (whose Testament spoke of a Fall from an idyllic existence) and many other early societies. Aristotle (384–322 B.C.) believed in a cycle of human affairs, by which all experiences were known, lost, and rediscovered by successive generations. Many others followed his view, although the prevailing pessimism of the ancient world still preferred the belief that civilization was declining from a fuller and happier age.

There was no idea of Progress; even the materialistic Romans looked back to a legendary time when life had been cleaner, purer, fuller and more heroic than their own life. Americans today have, in spite of their passionate belief in material advancement, the same sort of picture of their pioneering ancestors. The Roman conception of an idyllic past is illustrated in the verse of the poet of another materialistic age, Lord Macaulay (1800–1859) reporting in *Horatius* a fabulous Roman past when

> None were for the party, but all were for the state
> When the rich man loved the poor, and the poor
> man loved the great.

The same age, although dogmatically Protestant, managed to accept a picture of a medieval Roman Catholic 'Merry England'. True history – the chronicling and assessment of facts and societies – had been meanwhile initiated by Herodotus of Halicarnassus (485–425 B.C.) who has been called the Father of History, but is even more evidently the father of antiquarians and anthropologists.

The Middle Ages in Europe had an entirely different conception of Antiquity. The evidences of Roman material culture – bridges, buildings, roads and administrative procedure – survived. But whilst these were accepted, the spirit of the age rejected the Past as pagan and so immoral. The pagan beliefs still existed, the Church was still fighting them, and the Past was a thing of the Devil, godless and unredeemed. The official view of the Middle Ages was that the end of the world might arrive at any moment, that all events were dictated by a divine calendar, and that Antiquity was, on the whole, unimportant. This world was only a painful ante-room, from which a select few might proceed into eternal beatitude.

The Renaissance – the great revival of excitement and the arts – took a different view. Whilst its more daring spirits repudiated the theological beliefs of the Middle Ages, and it was a period (roughly from 1300) of adventure and discovery in ideas and the arts, it still looked backward for inspiration. It was not shocked by antiquity, but copied and enjoyed the past, adding its own vivid and personal contributions.

The excitement of the Renaissance subsided, in the realm of ideas, into the sensitive appreciation of the seventeenth century, proceeding to the cocky assurance of the men of the eighteen- and nineteen-hundreds. Antiquity still meant the classical world, but the Light of Modern Reason (a much used phrase) accepted it with cynical tolerance rather than adulation. Voltaire (1694–1778) had made it evident to his followers that history was the story of the sins and foibles of mankind. Later historians and philosophers made it more evident that in their view the past was a terrible example to the enlightened future – a future foreordained to success. For the idea of Progress had now been accepted.

The approach to Antiquity in England in the nineteenth century was not so cynical. It saw Progress ahead, but it also inculcated a strong sense of the past. Boys learnt, in the gentlemen's schools, their Greek and Latin, and also studied Gothic architecture. The classical education was the necessary basis of the upper classes, and its strict rules of organization and discipline still have their advocates. To them, appreciation of the past – a respect for antiquity and its views – is essential to true civilization.

This idea is by no means universal. Europeans and the Chinese, or at least Chinese thinkers, usually accept Antiquity as a necessary and positive ingredient of contemporary life. They respect tradition. To the vigorous societies of the United States (in spite of their pioneers) and the Russian republics, the past possesses overtones of restriction and of ignorant repression. The Idea of Progress is received by ordinary people as an ideal. They look to the future, and find that what is 'antiquated' is to be despised. It is likely that the emphasis will change, and already many thinkers, deploring that future they choose to foresee, are prepared to escape into history, which itself is inescapable. Clio, the Muse of History, was to the ancients the eldest daughter of Memory, and chief of the Muses. In spite of intellectual fashions, it is unlikely that she can be successfully deposed.

Antiquity, in a softer sense, is the occupation of antiquarians, to whom the past is an interest, not an instrument. They study 'antiques' – the physical remains of earlier days. The first of the great English antiquarians was John Leland, chaplain to King Henry VIII, at the crucial period of the English Renaissance. At this time began what are perhaps three of the most precious collections of medieval manuscripts in the world: the collection of Thomas Bodley at the Bodleian Library in Oxford, that of Archbishop Matthew Parker at Corpus Christi College in Cambridge, and that of Robert Cotton, which is the basis of what is now known as the Cottonian Collection in the British Museum.

The London Society of Antiquarians was founded in 1751, under a charter granted by that otherwise unenlightened monarch, George II. But as early as 1572 a society for the preservation of natural antiquities had been founded by William Camden, and the tradition had never really died. Indeed the great antiquarian, John Aubrey (1626–1697), has often been claimed as the real founder of county history. He lived in Wiltshire, which has perhaps more visible relics of the past – capped by Stonehenge – than any other county in the British Isles.

The present headquarters of the Society of Antiquarians is in London, at Burlington House in Piccadilly. Similar societies were formed in Scotland in 1780, and in Ireland in 1849. Most European countries, and the United States of America and elsewhere, now have bodies devoted to the same study of past custom, topography, social and political habit, and of physical remains. Today new processes of psychology, anthropology, etymology, archaeology and field work are called in to help recreate the world of the past.

It may not be unduly cynical to recall the reflection of the French critic Boileau (1636–1711) about Antiquity, that 'the ancients were moderns, but it is by no means certain that the moderns will become ancients'. Machinery for studying the past, however, is fuller and more precise than it has ever been before.

ILLUSTRATION: Pages 28 and 29.

Jew baiting

ANTI-SEMITISM as a term goes back to the eighteen-seventies, but in fact it is an old concept, the expression of the Dislike of the Unlike directed against a section of humanity which has had the glorious but uncomfortable distinction of being a dissenting or easily recognized minority in a succession of alien environments, for two thousand or more years.

In the course of this experience, as was inevit-

able, the Jews acquired specific characteristics – physical, economic, social – which were resented. But these characteristics were not the cause, though they were often used as the justification, of the prejudice. Basically, this was due to the fact that his religious principles made the Jew into the 'Eternal Protestant', who refused to conform to the creed of the majority and that afterwards, because of his historic experience, the Jew remained reluctant to accept the majority pattern – not in matters of religion only. The justification changed from one age to the other: sometimes with bewildering and even acrobatic completeness, but the underlying cause was always the same.

Anti-semitism goes back to the century *before* the beginning of the Christian era, in Alexandria, where this ethnic minority which refused to adopt the religion of the majority, found itself the object of a propaganda hardly distinguishable from that of the nineteenth century. Anti-semitism flourished in the same spirit in classical Rome, and for the same reason. The early Christians were also as much subject to it as the Jews, from whom they stemmed; but when they themselves attained power in the fourth century they illogically maintained this same attitude towards their former fellows in adversity. At this period, enmity was aroused only by the religion of the Jews.

Throughout the Middle Ages this ancient prejudice was intensified. It was now held that those who refused to conform should be thrust out of the normal structure of society, restricted to degraded callings, marked out for shame by the wearing of a special badge, prevented from having any normal contacts with true believers, and with this object be shut up in their own quarters (later to be called ghettoes).

A succession of Church Councils mark the stages in the degradation of the Jews, which could not fail to leave traces on their physique, their outlook and their mentality. The logical outcome was a loss of personal security, a succession of massacres and persecutions, and expulsions from one country after the other, culminating in the expulsion from Spain at the end of the fifteenth century. The Catholic Church suspected the Jews of a hand in the Reformation, and degraded them still more: the Reformers resented the fact that the Jews would not accept their new presentation of the Christian truth, and continued to treat them in the traditional fashion.

The modern age introduced the idea of religious toleration. But by this time habits of thoughts had become fixed. Previously, the Jew had been able to evade discrimination, and even to achieve an honoured place in society, if he adhered to the majority opinion in matters of religion – *i.e.* in Christian Europe, if he was baptized; and Jews in increasing numbers were willing to conform, with or without a ceremony – or at least to abandon their distinctive beliefs. Yet neither side could give up a traditional bias. The Jew who now professed Christianity, or had ceased professing Judaism, did not quite conform to the normal pattern, either in appearance, occupation, origin or – what was worse – opinions; his neighbour mechanically resented both his progress and his ideas, but could no longer justify his anti-semitism on religious grounds.

Hence in Germany – the land with which this process was especially associated – there grew up in the last decades of the nineteenth century the movement which received the name of anti-Semitism – nominally based not on religious but on racial grounds, and directed therefore against all persons, whatever their creed, who were traceably of Jewish extraction. This was, in fact, an absurdity from many points of view. The period saw a rapid weakening not only of religious loyalties, but also of separatism of every type among Jewish or ex-Jewish families; there can be little doubt that they would wholly have lost their individuality within a very short while if it had not been for this new movement. Also, since the time of the settlement of the Jews in Europe there had been a vast degree of conversion from Judaism to Christianity as well as a trickle of converts from Christianity to Judaism; inter-marriage had continued for centuries. Differentiation, therefore, on racial grounds was to a great degree fictitious. There must have been Jewish blood in almost every Central European family.

The new anti-semitism spread menacingly, but not (it seemed to most people) dangerously: because it sounded mad, and because some of its exponents were mad indeed. However, a transmutation of values in European life brought the maniac element to the fore. The atavistic prejudices, the petty jealousies, the individual resentments against the Jews which were summed up in the term 'anti-semitism' were one of the most powerful of the forces by which the Nazi movement obtained power in Germany. Forthwith the Nazis revived and put into effect once again all the medieval legislation against the Jews – now, however, applied against persons of Jewish extraction as well: separating them from society, excluding them from education, thrusting them out of economic life, branding them as pariahs: in the end labelling Jews once more with the Badge of Shame, and bringing into existence again vast ghettoes, compared with which those of the Middle Ages were gardens of delight. All this was achieved by slow degrees, so that the public conscience was not profoundly shocked even by the ghastly outcome – the deportation to Eastern Europe, and the deliberate extermination, in the gas-chambers and elsewhere, of no fewer than 5,000,000 Jews – one half of the total of those of all Europe, and nine-tenths of those of some countries. It is to this crime, unexampled in history, and even now imperfectly realized or even denied, that the almost plausible movement launched in the nineteenth century led inexorably.

It is too much to dignify anti-semitism by considering it an 'idea', for it is no more than a prejudice. But in the course of the past few years it has been of tremendous force in history. Without it, not only would the Nazi movement have failed to establish itself in Germany, but the triumphant expansion of German might throughout Europe, which followed an elaborate campaign of propaganda, could never have taken place so easily. And it is not dead. Hitler converted it into a potent instrument of policy; and there can, alas, be little doubt that it has established itself – together with its excesses, now taken for granted – as an instrument of reaction. It may not be an idea. But it is potentially, even now, a tremendous force for evil.

ILLUSTRATION: Pages 36, 37 and 38.

The lost paradise

ET IN ARCADIA EGO is on the whole a literary, Utopian concept which has meant 'I, too, have lived in Arcadia', *i.e.* I, too, have been happy in my time, although it may equally well be interpreted as 'I [Death] am also present in Arcadia'.

Arcadia geographically is a high, somewhat mountainous region in the interior of the Peloponnese. Barring Megalopolis, which was founded late in the fourth century B.C., there were no towns of real importance in Arcadia; land was only fertile in the valleys, and the population was mainly pastoral. Rather cut off from the rest of Greece, it retained a dialect slightly akin to Cypriot; both had preserved many characteristics of Greek speech before the Dorian invasion, which took place about 1100 B.C. The cults and mythology of the region had also kept a primitive character. As late as Plato's time – so he implied – human sacrifices were offered at the sanctuary of Zeus (who, the Arcadians claimed, was born in their country) on Mount Lycaeon. Pan, however, was the deity peculiar to Arcadia. He was the god of cattle and pastoral occupations, and was particularly associated with Mount Menalcus, where – according to Pausanias – he could often be heard playing on his reed-pipe.

The literary Arcadia, however, was largely a creation of Ovid and Virgil. Both poets had drawn on the *Universal History* of Polybius, himself an Arcadian, who lived in the second century B.C. According to Polybius, the people of Arcadia were hospitable and virtuous shepherds, men of a primordial simplicity, unconcerned with the doings of the world outside. They were an extremely musical people: 'among them music was considered an indispensable thing, instead of being merely desirable'.

In his *Fasti*, Ovid removed this actual Arcadia of Polybius into an ideal, archaic period, a golden age before gold had been invented or any of the arts: the time which was, according to a popular Greek proverb, 'before the creation of the moon'.

Virgil transported the manners of Arcadia into an ideal landscape inhabited by shepherds and nymphs, more reminiscent perhaps of the Sicily described by the Greek pastoral poet Theocritus than of the sterner Arcadia of Polybius. In all Virgil's pastoral poems, however, there is a new sentiment —a melancholy induced by the tension between the ideal environment and the inescapable human suffering.

The two great poets raised the bare and hilly

district to the status of a most powerful literary convention. The real Arcadia has no further literary history of any importance, and in fact it did not even retain its name into the Middle Ages; it ceased to be a social or political entity.

The Arcadian convention survived and gained new life whenever another vein of pastoral poetry was struck. At the Court of Charlemagne, for instance, in the circle of the scholar and poet Alcuin of York, who was the emperor's *arbiter elegantiarum* as well as ecclesiastical adviser, poets would take 'arcadian' pen-names, drawn from Virgil's eclogues and other bucolic writings: Thyrsis, Corydon, Menalcas. The Virgilian convention was revived by Boccaccio, who set his dialogue 'Ameto' in a real landscape of Tuscany, though he referred to it as 'Arcadia'.

This luxuriant and indolent pastiche of Virgil had little connection with Polybius's rusticity. But in the fifteenth century Italian poets made great use of the Arcadian invention. Arcadia became a retreat not only from hard reality, but also from the corrupt and violent present, into a lost country of simplicity and ancient virtue. It was in this sense that Lorenzo the Magnificent and Angelo Poliziano, the finest poet of the Tuscan Renaissance, celebrated the Medici Villa at Fiesole under the name of Arcadia.

The convention became accepted by painters, historians and romancers. By 1504 the Neapolitan poet Sannazaro had published his *Arcadia*, a loosely framed narrative which consists of alternate passages of prose and verse. The book celebrates the ideals of rural life; but it is filled with laments, dirges, and accounts of funereal rites.

During the sixteenth century mythological-pastoral writing – Spenser's *Faerie Queen* and Tasso's *Aminta* are good examples – became one of the main channels of poetic expression in practically all European languages. In England alone it was honoured by such poets as Drayton, and Sir Philip Sidney in his *Arcadia*. The sentiment associated with the convention inspires many madrigals which were so popular during the sixteenth and seventeenth centuries.

By the beginning of the seventeenth century the convention was losing its emotional power. At that time the North Italian Baroque painter Guercino (1591–1666) painted the picture in which the phrase 'Et in Arcadia Ego' first occurs. It is a landscape in which two shepherds have come, to their consternation, upon a skull resting upon a platform. The phrase is inscribed on the base. The context is the *memento mori* – the reminder of death in the fashionable pastoral scene. 'I am present even in Arcadia'; the skull is a personification of death. The phrase, once coined, acquired a great popularity. The great French painter Nicolas Poussin (1594–1665) painted two pictures with this title. The second of these twin paintings gave the phrase its current value by epitomizing the sentiment with which it is associated. In Poussin's painting, a group of rustics is gathered round a severely classical tomb, inscribed 'Et in Arcadia Ego'.

Although only the one translation of the phrase is possible, the whole tenor of the picture contradicts it. Poussin's second biographer (in spite of his predecessor's correct reading) mistranslated it: 'I, too, have been in Arcadia' – as if it were the person within the tomb who spoke. The mistranslation restores coherence to the image created by Poussin, but it is far removed from the meaning given to it by Guercino. For the Italian painter, the presence of death even in Arcadia meant the dramatic and terrifying confrontation of vigour and happiness with the cataclysm of sudden death, a theme frequently used in medieval moralities – in *Everyman*, for instance. Poussin had associated it with a new sentiment – the reminder to those in Arcadia that they cannot escape death, and, at the same time, a consolation in the knowledge that even those who are now in the tomb had once enjoyed the happiness which is to be had immediately.

The phrase soon became the device of a happiness once enjoyed and never to be experienced again, even though it is still living in the memory. 'Whenever, in a beautiful landscape, I encounter a tomb with the inscription "I, too, have been in Arcadia", I point it out to my friends, we stop for a moment, press each other's hands, and go on', writes the German poet Johann Georg Jacobi in the *Winter Journey*, a book published in 1769.

Jacobi was a writer of the hard, brittle and soft-centred neo-classical school, which had a particularly strong affection for the Arcadian convention. One of the most important centres of the neo-classical movement was the 'Arcadian Academy' of Rome which was founded in 1690 and exercised the greatest influence throughout the eighteenth century, and indeed much later. 'The wits of Rome', wrote Goldsmith in 1759, 'are united into a rural group of nymphs and swains under the appellation of Modern Arcadians.'

The Virgilian mood was in the ascendant in France. The sunsets of Claude (1600–1682), the most pastoral of the great painters, are suffused with it; Watteau (1684–1721) devoted more than half his work to the painting of scenes of pastoral life. In his pictures, however, the present is almost as melancholy as the past; decay crumbles the statues, and grass obliterates the paths in the great parks in which his *Fêtes Champêtres* take place.

The Arcadian convention was getting out of hand. Not only painting and literature – Tasso's *Aminta* went through ten translations before 1784 – but actuality was affected by the conceit of an ideal pastoral life. French nobility constructed Arcadian retreats, such as the Swiss dairy at Versailles, where they could withdraw into an artificial life of pastoral leisure among the scented cows. The convention became associated with the absurd artificialities of French court life rather than with primitive simplicity.

Arcadia was abolished by the Revolution. The critic Le Harpe wrote in 1799 of the pastoral eclogue: 'We have no poetry which is more discredited, nor any which is more alien to our manners and our taste. The genre is not to blame ... it is rather that our way of life is too far removed from pastoral nature and that we have never actually experienced the gentleness which tinges the ideal of bucolic existence.'

Le Harpe was only partly right. Although the convention was all but dead – it had occasional revivals at the most popular level, as in *The Arcadians* by Edward German – the sentiment has kept its hold. In England it had a strong influence on the development of landscape gardening, which in its early days was associated with the Palladian movement, sponsored by Lord Burlington (1694–1753). Landscaping, the taste for the picturesque which it entailed, and even the garden city movement, are still tinged with Arcadian predilections.

In France the movement, though not so influential in architecture and the visual arts, retained a strong influence upon literature. One of the masterpieces of contemporary literature,

Marcel Proust's *Remembrance of Things Past*, is an exploration of Arcadian melancholy: 'If a memory, thanks to forgetfulness, has been able to contract any tie, to forge any link between itself and the present, if it has remained in its own place, if it has kept its own distance isolated in the hollow of a valley or on the peak of a mountain, it makes us suddenly breathe an air new to us, just because it is an air which we have formerly breathed, an air purer than that which the poets have vainly called paradisaical, which offers that deep sense of renewal only because it has been breathed before, inasmuch as the true paradises are the paradises we have lost.'

ILLUSTRATION: Plate 1.

Not for edification

ART FOR ART'S SAKE – *l'Art pour l'Art* – as a declaration of independence dates no further back than the nineteenth century, and its origin may be sought in the great social and economic changes of that age, which created a gulf between the artist and a society that no longer supported him.

In any period when the arts had a hieratic, ceremonial or propagandist function such a declaration would be more surprising. One cannot, for example, imagine it as the watchword of sculptors in ancient Egypt, whose services were dedicated to the cult of the dead, or of the painters of the Académie Royale, whose duty it was to celebrate the glories of Louis XIV, or even of the Augustan writers, whose poems and pamphlets flattered or defended a Whig or Tory régime. On the other hand, it is easy to understand why artists in nineteenth-century France, deprived of their old aristocratic patrons and faced with a hostile or indifferent or uncomprehending bourgeoisie, should proclaim the intrinsic importance of their work and pursue it in a spirit of conscious defiance.

Charles Baudelaire (1821–1867) and Théophile Gautier (1811–1872) can jointly be credited with giving precision to the idea. The latter was responsible for the slogan 'L'Art pour l'Art', and both applied it in their work and expressions of opinion and purpose. Gautier wrote the poems of his *Émaux et Camées* (1852) in the spirit of an engraver of gems, concerned solely with the beauty of his verbal craft. 'Poetry', said Baudelaire, 'has no other end but itself, and no poem is so great, so noble, so entirely worthy of the name as that which has been written simply for the pleasure of writing a poem. If a poet has followed a moral end, he has diminished his poetic force and the result is most likely to be bad.'

To establish the existence of an essential or 'aesthetic' beauty in a work of art, distinguishable from moral, religious, idealistic or informative purpose, was undoubtedly of value at a time when this aesthetic element was disregarded. It became, and has remained, an influential idea in both the literary and visual arts. In music, it may be noted, it has always been taken for granted – no doubt since it was a characteristic doctrine of art for art's sake, as expressed by Walter Pater, that 'all the arts aspire to the condition of music'.

The tendency can be seen in a vigorous form in the development of French nineteenth-century painting. From the time of the Barbizon School (beginning 1830–1840) painters were discarding moral, religious, ideal or informative subjects in favour of the simpler themes in which they themselves took pleasure. Colour (the nearest visual equivalent to music) became, with the Impressionists and Post-Impressionists, increasingly important as a source of purely aesthetic sensation. The public was invited to enjoy the way a picture was painted rather than to be edified by any message it conveyed. This reversal of visual habit caused those storms of public anger which were a striking phenomenon of the time, and which greeted the simplest landscape or the most innocuous scene of everyday life, if the way of painting it was novel.

In literature the matter was more complicated. The freedom of the poet was not used merely to combine words beautifully or with a musical and pictorial suggestion, in the manner of Gautier, or Stéphane Mallarmé, whose 'eclogue', *L'Après-Midi d'un Faune*, may be considered one of the masterpieces of 'L'Art pour l'Art'. The complications lay in the freedom which the writer claimed to deal, if his art so required, with themes which were unedifying and taboo, according to accepted and conventional opinion. It is at this point that we find 'Art for Art's Sake' and 'Decadence' (q.v.) becoming interwoven. The poems in Baudelaire's *Les Fleurs du Mal* (1857) are not only exquisite in form, but are concerned with the emotional subtleties and sensations of vice. The feverish interest in excess governed by an austere and uncompromising devotion to art reappeared in others – Huysmans, for example – and towards the end of the century had its pictorial equivalent in Toulouse-Lautrec's studies of Parisian haunts of vice.

It was as an importation that the idea of 'Art for Art's Sake' gained ground in the later nineteenth century in Britain. The young Swinburne repeated the doctrine 'the art of poetry has absolutely nothing to do with didactic matter at all'. He expressed it in the *Poems and Ballads* (1866) and in defiant hymns to pagan beauty; with him the 'fleurs maladives' of Baudelaire become the 'roses and raptures of vice'. The spirit of both the aesthetic and 'decadent' trend is caught in his own remarkable fashion by Walter Pater in his famous description of Mona Lisa and the beauty composed 'of strange thoughts and fantastic reveries and exquisite passions'.

It is necessary to distinguish, from the thought or productions of the serious artist, the popularization and parody of 'Art for Art's Sake' that in the seventies and eighties took shape in the 'Aesthetic' craze incited in particular by Oscar Wilde. This fused, and was confused, with the ideas of William Morris, John Ruskin and Pater, with the vogue for Japanese prints and oriental pottery fostered by Rossetti and Whistler, with art, social improvement and interior decoration; all comically mirrored by W. S. Gilbert in *Patience* and by George du Maurier in *Punch*. A restatement of the essential idea (from a painter's point of view) was that made by James McNeill Whistler in the famous *Ten O'Clock* lecture of 1885, in which he brilliantly expressed the opinion that there is no such thing as an artistic age or an artistic nation, that the artist is an isolated being, independent of place and time, jealously cultivating his unique gift and quite indifferent as to the reception of his work by the world at large.

Whether the artist really gains by such an isolation remains a question, though in all circumstances he should be true to himself. Whistler's own art, exquisite and fastidious, is limited by a diffidence we do not find in more robust masters.

The new aesthetic perception cultivated by the great French painters of his time constitutes them forerunners of 'Modern' art; yet, in the latter, the fastidious cultivation of 'Art in itself' has been eventually merged into a passionate desire to express modern life and the feelings of the artist in relation to it. In the Post-Impressionist era, Maurice Denis already voiced a significant critical reaction when he found Whistler's painting 'sceptical' and dim. Wyndham Lewis later put on record in his 'Modern' manifesto *Blast* an opposition to 'Aestheticism' as a weary and outmoded cult. Picasso's *Guernica* belonged to a period in which the taste for the 'precious' and dainty has little place. Preciosity was one of the temptations to which the adherent of 'Art for Art's Sake' was prone; and in this respect it did not outlast the *fin-de-siècle*. Yet it may well be maintained that the artist's claim to free speech or expression (long so hotly contested) has had an enduring result.

ILLUSTRATION: Plate 15 and Page 33.

Arts and the machine

ART IN INDUSTRY as an ideal, as a marriage between two incompatibles, came in the very distant wake of the Industrial Revolution. At first, in aesthetic and political reaction to the values created by that revolution, the concept was expressed in terms of what were once known as the 'decorative' arts and the crafts; under the more proper term of 'industrial design' it has come to embrace the aesthetic control of production techniques throughout the whole of industry.

'We can try to get the artist to take an interest in those arts of life whose production at present is wholly in the hands of the irresponsible machines of the commercial system,' wrote William Morris in 1888, 'and to understand that they, the artists, however great they may be, ought to be taking part in this production; while the workmen who are now machines ought to be artists, however humble.' (*Art and its Producers*.)

During the long wooing, commerce remained cool, and the ardour, often muddle-headed enough, was all on art's side. Today, when the concept is more widely accepted than ever before, the official engagement may be said to have taken place, though real marriage remains – perhaps will always remain – an ideal.

The Industrial Revolution replaced the craftsman by the machine-hand and the engineer, and in so far as the later nineteenth century evolved forms which still seem to us beautiful, these were created for the most part by a new race of architect-engineers. Working in iron, steel and plate glass, men like Cubitt and Barlow and Paxton and Brunel created their bridges and ships and railway stations with minds splendidly unencumbered by the past. They were concerned more with the *function* than the *look* of the things they made, and it is this preoccupation with 'fitness for purpose' which relates them so closely with the beauty we have learned to see in our own contemporary architecture and design.

'Beauty' was a word much in use during the second half of the nineteenth century in Britain. Though never defined, it was associated in the public mind with the sham classicism of the academic painters, or some other form of idyllic past. It belonged, with 'art', in one pigeon-hole, while 'commerce', which was degrading man and countryside, belonged in another.

Thus the first articulate prophets of a new ideal, encouraged by the high priest Ruskin himself, and in particular by the chapter 'On the Nature of Gothic' in *Stones of Venice* (1853), looked not to their own architect-engineers, but to the past. Their gospel was compounded equally of political revulsion and a pre-Raphaelite medievalism. They wished to sweep away not merely this or that machine 'but the great intangible machine of commercial tyranny which oppresses us all' (Morris). It was not by such utopian ideas of a craftsman-society that the William Morris movement set the spark to the conception of industrial design as we know it today, but by its refusal to recognize a division between the 'fine' and the 'applied' arts. Morris stormed up and down the country: 'Have nothing in your house,' he said over and over again, 'which you do not know to be useful or believe to be beautiful.'

In the last two decades of the century a multitude of groups and guilds came into existence, all devoted to this same ideal – among them the Century Guild, the Guild of Handicraft, the Artworkers' Guild and the Arts and Crafts Exhibition Society. In these Voysey the architect, Cobden-Sanderson the publisher, and Walter Crane the illustrator were perhaps the leading figures – to be joined after 1896 by another architect, Charles Rennie Mackintosh with the *art nouveau* forms of the Glasgow arts and crafts movement. It must be admitted that, just as the wallpapers, textiles, furniture, books and stained glass that had come from Morris's own workshops since 1862 were bought by the wealthy few and not the democratic many, so the influence of these guilds marked, to some extent, merely another aspect of *fin-de-siècle* peculiarities. Nevertheless the influence was there. Crane took over the Royal College of Art; the London County Council founded its Central School; and in 1898 the young Ambrose Heal gave a new direction to the machine-made products of his family's furniture business.

The craft tradition was by no means dead. It was to inform Roger Fry's Omega Workshops and the whole life-work of men like Bernard Leach the potter; and it was to find a powerful propagandist in the sculptor-typographer Eric Gill. Yet it was on the continent of Europe that the ideas of Morris, Voysey and Mackintosh were given a new dynamism. 'Our guiding principle was that artistic design is neither an intellectual nor a material affair, but simply an integral part of the stuff of life. Further, that the revolution in aesthetics has given us fresh insight into the meaning of design, just as the mechanization of industry has provided new tools for its realization. Our ambition was to rouse the creative artist from his other-worldliness and reintegrate him into the workaday world of realities.' So wrote Walter Gropius of the Bauhaus, that wonderful school which, for fourteen years, first at Weimar and then at Dessau where under Hitler it died in 1933, was a laboratory of applied design for the whole world. Here worked architects, typographers, painters, photographers, stage-designers, sculptors, weavers, potters. 'The object of the Bauhaus was not to propagate any "style", system, dogma, formula or vogue, but simply to exert a revitalizing influence on design' wrote Gropius, '... we sought the vital spark of life behind life's ever-changing forms.'

Most of the Bauhaus work now seems mannered and dated, but it was through the Bauhaus

Continued on p. 39

ANARCHISM: Mikhail Bakunin (1814–1876).

ACADEMIC ART: 1. *Il-y-en a toujours un autre*, 1882, by Marcus
Stone, R.A. (1840–1921).

2. *A Favourite Custom*, by Sir Lawrence Alma-Tadema (1836–1912).

THE ABSOLUTE: 1. Immanuel Kant (1724–1804). The German Idealist philosopher.

2. G. W. F. Hegel (1770–1831), who described the Absolute as 'a night in which all cows are black'.

ANTIQUITY: 1. *Ruins of the Serapeon of Canopus.* From an etching by G. B. Piranesi (1720–1778).

2. *The Bank of England as a Classical Ruin*, by J. M. Gandy (1771–1843).

29

The presentation of Ani, the dead man, to Osiris. The god is enthroned within a shrine, and behind h

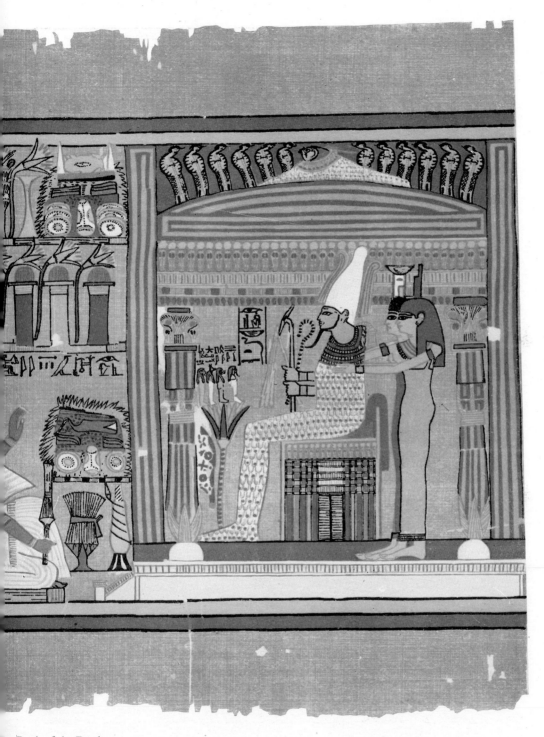

...e Book of the Dead.
...d Nephthys. In front there is a lotus flower, on which are the four children of Horus, genii of the dead.

ART IN INDUSTRY: William Morris (1834–1896) – on the right – with Burne-Jones. 'Have nothing in your house' said Morris, 'which you do not know to be useful, or believe to be beautiful.'

ART FOR ART'S SAKE: Algernon Charles Swinburne (1837–1909). A *Vanity Fair* cartoon by Ape. 'The art of poetry has absolutely nothing to do with didactic matter at all.'

ART IN INDUSTRY: *Early examples from the Great Exhibition, 1851.*

An engine in the Egyptian taste, by B. Hick & Son of Bilton.

Right : a sideboard of gutta-percha, made by the Gutta Percha Company.

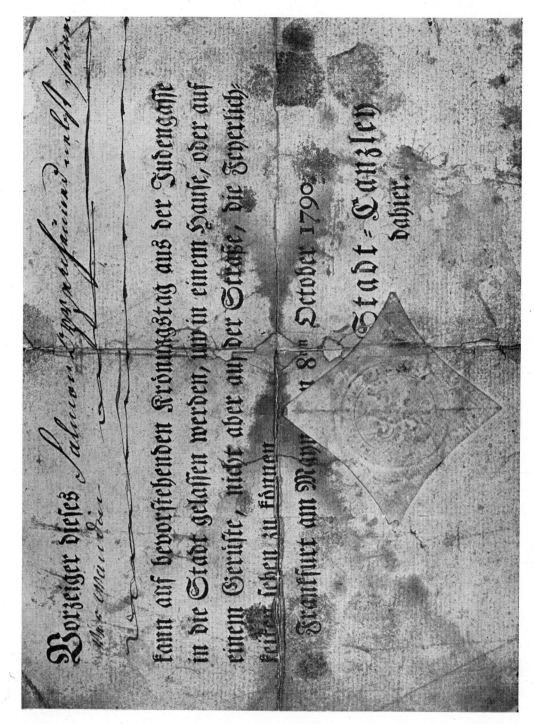

ANTI-SEMITISM: 1. A pass issued to Jews at Frankfurt in 1790.

2. Inscription on the town wall of Rothenburg, Germany. The placard shows a Jew clutching a bag of money, and the text reads:: *Making big profits, Greed & craftiness is my business. I like celebrating, eating & drinking and like buying nice girls. My oath does not mean a thing—in fact nothing is too low for me.*

ANTI-SEMITISM: 3. Jews being forced to scrub the streets of Vienna in 1938.

PLATE 1

that the profession of industrial designer came into being.

Reaffirmations of an ideal unity were not confined to Germany. The Bauhaus itself was reconstituted in the United States – where Louis Sullivan had first coined the phrase 'form follows function' and where Frank Lloyd Wright was creating a new, free architecture. It was to be seen in Holland, in the *De Stijl* movement, and in Scandinavia, where industrial units are small and a genuine crafts-movement produced furniture, glass and textiles that were the envy of the world. Individual firms, moved usually by individual owners or administrators, such as Frank Pick in the London Underground organization or Olivetti, the maker of typewriters in Italy, and individual designers such as Marcel Breuer, who made the first metal chairs, or Alvo Aalto in Finland who showed new uses for laminated ply-wood, have given the movement additional impetus.

Since the Second World War, it has become widely accepted that the designer should take his place as one of the production team responsible for all new manufactures, from aeroplanes to handbags, bus-tickets to park seats, kettles to carpets, and the training provided by leading art schools everywhere has become accordingly more technical. It seems fitting that Great Britain, first in the Industrial Revolution and first to voice dissatisfaction with its products, should be the first nation to sponsor an official Council of Industrial Design, set up in 1944 and charged 'to promote by all practicable means the improvement of design in the products of British industry'.

What are the tenets of this now-respectable ideal in the mid-twentieth century? First, design must be functional – not with the austerity of the 'twenties, when le Corbusier called the house 'a machine for living in', but nevertheless it must be conditioned by its purpose. Second, truth to material and to method – metal should not be made to look like wood, machine-turned ornament should not ape hand-made ornament. Third, acceptance of new materials and new techniques with all their challenge of new solutions to old problems. Design today is characterized by the freedom born of confidence, a fully plastic, three-dimensional sense of form, a sense of decoration that relies for its effect upon contrasts of material and texture, and bright, gay colours. Throughout

C

the Western world there is coming into being a common language of form in which painting, sculpture, architecture and the crafts meet. It is the beginning of a new tradition.

ILLUSTRATION: Pages 32, 34 and 35.

Alone with God

ASCETICISM – or the true asceticism – Evelyn Underhill has said, is a mental and spiritual gymnastic, not the mortification of the flesh; it remains close to its origin in *askesis*, the training of the athlete, and its exponents are *athletae Dei*, the athletes of God.

It need be no more of an obsession than the discipline recommended by Socrates in the *Phaedo*; as such, it is far removed from the extreme practices of some of the anchorites of the Egyptian deserts in the fourth and fifth centuries A.D., which aroused the malicious irony of Gibbon and moved Lecky to write of an 'ascetic epidemic', with its 'hideous, distorted and emaciated' practitioners who rejected all natural feelings and social responsibilities in favour of an interminable routine of 'useless and atrocious self-torture'.

It was a wiser life than this that had the effect of drawing men to the desert – the life, in fact, of St Anthony, who died in 356 and whose story came into St Augustine's hands thirty years later, with the result that Augustine describes in his *Confessions*: 'I had no mind to read further; nor was there need' – for to him it was the inner renunciation alone which counted. Augustine did not need a hermitage, or an eccentric perch like the pillar of St Simeon Stylites.

There were many to sing the praises of St Simeon, especially during his own lifetime, as a very angel upon earth, a miracle, the glory of Antioch and Syria. Even before he ascended the pillar to which he was chained in 423, he was so renowned for his sanctity that vermin dropped from his body as he walked, and he had already spent a period during which he was chained in a cave, with 'twenty fat bugs' lurking in the leather of his thong; and also for a while he buried himself daily in a trench.

Once aloft, St Simeon had the height of his pillar gradually lengthened from four cubits to forty, and at its top he is said to have been able to touch his feet with his forehead over a thousand times in succession – when he was not dictating letters on theological points to his disciples. Although Simeon was acknowledged to be the most holy martyr in the air, this exhibitionism was soon copied. Thalelaeus lived for ten years in a tub suspended from poles, bent double because of his corpulence. Others placed themselves on rock ledges so that if they fell asleep they would be in danger of falling.

The monks of Syria and Mesopotamia were especially vigorous in their practices. Some, under the theory that if they copied the madness of Nebuchadnezzar they would recover their lost likeness to God, became Grazing Monks and fed on grass. Acepsimas was eventually killed by a shepherd, who thought he was a wolf, for he had lived for sixty years alone in his cell. A certain Cyriacus used to stand for hours on one leg, until he fainted.

Amongst these extreme interpreters of muscular Christianity, whose lives were *pietatis palaestrae*, holy wrestling-rings, the one about whom the most fascinating stories are told is Macarius, in whom mere ardour was tempered both by geniune piety and occasional revelations of a competitive spirit. Having intemperately killed a gnat which stung him, Macarius punished himself by living for six months in the marshes of the Nile. An Arab writer recorded, at a much later date, the tradition that he never ate fresh bread, but dined instead off 'old shoes softened in a mess of palm leaves'. When he visited the monks of Tabennisi in disguise, he was first refused admission as too frail for their way of life. This annoyed him; and soon, having noticed the various austerities around him, he combined them with such success that the monks were so humiliated and enraged that they threatened to leave.

One can understand how those of humanist persuasion would be revolted by the ascetic way of life, killing the body because the body wishes to kill the soul. Thus some time after the fall of Rome the young pagan, Rutilius, was sailing through the western Mediterranean when he came to the island of Capraja, where a monastery had recently been built. His disgust caused him to write a fierce poem against this place, 'squalid with fugitives from light', where he saw only mental perversity, conscience and the black gall of dismal guts. Later he passed another island, Gorgona, where a friend of his now lived as an anchorite, lost to the world; he addressed him as a credulous fool, who believed that Heaven fed upon filth, and who followed a creed worse than Circe's, since it turned souls instead of bodies into beasts. Nor was this criticism merely that of the sensuous pagan against the ugliness of piety; it might be called that of the political and social man directed against those who run away from the awkwardnesses of life.

Classical philosophies and religions had long known various degrees of asceticism, from the discipline of Sparta to the rites connected with the Vestal Virgins of Rome; purification was an exceedingly ancient idea. To the Pythagoreans life was a continuous trial by which Man freed the divine spark within him and subjected his earthly impulses to his reason; the Stoics and the Epicureans alike demanded vigorous discipline; Plotinus wished Man to purge himself in order that he might achieve the divine union. But most classical attitudes were essentially social – Man existed in a community, and expressed himself through social action.

The rise of asceticism in early Christian times was a reaction against the corruption and insecurity offered by the world and its cities, since Constantine had accepted Christianity and made it official, altering its revolutionary and chiliastic emphasis; it was even a reaction to the Church itself, with its hierarchy of mediators and their ambitions and intrigues. So the curious situation arose that, when a saintly hermit became famous for his austerities, there was often a tug-of-war between the Church officials who wanted him for a bishop, and the man himself who wished to remain in solitude. The desert was enamelled with the flowers of Christ, solitude was paradise, the bliss of angels; to be visited often by men was to be deprived of the angelic society, to live in a city was as bad as imprisonment.

Yet these devotees, who believed that only God and themselves existed in the whole world, were answered by one of themselves when Anthony said: 'With our neighbour is life and death.' And it must at least be admitted that these Eastern searchers-out of the trackless places of the Thebaid, of Celle and Nitria, were often spiritual as well as physical gymnasts; magnanimity, humility and gentleness were their glories, as well as emaciated bodies and verminous heads.

When asceticism became absorbed into the great monastic orders it lost much of its individualism; it became a matter of chastity and frugality, of Trappist silence, of the routine of work and prayer and, in a different situation, of the arduous Jesuit training. Yet the exceptional man or woman still appeared, taking very seriously that remark of Origen that 'All evil which reigns in the body is due to the five senses'. The proud Thomas à Becket wore a hair-shirt next his skin, and when he lay on his bier in Canterbury Cathedral, the chronicler tells us, you could see on the flagstones the lice that had deserted his cooling body. To the monk, the body could scarcely be more than St Francis's 'poor Brother Ass', although it might be thought to be incorruptible, like the body of Father Zosima in *The Brothers Karamazov* by Dostoyevsky.

Puritan frugality grew parallel with Catholic, even if it never indulged in the transports of negation: there was an asceticism of the Presbyterian Sunday, of witch-hunting, of the making and keeping of money, of a strange ambivalence towards women. All through history human beings have found it necessary to come to terms with the body: primitive peoples have their initiation ceremonies, where maturity is signalized by the victory of the spirit over pain and mutilation, or where ordeals are suffered in order to confirm one's manliness (the Polynesian tattooing-ceremonies, the beating-games amongst the negroes of Sierra Leone); the same thing extends to the initiations in American college fraternities or to the hardening processes attributed to the public schools.

Often, however, these involve only a temporary deprivation and are not designed to condemn the body but to control it, to make it an effective instrument. Religious asceticism, which occurs in most human faiths, usually does more – as with the Indian Sadu, Fakir and Sannyasi, or in the ritual disciplines of Islam, the fast of Ramadan, the Salat, the Pilgrimage to Mecca and, more particularly, the special fanaticism of individual sects.

On the other hand, increasingly secular societies may invent new asceticisms. One of the more benign of these is that of the cowboy hero who sings, shoots, rides but never makes love to a girl; another is that of the tough, cynical and by no means conventionally moral detective who chooses a role of continuous violence and violent suffering, being beaten up and betrayed from day to day; and this in turn relates to the Hemingway character, with his elaborate code of honour, who stoically copes with the women, animals and drinking bouts he encounters. There is today an ascetic scientist, close to the magic of Superman, or an ascetic doctor, or an ascetic airman, all of whom partake of the nature of a *deus ex machina*. It is now more important to be expert than to be pious, and the modern cloister is a streamlined chromium affair, a space-ship or a laboratory or a clinic, over whose entrance is written not Rabelais' 'Do what you will', but 'Will what you do'.

To these super-terrestrial purlieus Romanticism in decay occasionally contributes the idea that sex is something to be *suffered*. We are made aware that sexual passion can be a torture-chamber; Aldous Huxley has devoted novel after novel to this special combination of science and nausea, of vomit and stainless steel.

ILLUSTRATION: Plate 13.

The existence of God

ATHEISM is a term applied accurately to the beliefs of those who deny the existence of God; inaccurately to those who merely deny current conceptions of deity.

In this latter use it is really a theological swear-word. So Socrates and the early Christians were both in their time accused of atheism because they questioned popular religious practices. Yet the connection between the two uses of the term is not accidental. The earliest criticism of religion is always a criticism of this or that conception of God as inadequate. It is a later development that sees all conceptions of God as inadequate and hence dismisses the notion of divinity as nonsensical. In the ancient world there is little or no denial of the existence of a supreme being, although Strato (c. 287 B.C.) seems to identify that being with Nature itself. It is only indeed in the eighteenth-century materialist philosophers that atheism became a self-conscious and aggressive doctrine. Here again it is important to distinguish between those who dismiss the idea of a supreme being altogether and those who quarrel with all orthodox conceptions of God, yet still cling to some view of such a being.

Spinoza (1632–1677) is the outstanding example of those philosophers with whom it is most difficult to make this distinction. For him God and Nature were ultimately one being, *Deus sive Natura*, and some have seen in him an atheistic thinker who makes 'God' merely another name for Nature, while to others he has been 'the God-intoxicated man' who saw in all nature the being of God. The issues raised by Spinoza were put sharply by the German thinker, Ludwig Feuerbach (1804–1872), who insisted that if God and Nature were one being, then the true name of that being is – 'nature'!

Feuerbach saw the idea of God as essentially a product of human experience, a misleading distortion of human ideals into theological form. In such an assertion as 'God is Love' Feuerbach held there was a true content, namely an assertion of the ultimate importance of love in human life. So he proceeded systematically to translate all theological assertions into statements about human life. In seeing religion as entirely a product of human needs and experience, Feuerbach put the essential atheistic position. His materialism was the most important influence upon Karl Marx's interpretation of religion as a product of man's experience of exploitation and a consolation for the sufferings involved—'the opium of the people.'

As a philosophical doctrine, atheism is not to be confused with agnosticism, a term coined by T. H. Huxley to describe the views of those who hold that we have not enough evidence to decide whether there is or is not a God. To this the atheist would reply that all the evidence is already available, and it is upon the basis of this that a decision must be made. A decision must be made because action depends on the belief that either there is or there is not a God. The choice therefore lies between atheism and theism. A sceptical thinker like David Hume (1711–1776), who re-

fused to accept that the absence of positive grounds for belief justified atheism, would do so because atheism seems to claim just such a knowledge of the ultimate nature of things as makes theism objectionable. Hume would also have argued that some belief in some kind of God seems to lurk in everyone. When he dined with Baron d'Holbach, the materialist philosopher, in Paris, he could say, 'As for atheists, I don't believe there are any, I have never seen one.' 'You've been a little unlucky,' replied d'Holbach, 'there are seventeen dining with you tonight.'

With eighteenth-century thinkers the criticism of religion was primary. They were atheists first, and then, because they rejected the religious account of the world, they sought another account. With later thinkers it has been otherwise. They give a non-religious account of the world and then, on the basis of such an account, reject religious claims. So contemporary Marxism is atheistic because it believes that it can settle all questions without recourse to religion, and contemporary Existentialism is sometimes atheistic because it believes that a true account of the nature of man makes belief in God impossible. This raises an earlier objection to God's existence – that which argues that if there is a God who rules the world, then man is a mere plaything of deity whose purposes are imposed on him from without. Bakunin, the anarchist opponent of Marx, put the argument for atheism thus: 'If there is a God, man is a slave; but man is free, therefore there is no God.' In such an argument there appears the conviction that human freedom is real only if there is no divinity, a conviction which made the loss of belief in God in the nineteenth century seem to many like the lifting of a burden, a genuine liberation.

Atheism is not necessarily synonymous with irreligion. Primitive Buddhism seems to have had within it a deep sense of wonder and reverence, and a religious view of human destiny, but to have lacked any belief in God and perhaps to have denied, positively, divine existence. In much modern atheism there is also an almost religious fervour.

Only within the last hundred years has atheism not been subject to civil disabilities. The need to swear religious oaths on taking public office meant that atheists could hold such offices only at the cost of hypocrisy. When in 1880 Charles Bradlaugh was elected to the House of Commons, his refusal as an atheist to take a religious oath led to a struggle of six years before he was finally allowed to take his seat. It was in the course of the debates on Bradlaugh that the case against atheism was re-stated by a member as, 'Mr Speaker, Sir, we all believe in some sort of a something.' It is, in fact, among the principal contentions of the atheist that religious belief must be reduced to a belief in 'some sort of a something', and that such a belief is practical atheism.

It is often asserted that the spread of atheism would lead to a decline in morality, since belief in God as the author of the moral law is the ultimate moral sanction. That there is no immediate connection between atheism and lack of moral sense is obvious from the high principles of such pioneers as Bradlaugh. But the gradual loss of religious belief in Western Europe has not yet become positive atheism. Only if it does so will it be possible to investigate the alleged connection between atheistic beliefs and moral practices. It is, of course, questionable whether religion in the West will continue to decline; but even if there is a revival of orthodoxy, it will be an orthodoxy which has had to learn from atheist criticism. It would be difficult to underestimate the debt of mankind to atheism as a purifying force in religion, as a source of criticism of fallacious argument, and as a doctrine productive of tolerance.

ILLUSTRATION: Page 86.

Atlantis and Shangri-La

ATLANTIS is the name of a large island supposed formerly to exist in the Atlantic opposite the Straits of Gibraltar. The story is one of the most ancient and certainly the most powerful of the legends of lost islands and lost paradises. If we examine this one legend in detail, we may see what lies behind all of them, and thus understand what makes their appeal to the imagination so great.

The first and indeed the only source of the legend is Plato who, in the *Timaeus* and the unfinished *Critias*, uses it to illustrate a moral: about 11,000 years ago there existed a large island oppo-

site the Pillars of Hercules called Atlantis, mountainous in places, but with a great central plain stretching on one side to the sea. The whole island was fertile, well-watered and temperate, and it abounded with precious metals, including one now unknown to us, called *orichalc*, which glowed like fire. On this island dwelt a race of men descended from the sea-god Poseidon, to whom the island was sacred. The Atlanteans were industrious and virtuous, and lived happily together for many generations. They were very wealthy. The capital city was adorned with temples and halls, and there were great dockyards, for, although inland, it was connected by a canal with the sea. The plain was irrigated by a complex system of canals which enabled the farmers to harvest two crops in the year.

At length, however, the divine strain in their blood grew weak, and the Atlanteans became corrupted by the sins of pride, lust and greed. They grew ambitious for empire, and thus came into contact with the Greece of that time and its inhabitants. Plato first describes Attica as being itself fertile and wooded, not bare and barren as it is today, and says that it was inhabited by a hard-working agricultural and pastoral people. In the war which followed, the Greeks were at last victorious; but before it came to an end, there was a great earthquake and deluge. Greece was denuded of its rich soil, and in one day the whole island of Atlantis was swallowed up by the sea. This terrible destruction was sent by Zeus as a punishment for the sins of the Atlanteans.

There are periodic references to the story later in antiquity, and in medieval times; but not until the early eighteenth century do people seem to have seriously asked if the story was true, and to have tried to locate the position of Atlantis. Olavus Rudbeck, a Swede, claimed in his book *Atland* (1702) that Atlantis was Sweden, and its capital Uppsala. He, and the French *philosophe* Jean Sylvain Bailly (1736–1793), who placed Atlantis in Spitzbergen, reasoned in part from the theory that the earth is rapidly cooling. The English antiquarian William Stukeley (1687–1765), for his part, argued in 1740 that Atlantis was to be identified with Britain and Ireland. Cadet, writing in 1787, first placed it where Plato says it was, and held that the Canaries and the Azores are the tops of the mountains of Atlantis.

Since that time books and pamphlets have multiplied. It was estimated in 1926 that there were no less than 1,700 extant works on Atlantis, and we may now reasonably suppose that the number is nearer 2,000. Of these perhaps the most famous is *Atlantis: the Antediluvian World* (1882) by Ignatius Donnelly, an American. He argued that Atlantis was the home of all the arts and sciences of mankind; that 'the gods and goddesses of the ancient Greeks, the Hindus, the Phoenicians and the Scandinavians were simply the kings, queens and heroes of Atlantis; and the acts attributed to them in mythology are a confused recollection of real historical events'; that Egypt was colonized from Atlantis; and that the destruction of Atlantis is the source of the Flood legends which are so widespread. Other authors have at one time or another identified Atlantis with America, with North Africa, with Nigeria or with Crete. The main interest in recent years has, however, remained with Atlantis as the Atlantic isle now sunk beneath the ocean.

The passionate intensity with which so many books have been written on so vague and uncertain a subject shows that Atlantis must express ideas of great potency. It must represent something which to many is important; in fact, there are not one but many constituents of the legend of Atlantis which have this compelling force. Some of these Atlantis shares with other legendary lands and islands.

To begin with, there is the idea of an innocent world where all were happy and good. This element is not explicitly present in Plato's account, but it has been added by more recent enthusiasts. In the words of Donnelly: 'It was the true antediluvian world; the Garden of Eden, the Gardens of the Hesperides; the Elysian Fields; the Gardens of Alcinous: the Mesomphalos; the Olympus; the Asgard of the traditions of the ancient nations; representing a universal memory of a great land, where early mankind dwelt for ages in peace and happiness.' Atlantis was, in fact, the site of the Golden Age, the kingdom of Saturn which we all believe in our bones to have existed.

In some of the other related legends this primeval world is still there, just beyond the horizon. St Brendan's Isle, out in the Atlantic beyond Ireland, or the Portuguese Antilia, the island of the Seven Cities, supposedly colonized by the Bishop of Oporto when the Arabs invaded Spain, were firmly believed in throughout the Middle Ages. Shangri-La, the secret valley where the treasures of the world will be preserved through the coming collapse of civilization, is still attainable if only we knew where to look; it is a haven still open to the seeker after happiness. And here it may be mentioned that many of the more mystical and less coldly rational advocates of Atlantis believe that the arcane secrets originally mastered in that country are still preserved by a group of initiates hidden somewhere in the world.

But Atlantis itself is lost for ever, drowned like the Breton valley of Ys, or like Lyonesse,

A land of old upheaven from the abyss,
By fire to sink into the abyss again,

which lay between Cornwall and France. It is irrecoverably buried in the remote past, denied to us like Eden. It is again like Eden in that it was lost to us as a consequence of sin, the sin of those who dwelt in it. But unlike Eden, it was not simply shut away from us: it was utterly destroyed. This destruction, like the destruction of Sodom and Gomorrah, provokes satisfaction at the punishment of transgressors, and at the same time awe at the terrible magnificence of its scope. Our secret terror of death by drowning, and our knowledge of the power of the ocean to drown the whole world, intensify our fascination.

Again, the legend of Atlantis gains by its very character of remoteness and uncertainty. Suppose it were proved that Atlantis existed, suppose we were to find a detailed account of its history and inhabitants, then most of those people who are now drawn to it would lose interest; they would move on to some still remoter mystery, such, for instance, as that of the Pacific continent of Mu, from which, according to some accounts, Atlantis itself was colonized.

ILLUSTRATION: Page 72.

Pioneers; and 'the advanced fool-farm'

AVANT-GARDE – *i.e.* 'advance guard' – is a term and a notion borrowed from warfare and applied to cultural, intellectual and artistic activities. It has been in general use, accepted and understood, having a definite meaning for both artists and public, since the latter half of the nineteenth century.

The idea of an *avant-garde*, of a group of artists who are in advance, in aims and technique, of their fellow-artists and of the public taste, grew up with the formation of new 'schools' of painting and writing (particularly in France) whose products it seemed impossible for the public to understand without first undergoing a radical readjustment of values. At the time of their inception it did not seem possible that these schools would ever be understood or accepted – least of all enjoyed as art should be enjoyed – since they did not sufficiently induce the public to make that necessary readjustment. The *avant-garde* shocks rather than soothes the sensibilities of its audience. But it is precisely in order to bring this about, to create a receptive body of taste and opinion in which it is possible to work, that the *avant-gardiste* makes himself apparently unacceptable.

To use the term at all implies a state of misunderstanding, almost a state of warfare, between artist and public, or artist and traditional critic, or between artists who wish to follow new ideas and those who are content to work within the bounds of theories already in existence, familiar and hallowed by use. The clash between the traditional and the experimental, the conflict which generates the energy of a new movement, is made clear in the review of a French art-critic, writing in 1876. 'The Rue de Peletier', he complained, 'is a road of disasters. After the fire at the Opéra, there is now yet another disaster there. An exhibition has just been opened at Durand-Ruel which allegedly contains paintings. I enter and my horrified eyes behold something terrible. Five or six lunatics, among them a woman, have joined together and exhibited their works ... These would-be artists call themselves revolutionaries, 'Impressionists'. They take a piece of canvas, colour and brush, daub a few patches of colour on them at random, and sign the whole thing with their name.'

This was a typical sally in the skirmish between artists and public: it was the voice of outraged tradition. The 'would-be artists', Monet, Manet, Dégas, Renoir and all the painters who filled the 'Salon of the Rejected' (opened in 1865, when the Salon proper refused to exhibit Manet), triumphed; and Impressionists are now highly respectable. Earlier, in 1855, Gustave Courbet had fired a broadside at tradition with a one-man show given in a Paris shack, and entitled simply: '*Le Réalisme*, G. Courbet.'

An *avant-garde* movement comes into being at a certain point in the development of an art. That point is generally when a tradition is being worked out, when it is growing stale or enervated, and is no longer capable of expressing fully the artistic needs of the age. The time is then ripe for experiment and progress based upon advances already made. By issuing proclamations, making a stir, enraging critics, catching the public eye (frequently by outrageous means), and by the familiar guerrilla tactics of artists thirsting for blood, an *avant-garde* movement can do valuable service in stimulating the discussion, argument and controversy which are essential to the healthy growth of art. They fling open windows and let fresh air in upon stale topics and wilting theories. On the other hand, an *avant-garde* movement ceases to be either effective or serious when its members overlook the vital continuity of art; it is the fact that however many offshoots there may be, only one painting, one poetry and one sculpture exist; their true development is in the nature of organic growth, it does not come by a series of cataclysmic upheavals.

The *avant-garde* mentality, the crusading desire to abolish shoddy standards, to encompass unknown territories of endeavour and to bring about a reconciliation between the artist and his public on the highest possible terms, finds its greatest opportunity for expression when tradition and experiment overlap, and both traditional and experimental elements require to be fused into a stable pattern, so that art may continue.

Genuine *avant-garde* movements, such as Impressionism in painting, or the group of very considerable writers, among them T. S. Eliot and James Joyce and Wyndham Lewis in the early years of this century, give full value to the importance of continuity in experiment, tempering their enthusiasm and eagerness to be ahead with a respect for tradition and scholarship. Such movements, after the initial stages of hysteria and excess which mark all 'new' movements, produce work of enduring value. The movement itself is regarded by its initiators as merely a part of the historical process of creation, and is disbanded as soon as its objective is achieved.

A second type of *avant-gardiste* aims simply to '*épater le bourgeois*'; W. H. Auden has warned the eager that the *avant-garde* is not always right, and frequently the *avant-gardiste* mistakes vigour for judgement and a bold statement of principle for an inspired practical application of that principle. His passionate desire to tabulate new, true and just laws for art often nullifies his ability to assess their value, and the value of those laws which they replace.

Frequently the *avant-gardiste* is something still worse: he is in the words of Wyndham Lewis, 'a scarecrow of an advanced fool-farm', a parasite, a minor figure concealing ineptitude in freakishness.

In a sense, of course, it is true to say that every age produces its *avant-garde*, the great originals who work twenty or thirty or fifty years in advance of their time, struggle for recognition, and at length receive the posthumous respectability always accorded to artists long enough dead. Wordsworth was as much of an *avant-gardiste* as Eliot; Gerard Manley Hopkins wrote far in advance of contemporary understanding or sympathy; and Chaucer was possibly the most daring inaugurator of them all.

B

Nymphs and milkmaids

'BACK TO THE LAND' has been a political catch-phrase, a literary and sociological aspiration, and a sentimental attitude.

> I sits with my feet in a brook;
> If anyone asks me for why,
> I hits him a whack with my crook –
> 'It's Sentiment kills me,' says I.

As a slogan it is first perhaps associated with the doctrines of the American writer on social and economic problems, Henry George (1839–1897). He was born in Philadelphia, went to sea, settled in California as a printer, and progressed into editorship and active campaigning in public affairs. In 1871 he published *Our Land Policy*, and developed his theme in *Progress and Poverty*, published in 1879. This had wide influence not only in America but also in Europe. He followed it by a work *Protection or Free Trade* in 1886. He had no political ambitions, but in 1886 received independent nomination as mayor of Greater New York, and was very nearly elected. He was immensely popular.

George's idea was that the land in each country belonged by right to the people of that country. Private ownership in land was no more appropriate than private ownership in air or sunshine. It had no foundation in morality or reason. But the private occupancy and use of lands were indispensable, and equal shares of land were unworkable. What was wanted was the general use of rent for the benefit of all, whether landowning or not. George proposed a tax on land so as to appropriate economic rent to public uses; he proposed also the abolition of all taxes falling upon industry and thrift. This theory he propounded in Great Britain as well as America, and also in Australia. He founded a paper to propagate his views. Politically, 'Back to the Land' became a catch-phrase for all politicians with a rural bias, and had some revival (after the war of 1914–1918) with English Liberals under the ex-Prime Minister David Lloyd George, seeking to re-establish the importance of the countryside in the eyes of what was by now a mainly urban electorate.

This special and local exploitation of a phrase is only an aspect of the recognition of the importance of agriculture which has existed ever since urban societies first came about. The city-states of Sumeria arose as a result of the invention of agriculture. London, the greatest city in the world, presumed an agricultural background, no less than Ur, Akkad or Babylon. This was recognized, and all early societies in Europe were based on land tenure; the possession of land, and its administration, were government.

Agriculture, or the land, is still fundamental;

but a break came in the eighteenth century, and in England. The Industrial Revolution brought with it a whole new society engaged in the mills and factories of the North and Midlands. The trees were blackened, the fields were dirty patches, and no longer unenclosed common land. Whole generations grew up living in back-to-back tenements, and had hardly seen the country at all. These people had no political influence. However, their masters, the mill-owners and the big manufacturers, did have an increasingly powerful influence. The wealthy agricultural oligarchs who ruled England ('the Country Interest') therefore sought to restrict this influence, and to them 'back to the land' meant a return to pre-industrial society.

Even when it had become evident that the British Isles had become a primarily urban and industrial society, there were still voices urging an attempt to make the United Kingdom provide enough food for its population from its own resources. Such voices came from the farmers (by then usually prosperous only in war-time), the Liberal Party, and such independents as G. K. Chesterton, riding back-forward into the future. In some respects they echoed the sturdy sentiments of William Cobbett (1804–1865), who had first christened London 'the Great Wen', and had denounced urbanization.

'Back to the Land' in its sociological sense took on a new reality during the bombing of the Second World War, when evacuation brought to the countryside, as refugees, thousands of town-dwellers. Reactions on both sides were mixed, but for a time this reversed the 'drift to the towns' and the picture of the country-dweller as an ignorant hayseed. This conception had run parallel, in the mass mind, with a sentimentalized view of rural life which had for long dominated much literature.

Admiration amongst authors for life in the country was first a genuine and justified feeling. It found early expression in the works of Virgil (70–19 B.C.). Of him the essayist Abraham Cowley (1618–1667) wrote: 'The first wish of Virgil (as you will find anon by his verses), was to be a good philosopher; the second, a good husbandman; and God (whom he seemed to understand better than most of the learned heathens) dealt with him just as he did "with Solomon" – that is,

gave him both. Many nations have lived', Cowley goes on, 'and some still do, without any art but this (agriculture); not so elegantly, I confess, but still they live; and almost all the other arts which are here practised are beholding to them for most of their materials. The innocence of this life is the next thing for which I commend it, and if husbandmen perceive not that, they are much to blame, for no men are so free from the temptations of iniquity.'

Yet by the time of Cowley, the courts and the poets belonged to the town. A note of artificiality crept into the approach to nature: nymphs and swains were idealized as something very different from real countrymen. Even Herrick, writing in a Devonshire he disliked, could say

> O happy life! if that their good
>   The husbandman but understood!
>   Who all the day themselves do please ...

The note, half false, half genuine, continued. Great poets, and many good minor poets, continued to look back to the land for inspiration; and the 'nature poets' sang its virtues gloriously against the growing domination of the town.

Their successors often lacked equal observation or sincerity, and by the beginning of the twentieth century a sentimentality and insincerity had crept into much 'nature-writing' and much poetry – sometimes by the 'week-end poets', who were townsmen escaping 'back to the land' for feeble and mannered inspiration. A bucolic school struck an even less convincing note with false heartiness of appreciation for a country scene already disappearing into the Folk Museum.

Cosmic events may force a change in society again, leading man back to the land. In any case its appreciation, and the desire to go back there, are basic, and necessarily so, in the human situation.

ILLUSTRATION: Page 167.

Between the scales and the see-saw

BALANCE OF POWER denotes power so evenly distributed among the leading nations that no one state, or group of allied states, is significantly stronger than any opposing group. It was a commonplace of international politics, before 1914, that this balance was desirable; and that if any state began to build up an overpowering force it was the duty of the other states to build up their own and, if necessary, combine to balance it.

The idea was familiar in ancient Greece, whose city-states made and broke alliances simply to prevent any one of their number dominating the rest. As a result, Greek wars were complicated and inconsistent; any state might suddenly decide that its own allies were winning too fast, and might accordingly change sides. Eventually the Greek states, balancing power between them to the last, were swallowed by Macedonia, which became stronger than all of them put together.

In the fifteenth century the balance of power again became an important feature of politics. The little Italian states of the Renaissance combined against each other to prevent any one of them becoming supreme; thus they delayed the unification of Italy by four hundred years, and handed over their country to the rule of Spaniards and Austrians. If they had all combined, they might have been a match for the enemy; but they were too busy maintaining the balance against their next-door neighbours.

From the sixteenth century the balance of power was an accepted principle of European politics. Any country that looked like becoming too strong was attacked by a combination of the others. This happened to Spain in the sixteenth century, France in the seventeenth and Britain in the eighteenth. Rather than allow one Christian state to become dangerously powerful, the Christian nations of Europe allowed south-eastern Europe to be conquered by Turkey, the Mohammedan enemy of all Christian states alike. Moslem pirates from North Africa were allowed to terrorize the whole Mediterranean as late as the French Revolution. All peaceful countries would have benefited if the pirates had been swept from the seas, as they easily could have been; but the principle of the balance of power made it necessary for one Christian state to make an alliance with the Turks against the rest.

During the nineteenth century the principle was still firmly upheld. It was simply to preserve the balance of power that Britain entered the Crimean War. Towards the end of the century the European powers began to form themselves into two big groups, which had become two hostile camps shortly after 1900. Neither group had any particularly aggressive intentions, but each was afraid of the aggressive intentions of the other; and each group piled up armaments to prevent the balance tilting against it. The result of this arms race, and of the fear and suspicion that accompanied it, was the First World War.

Most British statesmen were closely concerned with the balance of power. In the middle of the eighteenth century the philosopher Hume had laid down that it was founded 'on common sense and obvious reasoning'. In 1907 Sir Eyre Crowe wrote, 'The only check on the abuse of political predominance [by a powerful and ambitious state] ... has always consisted in the opposition of an equally formidable rival.' He went on to say, 'It has become almost an historical truism to identify England's secular policy with the maintenance of this balance by throwing her weight now in this scale and now in that, but ever on the side opposed to the political dictatorship of the strongest single state or group at a given time.' On the other hand, Sir Edward Grey, Foreign Secretary at that period, never used the phrase 'balance of power' if he could help it, and never consciously pursued the policy.

As an essential principle of European politics, the balance of power did not survive the First World War. It was superseded by the idea of 'collective security', the peace being maintained by all the nations acting together, embodied in the League of Nations. The League failed, because when it came to the point the nations would not act together; but the idea, after the Second World War, was given a new expression in the United Nations (q.v.). The working of the 'balance of power' depends on certain conditions, which do not obtain in the present-day world.

First, there must be a group of nations, each strong enough to make a material difference to the balance if it changes sides. Small states make practically no difference at all. United Italy contributed to the balance; the small, disunited Italian states were unimportant, and could in practice be ignored. At present there are two colossal states, and two others comparatively powerful, but not in the first rank; an insufficient number to operate the balance effectively.

Secondly, there must be a solid base of mutual

agreement between the states concerned. They must have, or think they have, so much in common that they are ready at any time to make an ally out of an enemy, or vice versa. When there is a fundamental cleavage of principle, states no longer aim at a balance; they aim at the supremacy of their own side, even if this means being overshadowed by one of their own allies. In the nineteenth century Britain could side with Russia against France, or with France against Russia, or with both against Germany, as the situation demanded, since the only real quarrel with any of them was the danger of their becoming too powerful. Nowadays our degree of co-operation with America may vary; but it is inconceivable that a free Britain should transfer its support from a free America to a totalitarian Russia. The idea, held by some people, of a 'third force' holding the balance between America and the Soviet Union, appears to many observers quite unrealistic, at least in Europe. If we had still believed in the balance of power, one or other of the allies would have made peace with a defeated but not crushed Germany in 1944 or 1945; but all the allies considered that the preservation of the balance was less important than getting rid of Nazism.

At its best, the balance of power was not a very successful means of ensuring peace. Often it meant that states that ought to have come together in unity were divided by suspicion and intrigue, and fell victims, one by one, to their common enemies from outside. When, as in the nineteenth century, there was no outside enemy strong enough to be dangerous, pursuit of the balance of power led to a world war, which impaired the civilization it was intended to defend. In the western hemisphere the principle has never been applied; no grouping of allies has been effected to offset the rising power of the United States; and the western hemisphere has had an incomparably more peaceful history than Europe. It is obvious that when one nation, such as Germany under Hitler, embarks on a career of ruthless conquest, the other nations must stop it; but it has become equally obvious that concern over the balance of power, as between normally friendly and civilized states, is a cure that is likely to produce the disease.

ILLUSTRATION: Page 124.

'Blubo' and the master race

BLUT UND BODEN, blood and soil, was part of the ideological terminology of the National Socialists' concept of race. Politics, society and law derived all meaning from the racial norm, according to which the accident of a man's birth was the sole determinant of his fitness to be a member of a community.

Hitlerism thus divided mankind into one superior race – the Aryans – and the other inferior slave-races such as the Jews, Slavs and Negroes. That teaching formed the root of Germany's expansionist foreign policy during the Nazi régime; it also inspired its educational, economic and social doctrines. The combination of the theory of race – that is, of 'blood' – as the chief factor in human destiny, with that of the German *Volk* rooted in the soil, gave birth to the slogan *Blut und Boden* or *Blubo*, as it was frequently abbreviated.

The phrase was first used by a German writer, August Winnig, in his *Befreiung*, published in Munich in 1926, in which he says: 'Blood and soil are the destiny of peoples.' The same sentence occurs in another book by Winnig, published in 1928. But the man who did more than anyone else to propagate the idea of *Blut und Boden*, and indeed to turn it into a cult, was Dr Walter Darré, Hitler's Minister of Agriculture. He was late in joining the National Socialist movement; Hitler had been impressed by the writings of this young agricultural economist, with whose ideas on race and soil he was in agreement. Darré was convinced that Germany's salvation lay in the combination of a revival of agriculture and a strengthening of the Nordic type of peasant. Hitler had read Darré's books in which these ideas were developed: *The Peasant as the Life-source of the Nordic Race* (1928) and *The New Nobility of Blood and Soil* (1930). In June 1930 the author was invited to outline his theories at a meeting of Nazi Party leaders, and he did this so impressively that Hitler commissioned him to organize the agrarian policy of the party.

The German peasants had so far shown no inclination to swallow the Nazi teaching. Darré promised them better farming conditions, and at the same time tickled their racial pride by appealing to the peasant's pride of family. 'If this régime can carry through the objectives which I have laid before you,' said Hitler in the Reichstag in March 1933, 'then the peasantry will become the supporting foundation for a new Kingdom of Blood and Soil.'

On 29 September 1933 the Nazis passed a new 'Hereditary Farms Law' (*Reichserbhofsgesetz*) which implemented these ideas. Its preamble stated: 'The indispensable link of Blood and Soil is the indispensable prerequisite for the healthy life of a people.' The law was devised to 'purify' the bloodstream of the peasantry, to fix the peasant's status in a rigid social-economic class hierarchy unalterable except at the discretion of the state, and also to fix his immutable attachment to the soil. The law was supported by two other measures, the institution of a 'National Food Corporation' (*Reichsnährstand*), centralizing all agricultural production and distribution, and of a 'Settlement Programme' by means of which the depopulation of the countryside was to be stopped. Blood and soil were to become the Alpha and Omega of German agriculture. The blood of the peasantry, the Nazis argued, is the principal lifespring from which flows the ever-renewing supply of men to the expanding glory of the Fatherland. The soil tilled by the peasants nourishes all in the tasks which the 'divinely inspired Leader' lays before them.

Hitler's crusade of Blood and Soil was a poor substitute for an economically sound system of agriculture which Germany needed. But its disastrous effects were not merely felt in the realms of economics and agriculture. Darré had studied the breeding of animals, and thought that the experiences gained in improving livestock could be profitably applied also to the improvement of the human race. The 'Hereditary Farms Law' declared that whoever aspired to hereditary farmholding must observe certain selective conditions in mating. The bride must possess certain minimal mental and physical requisites. The male heirs to peasant holdings must satisfy certain racial standards. Darré also introduced a new type of professional man, distinct from doctors, the *Zuchtwart*, or breeding expert, whose task it was to guide and control 'the preservation of Nordic Blood for the improvement of the race'. In a later publication Darré mentioned a new type of functionary, the 'Assistant Generator' (*Zeu-gungshelfer*); he 'has to provide for progeny in the place of a husband who, by reason of illness or owing to any other cause, proves to be incapable of generation'.

Special matrimonial legislation and the institution of 'breeding experts' were enacted for members of the Nazi Party aristocracy, particularly the S.S.; and German girls were grouped in four classes in relation to their racial and eugenic fitness for marriage and child-bearing. The Nuremberg Laws prohibited 'racial disgrace', *i.e.* connubium and extra-marital intimacy between Aryans and 'inferiors' and 'alien' races such as Jews and Negroes. It was entirely in the logic of the sterilization laws and other measures for the 'planned breeding of men' that the ultimate ideal from which Germany and the world were fortunately preserved was what a Berlin physician, Dr Dupré, had called the 'breeding state' (*Züchtungsstaat*), in which procreation and the rearing of children were to be withdrawn from the competence of individual decision and submitted to public regulation.

The whole body of ideas expressed by *Blut und Boden* was deeply rooted in German history. The cult of the soil was a constant theme of German poets and mystics. 'The love of nature is the highest joy of life', wrote Nikolaus Lenau, one among many poetic nature-worshippers. The cult of the land found its peak in the old Germanic mysteries of twilight and darkness, in the sadness of oak and juniper trees, in the macabre pantheism and mysticism of the *Walpurgisnacht*. The Nazis merely extended, and gave a pseudo-scientific form to, popular beliefs long held in Germany.

Rosenberg, the official high-priest of Nazi ideology, wrote in his *Myth of the Twentieth Century*: 'Today a new faith is coming into being: the myth of blood, the faith that the cause of the blood is the cause of the divinity of man. We must recognize that the most profound law of every genuine culture is to give conscious expression to the vegetative vitality of a race.' And he went on to quote the heretical medieval German mystic, Master Eckhart 'The noblest thing in man is his blood, if it wills rightly. If it wills wrongly, it is the vilest.' Master Eckhart was certainly no racialist of the modern kind, but the quotation illustrates the affinity between *Blut und Boden* and mystical spirituality.

It was the special strength of Hitlerism to have identified a transient political movement with the age-old characteristics of the German people. Moreover, the creed of Blood and Soil was calculated to appeal, and did appeal, to the activism and vitalism of modern man, to his impatience with rationalist speculation, and his restlessness. National Socialism claimed to rebel against a liberal democratic society, with its empty formalities, vague catchwords and impotent sentiments. Blood and Soil expressed a *Weltanschauung* of living and doing, of risk, action and conflict, a kind of cosmic energy, both world-creating and world-renewing, which could inspire youth with a belief that the very force of life itself was with them.

It will hardly be denied that several of these Nazi ideas within the idea of *Blut und Boden* express certain aspects vital to any truly human life. Where the Nazis went wrong was in confusing, as it were, 'soil' with 'plant', in regarding the plant as the product of the soil rather than of a seed distinct from the soil and belonging to a higher order. *Blubo*, therefore, became a goddess in her own right, an ultimate reality, the absolute negation of all Christian values enshrined in the concept of man as a free person. Against this *Blubo* declared that the individual was nothing, the state everything.

The mental climate in Germany had been prepared for *Blut und Boden* by Hegel's doctrine of the state, as well as by Nietzsche's cult of natural strength and of the Superman. National Socialism exploited their teaching for its own entirely different ends. But the attack against rationalism, humanism and liberalism to which *Blut und Boden* gave a German form and name was in fact a universal phenomenon of Western society in the late nineteenth and early twentieth centuries. In England George Bernard Shaw extolled what he called the 'life force', and D. H. Lawrence discovered a mystical religiosity in the impulse of the blood and in the vital union of sex. In France, Henri Bergson, the philosopher of the *élan vital*, invested vital instinct with qualities proper to the higher intuition of spirit. Far removed though these writers were from the Teutonic crudities of Blood and Soil, they nonetheless shared in the rebellion against an age that had exalted mechanism to the detriment of life. (See also *Vitalism, Superman, Herrenvolk, Back to the Land.*)

The 'Suspicious Stranger'

BOHEMIANISM was first introduced to the general public as an attractive and amusing way of life by Henri Murger, whose *Scènes de la Vie de Bohème* was published in 1847–1849.

Murger was a renegade bourgeois (he had formerly been a lawyer's clerk) who sentimentalized the disorderly life of artists in the Latin Quarter and made a virtue out of the peculiarities of 'genius', usually as ineffective as it was misunderstood. He thus vulgarized the very real break between the artist and society which was the result both of Romanticism itself and of the relative failure of the revolutionary epoch, enshrined first in the restoration of the monarchy and later in the Second Empire.

Gautier's *Mademoiselle de Maupin* (1835) had declared war on philistine respectability, and Daumier was now caricaturing the commercial classes in his lithographs for *Le Charivari*. In this context Murger's artists lived gaily and irresponsibly with their dreams and their *grisettes*; Schaunard, the composer who would never complete his symphony, 'The Influence of Blue on the Arts', symbolically struck the cracked note on his piano; much of the time was spent on practical jokes and the ingenious cadging of meals from the proprietor of the Café Momus.

Nevertheless, it was Murger's book which drew the Anglo-American artist Whistler to the dilapidated Hotel Corneille, near the Odéon, in 1855. Enthralled with the *vie de bohème*, occasionally visiting Gleyre's studio, spending evenings watching the can-can at the Jardin Bullier or attending a performance of the *Dame aux Camélias*, Whistler found Murger's Mimi in a girl he called Fumette, whose singing her artist friends loved '*si artistement*'.

This phase of Whistler's life can be examined in his fellow student George Du Maurier's *Trilby*, in which he had figured as Joe Sibley 'the idle apprentice, the King of Bohemia, *le roi des truands*' who was 'always in debt', 'eccentric in his attire', and 'like Svengali' vain and witty. But Du Maurier's description of life in the studios went no deeper than Murger's, for his students spent much of their time in gymnastics and boxing-matches; a trapeze, foils and fencing masks were as prominent in their rooms as 'Dante's face and Michelangelo's Leda'.

It was left to George Moore, influenced by the 'mad and morbid literature' of symbolist decadence before he deserted Paris for the 'Fabulous Bohemianism' of Curzon Street, with its 'triumphant champagne, debts, gaslight, supper parties', to add the essential satanic note. Attired in a Japanese dressing-gown, Moore was in the habit of calling his python Jack to feast on a guinea-pig tied to the 'tabouret, pure Louis XV' when he woke in the morning, in order that he might appreciate 'with what exquisite gourmandise he lubricates and swallows'. Perverse fastidiousness and dandyism influenced the bohemian from one side, while, on the other, absinthe, venereal disease and police censorship dragged him down into sordidness.

No one was more bohemian than the French poet Paul Verlaine, the purest of lyricists, who drank himself through a decrepit middle age in filthy lodgings, preyed upon by two prostitutes long past their prime, and who was forced, as winter came on, to seek the shelter of a hospital, where he oscillated between self-pity and mischievous exhibitionism. The bohemian has always sought to excuse himself and to justify himself, his fidelity to his Muse being that of Ernest Dowson to Cynara, to whom he was faithful only in his fashion.

A searching, if somewhat morbid, examination of the relation between bohemianism and art has been attempted by the German novelist Thomas Mann, himself a product of good merchant stock. In story after story Mann harps on the fact that the artist is the result of a decline in the vitality of a family, that he is perverse, incapable of normal feelings and close to the criminal, and yet sometimes poignantly desirous of returning to the flock. In his family chronicle *Buddenbrooks*, the faulty strain produces first a bohemian-dilettante, Christian, and then, in the next generation, a truly gifted boy who dies partly as the result of his devotion to music.

The same type of pretentious, but in a way pathetic and moving, dilettante is caricatured by Mann in his *Tristan*, while the perverse nature of magic and make-believe leads to the tragic ending of *Mario and the Magician*. Von Aschenbach, in Mann's *Death in Venice*, finds that the moral

discipline he has always imposed upon his creative temperament has been contrary to its true bent; dreaming of a sinister jungle, he soon turns into a rouged homosexual following a boy through cholera-infested streets to his death. It is in *Tonio Kröger* that Mann's theory has its sharpest expression. Tonio dresses aristocratically because 'Every artist is as Bohemian as the deuce, inside! Let him at least wear proper clothes and behave outwardly like a respectable being.' Declaring that only beginners imagine that a creator must *feel*, since they are happily unaware of his corrupted nervous system with its 'irritations and icy ecstasies', he nevertheless confesses that he prefers life in all its 'seductive banality' to the gulf of irony that his temperament has granted him. He is, in fact, a '*bourgeois manqué*', and as such, revisiting his boyhood town and home, is arrested as a suspicious stranger.

Although the concept of bohemianism has been long ago taken over by the tourist agencies, and many writers and artists today prefer, as did Tonio Kröger, to dress like Mr T. S. Eliot, who might in appearance be a bank manager or a public trustee, rather than like the late W. B. Yeats with his flowing tie and poet's hair, there is little reason to suppose that bohemian tendencies are in danger of disappearing entirely. The madcap expatriates of the Parisian twenties have surrendered to the cost of living, but the publication of Joyce Cary's *The Horse's Mouth* draws attention to a comparatively recent outbreak of bohemianism in England.

For reasons rather less sinister than those of Thomas Mann, it is probable that creative people will not accept the Welfare State wholesale, any more than they accepted its bourgeois predecessor, while intense concentration on their far from lucrative work may keep them in that state of 'vital mess' which 'outsiders' consider appropriately artistic. They may not be as gay as Murger's characters, or Du Maurier's. No doubt it will always be possible to accuse them, in Emerson's words, of being 'open to the suspicion of irregular and immoral living', but they will almost certainly be more culture-conscious, and even public-spirited, than is suggested by Thackeray's definition: 'A bohemian is an educated hoss-thief.'

ILLUSTRATION: Pages 74 and 75.

Without a head or a tail

BOURGEOISIE, like capitalism, is a word which has become a political symbol and which is so battered by the usages of time that its significance has been destroyed for the present generation.

Its most general meaning is now the 'middle class'; and at this point argument and confusion begin, and indeed are invited, for the term is merely relative to those below and those above the middle, saying nothing about the content of that middle position.

In the Middle Ages the men of a town (*burg*) were its 'bourgeois' or burgesses: collectively its 'bourgeoisie'. The word became widespread with the rise of town life after the tenth century to distinguish the men of the town from men of the country, these tiny urban communities being islands in a feudal, rural sea. The 'bourgeois' in them were small pockets outside the great feudal pyramid, where all men holding land, or living by working the soil, owed allegiance to some feudal superior and came under the jurisdiction of a manorial, or feudal, court; the landholders themselves forming a pyramid of obligation and allegiance which culminated in the king – or, for most practical purposes, in some great feudal magnate whose lands were comparable in wealth with those of his lord the king.

The bourgeois did not come under this feudal discipline, although their town would claim its 'freedom' and the right to hold a market and a court from the charter of the king, or a magnate; traditionally a serf escaping from his lord might himself claim that freedom, having breathed the free air of the town (or eluded his pursuers there) for a year. The men of the town, who were technically speaking the bourgeois or the burgesses, would be, in the main, the merchants and masters who accepted apprentices and employed the journeymen in the various trades of which the names of the guilds and companies of London still remind us.

In this way the word 'bourgeoisie' began gradually to apply to the economic functions of the townsman, whereas originally it had distinguished those people who lived in the town. It was used in the seventeenth century in France to signify particularly the *class* of small master who owned the skilled workshops in which manufactured articles were made. This was at a time when the towns had not swollen, and the bourgeois were mainly local merchants and manufacturers. Growing wealth brought a greater specialization of function and a growing complexity to the society prospering upon this wealth in the towns. In England the term 'middling orders of society' became common in the eighteenth century, its very vagueness indicating the need for a wide umbrella beneath which to shelter many sorts and conditions of men, growing both in numbers and in prosperity; neither the peasants, the labourers nor the simple urban workers, neither the nobility, the rich gentry nor the owners of great estates, but those somewhere in between, both in wealth and status.

These middle classes were always rising. In France the change was seen in the division of the 'bourgeoisie' into the 'grande bourgeoisie' and the 'petite bourgeoisie'. The implication was the same. The first group included the rich lawyers, bankers and merchants, particularly those rising to great fortunes upon foreign trade, now often having a country estate as well as a town house; the 'petits bourgeois' were still the small masters and those in commerce in a humbler station.

To the first class was added a new man – the industrialist, owning the factories which the Industrial Revolution was bringing into existence, and with him, many others also rising upon the wealth created by the Industrial Revolution in finance and trade in all its aspects, whether of commodities, credit, insurance or property.

To the ranks of the 'petite bourgeoisie' were added, in great numbers, retail shopkeepers and clerks. The virtues of the 'petite bourgeoisie' were supposedly integrity, thrift and hard work; the 'grande bourgeoisie' showed initiative, organizing ability and the aggressive drive suited to captains of enterprise out to conquer the unmapped continents of economic expansion. In fact, one set of qualities complements the other so that he who has both in abundance – and good luck as well – may aspire to the ranks of the 'grande bourgeoisie'.

As the middling classes were thus accepting many recruits, the same economic movements were producing a new army of urban factory workers, owning only their labour, and being in these industrial circumstances as clearly distinct from the owners as the journeymen had been from the medieval bourgeois masters. It was this partial pattern of an industrialized society which was given systematic form and claimed as the complete truth by Karl Marx.

Capitalism was inevitably driving society into two camps. The smaller, the 'bourgeoisie', owned the means of production, the factories and the machines which gave work to the others, thus controlling the economic life of the country directly, and the political and cultural life indirectly. Their interests were unalterably opposed to those of the workers in the other camp, who had nothing to sell but their labour, and would eventually realize that they had nothing to lose in revolution but their economic shackles and bonds.

Such a theory, which claimed to set out the final truth about the social and economic process by throwing the word 'bourgeoisie' into the political arena, charged it with a new technical meaning. From Marx onward, 'capitalism' and 'bourgeoisie', as words and concepts, have been on the defensive, with an air of suspicion and opprobrium about them, even for most undisputed members of the middle classes themselves.

With the word 'bourgeoisie' now vaguely implying exploitation, and its adjective 'bourgeois' meaning dull, materialistic and unexcitingly suburban, the reality behind the term has once more been changing rapidly. The decline of the *laissez-faire* state, as democratic governments concerned themselves more and more with the general standard of living, has been a part of a profound change in the structure of society. In the gap Marx established between workers and owners there has appeared a new category – the white-collar class. Selling their brains and orderly minds rather than their labour in the Marxian sense, the white-collar men are certainly not owners themselves, yet they are distinguished from the workers on the floor of the shop; they consider themselves set apart from the working classes; and in their habits of life they strive towards middle-class status. In recent years they live in an uncomfortable social stratum.

With the rise of the joint-stock company in the nineteenth century, control has now largely been split off from ownership in enterprise, so that the professional managers in the larger concerns seldom own much, if any, of the capital they direct. They are themselves the employees of the shareholders (as may be proved if the board of directors submit many unfavourable reports at the annual meetings) and they are no longer owners and entrepreneurs in the Marxian sense of being members of the 'bourgeoisie'. The 'managerial revolution' has produced unalterable changes.

In so far as capital and control are now divided, in this rigid interpretation the 'bourgeoisie' has ceased to exist. Similarly, workers in the new industries have not shown the class consciousness which Marx saw rising in the old basic industries of coal, iron, textiles and shipbuilding. The 'bourgeoisie' has been shattered as a concept as much as that of the proletariat. Most people who have the slightest doubt about their economic position will regard their social status as that of the middle class; and in America, where neither 'proletariat' nor 'bourgeoisie' as terms have had much currency, recent polls have shown that almost ninety per cent of the people questioned consider themselves to be members of the middle class.

Not unnaturally the changes in the hundred years since 1850 have burst the strait-jacket of a set of terms which even then had to be forced to include many ill-fitting facts. There must always be a crowded gap between those undisputably at the bottom of society and those who are, with more doubt, at the top. All changes in society mean new migrants through these middle regions. These successive changes in the content of the middle class and the 'bourgeoisie', and consequently in the real significance of the concept, have enabled the 'bourgeoisie' to keep floating perpetually through history. Yet the word has lost its formal meaning; and history deals roughly with those who try to ignore change by catching a meaning and imprisoning it in the unchanging cell of a single form – though they may confuse succeeding generations, and give slogans to the demagogue.

ILLUSTRATION: Pages 76 and 77.

C

Death and law

CAPITAL PUNISHMENT is the taking of a man's life by legal process. It is found as a penalty in the earliest codes of law which are known to have existed; and notably in the Code of Hammurabi (c. 2100 B.C.), which systematized and clarified a vast body of older Sumerian law, was studied for 1,500 years, and influenced permanently the whole conception of law and justice.

This code is deceptively modern in its appearance; in early law death is the penalty for sacrilege rather than for offences against the state. Murder as a crime has in all early law much less than its modern prominence. It is a private matter between the families concerned; the wider community interferes cautiously and often unsuccessfully to limit the destructive force of private vengeance. That is the point of the *lex talionis* in Babylonian and Hebrew law; the literalness of 'an eye for an eye, a tooth for a tooth' was intended to limit the amount of retribution. In Anglo-Saxon law the *wergild* operated in a similar manner; the price of a man's life was fixed in cash according to his rank, and if his family accepted the payment, the feud was at an end. The Crown in times of strength brought pressure on the contestants to accept, and took one-third of the price. But some crimes were 'boteless': beyond the reach of a fine.

In the *Eumenides* of Aeschylus (458 B.C.), the Furies tell Orestes that the sin which cannot be forgotten and for which there is no payment is that against parent, guest or God; and that in the realm below, the Kingdom of Night, Death waits to scan all life and to straighten the crooked. This was widely true outside Greece also; treason was a crime against the king in his divine aspect; offences such as cursing father and mother or sabbath-breaking (in the Hebrew code) stood with rape and sodomy and incest as capital crimes; in Roman Law parricide had reserved to it a penalty of strange and primitive character,

alluded to both by Cicero and Juvenal. The offender was sewn up in a leather sack (called *culeus*, from Greek *koleon*, a sheath) with a dog, a cock, a viper and an ape – and drowned. (The murder of other relations was punished only by exile.)

Death is envisaged, also, not merely as a punishment in itself, but as a means of giving the offender into the hands of the Gods or the rulers of the underworld; Death is a person as well as a thing. Deep beneath the apparent calm of modern abstract justice, these ancient sanctions still flow like a forgotten river in a sewer under a modern city. But in ancient times the logic of reason had also begun to operate; the penalty of death was used as a deterrent; and for that purpose it was necessary to make it conspicuous and horrifying. Before hanging was used to kill, it appears that it was used to expose dead criminals so that others might take notice. This was the fate of Pharaoh's chief baker in *Genesis*, as in England robbers and pirates were 'gibbeted' in iron frames down to the nineteenth century.

Among the methods of legal execution which have been commonly used are drowning (Babylonian), impaling and beheading (Assyrian), stoning and burning (Hebrew) and crucifying (which the Romans found too horrible and degrading for their own citizens, and reserved for others). For the Jews, the hanged man was 'the curse of God', and the land was desecrated by his presence. In England, hanging was supplemented by burning for heresy, including witchcraft; and beheading, for high treason committed by a person of noble birth; while for treason by lesser men, hanging itself was supplemented by drawing, quartering and subsequent exposure.

During the Middle Ages capital punishment was already claimed as a prerogative of the king; but in the thirteenth and fourteenth centuries the right 'of pit and gallows' was given (at first freely, and then reluctantly) to great lords, abbeys and towns; men felons were hanged, and women drowned in the pit. The Church fought against the extension of the death penalty, and claimed immunity for those in holy orders, and later for all who were literate; this 'benefit of clergy' was not formally abolished in England until 1829.

By the end of the seventeenth century, burning, beheading, drowning, drawing and quartering had disappeared; and transportation to the

American and West Indian colonies had begun
to take the place of hanging for a very large number of felonies, and even (as in Monmouth's Rebellion of 1685) for some who were guilty of
treason. But hanging was still the punishment for
a great and growing number of offences; from
about fifty in late Stuart times, the list grew to
over 200 in the early nineteenth century. The first to
question this indiscriminate policy were the early
Quakers. George Fox, their founder, protested
to the Commonwealth Parliament in 1659 and
again to the Restoration Parliament in 1660 that
no one should be put to death 'for cattle or money
or outward things'.

More systematically, his follower John Bellers
gave in 1699 '*Some reasons against putting of Fel-
lons to death*', arguing that it was a mockery to
pray, 'Forgive us our trespasses as we forgive
them that trespass against us', and then to prosecute a man to death for twenty shillings; that the
life of a man was of greater value with God than
many pounds; that it was a great defect in the
law to make no difference between theft and murder; and that felons might be made honest and of
value to the State by being sent overseas for a
term of years, or given useful work in prison.
True to Quaker principles, William Penn and his
friends wrote into the *Act of Union*, the foundation law of Pennsylvania (1682), that only murder
and treason should be capital offences, and that
prisons were to be considered as workshops,
where offenders might be 'industriously, soberly
and morally employed'. So long as Quakers
governed Pennsylvania (about seventy years) this
law was unchanged.

Years had to pass before other voices were
raised in support of the Quaker view, either of
prison reform or capital punishment. Goldsmith
wrote in 1766: 'It is the duty of all of us, from
the laws of self-defence, to cut off that man who
has shown a disregard for the life of another.
Against such all nature rises in arms; but it is
not so against him who steals my property'.
Humanitarian feeling and Evangelical zeal now
fought a century-long battle against fear. The
State, without an efficient police force, faced the
profound disturbance of the Industrial Revolution and the terror of political revolution; and
hoped that by severity it could defeat anarchy.
The list of capital offences became extraordinary:

picking a pocket of more than one shilling, shop-
lifting of more than five shillings, cutting down
growing trees, destroying silk or velvet on the
loom, sending threatening letters, damaging a
lock or sluice or maliciously wounding cattle.
Utilitarians and socialists like Bentham, Robert
Owen and Francis Place, attacked the stupidity of
this legislation; Evangelicals its wickedness.

Quakers were in the van: Elizabeth Fry,
Stephen Grellet and Peter Bedford, who got to
know criminals as personal friends and shared
their confidence. One of them, William Allen,
comments on a typical case:

Shall a person, to whom, be it remembered, society has
failed in its duty by suffering him to grow up in ignorance, for the crime of stealing but a few shillings and without any aggravating circumstances, be cut off in the prime
of life, and endure the greatest punishment which one
human being can inflict upon another ... Everything seems
planned to *avenge* society of its injuries, while the means
for preventing their increase are almost completely over-
looked. To reform the guilty, and to restore them as useful
members of the community, is a glorious triumph of
humanity, and marks a state rising in the scale of civilization; but to have no refuge other than the punishment of
death, reminds me of the miserable subterfuge of a barbarous age, barren in expedients to save, strong only to
destroy.

The reforming policy prevailed; the list of
capital crimes was gradually diminished until, in
1861, only murder, high treason, piracy and
(oddly) the burning of dockyards remained as
capital crimes; and, in fact, since that date no one
has been hanged in England except for murder,
with certain exceptions for treason. Other countries were pursuing a similar policy: some ahead
of England, and some a little behind.

All the prophecies of disaster that had been
made proved false; the fear of death had not
proved a deterrent, and felonies did not increase.
The reasons for this were variously diagnosed: the
efficiency of the 'New Police', improved social
conditions, education. But whatever they were,
the reformers were emboldened to press for a
complete abolition of the death penalty. The
arguments for abolition are that the penalty is ineffective, and may even prove an incentive to
murder for the neurotic and exhibitionist; that it
is barbarous, a stigma on society's own failure,
and particularly horrible because it has to be

carried out in cold blood by a body of officials; and that, with every safeguard, it may involve a miscarriage of justice that can never be rectified.

The arguments for retention are that violence must be met with violence; that swift retribution is the language which the criminal understands; that pity and consideration for the criminal involve injustice to the victim and to society as a whole.

A good deal of evidence has been produced from countries where capital punishment has been abolished, that crime against the person does not increase on that account. On the other hand, many feel that conditions, after two wars and in an age of violence, make ours a bad time to try experiments: in Great Britain the movement which, at the end of 1945, seemed likely to assure at least an experimental abolition of hanging for five years, has lost its impetus. The whole position might be summarized by saying that expert opinion on the whole is *for* abolition, and public opinion on the whole is *against* it; the two must march together before any decision can be reached. But more than argument is needed, as the curiously mixed feelings of society show; the hangman is shunned, the condemned man pitied, by those who staunchly proclaim their faith in the remedy of violence.

ILLUSTRATION: Pages 78 and 79.

Economic or social organization?

CAPITALISM has meant different things at different times and has had different meanings for different people. Since the early socialists in the nineteenth century, especially Marx, attacked the whole basis of capitalist society, the sins and virtues of capitalism have been fought over in the hurly-burly of political argument, whereas its meaning should have been allowed to slumber in the quiet objectivity of a technical economic term.

Capitalism is a mode of economic production requiring the use of capital, or being dependent in any great degree on the employment of capital; yet this is a definition which avoids a precise significance. Most production, even in its simplest

forms, as Robinson Crusoe found out, needs some use of tools (or 'capital equipment') created from resources saved from the energies which are devoted purely to subsistence. And so the search to discover the origins of capitalism – in this sense – can end in classical or medieval times.

Some of the medieval wool merchants in the thirteenth century, for instance, had large capitals tied up in stocks of raw materials or cloth, even if little or none in buildings and machines (since the yarn was spun by hand and the cloth woven in cottages). Capital did accumulate in Flanders, Italy and the southern German towns with such great merchant and finance families as the Fuggers, who were indeed capitalists in this sense of laying out large sums in their trading and lending.

But such examples as these are isolated instances of large values employed in enterprise, when the *general* pattern of activity was local, personal, and carried on with small resources, and when the economic strength of Europe was still unmobilized.

Apart from the physical growth and use of capital in enterprise, capitalism may be defined by and identified with the *spirit* typifying this use of capital. Capitalist enterprise showed a deliberate search for acquisition and accumulation of wealth, in place of the mere effort to maintain a traditional livelihood. It sought freedom from restriction, it used rational methods to adapt means to its own ends. In this way the spirit of capitalism engendered the bourgeois virtues of industry, initiative, thrift and stability. And the Protestant religious spirit of those men who led the economic advance of the seventeenth and eighteenth centuries often did reinforce those qualities: idleness and profligacy were followed, in their view, by damnation and bankruptcy.

Employment of capital in production and trade, that is, the conscious use of capital resources in enterprise, appeared amongst merchants in foreign trade, and became dominant in foreign trade in the eighteenth century, as one may see from their houses and their estates. At the end of that century, the new factories of the Industrial Revolution began also to demand much investment. A merchant supervising the production of cloth might have owned the simple tools in weavers' cottages, and the yarn he distributed to them. But the capital he had employed was mainly in the value of the materials; in the technical phrase, it had been 'circulating capital' rather than 'fixed capital'. When production in various industries began to move into the factories, manufacturers had to get vast sums of fixed capital in plant and machinery in order to employ workers. They became known, therefore, as 'capitalists' – men employing capital in this way – before the new economic system was named 'capitalism'. About this specific definition of the word there is no problem, and there is little questioning the advantages which come from increasing investment in this way. State socialism is capitalist in this sense.

Marx, however, developed a theory of society which brought 'capitalism' into the political conflict. A further meaning (the one most common today) derives from Marx – capitalism not as a technical term indicating the dominance of capital in economic organization, but capitalism signifying that organization of society and the state which is favourable *to* capitalists – *i.e.* the free enterprise economy and the *laissez-faire* state. To Marx the state was identical with the economic group which controlled the production of wealth. In the capitalist state, or 'under capitalism', the institutional order remained free to a predominant degree, and individuals, as economic agents, were free to employ their capital in their own way, to run the full risks of failure and to enjoy the full opportunities of success. Thus profits, or the expectation of profits, became the criteria for activity, initiative following the drive of capital for profit and efficient employment.

Such a free enterprise economy, being also a form of political organization, and almost a way of life with its own system of values and attitudes of mind, is opposed by the socialist thesis in its various forms. Socialists maintain that the state should plan the sowing and the harvesting of the fruits of economic activity in the interests of all its citizens, by directing the system of production and distribution consciously; they should not rely on 'natural' economic forces – upon Adam Smith's 'invisible hand' – to control matters automatically. The socialist thesis does not acknowledge that harmony of interests between the individual pursuit of gain and the common interest posited by those who support *laissez-faire* and 'capitalism'.

In this sense, though, capitalism, has never been entirely unrestricted; it has been controlled by law, by custom and by social usage. It is the silent conjuring trick performed by Marx of changing the content of the word capitalism from meaning an economic system dependent upon capital, into meaning a society run in the interests of capitalists (which may, or may not, be in the interests of all) without changing the word, which has confused the unwary. Now for good or ill, the use we have to contend with is 'capitalism *versus* socialism'.

ILLUSTRATION: Pages 80 and 81.

All passion spent

CATHARSIS is originally a Greek medical term meaning literally 'purification' and hence 'purgation'. But the doctrine of catharsis is a psychological theory, teaching that the function of certain kinds of art is to act as a hygienic 'release' of certain emotions.

The doctrine orginates with Aristotle, who in his *Politics*, when discussing the place of musical training in the educational curriculum, mentions incidentally the 'cathartic' effect of certain kinds of music, which he promises to explain in the *Poetics*. In the present text of the *Poetics* he does not fulfil this promise, and the term again appears only incidentally as one of the defining characteristics of tragedy; a form of art which acts 'through pity and fear effecting a catharsis of these emotions'.

The clue to Aristotle's meaning is given by a theory of Plato's, which Aristotle is criticizing. Plato in the *Republic* had attacked the dramatists and proposed to exclude them from his ideal state. One reason was that the drama panders to the satisfaction of 'passions which should be allowed to wither away, and sets them up in control, although the goodness and happiness of our lives depend on their being held in subjection'. This was a moral accusation based on psychology. Aristotle admits the psychological facts, but reverses the moral conclusion. Passions cannot be suppressed, but they can be harmlessly discharged in a make-believe situation, and this is the proper task of the dramatist.

Moreover, the process is not merely one of social hygiene. It affords positive pleasure as well; even more, it affords aesthetic insight. In the European literary tradition these two elements were lost sight of, and critics such as Corneille, Racine and Lessing interpreted Catharsis as a purely ethical doctrine of the function of drama. Milton was a rare exception; he appreciated all three elements. In the preface to *Samson Agonistes* he says:

Tragedy, as it was anciently composed, hath been ever held the gravest, moralest, and most profitable of all other poems: therefore said by Aristotle to be of power, by raising pity and fear, or terror, to purge the mind of those and such-like passions; that is, to temper or reduce them to just measure with a kind of delight, stirred up by reading or seeing those passages well imitated. Nor is Nature herself wanting in her own efforts to make good his assertion: for so, in physic, things of melancholic hue and quality are used against melancholy, sour against sour, salt to remove salt humours.

And the last lines of the poem itself are cathartic:

His servants he, with new acquist
Of true experience, from this great event
With peace and consolation hath dismissed,
And calm of mind, all passion spent.

These three elements of catharsis – moral, hedonic and aesthetic – are all related. Since the original doctrine is concerned with tragedy, the emotions discharged therefrom are, according to Aristotle, 'pity' and 'fear'. Both are painful emotions – fear being the pain of anticipated calamity, and pity transferred fear, not compassion – that is, the pain felt by contemplating misfortune, which might have happened to oneself, happening to others. Dramatic tragedy relieves these emotions by deliberately evoking them. It does not 'set them up in control', as Plato thought; it discharges them harmlessly. The cure is homoeopathic: but it is a cure.

But the fact that catharsis is also pleasant is dependent on Aristotle's conception of the tragic hero, who does not deserve his calamity, yet is not entirely blameless. His imperfections give him human stature, which permits sympathy; yet, having heroic stature as well, he symbolizes the human race. Emotions are 'purged' in a second way: even in the act of indulgence they are re-

fined or sublimated by casting off the self-regarding element. But this is just what makes them painful in ordinary life. In the theatre the pleasure is unmixed with pain.

And this is where the third element (aesthetic insight) also enters. Poetry, for Aristotle, concerns 'the universal' as opposed to 'the particular'. Just as the tragic hero is not just a man, but a symbol of Man, so depersonalized emotion is not just feeling, but an experience of something which is true and valid universally.

Yet catharsis is a theory of tragedy, not of art in general. Indeed, according to R. G. Collingwood (*Principles of Art*, 1936) it is not even a theory of dramatic art: 'Aristotle's analysis is perfectly correct and highly important, though (of course) not as a contribution to the theory of art, but as a contribution to the theory of amusement.' Art cannot be described by prescribing functions for it, as the 'safety-valve' theory of catharsis would do. Entertainment is a means to an end (pleasure), and it is perfectly legitimate to add social hygiene as a further end. But art is not a means to an end. The doctrine of catharsis is primarily pathological, though it contains some incidental aesthetics. Confusion between these two elements is not surprising; for its subject-matter, drama, is a very complex art form, in which it is not easy to separate aesthetic value from entertainment value.

A political abstraction?

CENTURY OF THE COMMON MAN, more an Invocation than an Idea, and more a catch-phrase than either, belongs to the politician's platform: it may not actually have been invented by Henry Wallace, then Vice-President of the United States, in 1944; but the appeal of 'We, the People' – or of 'You, the People', depending on the speaker's position, on or off the dais – is certainly an old one, long accustomed to meet with applause.

Count Mirabeau commented in 1789 that the people, in order to be formidable, had only to stand motionless. But that is a negative stance at best: and the people can also be formidable when they take to action and destroy a great many things, persons and institutions which they do not favour, which have, they feel, oppressed them in the past. The problem is the principles and foundations upon which they will build thereafter. The ground of the twentieth century is cumbered with much wreckage, some of it the consequence of courageous assault; but there is not, as yet, a universally accepted home for the brave built upon the ruins. How far, then, does common man rule his own destinies in this, his own age?

Assuredly he has very much more political influence than his grandfather had. In his grandfather's day he was already observed as a phenomenon and a portent, and the time of his power was foretold in distaste and dismay. Here is *The Economist's* view, put in 1848, when aristocratic absolutism in Europe seemed likely to fall before the attackers:

Granting to them [that is, common men] the best intentions and the most unselfish views, their haste, their impressibility, their openness to deception, and their inevitable ignorance, must ever make and has ever made the government of the lower classes fatal beyond all others to freedom, to prosperity, and to peace.

The alarm faded, for common men did not seize the reins in Europe; the Right returned, restored with constitutions. Liberal England continued to measure its tread to the easy pace of John Locke, and cheerfully consigned Marx and his ideas to a museum. Lord John Russell, a reforming statesman who stood well to the left of his Whig connexions, thought that 'Universal suffrage is calculated to produce and nourish violent opinions and servile dependents'.

John Stuart Mill disagreed with this, and with Tennyson's glowerings about 'a tyranny of extremes', but only on the ground that the middle class was and would remain strong enough to hold the balance, to neutralize the obvious evils inherent both in aristocratic and in democratic control – using this last adjective pejoratively, as it was always used in Victorian intellectual argument.

The middle class itself thought Mill was right, and confidently backed the extensions of the franchise that took place in England in the nineteenth century. After the Reform Act of 1867, one

in twelve had the vote; after that of 1884, one in seven. The pale of the constitution opened wide: Demos was summoned to swell the party ranks – to the dismay of the older school of party-leader.

Were the commonalty interested in measures, or in men? In men, and, from the orthodox view, in the wrong men. In particular did the general election of 1880 cause much heart-searching about the common man and his political role. After a spell of six years' highly active rule, the Conservatives were suddenly extinguished, and Gladstone, 'on the shoulders of Midlothian', was swept in with no policy, it seemed, but the reversal of all that his opponents had been doing. A sad Conservative analysed the position, and its implications, in *The Nineteenth Century*:

That the government of this country, whether Liberal or Conservative, should be at the mercy of a popular opinion, working as it were underground, invisible, inaudible, inscrutable, and throwing up no indications whatever to mark the course it is taking – that it should be possible both for political parties and for the general [that is, the educated] public to remain to the last in total ignorance of the intentions of that great lower class which can turn elections at its will – is not only so remote from the commonsense of politics, but so manifestly inconsistent with the maintenance of any dignified or regular system of government, that it is not necessary for a man to be on the losing side to make him anxious about our political future.

It seemed that the majority were of the view that, 'after one party has been in office six years, it is time the other had its innings'. Thus the doctrine of 'time for a change', so potent in our generation, caused this analyst to shudder.

Yet common man could not be prevented from climbing up the political structure. He swung in the Liberals in 1905; swung out the Conservatives in 1945; in America he made Woodrow Wilson a hero and demoted him later (not to villainy, but to folly), and elected Franklin Roosevelt President four times running, in the teeth of every organized body of opinion in the country. On the continent of Europe the story was the same; the French democracy, keeper of the keys of the great Revolution, spent its time hunting for leadership by candlelight; in Germany the seekers, after some false starts, were more successful, and found a common man indeed and enthroned him as their Leader. The Russians, wiser perhaps in their generation, had no truck with the common man except on paper, where he might be allowed to possess the Order of Lenin and all the virtues of the noble savage. Italian Fascism was an odd comment on Mill's theory that the middle class could hold the balance.

Nowhere, in fact, could democracy and power be properly equated. In Scandinavia politicians had no political ambitions for their country, and in Great Britain common men desired their political chiefs to lead them while the chiefs desired to be told what to do; in both, therefore, a vacuum existed. Common man as a political figure has no very impressive record. His politics have led him to war, and very often he has shouldered his rifle with some feeling of mental relief.

But is he happier in his social sphere? His greatest charter says he must pursue happiness, and he has done his best. Is it yet in his net? He lives longer, lives better, eats more, marries younger, fathers fewer, works less, spends more. Since he has been to school he knows more and is less gullible; he is fascinated by himself, and will plough though unreadable manuals on sex, behaviour, and personality in order to be up to date with modern thought on all three.

He wishes to be 'of' his age and generation; in America, at least, he wants to graduate, to win friends and influence people, to become a man of distinction. She wishes to marry him, on his way up, or when *there*. In Britain the common man has not so many ladders available, and so has tended to equate success, particularly success in commerce, with sin. He wishes to have more time off, but does not know for what; hence the rise of the merchants who deal in what George Orwell in his terrible tract *1984* called 'prolefeed'. He has demoted authority because he is as good as the next man, and he becomes a ready enemy to the next man if the next man proves to be better than he. For this reason he distrusts especially the man who knows more than he does, sees further, has more sense and is thus more conceited; scientists and priests alike are 'experts', minders of the machine that employs common man and that common man must tend – but they stir his fears too much, and they do not appear to respect him as politicians do. And even when at ease, and undisturbed by 'Them', it may enter his head to feel guilt that others, in Africa, China, half the world,

are supporting that ease with their labour. No expert can rid him of this guilt, and so he rails at the society which has implanted it. Thus happiness continues to elude him.

But we need not pity him, for he is not there, after all. No one feels the sum of pain in your toothache and his headache. Common man is a political abstraction. A man may still make his own soul, in his own time, in any century.

ILLUSTRATION: Pages 82 and 83.

'But all mankind's concern is charity'

CHARITY in its original and highest sense signifies a Christian love that 'is its own fruit' (St Bernard); and also a love of one's neighbour which may manifest itself in good works and alms-giving.

The word 'charity' in the Authorized Version of the New Testament represents *agapē* of the Greek text; *agapē* signifies disinterested love seeking no reward, nor allowing itself to be diminished by any return of evil for its good. The most famous account of charity, or Christian love, is given by St Paul in I Corinthians, XIII: 'Charity suffereth long, and is kind; charity envieth not; charity vaunteth not itself, is not puffed up, doth not behave itself unseemly, seeketh not her own, is not easily provoked, thinketh not evil; rejoiceth not in iniquity, but rejoiceth in the truth, beareth all things, believeth all things, hopeth all things, endureth all things.' And finally St Paul says, 'And now abideth faith, hope, charity, these three; but the greatest of these is charity.'

Charity can be distinguished from other forms of love in that it is disinterested. God is to be loved for himself, not for his gifts, and persons and things are to be loved for God's sake, because they are temples of the Holy Ghost. 'Some people want to see God with their eyes as they see a cow,' wrote the German mystic Eckhart, 'and to love him as they love their cow – for the milk and cheese and profit it brings them. This is how it is with people who love God for the sake of outward wealth or inward comfort.'

The second distinguishing mark of charity is that it is not an emotion, but rather an act of the will, a purposeful turning away from the self and its cravings towards that love of God which asks nothing and refuses nothing: to those who seek first the Kingdom of God all the rest will be added. 'The worth of love does not consist in high feelings, but in detachment, in patience under all trials for the sake of God whom we love.' (St John of the Cross.)

Charity is love, but unlike other forms of love it is without greed or fear; it is tranquil, having no craving or aversion in it; it is free from all glorification of self at the expense of others. 'Charity is both the means and the end, the only way by which we can reach that perfection which is, after all, but charity itself ... Just as the soul is the life of the body so charity is the life of the soul.' (St Francis de Sales.)

Originally there was no breach between charity in the sense of divine love and charity in the sense of alms-giving. In the latter sense charity was simply the love of one's neighbour in God, manifesting itself in the form of good works.

In the early Christian Church the poor were loved as neighbours and were not regarded as a social problem. Each church was a centre of voluntary and personal relief. Before the priest sat at table, a portion of his meat was separated and sent to the hungry. Offerings of money were placed before the altar and used to help the poor. Acts of charity were not yet divorced from loving-kindness, and, undertaken in a spirit of humility, they blessed those who performed them and those who received. In the early Church charity created a community bound together by love, outside the normal life of the Roman Empire.

Under the Emperor Constantine (288–337), Christianity became the established religion of the Roman Empire, and the ideal of Christian charity began to have a wide social importance. St Chrysostom (347–407), speaking of the social duties of the Church, said: 'If there were no poor, the greater part of your sins would not be removed; the poor are the healers of your wounds.' As a result of this teaching, there arose, for the first time among Christians, the view that alms were a kind of investment to be realized in the next world. The conception of charity began to grow shallower.

A system of relief independent of the churches began to develop. Hospitals were founded, and

almoners were appointed to distribute alms. St Basil (329–379) founded poor houses, orphanages and homes for infant children. There were many bequests for such institutions, and in time the clergy became the owners of large properties and administrators of endowed charities which continued throughout the Middle Ages, and still exist today.

As the power and wealth of the Church increased, the feeling of brotherly love that had united all Christians within the early Church began to weaken. The poor then took on the aspect of a burdensome social problem to be tackled by professional administrators, rather than by men actuated solely by Christian love and charity. And yet the name of charity continued to be associated with the doings of the officials and the bureaucrats.

During Henry VIII's reign the system of relief from endowed charities began to fail in Great Britain, and when the monasteries and religious houses were dissolved, it became impossible any longer to help the poor by voluntary means. Thus in 1601 the celebrated Poor Law of Queen Elizabeth (43 Eliz. c.2) was passed. Under this statute 'overseers of the poor' were appointed in each parish and were authorized to levy a compulsory rate for the support of the aged, invalid, and deserving poor, who were to be fed and lodged in workhouses. The sturdy beggar who avoided work was imprisoned.

The Poor Law, amended, but in spirit essentially unchanged, remained on the Statute Book until it was superseded by the National Assistance Act in 1948.

In the sphere of voluntary charity, the two bodies most active in modern times have been the Charity Commission and the Charity Organization Society. The Commission was set up in 1853 by the Charitable Trusts Act, and was made responsible for reorganizing the voluntary charities for the poor, many of which through mismanagement had fallen into decay. The Charity Organization Society (1869) typified the attitude of the Victorian middle classes to the poor. It organized a relief system based on careful enquiry into the morals of those in trouble, and only helped the 'good poor'. It set itself to prevent any alms-giving that it considered wasteful and indiscriminate. W. H. Davies, the distinguished poet, who suffered at the hands of the Society, says that its main purpose was 'to prevent charity from being done' (*The Autobiography of a Super-Tramp*). The Society never succeeded in winning the confidence of the poor.

Today voluntary charities continue to exist, but as far as the relief of the poor is concerned, they have been made unnecessary by the activities of the Welfare State.

In modern English the word 'charity' is seldom used in its original sense as signifying the highest and most divine form of love. The word has been debased more thoroughly than any other word in the language. It has become associated in most people's minds with an all-too-human way of dealing with the poor, with the overseers of the poor, with the Poor Law, with workhouses, with charity children, with the odious forms of bumbledom pilloried by Dickens and with the pharisaism of the Charity Organization Society. The progressive debasement of the word is an illustration of the truth of St Paul's saying: 'And though I bestow all my goods to feed the poor ... and have not charity, it profiteth me nothing.' (See also *Concern*.)

ILLUSTRATION: Pages 84 and 85.

Chivalry and courtly love

CHIVALRY was a social code which grew out of an economic situation in Europe; and COURTLY LOVE was the application of that code to the relationship of the sexes.

The economic situation was one of anarchy and disintegration, in a society where trade hardly existed, where central government was ineffective and where land was the only important form of property. This situation arose in Western Europe about the tenth century, after the failure of Charlemagne's attempt to recreate a European Empire and to find means of administering it; and it arose above all in France, so that France is the country which supplied the terminology of feudalism, chivalry and courtly love.

Spain had the Moors; Italy had cities (and city life and feudalism are incompatible, bourgeois and chivalrous ideals irreconcilable); Germany had some strong kings who used the Church to establish local administration, and by their prestige and their great estates held feudalism in check; England was a country in which independent peasant proprietors still counted until the Norman Conquest. Only France, therefore, could produce the ethos of chivalry, its ritual in fealty and knighthood, its symbols in heraldry, its diversions in the chase and the tourney, its gospels in the poems of the *langue d'oc* and the *langue d'oil*, its missionaries in those second-generation immigrants, the Normans, who came out of Scandinavia to invade north-west France in the tenth century.

Having accepted Christianity, the French language and the feudal code, they carried them to England, to Sicily, to Jerusalem, to Constantinople. But their borrowing was reciprocal; on the farthest edge of their English conquests in the marches of Wales and Cornwall they picked up the stories which they carried back to France to be developed into the central myth of chivalry: the *Matière de Bretagne*, the Arthurian cycle. By the thirteenth century, Arthur and his Knights had become the favourite heroes of every European country as far east as Hungary.

Chivalry, then, is the dream of a society based on the personal relationship of service and protection; its key virtue, fidelity, its abhorred vice, treachery. The dream is coloured by Christian ideals, by Celtic myth and by pagan philosophy (Latin through Virgil, Ovid and Cicero; Greek through the Moors of Spain, Sicily and Palestine). Like all dreams, it has points of contact with reality and of startling divergence from everyday fact. The oath of fealty was solemnly sworn, as it is to this day in the English Coronation Service. Noble families sent their children (of both sexes) to be trained in the households of friends or kin, as pages and esquires, gentlewomen and maids of honour.

The boys, besides fagging as humbly as nineteenth-century public schoolboys, learnt the technical terms and 'manage' of horse, hound and hawk; the use of sword and lance, the rules of siege warfare, of battle and tournament; a little law and some estate management. They learnt also elaborate parlour games, singing, dancing, music, stories and poems, for it was their duty to provide amusement. In these things the girls shared, learning as well how to provide for the needs of a great household all the year round (a task requiring as much skill and resource as any company director's, in an age when nothing to speak of could be bought at a shop, and the keeping of food in winter was problematical).

Since status was bound up with the holding of land, the loss or division of estates was most to be feared. Hence the laws of primogeniture; the eldest son must succeed, but this left the problem of younger sons. The myth of knights wandering in search of adventures is rooted in this situation, and bolstered by the fact that in Spain, against the Moors, in Egypt or Syria, against the Turks, in Byzantium as a mercenary, and in East Prussia with the Teutonic Knights, there was a living to be had. Chaucer's Knight, who had been to most of these countries, was closely observed from life.

Sometimes opportunity came nearer home, in the Crusade against the Albigenses of Provence, or in the Welsh marches. There were wars, or civil wars, or the snatching of land for which the small gentleman needed the protection of the great lord, and the great lord the backing of the small gentleman. This kind of life was the background of Sir Thomas Malory himself, the chronicler of Arthur (if he has been correctly identified) – except that by getting caught and choosing the wrong backers Malory had to suffer long in prison, and had time to translate King Arthur 'out of certain books of French'. 'I pray you all, gentlemen and gentlewomen that readeth this book of Arthur and his knights, pray for me while I am on live, that God send me good deliverance ...'

'Gentlemen and gentlewomen' are the only audience the author addresses himself to. The printer apologizes for standing in their light – 'I, William Caxton, simple person' – since the code of chivalry is for gentlemen only. The Black Prince, the flower of chivalry, having taken King John of France prisoner at Poitiers ('To whom shall I yield me? Where is my cousin the Prince of Wales?') served the King at supper that night in his tent, 'as humbly as he could, and would not sit at the King's board, but said he was not sufficient'.

It was a different matter when it came to a city. 'The city of Limoges was pilled, robbed and clean brent [burnt] and brought to destruction ... it was left clean void as a town of desert,' says Froissart; but no criticism of the Black Prince can be sustained. On the other hand, when Lancelot (in Chrétien de Troyes's poem) is seeking Guinevere, who is captive in the Land of Gorre, and, having lost his horse, accepts a ride from a dwarf with a cart, he is so shamed by being put in the position of a common criminal that even his friends admit that he will never get over the disgrace. Even the rabble in the streets, and the keeper of the bridge taunt him.

The same consciousness of rank and the distinctions it brings prevails in *courtly love*. (The name is a nineteenth-century invention of Gaston Paris.) In the famous treatise written by Andreas the Chaplain about A.D. 1180 at the same court of Troyes and for the same Countess Marie (daughter of Eleanor of Aquitaine) who was Chrétien's patroness, the author makes short work of love among peasants. For the men, it gives them ideas above their station (like education, later on) and makes them neglect their farms, which then become useless *to us* (their lords). For the women: if you fancy them, when you find a convenient place, take what you want and embrace them by force (it was in this manner that the poet William Langland is said to have been born on a farm under the Malvern Hills).

Boccaccio, for all his loyal love of 'Fiammetta' (Maria d'Aquino, herself a love-child of the King of Naples) thought it no treachery to her to keep a peasant mistress. A citizen, however, might aspire to love, so long as he chose a mistress above him. For love is a relationship of fealty; a lover, having chosen his lady, becomes her sworn man; she is his 'lord' and his obedience is to her only. But this fealty is no public ceremony; it is secret. A man who cannot keep silence cannot be a lover.

Because a lover's relationship is one of obedience, it follows that a man cannot love his wife. On the contrary, it is the wife's duty to obey her husband, as she has sworn to do in her troth-plight. There is every other good medieval reason why married people cannot be lovers. Ovid says they cannot, and that is one form of authority. The Church says they cannot, and that is another kind of authority. For marriage is a sacrament; and the sacrament would be defiled by using the sexual act for pleasure. Sex in marriage is used to beget children, and to symbolize the mystic union of Christ and his Church. An uxorious husband is capable of committing adultery with his own wife (a view still held by Jeremy Taylor in the seventeenth century.) There were also substantial practical reasons as well as the theological ones. Marriage among the gentry was a business arrangement made between families to sustain or augment their estates. It had nothing to do with love.

Nor could love exist for an unmarried girl. She was in the state of virginity, and that state, the highest known to a mortal, must be respected. A knight who touched her (whatever his feelings) was therefore not a lover, but a cad; his duty if he finds her in the forest is to protect her from being molested and restore her intact to her family. Sir Lancelot (whatever his faults) knew better than to take the Maid of Astolat when she begged him to marry her or be her paramour. 'Fair damosel, said Sir Lancelot, of these two things ye must pardon me', and he went to her father and cleared himself: 'She is a clene maiden for me, both for deed and will.' Chaucer remembered the rules when he made his Criseyde a widow; if she had been a maid, not even Pandarus could have schemed for Troilus.

Courtly love, then, demanded certain conditions. It must be heterosexual (this does not quite go without saying; Andreas makes it Chapter II of his treatise). It must be adulterous; it must be secret; and it must be faithful. No man can be a lover of more than one woman, and she must be his equal or superior in rank. She is entitled to treat him with scorn, contempt, contumely or utter indifference; this will not alter his love; he will persist until his love is rewarded, and the reward he looks for is a fleshly one – sexual satisfaction; he will not, in general, be content with the union of souls, although this solution, too, was known.

Two medieval sanctions were thus defied by courtly love: those of feudalism and the Church. The woman beloved may be, and in fact and literature often was, the wife of the lover's feudal lord; as Iseut was the wife of Tristan's uncle and king, Mark; as Guinevere was of Lancelot's king, Arthur. The lover is then betraying his lord for the sake of his lady. From the Church's point of view, the fact of adultery was a direct defiance of the Ten Commandments, and so sufficient condemnation. It need not be said that these matters troubled both lovers and poets. Andreas, having written three books to instruct his pupil Walter in the art of love, wrote a fourth to persuade him to resist love and its blandishments, now equipped as he was with full information about it.

Courtly love poems, such as Chaucer's *Troilus and Criseyde*, or even Sir Philip Sidney's sonnet sequence, *Astrophel and Stella*, end with a palinode renouncing love. Chrétien de Troyes would not finish *Lancelot*, and left the end to Godefroy de Laigny. Good clerics tried to turn the themes of courtly love to the service of Our Lady. More subtle moralists, like the author of *Sir Gawain and the Green Knight*, played the game to the full, but put a moral sting in the tail of it (Sir Gawain refuses his hostess's advances with full *courtesy*, without ever rebuking her or putting her to shame; but he sinks himself by accepting a gift from her and concealing it from her husband).

Yet it is just in these tensions that the appeal of courtly love consisted. Whatever its sources in the poems of Ovid, and particularly his *Art of Love*, or in notions from Moorish Spain during the peaceful period before the fanatical Almoravid invasions of 1086, there can be no question that courtly love was in the first place a social phenomenon of southern France in the twelfth century. It can be no accident that this same part of Europe cherished heterodox notions in religion which eventually brought on it the condemnation of the Church and the scourge of a Crusade beginning in 1209, which smashed its life and culture. The heresy of Love (for he was thought of as a God) was one more heresy to set with those of the Waldenses of Lyons and the Cathari of Albi; but it was a heresy that infected the conquerors, and has lasted as long as Christendom.

ILLUSTRATION: Plate 12.

Cold and clear, warm and vague

CLASSICISM and **ROMANTICISM** form a fundamentally antithetical pair in art and life, although Emerson wrote in 1841 that 'the vaunted distinction between Classic and Romantic Schools' seemed 'superficial and pedantic'.

Yet few critical terms have changed their meaning more often or have provoked more acrimonious controversies. The world 'classic' was first used by Aulus Gellius, a second century grammarian, who spoke of *classicus ... scriptor, non proletarius*. In this context *classicus* signifies a correctness of language and style, an aristocracy, almost, of literature. A 'classic' writer wrote in Latin for a civilized élite. The word was later used to describe Greek and Latin literature, and in consequence those periods of English and French literature which derived their basic principles from Greek and Roman authors. It still retained its original meaning, however, Pope in his second Horatian Epistle writing

> Who lasts a century can have no flaw;
> I hold that wit a classic, good in law.

'Romantic' comes from the Old French *romanz – escrire romanz*, meaning primarily to write in the vulgar tongue instead of Latin, which was the language of the educated classes. From the first, therefore, it stood for works which were popular, formless, fanciful and the reverse of classical. In the eighteenth century it was employed in the sense of 'strange', 'wild', appealing to imagination and feeling.

The contrast was sharply accentuated by the Battle of Ancients and Moderns in the seventeenth century, when 'Romantic' became identified with 'modern'. It was used in this sense in the nineteenth century by Stendhal in *Racine et Shakespeare*, and by Baudelaire, who remarked in *Curiosités esthétiques*: 'For me Romanticism is the most recent, the most actual expression of the beautiful', and in the same work: 'Whoever speaks of Romanticism speaks of modern art.'

The identification of 'Romantic' and 'modern' probably accounts for the violence of the Romantic Movement in France. One of its most striking manifestations was 'la bataille d'*Hernani*' in 1830, when the première of Victor Hugo's poetic drama caused an uproar at the theatre because the author broke one of the most cherished rules of classical French prosody: he used *enjambement*; also he discarded the classical forms of address and replaced the formal 'Seigneur' of Corneille and Racine by the expression 'Mon Lion'.

The controversy, which had never come to an end, broke out with fresh vigour in England and France after the First World War. French writers denounced Romanticism on the grounds that it was of Germanic origin and fundamentally unFrench. In England T. S. Eliot emerged as the champion of a new Classicism, and Middleton Murry as the champion of a new Romanticism. 'There may be a good deal to be said for Romanticism in life,' wrote Eliot in *The Sacred Wood* (1920), 'there is no place for it in letters,' while his preface to *For Lancelot Andrewes* (1928) contained the famous declaration that his position was 'classicist in literature, royalist in politics and anglo-catholic in religion'.

Controversy has tended to obscure the issues, yet there is no doubt that Classicism and Romanticism stand for certain well-defined stylistic differences. Classicism is based on reason, order, clarity and on the belief that discipline is an aesthetic as well as a moral virtue. Romanticism insists on the primacy of feeling, freedom, colour and the power of suggestion. These stylistic differences are themselves the outcome of different philosophies and different conceptions of the nature of man.

In *Speculations* (1924) T. E. Hulme said that Classicism regarded man as 'an extraordinarily fixed and limited animal whose nature is absolutely constant. It is only by tradition and organization that anything decent can be got out of him.' For Romanticism 'the individual is an infinite reservoir of possibilities; and if you can so rearrange society by the destruction of oppressive order, then these possibilities will have a chance and you will get Progress'.

Classicism, indeed, implies the existence of a stable order and an intellectual élite. It sees man as a member of the community and is the expression of a *social* experience. Romanticism, on the other hand, is essentially individualist and is concerned to exploit what Hulme called the 'infinite reservoir of possibilities'.

The opposition between Classicism and Romanticism therefore resolves itself into a conflict between the community and the individual, between a static and a dynamic society. We are accustomed to think of the Romantic as a 'rebel' or a 'revolutionary'. The desire for absolute freedom and an impatience with every form of rule or restriction are perhaps the most important characteristics of the Romantic. The weakness of Classicism is that through a respect for rules for their own sake it hardens into a dogmatism which is divorced from living experience. The danger of Romanticism is that contempt for rules leads to anarchy in life and formlessness in art.

A Frenchman once wrote a book called *Le Classicisme des romantiques*, and it would not be difficult to write a companion volume on *Le Romantisme des classiques*. For Classicism and Romanticism are something more than literary and artistic movements. They stand for two conflicting tendencies in the human mind – the need for order and the desire for freedom. In periods known as Classic and Romantic one of these impulses is clearly predominant, but in other periods the balance is more evenly distributed. The two impulses sometimes co-exist not merely in the same period, but in the same man; and it is arguable that the greatest writers and artists are those in whom the balance is most perfect.

We think of the seventeenth century as the great age of French Classicism, but it was also the Age of Baroque in Europe. It is now recognized that Baroque opulence and extravagance have affinities with Romantic wildness and individualism. Scholars have detected Baroque elements in Corneille, and one has gone so far as to describe Racine's *Phèdre* as the dry type of Baroque tragedy. A more extreme view was put forward by the German art historian, Heinrich Wölfflin, in his *Principles of Art History* (1915). Instead of the old division into Classic and Romantic, he divided European art into Classic and Baroque. He went on to say that the principle of Impressionism was already apparent in a 'Baroque' artist like Rembrandt.

The implication of this remark is clear: Impressionism was not a movement which originated in the nineteenth century or a mere development of Romantic painting; it was part of a much older and much larger movement in which Romanticism itself was simply a comparatively late stage.

It is characteristic of Romantic movements that they are always preceded by what the French call 'pre-romanticism' – periods in which aristocratic societies are breaking up, in which 'the rules' are undermined and in which the emphasis shifts from reason to sensibility. This happened in the eighteenth century, and the process was hastened by the French Revolution. The nineteenth century began with Romantic Movements in England, France and Germany, but it was not exclusively the century of Romanticism, any more than the seventeenth century was exclusively the century of Classicism. A Swiss writer, Professor Jean Rousset, has claimed in his *Littérature de l'Age Baroque en France* (1953) to have discovered 'several parallel seventeenth centuries', and the claim could be made with still greater force for the nineteenth century.

The pattern of that century is highly complex. Romantic poets like Lamartine and Hugo did not jettison the classical alexandrine; they continued to use it with modifications, and it was not until the last quarter of the century that it was dislocated by the invention of *vers libéré* and *vers libre*. Baudelaire was certainly influenced by the Romantics, but Remy de Gourmont found in his work 'a return to traditional French versification', and T. S. Eliot has described him as a counter-romantic. Other critics have emphasized the gap between his work and Romanticism, and have treated him as the father of the Symbolist Movement which began officially in 1886.

In painting, the position was somewhat different. 'The great fault of M. Ingres', wrote Baudelaire, 'is to try to impose on everything he sees a perfection which is more or less despotic and borrowed from the repertoire of classical ideas.' Impressionism was a reaction against Classicism, and the Impressionists substituted what Wölfflin called 'the broken line of the painterly style' for the classical line of Ingres. Impressionism and Symbolism were both movements of liberation. There is a parallel between the disuse of the alexandrine and the disuse of the classical line, between 'the broken line' of the Impressionists and the broken rhythms of free verse, between the Impressionists' experiments with light and the Symbolists' search for more and more subtle combinations of feelings.

In literature the close of the century was dominated by two contrasted movements – Symbolism and Naturalism. They correspond in a sense to the Classicism and Romanticism of an earlier age. Mallarmé declared that the aim of the poet was 'to paint not the thing, but the effect it produces'. The Naturalists were concerned through elaborate documentation to restore 'the thing', to present the reader with a 'slice of life'. In this respect they were not simply anti-Romantic, they were trying to return to the objectivity of Classicism, and it can even be argued that the philosophical positivism on which their work was founded was the final stage in the disintegration of the classical metaphysic which was the foundation of Classicism, just as subjective idealism was the foundation of Romanticism.

Surrealism, which grew out of Symbolism, is an extreme form of Romanticism, and demonstrates the emotional and linguistic anarchy to which the pursuit of absolute freedom leads inevitably. A French critic's description of the style of Marcel Proust – another of the heirs of Symbolism – as *classicisme impressionniste* is a remarkable example of the permutations of which the terms Classicism and Romanticism are capable.

Classicism and Romanticism are words which need to be used with the greatest circumspection, but undoubtedly they stand for two of the deepest tendencies of all art and literature.

ILLUSTRATION: Pages 132–134 and 363–365.

Protection of Trades Union workers

A **'CLOSED SHOP'** indicates that a particular trade or employment is open only to trade unionists, and that those who are not members of a trade union are not allowed to obtain employment in it; it is also used where employment is open only to members of a particular union to the exclusion of other trade unionists.

The Closed Shop can be traced back through the history of the unions to the guilds of the fourteenth century. The Statute of Labourers in 1351 fixed wages and conditions of work, and in many guilds no guild journeyman was allowed to work with non-members. This was particularly so in the sixteenth and seventeenth centuries, and the Statute of Artificers in 1562 introduced a system of compulsory apprenticeship.

The Closed Shop is recognized by law, though this is only a recent development; attempts to

force men to join a union as a condition of employment or to force employers to employ only union men have always been viewed with suspicion by the legislature; thus the Combination Act of 1799 declared illegal any contracts between any journeyman or other workman designed to prevent or hinder any person from employing whomsoever he shall think proper to employ in his trade or business. In 1825 it was provided that violence or threats for the purpose of forcing or inducing a worker to belong to a union or to contribute to any common fund were illegal. To fine a person for not belonging to a union was also forbidden.

A further Act of 1871, the Criminal Law Amendment Act, introduced a clause forbidding obstruction to compel an employer to discharge a worker, to refuse employment or to alter the mode of carrying on his business. Under the Trade Disputes Act of 1906, neither the furtherance of a labour dispute nor threats (unaccompanied by violence) that work will be stopped by concerted action are illegal, though it is possible that a charge of conspiracy will be brought. Several decisions of the House of Lords (Allen v. Flood, Quinn v. Leathem and Crofter v. Veitch) have laid down the principle that it is entirely within the rights of the workers to take any steps not unlawful to prevent any of the work which they had regarded as legitimately theirs being entrusted to other hands.

By the Trade Disputes and Trade Unions Act of 1927 (passed as a direct result of the General Strike in 1926) certain strikes were made illegal, and local and public authorities were prohibited from making union membership or non-membership a condition of employment, and from discriminating against workers because they were or were not organized. Public authorities were not allowed to make it a condition of a contract that persons should or should not be members of a union. There was also a provision that workmen who wished to become members of a union should have to contract expressly into membership in writing and could not become members by failing to contract out of membership. This was aimed at the passive workmen who did not bother to join a union and who had automatically become members in the days before the Act. This whole Act was repealed in 1946.

The purpose of trying to establish a Closed Shop is to give the union greater bargaining power and solidarity. Unionists can see no reason why non-unionists should be able to contribute nothing and yet obtain all the advantages for which the unionists have often made considerable sacrifices. The non-unionist sees no reason why he should contribute to funds which might be used for political work with which he has no sympathy. Therein lies the conflict. Employers, too, are divided about the Closed Shop. Some prefer to bargain with recognized unions whom they know well and who can control their members. Other employers have gone so far as to refuse to have any union men in their employment at all.

The desire of a union to establish itself to the exclusion of other unions has led to a type of Closed Shop better known in America – the refusal to work with members of any other union. In Great Britain the official policy of the Trades Union Congress was laid down in the report of the executive council in 1946: 'The Closed Shop in the sense of an establishment in which only members of a particular union can be employed to the exclusion of members of other unions is alien to British Trade Union practice and theory. Congress has never consented to the recognition of an exclusive right to organize by one union where other unions have built up their organization side by side.'

In the United States of America the Closed Shop is of long standing; there was a case as long ago as 1794 in which the shoemakers of Philadelphia compelled employers to hire only union members. Before 1947 Closed Shops were regarded by most States and by most courts as legal. They were viewed with suspicion, but the National Labour Relations Act of 1935 expressly laid down that nothing in any Federal Statute made a Closed agreement between an employer and the union illegal. Since 1947 – and in particular since the Labour Management Relations Act which was passed despite the President's veto – the position of the union which seeks to establish a Closed Shop has worsened. Most States have introduced legislation reaffirming the principle of freedom of employment and freedom to refrain from joining a union, and in fact many States have introduced into their Constitution laws prohibiting the Closed Shop. Closed Shops have not been wiped out, but the powers of the unions to insist on them have been largely curtailed and the phrase 'freedom to work' is given a very wide scope.

A lake of stew and of whiskey too

The **LAND OF COKAYGNE** is described by the late sixteenth-century lexicographer John Florio as 'the epicure's or glutton's home, the land of all delights, so taken in mockerie'.

Where Heaven is the moral and spiritual ideal, and Utopia the social and intellectual ideal, Cokaygne is the sensual ideal, the land 'where the living is easy', where the only law is the absence of compulsion to do anything at all, where physical delights are indulged without fear of recrimination and without any after-effect but renewed appetite.

This was the ideal of the serf, the common man of the Middle Ages who laboured year in, year out, with the most meagre reward for his work, and without hope of improvement in his lot in this world, where his nose was firmly held to the ground by the nobles, or in the next, where the Church promised him eternal fire if he departed so much as an inch from his prescribed course of behaviour. Even the abortive peasant revolts that flickered across Europe brought no hope of relief from the necessity to work, for had they been successful, man would still be bound to the soil, from which he seemed to have come such a little way.

Out of this despair sprang the image of a land where work should be no more, where the poor man should have the delights he most prized without even the trouble of asking for them, a land in which the rich man should have no place. Yet there is no bitterness in the concept: wealthy nobleman and fat monk doubtless had their own paradises; this was simply something that was at last exclusive to the poor. All subsequent and related Cokaygnes are marked by the emphasis on idleness – 'plus i dort, plus i gaaigne' – 'more sleep, more profit'. They are passively hedonistic, not actively vengeful on past injustice.

The vision was new to the Middle Ages: the form it took was old. For centuries legends had told of the Isles of the Blest beyond the setting sun, and it is in this direction that Cokaygne was supposed to lie.

Fur in see bi west Spayngne
Is a land ihote Cokaygne

begins the long early fourteenth-century English poem which is one of the chief literary sources, and it goes on to compare Paradise unfavourably with the delights of Cokaygne, all of which are set out in great detail. No quarrelling there is, nor sickness nor death, nor harsh weather, nor are there any of the beasts which were the serf's daily care, except in a ready prepared edible form. It is particularly in the abundance of food and drink that Cokaygne excels:

Ther beth rivers gret and fine,
Of oile, melk, honi, and wine;
Watir servith ther to no thing
Bot to sight and to waissing.

The main section of the poem is a description of the attractions of the abbey, clearly a tilt at the gluttonous monks about whom Chaucer also had some harsh things to say. The walls are made of pastry, fish and rich meat, in the meadows of the cloister grow trees with every manner of spice upon them (an imported Eastern luxury that normally graced only the rich man's table), precious jewels deck the banks of healing springs, and birds sing in every bush, while geese dressed in garlic sauce fly on to the spit, crying, 'Gees al hote, al hot!' and stewed larks fly straight into lazily opened mouths. Close by stands a nunnery, providing yet further delights for the happy monks, and the poem ends with an admonition to the rich that only by wading in swine's dirt for seven years, a symbol of the poor man's daily round, could they hope to come to this land and enjoy its pleasures.

More than a few of the details in this meticulous account recur in other Cokaygne stories. The geese flying to the spit, the description of a roast pig running about with a carving-knife in its side, the house of pastry, and the rivers that flow with good drinks are the most notable elements, the drinks modified according to local taste. The English poem makes the rivers run simply with wine (as well as the more basic oil, milk and honey), but the French are naturally more specific about vintages. In a charming thirteenth-century account, printed in Méon's *Fabliaux et Contes* in 1808, there are two rivers mentioned, one running red wine 'du meillor que l'en puist trover en Biaune', the other a superlative white unparalleled in Auxerre, Rochelle or Tonnerre.

This sensual ideal may be laughable, but there are in the accounts of it curious echoes of more spiritual concepts. The dream of a contented, warless society is in no way laughable, and it is basically the same as Traherne's ecstatic innocence – 'I knew not that there were any sins, or complaints or laws. I dreamed not of poverties, contentions, or vices ... Everything was at rest, free and immortal' – and it is, of course, foretold by Isaiah and in the Revelation of St John in famous passages. But even the incidental trappings of Cokaygne crop up in unexpected places: the appearance of the Holy Grail at the Round Table caused every knight to taste 'such meats and drinks as he best loved in the world' (as A. L. Morton has pointed out in *The English Utopia*); and the frequency of feast-days (four times as many a year, with Lent only every twenty years, in the French fable) carries a reminiscence of Peter Abelard's hymn 'O quanta qualia sunt illa sabbata'.

The Church viewed this legend with disapproval. The westward location of Cokaygne was a contradiction of Genesis ii, 8, 'And the Lord God planted a garden eastward, in Eden': and the whole concept of the intensification of 'this worldes joie' instead of its renunciation was directly opposed to the Church's teaching, and was anathema to the later Puritans. It was especially the anti-clerical satire that rankled. None the less, Cokaygne flourished, and when it did fade it was through an advance in the conditions of life and work. Harsh life in the nineteenth century had kept it alive in such songs as the American *Rock Candy Mountains* (now, with its sprightly yet sad tune, to be had on gramophone records). It harks back to the medieval poems:

In the big Rock Candy Mountains
You never change your socks,
And the little streams of alcohol
Come a-trickling down the rocks.

Continued on p. 87

PLATE 2

CULT OF THE INDIVIDUAL: Self-portrait by Salvator Rosa (1615–1673).

ANCESTOR WORSHIP: Sadahide, dancing before a Shinto shrine. The Japanese are believers in ancestor-worship.

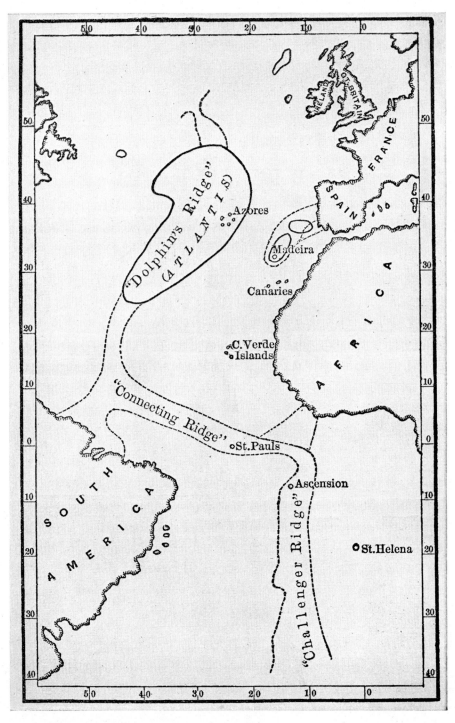

ATLANTIS: A 'Map' showing its islands and connecting ridges, from deep-sea soundings, from Donnelly's *Atlantis*.

Amaurotû vrbs.

fons Anydri. Ostium anydri

hythlodaeus.

UTOPIA: The frontispiece to *Utopia*, by Sir Thomas More (1478–1535).

BOHEMIANISM: 1. A Parisian poet wearing the garb of Bohemia.

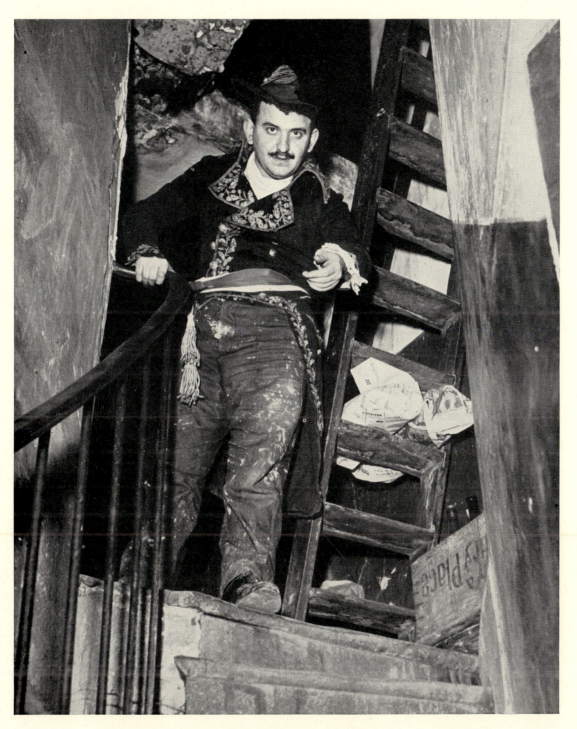

2. A painter in Paris in 'art uniform'.

BOURGEOISIE: 1. *An English Family at Tea.* The solid English aristocratic home, eighteenth century.

2. The solid English bourgeois home, nineteenth century. *Mr Wyatt and his granddaughter*, by Sir J. E. Millais (1829–1896).

CAPITAL PUNISHMENT: 1. A public hanging in Kentucky, U.S.A. A twenty-two-year-old negro convicted of the assault and murder of an old woman is led up the gallows steps.

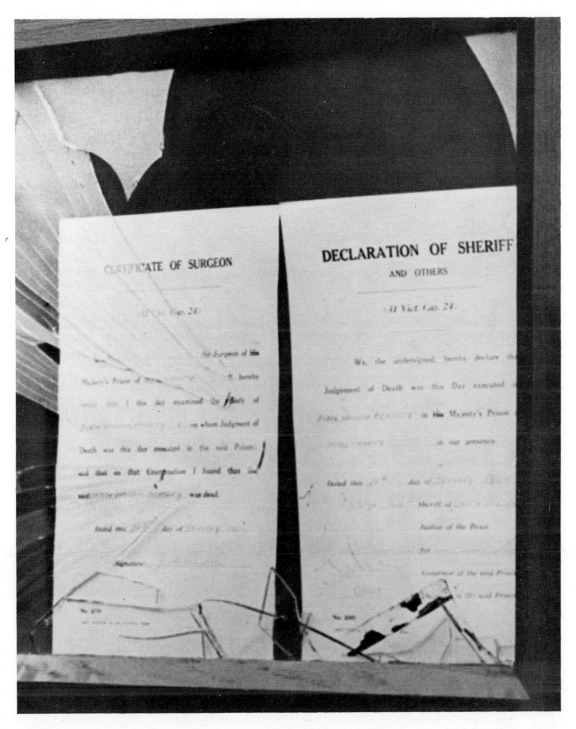

2. Capital punishment arouses violent reaction; demonstrators have smashed the glass on the certificate outside Wandsworth prison announcing an execution.

CAPITALISM: 1. The frantic capitalist world in the Paris *Bourse*, by Gustave Doré (1833–1883).

2. Reading the stock-market news. *Going to the City*,
by J. J. J. Tissot (1836–1902).

BEFORE THE CENTURY OF THE COMMON MAN: *The Derby Day* (1858), by W. P. Frith (1819–1909). The poor child turns to look at the racegoers' picnic.

THE CENTURY OF THE COMMON MAN today—a view of Blackpool beach with the famous tower in the background.

83

CHARITY: 1. *The Beginnings of Charity for Children,* by B. Nebot (1741).

2. *Charity*, by Lucas Cranach the Elder (1472–1553).

ATHEISM: Charles Bradlaugh (1833–1891), whose refusal to take the religious oath after his election to the House of Commons in 1880 led to a six-year struggle. Drawing by W. R. Sickert.

PLATE 3

MIRACLES: The Legend of the Wolf of Gubbio by Sassetta (*c*.1392–1450).

Some elements have changed. The bulldogs all have rubber teeth, the cops have wooden legs, cigarettes grow on trees, there are

> . . . lemonade springs
> Where the blue bird sings

and into the bargain

> A lake of stew and of whiskey too,
> You can paddle all about 'em in a big canoe.

The *Poor Man's Heaven* also has a lake of beer; while an Irish description gives the land of bliss sheaves of whiskey and porter. So have the idea and its elements echoed down from the Middle Ages; and there are new politicians and wiseacres who see the land of Cokaygne disgracefully re-alized at last in Great Britain's Welfare State.

In Bruegel's painting, cakes or pies are on the roof and grow from the ground like a prickly pear, the roast pig runs about ready cooked, the roast goose lays itself on the plate, a man with a spoon crawls out of a soft pudding; and prominent among those who dream of this Schlaraffenland is the peasant in the foreground, asleep on top of his flail, symbol of symbols of the hard work and sweat involved in the pursuit of daily bread. Yet his characters who desire Cokaygne include the clerk, the soldier and the knight. Bruegel's picture is one of mankind.

ILLUSTRATION: Page 217.

Cold and hot war

COLD WAR is defined by contrast with a 'hot' or 'shooting' war; it is a condition of hostility between nations exclusive of friendly intercourse and co-operation, and marked by minor acts of violence and intimidation, but stopping short of large-scale armed conflict.

It is a new name, but not a new phenomenon in history: to a great extent it was characteristic of earlier times of border raiding and skirmishing and ill-treatment by rival states of each other's citizens without full regular warfare. In the inter-national law and convention of modern Europe, however, peace and war came to be clearly and sharply differentiated, and in time of peace civi-

E

lized nations were supposed to observe a number of rules in dealing with one another, and with alien visitors or residents in their territories, on a basis which assumed that normal relations be-tween states were trustful and friendly.

Behind this assumption was the fact that the principal European powers during the eighteenth and nineteenth centuries accepted certain com-mon standards of behaviour in international re-lations, one of which was that governments as such did not carry on campaigns of public abuse against one another, but tried to promote their policies through diplomacy, while the more emotional forms of antagonism were left to un-official organs of the press.

Two factors in recent times have modified this state of affairs and have blurred the line of dis-tinction between war and peace. In the first place, the increasing importance of pre-war military preparation for deciding the issue of war when it breaks out, has made both governments and public opinion increasingly alarmed by moves of other nations which, whether by armaments, mili-tary alliances or construction of bases, appear to be threatening the security of their neighbours. There is less and less of the old leisurely sense that, apart from a small permanent military and naval establishment, it is time enough to think about waging a war when it has actually been de-clared; there is less of the mood expressed by the legendary words of Drake that 'there's time to finish this game of bowls and beat the Spaniards too'.

Today there is always the threat of the *Blitz-krieg*, the fear that a war may be lost before a shot is fired. The question how much to arm, and against whom, becomes a predominant considera-tion in peace-time economic policy, and an at-mosphere of warlike tension is kept up, so that peoples cannot relax and forget about war to the extent that they could during most of the nine-teenth century after the fall of Napoleon.

The second factor is ideological cleavage of a kind which affects fundamentally the conditions of international intercourse. Differences of cul-ture or of social and political institutions do not of themselves have this result. But ideologies which separate humanity into two basically op-posed categories, such as the revolutionary inter-national class-war doctrine of Marxism–Leninism or the racialist *Herrenvolk* concept (q.v.) of the Nazis, make it extremely difficult for governments based on them to have normal, friendly relations with other governments which by definition represent forces wholly evil and antipathetic. Further, as these ideologies are virtually 'secular religions' inspiring a fanatical belief in a historical destiny to be attained through worldwide conflict, it becomes impossible to contain them within the bounds of laws and conventions designed to regulate the intercourse of national states with limited and calculable material interests; thus the traditional procedures of diplomacy tend to break down and give way to permanent attitudes of antagonism in which particular clashes of interest are merely occasions for expressing hatred and condemnation.

Finally, the enormously increased importance of popular appeal through media of mass communication, as compared with international relations through professional diplomats, and the monopoly of all such media by the governments of totalitarian states, has brought into world politics an element of systematic official abuse and vituperation such as was quite unknown fifty years ago. When all means of publicity are controlled by the government, everything said in a newspaper or broadcast becomes an official utterance; it is impossible to maintain the old courtesies of international intercourse when states are competing with one another in the most rabid kind of mob-oratory.

The Russian Bolsheviks, seeking to appeal to the masses over the heads of their governments throughout the world, were pioneers in the disregard of traditional restraints; the Nazi Propaganda Ministry under Goebbels carried on the process; and since 1945 the extreme hostility and offensiveness of Soviet propaganda have brought exasperated counterblasts from the West. International conferences have tended to degenerate into slanging matches, with each side rhetorically appealing to a world audience outside the conference chamber rather than to the persons with whom they are supposed to be negotiating. These are conditions adverse to any relaxation of tension or to peaceful settlement of disputes through ordinary diplomacy.

The present phase of 'cold' war is one which is likely to continue as long as there are borderline countries disputed between the Communist and anti-Communist power groups. The character of Communism as a movement which combines principles of revolutionary violence and dictatorship with the international solidarity of the Soviet bloc of states, makes it impossible to regard a Communist revolution simply as an internal matter of the country in which it occurs. The Soviet–Communist challenge has thus evoked in America, and to a lesser extent in Europe, a will to counter-action which can lead at any time to sharp collisions. So far, however, the outbreaks of shooting war have remained strictly localized; the greatest crisis – that produced by the blockade of Berlin – did not lead to war, and the indications are that neither side wishes to precipitate a general conflict of arms. So cold war may become a normal condition of world affairs over a considerable period of time, just as feuds and forays were normal on the English–Scottish border for hundreds of years.

ILLUSTRATION: Page 123.

A notion of the state

COLLECTIVISM is the opposite of individualism. The earliest authority for this word dates to 1880, and three strands of meaning may conveniently be picked out for comment, of which the latter two are clients of the first.

The first is the belief that state action can be beneficial to the mass of the people even in matters which might well be left to the management of individuals. This implies a disbelief in the principle of individualism or *laissez-faire*, and a willingness to tolerate the circumscription of individual rights by extending the intervention of governments.

The second is the belief in the virtues of state ownership of the means of production, distribution and exchange. This is in essence the foregoing belief translated into economic terms, a translation which is largely a step-child of Marxism and which acquired its widest currency only after 1917. However, this is the principal meaning of 'collectivism' given in some modern dictionaries and in the fourteenth edition of the *En-*

cyclopaedia Britannica. Yet in England, at least, this was not originally, and is not now, the chief meaning of the word, which 'can cover a wide variety of state action and is indeed the vaguest term in use to cover the many forms of socialism and co-operation'.

The third meaning is more restricted still; collectivism is applied to certain types of socialistic experiment; *e.g.* the collectivization of peasants in Russia and Yugoslavia, the co-operative farms of Israel and as well as most workers' co-operatives in general.

The rise of collectivism in England was analysed at length by A. V. Dicey in *Law and Public Opinion in England*, which includes a commentary on collectivist legislation, but contains, interestingly enough, no single reference to Marx or Marxism. Dicey detects three main currents in nineteenth-century opinion: (*a*) the period of old Toryism or legislative quiescence (1800–1830), (*b*) the period of Benthamism or individualism (1825–1870), (*c*) the period of collectivism (1865–1900).

Jeremy Bentham (1748–1832) was not a social prophet or seer like Carlyle, he was not a philosopher or moralist like Mill, nor yet an economist or humanitarian like Marx. His aim was reform of the law, and his doctrine possessed the merits of being intelligible, reasonable, cogently argued and practicable. 'Not only was he thus eminently original among the lawyers and the legal philosophers of his own country; he might be said to be the first legal philosopher that had appeared in the world,' said Brougham in 1838. 'His genius was of the rarest quality,' adds Dicey; 'in Bentham's intellect were united talents seldom found in combination.' And few visionaries have been so practical and hard-headed. Not many men have exerted such a positive and practical influence after death as did Bentham. His ideas are still being profitably quarried.

Bentham laid before himself three principles of law reform: (*a*) that legislation is a science, for the law is an instrument for a purpose; (*b*) that purpose is the promotion of the greatest happiness of the greatest number (the principle of utility, or utilitarianism); (*c*) that the individual is in the main the judge of his own happiness. It is this last principle which is the stumbling-block to collectivists; it is the principle of *laissez-faire*,

which Herbert Spencer claimed to be the proper basis of sound legislation (*i.e.* rather than the principle of utility); and it is this principle of which John Stuart Mill's famous book *Essay on Liberty* (1859) is a defence.

Benthamites conceived that a programme based on these principles would aim at extending individual liberty taken in a wide sense, which would mean removing every restriction which law imposes upon the free action of the citizen, so as to secure to any individual as much freedom of action as was consistent with everyone else having the same amount.

The working out of these aims can be studied in the Acts of 1833–1854 under which usury ceased to be a crime; the years 1846–1849 saw the repeal of the Navigation Laws; in 1824 and 1825 the Combination Acts repealed all laws prohibiting workmen or employees from combining in matters pertaining to their work. Other Benthamite legislation includes the Companies Acts of 1856–1862, the Poor Law Act of 1834, the Roman Catholic Relief Act of 1829 and the Oaths Acts.

These acts embody the essence of individualism. They enshrine the Victorian self-confidence, the belief in self-help and hard work, of that intensely acquisitive society. Of the evil consequences for those unable to help themselves, whether through lack of desire, of industry, of intelligence or of opportunity, we have since been incessantly reminded; and it was the desire to combat these consequences which gave collectivism its first impulse. As Wheare implies, you cannot tell nowadays where collectivism leaves off and socialism begins. As for socialism, 'The masses approve of it,' gloomily remarks von Mises, 'it expresses the thoughts and feelings of all; it has set its seal upon our time. When history comes to tell our story, it will write above the chapter, "The Epoch of Socialism".'

Nineteenth-century collectivism had little in common with Marx – it was not an economic dogma – except humanitarianism, and its instruments of reaction against Benthamism were those prepared by Bentham: the principle of utility (which it fell in with), the doctrine of the sovereignty of parliament (originating with Sir William Blackstone), and the tendency or habit of extending legislation to improve the mechanism

of government. Its leaders were the Tory humanitarians, Richard Oastler (1789–1861), Michael
Thomas Sadler (1780–1835), the poet Southey
(1774–1843), and above all, Lord Shaftesbury
(1801–1885). These men had gradually come to
the view that the state ought to interfere to protect certain members of the working class from
the excessive pressures of the system, and this is
a collectivist notion.

The defeat of the Chartists in 1848 was perhaps
the first big step away from individualism, for its
consequence was an increasing interest in trade
unionism with its taste for collective bargaining.
The unions contended that they were entitled to
legal recognition, although they admittedly aimed
at the restraint of trade, and claimed the right to
bring pressure to bear on any artisan in a given
trade to prevent his following his inclination,
should that be contrary to union rules or wishes,
although this admittedly circumscribed his freedom of action. There was a collectivist tinge
about the Railway Companies Acts, of which the
first was passed as early as 1823.

The abandonment of the Charter and the moderation of the unionists ensured them plenty of
sympathy from those who did not care for Benthamism. Disraeli's friends may have had little in
common with the struggling millhands, but they
liked the millowners' radicalism even less. Other
signs of changing opinion were the publication in
1848 of Mill's *Political Economy*, which tries to
harmonize Benthamite teaching with certain
working-class aspirations, to be followed in 1849–
1850 by Carlyle's *Latter-Day Pamphlets* containing tremendous assaults upon *laissez-faire*
principles, and in 1850 by Charles Kingsley's
Alton Locke. Thus, four factors point the decline
of individualism: the rise of Tory philanthropy
(Shaftesbury and the factory movement), the gain
of collectivist dogma in the working class (unionism), the changing current of thought (Mill and
Carlyle), and the advance of industry which called
for such measures as the Railway Companies and
Joint Stock Companies Acts.

No change in legislative opinion can be found
till after 1867, the year of the Reform Act by
which the Tories gave the vote to the urban workers. Before this Act parliament represented the
essentially Benthamite middle classes. Mill had
written in 1861, 'In this country ... what are called

the working classes may be considered as excluded from all direct participation in the government,' and he went on to speak of the 'too lavish
and indiscriminating beneficence' of the governing classes.

It is today easy to forget that the Reform Act
of 1867 passed because many Tories believed that
the working-class vote would diminish the power
of individualistic liberalism. A prerequisite of this
belief was, of course, the lack of extremism in the
working-class movement. One may note, too, the
fading of the political in favour of the social or
economic overtones of collectivism.

The history of collectivist legislation is not yet
complete, for collectivist enthusiasm probably
reached its zenith during 1945–1950, the period of
office of the Labour Government in Great Britain. No theorist should be so simple-minded as
to be surprised by the ease with which collectivism in England surmounted the discredit into
which Russian methods had fallen. The roots of
the adulation of Leninism common in the Labour
Party after 1917 must obviously be shallow compared with the long and honourable tradition of
interventionist legislation handed down from
Lord Shaftesbury. Continental socialism is a doctrine of revolution, and the Welfare State owes
far more to Tory philanthropy than to any such
teachings. Today the paradox is that it is the
Labour Party, with its collectivist traditions,
which has inherited the legacy of Tory philanthropy, while the Conservatives have without any
embarrassment inherited the legacy of Benthamism and that of nineteenth-century middle-class
radicalism.

It is doubtful whether the number of genuine
socialists in Britain is large; few people are anxious about the fate of the specifically socialist
parts of the Labour Party's programme, and not
many individualists are so enthusiastic that they
would welcome the disappearance of the Welfare
State even in return for the resultant gains in freedom from regulation and taxation. The unions in
a nationalized industry dislike striking, especially
when a Labour Government is in power; while
in the Conservative Party the new Benthamites
dislike such things as protectionism, social services and the restrictive practices of big business.
Neither party has swallowed its inheritance whole.
Government must compromise.

Black, brown, yellow, white

COLOUR BAR represents those policies, laws, customs and personal attitudes by which a group is discriminated against because it differs in the colour of its skin from another dominating group. The two most notorious instances today are the *apartheid* policy of the South African Nationalists and 'Jim Crow' in the southern states of America.

The same general pattern is followed in both these regions: political rights are denied either directly or by a poll-tax, by 'white primary' or other restrictions, reinforced by intimidation; educational facilities are limited and higher education is discouraged; the groups concerned are segregated in special areas, which tend, through the poverty of their inhabitants, to become slums; they must behave in particular ways when they enter the territory of their oppressors.

The philosophy behind this discrimination rests upon the belief that the coloured people belong to an inferior race. They are variously considered to be backward, lazy, childish, dirty, animal-like or merely different. Two forces in particular support this view: first, the tendency of an 'in-group' to despise those outside it; secondly, the desire to prevent economic competition and to keep available a cheap supply of labour. Very complicated psychological attitudes are also involved.

However, this wholesale discrimination is not the only form of colour bar. In British colonies, for instance, in which some encouragement is now given to the gradual development of a democracy, discrimination may be tacit and subtle; it may function more as a general atmosphere than as an explicit policy, leading to little more than the exclusion of 'natives' from certain public places, such as hotels and restaurants, together with their absolute exclusion from private clubs.

There is a marked difference in this respect between the social status of the negroes in East and West Africa (Kenya and Nigeria or the Gold Coast). In Malaya the High Commissioner spoke recently against the colour bar, particularly unreasonable in a country 'governed' by Malay sultans and protected by a vastly enlarged native police force – nevertheless it would be strange to see a yellow or brown-skinned person in a Singapore club, however prosperous or politically important he might be. 'They have their own clubs and we have ours', is the usual explanation, though it is not difficult to see that in a colonial setting, where the club is likely to be a secondary administrative centre, exclusion will be very much resented.

Few travellers to the British-administered East will fail to meet highly cultivated natives who remember, and sometimes cherish, at least one slight of this kind. Sometimes it is difficult to separate colour discrimination from economic patterning. In Singapore to be a first, second or third-class patient in a hospital is a matter of money; but this does not apply to the administrative regulations, which cause long queues of natives at the Food Office while the whites, fewer in number, are dealt with briskly. In its subtler aspects the colour bar need be no different from anti-semitism (q.v.). Indeed, it is quite possible that a negro would be more acceptable in French-Canada than a Jew.

Anthropologists suggest that all civilizations originated with 'coloured' people, whether the yellow skins of the Chinese river valleys, the browns of India, Mesopotamia and Egypt, or the swarthy countenances of the Mediterranean coasts. Certainly no difference of intelligence has been found between negroes, emotionally today's most 'coloured' and colour-barred people, and other races. In this matter science finds cultural conditioning more important than hereditary factors, and if certain negroes are more 'childlike' than whites of the same age, it is due to the circumstances in which they have been brought up. Thus the Arabs – scarcely a progressive force today – were in fact the transmitters of Greek culture to the West.

Colour consciousness is not a modern invention, although its emphasis seems one of the least pleasant features of the last hundred or so years. There is evidence that the Indian caste system originated as an attempt to keep colour differences well marked. Chinese exclusiveness, and the superiority felt by many Greeks, notably Aristotle, may have involved colour to some extent. In fact Aristotle quarrelled with the sophists over his belief that an eternal law required that certain peoples should be inferior to others. On the other hand, Alexander treated Greeks and Barbarians alike, permitted inter-marriage, and thus laid the foundations of that broadening sense of community which was to be a feature of the Roman Empire and to some extent of Christendom. However, one cannot say of the Crusaders, as one can of Islam, that they had no sense of colour at all.

The spread of imperial conquest was not entirely to blame, for the Portuguese and the Spaniards, whatever their other faults, mixed freely with the South American peoples. Nor were the English always susceptible to colour; there are many charming stories of American Indians and Polynesians brought home and treated with honour, as well as great interest, despite the slave-markets in the ports. But as empire spread, and became administrative as well as commercial, requiring an ethos and a rationale, the northern Europeans felt it necessary to demonstrate their superiority. Bureaucrats and military men succeeded adventurers. One 'Noble Savage' (q.v.) might be exceedingly picturesque, but a teeming Indian community of noble savages must be governed with aloofness.

Recruits for government were drawn from the less tolerant classes; they brought out wives more conventional than themselves, were faced simultaneously with a tempting luxury and a tedious loneliness, and developed the 'White Man's Burden' as a result. *You must not go native; you must not let down the side.* Unfortunately this co-incided with much 'Nordic' theory, perpetrated by Gobineau in his *Essai sur l'inégalité des races humaines* (1853) and by Anglo-Saxon devotees on each side of the Atlantic. The age of the solar topee and the cholera belt regarded its native charges as 'lesser breeds without the law', and saw to it that they were provided with the accoutrements of modesty. Between the Black Hole of Calcutta and the massacre at Amritsar there reigned an unimaginative propriety which would have astonished Warren Hastings.

As conditions worsened, racial assertiveness seems to have grown more acute on both sides. The defeat of Italy by Ethiopia in 1896, of Russia by Japan in 1904, the Boxer Rebellion, the revolt in Mexico – there were a dozen indications that the coloured peoples were on the march. Throughout the West one heard of the 'Yellow Peril'.

About the turn of the century the American negroes reached the nadir of their fortunes. At the end of the Civil War they had enjoyed a brief period of social equality, during which they entered state legislatures and government positions, but it was soon clear that both the white planters, and even more the illiterate 'poor whites', who often found themselves in competition with their coloured neighbours, were determined to evade the provisions of the American Constitution. The Ku Klux Klan formed the shock troops in support of this policy. From the 1880s to 1930 over four thousand people were lynched in the United States, of whom more than three thousand were negroes. During the same period race riots occurred in various northern cities where colour feeling was always in danger of flaring up. The novelist Richard Wright has described what it felt like to be a negro just before the Second World War both in a backward southern state and amongst the communists and liberals of Chicago, and there does not seem to have been a great deal of difference between the two.

Feeling against minority groups is still strong in the United States, whether colour is involved or not, and Italians, Mexicans and Puerto Ricans have had to suffer as well as negroes and Orientals. It is hard to say whether anti-negro feeling is strongest because the negroes form such a large part of the population or because they are held to be most markedly different from the whites, both in their physical appearance and in their supposed possession of certain gifts which other people secretly envy. It may be that Anglo-Saxon puritans are conscious of repressing their drives towards the freedom and innocence implied by a Garden of Eden and that they make the negroes their scapegoats. It would be ironic, indeed, if the colour bar were an expression of our bitterness at lost childhood, lost passion, lost gaiety, and at the fact that there is so little colour in our lives.

ILLUSTRATION: Page 180.

Robert Owen to Joseph Stalin

COMMUNISM is an old idea, but a new word. Meaning a theory of society by which all property should be vested in the community and all labour organized for the common good, 'communism' first appeared in English literature in 1843.

Utopian communities which would answer this description were dreamed of by Thomas More in the sixteenth century; and indeed existed amongst early Christians, and in medieval monasteries. In the eighteen-twenties communist communities founded on the principles of Robert Owen (1771–1858) sprang up and withered away on the eastern seaboard of the United States.

Nobody, in the English-speaking world at any rate, took communism or communists very seriously in the early years of the nineteenth century. Most would have agreed carelessly with the Corn Law jingle;

> What is a Communist? One that hath yearnings
> For equal division of unequal earnings.

The theorizing of Karl Marx (1818–1883) transformed the situation, and it is to Marx, then to Lenin and Stalin that the idea of communism owes its meaning.

Marx wrote at a time when the Industrial Revolution was rapidly developing man's wealth, but at the same time condemning large numbers of workers to a soul-destroying labour under terrible conditions. Europe, too, was still seething with the political ideas which had been loosed by revolutionary France.

Under these influences Marx evolved 'dialectical materialism' (q.v.). By 'dialectics' is meant the conflict of opposites and, from this conflict, the emergence, by a final reconciliation, or synthesis, of a new idea. Marx believed, too, that man's dominant motives are materialist: that man's actions are governed by a struggle to control the means of production (*i.e.* land, labour and machinery or tools) for his own material benefit. In this struggle some groups triumph over others, and there emerge two classes: those who own the means of production and those who do not; history was a perpetual struggle between these two opposing classes (the dialectical clash of opposites) for control of the means of production. This conflict would be resolved by a final synthesis producing the communist society in which private property would be abolished.

According to Marx, the conflict would take the form of a revolution in which the working class, who created all of value as a result of their labour, would be victorious; in the same way the capitalist class in many European countries had recently ousted the landowning aristocracy from their position of supreme power. In due course the workers would set up a dictatorship of the proletariat to establish the communist regime. Eventually this dictatorship would 'wither away', leaving true communism.

Marx believed, too, that all institutions of the capitalist state, including the churches, the administration of justice and parliament, were simply methods whereby the dominant property-owning class kept the others in subjection, so that all would be overthrown in the revolution.

Marx was not only a theorist. He was instrumental in founding working-class societies in Germany to work for the revolution, which, although inevitable and predestined, required organizing. But he was banished from Germany in the wave of repression which followed the rising in 1848, and thereafter came to England, where he founded the International Working Men's Association. The revolution, which he expected yearly in one of the highly developed capitalist countries, never happened, but his ideas took root, and his followers increased in all the countries of Europe. Some of them became social democrats, believing, that is to say, in an ultimate communist or socialist society, but aiming to achieve that end by peaceful methods, working through existing political institutions. Others stood firm by the revolutionary method. Among these was Vladimir Ilyich Lenin (1870–1924), who in his exiles from Russia schemed and organized and prepared in London and Switzerland.

Lenin made a number of contributions to communist theory, of which the most important was his doctrine of Imperialism. He wrote: 'Imperialism is the eve of the proletarian social revolution', when 'capitalism arrives at the threshold of the most complete socialization of production'. Capitalism, he thought, developed until the great monopoly firms controlled their governments and forced them into a struggle for markets, compelling them to exploit colonial peoples for raw materials. So inevitably Imperialist wars would arise out of the struggle for markets between great capitalist states.

Lenin's expectations were to some extent justi-fied, for it was the First World War which gave the Bolsheviks (the revolutionary wing of the Russian Socialist Party) their chance to establish a communist dictatorship – the Union of Soviet Socialist Republics.

It would have seemed curious to Marx that Russia should have been the first communist country. Yet much of what we now mean by com-munism is in fact more Russian than Marxist. Russia was a backward country; she had avoided that emphasis on the freedom of the individual which came out of the Renaissance and the Re-formation. Thus a ruthless disregard of human life and rights was a common feature of Russian history. So, too, it was less difficult to persuade and coerce the Russian peasants into collective farms (where there is no private ownership) be-cause of the traditional village organization of the Mir, which until the nineteenth century had held and organized the peasant's land in common. Lenin's task was made easier by the absence of an effective middle class, for Tsarist Russia was still in the main a land of land-hungry peasants and landlords with no effective parliament and little local self-government.

In 1917 the Russian army had suffered a series of shatteringly expensive defeats at German and Austrian hands, and its supply system, in cor-rupt and inefficient hands, had virtually broken down. It was not surprising, therefore, in Lenin's words that 'the Army voted for the Revolution with its feet'.

By 1924, when Lenin died, the Revolutionary régime was consolidated. But there was no sign of the state withering away. On the contrary, the dictatorship became ever more rigid under the leadership of Joseph Vissarionovich Stalin (1879–1953) and the politically élite members of the Communist Party. There were perpetual strug-gles within the party, struggles for power and struggles on policy. Of these, the most significant was the struggle between Trotsky and Stalin, which led to the former's banishment from Rus-sia. This centred round an important point of communist theory. Marx and Lenin had always regarded the aim of communism as world re-volution, and had thought that a communist régime in one country would be followed im-mediately by others all over the world. The early

Bolshevik leaders, including Trotsky, had worked for this spead of the revolution, but although soviets were set up in Hungary and Bavaria for a short time, it was clear by the end of the nineteen-twenties that the world revolution was far away. Stalin therefore adopted the slogan of 'Socialism in one country', and started the process of isolat-ing Russia from the rest of the world and at the same time building up Russia's industrial strength.

Stalin's other contribution to the development of communism was his handling of the question of nationality. By ensuring that those commun-ists governing the outer provinces of Russia – e.g. Kazakhstan, or Mongolia – were natives rather than Russians, the communists have been able to avoid the upsurge of national feelings. Added to a genuine absence of racial superiority, this is a valuable weapon for communists inciting colonial peoples against their overlords. The col-lective farm, too, provides hope for the Far East-ern peasant condemned by the pressure of num-bers to struggle for his living on a wholly inade-quate plot of land, without modern equipment.

Communism in brief, is a 'secular religion', a political faith which gives its devotees a key to all sections of human endeavour, since politics, re-ligion, literature, art, music, biology, etc., can all be interpreted in the light of the class struggle. Thus, a dock strike in the United States, or the discovery of an Indian wolf child proving not only the triumph of environment over heredity but the degradation of capitalist society, all point the way to the communist society.

ILLUSTRATION: Pages 126, 127, 128, 129 and 131.

Concern among the Quakers

A CONCERN (in the Quaker sense, now bor-rowed also by others) means the recognition of a course of action as laid upon an individual by 'the motion of Love' (John Woolman's phrase for the will of God); and the carrying out of this action through a particular discipline.

Thus a 'concern' overrides the motives both of duty and desire; a man cannot 'have a concern' for something which he *thinks ought to be done*, nor yet for something which he *would like to do*: a concern can arise only from the 'motion of Love'; but when that is felt it must be followed, however trivial or outrageous its expression may appear. It may involve no more than a call on a neighbour; it may involve going to the Sultan of Turkey or the Tsar of Russia.

Both these instances are historical: Mary Fisher, bred a servant girl at Selby in Yorkshire, went alone in 1658 to Mohammed IV, who received her with state ceremony in his camp near Adrianople; Thomas Story in 1697 went to Peter the Great, to plead for Friends in Danzig; William Allen and Stephen Grellet went to the Tsar Alexander in 1818, to lay before him the condition of Russian prisons and the defects of Russian education. A concern may involve something personal like keeping a Journal (John Woolman kept his 'to leave some hints of my experience of the Goodness of God'); it may involve a complete change in the way of life: William Tuke, tea merchant of York, and his wife Esther in 1796 opened The Retreat, the first mental hospital (as opposed to madhouse) in England.

Concern in this sense is clearly not a Quaker prerogative; Florence Nightingale was 'under concern' in the strictest sense, and even had it laid upon her 'by the audible voice of God' that she should serve the sick. The Quaker conception, however, provides also a discipline for the testing of the concern and machinery for carrying it out: it is obvious that many people have 'heard voices' ordering them to do things who have not proved to be Florence Nightingales; and equally certain that Miss Nightingale would have been helped by being able to use a sympathetic and powerful organization.

To recognize concern at all, it is necessary first to submit to 'the refining hand of God's power'. Love cannot move except through a channel prepared for it. This process is painful; but danger comes with the first success; the novice is then liable to 'outrun his guide'. 'O thou called of the Lord, thou canst never become his chosen unless thou obey his call ... if thou art not faithful in the little, thou wilt not be made ruler over much' (Job Scott, 1751–1793).

Though any concern comes first to an individual, he is bound, if it is anything more than trivial or personal, to submit it to the group – the particular Meeting of which he is a member. 'The fleece must be tried wet and dry' is the Quaker expression, alluding to Gideon's insistence that God should give him a double check of the sign miraculously sent him before the attack on Midian (Judges vi. 39). Over-insistence is taken as a bad sign: 'Let the baptizing power of the Spirit of Truth be its own witness.'

If the concern in question receives the approval of the Meeting, the decision (which must be unanimous, since Quakers never vote) is recorded in a Minute drawn up by the Clerk (who is both Chairman and Secretary), according to the 'sense of the Meeting'. This Minute is more than a record; the Meeting which accepts a concern now shares it; if money is required, the Meeting must help to find it, and must take any other action, including prayer, that is required. In a matter of importance, the Minute goes in ascending order to the Monthly, Quarterly, and at last to the Yearly Meeting (an Annual Conference with final authority). If the concern involves travel, the Friend under concern carries the Minute with him as a passport and explanation; and returns it, endorsed by the Meetings he has visited, at the end of his labours, or, in Quaker phrase, 'when he is clear'. ('Now I am clear; now I am fully clear,' said George Fox as he died.)

The whole process may be seen at its best in the life of John Woolman of New Jersey (1720–1772). In 1763, for instance, he felt 'inward drawings' to visit the Red Indians at a time when war threatened between them and the Whites. He told no one ('except my dear Wife') until it came 'to some degree of ripeness'. He then laid the concern before Friends, 'at our Monthly and Quarterly and then at our General Spring Meeting'. 'Having the unity of Friends', he prepared to go; but on the night before his departure he was awakened by a man from Philadelphia with the news that 'the Indians had taken a fort Westward and Slain and Scalped English people in divers places'.

'It was a humbleing time to me,' says Woolman. 'In this Conflict of Spirit there were great Searchings of Heart, and Strong Cries to the Lord, that no motion might in the least degree be attended to, but that of the pure Spirit of Truth.'

He then set out with one companion, and when they lay at night under the stars, Woolman thought over his motives while this friend slept: 'I grew jealous of myself, lest the desire of Reputation, as a man firmly settled to persevere through dangers; Or the fear of a disgrace ariseing on my returning without performing the visit might have some place in me.' The trees near their tent had been peeled, and painted in red and black by the Indians with war scenes. 'Thinking on the innumerable Afflictions which the proud, fierce Spirit produceth in the world ... the desire to cherish the Spirit of Love and peace amongst these people, arose very fresh in me.'

Arrived at the Indian township which was his destination, John Woolman was received in a friendly way. He showed the Indians his certificate and spent four days with them 'that I might feel and understand their life, and the spirit they live in, if happily I might receive some Instruction from them, or they be in any degree helped forward by my following the Leadings of Truth amongst them'. Then, feeling his mind 'at Liberty to return', Woolman went safely home.

It would have been useless to ask Woolman what good his visit did. The Quaker attitude to this question is best expressed in the story of Stephen Grellet, a French nobleman who fled to America from the French Revolution, and there became a Quaker. Travelling in the woods, he felt impelled to return on his tracks with great difficulty to a lumberjacks' hut which he had noticed, and to preach there. The woodmen had departed, but, feeling the foolishness of it, he preached to the empty hut. Years later a man stopped him to tell him that he had heard the sermon and had been changed by it; he was one of the party of lumberjacks returning for something he had left, but had remained hidden from the extraordinary preacher. This story is probably legendary; but much of the truth about 'concern' is in it.

War and the C.O.

CONSCIENTIOUS OBJECTION is the refusal to perform compulsory military service, stemming from a religious or ethical belief that warfare is quite simply wrong. The earliest re-

cords of the Christian religion reveal that many Christians refused to become soldiers in the Roman legions and accepted the penalty of death. The first known conscientious objector was Maximilianus, a Numidian Christian who was conscripted for the army in A.D. 295, when he was twenty-one. He said: 'I cannot serve as a soldier, I cannot do evil, I am a Christian', and was executed. Afterwards he was canonized.

Three years later, Roman records report that a centurion, Marcellus, cast off his military belt on the occasion of the Emperor's birthday and cried out, 'I serve Jesus Christ, the eternal King'. Marcellus objected to sacrificing to the gods and to the Emperor, and also regarded military service as incompatible with the practice of Christianity. Not only was he put to death; the clerk to the court, who protested against the sentence, was also executed. These were not isolated instances. In the years preceding and following the outbreak of the Roman persecution of Christians in A.D. 303 there were many cases of Christian soldiers leaving the army and suffering martyrdom.

The grounds of objection to military service on the part of these early Christians were three. They objected, like Marcellus, to sacrificing to the gods and to the Emperor, an objection which led many Christians, other than soldiers, to be thrown to the lions. They objected to joining the Roman legions, because in their view the Christian Kingdom was 'not of this world'; they looked forward to the Second Coming of Christ and his Kingdom. And it would appear, as instanced by Maximilianus, that they also regarded military service itself as 'evil', as incompatible with Christian conduct.

The first of these grounds is no longer relevant, though before the First World War conscientious objectors in Great Britain were concerned that they would be required to take the military oath, which they regarded as the modern equivalent of sacrifices to the gods and the Emperor. That issue was decided for them, however, by the terms of the Military Service Act, which 'assumed' that they had taken the oath. For Christian objectors, the two other grounds remain.

One group of conscientious objectors, known as Jehovah's Witnesses, still literally take the view that they must not fight for the kingdoms of this world, because they anticipate the Second

Coming. They even believe that they will be justified, when the great moment comes, in taking up arms to establish the new Kingdom. But beyond this sect there are considerable numbers of Christians who in a more fundamental way advance Christ's declaration that his Kingdom is not of this world as the ground of their refusal of military service.

They attach to it the injunction that it is the duty of Christians to give unto Caesar the things that are Caesar's and unto God the things that are God's. They interpret this as meaning that they are in duty bound to pay the taxes which the state demands (which was, indeed, the very problem which stimulated Christ's command), but that they would be wrong to surrender their personalities, their *spirit*, to the state for purposes which they regard as un-Christian: their essential selves are not Caesar's, but God's.

This raises the question whether military service is un-Christian. The religious objector holds that the Christian obligations to love your neighbour as yourself, to forgive your enemies and to regard all human beings as the sons of God are incompatible with war. He holds that love of others should be the Christian way of life in all circumstances. If he is true to his convictions, he does not apply this only to military service, he applies it to all his personal relations. It is a difficult faith to live up to.

He accepts the political implications of this faith, and believes in unilateral disarmament. He would, if he could, abolish the army, the navy and the air force. He would have his nation approach other nations in international affairs with the moral appeal alone. In the final resort he would be prepared for hostile forces to invade his country and to occupy it rather than defend the nation by force of arms. His opposition to any government which he regarded as unjust would be limited to non-violent means, exemplified by the movement of 'non-co-operation' which was initiated by Gandhi (1869–1948) in India. Even such resistance would be carried on without ill-will.

The pacifist interpretation of Christianity has been the special characteristic of the Society of Friends, the Quakers; but it has its adherents within all Christian denominations. The Anglican Church, the Roman Catholic Church, the Free Churches – all have their pacifist groupings which contribute to the ranks of conscientious objectors.

But conscientious objectors are not limited to those who are motivated by religious principles. In Britain, at least, it has been recognized by some tribunals that men may be conscientious in their objection to military service on ethical, intellectual or political grounds, irrespective of religious faith. This recognition of conscience has even gone to the point of exempting from military service men who have said openly to the tribunals that they would fight in a social revolution. There is one case on record of the granting of exemption on conscientious grounds to an Indian who declined to fight in the Second World War because his country did not then possess self-government.

The Military Service Acts do not define conscientious objection. Many of the tribunals regard it as a conviction, whatever its basis, held so deeply that to the individual concerned it is a matter of right or wrong, a conviction whose denial would be a debasement of personality.

Britain has gone further than any other nation in the liberality of its interpretation of conscience. Between June 1939 and December 1952, 44,789 youths and men were exempted by the local tribunals out of 63,907 who registered as conscientious objectors. These figures do not necessarily mean that the tribunals were easy-going in granting exemptions. During the same period 1,129 men were court-martialled in the armed forces on conscientious grounds after failing to obtain exemption, and 5,576 underwent civil prosecution for refusing to be medically examined for military service, or for other offences against the conscription laws. These have often involved long terms of imprisonment.

Conscientious objection to military service is not, of course, confined to Great Britain. The War Resisters' International has members in twenty-eight countries and contacts in sixty others. Under many governments the refusal of military service involves imprisonment; in some it involves death.

Whether it be in America or Russia, the same spirit animates these men. 'Surely we belong to one family,' wrote a Russian objector in 1949. 'It is the one spirit which is working through us. We begin to be encouraged that even our very small strivings are not in vain – we have added our little brick to the great cathedral of the unity of mankind.'

There speaks the best in conscientious objection from the early days of Christianity to our present time.

States within the state

The **CORPORATIVE STATE** was the term adopted by the Italian Fascist dictator, Benito Mussolini (1883–1945) to give concrete form to certain ideas about the nature of the totalitarian state. For totalitarian states the word 'state' has become charged with a special meaning. It is not conceived only as a necessary instrument to enable society to run smoothly – as a machine – but absorbs into itself all patriotic emotions and allegiances. Only the state and its servants know the true mission of the people, so the state alone has the responsibility and the power to guide the people towards this appointed end, uncurbed by any constitutional check, with claims to unqualified obedience and the right to organize all forms of individual and group life needed to further the people's destiny.

The state, in Fascist theory, became the entire expression of nationhood, owning a total allegiance from its members, so that it was unpatriotic or treasonable to oppose the group which controlled it. As Mussolini said, the nation is created by the state, and outside the state there can be neither individuals nor groups – political parties, associations, syndicates or classes. The totalitarian organization of the corporative state is thus an organic part of Fascist political theory, giving to the institutions of the nation the unity which the state holds over it in theory. Through it the authority of the state is carried into all the important forms of association, which become inspired by the state, from which all life and initiative flow to the nation.

All absolutist states have had to deal with the problem of the associations and 'corporations' living a group life within their boundaries. These groups are potential centres of opposition to the central government (for no individuals have power in isolation). So for Thomas Hobbes, in his *Leviathan* (1651), they were lesser commonwealths within the bowels of a greater – sapping its strength 'like worms in the entrails of a natural man'. The absolutist states of the seventeenth century found a weapon in Roman Law against these groups – under what was called the Concession Theory all associations needed the permission of the state to exist. Where this was not granted – or conceded – they might legally be broken up. It is to this tradition that the totalitarian states of the twentieth century look back, but the corporative state went further, in that the state did not merely give permission for certain associations to exist, but actively organized them and controlled them: sanctioned by the state, they become welded into the body of the state.

In this manner the long shadow of the Italian state fell over the complexities of Italian social life. The recognized trade unions became the official bodies for organizing the labour force in the national interests, just as the employers' associations became councils directing industry and commerce in conjunction with the state. The Italian Charter of Labour, which organized both capital and labour, decreed, in Article 3, that '... only the juridically recognized syndicate which submits to the control of state has the right to represent legally the entire category of employees and workers for which it is constituted'. The army became, from principle rather than necessity, a national, not a professional one; youth movements became fused into a single public monopoly – another creature of the state – while press and radio formed other controlled adjuncts of government.

In totalitarian states such associations become part of the official fabric of the state – so it was with the Charter of Labour in Italy or the Reich Labour Service in Germany, and with the youth movements in both countries – or else they are unofficially infiltrated by members of the one political party which has the right to exist. In either case the purpose and function of the control is clear; and associations which were reluctant to be embraced by the state were outlawed, or deprived of their leaders. Thus the tentacles of the state spread down through all the important aspects of social, communal life – except for a certain freedom in religious life – controlling citizens as children, conscripts, workers and employers.

ILLUSTRATION: Page 130.

___

And God saw everything that he had made ...

CREATION is the beginning of the world, whether it be the whole universe or only the terrestrial globe; and the term naturally implied a creator.

What is, must have been made: this idea that the world had a beginning is presumably as old as man, and the inconceivability of anything not having a beginning must have led men from the time they first thought about the subject to postulate a creator. There is no need to recount the resultant myths in detail, but they have certain features which are worth mentioning.

In the first place they all presuppose a *personal* creator. This is usually a god, but he may also be a god-like man, or even a god-like animal. The actual mechanism by which the world is created frequently involves an egg, but otherwise varies so widely as to make it certain that there is no revelation in this respect and that fancy has been given free rein.

In the primitive as in more sophisticated myths, the creator sometimes makes the world out of already existing material, and sometimes engenders it, so to speak, out of himself. The first view is expressed in *Paradise Lost*, and in Dryden's picture of Nature lying 'underneath a heap of jarring atoms' before creation, but the more official Christian and Mohammedan view, derived from the Jewish belief, is that God created the world out of nothing.

In the Bible there is a detailed account of the process of creation, followed by a continuous genealogy from Adam down to historical times. This makes it possible to calculate the Biblical date of creation, and in the seventeenth century Archbishop Ussher, the Irish Primate, worked out the accepted date, 4004 B.C. This of course referred only to the creation of the earth, though it was intended to have a universal application.

Present-day scientific opinion on the creation of the world, when by this we mean the earth, is not at all settled. One school holds that the earth, together with the other planets, condensed out of a filament of gas drawn from the sun. How it was drawn out is a matter of opinion. Another school holds that the planets are the remnants of the hard core of a companion to the sun which exploded and, except for these remains, was entirely dissipated. Another again believes that the planets condensed at the same time as the sun from the same gaseous cloud, and are thus, so to speak, not children but brothers of the sun.

All agree that the earth first condensed somewhere about 3,000 million years ago. From there on, the scientific view is that the creation of the earth as we know it today is a serial and unending process. The oldest rocks solidified perhaps 2,000 million years ago, and life emerged perhaps 1,000 million years ago. Fish are about 300 million years old, reptiles 200 million, and deciduous trees and grasses about 100 million. Mammals first became predominant about 50 million years ago. As for man, it is estimated that creatures more man than ape have been in existence for a million years, and that *Homo sapiens*, true man, is at least 100,000 years old. This is a far cry from Archbishop Ussher's 4004 B.C.

The question of the creation of the whole universe is a very different one. Certain cosmological theories, such as that of Milne, demand a starting point for the history of the universe as we know it. This beginning is also implied in one version of the theory of the 'expanding universe'. On the other hand some cosmologists, such as Hoyle and Gold, believe that the universe, while expanding, is infinite in space and time. That is to say, there is no reason for postulating by their theory a particular moment when the whole universe was created. They suggest on the contrary that there is and always has been a 'continuous creation'. But the whole topic is extremely open, and indeed it is one in which science is at the moment not much interested, regarding it as outside its province.

It is indeed possible that nothing useful will ever be said about the creation of the universe, because of the philosophical problems which are involved in any approach to the subject. These crop up as much when a personal creator is postulated as when he is not.

Consider this argument. Suppose God exists, and created the universe. He must have done it for a reason. Since He is omniscient, he must always have known this reason, and since before the universe was created there was no such thing as time and change, this reason must always have been a good one. Therefore if he was ever to create the world, he must have done it the first moment he was able to: therefore God and the world must have come into existence at the same time.

It may be objected that it is improper to talk about time before the universe was created, as St Augustine thought; since time is no more than a part of the universe, and God is timeless. But if this is so, then it becomes literally meaningless to talk of God existing before the universe was created. Nor can we imagine in the faintest degree what a timeless existence is, and thus we ought not to attach any meaning to the words.

Another question already mentioned is: If the universe was created, was it created out of something or out of nothing? If out of something, then we must ask what this something was created out of. If out of nothing, then the process is unimaginable, and it becomes futile to try to make any statement about it at all.

Again, there has been no satisfactory answer to the argument that if the world must necessarily have a creator to engender it and start it off, then this creator must himself need a creator. An infinite regress of this kind can only be avoided by juggling with the notion of time; which leads to the complications outlined above.

The truth is that clear thought about the idea of creation is almost impossible. Kant pointed this out more than 150 years ago. It is inconceivable, as he said, that the universe should not have had a beginning, that it should just stretch back into the past for ever. But it is also inconceivable that it should have a beginning, because we cannot imagine anything genuinely without a preceding cause, and this is what the universe in its first moment of existence (or God in his first act) would be. This, said Kant, is a contradiction which springs from the fact that we are trying to think about something which we cannot think about, because it lies outside the world by its very nature, whereas we can only think about what we have experienced in some way or another. This just argument applies equally to ra-

tionalists and to theologians. In this, as in many other things, we should be wiser if we followed Wittgenstein's maxim: 'Whereof we cannot speak, thereof we must keep silent.'

What is culture?

CULTURE is a word involving a number of concepts of the greatest importance to modern man, who may wish to 'defend Western Culture' or to 'spread culture amongst the masses' or to appreciate the 'culture of primitive peoples', while depending upon a 'culture' of penicillin when he falls ill and presenting his wife on her birthday with a string of 'cultured' pearls.

Unfortunately, as these phrases show, the examination of culture can easily become bogged down in the rival definitions of archaeologists (see the *Three Ages System*), to whom the word may apply to a variety of stone implements, or of anthropologists, who use it in their explanations of exogamy or cannibalism, or again of sociologists, who, examining the mixed and complex ways of urban peoples in such a study as *Middletown*, find culture patterns in the statistics of club-membership or cinema attendance.

It may still be agreed that 'culture is that complex whole which includes knowledge, belief, art, morals, law, custom and any other capabilities acquired by man as a member of society' (Tylor) or that it is an 'organized body of conventional understandings manifest in art and artifact' which persists through tradition (Redfield). But this has clearly little relation to Sir Thomas More's 'culture and profit' of the mind (1510), or to the Authorized Version's 'give us seed unto our heart, and culture to our understanding', let alone Matthew Arnold's study of perfection – that 'sweetness and light' which arose from 'the acquainting ourselves with the best that has been known and said in the world, and thus with the history of the human spirit'.

Man's social life is not, like that of the ants, biologically determined. He has to learn his behaviour from the group into which he is born, and if his infancy is spent among wolves, then he will crawl on all fours and utter inarticulate cries, as exemplified by the 'wolf-children' of India. He is no longer regarded as coming into the world with the formidable array of instincts once attributed to him; he has certain basic physical requirements, and since several of these depend on the presence of other beings, they activate 'cultural imperatives', for they involve social acts. These minimum needs and relationships develop into a great series of secondary activities, such as kinship stratifications, taboos, religious practices and arts, which it is the business of the anthropologist to examine in so far as they are characteristic and meaningful.

In the world today some five hundred 'preliterate' peoples have been listed, and their general cultural activities have been reduced to an absolute minimum of eleven (including family and social system, mythology and scientific knowledge, property arrangements and war). It is often difficult, of course, to assess how 'primitive' a modern tribe may be; some authorities would describe the life of the Eskimo as approximate to that of Upper Palaeolithic man, living over twenty thousand years ago, but in many cases we have to deal with peoples of considerable development. At the root of culture lies, obviously enough, the discovery of language, although there has been some controversy as to whether culture of a sort can exist among the higher animals. Thirty-two cries have been distinguished amongst the apes (and a gorilla's brain is less than half the size of a human being's). On the other hand, one of the surprising things about primitive languages is their great variety and complexity.

Nowadays the study of primitive culture has turned away from the methods of pioneers like Sir James Frazer (1854–1941), who selected what interested him from the customs and folklore of different parts of the world and built up what Ruth Benedict (1887–1948) called a composite dummy formed out of the fragments of many bodies. An artifact can be understood only as a function of the institution which uses it, an institution as the expression of the real needs or fantasy needs of its originating group. Primitive Man has thus tended to disappear amongst primitive man, remarkable for their variety.

Margaret Meade has shown in her *Sex and Temperament in Three Primitive Societies* (1935)

how the Arapesh, Mundugumor and Tchambuli, who all live near each other in New Guinea, have quite different social ideas and quite different relations between the sexes; Ruth Benedict did much the same for the Hopi, Zuni and Navajo Indians in *Patterns of Culture* (1934). On such grounds the Anglo-Polish anthropologist Bronislaw Malinowski (1884–1942) felt he could dispose of great generalizers like Freud and Jung, who follow totem complexes from region to region or see myths as archetypal expressions of some 'collective unconscious'. He regarded current attempts to explain the growth and spread of cultures as equally controversial; the evolutionists, who see development as a series of spontaneous metamorphoses, and the diffusionists, who split cultural activities into units capable of being carried from place to place, are both disapproved.

Indeed, it is in the historical field, and notably in the relation of culture to civilization, that much confusion exists. Although culture and civilization are sometimes used almost as interchangeable terms, others insist that a civilization may well involve a series of cultures or suggest that it should be reserved for 'a special aspect of more advanced cultures'. There is much support for the Kantian description of culture as an inward state, with civilization as a possible exterior form, while Spengler regarded civilization as the aspect of a declining culture. R. M. MacIver holds that 'our culture is what we are, our civilization is what we use'.

The much-criticized Arnold Toynbee, in his *Study of History*, rejects the theory that cultural development has been due either to some superior biological inheritance (for instance, the myth of Aryan blood) or to a particularly easy geographical environment (conditions along the Nile and Euphrates rivers). Deciding that out of the twenty-one civilized societies that he classifies as such within the last six thousand years, only six emerged directly from primitive life, he has sought for the explanation of this emergence in the 'realm of mythology, as the enshrinement of human wisdom', and has concluded that societies move as the result of response to a challenge. Thus the suggested drying-up of the grasslands which are now the Sahara and Arabian deserts, was variously responded to by those who became nomads, those who followed the retreating vegetation into the tropics and those who, arriving at a second challenging situation in the marshes of the Nile Delta, evolved the Egyptian Civilization. Similarly the Mayan Civilization resulted from the challenge of the jungle, and that of the Andes from harsh plateau conditions.

It is thus, almost imperceptibly, that biological considerations (the size of the brain or the shape of the larynx) pass over into tribal organization to be followed by the development of territorial groupings in place of kinship clans, and then, via the comparative study of advanced societies and the kind of moralism implied in Toynbee's theory, or the ultimate spirituality of Malinowski's, finally enter the disputed area of 'ways of life' in the muddled societies of today. Anthropology itself is at once a tool of the culture which uses it, and a scientific corrective of that culture's least founded myths.

In the last fifty or so years it has, amongst other things, clarified the concept of *race*, demonstrated the habitual danger of an *in-group* despising those outside it as barbarians, and fostered an interest in the variety of cultural adaptations; but, of course, in doing this it has provided new material for the primitivists amongst us (from D. H. Lawrence to Picasso). But it has not been the business of anthropologists and sociologists to decide what culture is suitable for a democracy, or how the two principal meanings of culture can be bridged and integrated.

It is probable that Westerners today are aware of the very mixed nature of their cultural inheritance and of the degree to which objects and attitudes have been diffused amongst them (as coca-cola, dance-tunes, tractors, etc., flow back to where tea, rubber, silk and sarongs, etc., originated). This mixed culture of theirs, with its economic power and its ability to diffuse and control, probably cannot satisfy them while science is still utilized in hot and cold wars. In the light of their insecurity, and resultant self-consciousness, they attempt to reassure themselves about their 'way of life', which communism challenges, and now and then their 'standard of education', which can grant them status in a fluid society. But no one, unless perhaps T. S. Eliot in his *Notes Towards the Definition of Culture* (1949), has made clear the relation between the culture of milk-bars, be-bop haircuts and football pools on the one hand, and that of paintings, poems and the development of 'manners' on the other.

E. M. Forster in his novel *Howard's End* (1910) drew the picture of an aspiring culture-conscious insurance clerk, Leonard Bast, who finally died under a pile of the books he loved so much and understood so little. Forster's point was that the mere reverent accumulation of knowledge, by reading Ruskin's *Stones of Venice*, for example, was no substitute for an organic cultural relation with the work in question. Multiplied a thousand-fold, the Leonard Basts (or Hyman Kaplans) of England and America are today engaged in taking introductory and outline courses at universities and extension classes, joining clubs and attending exhibitions – with this difference, that, while in the United States the 'trend of culture' is at least bitterly critical of the American Way of Life, in England the Third Programme and Arts Council seem no more than over-discreet, because semi-official, agencies for the diffusion of high-brow entertainment.

ILLUSTRATION: Pages 119, 120 and 121.

D

'I cried for madder music and for stronger wine'

DECADENCE generally speaking, implies a decline, deterioration or falling away (Latin, *de-cadere*) from some approved standard. This, in one use of the term, may be a decline from what is natural, healthy and vigorous in life.

In another sense it refers to the condition of literature and other arts at the end of a great period or in an interim period of change. This is a complex subject of enquiry. It introduces the question of *style*, which may be considered apart, as a development not necessarily bad because it is 'decadent'. Some critics, like John Ruskin, have simplified the matter by analogy with youth, maturity and old age, 'Never', says Ruskin, 'when you have to judge of character in national styles, regard them in their decadence, but always in their spring and youth. Greek art is to be studied from Homeric days to those of Marathon; Gothic, from Alfred to the Black Prince in England' ... and so on.

The faultiness of this system is plain. Where a medium of expression is concerned, the end is often a beginning. Is Byzantine art a form of senility after the great period of classic art? On the contrary it brings with it (from the modern point of view) something new and splendid. Medieval Latin is in one sense the second childhood of the classic tongue – but it is also the source of the Romance languages of today.

In a particular sense, 'Decadence' is mainly a literary movement, influential in France and England during the latter half of the nineteenth century. Its partisans were not entirely precise or consistent in reconciling the possible meanings of decadence, as the late Holbrook Jackson showed in his celebrated book *The Eighteen Nineties*. He set side by side two quotations from Arthur Symons, interpreter of the 'movement', in which Symons hesitates between moral and aesthetic implications. Thus, in his essay *The Decadent Movement in Literature* (1893), he observed that the representative literature of the day 'has all the qualities that mark the end of great periods, the qualities that we find in the Greek and Latin decadence; an intense self-consciousness, a restless curiosity in research, an over-subtilizing refinement upon refinement, a spiritual and moral perversity. If what we call the classic is indeed the supreme art – these qualities of perfect simplicity, perfect sanity, perfect proportion the supreme qualities – then this representative literature of today, interesting beautiful, novel as it is, is really a new and beautiful and interesting disease.'

Yet some years later, in his Dedication to *The Symbolist Movement in Literature*, Symons gave another definition in terms of style, instead of spiritual and moral perversity. He now says: 'It pleased some young men in various countries to call themselves Decadents with all the thrill of unsatisfied virtue masquerading as uncomprehended vice. As a matter of fact, the term is in its place only when applied to style, to that ingenious deformation of the language, in Mallarmé,

for instance, which can be compared with what we are accustomed to call the Greek and Latin of the Decadence.'

We must be content to accept the fact that all these ingredients appear variously in the work of a number of writers, Gautier, Baudelaire, Verlaine, Rimbaud, Mallarmé, Huysmans, in France; Pater, Wilde, Beardsley (both as author and draughtsman), Swinburne and Dowson in England. 'Decadence', historically and with the French writers especially, was the outcome of the romantic spirit that reached its height about 1830. This left behind, in an artist minority, the defiant mood, the love of excess, the disdain of prosaic bourgeois life and rectitude, the nostalgia for a vanished aristocratic age, that were typically romantic. Thus Gautier's *Mademoiselle de Maupin* (1835) was written with the deliberate intention of offending against bourgeois morality. The sickness of spirit that comes of excess is interpreted by Baudelaire in *Les fleurs du mal* (1857). The idea that civilization was old and weary, that the artist, or person of sensibility, was at once its enemy and its product stimulating jaded senses with pleasure ever more curious, subtle and perverse, is a recurrent theme. Baudelaire found the essence of it in the work of Edgar Allan Poe, whom he so much admired; in, for example, the curiously macabre connoisseurship of Roderick Usher (in books, scents, liquors) in Poe's tale *The Fall of the House of Usher*. The same theme is elaborated in the *À rebours* (1884) of Joris Karl Huysmans; and the decadent yearning for sensation is echoed in the cry 'for madder music and stronger wine' of the poet Ernest Dowson (1867–1900).

Where the Decadent differs from the Romantic (in one point, at least) is in coupling exhaustion with excess. Walter Pater (1839–1894) evoked the atmosphere in the passage in his study of *Aesthetic Poetry*, where he imagines 'poetic flowers of sentiment [to] expand among people of a remote and unaccustomed beauty, somnambulistic, frail, androgynous, the light almost shining through them'. He anticipates the spirit in which Aubrey Beardsley (1872–1898) wrote his erotic romance *Under the Hill* and illustrated *Salome*. By the same token it is significant to note that a picture by Whistler could be praised in Paris as 'convalescente' which was indeed a 'decadent' term of aesthetic approval.

Huysman's *À rebours* is a key-work, a 'bre-viary of decadence' as it has been called, a re-search to the utmost and most bizarre limits of sensation. How far it inspired Oscar Wilde to write *The Portrait of Dorian Gray* (1891) may be judged from the passage in the latter work which refers to it as 'the strangest book he had ever read. It seemed to him that in exquisite rai-ment and to the delicate sound of flutes, the sins of the world were passing in dumb show before him.' The comment relates not only to the subtle pleasures of the hero Des Esseintes but to the style of decadence as represented by Huysmans, that 'curious jewelled style, vivid and obscure at once, full of *argot* and archaisms, of technical ex-pressions and of elaborate paraphrases ...' 'Here indeed', in the words of Verlaine, decadence 'shimmered in purple and gold.'

On the whole, Decadence was not the fated and inevitable end of anything – except the nineteenth century. Two great wars have since effectively eliminated languor and luxury from both life and art. The idea of Decadence has become 'period'; the 'faint lights, and faint colours and faint out-lines and faint energies', which William Butler Yeats considered of its essence, have been roughly revitalized. Yet behind much artificial-ity and pose, there was a valid spirit of discovery about life (and art also) contained in it. At the present day, for instance, we can separate the great poets Baudelaire (1821–1867) and Rimbaud (1854–1891) from the period context and regard them as pioneers in emotional expression.

ILLUSTRATION: Pages 168, 169, 170 and 171.

How to know God

DEISM postulates belief in a God who is known by human reason, as distinct from divine revela-tion. In the seventeenth and eighteenth centuries this concept was powerful in European thought. At first the emphasis was on the positive aspects of the idea; Deism was the opposite of Atheism. Thus in the middle of the sixteenth century we find Viret, a Swiss reformer and a colleague of Calvin, referring to it as a name 'tout nouveau le-quel ils veulent apposer à Athéiste'. A hundred and fifty years later it was the title adopted by self-styled freethinkers, who were to all intents and purposes Atheists.

The pioneer of Deist thought was Lord Her-bert of Cherbury (1583–1648), the elder brother of George Herbert the poet. In his *De Veritate* (1629) he sought (*a*) to show that 'natural religion' does not require to be crowned by revelation, with the corollary that man's own moral and intellectual powers are sufficient for his salvation, and (*b*) to define the content of this natural religion by specifying a number of principles which he thought common to all religions and to all men. These principles Herbert called 'notitiae com-munes' or 'common notions'; they were, he held, true principles innate in the mind of every man. He was not original in attempting to find com-mon factors in all religions; the first thinker to try to formulate a universal religion was Cardinal Nicholas of Cusa in *De Pace Fidei* (1476).

But it was in the five basic articles of his natural religion that Herbert broke new ground. They are: that a supreme Being or God exists; that he ought to be worshipped; that the most important ele-ment in this worship is moral virtue; that human faults are to be expiated by repentance, and that God rewards and punishes us in both this life and the next.

Herbert and all the later Deists believed natural religion to be vastly more important than revela-tion, on the ground that in human nature we can find eternal truths universally necessary to salva-tion, while revelation was taken to be of only temporary or local significance. What is original and revolutionary in Deism is to be found in this reversal of the traditional medieval doctrine of the supremacy of revelation over reason. Yet one must not underestimate the extent to which Her-bert retained the common beliefs of Christen-dom; he firmly believed in the freedom of the will and in a 'particular providence'; and, al-though he rejected traditional revelation, which was essential neither to true religion nor to per-sonal salvation, he was convinced that God can and does communicate his will to individuals. Indeed, he believed that such a communication was made to himself concerning the book *De Veritate*.

Although distinguished scholars such as Grotius had advised him to publish the book, Herbert hesitated because of its controversial nature. He therefore prayed for a sign of the Divine Will; and reported: 'I had no sooner spoken these words than a loud though gentle noise came from the heavens, for it was like nothing on earth, which did so comfort and cheer me, that I took my petition as granted; whereupon also I resolved to print my book.'

Herbert has been accused of inconsistency in rejecting a traditional and general revelation while admitting a particular and personal one. Yet the incompatibility between these two views is only apparent, for Herbert refused to admit the received authority of a record of revelation precisely because he held that the essential truths of religion are written in the heart of every man and, further, that at need every man can receive special supplementary communiqués from God. Herbert and the other Deists certainly emphasized the independence and transcendence of God in respect of the created world, but it would be an exaggeration to ascribe to them the view that God does not care about man or the Creation as such. Thus Charles Blount, who called himself a 'Christian Deist', roundly asserted in his book *Religio Laici* (1682) that 'God governs the world by Providence'. Nowadays perhaps the best-known, but certainly the least systematic, of the early Deists is that magnificent artist in prose Sir Thomas Browne (1605–1682), who refers in *Religio Medici* to the 'two books' on which the Christian religion is based, one written by God, the other by Nature.

The later developments of Deism were decidedly 'left-wing' – that is, towards a progressive dilution of the doctrines of traditional Christianity. Here the first important name is that of John Toland (1670–1722), a political radical and one of the first men in history to describe himself as a freethinker. In 1702 he anonymously published a book called *Christianity Not Mysterious*, in which he described the truths of natural religion as 'Enacted by the All-wise and Supreme Being from the beginning of the World, and therefore not to be destroyed or altered by every whiffling Proclamation of an Enthusiast'. Toland invented the word 'pantheist' to describe his standpoint, but now he would be called a materialist. He claimed

as his spiritual forebear John Locke, the first of the English empirical philosophers, but Locke, a cautious middle-of-the-road thinker, disowned the radical Toland.

The disintegration of religion was carried a stage further by the most influential of all Deists, Matthew Tindal (1656–1733), who found it essential to dedicate himself to a belief of some kind. He was converted to Roman Catholicism, but left the Roman Church after two years. Later he anonymously published a book which came to be known as the Deist's Bible, *Christianity As Old As Creation* (1730), which had the even more heterodox sub-title *The Gospel A Republication Of The Religion of Nature*.

In this Tindal represents Christianity as a restoration, and all other positive religions as distortions, of natural religion; which, in turn, is defined simply as the practice of morality, that is to say, the production of the greatest amount of happiness. There is no other legitimate way of praising God, for since God is perfect and self-sufficient, it is both sacrilegious and superstitious to suppose that he requires our services. This standpoint is far from the moderate point of view of Herbert of Cherbury, though Tindal's thought develops logically from the thought of his predecessor. If a religion is purged of its supernatural elements, then it no longer has the character of a religion.

The Deists, like the rest of their contemporaries, laid so much emphasis on the powers of human reason that no place was left for faith, which must always be an ingredient in genuine religious belief. In fact, it could be argued that in the Deist sense the expression 'natural religion' is a contradiction in terms.

There is another reason why Deism inevitably developed into atheism. A system of religious thought is a unity. Once this is broken, and certain elements are rejected as unimportant, there is no conclusive reason why the process of corrosion should stop short of the total abandonment of the religion. As Hobbes saw, the dogmas of religion must be swallowed whole or not at all. This the Deists refused to accept. They found it impossible to hold an orthodox religious faith, firstly because the squabbles of the sects had discredited all religious doctrines, and secondly because the growth of the natural sciences had created the impression that human reason was all-powerful.

On the other hand, they found atheism unacceptable, in part because it seemed to them that scientists like Galileo, Harvey and Newton had found further evidences that the universe is the work of a Divine Architect.

Although the English Deists were not themselves engaged in scientific research, they were much affected, perhaps more than they knew, by what has come to be called 'the scientific outlook'. The investigations of science are based on the presupposition that nature follows uniform courses discoverable by human reason. If the possibility of a completely random event is admitted, *i.e.* a miracle, then science is no longer possible. A revelation in the religious sense is a miracle, since it is a direct intervention of God in the world. The refusal of the Deists to admit revelation originated in apprehending that this concept was fundamentally inimical to the researches of the 'natural philosophers', or scientists.

Deist thought in England contains in germ the doctrines of atheism, mechanism and anti-clericalism; under Deist influence these ideas were rapidly taken up in France. Diderot, La Mettrie and Holbach claimed to be inspired by the English Deists, but were all out-and-out atheists. Why did these French thinkers refuse to compromise in the English fashion? In his *Système De La Nature* (1770) Holbach gives an explanation. He points out that in England the bourgeois revolution had already taken place and a degree of tolerance and enlightenment had been achieved, whereas in France the enemies of feudalism and superstition were still in power. Unlike their English counterparts these French writers were actively interested in the natural sciences, which also accounts for the alacrity with which they embraced materialism and mechanism. Many of the doctrines of Deism have been embodied in the theory and practice of Freemasonry, and the same factors that made French Deism so militant account also for the anti-clericalism which is characteristic of Freemasonry in France.

In Germany the influence of Deism was different. It was transmitted chiefly through the agency of the philosopher Alexander Gottlieb Baumgarten, of Halle (1714–1762). Baumgarten's brother was a theologian who, like others, was influenced by Deism to prosecute new researches into Biblical criticism.

ILLUSTRATION: Page 177.

Every event has a cause

DETERMINISM is the theory that every event has a cause, and that every event is completely determined by its causes; and therefore that one can exactly predict any future event if one knows everything that will go to produce it.

There are two spheres in which determinism is thought to operate. The first is the whole world of nature, or at least of inanimate things. Here the belief that every event has a cause, which can in theory be discovered, is generally accepted. The second is that of living things, and in particular of human beings. Here a strictly deterministic attitude is fiercely resisted by many people.

The idea of an ordered world of nature has been established only in modern times. It had been current for several thousand years, but had to compete with the idea of the world as a capricious place where anything might happen without cause or reason, a world of spontaneous generation and metamorphoses. The growth of the idea was helped by the Christian doctrine of a universe ordered under God, but only in the last century or two have people in general come to accept the fact that nothing whatever happens without a cause; or, conversely, that everything which happens can be explained.

This has come to appear to us so reasonable and essential that when (as with the deflection of light in gravitational fields or with psychical phenomena) we cannot provide an explanation, our natural reaction is to assume the reason to be our own ignorance. Much play was made some time ago over the 'principle of indeterminacy' in quantum physics, and thinkers attempted to deduce the unpredictability of human behaviour from the unpredictability of individual electrons. Yet regularity of pattern and sequence hold good in micro-physics as they do elsewhere, and the difficulty is rather one of applying our ideas of a 'thing' to the ultimate constituents of matter.

The growth of scientific knowledge is still entirely based on the assumption that the world is ordered: that we can provide explanations and make predictions.

Determinism in its most usual sense extends this belief in dependability, causality and regularity to living things, and in particular to ourselves. It is the view that if we know a man's character and the influences operating on him at any given time, we can predict exactly what he will do next. It is also the view that if we know the character a man was born with (the methods of thinking, and the capacities he inherited from his parents), and all the relevant influences of his environment on him, we can predict exactly what his adult character will be.

The reasons for this extension of determinism to cover living and intelligent beings are numerous. In the first place, it is reasonable to suppose that a hypothesis successful in natural science may be fruitful here as well. The evidence of biology also shows that at least in its simpler aspects life is determined and determinable. Again, it has never been thought a matter of reproach that a man should be dependable, or in other words that one could predict what he would think or do. In any case, it is hard to imagine in detail what it would mean to reject a determinist viewpoint. If one's character is not determined by the interplay of heredity and environment, how is it determined? If one's character is not delimited at all in this way, can one be said to have a character?

Undoubtedly determinism as applied to human beings is largely theoretical at the moment. No one knows a man's character really well, whether at birth or in maturity, nor does anyone know all the factors which would affect a man's choice at any particular time. The reason for this, say the determinists, is simply that human beings are much more complex than, say, a lump of rock; therefore the factors governing their movements are much more difficult to discover. But there are these factors, and they are discoverable. One only has to look at practical psychology to see how much can be discovered about people's characters, and how accurately the behaviour of at any rate a group of men can be predicted.

The opponents of determinism, who maintain that the human mind is fundamentally unknowable, and that it will never be possible to predict a man's decision with the assurance with which we can predict the movement of a lump of rock in flight, occupy a position equally theoretical, there being no good evidence which compels us to say that they must be right. Both parties are arguing over a future possibility, one asserting it, the other denying it; the question is which of the two is more reasonable.

The upholders of a belief in determinism have often combined it with other beliefs. Democritus, the Greek cosmologist, and Epicurus, the moral philosopher, who shared his views on the nature of the world, both combined determinism with materialism, the belief that matter is all that exists. The Roman poet Lucretius, whose *De Rerum Natura* is an exposition of the Epicurean philosophy, and who coined the classic motto of determinism: *Nil de nilo fit* ('nothing is produced out of nothing', or in modern terminology 'every event has a cause'), also believed passionately in materialism, and thought that it could be the salvation of men, ridding them of the terrors and false hopes of superstition and religion. In Swinburne's words:

> From too much love of living,
> From hope and fear set free,
> We thank with brief thanksgiving
>   Whatever gods there be.
> That no life lives for ever;
> That dead men rise up never;
> That even the weariest river
>   Winds somewhere safe to sea.

Again, determinism has been associated with fatalism, which is the belief that what is fated to happen *will* happen, whatever we try to do about it. This is to picture life as an inexorable process against which we can struggle if we like, but against which we will struggle in vain. Determinism is very different, since determinists hold that what we do matters a great deal, but that what we want to do and what we will actually do can be predicted in advance by anyone who knows all the facts. Thus the essential fatalist attitude 'There is no use in struggling against Fate' is not implied at all in the determinist position.

Some determinists have indeed gone further

than the position outlined here. The *Concise Oxford Dictionary* defines determinism as a 'theory that human action is not free, but determined by motives regarded as forces acting upon the will', and some controversialists did hold this view, particularly in the nineteenth century. It is inadequate, and it involves more than one fallacy – for example, the belief that one cannot be free if one is determined (in this sense). The only sense of freedom in which this would be true is that of capriciousness and irresponsibility. In all other cases it is obvious that when choosing freely, one is still determined by one's nature and by the facts. Again, it involves a false analogy with the physical world, where except in atomic physics all forces are external to the thing acted upon. It pictures the mind as a kind of weathercock, and ignores the kind of determination which comes from the inherited and developed structure of the mind itself.

The most persistent opposition to determinism comes from those who believe that to accept it means to deny 'free will' – that term, originally theological, used to express the fact that we often appear to be able to choose freely between one course of action and another. It will be clear from what has been said above that this freedom of choice does not conflict with determinism. Freedom of choice means freedom to choose whichever of two course of action we want to take; a determinist does not deny this, but only holds that taking one or the other will in fact be a consequence of what we have been and what we have experienced, and can thus be predicted. To deny this can only mean that our important acts, the ones which the whole discussion is about, are always inconsistent and out of character; which is absurd.

The motive behind this insistent opposition, apart from the sense of freedom in our decisions, is the feeling that praise for good acts and blame or punishment for bad acts would be inappropriate if determinism were true. Except that praise and blame, reward and punishment would remain essential as encouragements and deterrents, helping to mould the character, this is probably a true conclusion. And indeed it is an obvious fact that blame and punishment are today increasingly being used only for their corrective effect. (See also *Free Will*.)

Satan and his brood

The **DEVIL** hardly comes into the Old Testament at all. He does not appear in the Creation story in Genesis, where the tempter, so far as the text goes, is the serpent 'more subtil than any beast of the field which the Lord God had made'. In the prologue to Job he is still included among the sons of God; his presence in heaven is accepted, and he is set the task of testing the 'perfect and upright man'.

In one or two other passages where the word *Satan* is used, it has only its literal meaning of 'adversary' without diabolical implications. 'Baal-Zebub' is mentioned, but only as a local deity; like Apollo among the Greeks, he is 'the master of flies'. But perhaps the most important passage, from the use made of it later, is Isaiah's shrill song of triumph over the King of Babylon. The prophet imagines the tyrant's sceptre broken and sees him going down to Hades (Sheol), where the shades of the dead come out to wonder that he has become as weak as they: 'How art thou fallen from heaven, O Lucifer, son of the morning' – and *Lucifer* here means shining one, day-star perhaps; but the Hebrew word *hêlēl* is not a proper name. Isaiah is quoting against the Babylonian kings, with their claim to divine honours, the Sumerian myth of the falling star; a use of foreign mythology which can be paralleled in Ezekiel.

It is this use of foreign myth which explains the vastly greater importance of the Devil in the New Testament, and his emergence into personality. The tribulations of the Jews, the Exile, the influence of Assyrian, Babylonian, Egyptian and Persian ideas, brought them into contact not merely with fresh Gods, but with fresh attitudes to God. The universe became peopled with angels and demons; and as the Jews advanced the uncompromising monotheism of Jahweh, Lord not merely of heaven and earth but even of Sheol, so the figure of the enemy, Satan, rose to oppose him, to transform Sheol into Hell, his own kingdom, and to dispute with God the mastery of earth. For the Iranian universe was dualist; in Persian religion Ormuzd and Ahriman, the powers of Light and Darkness, Good and Evil, are locked in a perpetual struggle. Neither Jewry nor Christianity accepted this philosophy; it came to be, for both, one of the subtlest and most powerful of heresies. But in the centuries just before and just after Christ it produced a turmoil of new thought and a proliferation of myth, expressed in the Talmud and the New Testament, and more exotically in the Apocryphal and Apocalyptic Books, as later in the Kabbala.

The conception of a *Devil* is possible only in a religious system where God has become a being of infinite goodness concerned for the well-being of the world. In most early religions the gods with whom one deals from day to day are neither good nor evil, but capricious; they may be propitiated or antagonized by breach of taboo or appropriate sacrifices or formulae; and if behind them there is a single God, he is aloof, indifferent or at least unapproachable by any human means.

Yet, according to some modern anthropologists the Devil is more than a religious concept or a being existing in the spiritual realm or in the poetic imagination. Dr Margaret Murray, in *The God of the Witches* (1933), claimed, without a glint of genuine evidence, that a form of religion opposed to Christianity and persecuted by it, survived until recently in Western Europe, practising its rites in secret but very widely. These witch rites were those of pre-Christian cults, driven underground but never destroyed, and particularly liable to recrudesce in times of disaster (such as the Black Death in the fourteenth century) or of religious disturbance (such as the aftermath of the Reformation). The rites involved initiation ceremonies, sympathetic and imitative magic, sacred feasts, dances, orgiastic ceremonies and sacrifice. They were conducted in *covens* of thirteen members by the Horned Man, a priest-god in animal form – that is, wearing the skin and horns of a beast.

This, then, was the Devil; and upon him, although the worship over which he presided might be joyous, liberating or even beneficent, the Christians projected all their fears and hatred, and the multifarious notions of evil which they had inherited. So far, Dr Murray argues an identity between the Horned Man and the original God of palaeolithic man, and asserts a continuity of cult and tradition over much vaster periods than historic time. Too little can ever be known of palaeolithic culture to justify such a claim, and the gaps to be covered are too vast to be bridged

by speculation. Moreover, Dr Murray's presentation of witchcraft is altogether too sympathetic. It is clear that those who embraced witchcraft did so with a consciousness of its being evil (from their point of view as well as posterity's). The sealing with a secret mark, the use of blood and excreta, were meant to degrade, and they did degrade; they were meant to isolate the initiates, and they did isolate them. Evil-wishing and harmful magic practised through wax images identified with the victim were intended to be destructive, and they were destructive. Perhaps we, who have lived with Belsen and the Mau-Mau, may more readily understand than some previous generations the position of a man in the Middle Ages, to whom the Devil was not a remote, and still less an outmoded, abstraction, but a man in black whom one might meet in the village, or a horned and cloven-footed monster who might appear on moor or heath, and not only be frightening, but also attractive and likeable, and therefore more frightening for that.

The fascination of the Devil and his brood is everywhere in the Middle Ages: in wall-paintings of Doomsday; on the capitals of columns in churches and under misericords; in jovial anecdotes and nicknames and the elaborate horseplay of mysteries and interludes; in Hell-mouths gaily painted and spouting sulphurous fumes whence the little Devils emerge with pitchforks to gather in their victims; and in the ingenuity of theological speculation. Thus, for instance, in the hierarchy of heaven there were originally not nine orders – the triple three of seraphim, cherubim and thrones; dominions, virtues and powers; principalities, archangels and angels. There was one other: that of the light-bearer, Lucifer, the beautiful one who originally sat above all the others, till in his pride he claimed the northern part of heaven, and was thrown out by the (much lower) archangels. (The Franciscans later claimed his vacant throne for their founder, 'above the seraphim'.)

His rout of rebels were given names and identities: Satan was distinguished from Lucifer, ancient and fallen Deities like Beelzebub and Ashtoreth rubbed shoulders with new pretenders like Mahound, and with Ragomoffin, Titivullus, and homebred demons like Puck (who was not always so harmless as he appears in Shakespeare). The dying man saw them gather at his bedside, waiting for him to despair so that they might carry off his soul. Whole orders like the Knight Templars, whole districts like Provence in the thirteenth century, might become infected by the Devil and lapse into heresy.

There are, moreover, curious links between these medieval aberrations and the nineteenth-century revival of Satanism. The Palladians or Palladistes, whose leader had the un-diabolical name of Albert Pike, claimed that they possessed the Baphomet, the idol worshipped by the medieval Templars. It had been carried in 1801 to Charleston, U.S.A., by Isaac Long, who hid it in a cave together with the skull of the last Grand Master of the Order, Jacques du Molay and on the worship of these relics a cult was established. The Palladistes, who were taken seriously by the Vatican, were discredited by the antics of their chief publicist, 'Bataille' (C. Hacks), who announced as his High Priestess Diana Vaughan, a fascinating and circumstantial person who claimed descent from Thomas and Henry Vaughan, the seventeenth-century poet and mystic. Unfortunately, Bataille revealed later that he had invented her.

Yet even in the mixture of folly and terror, the grotesque and the absurd, the hysteria of romantic decadence, the true diabolic note is heard again. In Blake's *Prophetic Books*, in Baudelaire's *Les Fleurs du Mal*, in Rimbaud's *Une Saison en Enfer*, even in Huysmans' *Là-bas*, the Dark Principle showed that it still had revelations to offer. But Blake has the last word: 'To be an error and to be cast out is a part of God's design.' This view, by which Evil had its birth in heaven itself, its rebirth in Paradise, its consummation at the Last Supper and the Betrayal in the Garden, is more troubling and more difficult to accept than the Manichean view which makes Evil an independent and equally powerful principle with good. But in the end it is a profounder and more subtly satisfying one.

ILLUSTRATION: Page 230.

Toeing the party line

DIALECTICAL MATERIALISM is the philosophy and world-outlook of the Communist Parties which now control a very large portion of the globe.

Although it was worked out by Germans in the security of the British Museum, and has a respectable if remote ancestry amongst the Greeks, both in the method of Socrates and the ideas of Heraclitus, this neo-Hegelian apparatus is seldom discussed, let alone controverted, in the non-Marxist West. It seems either to be regarded as an Oriental mystification, a dance of the seven revolutionary veils, or to be ignored as the screen behind which duplicity and opportunism occur, as in the notorious changes of the 'party-line'. Whatever its demerits, which are without doubt numerous and crucial, it is worth a diligent examination.

This philosophy is materialistic because it believes that matter preceded mind, and hence it dismisses all supernatural deistic explanations of the universe ('Idealism is clericalism', Lenin). But it also opposes the mechanistic view of nature as consisting of separate material particles interacting with each other according to the laws of mechanics: the 'clockwork' universe of Newton, or Harvey's description of the circulation of the blood, where change was interpreted rather as repetition than development, and where, however dimly and tentatively, a Supreme Being was posited.

In its day this mechanistic materialism was an ideology of progress; but when it was taken over from the bourgeoisie, by the utopian socialists, or applied by the realists to the study of heredity and environment, it lost its usefulness. (Dialectical materialism thus recognizes that ideologies are the result of social-economic conditions and may be weapons of progress in one age, of reaction in another.) Metaphysics is criticized in a similar way, for the metaphysician deals with abstract concepts and fixed forms, which must be either one thing or the other ('He thinks in absolutely irreconcilable antitheses', Engels). Marxists have demonstrated the error of this rigidity by referring to the association of British and American imperialisms, which both collaborate *and* conflict, or to the possibilities of the co-existence of the Soviets and the West.

When Engels wrote that 'The world is not to be comprehended as a complex of ready-made things but as a concept of processes', he pointed out what is *dialectical* in communist materialism, what was extracted from the idealist Hegel and 'turned on its head' – namely, that everything in the universe, every object, every event, is full of contradictions, and that it is through these contradictions that development takes place. Lenin speaks of the 'contradictory, mutually exclusive ... tendencies in all phenomena', and Marx of 'recognition of the existing state of things [and] recognition of the negation of that state, its inevitable breaking up'.

Dialectics sees everything in constant motion and change and, although it does not expect nature and social life to yield a series of Hegelian triads (thesis, antithesis, synthesis), much emphasis is laid on the universal presence of pairs of opposites (whose unity is only temporary) and on the revolutionary leap by which quantitative change suddenly becomes qualitative. The student will find many illustrations of this latter point in the pamphlets he reads: water turning to steam or solidifying into ice are examples now supplemented by the manufacture of uranium 235 out of 238 and by the critical mass necessary to start a chain reaction. In history, Marxists will say that the 'leap' into industrial capitalism could take place only when sufficient wealth had accumulated in private hands and a sufficiently large property-less proletariat had been formed by enclosures.

It is in the study of history that the most dramatic application of dialectics occurs. Materialism demands that economic and social forces should generally manipulate individuals and ideas, although Engels allows some importance to what he calls the superstructure; dialectics exposes the method by which change takes place. In broad outline, Marxists believe that society developed from primitive communism through slavery to feudalism and then capitalism, each state being born out of the contradictions in the previous one and finally negating it. The root condition of modern times has been that of the class struggle, the movement towards the dictatorship of the proletariat, and the distant goal of a classless communist society in which the State itself shall 'wither away' – what Engels calls humanity's leap from the realm of necessity into the realm of freedom.

Capitalism had first to create its opposite be-

fore that opposite could negate it. In its days of expansion it was a progressive force; now in its decline the shadows of negation lie full upon it, monopoly replacing the free enterprise in which it claims to believe, autarkic states rendering free trade impossible, and the industrial unrest consequent upon recurring depressions making its downfall even more obvious. Since, unlike liberal reformers, Marxists do not believe that evolution is a gradual uphill development, but a series of abrupt leaps, the change to a truly socialist society must involve the complete break-up of the previous apparatus. Pure communism is an ultimate ideal, reproducing on a higher plane the primitive organization with which the progress of Man began.

It is important to realize that *inside* communist parties a great deal of dialectical analysis is carried on and great pains are taken to justify political changes theoretically, to differentiate between strategy and tactics, to quote relevant passages from Marxist scripture while the analysts also remind each other of the dangers of being doctrinaire. The recent convert is likely to be exhilarated by the grasp of world problems shown by his new friends, who can generalize so broadly and condemn so confidently all opposite points of view as either lies or the expression of class interests. He will find himself in a mental climate as insulated as that of the Freudians or the Catholics.

Outside the party, on the other hand, criticism deals with an entirely different subject matter: Russian power politics, the personal intrigues of various leaders and so on. The scientific pretentions of communists are rarely taken seriously by those who are conscious of the distortions inserted into revolutionary history (as in the suppression of Trotsky's career) or the seemingly faked evidence produced during the various purges. Whatever the eventual significance of all this, it does seem that Marxist politicians, when faced with the vagaries of human nature, are not prepared to be purely scientific. They are always inclined, since they are expert propagandists, to reinforce a tactical change with a mass of emotional material (Russian patriotism during the war, for one example). From this intellectual elasticity much confusion has resulted. (See also *Communism*).

Who begins?

DISARMAMENT as the limitation of national armaments by international agreement has become a political slogan of the utmost potency, an ideal, it seems, of Cloud Cuckoo Land, or the Golden Age.

The term came into being in the last century, when the character of warfare had been profoundly changing. Nations were beginning to rely on mobilizing large numbers of civilian reservists as well as the professional soldiers, thus vastly increasing the sources of manpower. At the same time science and industry were producing more and more lethal and expensive weapons of war. Metal-clad warships were first used in the Crimean War (1854–1855) and by the eighteen-nineties a new machine-gun, the Maxim – so revolutionary and deadly that its inventor believed it would lead to the abolition of warfare – had come into mass-production.

The ideals of modern nationhood released by the French Revolution were also working their effect in Europe – principally in the unification of Germany, the creation of modern Italy and the disintegration of the Ottoman Empire in the Balkans; in the Far East Japan was undergoing a renaissance. Elsewhere the last of the struggles for colonies by the European powers was still being waged. These fundamental convulsions had brought about a widespread consciousness of change and insecurity; after the Franco-Prussian war of 1870–1871, which established the new power of Germany, Europe began to drift apart into rival 'armed camps', competing lavishly in armaments to secure military and political advantage.

In the Anglo-Saxon countries the reverse of the picture had also been appreciated. Through the Industrial Revolution and growth of international trade the known area of the world had enlarged; with the development of new means of communication, the steamship and the telegraph, the world had become more compact and the parts more interdependent. So there grew up a school of practical, and often radical, internationalism, which deplored the waste of resources upon armaments, arguing, as Cobden and Bright argued in England, that the real interest of the world was in peace and the development of commerce. A widely read book on this subject, *The Great Illusion* by Sir Norman Angell, was published on the eve of the First World War.

These thinkers were supported by the Quakers, for example, and by the Socialist International, both opposed to war on religious or on ideological grounds.

The idealists were not powerful enough to win the day. Disarmament was discussed abortively at a 'Peace Conference' called at the Hague in 1899 by the Tsar of Russia. The tension increased until in 1914 a spark in the Balkans set war ablaze in Europe, and involved all the great powers of the world.

When the war was over, Germany was forced by the victorious Allies to disarm. It was widely believed that the pre-war armaments race had combined with general insecurity and German aggressiveness to bring about the catastrophe of war. So when revulsion against international anarchy and longing for world peace brought into being the League of Nations, the following article (No. 8) was written into the Covenant of the League:

The members of the League recognize that the maintenance of peace requires the reduction of national armaments to the lowest point consistent with national safety and the enforcement by common action of international obligations.

Public opinion looked forward to the establishment of lasting peace by this means. The 'enforcement ... of international obligations' referred to the attempt to establish 'collective security' through the Covenant of the League. It was believed that the common obligation of League members to combine their forces to resist an act of aggression against one of their number would mean that an individual nation need no longer rely on its own unaided strength to defend itself; therefore it would be possible for all to reduce their armaments.

France, Belgium and Poland, Germany's neighbours, were not satisfied that their security was guaranteed; the Locarno treaties of 1925 were accordingly aimed at preventing aggression by Germany.

Disarmament negotiations lasted from 1921 to 1933, and attempts were made to define classes of armaments and methods by which they could be reduced to equitable levels. By the time that some items had been agreed on the situation had changed. Japan was fighting China, militarism was resurgent in Germany and the world was struggling with an unprecedented economic crisis. France began to press for the redefining of 'collective security'. In 1933 the Nazis came to power and Germany withdrew from the League of Nations; the Disarmament Conference was now adjourned *sine die*.

As the Second World War ended, it became evident that the military and economic strength of Germany and, it was hoped, the spirit of German militarism, which had been the instruments of Hitler's policy, would be utterly crushed. Hopes of disarmament revived at the conferences which led to the formation of the United Nations Organization, culminating in the wording of Article 26 of the UNO Charter:

In order to promote the establishment and maintenance of international peace and security with the least diversion for armaments of the world's human and economic resources, the Security Council shall be responsible for formulating, with the assistance of the Military Staff Council referred to in Article 47, plans to be submitted to the Members of the United Nations for the establishment of a system for the regulation of armaments.

Under Article 47, the Military Staff Council is to give advice, *inter alia*, about 'the regulation of armaments, and possible disarmament' – functions since taken over by the Commission for Conventional Armaments and the Disarmament Commission, whilst the Atomic Energy Commission deals with problems arising from nuclear fission, and with means 'to ensure its use only for peaceful purposes'.

How can disarmament turn from pious hope, or slogan, into fact? The difficulties are great. First, the means of making war may include huge segments of industry, civil aviation and merchant shipping, even the birthrate, determining the supply of manpower for the armed forces, enters into the calculation of relative strengths. Secondly, a general reduction in armaments on a percentage basis is hard to achieve, if the nations do not consider themselves to be on an equal military footing before it takes place. There may be special reasons why one nation is maintaining a higher level of armaments at a particular time than the others; or one nation may have a military preponderance, which an *equal* reduction in armaments all round would perpetuate.

Thirdly, opinions differ on the minimum of armaments which may be retained for defence and policing. Great Britain, for instance, may argue her need for large capital ships to maintain Commonwealth communications, and that the submarine is an instrument of aggression; small powers may argue that submarines are necessary for their naval defence.

Finally disarmament would involve inspection of military establishments, industry and national budgets; and in a world where the need for disarmament is greatest – *i.e.* where the motives of all are held in suspicion – inspection has no friends. Between the two wars limitation of naval armament was actually agreed between five powers – Britain, the United States, France, Italy and Japan. This involved only one type of warfare, the instruments of which could be defined; and the relations between the three countries most concerned, Britain, U.S.A. and Japan, were then reasonably good. The general problem for the world was summed up by UNO's Commission for Conventional Armaments in a majority report of August 1948: 'A system of reduction of armaments and armed forces can only be put into effect in an atmosphere of international confidence and security.'

There being no such confidence and no such security, pacific powers were compelled into the paradoxical situation described by Churchill, when he said of his own country 'We arm to parley.'

ILLUSTRATION: Page 125.

'Thy silk twist let down from heaven to me'

DIVINE GRACE is the means by which (in Christian doctrine) a connexion is re-established between God and man, after the breach made by Original Sin (q.v.).

Its nature and operation have provided the central debate of Christianity from the fifth to the twentieth century A.D.; a debate which can never be finished because it runs through all churches, and through the heart of man himself. Augustinians and Pelagians, Thomists and Scotists, Calvinists and Arminians, Jesuits and Jansenists, Deists and Evangelicals, Liberals and Barthians: the parties are innumerable. Yet often the leader renounces his label, as Karl Barth denies that he is Barthian, and St Augustine was no true Augustinian.

Nor has the debate been confined to the professional theologians. From Pelagius himself, the humbly born Briton who began the whole thing, and his ally the young Roman barrister Coelestius, who so brilliantly publicized it, the debate might be described as a series of raids into theological territory by marauding laymen. These included John Scotus Erigena from Ireland in the ninth century, who amazed the Pope and the Carolingian Court with his knowledge of Greek; Peter Waldo, the poor man of Lyons, in the twelfth century, whose followers survived to Milton's time to be celebrated in a famous sonnet ('Avenge, O Lord, thy slaughter'd saints ...'); Juan de Valdes from Castile, in the sixteenth century, whose *Divine Considerations* were translated into English by Nicholas Ferrar of Little Gidding, and annotated by George Herbert; Hugo Grotius, father of international law; the Scots laird Robert Barclay, who became the spokesman of the early Quakers (*An Apology for the True Christian Divinity*, 1678); above all Blaise Pascal, scientist, mathematician and Jansenist (1623–1662), whose *Provincial Letters* (against the Jesuits) and *Pensées* (the posthumous fragments of an intended *Apology for Christianity*) are the finest monuments of one phase of the debate.

Equally profound, in the nineteenth century, are the observations of Coleridge in the *Aids to Reflection*, and the writings, particularly the *Journal*, of the Danish philosopher Søren Kierkegaard (1813–1855) who sought assurance of grace in the ultimate pit of guilt and despair. In a time of easy optimism, progress and perfectibility, he prepared for the mood of our age when the theme of grace has become at least as topical as in the twilight of the Roman world when it was shaped. So now we have Barth, Heim and Brunner; Maritain, Gilson and the Neo-Thomists; Berdyaev, Simone Weil and Kafka continuing the tradition of the lay raiders; and in literature we have echoes of the debate everywhere.

Not that there is anything new in that; how would we understand *Othello* unless we marked Cassio's greeting to Desdemona, newly arrived in Cyprus:

> Haile to thee, Ladie: and the grace of Heaven,
> Before, behinde thee, and on every hand
> Enwheele thee round ...?

And out of the stews of Vienna, in *Measure for Measure*, comes Shakespeare's other saying, that might properly end this paragraph: 'Grace is Grace, despight of all controversie.'

What, then, is the controversy? When Karl Barth himself, greatest and best-equipped of Augustinians in our time, has declined to paraphrase the attitude of his predecessor, John Calvin, lesser men may be excused from attempting to cover the ground of the whole debate. Yet essentially the issue is simple enough: is there any good in man's nature? Can he help himself, or is he so utterly cut off from God by the Fall that he can do nothing without Divine assistance? Must God take the initiative in saving man by GRACE, defined (prosaically by A. Raleigh) as 'the free and unmerited favour of God', or (poetically by George Herbert) as 'thy silk twist let down from heaven to me'? And if God takes the initiative, does he not inevitably bless or damn by doing so; and hence remove free will, man's highest prerogative?

The debate began in the fifth century at the very moment when Alaric and his Goths sacked Rome, in A.D. 410.

The disputants were men from the opposite rims of the Western world: Augustine, Bishop of Hippo (about 200 miles from Carthage, in North Africa), and Pelagius, from Britain, who, although he lived an ascetic life, was not an ordained priest; a quiet man, with a great reputation for sanctity and scholarship. Already elderly, tall and stout (as the gibes of his adversaries tell us), he had long lived in Rome where, in a perennially British way, he was utterly shocked at the depravity of its inhabitants, Christian as well as pagan. The Romans excused their weakness, in a perennially *Roman* way, by pointing out that (since the Fall) sin and corruption were man's natural state. 'What they lack', said Pelagius, 'is not the power but the will.'

He was now joined by Coelestius, the young

Roman lawyer with demagogic gifts and a flair for publicity, and in the last days of Rome, with the Goths at the gate, they were beginning to win adherents and to give concern to the orthodox by their views. Augustine, who had been Bishop of Hippo since 396, had heard good things of Pelagius personally, and heard only rumours of his heresies; he had his hands full and did not wish to intervene. However, the sack of Rome scattered Pelagius, Coelestius and their followers and spread their ideas through the Mediterranean. Pelagius himself, after passing through Hippo while Augustine was absent, reached Palestine, where formal complaints were laid against him. The dispute went on until his views were finally condemned at the Council of Ephesus in 431. They re-emerged in the form of Semi-Pelagianism, and were condemned at the Council of Orange in A.D. 529. Since then they have had what James Joyce called 'a commodius vicus of recirculation' – a tide of times, and many returns.

The Pelagians held that God is, above all, just; therefore the notion of inherited sin is blasphemous; men are not *born* in sin, but in Adam's state before he fell; creation itself is an act of mercy, and the desires of the flesh are not in themselves evil. So man's nature is not utterly corrupt, his chief glory is in his reason and free will, and of himself he may seek and find God; even some heathens have fulfilled the law of God; Adam, like other men, sinned through his freedom, but his sin does not bind posterity (which would be unjust); and grace is always bestowed according to merit, even though the merit may not always be discernible by human eyes.

The Augustinians began the other way, not with God's justice, but with man's fault:

> By Adam's Fall,
> We sinned all.

Although by God's mercy it might be a *felix culpa*, a blessed fault, since it led to the Incarnation, it was nevertheless from the human point of view a cosmic catastrophe, because it cut man off for ever from seeking God for himself, and from renewing that direct and easy familiarity in which God walked with our first parents in the garden in the cool of the day.

In the Augustinian view, the corruption runs through all nature, so that even man's best gifts are tainted with it. He cannot trust his reason, his imagination, or his will. He cannot hope to accumulate merit by good works; for even good works begun in man's own strength will be corrupted. He cannot even pray, until God teaches him how ('Heare us, for till thou heare us, Lord, We know not what to say', as Donne put it).

What, then, can man do? God has provided a bridge between earth and heaven: the Church, instituted and guided by Christ. Through the Apostolic Succession the contact is unbroken, the *grace of orders* is bestowed. Through the Sacraments the priest is the intermediary, to enable Grace to reach the worshipper. The sacrament of Baptism snatches the infant from the corruption of nature into the circle where he can at least be reached by *prevenient grace*, that first portion of Divine light which enables the suppliant to co-operate in seeking more, by the *grace of perseverance*, through which he will endure to the end. At this stage, and only now, are prayer, good works, a holy life, and penance, of value. For although there is *sufficient grace*, it is not always *efficacious*, because only the elect will persevere. So there is no salvation outside the Church, at least so far as we are concerned in the Western world and in the ages since Christ's coming, whatever exceptions God may have been pleased to make for them of old time.

Fortunately, the literature of Grace is not merely a series of bald propositions. 'Too late have I loved thee, O thou beauty, so ancient and so new! late have I loved thee, and behold thou wast within, and I was without, and there seeking thee! Thou didst call, thou didst cry, thou didst break my deafness; thou didst glance, thou didst shine, thou didst chase away my darkness.' The mysterious and moving poetry of Augustine is found again in those that came after. 'Man is only a reed, the weakest thing in Nature: but a thinking reed. It needs no universe in arms to crush him; a vapour, a drop of water, is enough. And, if the universe should crush him, man would still be nobler than that which destroys him; for he knows that he is dying and that he is beaten, but the universe knows nothing of it.' So Pascal.

And when we have done with the 'thin airy knowledge of syllogisms' (as John Smith, the Cambridge Platonist, called it) there is still the

Grace to be seen in men's lives. Robert Barclay quotes the 'simple old rustick' who converted the heathen philosopher who had successfully disputed with 'the Christian Bishops in the Council of Nice': 'They contended with him in his own way, and he could still give words for words; but there came from the old man that virtue, which he was not able to resist.'

The king's divinity

The **DIVINE RIGHT OF KINGS** in Western Europe is an idea of pre-Christian origin.

Early Germanic and Celtic kings were accustomed to begin their reigns with a series of elaborate and magical ritual actions, some of which survived to influence the English coronation rite. The new ruler was above all else a warrior, his duty to his people was to protect them from the forays of their enemies and take war to the enemy's territory if he could; so it is not surprising to find that it was usual to gird a new ruler ceremonially with the sword and armour of his predecessor. The climax of the ceremony was to cover the new ruler's head with a golden helmet which in the course of time became a crown.

The importance of this ceremony and its implications are well brought out in the Anglo-Saxon poem *Beowulf*. Beowulf, the old warrior-king, having been mortally wounded and lacking a son, designated as his successor the one warrior who had stood by him in his last fight. 'The prince brave of mind took from his neck a golden ring, gave to the young spear-warrior his helmet bright with gold, his ring and corslet, bade him use them well.'

The pagan king seems to have been the focal point of the religious sentiment of his people. His priests were strictly there to perform the rites and to advise their lord, they were not an independent 'clerical corporation', and no conflicts between 'church' and 'state' were possible.

The king was normally expected to have 'kin-right', to belong to the royal family, which usually claimed direct descent from the gods. Other things being equal, he might well, but not neces-

sarily, be the eldest son of the last ruler. Early medieval society could not stand either a weak king or a minor without political and economic disaster; suitability, therefore, played a part in the choice of a king. In the midst of the Viking wars in Wessex, King Ethelred died, leaving two young sons; they could not possibly succeed at such a time. Therefore his co-general and brother, the great Alfred, succeeded instead.

Whatever the circumstances, no one had an inalienable right to succeed; the king must be elected by the council of the great men of the kingdom. Election meant no more than acclamation in most cases, though not in all. A later Ethelred, the famous Unready, was driven out of his kingdom by the Danes. But his English subjects wrote to 'their dear lord' offering to have him back 'if he would govern them better than he did before'.

The conversion of the Germanic tribal kingdoms to Christianity made at first remarkably little difference politically and constitutionally. Conversion everywhere depended on the support of the ruler, without which the missionaries were powerless. The new bishops replaced the old priests in the council of the notables, and they performed the old rites with a Christian gloss on them. Thus many of the pagan notions of kingship penetrated Christian thought.

Ælfric, the greatest writer of English prose in the early Middle Ages, in his life of St Oswald, king of Northumbria, records how Oswald conquered many of Northumbria's neighbours and claims this as a proof of merit. Notions about the wickedness of aggression were only slightly understood. Even the divine descent was preserved, in a slightly doctored form. A genealogy of King Alfred, a model Christian king, still included Woden amongst his ancestors, although Woden was no longer claimed as a god, occurring only in a string of names going back to 'Adam son of God'.

In the long run, nevertheless, Christian influence extraordinarily exalted the status of kinship. In 751 the real ruler of the Franks, Pepin, persuaded the Pope to allow him to overthrow the titular king and take the title as well as the reality of rule. In order to counter his manifest lack of blood right, Pepin persuaded the Church to demonstrate his title by a ceremony drawn from biblical precedents – that of anointing him with holy oil.

From now on the anointing or consecration of a king became more and more popular, and was soon recognized as the ceremony by which the new king was set apart from other men and marked out by God as the ruler of his people. It made him much more than an exalted warrior, it set him apart from ordinary laymen, and as late as the twelfth century men could still be found to argue that a king had all the powers of a sacramental priesthood. He was 'the Lord's anointed'; early medieval kings frequently styling themselves vicars of Christ or God, without causing offence to anyone.

In a society in which symbolism did service for political and social thought such ceremonies were tremendously influential, the history of the Christian Middle Ages being largely that of a steady growth in royal dignity and power. Some attempt was made to exalt the idea of royal responsibility at the same time. The old idea of election was incorporated in the coronation service, the new king had to promise, before he could receive consecration, that he would maintain justice, equity and true religion. Now and again the new king was forced to amplify his promise with a charter promising to reform specific abuses; as late as 1199 King John on his coronation day had to submit to a homily on the duties of an elected king from the Archbishop of Canterbury. But there is no doubt that in the later Middle Ages the authority of the king grew at the expense of all else.

Until the death of Henry III in 1272, an English king did not begin to rule until he was crowned. After 1272 the accession of a king was deemed to follow at first four days, and later one day, after the death of the old king. From the death of Henry VIII even this interregnum disappeared, and it has since been true to say of the English constitution that the king never dies – *i.e.* election has been completely displaced by the notion of hereditary successions by right of primogeniture. This was indispensable to an absolute monarchy, since it meant that a new king could reckon on succeeding without having to make any embarrassing concession to the more powerful of his subjects. At the death of Henry VIII it looked as though the English monarchy was on the way to becoming the most absolute in Europe, but the accident of a minority, a disputed succession and a long period of female rule prevented this from happening. The Stuart kings of England did their best to create and promote sentiment in favour of a divinely appointed and commissioned king, but the victory of parliament and the execution of Charles I witnessed to their failure.

But since the parliamentary party could provide no better alternative to despotic kingship than military dictatorship, a fund of royalist sentiment and sympathy endured in England. But it was sympathy for a limited and controlled kingship.

At the end of the seventeenth century the university of Cambridge could say, 'We still believe and maintain, that our kings derive not their title from their people, but from God; that to him only are they accountable; that it belongs not to subjects, either to create or censure, but to honour and obey their sovereign.'

Few outside the ancient universities would have agreed with them. Some years later Alexander Pope expressed a more widespread opinion on the divine right of kings when he dismissed it in one scathing sentence as:

The right divine of kings to govern wrong.

ILLUSTRATION: Page 172.

Love, rebellion, retribution

DON JUAN, lover and blasphemer, has inspired more literary and musical works than any other legendary figure. Once a poor theatrical joke, cruder than Punch, Pierrot, Scapino, Till Eulenspiegel, the Devil of the medieval mystery plays and others of that fantastic company, he alone has survived and grown in stature down the centuries, reflecting in his story the ideal of love and the imp of rebellion that are in every man.

His freedom is complete; and yet we must satisfy our *amour propre*, and so in the end he is dragged off to Hell, or rather, he walks out with his head high and a kiss still warm on his lips, and moral order regains its balance after the blow he has given it. 'A very pious entertaining tale,' he

sneers in Flecker's play *Don Juan* (1911). He opens
the magnificent speech which concludes Act II of
that uneven drama with the same aristocratic
contempt:

> I am Don Juan, curst from age to age
> By priestly tract and sentimental stage.
> Branded a villain or believed a fool,
> Battered by hatred, seared by ridicule.
> A lord of earth, all but a king in hell:
> I am Don Juan with a tale to tell.

It is a tale of seduction and murder. Don Juan
Tenorio, a name he acquired from a real person,
woos and wins woman after woman, none resisting his passionate siege. During a night escape
from the room of one of his willing victims he is
involved in a duel with her angry father, the Com-
mander, and kills him. Later he brashly invites
the statue of the old man to dine with him, and in
the middle of the meal a thunderous knock an-
nounces the arrival of the stone guest. Don Juan
is led away to damnation.

Such are the basic ingredients of the story. A
later version, in which he is given the surname of
Mañara (or sometimes Maraña), holds that he
repents at the last and dies in the odour of sanctity in a monastery. Moral justice is thus satisfied by repentance instead of punishment; the
true Don Juan would have preferred a medieval
Hell with all its racks and fires and grinning
demons to this pious emasculation.

Stories of libertines are universal and ageless;
the first person to name Don Juan, set him in
Spain, and tell his tale, was Gabriel Tellez (1571–
1648), a Catholic priest of Madrid who wrote
numerous plays under the name of Tirso de
Molina – especially *El burlador de Sevilla* (1630)
– 'The seducer of Seville', which is a basically
comic presentation of Don Juan with an ending
that is unexpectedly tragic and moving. It seems
to have been the source of a flood of stories and
stage pieces, for the seventeenth century was rich
in Don Juan plays.

Molière's *Le Festin de Pierre* (1665) emphasizes
the atheistic tone of the character, preserving the
skeleton of the legend and adding a wealth of wit
and worldly wisdom. Don Juan is also provided,
as in the *Burlador*, with a foil, the Sanchoesque
servant Sganarelle, who cannot approve his master's goings-on but clings to him faithfully; this

subsidiary character is nearly always in attendance. In Tirso de Molina's play he had been
called Catalinon; in da Ponte's libretto for Mozart's *Don Giovanni* (1787) he is Leporello, and he
follows his master even to the extent of imitating
him at one point. Da Ponte based his book on
Bertati's libretto for Gazzaniga's opera *Il Con-
vitato di Pietra* (1787); it inspired some of Mozart's most lovely music, but it is in itself a weak
story. Don Giovanni is shown at his worst, the
rather ridiculous figure in two unsuccessful se-
ductions; it was only because audiences by this
time were prepared to take the Don's reputation
for granted that the story stands at all. Before Mozart, many operas by minor Italian composers had
been written on the subject, Gluck had composed
a ballet *Don Juan* (1761), Shadwell's mediocre
The Libertine (1676), with music by Purcell, had
taken the legend to England, and Goldoni's *Don
Giovanni Tenorio* (1736) had swelled the rising
deluge of plays in Italy.

So far there is scarcely any attempt to provide
Don Juan with a philosophy (except in Molière),
or indeed even with a character other than that of
a thoughtless seducer: as a two-dimensional figure
his brilliant scarlet was not enough, and he was
threatened with a fate more terrible than his legendary punishment – a humiliating neglect.
Suitably, it was Byron who fostered a new interest in the Don, even though in his poem *Don Juan*
(1819–1824) the youthful, easy lover of Julia,
Haidée and the other more distinguished ladies is
scarcely the Don Juan of old: he seduces, but he
loves each one as well, and when he passes on, it is
more through circumstances than inclination.

The importance of the poem from the legend's
point of view lies in this romanticism. Byron
probably knew of the conventionally told English pantomime *Don Juan, or the Libertine Destroyed* (c. 1790), but he infused his character with
a new life by the new idea.

Vogt's *Der Färberhof* (1809) and Hoffmann's
tale in *Phantasiestücke in Callots Manier* (1814)
also help to establish the idea of a romantic Don
Juan. Here at last, too, are the stirrings of the
idealism which helped to save him from literary
death. He is filled with longings which no one
woman can still, and in lyric voice as well as the
old dramatic voice he cries for a love that will
cool his desire instead of inflaming it to the next

Continued on p. 135

PLATE 4

INSPIRATION: Inspiration of the Poet by Nicolas Poussin (1594–1665).

CULTURE: 1. A woodcut by Eric Gill (1882–1940), showing one aspect of 'culture'.

CULTURE: 2. Students at the University of Copenhagen.

SMOKING
IS STRICTLY PROHIBITED
IN THIS BUILDING

THE LECTURE TODAY

IS AT
SUBJECT
ITALIAN
LANDSCAPE

ROOM   FREE

3. Outside the National Gallery, London, before a lecture.

121

IRON CURTAIN: The separation of the American and Russian zones in Austria.

YOU ARE NOW ENTERING THE AMERICAN ZONE

COLD WAR: The Brandenburger Tor, Berlin.

THE BALANCE OF POWER: Lithograph by Honoré Daumier (1808–1879).

DISARMAMENT: *After You.* Lithograph by Daumier.

COMMUNISM: 1. Karl Marx (1818–1883).

2. Commemorative Russian stamp, 1933, showing Karl Marx's grave in Highgate Cemetery, London.

COMMUNISM: – as the opiate of the people. 1. Peasant women at a Communist meeting in Hungary. (*See* also 366 and 367).

2.

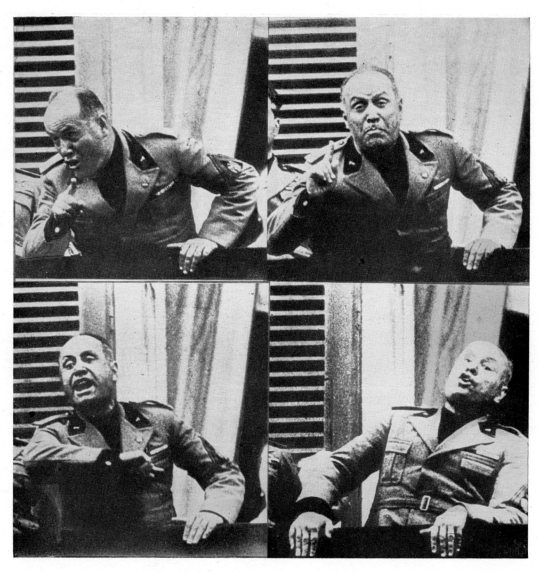

THE CORPORATIVE STATE: Benito Mussolini (1883–1945), in action.

COMMUNISM: Lenin (1870–1924), lying embalmed in his coffin.

131

CLASSICISM: 1. The Villa Badoera at Fratta Polesine, Rovigo, by Andrea Palladio (1518–1580).

2. Osterley Park, England.

133

CLASSICISM: 3. *A Dance to the Music of Time*, by Nicolas Poussin (1613–1675).

PLATE 5

EQUALITY OF THE SEXES: Le Bas Bleu by Honoré Daumier (1808–1879).
'Goodbye, my dear, I am going to see my publishers and shall most likely be late home. Don't forget to give
Dodore his pap twice again.'

conquest. Sometimes he fails, and rides with gay aspect but sodden heart to Hell on the back of his own sensualism; sometimes he finds his ideal in a simple unspoiled country girl, but is overtaken by retribution from a past adventure – the knocking of the stone guest echoes his passionate heart. Modern psychology knows many cases of the rake who falls for the purity he has so often despised. Pushkin, de Musset (in *Namouna*), and Tolstoy added their say to the reviving legend, and in Nikolaus Lenau's unfinished *Don Juan* (1851) the grand idealist stands forth at last:

Fain would I run the circle, immeasurably wide, of beautiful women's manifold charms, to die of a kiss at the mouth of the last one ... I shun satiety and the exhaustion of pleasure; I keep myself ever fresh in the service of beauty: and in offending the individual I rave for my devotion to her kind. The breath of a woman that is as the odour of spring today, may perhaps tomorrow oppress me like the air of a dungeon ... Passion is always and only the new passion; it cannot be carried from this one to that; it must die here and spring anew there; and, when it knows itself, then it knows nothing of repentance. Forth and away, then, to triumphs ever new, so long as youth's fiery pulses race!

These full-blooded sentiments were the inspiration for Richard Strauss's superb tone-poem (1888), but this was the last of the great Don Juans. Shaw's John Tanner in *Man and Superman* (1903) is a Shavian reversal – he is *sartor resartus*, the amorist pursued to Spain by a woman, where, in the third act, John Tanner and the other characters leap back across time to Don Giovanni Tenorio's circle and discourse wit and metaphysics in rolling prose. Here is no Don Juan, although the author's reasons for this are brilliantly set forth in the Preface. Flecker's play *Don Juan* (1911), which Shaw admired, has some fine poetry, but it twists the legend too ingeniously to a purpose that does not suit it.

Don Juan would seem to be dying. His adventure is at once too strong and too weak for an over-organized age: there is an inherent improbability in the story that crumbles in the face of scepticism, and the spirit of the times is one from which he can take no inspiration. Medieval moralities and the high tide of romanticism each gave him their inspiration; today he would be bewildered by confused ideals, and would scorn a law and order based on social necessity too much

G

to break it. His blasphemy was founded on burning faith in a simple right and wrong. In Baudelaire's fine poem *Don Juan aux Enfers* (also finely translated by Flecker) he stands in Hell aloof from pettiness and mocking:

... le calme héros, courbé sur sa rapière,
Regardait le sillage et ne daignait rien voir.

And Sancho Panza

DON QUIXOTE, the supreme masterpiece of Cervantes and of Spanish literature, is the story of a man who tried to make reality conform to his dreams.

Its hero – Sir Lanternjaws is the implication of his name – was a poor gentleman, whose habitual diet consisted of 'a stew, more beef than mutton, of hash most nights, boiled bones on Saturdays, and a young pigeon as a Sunday treat'. He had a tough constitution, was 'lean-bodied, thin-faced and a great early-riser', and, to supplement the spare dishes that his author detailed, he had been nourishing himself for years on the most highly spiced of fiction.

In the days when his creator, Miguel de Cervantes, wrote, romances of chivalry were the most fashionable reading. Charlemagne and his Peers, Roland's defence of the pass at Roncesvalles, King Arthur and his knights, the great Spanish heroes of old, and the Portuguese tale of Amadis of Gaul – all these filled the unfortunate gentleman's imagination to such an extent that he, too, set out one morning in search of adventures. And adventures he found in plenty. For such was the power of his imagination that he succeeded in transforming the most ordinary events into the stuff of romance.

He rode up to a wayside inn, on the bare Spanish tableland, and assumed that it was a nobleman's castle, of which its landlord was the warden; and a couple of wretched sluts who were lounging near the gate heard themselves to their great surprise addressed as high-born ladies. What is more, he insisted on being dubbed knight by the landlord.

Such was the conviction of Don Quixote that he lived in the world of chivalry that he compelled other people to play up to him. Many times he was beaten and mocked and met with other reverses. But even Sancho Panza, whom he took as his squire, a shrewd, cunning peasant who shared his disasters, came in spite of himself to believe in his master, and to trust his promise that one of these days Don Quixote would win a kingdom or an empire, and would confer on him the governorship of at least an island.

Sancho, who 'rode on his ass like a patriarch', is a complete contrast to his master, who sat his bony, broken-down steed Rosinante with a crazy dignity. Don Quixote's language is involved, old-fashioned, and high-flown: Sancho's is pithy, realistic, and chock-full of proverbs. Don Quixote creates in his imagination the fair lady Dulcinea, the mistress of his heart, and sends Sancho off to find her. Sancho then sets his imagination to work and succeeds in persuading the knight that a certain 'round-faced, flat-nosed', and, incidentally, foul-tongued country girl is actually the lady of his dream, though temporarily transformed owing to the machinations of certain hostile magicians. One of the happiest touches in the whole book is Sancho's amazed self-satisfaction when he finds that he has brought off the trick.

The first part of *Don Quixote*, which Cervantes published in 1604, is full of such incidents, interspersed with tales of shepherds and lovers which have little to do with the main narrative and which the reader who comes to the book for the first time may conveniently skip. *Don Quixote* met with great success, and ten years later its author led his hero out again, on another expedition. The second part of the book, though containing fewer of the well-known incidents than the first, is the greater of the two. For it contains no irrelevant stories, and in it the strength of Don Quixote's romantic imagination seems to have grown.

His murderous assault on the puppets of a certain Master Peter, who is performing one of his favourite stories, his journey in the enchanted boat, and his descent into the pot-hole known as the Cave of Montesinos, at the bottom of which he finds the heroes of old, are the grandest adventures in a book full of adventures. In this second part the Don meets a wealthy nobleman who deliberately encourages him in his illusions, and who contrives situations which will give them play. But in the end Don Quixote is beaten in battle by a friend who has disguised himself as the 'Knight of the Moon'; he can in fact only be cured of his folly by one who will lend himself to that folly. Then as he travels back in a ramshackle cage, perched on the top of an ox-wagon, resigned to fulfil his promise to the knight who has conquered him and to give up chivalry, it is Sancho who wants the adventures to go on and urges him to break loose. But the Don has resolved that he will now lead the life of a peaceful shepherd. He dies, though, before he can set his crazy brain working on this new theme.

Cervantes' subject is really the triumph of the imagination over reality. Almost from the start the reader's sympathy is with Don Quixote and against all the sordid world of inn-keepers, convicts, windmills, priests, barbers, and goatherds, which seems on countless occasions to be just on the point of waking him out of his dream. One is on the Don's side because of his generosity and the vein of poetry in him that transforms the ordinary into the extraordinary, the commonplace into the rare. There must be few who read of the fair Dulcinea of Toboso who do not believe in her as fervently as did her enamoured knight; few who are not convinced that all the amazing things he claimed to have seen when lowered on a rope down the Cave of Montesinos were not the soberly reported truth.

Cervantes' book has added to the languages of the world the noun 'quixotry' and the adjective 'quixotic', which have come to stand for actions and behaviour that are extravagantly disinterested or chivalrous. The Don's famous release of the convicts whom he found dragging their heavy chain on the road to servitude in the galleys is a typically 'quixotic' action, since all that *he* gained by it was a hail of stones from those ungrateful rascals, which cost him several teeth. But one must not forget, when using the word, that 'quixotry' always has a strand or two of poetry intertwined with its commoner constituents of generosity and craziness.

ILLUSTRATION: Page 179.

Rules for playwrights

The **DRAMATIC UNITIES** – of Time, Place and Action – do not derive from Aristotle, as is still widely supposed, but from a misinterpretation by sixteenth-century Renaissance scholars of Aristotle's treatise, the *Poetics* (c. 330 B.C.) in which he considered the nature and function of poetry with particular reference to drama and epic.

The fascination which the rediscovered antique learning exercised over Renaissance minds led to a cult of classicism and to the laying down of 'classical laws' for the control of the creative arts. These 'laws', though they owed more to Renaissance pedantry than to Greek precept, took firm hold in the modern world, sometimes to predominate in seventeenth-century France, sometimes to meet rejection, as in Elizabethan England, but always to act as a stabilizing influence to which the human imagination returns after a period of Romantic excess. The free spirit of ancient Greece worked according to its own innate sense of balance and proportion, a true classicism which the later classicists were compelled to press into a restrictive code which produced its own reaction and the subsequent centuries of alternation – a continuous swinging of the pendulum – between the Classical and the Romantic (q.v.).

The Dramatic Unities in their modern codification can be defined as follows: first, the *Unity of Time* requires that the period covered by a play shall be little more than twenty-four hours. On this point Aristotle says nothing more than that 'Tragedy endeavours to keep as far as possible within a single circuit of the sun, or something near that'. He was recording the usual practice of the Greek tragic poets, not formulating an invariable rule.

Secondly, the *Unity of Place* requires that a play shall be confined to a strictly limited area, preferably to a single location. On this Aristotle says nothing specifically, pointing out only that epic poetry has the advantage of a play in being able 'to describe a number of simultaneous incidents', where 'in a play one cannot represent an action with a number of parts going on simultaneously; one is limited to the part on the stage ...'

This does not, however, touch upon the question of whether it is valid in drama to effect changes of scene or to move the several parts of the play from place to place.

Thirdly, the *Unity of Action* requires that a play shall confine itself to a single close-knit plot and not complicate the action by introducing sub-plots. This is the only one of the three unities which can be traced definitely to the *Poetics*: 'the story, as an imitation of action, must represent one action, a complete whole, with its several incidents so closely connected that the transposal or withdrawal of any one of them will disjoin and dislocate the whole. For that which makes no perceptible difference by its presence or absence is no real part of the whole.'

Shakespeare and most of the other Elizabethan playwrights ignored the Unities. Dryden (1631–1700) established more firmly the belief that it was incumbent upon playwrights to conform to the rules. Though Dryden himself had the genius to surmount artificial restrictions even while observing them, such eighteenth-century English 'classical' tragedies as Addison's *Cato*, the plays of Nicholas Rowe and Samuel Johnson's *Irene* prove that the formula was exhausted.

Corneille and Racine, between 1636 and 1690, had produced within the limits of the formula the supreme masterpieces of French tragedy, having the advantage of a language which can charge rhetoric with passion and power sufficient to override the static effect imposed by the Unities. In the comedies of Molière and others the hampering artificiality of the Unity of Place is seen in the frequency with which the setting is bounded on three sides with houses from which the characters appear to conduct the action in a public place or street, without regard for probability.

ILLUSTRATION: Page 174.

'Dulce et decorum ...'

'DULCE ET DECORUM EST PRO PATRIA MORI' – 'It is pleasant and fitting to die for one's country' – is taken from the Odes (III. ii. 13) of the Roman poet Horace (65 B.C.–8 B.C.).

The sentence expresses a kind of patriotism which can exist only where the citizen is conscious of a duty to his country which overrides loyalty to any individual within or outside it. The conception was familiar to the classical mind, Greek as well as Roman. Pericles, for instance, in his funeral oration for men killed in the Peloponnesian War, is reported by Thucydides as having closed a passage praising the city-state of Athens with the words 'Such is the Athens for which these men ... nobly fought and died.' The classical mind was also familiar with the contradiction of the idea in practice; Roman history, from the time of the Republic right through to the fall of the Western Empire, is a record of generals who convulsed the state by persuading their troops to exchange loyalty to the state for loyalty to their leaders.

With the success of the barbarians, whose only idea of the state was derived from the Empire which they destroyed, and who amongst themselves recognized loyalty only to their war-leaders, the classical notion of patriotism was eventually overthrown in theory as well as in practice, and as a more or less orderly political structure emerged in Western Europe after the Dark Ages, it took the form of a network of personal loyalties from tenant to lord, from lord to king, and – very tenuously – from king to emperor. To venture one's life for one's lord was an accepted medieval duty; to venture it for one's country was scarcely accepted as a duty at all until the Middle Ages had begun to pass away.

The Middle Ages are conventionally regarded as having come to an end during the Renaissance, and the political expression of the Renaissance in Western Europe was the monarchical nation-state, in which the king strove to attract all power to himself away from the great nobles who had been almost the equals of his predecessors and who, while their strength remained, continuously threatened his own safety. A revival of the classical doctrine of patriotism, with its insistence on the paramountcy of the state over the individual, was therefore highly convenient.

At the same time it was equally convenient that the medieval doctrine of personal loyalty should be cultivated in so far as it related to loyalty towards the king. The Tudors destroyed those families who had survived the Wars of the Roses and were still strong enough to threaten the Crown; by their statutes against livery and maintenance the Tudors also tried to extirpate the feudal loyalty to those families. But they were careful to draw directly to themselves the personal loyalties of their subjects which had formerly been filtered through the channels of the feudal system. Partly for this reason, Henry VIII carefully made his Parliaments partners with him in his attacks on the fabric of the medieval kingdom – especially in those attacks which, like the dissolution of the monasteries, promised great material benefits to the classes mainly represented in Parliament. For this reason, also, Elizabeth I so courted her subjects' affections that at the end of her reign she claimed in front of Parliament '... this I count the glory of my crown; that I have reigned with your loves'.

Presumably it was out of the union of these ideas that there gradually arose the very strong hybrid variety of patriotism which in England came to be identified with the phrase 'King and Country' – 'King' representing the strain of medieval thought, adapted to the uses of the new monarchy, and 'Country' representing the strain of classical thought revived at the Renaissance. It is this kind of patriotism, with the emphasis on 'Country' rather than on 'King', which provides a latter-day setting for the ancient thought of Horace – 'dulce et decorum est pro patria mori' – and which has prompted English poets to echo the Roman.

Three examples will illustrate English adaptations of the Roman idea. First, William Collins (1721–1759), writing after the defeat of the last Jacobite rebellion:

> How sleep the Brave who sink to rest
> By all their Country's wishes blest!
>
> (*Ode written in MDCCXLVI.*)

Next, Sir Henry Newbolt (1862–1938), in the chapel of a public school with a strong military tradition, addresses his son in the full ripeness of late Victorian Imperialism:

> God send you fortune, yet be sure,
> Among the lights that gleam and pass,
> You'll live to follow none more pure
> Than that which glows on yonder brass:

'Qui procul hinc', the legend's writ –
   The frontier grave is far away –
'Qui ante diem periit:
   Sed miles, sed pro patria.'

(Clifton Chapel.)

Finally, in the disenchantment of the First World War, Wilfred Owen (1893–1918) describes a man stricken by gas, and ends his poem:

If in some smothering dreams, you too could pace
Beside the wagon that we flung him in,
And watch the white eyes writhing in his face,
His hanging face, like a devil's sick of sin;
If you could hear, at every jolt, the blood
Come gurgling from the froth-corrupted lungs,
Bitter as the cud
Of vile, incurable sores on innocent tongues,
My friend, you would not tell with such high zest
To children ardent for some desperate glory,
The old Lie: Dulce et decorum est
Pro patria mori.

(Dulce et Decorum est.)

There can be no question which of the three extracts is closest in feeling to present-day thought. Patriotism is not out of date, but after two disastrous wars the more flamboyant expressions of it are out of date, decidedly.

ILLUSTRATION: Page 266.

'The Philosopher's Stoon, Elixir clept'

The **ELIXIR OF LIFE**, usually a synonym for the Philosophers' Stone (q.v.), could, like the Stone, transmute base metals into gold. Its particular function as a symbol, however, was to convey the idea that the Stone was a Universal Medicine, bringing rejuvenation and eternal life. 'Our Medicine', wrote Arnoldus of Villanova (c. 1235–1313), 'has also power to heal all infirmity and diseases ...; it turns an old man into a youth. If the illness be of one month's standing, it may be cured in a day; if of one year's standing, it may be healed in twelve days; if of many year's standing, it may be healed in a month.'

The Elixir was said to be a liquid, whereas the Stone itself was more often called a red, or red and white, powder. It might either be drunk, or used to assist in the alchemical operations. As a liquid, it was also called *Aurum Potabile*, drinkable gold. 'I have received', says one writer, 'an *aurum potabile*, enjoyed an imperishable drop, which fashions me – as my head is fashioned at the right hand of Majesty.' The ingredients needed for the Elixir were as diverse, and probably as much a matter of guesswork, as those for the Stone. Since the first essential was the mysterious Primal Matter, and none could say in practical terms what this was, the wildest suggestions were made. As Chaucer said in the Canon's Yeoman's Tale:

Nat nedeth it for to reherce hem alle,
Watres rubifying and boles galle,
Arsenik, sal armoniak, and brimstoon;
And herbes coude I telle eek many oon,
As egremoine, valerian, and lunarie,
And othere swiche, if that me liste tarie ...
Unslekked lym, chalk, and gleyre of an ey,
Poudres diverse, asshes, dong, pisse, and cley,
Cered pokets, sal peter, vitriole;
And divers fyres maad of wode and cole;
Sal tartre, alkaly, and sal preparat,
And combust materes and coagulat,
Cley maad with hors or mannes heer, and oile
Of tartre, alum, glas, berm, wort, and argoile.

It is noticeable, however, that a number of these ingredients are, in fact, poisons, and there was a tradition that some form of poison was an essential. To quote the English alchemist 'Eirenaeus Philalethes' of the seventeenth century, 'This Water is by Philosophers called their Venom, and it is indeed a very strong poison. But as concerning the Medicine that is made of it, it is certain that of all Medicines in the World it is the highest, for it is the true Arbor Vitae.' The use of small quantities of arsenic for medicinal purposes dates back to this paradoxical conception.

As with many receipts for attaining eternal life (cf. the closing scene of Rider Haggard's *She*), it was sometimes held that the Elixir must be taken twice over. 'He takes the mercury as a poison,' it is said of one adept, 'and dies; drinks it again and becomes alive, and thus he casts off all impurity, for he becomes white and lives.' Possibly this was connected with the idea that men must taste a second time the fruit of the tree of knowledge before they could achieve salvation.

The notions underlying the Elixir have much in common with the Gnostic heresies of early Christianity, especially with the belief in the fall of the Godhead into the world of matter. Like the Philosophers' Stone, the Elixir was capable of releasing the 'seed of gold' hidden within the base metals or within man. It was, in fact, this vital, dynamic seed concealed beneath the surface, like some unconscious driving force, that was to bring about rejuvenation.

Modern psychologists of the Jungian school tend to equate it with libido. In the alchemical texts, however, the associations were often religious. The seed was referred to as 'a small spark of the invisible, eternal fire', as 'the faded image of God', or 'the tincture which is Christ Jesus himself, the beginning and the end, the centre of the revealed divine eternity'. That is to say, God was thought of as being himself imprisoned in the base matter which he had created, and into which he had fallen from the state of grace. The task of the alchemist was thus to release the divine spirit from the darkness of the material world, and at the same time to release himself from his own bondage to that world.

This he accomplished by submitting himself, as it were, to the divine pattern of things. By accepting the poison of the Elixir, he too entered the way of death and resurrection, he too descended into the abyss in order to emerge triumphant. Only by total renunciation could the world be totally accepted. The alchemical quest was often for more than total acceptance, it was also for total knowledge, total power and eternal life in which to enjoy them. The alchemists were constantly open to the temptation to which Eve succumbed: 'Ye shall be as gods, knowing good and evil.' Both Elixir and Stone held out a promise of godlike splendour. The quest for them, in the West, was more than an *imitatio Christi*, it was an attempt at self-identification with the Godhead.

The origins of the Elixir are as obscure as those of the Stone. At no recorded period was one ever mentioned without the other. The name itself of the Elixir is Arabic in form, but is probably de-

rived from a late Greek word for a desiccative powder. This, however, does not necessarily point to a Greek origin, for the Elixir was also known in China at a very early date, under the name of 'huan-tan'. There the belief existed that alchemical preparations not merely conferred immortality, they had already created a band of supernatural beings, formerly mortals, who favoured later adepts with their benevolence.

In the West, according to tradition, the long life of Adam was due to his having tasted the Elixir. In medieval times the most famous of the adepts said to have discovered the secret was Nicolas Flamel (1330–1418), who, chancing on a mysterious treatise by 'Abraham the Jew', after much labour and travelling succeeded in fathoming its depths. According to his own account, he succeeded with the aid of his wife Perrenelle in making the Stone on 25 April 1382; part of the house in which he did so can still be seen in Paris.

According to legend, both he and his wife became eternally young, and migrated to Asia (for reasons not stated), where they were still living three hundred years later.

A century after Flamel, similar claims were made by Isaac of Holland, who prescribed a dose of the Elixir of the size of a grain of wheat every nine days. Others, like Salomon Trismosin, asserted that they had administered the Elixir to aged women, who had at once been restored to perfect youth and beauty. But of all who ever used or claimed knowledge of the Elixir of Life, the most famous are certainly Goethe's Faust, the charlatan and impostor Cagliostro (1743–1795) and the fatuous Sir Epicure Mammon of Ben Jonson's *Alchemist* (1610). The three fairly represent the odd mixture of high mystic lore, humbug and quackery that entered into the alchemical quest.

ILLUSTRATION: Page 216.

The enthusiast

ENTHUSIASM means the state of being possessed or informed by a divine spirit, and is thus closely related to Inspiration (q.v.).

Originally, it may be supposed, this was a state reserved for religious manifestations; the Delphic oracle, the Bacchantes or Maenads, were moved by an 'enthusiasm' which we would be more inclined to describe as hysteria. When Plato used the word, he did so with more than a hint of sarcasm about politicians, whom he described as no less divine, no less enthusiasts, inspired divinely, and possessed by the divinity, when in their speeches they direct aright many and great affairs, without any real knowledge of the subjects they are discussing. The expression had almost lost its proper religious meaning. 'Enthusiasm' has suffered from a like suspicion in the Christian society; an expression which might well be applied to the Apostles or to Joan of Arc was already a term of ridicule when it was used to describe the Quakers; and nowadays it serves for hot-gospellers as well as football fans. Indeed many modern revivalists are at their best when in a sports stadium; Enthusiasm loves a crowd.

In England, 'enthusiasm' remained interchangeable with inspiration until the turn of the seventeenth century. Dryden the poet (1631–1700) described St Cecilia as 'the sweet Enthusiast', and gave a description of poetic imagery (anticipating Bergson's) which contains a far from pejorative definition: 'Imaging is, by itself, the very height and life of poetry, which, by a kind of enthusiasm, or extraordinary emotion of soul, makes it seem to us that we behold the thing, which the poet paints.' Yet Dryden's generation also dismissed with contempt a state of mind which defied the processes of logic. John Locke (1632–1704) wrote: 'Let an enthusiast be principled that he or his teacher is inspired, and acted by an immediate communication of the Divine Spirit, and you in vain bring evidence of clear reason against his doctrine.' He also denied that it was founded on divine revelation and said, 'It rises from the conceits of a warmed or overweening brain'. Dr Johnson, accepting this valuation, defined it in his Dictionary as 'a *vain* belief of private revelation', while Boswell, reacting against Methodism, wrote in a footnote: 'Let it be remembered that these are not the words of an antiquated or obscure enthusiast, but of a learned and polite prelate, now alive.'

The fluctuations in the value set on this notion indicate the uncertainty beneath so-called serenities and certainties of the eighteenth century. Enthusiasm, passionate elevation of soul, was lauded as a virtue by Jean-Jacques Rousseau, in the face of the Encyclopaedists in France, who were doing their best to bring about a more rational outlook; and even the austere Kant, overwhelmed by Rousseau's great fervour, had to introduce enthusiasm into his conception of the Sublime.

The war of enthusiasm against 'reason' was pursued at the same time in religion, and is not yet over. John Wesley discovered his mission in a moment of 'enthusiasm' at Aldersgate Street in 1738, and in the following year he and Whitefield began to attract the masses by their preaching in the fields. Further revivals of this kind were stirred by Edward Irving (1792–1834), the friend of Carlyle, and, in our own time, by the Oxford Group or Buchmanites. But Émile Durkheim (1858–1917) and Gustave Le Bon, in their scientific studies of mass-hysteria (Le Bon: *La Psychologie des foules*, 1895), closely followed by MacDougall in England, began to throw a light on the manifestations of enthusiasm. The demagogy of Mussolini and Hitler has rightly made us contemptuous and afraid of the inspiring individual and the irrational mob. On the religious plane, too, such works as Aldous Huxley's *The Witches of Loudun* show beyond doubt that claims to possession may lead, even in the name of religion, to a destructive excitement hardly to be distinguished from that which causes pogroms against Jews, the tarring and feathering of negroes, the righteousness of the witch trials at Salem under Cotton Mather, and the lynching of the scapegoat, or the unpopular.

In a much-diluted sense, enthusiasm is still recognized as a desirable quality. It is true that no amount of enthusiasm will turn a fool into an artist (though Rousseau himself is a possible exception); yet books without some trace of it have little life. The twentieth-century mind will permit enthusiasm when it is governed by intellect. When Valéry said, 'Enthusiasm is not a proper state of mind for a writer', he did not mean to exclude it entirely, but 'in order to build a locomotive an engineer isn't obliged to be travelling at 120 miles an hour'.

ILLUSTRATION: Page 176.

Good for what?

EQUALITY OF THE SEXES, it is tempting to say, is a slogan invented by women to achieve the subjugation of men.

Whatever its purpose, it sums up in a few words some fundamental problems in politics, social status and economics that have arisen since the eighteenth century, and which can only be thought of and solved in a civilization of the highest level.

Equality of the sexes implies the abolition of all differences between men and women in education, electoral rights, the disposal of property, in opportunities for work and remuneration and as partners in marriage. It ought to imply the liability to the same duties (such as military service); but here the test of civilization is to make allowance for physical differences which only the least desirable male would regard as constituting unfair privilege. It certainly implies the same moral responsibilities, and the whole notion is indeed a moral one, based on the nature of human persons; it is a pity, indeed, that the term 'sexes' came to cloud the issue. The human male and human female cannot be regarded as equally endowed (in physical characteristics), so that the idea amounts largely to a social aspiration.

It is astonishing that the French revolutionaries, in their *Declaration of the Rights of Man* (1790) and their enlightened constitutions of 1791 and 1793, did not intend woman to benefit from any of their pronouncements. The challenge was taken up by the grandmother of feminism, Olympe de Gouges, who in her *Declarations of the Rights of Woman and the Female Citizen* (1791) declared that 'since women share the right to the guillotine, then they have the right to the hustings'.

The year after, in 1792, Mary Wollstonecraft published her *Vindication of the Rights of Women* (a work perhaps influenced by Condorcet's essay *Sur l'admission des femmes au droit de cité*). Her claims were modest enough, though firm: she was prepared to admit the superiority of the male in certain respects, and demanded reforms in education, legal status and, much too theoretically, a recognition of women's equality as persons; repeating many times that 'It is not empire, but equality and friendship which women want.'

She was closely followed by Mme de Staël, whose demonstrations were on the whole negative: in *Literature and Social Institutions* (1800) Mme de Staël declared 'Examine the social order and you will soon see that it is armed to the teeth against any woman who seeks to rival the reputation of men', while her *Corinne* (1807) is a novel written to demonstrate the misfortunes of the woman of superior intellect.

Feminists have perhaps done more harm than good to the cause of emancipation, from Mme de Staël to Virginia Woolf and Winifred Holtby, by insisting rather loudly on historical grievances. Certainly the history of woman has been sordid. She has been held as unclean or bewitched in many primitive societies, she has been bought and sold until comparatively recent times. If she has been deified and sanctified in almost every religion, if she has held power in matriarchies, in temples and in palaces, she has been treated certainly as a *minor* throughout Europe until the twentieth century; her labour and her body have been exploited, she has always suffered from man.

But the history of man has been no better. The common man has always been the sport of kings and lions, the victim of witch-doctor, priest, squire and captain. He has enjoyed theoretical liberty while being the victim of the press-gang, the noose and the galley—until very recently. Man has suffered crucifixion and burning at the stake for his beliefs; he long had, in the mass, the same educational, electoral and economic disabilities as women. Even now he may be conscripted and forfeit his life as soon as he is eighteen, at an age when he has no right to vote. The sexes have certainly been equal in misfortune, and the sufferings of women at any moment of history may be paralleled by those of their sons and husbands. Both have suffered equally from the power and greed of the few.

Biologically there is no equality, and it is now plain that woman is the better endowed sex. More males than females are conceived; more males than females die before birth, more die from the age of one to five, and by the age of ten there are already more girls than boys. Women have a greater expectation of life. More men than women are victims of cancer, tuberculosis and insanity: women are both physically and mentally the more stable, though not necessarily stronger or more intelligent. On the other hand, though there have been distinguished women writers and thinkers in every age, they cannot be said to have excelled in creative work either in the arts or in the sciences. Since (in Britain) compulsory education for the masses, both male and female, was enforced only after 1870, it is too early perhaps to say whether this particular inferiority is natural or environmental.

The problem, then, is social. Perhaps the crudest statement ever made of the doctrine that woman's place is the home, was that of Euripides: 'A woman should be good for everything at home; but abroad, good for nothing.' That is what many men secretly think and hope, and what many women are openly content with. From Saint-Simon, Cobden, F. D. Maurice and John Stuart Mill onwards, the liberation of women has been accomplished by both men and women of the upper and educated class: there was no revolution from below.

In Great Britain women have substantially the same opportunities for higher education as men (except at Oxford and Cambridge where they have insufficient colleges). They have the same electoral rights, substantially the same rights before the law, both criminal and civil. They are still, however, excluded from the House of Lords, from certain diplomatic appointments, and from the Catholic and Church of England ministries.

Inequalities still exist in many departments of life for which it is not easy to legislate. The demand for 'equal pay for equal work' was first made by the Trades Union Congress in 1887, and was recognized in principle by the British Government in 1947. But while it is possible to lay down minimum rates, it is not easy to compel employers to pay the same rates at all levels. Further, equal wages leave the male at a disadvantage at the beginning of a career, for on the one hand apprentices are paid a nominal wage (and few women are apprenticed), while during the two years of military service both skill and increments are lost by the men.

At the same time the abstract moral argument is clear: a job of work must be worth so much and no less, and the man or woman performing it should be paid the same rate. At present many employed women (in the civil service, teaching, etc.) are certainly performing the same type and amount of work, at rates of pay and superannuation inferior to men's. The legal obligation of a man to support his wife and children does not necessarily enter the argument, for allowances can be and are to some extent already made in the way of income tax and subsidies, both in France and in Britain.

If women are still at some disadvantage socially and economically, their liberation has certainly entailed some possible upsetting of the balance in the other direction. Men's careers are hampered by military service, while there seems small reason why young women should not perform some public service, such as training in nursing, which would be for the benefit of the whole community. There is no valid reason why husbands should be responsible for their wives' income tax, or be imprisoned for their debts. It is surprising that a man has no legal claim whatsoever on his illegitimate children, and here the civil law is harsh upon paternal feeling.

As women can now sue equally with men for divorce, there seem to be no grounds remaining why a rich wife should not pay alimony to a former husband. Women, but not men, can sue for breach of promise. Divorced husbands are often given the guardianship, but refused the custody, of their children, even when the wife is the guilty party. Women, though not men, may in many cases achieve dual nationality by marriage with a foreigner. No married woman is legally responsible for her husband's support, though she may be rich or he may be sick.

In other words, many anomalies have arisen which show that the process of equalization is, for society as a whole, a painful one which will need increasing corrective legislation. Fortunately, common sense and moral decency usually come to support both men and women when the legal ass is inadequate.

ILLUSTRATION: Plate 5.

Better babies

EUGENICS, or SOCIAL BREEDING (coming from the Greek word *eugenes* – 'well-born') is an idea which was first introduced into

English by Sir Francis Galton in 1883. The adjective 'eugenic' means – 'pertaining to the production of fine offspring' and Galton defined 'eugenics' as 'the study of the agencies under social control that may improve or impair the racial qualities of future generations either physically or mentally'.

Eugenics was therefore thought of by its founder as a study or science, but it has not become one of the conventionally accepted sciences. 'Eugenists' do not exist with psychologists, statisticians or geneticists. A person described as a 'eugenist' would probably be interested in certain branches of psychology, statistics and genetics and he might be a specialist in one of them. But he might equally well be a business man or a lawyer or a housewife specially interested in proposals for the improvement of the racial or inborn qualities of human beings.

The questions to which these people want to find answers are: what human qualities, physical or mental, are inborn as opposed to being the result of environment? How are these qualities transmitted? How can they be detected and assessed? Which of them will impair or improve the race? How are they distributed in the community? By what social policies can the improving qualities be propagated and the impairing checked?

The history of the systematic study of these questions begins with Galton but the idea of influencing human breeding by state policy had occurred to Plato. In Book V of the *Republic* Socrates asks Glaucon about the breeding of sporting dogs. 'Do you breed from all alike,' he enquires 'or, as far as possible, from the best?'

'From the best.'

'And at what age? When they are very young, or very old or when they are in their prime?'

'When they are in their prime.'

The same principles, Socrates suggests, might be applied to human beings. The best should have as many children as possible, the worst should have few and those they have should be left to die.

Aristotle also favoured the idea that only the best human beings should be allowed to have children; but the Greeks, though they allowed unwanted children to die, never took any steps to enforce good human breeding.

In 1859 Charles Darwin published *The Origin of Species* and in 1871 the *Descent of Man, and Selection in Relation to Sex*. The latter book argued that, since higher species had evolved from more primitive types by operation of natural selection, even greater changes might be secured by practising deliberate selection. Darwin's work roused his cousin Galton to the study of heredity. But Galton intended eugenics to be a faith and a policy as well as a science. Galton, in fact, went so far as to write that eugenics must be introduced into the national consciousness as a new religion. In the last ten years of his life (1901–1911) he was concerned to mould public opinion on the matter and a Eugenics Education Society was founded.

At this time there was some reason to suppose that science might soon answer the questions of *What human qualities are inborn?* and *How are they transmitted?* Weismann had already suggested that the determinants of inherited characters were located in the chromosomes, and in 1900 Mendel's study of inheritance in plants and animals became known. Shortly after Galton's death T. H. Morgan published his researches into the hereditary characters of the fruit fly (which has only four chromosomes as opposed to man's twenty-four). 'Genes' first appear in 1913. They are the particles of the chromosomes and it is to them that inborn differences are now thought to be due.

Despite the great advances that have been made in animal and plant genetics, we are still far from any certainty in matters of human inheritance. There are minor exceptions. We know rules about the inheritance of colour-blindness, haemophilia and a number of physical deformities, and there is some evidence that mathematical and musical abilities are inherited. Yet even if the scientific problems of human inheritance were solved, the moral problems would remain. Who are the best people? What qualities do we want to be reproduced? Who are the worst people, so bad or so sick that they ought to be prevented from having children?

It seemed for a time that the last of these questions could be answered in part. Certain of the states of the U.S.A. passed laws on the sterilization of mental defectives; but once again the problem of deciding just who is so defective that his fellow-citizens are entitled to deprive him of children has proved too great. There has not been a general movement towards legal sterilization. On the contrary, the ferocious race theories of the Nazis in Germany have made people more cautious than ever of such steps.

Honesty to experience

EXISTENTIALISM ought to have a perfectly straightforward meaning. This was obscured first by German philosophers, then by a group of French writers, next by the bright persons of the Left Bank; and finally by journalists and literary critics in England, who decided that the bright persons were tiresome, and that existentialist ideas must be bad, thus saving themselves much trouble.

One *could* say that existentialism began with the poet William Blake, who condemned abstract thinking on the ground that it was something other than human existence. The agreed founder, however, was Søren Aabye Kierkegaard (1813–1855), the Danish religious philosopher, who was little known in Anglo-Saxon countries until the nineteen-thirties, by which time his influence in Germany and German Switzerland had divided into two streams – on the one hand, the systematic *Existenzphilosophie* of Heidegger and Jaspers, on the other the 'theology of crisis' of Karl Barth and Emil Brunner. Heidegger talks about 'the gods', but may be regarded as an atheist. Jaspers allowed loopholes for religion. In France before the war, Gabriel Marcel invented Catholic existentialism. Jean-Paul Sartre, its best-known contemporary exponent, derives mainly from Heidegger.

Kierkegaard was in philosophical revolt against Hegel and in spiritual revolt against the Lutheran state church of Denmark. He condemned Hegel on Blake's grounds. Hegel's philosophical system took no account of, or too easily resolved, the complexities and contradictions of individual human life. In much the same way, official religion smoothed everything out with its meaningless pieties. A simple way of saying what Kierkegaard said about both, would be that people are liable to hold opinions which are not based upon their own experience and whose implications they make no attempt to work out in practice. To think *existentially* is to be absolutely honest with oneself, and not to indulge in the holding of a set of mere opinions.

A divorce between thought and action is particularly likely to take place in Protestant and perhaps most conspicuously in Lutheran countries, where it is an article of faith that one is saved by faith alone, that works are futile and that divine grace is coercive.

The difficulty existentialist thought has had in obtaining a hearing in England seems due in part to temperamental reluctance to think either existentially or abstractly (the mind of the English-speaking world seems to be concentrated on *things*), and in part to language difficulties. The German language, on the other hand, has proved only too accommodating, In any discussion of existentialism, language peculiarities quickly become the object under consideration.

'*Angst*' (q.v.), the 'dread' of the Kierkegaard translations, the '*angoisse*' of Sartre, is the same as the Freudian 'anxiety'. '*Existenz*' is only one of a number of German words which would tend to get themselves translated by 'existence' in English. Two other such words are '*Dasein*' and '*Vorhandensein*'. The German philosophers make play with all three. '*Vorhandensein*' is a mere objective, inanimate 'givenness'. '*Dasein*' is human existence as we understand it when we say that the dog's life we lead is not a life, it's an existence. '*Existenz*' is thought of etymologically as that which 'stands out'. It is already significant, like our 'life' when it is better than a mere existence. Also to be taken into account is the '*Sorge*' (preoccupation, care) with which we inwardly reflect the banal reality of our everyday lives ('*Alltäglichkeit*'). If we want to speak of a truly Kierkegaardian inwardness ('*Innerlichkeit*'), we might do well to learn the original Danish word, which is '*Indesluttethed*'.

In France, existentialist thought has been at its best when it was not theorizing about itself but using itself practically. Applied existentialism has its triumphs. Sartre's *Portrait of the Anti-Semite* is compulsory reading for any political columnist. A novelist who does not read Sartre's analysis of love-hate relationships in *L'Être et le néant* (1943), or an aesthetic theorist who does not look at what he has to say about the nature of images in *L'Imaginaire*, is handicapping himself unnecessarily.

The best thing for English people to do is probably what they were doing already – *viz.* to ignore systematic existentialism. There are, however, different ways of doing this. The bad way is to pretend that you have studied the whole matter thoroughly and decided against it (most of our literary critics have tried this at some time or another). The good way is to think 'existentially' because you are a truthful person, but without using the word. It is, moreover, possible to read Kierkegaard without giving a thought to Heidegger, Jaspers, Marcel, Sartre, Barth, or Brunner. Reading Kierkegaard is frequently a pleasurable activity, and a certain amount of it will no doubt become *de rigueur* towards the end of 1955, when his centenary falls due.

ILLUSTRATION: Page 218.

F

It's not cricket!

FAIR PLAY denotes equitable dealing and upright conduct, particularly in any rivalry or dispute. It is a phrase of long standing (it is found in Shakespeare), and originally was used as the antithesis of 'foul play', which had not then acquired its special signification of violence. The saying 'Fair play is a jewel; Lucy, let go of my hair!' was at one time a popular proverb in Kent.

The ancient world seems to have had no conception of 'fair play' at all. Samson attempted to defray the expenses of his wedding by betting his guests that they could not solve a riddle. Rashly they agreed to the bet before they knew what the riddle was; and, when they found that it was indeed incomprehensible, they threatened to burn down the bride's house unless she wormed the secret out of her husband and passed it on to

them. When she did this, and they were able to tell Samson the answer, he protested that they could only have found out the answer by cheating – thus admitting that the riddle had been outrageously unfair in the first place.

Losing the bet did not leave Samson out of pocket; he attacked the town of Ascalon, killing thirty men, and paying off the debt by handing over their clothes. There is no indication that anyone saw anything irregular in all this.

The Greeks were no better. Before there was any question of a complicated return to his home, Odysseus had already won a reputation for ferocious and unscrupulous tricks. The champion of the Trojan War was the hero Achilles; having been dipped in the Styx as a baby, he was completely invulnerable except for one heel; but when he challenged to mortal combat Trojans who had no such protection, his heroism was established in the eyes of all Greeks, himself included. In fact, the only unfair part of the story, to the Greeks, was the Trojan arrow that eventually struck him in the heel.

Siegfried, the great hero of German legend, was a paladin of exactly the same type. In his case the protection came from the fat of a slain dragon; and Siegfried, supremely confident that this fat protected him all over, denounced as a coward anyone reluctant to fight him to the death. The belated discovery that there was one place on his body not covered with this fat, through which he could be, and was, mortally wounded, is treated by the teller of the legend as a tragedy.

The notion of fair play had to wait for a Christian Europe. Legend and history even then are full of stories of sharp practice, but almost always with the suggestion that this sharp practice is regrettable; even the fact that it was completely successful does not excuse it. Irritated at the behaviour of the Douglas family, King James III of Scotland (1451–1488) invited the two boys at the head of it to dinner in a royal castle. The nature of the entertainment arranged for them was indicated by the first course, a black bull's head – the sign of death. The boys were seized, and executed in the courtyard. This became known as 'The Black Dinner'; it was widely censured as a gross violation of the rules of fair play.

However, the application of these rules was, and still is, arbitrary. To the medieval baron of Western

Europe fair play applied only to another baron of Western Europe; Saracens, Byzantines, and people not of noble birth were capable of any villainy; the only safe thing was for the baron to be first in the field with his own villainy. The gentleman's code of the seventeenth and eighteenth centuries imposed little restriction on his treatment of anyone who was not a gentleman. Quarrels between gentlemen were settled with swords; and provided one observed the correct procedure, it was perfectly legitimate to kill one's enemy in cold blood – he might be a totally inept swordsman – at no risk to oneself. The Duke of Buckingham, who first seduced the wife of the Earl of Shewsbury, then goaded him into a duel by his jeers, and then deliberately killed him, was playing perfectly fair by the code of his time. A later generation of Englishmen was inclined to believe it to be in order for a gentleman to beat up a 'cad', provided he fought according to the rules of boxing – with which, of course, he was familiar, while the cad, with any luck, was not.

Always there is a tendency to regard the type of war in which one excels as perfectly fair, and the type in which one does not excel as diabolical. To the British, long supreme on the surface of the sea, the sinking of a destroyer by a submarine is thoroughly unsporting; while the Germans, in the late war, reacted to Commando raids by shooting captured Commandos out of hand. In war-time it is tempting to denounce as a violation of 'fair play' almost anything done by the enemy, particularly if it should be successful. Thus the battle of Flodden appears to have been fought with unusually high respect for the rules by both sides; but the song, in an attempt to console the Scots for having lost it, says 'The English, for ance, by guile won the day'. However, in war it is always difficult to decide who has broken the rules; partly because it is seldom clear just what the rules are, and partly because few people will hesitate to break them if they think they can ensure victory by doing so.

The expression 'fair play' suggests that what is at stake is simply a game – something in which victory is desirable, but not all-important. The expression 'All's fair in love and war' means that nobody bothers about fair play, at least on his own side, when the issues at stake are sufficiently important.

God and the First Cause

The **FIRST CAUSE** as an idea is at least as old as the philosopher Anaxagoras, who lived in Athens about 450 B.C., and who was the earliest known example of a thinker persecuted for religious unorthodoxy. His astronomical theories, like those of Galileo, involved him in accusations of impiety, for saying that the sun and moon were made of the same stuff as the earth.

Earlier speculators on the origin of the universe had already linked the process of creation with the revolution of the heavens; they worked on materialistic lines and introduced the basic principle of Matter and Motion. Anaxagoras was dissatisfied with the assumption that matter moved itself. He postulated *Nous* or Mind as the prime mover. Thus he introduced into cosmology an element of anthropomorphism which persisted throughout the history of the idea of a First Cause. The question 'What causes motion?' is answered in terms of familiar human experience: just as man's mind initiates bodily movement, so cosmic Mind initiates the movement of the universe.

Both Plato and Aristotle strongly commended the idea of a cosmic Mind, but criticized Anaxagoras for misusing the idea. They complained that Mind ought not to be described as a mere originator of motion, something to be dispensed with once the problem of getting the universe started has been solved. Mind is intelligence; and if there is a cosmic Mind, it is not merely a kinetic principle but an intelligence which orders all things for the best, which foreshadows a similar criticism made of the idea in Christian theology.

With Aristotle the doctrine of a First Cause takes definite shape. Aristotle saw clearly that the force of the doctrine depends on a precise analysis of the word 'cause'. He distinguished four different meanings, two of which are relevant here: (*a*) *efficient cause*: this gives the answer to 'What made such and such a thing happen?'; and (*b*) *final cause*: this gives the answer to 'Why [for what purpose] did it happen?' In his own theory of the First Cause he differs from Anaxagoras by substituting (*b*) for (*a*). There must be a prime mover, which is itself unmoved: otherwise its own movement would be just as much in need of explanation as any other movement. But there is only one kind of thing in the world which produces motion without itself being in motion: namely, the object of desire, purpose or love. Thus the First Cause is a final cause, and is identified with the Aristotelian God, who moves all things by being loved, by supplying a purpose for the activity of the universe, a 'reason' why things are as they are.

In the thirteenth century the great philosopher St Thomas Aquinas (1225–1274) succeeded in establishing Aristotle as the chief authority in official Catholic philosophy. Aquinas used Aristotle's argument of the unmoved mover and of the First Cause in two of his famous five proofs of the existence of God. But the Christian's God differed in some important respects from Aristotle's, and the final cause became less appropriate. By the time Leibniz and Kant were using the argument of the First Cause, the final cause had been dropped and replaced by something closer to the efficient cause. The argument takes on a more modern dress. Everything has a cause, which in turn had its cause, and so on. But this series of causes and effects cannot be infinite, and must have a first term. The first term must be uncaused; otherwise it would not be the first. All other causes are also effects: the First Cause alone is not also an effect.

The idea of a First Cause must be assessed in the light of the criticisms which have been made of this type of argument. The following are typical.

(1) Even if the argument proves the existence of a prime mover or First Cause, it does not prove the existence of a God. To identify the First Cause with God is to endow it with attributes of a divine being, which the argument itself does not warrant. This is reminiscent of Aristotle's criticism of the cosmic Mind of Anaxagoras.

(2) It does not even prove the existence of a First Cause, except on the hypothesis that a series of causes and effects cannot be infinite. But such a hypothesis is not self-evidently true. On the contrary, the possibility of an infinite series is demonstrated by (for example) the series of natural numbers 1, 2, 3, etc.

(3) Even if the series of temporal events is in fact infinite, it still does not follow that the first event must have been a cause of all the rest. Although it may be true that everything has an (efficient) cause, it does not follow that the total-

ity of things has a single cause of its own. Leibniz saw this weakness and tried to strengthen it with his Principle of Sufficient Reason (roughly, that whatever exists, there must always be a reason why it exists), but this, though it applied to the totality of things, was a departure from the strictly causal argument.

(4) The most serious objection of all depends, like Aristotle's theory, on an analysis of the term 'cause'. Nowadays 'cause' is nearly always taken to mean something close to 'efficient cause'; but further analysis has eliminated the anthropomorphism latent in Aristotle's notion of 'what *makes* things happen'. For example: heating a piece of metal causes it to expand. If we say that heat 'makes' it expand, we speak in terms of a model like Aristotle's, such as the potter 'making' a pot; but what we really mean is something very different. 'Heat causes expansion' means only that whenever the metal is heated, it expands. Causal connexion is merely 'uniformity of succession' (J. S. Mill). The consequences of this are fatal for the First Cause doctrine, since it follows that we cannot say that A is the cause of B, unless we can say that A is or could be regularly followed by B. If it is logically impossible for A to happen more than once, it cannot be spoken of as a cause. But the First Cause is by definition something that can happen only once.

According to modern logic, the expression 'first cause' is self-contradictory, so long as 'cause' is taken in its most widely current usage. Of course it is still open to the First Cause philosopher to invoke some other kind of cause, such as Aristotle's final cause. But the appeal of the First Cause argument today rests on psychological rather than logical considerations: for example, the prestige of scientific causal explanation; the anthropomorphism of efficient causes; and the psychological difficulty of conceiving an infinite series. (See also *God*.)

Four roots

The **FOUR ELEMENTS**: Earth, Water, Fire and Air, first appear in philosophical think-

ing in the work of Empedocles, the Sicilian philosopher of the fifth century B.C.; and he used them
in his attack on Parmenides, who held that the
world of the senses, and our notions about it,
are illusory; and in particular that we are deceived in thinking it a world of change.

Parmenides thought that behind this appearance there is a pure essence which is limitless and
changeless, undivided and imperishable; this
alone is real. Empedocles, on the contrary, explained that change *is* the essence of the universe.
There are four 'roots', the elemental masses of
earth, air, fire and water, and from them all
other things are derived by the operation of two
contrary forces: *love* and *hate*. What appear to us
as generation and destruction are, in fact, com-
pounding and dissolution. From these two forces
and these four roots, Empedocles, and Aristotle
following him, and the Arab doctors translating
Aristotle, and the medieval philosophers translating the Arab doctors to get at Aristotle, and
the Renaissance 'fundamentalists' like du Bartas,
were able to elaborate an astronomy, a chemical
and physical theory, and a medical theory, which
explained the nature of the universe, the earth,
and man himself.

The medical theory developed through Hippocrates, a contemporary of Empedocles who was
born in the island of Cos about 460 B.C., and his
enthusiastic follower Galen, born at Pergamon in
c. 129 B.C., who after doctoring gladiators rose to
be court physician to Marcus Aurelius and Com-
modus. The chemical theory developed through
the alchemists, whose origins are lost in legend,
but whose notions were spreading in the dark
ages through the whole land mass from China
to the Atlantic coast, and taking up local colouring and supplementary material as they went.
The astronomy began with Empedocles himself,
who held, for instance, that *day* and *night* were
produced by the separation of fire and air, from
which came two hemispheres, the bright and the
dark. Their movement round the earth is explained by the loss of equilibrium caused by the
pull of the opposing forces; the presence of the
stars by the fact that the dark sphere still contains
a little fire.

These notions were later ousted by the more
elaborate and systematic astronomy associated
with the geographer, Ptolemy, who lived in the

second century A.D.; but they were not abandoned entirely, and down to the seventeenth
century an interpretation of creation in terms of
the four elements was still current. It was popularized then by du Bartas, the French Protestant
encyclopaedist, whose *Divine Works and Days* was
translated into English in 1592–1599 by Joshua
Sylvester:

> Earth as the Lees and heavie dross of All
> (After his kinde) did to the bottom fall;
> Contrariwise, the light and nimble Fire
> Did through the crannies of th'old Heap aspire
> Unto the top; and, by his nature, Light
> No less than hot, mounted in sparks upright:
> But lest the Fire (which all the rest imbraces)
> Being too near, should burn the Earth to ashes;
> As Chosen Umpires, the great All-Creator
> Between these Fires placed the Aire and Water;
> For one suffiz'd not their stern strife to end.
> Water, as Cozen did the Earth befriend,
> Aire, for his kinsman Fire as firmly deals.

It is curious to see the Four Elements, at the
end of their long life, returning to this connexion
with the Creation Myth, for it is quite possible
that they started there, before any of the philosophers got to work on them. It is at least note-
worthy that they play a prominent part in the
Creation Story as told by Ovid at the beginning
of his long poem, the *Metamorphoses* (finished
in A.D. 7). In the void, he tells us, before sea and
lands were, no form of things remained the same;
cold strove with hot, moist with dry, soft with
hard, things which had weight with those that had
none. Then God ('whichever of the gods it was',
says Ovid) composed this strife; all was bound in
harmony. Fire, having no weight, leapt up to
form heaven's vault; air was next in lightness and
place; earth sank to the bottom, and water took
the last place, holding the solid land in its embrace.

So the Four Elements made their progress
from Myth to Science, and then sank, apparently,
into a mere poetic device of playful metaphor:

> For when the Fair in all their Pride expire,
> To their first Elements their Souls retire:
> The Sprights of fiery Termagants in Flame
> Mount up, and take a *Salamander's* Name.
> Soft yielding Minds to Water glide away,
> And sip, with *Nymphs*, their Elemental Tea.

The graver Prude sinks downward to a *Gnome*,
In search of Mischief still on Earth to roam.
The light Coquettes in *Sylphs* aloft repair,
And sport and flutter in the Fields of Air.

These lines from Pope's *Rape of the Lock* (1714) might appear trivial if it were not for their exquisite music and wit; but there is a whole world of learning and millennial tradition behind them. Pope entered it through the Rosicrucian *Comte de Gabalis* (1670), but in that work the Abbé de Villars was merely tapping the serious studies of Hermetic philosophy, the occult world of Jewish and Christian heresy, to which other English poets (notably Milton and Blake) owed so much.

These occult studies were the children of alchemy. Down to the time of Newton, Boyle and Leibniz, the fundamental beliefs of alchemy could still be taken seriously; but in the eighteenth century the discoveries of Lavoisier and Priestley discredited them; Priestley isolated the oxygen in air, Lavoisier (in 1789) published the first table of elements in the modern sense, for which search had been made since Boyle (1661) defined them as 'primitive and simple or unmixed bodies, not made of other bodies or of one another'. But the revival of the belief in transmutation, brought about by nuclear physics, and the revival of interest in alchemy itself through Jungian psychology, which treats it with great respect, may yet rehabilitate the Four Elements. It is certain that vast tracts of the past are incomprehensible without them.

Alchemy did not, as a matter of fact, regard the Four Elements as the primal substances. Behind them lay the *prima materia*, primitive matter itself, *tao* as the Chinese called it. The dream of the alchemists was that they might some day be able to separate this primal substance in the laboratory. Thus from gold or mercury they would prepare 'the mercury of the philosophers', the essential element freed from its drosses – the earthy quality, the liquid quality, the volatile principle so that it would then be fixed; and in this process they used the fourth element: fire.

But the elements are not only outside man, they are also in him; for man is a microcosm, a small model of the great universe, the macrocosm (a notion which goes back to Egyptian and Babylonian thought). Galen had brought the Ele-

ments into medicine by uniting Hippocrates' theory of fluids – blood, phlegm, yellow and black bile – with earth, water, fire and air. Health and temperament depend on the blending and balance of them all. Fire was hot and dry, air hot and moist, water cold and moist, earth cold and dry. Fire predominated in the choleric man, air in the sanguine, water in the phlegmatic, earth in the melancholy. There are diets and treatments for each humour.

Thus the striking thing about the Four Elements is their universality. They belong to a view which sees correspondences everywhere; which can attribute passions to substances, and accept metaphor literally. This is a world which can proliferate into extraordinary structures of credulity, in which one thing turns into another and is equated with another until the brain reels, and Empedocles' principle of change seems to reduce all to the primal chaos again. But it is a world in which the poet is, by nature, a citizen; and therefore the poet has turned to plunder it in times of supreme need: Shakespeare's *Antony and Cleopatra*:

> I am Fire, and Ayre; my other Elements
> I give to baser life ...

Donne's *Parting from Her*:

> I will not look upon the quickning Sun
> But straight her beauty to my sense shall run;
> The ayre shall note her soft, the fire most pure;
> Water suggest her clear, and the earth sure.

down to a lovely straightforward statement in Dryden's *Song for Saint Cecilia's Day, 1687*:

> From Harmony, from heavenly Harmony,
> This universal Frame began;
> When Nature underneath a heap
> Of jarring Atomes lay,
> And cou'd not heave her Head,
> The tuneful Voice was heard from high,
> Arise, ye more than dead.
> Then cold and hot and moist and dry
> In order to their Stations leap
> And MUSICKS pow'r obey.
> From Harmony, from heavenly Harmony,
> This universal Frame began:
> From Harmony to Harmony
> Through all the Compass of the Notes it ran
> The diapason closing full in Man.

Freedom and politics

FREEDOM is an essential attribute of human nature and a reflection of its rational character. Man appears to be a slave to necessity: he is born and he dies, he must wash and dress and eat and drink and move from place to place. He cannot escape a thousand obligations that nature imposes upon him. Yet he is essentially a free being because he can rise above these necessities.

Man can resist the tendencies of his instinct because of motives which his intellect offers him. He can freely choose between different possibilities, whereas no such choice is to be found in animal instincts. There may be many reasons or none why a man will prefer one course of action to another. What matters is not that he may make the best, or a good, choice, but that he does not choose blindly.

Freedom is concerned with the means and ends of human conduct and as such is as old as human society. In its political aspect, all the same, it is not part of the common stock of humanity, but the fruit of a mature civilization, the result of a long, often interrupted struggle, the beginnings of which lie in the free city-states of ancient Greece. Solon's constitution in Athens, six hundred years before the birth of Christ, established the basis of political freedom as it later became characteristic of civilization in Europe.

The new thing was government by law and consent instead of compulsion, and the division of power instead of its concentration in the hands of one man. The Greek experiment in freedom did not last. The supremacy of law and constitutional government, the rights of the individual vis-à-vis the State, the necessity of effective standards of right and wrong which Plato and Aristotle and the Socratic and Stoic philosophers evolved, could not find the safeguards in the ancient world which they required. True freedom excludes all absolute power and arbitrary action, and the republics of antiquity were as incapable as the Oriental despotisms of satisfying that condition; absolutism, whether of one man or of the majority, and slavery, remained the basis of their power.

Christianity provided the new law, the new spirit and the new authority for freedom which Greece and Rome had been unable to supply. 'Render unto Caesar the things that are Caesar's, and unto God the things that are God's', was the precept, and, inheriting her power from the dying Roman Empire, the Christian Church created the force to execute it. Christianity countered the State's claim of absolutism with the higher claim of God. It affirmed the infinite worth of each individual soul. Each man is a child of God and as such has an inherent dignity. Society exists to further the good of individual souls. A new relationship arose between governors and governed which recognized that there are rights and duties superior to those imposed by men – the law of nature, which is the law of reason, and of God.

Civil liberty was born in the Middle Ages out of the collision between the temporal and the spiritual power. The cities of Germany, Italy and Flanders won their emancipation, Switzerland obtained its independence from Austria, parliamentary government was developed in France and England. Magna Carta limited the powers of the king if only in favour of one class, the barons. It was recognized by medieval thinkers that political authority derived from popular suffrage and that unjust rulers could be deposed by the people. The Church defended the rights of the people against the encroachments of the princes and the feudal nobility, but became herself an absolute power in that struggle.

The decline of religion in the later Middle Ages strengthened the absolutism of the State. The doctrine of the divine right of kings (q.v.) received a strong impulse from Macchiavelli's teaching that the ends of government justify the means employed. There was little freedom in Europe in the sixteenth century, when the kings of France, Spain and England made themselves masters of the Church. The Reformation movements, instead of emancipating the nations and making for freedom, as their founders claimed, strengthened the despotism of kings and princes. 'Calvin preached', Lord Acton wrote, 'and Bellarmine lectured, but Macchiavelli reigned.'

Power was the test of religious toleration in the sixteenth and seventeenth centuries; rulers decided the religion of their countries and the dissenters had to leave or to renounce their religion. It was only through curbing the authority of states that religious and civil freedom was to become possible in modern Europe, and that not fully until the twentieth century.

Europe seemed incapable of becoming the home of free states and it was from America that in the eighteenth century freedom began its triumphant journey. Liberty was one of the watchwords of the French Revolution, but the passion for equality destroyed all hope for the realization of freedom.

The impulse of nationalism which the French Revolution bequeathed to modern Europe again acted as a force rather towards despotism than freedom. Freedom requires the division of power. Just as religious freedom is possible only where the co-existence of different religions is admitted, with an equal right for participating members to govern themselves according to their own principles, so the centralizing unifying force of the national state became the enemy of true freedom within its own society as well as within the society of nations. Political and religious freedom will be most complete where unity exists as the triumph of truth, not of force, and where diversity is conceded. This is what one historian of freedom, Lord Acton, regarded as the great lesson of European history.

Two concepts of freedom stand opposed since the nineteenth century and the conflict between them is not yet concluded. The one understood freedom as an end in itself. John Stuart Mill, who was its chief protagonist, held that man's freedom is absolutely sovereign over all conduct that concerns himself, that is, his body and mind, and he made an absolute division between the individual and society. The only purpose, he said in the *Essay on Liberty* (1859), for which power can be rightfully exercised over others is to prevent harm to others. A man's own good, physical or moral, is not a sufficient warrant for interfering with his absolute freedom.

However, purely self-regarding actions are impossible. Man does not exist except as a member of some society whose laws have made him what he is. What Mill failed to see was that man as a self-conscious independent individual emerges only at a later stage of his development. The individual is no more thinkable without his social, than without his physical, environment. Both are mutually responsive; there is no change in the

one without a corresponding adjustment in the other.

This view of freedom led to the extraordinary conclusion that the best way to serve society was for man to serve his own interests. It installed the profit motive as the guiding principle of economic conduct. Against this system of naked materialism and the crying social injustice which it created, Karl Marx protested. The nineteenth century prided itself on the political rights which man as an individual had achieved: Marx believed that political rights in such a society were a sham, as undoubtedly to some extent they were. But he included in his attack against the capitalist society of *laissez-faire* the whole of Europe's hard-won heritage of freedom and political responsibility. He set up the proletariat instead of man, the State instead of the individual. A new despotism took the place of the old.

The basis for Marx's protest had been provided by Hegel's dynamic view of freedom, not as an end in itself, but as a means for the realization of power and dominion over the external forces of nature and history.

Soviet communism, which adopted this philosophy, holds freedom to be identical with necessity. The revolutionary is an instrument of the process of historical necessity who cannot act other than he does act. His situation will be like Luther's when he said: 'Here I stand, I cannot do otherwise.'

It is of course true that in many cases freedom may amount to no more than electing to adopt what cannot be avoided. The conscript and the volunteer are both caught in processes which they cannot halt; nevertheless, psychologically and morally, the situation is different. It is the act of self-determination that makes the difference between the subject and the citizen. The problem of freedom in the last resort cannot be solved apart from the problem of man as a responsible person. As such he is a part or a member of a political society, but not to the whole extent of his being. In so far as he is part of the community, the common good is higher than the good of the individual citizen, and it is in the nature of things that social life should impose upon him as an individual many restraints and sacrifices.

But as a person endowed with a spiritual life and called to a destiny outside time, society has no claim upon man. The problem of freedom which faces the modern world is not the choice between man or the State, or between individualism or collectivism. The tension between these opposites is as healthy as it is necessary. The real problem of freedom is the preservation of spheres where man can fully be a person, and is not forced to be a slave.

ILLUSTRATION: Page 178.

Two major freedoms

FREEDOM OF SPEECH and **FREEDOM OF THE PRESS** are expressions used to describe the absence of any official restraint on the publication of books and printed matter, or on speaking.

Underlying this definition there is the deeper meaning of these freedoms, the liberty to think and express one's thoughts as one wishes. This is considered in many countries to be among the most fundamental and valuable of constitutional liberties, though in others these freedoms are rejected and refused by government.

There are many reasons why freedom of expression in books and in speech should be so highly valued. Perhaps the strongest argument is that liberty is valuable for its own sake. In every branch of activity it is better that individuals should be left free; and the government is justified in interfering only where it is clear that to do so does more good than harm. As we have seen, John Stuart Mill defends freedom of thought in this way in his *Essay on Liberty* (1859). 'We can never be sure' he wrote, 'that the opinion we are endeavouring to stifle is a false opinion; and if we were sure, stifling would be an evil still.' This is the classic liberal argument for the restriction of state power, but the love of liberty is an ancient and deep-rooted emotion as well as a rational belief.

There is also a more specifically political argument for freedom of expression. If one holds that there can be no true democracy without an opposition, to persecute opponents of the government is to stultify the nation's political life. Belief in democracy rests partly on faith in the consequences of open discussion; only in the free give and take of argument, in print or in speech, will the best policy be worked out.

Equally, if the ultimate aim of society is to enable every individual to realize his powers and develop to the best of his ability, he needs freedom in order to do this. Free expression and exchange of ideas, and free choice in matters of belief are means towards this end.

Belief in the need to find and uphold the truth is another reason for attacking government control of opinion. No state is justified in pointing to a set of beliefs, either political, religious, economic or social, and saying they are true and all others are false. Experience has shown that what is truth to one generation is falsehood to the next, and no government is justified in coercing belief in its definition of truth.

Although freedom of speech and freedom of the press have so much to recommend them, the government's right to control the expression of opinion was never questioned until the seventeenth century.

Since then these freedoms have been denied on both political and moral grounds. Non-democratic governments fear that attacks in the press and at public meetings will weaken them or cause their downfall; no despot tolerates criticism. Churches have enlisted state aid to prevent the propagation of views considered wrong or blasphemous, and some churches still extend a voluntary censorship over their members.

Freedom of the press can be limited either by a censorship or by prosecution after publication, the former being the commonest and most efficient method. Censorship goes back to the earliest days of printing. The first censor's office was established at Mainz, where Gutenberg had opened his press, in 1486. When the art of printing was introduced into England, presses were put under Crown control. No one was allowed to print except under licence, and in Queen Elizabeth's reign licences were issued only to presses in Oxford, Cambridge and London. All offenders came under the jurisdiction of the Court of Star Chamber.

When the Long Parliament abolished the Star Chamber in 1641, some people hoped that its control over opinion would cease as well, but censorship was continued. Among its bitterest opponents was John Milton, who attacked the censorship in his *Areopagitica* of 1644. He saw that criticism of the government is the way to reform and the righting of wrongs; but it was his passionate love of truth – truth reached after battle with falsehood – that fired him to attack control of thought so vehemently: 'Though all the winds of doctrine were let loose to play upon the earth, so Truth be in the field, we do injuriously by licensing and prohibiting to misdoubt her strength. Let her and falsehood grapple; who ever knew Truth put to the worse, in a free and open encounter.'

The censorship was given a statutory basis after the Restoration, but in 1695 Parliament refused to renew the Licensing Act, and it has been in abeyance ever since. The law also ceased to apply to the American colonies, and since they became the United States of America the censorship has not been renewed. France, on the other hand, which proclaimed liberty so bravely in 1789, did not relax control of the press until 1881. By then almost every country calling itself a democracy had ended censorship, though all have reserved the right to renew it in time of war.

Freedom of speech has usually been a parallel right to freedom of the press, and one is seldom found without the other. A government that prosecutes opposition when it is in the form of books and papers will hardly allow it to be spoken freely. Since there can be no censorship of speech, the precise point at which speaking was freed in a particular country is hard to distinguish. One can only consider that freedom of speech has been granted when prosecutions for attacks on the government cease and when there are no hindrances to public meetings.

Yet no country that allows free speech and a free press gives completely unrestricted liberty of expression. Every country has laws against libel, slander, blasphemy, obscenity and sedition. In England both libel and slander are offences, since freedom of expression must stop short of defamation of others. In addition, it is a crime to publish obscene books and to use obscene language.

This attempt to protect the nation's morals is carried even further with regard to plays, and over the public theatre there remains a vestige of the old censorship. No play can be given public performance in England without the Lord Chamberlain's permission, as a protection against moral (and sometimes political) abuse.

There is also protection against seditious material. The term 'sedition' embraces everything – whether by word, deed or in writing – which is calculated to disturb the tranquillity of the State. In England today the government uses its power to punish sedition very seldom, common as such prosecutions were in the past. Blasphemy and attacks on Christianity used to be punishable offences, and profane cursing and swearing are still forbidden by an Act of 1745. This is another field in which the government has virtually ceased to exercise its powers on prosecution; it is no longer considered the State's duty to uphold religion and morals by the threat of punishment. This is left to the Churches, and the Roman Catholic Church protects its members from books attacking the faith by putting them on the Index of forbidden reading.

It can be seen that in England the government could, if it chose, use all these laws to threaten freedom of speech and freedom of the press. In fact it exercises its powers with great discretion; only outrageous cases of obscenity or sedition are punished. Some countries have wished to make liberty more certain than this, and guarantees of freedom of speech and freedom of the press are written into their constitutions. Although the efficacy of these written safeguards is doubtful, the fact that they are included shows how highly they are valued.

ILLUSTRATION: Pages 181, 182 and 223.

'Night, sleep, death and the stars'

FREE VERSE, verse of irregular rhythmical pattern, has a somewhat dated sound today, for there is nothing staler than a successful revolution, and the wish of poets to break free from modes of expression which were too rigid, to reflect what they conceived to be the modernity of their age or to be personal in their own particular way, has long been recognized and appreciated in the work of an Eliot, an Eluard or a St-Jean Perse.

Free verse is often referred to by the equivalent French words *vers libre* since it was in France that an important part of the battle was fought by the Symbolists. The French lacked an exuberant and experimental sixteenth century; they had to free themselves from the classical ideal and the dominance of the alexandrine. It has been suggested that Arthur Rimbaud (1854–1891) derived the free rhythms of his *Marine* and *Mouvement* from Judith Gautier's translations of Chinese poetry published in 1869. His friend Verlaine (1844–1896), in the words of Lytton Strachey, expressed 'the delicate, shifting and indecisive feelings which he loved so well' by relinquishing the last shreds of orthodox pattern and turning his verse into 'a perfectly fluid substance'.

The immense vitality of the 'free' poems of Walt Whitman (1819–1892) had made the decisive Anglo-American contribution between 1855 and 1871. There had, of course, been free verse before Whitman and before the Symbolists. According to William Blake's preface to *Jerusalem* (1804), the spirits who dictated that poem preferred it. Although Blake had at first considered the 'monotonous cadence' of blank verse 'necessary and indispensable', he 'soon found that in the mouth of a true Orator such monotony was not only awkward but as much of a bondage as rhyme itself'.

It was with the school known as Imagism that free verse came into its own in England and America. T. E. Hulme, whose theories were influential in the formation of the group and whose fine poems were much admired by it, had prophesied a period of 'dry, hard, classical verse' which would be a welcome departure from the outrush of Swinburne. The anthology *Des Imagistes*, appearing in 1914, did its best to provide the answer by echoing the naked clarity of Ancient Greek verse and the clear images of Chinese verse.

A year later a characteristic manifesto declared one of its objects to be 'To create new rhythms – as the expression of new moods – and not to copy old rhythms which merely echo old moods. We do not insist on "free verse" as the only method of writing poetry. We fight for it as for a principle of liberty. We believe that the individuality of a poet may be often better expressed in free verse than in conventional forms.' Thus F. S. Flint, a minor poet and Imagist, felt that rhyme and metre

were artificial excrescences whose nature was to grow more and more insipid until they eventually became 'contemptible and encumbering'. The minor verse of the minor Imagists has not worn particularly well, but the atmosphere around Imagism, and free verse generally, proved stimulating to a number of poets.

A case in point was D. H. Lawrence (1885–1930). Beginning as a Georgian, capable of writing ably in traditional forms, he felt by June 1916 that 'the essence of poetry with us in this age of stark and unlovely actualities is a stark directness, without a shadow of a lie, or a shadow of deflection anywhere'; this attitude brought him to his major successes in *Birds, Beasts and Flowers*, as well as to the rather slipshod bits of satire and epigram in *Pansies*. Indeed, it may be felt that the most effective free verse is not really so free after all, for a kind of inevitability of cadence gives it weight and formality (at the least it sounds like a sensitive translation); and when it falls into long rhythms, as so often with T. S. Eliot, and others including Robinson Jeffers, the reader soon discovers a degree of regularity.

It is in America rather than Britain that free verse remains something of a revolutionary doctrine. The influence of Whitman reinforced a natural desire to speak with a new voice, rejecting the 'genteel tradition' of Longfellow and Whittier. The nationalist intention of American poets wishing to assert their own language, which is exemplified in Carl Sandburg's *Chicago Poems* (1914) 'Hog Butcher for the World ... City of the Big Shoulders' – or in the *Spoon River Anthology* (1915) of Edgar Lee Masters, exists simultaneously with the subtle effects, and often acidly satirical criticism of the American way of life, to be found in the even freer poems of E. E. Cummings, as in *Tulips and Chimneys* (1923) or *Is* 5 (1926). Cummings never shouts, although he can jeer deliciously; his use of free verse achieves new things by exploiting the irony and ambiguity implicit in the waywardness of language; by a strategic arrangement of words and parts of words he emphasizes their frequently conflicting charges of meaning and casts a glow of liveliness over what would have been self-consciously pure or self-consciously hearty in others. Free, or freeish verse, delicate, witty, subtle and wiry, has also come from the great Marianne Moore, born, like

T. S. Eliot, in St Louis, Mo., and associated in her early days with Imagism.

Free verse was decisively checked by the emergence of the poetry of W. H. Auden (b. 1907), a virtuoso in formal writing, who has insisted that severity of form tests the authenticity and strength of impulse.

Unpredictable

FREE WILL is the hypothesis that the behaviour of an individual human being at a given moment is in part determined by the activity of a metaphysical entity, the Soul. This activity is neither random nor in any way determined by the previous physical states of the body. Thus Free Will must be sharply distinguished from 'freedom of choice'. The extent to which the latter may be said to obtain for a given individual at any moment is equivalent to the amount and nature of the information required to predict his behaviour. Thus, in order to predict a knee-jerk reflex when the patellar tendon is tapped, we need only know that the subject is alive and in good health. To predict the behaviour of a wealthy and leisured person at some moment on a summer's day, with no such clear-cut stimulus situation, far more detailed and copious information would be required about the present state or past history of his central nervous system. These examples do not contradict subjective common-sense ideas, the former extreme example being commonly called an involuntary movement. This way of looking at it in no way conflicts with the basic scientific postulate that the behaviour of a man is wholly deterministic, like that of any physical system, and can wholly be explained by means of the two concepts of causality and chance on randomness (the second concept probably not being required in this case).

The metaphysical notion of free will arises as a result from a purely irrational and emotional rebellion against these two principles, falsely interpreted as though they constituted a restriction of the individual's freedom of choice by the dominating behaviour of other human beings and also the physical world.

The Greeks, in their cultural prime, expressed this feeling by personifying the concepts of Chance, Fate, Destiny and Necessity. They did not, however, feel compelled to deny the inevitable effects of these two principles, and hence the work of Thucydides, for instance, is almost modern in its clear distinction of the relations between causality in general and social interaction of human beings in particular.

The collapse of the Athenian culture under stress of plague, war and internal conflicts produced a reduced sense of freedom on the part of its citizens. There then began a preoccupation – chiefly expressed by Plato – with the metaphysical concept of the soul. The way was thus open to endless sterile debates about the nature and limits of free will.

This trend became still more marked under the influence of Christianity, with its single omnipotent personal deity. The Christian theologians repudiated altogether the notion of Chance, so that Augustine, for instance, regarded it as sinful to indulge in superstitious practices, such as the interpretation of omens: divination and astrology were acknowledgements that the workings of destiny would render prayers useless. They appear to have connected chance with the will of another personal deity, the devil – a personification of Chance in amounting to a complete denial of the nature of the principle.

Determinism (the counterpart of free will) appears, in the Christian scheme, as the tyrannical control of all natural events, and of human behaviour in particular, by God, conceived like a human individual. There now arose an endless series of debates as to the degree of freedom of choice permitted to human beings by this dominant individual (who may be visualized as the overlord of a colony of baboons). Needless to say, all this was heavily disguised and emerged in the form of metaphysical debates. Volumes were written in this way about free will and predestination by God, though the results were naturally as inconclusive as those of Milton's devils.

Others sat apart on a hill retired,
In thoughts more elevate, and reasoned high
Of providence, foreknowledge, will and fate,
Fixed fate, free will, foreknowledge absolute;
And found no end, in wandering mazes lost.

The arguments centred on the infinite omniscience and predictive accuracy of God, who must be supposed to have complete foreknowledge of all events; a state of affairs which, it was uneasily recognized, was incompatible with the notion of free will which should imply a large element of complete unpredictability in human behaviour. Attempts were made to reconcile the conflicting positions by insisting on the illusory nature of time. An example is the system of Boethius recently revived by C. S. Lewis, the Christian apologist, according to which God, situated outside time in eternity, can see the whole course of events spread out before him as though on a purely spatial map. In this way the predestination implied by foreknowledge can be by-passed. Such a system is like the scientific ones of Newtonian classical mechanics and Einstein's relativity theory in that there is no direction associated with time, and 'predictions' may be made in any direction.

The controversies about free will and predestination in the Christian culture of the Dark and Middle Ages and the Reformation period was lively and bitter, the first major dispute being that between Augustine and Pelagius. Pelagius did not recognize the necessity for grace – which can be regarded roughly as a 'helping hand' from God towards our salvation – grace being regarded as an interference with our free will as well as a predestination of man. As Aldous Huxley has pointed out, the protagonists of predestination and grace – the latter being the idea that an individual's achievements are predetermined by his endowments – are at least one stage nearer a realistic view of the universe. But of course the fundamental error of personification greatly confused the whole issue; the attractiveness of Pelagianism lay in its comforting assertion that God is not an unmitigated tyrant.

At the Reformation, the dispute assumed considerable sociological importance, and greatly embittered the quarrels of the Catholics, at that time moderately Pelagian, and Calvinists, extreme protagonists of predestination. Interestingly, the latter group asserted the right to rebel against merely human overlords. The controversy reappeared in the seventeenth century within the Catholic church in the form of rivalry between the Jesuits (moderate free will) and Jansenists (extreme predestination), and within the Protestant churches as the rival doctrines of Calvin (extreme predestination) and Arminius (extreme free will).

By the present century the decline of Christianity and the exposure by the positivist philosophers of the imprecise nature of metaphysical thinking seemed to presage the end of the sterile controversy. It was given a new lease of life by the appearance of Heisenberg's principle of indeterminacy (1927), which asserted the impossibility of simultaneous measurement of the momentum and space-time position of an electron. Its utter irrelevance to the controversy has often been pointed out (*e.g.* by Max Born), but it is most significant that a formulation which, however distorted and over-generalized, could only be supposed to increase the element of Chance in the course of events (this is in itself, of course, a misunderstanding), was used to re-assert free will. A similar naivety colours the physics of the Greek Atomist Epicurus (341–270 B.C.), who tried to gear free will to an hypothetical, arbitrary 'swerve' from a straight path of some of his atoms. His exact theory of the 'swerve' is not fully clear but it is obvious that Epicurus is trying to avoid the inexorable necessity of older atomic theories. This shows the strong emotional weighing behind these theories.

While the motives of the Pelagians are obvious enough, those of the predestinationists remain obscure until it is realized that they were in extreme revolt against what they felt to be the tyranny of Chance (a feeling expressed openly by the ancients). The revolt against predestination itself was secondary. (See also *Determinism*.)

Word by unchallengeable word

FUNDAMENTALISM is an attitude of mind rather than a single idea and is most commonly found as a set of opinions about the inspiration of the Bible. Fundamentalists say that a believing Christian must accept the divine

158 IDEAS

authorship of every sentence of Scripture, in the sense that the documents were no more written by the man whose name they bear than a best-seller is written by the novelist's typewriter.

The truthfulness and credibility of God are equally involved in the assertion of the author of the epistle to Titus that he left his cloak behind at Troas, as in the account of the Resurrection. A fundamentalist, therefore, cannot accept the assumptions of biblical criticism – that, in part at least, the documents are human documents which can be studied like other human documents. For the fundamentalist to admit this would be tanta-mount to giving up his faith. If apparent dis-crepancies are pointed out, or manuscript diffi-culties are shown, it is an illusion of the Devil; in the nineteenth century, fundamentalists ex-plained away fossils and the antiquity of the earth. They maintain also that the Bible is as easy as it is truthful, requiring no aids. This is a posi-tion belonging to the nineteenth century. Similar opinions can be found in earlier periods, but mainly when knowledge of natural science was slight and confined to a few, and among simple people. Even in the Middle Ages a more critical attitude to the text of the Bible could be found wherever there were scholars to cope with it.

In the eighteenth century the new physics had hardened into a widely acceptable 'scientific ideology' – the mechanistic deism of the En-lightenment. On this view God was kicked up-stairs to the lonely dignity of First Cause and Great Architect of the Universe: once begun, the universe must run along precisely determined lines to an exactly calculable time-table; God could not intervene in human affairs, so that there was no place for revelation and there was little interest in the Bible. When to all this was added, a few generations later, the theory of evolution, it seemed to many honest minds that Scripture was utterly discredited.

Some could not accept this but would not argue for an alternative: some placed their faith above their integrity and the characteristically nine-teenth-century form of fundamentalism was created, an impregnable mountain of sand in which the intellectually feeble could comfortably bury their heads.

Both the new science and the new fundamental-ism provoked another reaction amongst Chris-

tians. Some of them felt that they could neither reject the empirical discoveries of science, nor accept the unpleasant moral doctrines frequently canvassed as equally true. Their attitude was summed up in the words attributed to St An-selm, 'All truth by whomsoever uttered, is from the Holy Spirit', and in this light they turned to the Bible and they helped to create a new science of the exact study of historical MSS – the science of textual criticism.

It is now possible to say that a Christian may both assent to orthodox doctrine on the inspira-tion of the Bible, going so far with the funda-mentalist, and yet retain his intellectual integrity. It is recognized that the Bible is a human as well as divine work. Nowhere does the Bible itself claim to be infallible. The canon of Scripture, what went in and what stayed out, is the work of the Church on earth. The men whose sayings and deeds are recorded in Scripture claim only that they bear witness to what is true, to the power, mercy and goodness of God. Few would now claim that the first chapters of Genesis are historically accurate, yet the doctrine they reveal that Man has the power of moral choice, the freedom to exercise it and the corrupt nature to misuse it, is not thereby diluted.

Christians realize that when God speaks with men, he uses the language and ideas that they can understand; that God can and does use the methods of poetry and fiction as well as history in order to reveal himself to men. Thus the chal-lenge of science, natural, biological, and histori-cal, has given Christians a deeper understanding and love for the Bible wherever that challenge has been honestly met. Fundamentalism in the old sense has no claim on anyone's allegiance; but a chastened orthodoxy is still a living intellectual force.

Fundamentalism has recently impacted strong-ly into American religious thought. Before the First World War a series of tracts in the U.S.A. heralded much controversy inside religious bod-ies. As late as 1925 a schoolteacher in Tennessee was put on trial for teaching Evolution in a school. He was found guilty though no measures were taken. Fundamentalism can still be a strong undercurrent.

ILLUSTRATION: Page 228.

G

Genius of all sorts

GENIUS, in modern English usage, means 'the highest conceivable form of original ability, something altogether extraordinary and beyond even supreme educational prowess'. It did not develop this connotation, now its major meaning, until the eighteenth century.

In classical times the *genius* of the Roman house-father and the *iuno* of the house-mother represented the male and female forms of the family's power of continuing itself by reproduction, and were worshipped as such in private cults.

Later, under the influence of Greek individualism and the idea that every person had a guardian spirit or *daimon*, the *genius* lost its original meaning and came to mean first a personification of the individual's desires and appetites, and then the guardian angel or higher self of the individual. (Hence, later still, the use of the terms good and evil genius.) It was also sometimes rationalized into the individual's character or temper.

A further development of the word, again following that of the Greek *daimon*, enlarged it to embrace not only the guardian spirits of individuals, but also of places (*genius loci*), buildings, guilds, corporations, and the state.

In English the word *genius* has never had its earliest Latin meaning, but all its later meanings have come down to us, and it has developed from these some other specialized usages.

As early as 1390 genius was used as the proper name of an allegorical character representing the native moral instincts of man. The word, however, was rare even in the sixteenth century. It comes occasionally in Ben Jonson, notably in *The Poetaster*:

> Ramp up my genius, be not retrograde;
> But boldly nominate a spade a spade.

Shakespeare employs it no more than six or seven times – in *Macbeth*, for example, when Macbeth says of Banquo,

> There is none but he
> Whose being I do fear; and under him
> My genius is rebuk'd, as it is said
> Mark Antony's was by Caesar,

in *Julius Caesar*, when Brutus soliloquizes,

> Between the acting of a dreadful thing
> And the first motion, all the interim is
> Like a phantasma or a hideous dream:
> The genius and the mortal instruments
> Are then in council,

and in the Second Part of *Henry IV*, when Falstaff describes Justice Shallow as 'like a man made after supper of a cheese-paring: wen 'a was naked he was for all the world like a forked radish ... 'a was the very genius of famine'.

In the middle of the seventeenth century 'genius' became a synonym for talent. Thus Dryden wrote:

> Our builders were with want of genius curst;
> The second temple was not like the first.

John Evelyn, in speaking of Christiaan Huygens, says that he was 'so worthily celebrated for his universal Mathematical Genius'.

In the eighteenth century genius less often meant the guardian spirit of a man than his essential character or talent; and, developing from this, it acquired the sense of the prevalent feeling, spirit or trend of a nation, age or language. Dr Johnson in his *Dictionary* (1755) does not recognize its modern meaning, but speaks in his preface of 'such [words] as are readily adopted by the genius of our tongue'.

Fielding in *Tom Jones* (1749) had mentioned 'the wonderful force of genius only, without the least assistance of learning'. Goldsmith, too, and Horace Walpole gave genius its already modern sense.

The contrast between genius and talent was much written of in Germany and France, though it was the Italian, Cesare Lombroso (1835–1909), in his *Man of Genius* who came near to what appears the fundamental difference between talent – or ability – and genius. He quoted from

Jurgen-Meyer that 'the imagination of talent reproduces the stated fact; the inspiration of genius makes it anew. The first ... repeats; the second invents or creates. Talent aims at a point which appears difficult to reach; genius aims at a point which no one perceives.' In other words, genius is the innovator, the path-finder, the maker of departures; and Lombroso went on to describe the intuition which is the hallmark of genius by saying that 'genius divines facts before completely knowing them'. Voltaire wrote charmingly of Corneille that he 'composed *Horace* as a bird composes its nest', and the genius may often manifest his qualities very young. Mozart played the harpsichord at three and composed at four; Dante wrote a sonnet at nine; Goethe wrote a story in seven languages when he was scarcely ten. On the other hand, as genius has its contradictions, there are others who have appeared very stupid as children – Goldsmith, Chatterton, Newton, Flaubert, Einstein, for example.

The genius usually antagonizes the world with his new ideas. He goes like a thunderstorm, Kierkegaard remarked, contrary to the wind. Havelock Ellis pointed out that the genius meets with everything from passive refusal to have anything to do with him to torture and death; also he often antagonizes people by his personal peculiarities; his being, as it were, a misfit in everyday life. He is liable to stammer, to shuffle in his walk, to be hopelessly clumsy, to twitch in face or limbs; he falls into deep moods of melancholy, is odd or stupid about the most ordinary things – Mozart could not carve meat without cutting his fingers – and is hyper-sensitive himself, but insensitive or even cruel to others.

It is such characteristics that have led men all down the ages to confuse genius and madness. Lombroso and his school, indeed, regarded genius as fundamentally a pathological condition, closely allied to madness. Havelock Ellis, in his *Study of British Genius*, points out that the tendency to muscular inco-ordination, clumsiness, and speech difficulties mark two classes – the genius and the idiot; and he considers that there is an affinity between the two.

Galton assumed that genius is a natural variation; and showed that men of ability, if not of genius, tend to come from able families.

Some curious artificial means are said to have been used by different geniuses to stimulate their powers. Schiller plunged his feet into ice; Paisiello composed beneath a mountain of coverlets; Rousseau meditated with his head in the full glare of the sun; Bonnet retired into a cold room with his head wrapped in hot clothes; Shelley lay on the hearth-rug with his head close to the fire; Descartes buried his head in a sofa; Milton composed with his head leaning over his easy-chair.

Studies of the families of geniuses have shown that geniuses tend to be eldest or youngest children, to belong to large families, to come of elderly parents, to be the offspring (in the case of male genius) of predominantly boy-producing parents, and (in the case of female genius) of predominantly girl-producing parents; and that they are as likely to inherit ability through the mother as through the father.

The ideal of the gentleman

The **GENTLEMAN** originally meant a man of gentle – *i.e.* good – birth. Gentleness referred to descent, in this sense remaining close to its Latin root (*gens*, tribe or race).

When one thinks of how in contemporary usage 'gentle' connotes kindliness and mildness, so that one can speak of a gentle wind or rain, it is apparent at once how much 'gentleman' has enlarged its meaning. A term standing for a certain kind of rank by birth has come to symbolize general qualities associated with such birth. This is a very common process with terms of rank. Villain or villein, originally a menial in the feudal manor, is another term which has changed in a like way from its first meaning.

In part, nevertheless, the word gentleman still has its earlier significance in England. This is so particularly among those who use the term in a casual manner to indicate descent. The precise qualifications of families to which gentlemen belong include, formally, the right to bear arms. This in turn rested upon wealth – specifically upon landed wealth. The leisured mode of existence which only the wealthy landowner could maintain, together with his exercise of local authority in such offices as Justice of the Peace, no less symbolized his gentle rank than inclusion in volumes which registered those with titles and estates.

It was a rank which one could acquire. If the wealthy merchant of Elizabethan times, after having induced a herald to discover an appropriate coat of arms, was still not quite a gentleman, his descendants would surely be. Gentility, like nobility, was sarcastically defined as 'antient riches'. Or, in Thomas Fuller's words, 'Manners and money make a gentleman'.

But yet this begs the question of what is a gentleman – a question which fascinated Europeans, particularly at the time of the Renaissance, and has produced a large literature of courtly manuals or conduct books. Many of these are simply instruction books in manners. Among those which gave serious thought to analysing the concept of nobility and gentility were *The Refined Courtier* (1560) by Giovanni della Casa and *The Courtier* (1518) by Castiglione. Both were translated into English and widely read in Tudor England. Among English writers one may mention Henry Peacham for his *The Compleat Gentleman* (1622), and Richard Brathwaite for his *The English Gentleman* (1630) and *The English Gentlewoman* (1631).

An important, if not the main, problem which arose in this discussion was the tension between status by birth and status by manners. Did a man who was a gentleman by birth have to behave in a gentlemanly way in order to qualify as a gentleman at all? Equally could one who was not born a gentleman become one by acquiring the manners and the education of a gentleman? This is a serious problem for a society whose moral foundations are Christian, since these are universal morals, applying to all men irrespective of birth and rank.

To answer no to the first question is to admit that no matter what the well-born did they would still enjoy esteem and to put oneself as Professor Ernest Barker has said, on the side of Lucifer, once the conception of a gentlemanly standard of behaviour has taken root in the culture.

The writer of an anonymous sixteenth-century book called *The Institucion of a Gentleman* perceived the tension. He divided men into four classes. The first were the 'gentle-gentle': gentle by birth, gentle in manner. The second were the 'gentle-ungentle': gentle by birth, ungentle in manner. The third were the 'ungentle-gentle': ungentle by birth, gentle in manner. The fourth were the 'upstart unworthy'. The last evidently referred to the *nouveaux riches* of the time, who, with no evident claim to gentility on the grounds of either birth or manners, arrogantly demanded recognition and appropriated for themselves titles and perquisites of honour that they were unqualified to possess.

The distinction between ungentle-gentle and upstart unworthy enables us to see in the clearest possible focus the assumptions of this whole school of thought: a gentleman is a *naturally* superior being. In this these writers were following the conceptions of the Greeks – particularly Aristotle – for whom mankind could be divided into those who were freemen or slaves by nature. The upstart unworthy is excluded from gentility for lack of superior moral qualities. The issue then remains: is this natural superiority dependent upon one's birth (*i.e.* are all who are born slaves by nature slaves)? Castiglione would have said yes, and in fact would have regarded 'quality' as inheritable. Peacham had no doubt that the nobleman and common people were made out of different clays. Peacham's problem was what kind of education could best bring out the true qualities of nobility; in his view an uneducated nobleman or gentleman was incomplete.

It was easier to say what a gentleman was *not*. He was not a warrior, he was not a courtier. He was essentially a civilian, to whom military duties were an intermittent obligation, to be taken up only in times of national stress. Furthermore, he was not a fop and he was not a dandy living a life of useless elegance in a court cut off from the rest of the society; he was a man living, for the most part, in the country amongst his tenants and taking his responsibilities as a landlord and as a judicial official seriously. In the development of the ideal of the gentleman in England – which, it should be noted, is the only country in modern times in which it has developed – a sense of social and political responsibility was integral.

The gentleman was not a menial; obversely he needed a sense of his own dignity, so certain occupations, particularly those involving manual labour, were beneath him. He was marked by self-confidence, as well as education, whereas the *parvenu* was nervous and uncouth and lacking in dignity.

Yet dignity, by itself, was not sufficient; by itself it may become an extreme fanatic pride in 'blood'. What also distinguished the gentleman was rather dignity and pride, together with a sense of social responsibility – a proper respect for other persons. He was neither servile nor arrogant. This explains why the ideal of the gentleman has been so respected and imitated throughout English society. By contrast European aristocrats are, from an English point of view, 'not quite gentlemen'. The Prussian Junker who dreams about the number of quarterings that he has on his coat of arms, is, by English standards, slightly ridiculous. One might also add, parenthetically, that it is because the English gentleman is what he is that there has never been an anti-aristocratic revolution in Great Britain. Was it because he has unknowingly followed Cardinal Newman's definition of a gentleman, one who never inflicts pain?

The gentleman, too, was an amateur skilled in all things – that is to say, a rounded man as contrasted with a specialized tool. Peacham's programme of education was conceived precisely in these terms; it included archery and hawking as well as the classics. In recent times, however, with the break-up of inherited wealth, this element in the conception of the gentleman is beginning to dissolve.

In the United States the conception of equality is so entrenched in the culture that the idea of natural differentiation of gifts can hardly be mentioned. The gentleman in America is a person who is kind and unselfish in his relations with other people. To give a somewhat crude example, a person who holds a door open for a lady is doing what is called a gentlemanly act. When the American boxer John L. Sullivan was advising some rowdy to quieten down he said: 'It don't cost nothin' to be a gentleman.' The ideal of the gentleman in America is no longer based upon the dignity of superiority, and it has in consequence little to do with social rank. Outside a few aristocratic enclaves, it has become a 'universalized' ideal, one which anyone can attain, irrespective of his birth and education.

I am that I am

GOD as one supreme being who created the world – the belief in monotheism – is sometimes said to emerge historically from polytheism and pantheism, from ideas of many gods mutually competing for power in the world, or of a god inherent in all things. But Christian monotheism is unique and presents a sharp contrast to all other religions. It grew out of the also practically unique monotheism of the Jews, with its origin in the worship of Jahweh, in the Old Testament, emerging in the Deutero-Isaiah into a clear-cut conception of the one God to whom man owes his being.

Greek mystery religions and the mystical developments of oriental religions tend towards an emphasis on individual experience and communion which seems to imply the existence of a single personal being with whom union is to be achieved; but the actual teaching of these religions is agnostic or pantheistic, and impersonal. The only monotheism comparable with the Judaic-Christian conception is the isolated pre-Christian religion of Zarathustra.

Elsewhere there is an attempt to put one god as a ruler over other gods; the Egyptians put Ra in this position, and the Babylonians put Marduk. But the unitary conception of the Jews and the unitarian and trinitarian ideas of Christianity stand out as something in a totally different category.

Today there is in Hinduism a sense of power and an inflexible law behind all other phenomena; but its doctrine remains pantheist. Tao contains the idea of an eternal order, but it is impersonal and vague. Buddhism is agnostic. Mohammedanism alone today shares a monotheistic religious doctrine with Christianity, and it is derived from the same Judaic and early Christian source. In a sense it is a Christian heresy.

Once Christian monotheism was established, thinkers began to probe the idea and to fill it out, to work out by one means or another just what this one God was like. For this purpose they relied to a considerable extent on the philosophical speculations of the Greeks of the fourth century B.C. In the thirteenth century St Thomas Aquinas welded together the Platonic and the Aristotelian conceptions to form a complete philosophical approach, integrated into and usable by the Christian revelation. He set out the proofs for God's existence under five different headings.

From this philosophical achievement there developed a complete, self-sufficient approach to philosophy, in which the purely rational Aristotelian approach received the strongest emphasis and in which the concept of God may perhaps be best summed up as the Uncaused Cause, the origin of every chain of causality. The logical proofs of this idea can be put under the three headings – the Ontological, the Cosmological and the Teleological. All this was questioned by Immanuel Kant in his *Critique of Pure Reason* in the eighteenth century; he placed the concept of God in a different light, as a moral intuition.

From that time the certainty of God's existence, already deprived of a deep reverent and experiential approach, steadily lessened in the minds of western people. Today, against the background of a shallow secular agnosticism and atheism, there is a verbal battle ensuing between the Thomists and the metaphysicians on the one hand, and the logical positivists on the other. The Thomists maintain that the objective logical proof is still valid; the non-Thomist metaphysicians maintain that the existence of God is indeed comprehensible to human reason, but not necessarily or primarily by means of a logical proof; the logical positivists maintain the impossibility of attributing any factual meaning to the word God, and the futility, therefore, of maintaining either a logical proof or a metaphysical intuition of him.

The atomic scientists have added a further complication by stating that the explosions of the electrons in radium atoms occur at times inherently unpredictable, that is, by pure chance; at first sight, this adds further doubts of the validity of the idea of God as the Uncaused Cause. But causality in fact remains the law by which every man lives, and one reasonable way from which God's existence may be deduced.

It is true, however, that no logical method will satisfy the human mind, which is hungry to reach beyond a logic confined within space and time. So there is the modern emphasis on knowing God through experience, the possibility, in fact the inevitable experience, of knowing God in every mo-ment of experience, implicitly. This may be a direct intuition or an indirect intuition of him behind some created thing.

This philosophical concept is echoed by the affirmation of the psychologist, working from a purely empirical point of view, that the idea of God has a useful, even an essential, function in mental therapy. C. G. Jung reached the conclusion that he could only enable his patients to accept themselves – to accept life – when they were able to tie themselves back to or to project themselves into what they call God, the bigger unity, the ultimate. Only in this way could they become what they needed to become, humble yet responsible. Jung, speaking as a technician, refuses, with what may be sound scientific integrity, to say that his therapeutic experience is in any sense a proof of God's existence. He leaves that to the philosophers, or to those who are prepared to make an act of faith.

But the Roman Catholics maintain (it is an article of faith defined by the Vatican Council) that it is in fact possible to know that God exists, without any act of faith. An abstract analysis of the Christian act of faith describes it as built on this natural knowledge; it is a belief in the revelation of Jesus Christ, a revelation about the nature of God, of whose existence we already know.

In practice it is difficult, and not always convincing, to separate the natural and the supernatural. Indeed, the Christian religion puts forward a conception of God in which the supernatural is built inextricably into the natural. It is a synthesis and, more, a hypostasis of the two basic philosophical conceptions of a God as either entirely transcendent, or entirely immanent. Christianity speaks of God who created the world, and maintains the world, and is present in power in every part of creation, but who was also at a particular time incarnate as a real man, and now remains incarnate both sacramentally in the form of bread and wine, and mystically, in the members of the Church, and in all men who are destined to be members of his Church and to be brought by it to the happiness of eternal life.

'God is love', says St John, in whose epistles may be found the simplest and yet the most profound statement of Christianity in practice and in theory: 'He who loves not his neighbour whom he can see, how can he love God whom he cannot see?' The mainspring of the idea of the incarnation carried through to the crucifixion, the resurrection, the ascension and the coming of the Holy Spirit, is love. This same love is seen in some form or other at the heart of every religion. But in no other religion is there the claim that God, out of love for man, became man and suffered man's own particular unhappiness and, without sinning himself, in some sense actually took on himself the suffering of all men's sins.

The Christian conception of God as a Trinity, composed of three persons, God the Father, God the Son, and God the Holy Ghost, was taught by Jesus Christ and is now held by the majority of Christians. God the Father proffers the idea of a transcendent God, the creator and sustainer who is outside the universe; God the Holy Spirit proffers the idea of the immanent God, the spiritual power and inspiration perpetually present in men's souls. These two ideas are held together, crystallized and made personal in the third idea, that God became man in Jesus Christ.

Christianity yet holds these three persons to be one God. God is wholly present, it teaches, in the Blessed Sacrament when Jesus is sacramentally present. God is wholly present in the soul of the just man whom the Holy Spirit inspires. Three persons in one God is the Christian idea of God. The relationship of the three persons takes the form of an analogy with a human family; God the Father perpetually generates God the Son; the Son offers himself back to the Father, and there proceeds from this relationship the Spirit of Love.

ILLUSTRATION: Pages 220 and 221.

'O lovely age of gold'

The **GOLDEN AGE** in classical mythology was the first and best age of the world. Mankind lived in ideal prosperity and happiness. Everything in the garden was lovely: there was no disorder, no crime.

The Golden Age is a term that is often used as a ticket for any 'best period' – of a nation, of a literature, of a political movement. Shakespeare's time is held to be the Golden Age of English literature. 'With Ovid', wrote Dryden, 'ended the Golden Age of the Roman tongue.'

To Edward Gibbon, the Golden Age of mankind was the Roman Empire under Antoninus Pius and Marcus Aurelius Antoninus, from A.D. 138 to A.D. 180. The latter half of the nineteenth century can be referred to as the Golden Age of English liberalism.

The idea of a Golden Age, a Utopia that might have existed in the past, and not one that is planned only for the future, has most strongly appealed to three poets: a Greek, a Roman and an Italian. It was the Greek pastoral poet, Hesiod, who first coined the term Golden Age; and he painted its picture in the fanciful colours that have since become its mark. Hesiod flourished sometime in the eighth century B.C., after Homer. In his *Works and Days* comes this passage:

> When gods alike and mortals rose to birth,
> A golden race th' immortals form'd on earth
> Of many-languaged men: they lived of old
> When Saturn reign'd in heaven, an age of gold.

The people of Hesiod's Golden Age had an idyllic life. Their minds were calm and untroubled, he says. Years never wearied them, and they were never ill. Their days were a pleasant whirl of feasts. Though they had wealth, they shared it all. They did no work; but the earth gladly yielded its fairest fruits to them. Death came to them as a gentle sleep; and, because their lives had been so good, Zeus raised them up again, to become daemons. In this guise they wandered the earth as ministers of good and ill, unseen dispensers of justice.

Ovid, who lived from 43 B.C. to A.D. 18, was the great Roman poet of the Golden Age; he brought to his account of it, in the first book of his *Metamorphoses*, great beauty of expression.

Most of all, Ovid was taken with the absence of compulsion in the Golden Age. Without laws, without people to compel others, he says, it still kept faith and did right. People lived safely without judges and there was no fear of punishment. It was a self-contained world: for no one ever travelled. There were no ships, no moats round towns; there were no trumpets or swords. And Ovid, like Hesiod, dwells on the fact that the earth, without compulsion, gave all that was needed for sustenance.

He ends on a beautiful passage, to which only the original Latin can do full justice:

ver erat aeternum, placidique tepentibus auris
mulcebant zephyri natos sine semine flores;
mox etiam fruges tellus inarata ferebat,
nec renovatus ager gravidis canebat aristis;
flumina iam lactis, iam flumina nectaris ibant,
flavaque de viridi stillabant ilice mella.

(The spring was everlasting, [he says] and gentle zephyrs with warm breath played with the flowers that sprang unplanted. And the earth, untilled, brought forth her store of grains, and the fields, though unfallowed, grew white with the heavy bearded wheat. Streams of milk and streams of sweet nectar flowed, and yellow honey was distilled from the verdant oak.)

But the most effective poet of the Golden Age was the Italian, Torquato Tasso, who was in the service of the Cardinal d'Este, at Ferrara. His vision of it comes in his pastoral drama, *Aminta*, which was first performed in 1573.

O bella età dell'oro, [it begins]
Non già perchè di latte
Se 'n corse il fiume e stillo mèle il bosco ...

O beautiful age of gold,
Not because the streams ran
With milk, not because the wood
Distilled honey ...

Tasso is not so interested in the fruits and flowers. The Golden Age is beautiful he says, not because the streams flowed with milk and nectar, but because 'that empty name without a substance, that idol of deceit and hypocrisy, which by the mad crowd was afterwards called Honour and made the tyrant of our nature, had not yet mixed its dark conceits with the blessed sweetness of the loving crowd of the human race'.

Like the others, he laments the blithe joy of those happy, far-off days:

Then among the flowers and streams the winged little Loves led up their dances and carols, without their bows and without their torches. The shepherds and nymphs sat together mingling whispers with their charms, and with their whispers fond and clinging embraces. The naked maid displayed her blooming roses, and the treasures of her virginal and firm bosom which she now keeps concealed, and oftentimes in stream or lake the lover would play with the maid he loved.

But Honour comes along to teach lovely women to keep their beauty from others' eyes. And Tasso upbraids Honour for making what used to be the gift of love into a theft. He asks to be left alone, to live 'after the manner of the ancient race of men'.

Let us live, since the life of man has no truce with years and soon departs; let us love, for the sun sinks down and rises again, while its short light dies unto us once for all, and sleep brings on eternal night.

We can never say that there was, or that there was not, a Golden Age. If we found a people living in the conditions which the poet makes the background of the Golden Age, to our eyes it would be a very dank and squalid place. Dreams of a Golden Age are probably no more than the fond wishes of oppressed mankind. According to mythology, after the Golden Age came the Age of Silver, then of Bronze, the heroic, and finally, our own age, the Age of Iron, nadir of the decline. Mankind always looks forward to some ideal state in the future, or back to a Golden Age. Whichever way he looks, the ideal state is a long way off.

ILLUSTRATION: Page 265.

Steering the middle course

The **GOLDEN MEAN**, 'Aurea Mediocritas', is a phrase which occurs in an Ode of Horace (II x):

The man who loves well the golden mean escapes the squalor of a tumbledown shack – escapes too the envy which the grand style of living provokes.

The idea has long been a favourite one among the English, and has become quite domesticated. '*Household happiness, gracious children, debtless competence, golden mean*', wrote Tennyson. 'Greatness, with private men esteemed a blessing,' says one of Massinger's noble characters,

is to me a curse;
And we, whom, for our high births, they conclude
The only freemen, are the only slaves.
Happy the golden mean.

Better, then, to be one of Cowper's

> Tenants of life's middle state,
> Securely placed between the small and great.

This comfortable middle-class application of the notion of the mean or middle way has a very English flavour to it; yet it corresponds closely in spirit to the precept which in ancient times was to be found inscribed in the temple of Apollo at Delphi, the religious centre of the Greek world: NOTHING IN EXCESS – or, as we say, Moderation in all things.

Modern historians and critics have seen in this principle the golden thread running through all that is truly classical in art and literature. The delicate compromise between nature and convention which distinguishes Greek sculpture at its most perfect moments, the grave balance of vertical and horizontal in a classical temple, and the generous combination of patriotism and individualism revealed in the funeral oration of Pericles – all these and more have seemed to owe their strength and sanity to the regulative influence of the idea of the Mean.

Yet the principle itself, like most gnomic utterances, is far from being self-explanatory. For as soon as we come to apply it to a concrete set of circumstances we are faced with the question, what *is* 'enough, but not too much or little' in the particular case we have to consider? How do we discover which line of thought or policy or action is mid-way between the various possibilities of excess?

Happily this question is discussed by Aristotle (384–322 B.C.) in his great work on ethics – happily, since no subsequent thinker has brought so much perceptiveness to bear on the problem. Indeed, it was Aristotle who first formulated the theory that every good quality is a mean between two extremes.

Aristotle is trying to find a satisfactory answer to the question, What acts are right? To be right, he says, an action must be in accordance with right reason, and must neither fall short nor be excessive. As an example of what he means by the second requirement, he instances the case of an athlete in training: if ten pounds of food is too much for him, and two pounds too little, then the right amount will be something *between the two extremes* – though not necessarily the arithmetical mean between them, but rather *the mean relative to his needs*, to be determined by right reason.

Aristotle now applies this to virtue, which, he correctly points out, is concerned with our feelings as well as our outward acts. In every situation, he says, we can feel whatever we do feel more or less intensely: for example, on the field of battle a soldier may feel great fear, moderate fear or no fear at all, and may in each case act accordingly. Now what we require of a soldier is bravery, not cowardice, and not rashness. And the brave man is one who feels not too much fear (that is what makes a coward) nor too little fear (for then he would become rash instead of brave), but a moderate amount of fear, sufficient to deter him from taking unnecessary risks, but not so great as to prevent him from braving necessary ones. In other words, Aristotle concludes, the virtue of courage is a mean between the extremes of cowardice and rashness.

This is generally the case. Every good quality of character or action can be shown as striking the happy medium between two extremes. Aristotle gives many examples. To be liberal in money matters is to steer between meanness on the one hand and extravagance on the other. Praiseworthy ambition is a mean between a thirst for power on the one hand, and lack of enterprise on the other; modesty falls between boastfulness and self-depreciation, tact between saying too much and saying too little.

It will be seen that the doctrine is quite in accordance with modern ways of thinking. Furthermore, it is of particular relevance at a time when there is great uncertainty about the moral standards we ought to adopt. The same problem faced Aristotle, whose teaching was delivered in the form of lectures to young men who would one day be the rulers and leaders of the society in which they lived. His conclusion is that our standards must accord with the doctrine of the mean – so that in living by them we avoid the evils of excess and defect, and tread the golden middle of the road. But we must always remember Aristotle's warning that there is no *formula* or *mechanism* which will enable us to work out where, between the extremes, the mean lies. That task, he reminds us, needs to be performed afresh in

Continued on p. 183

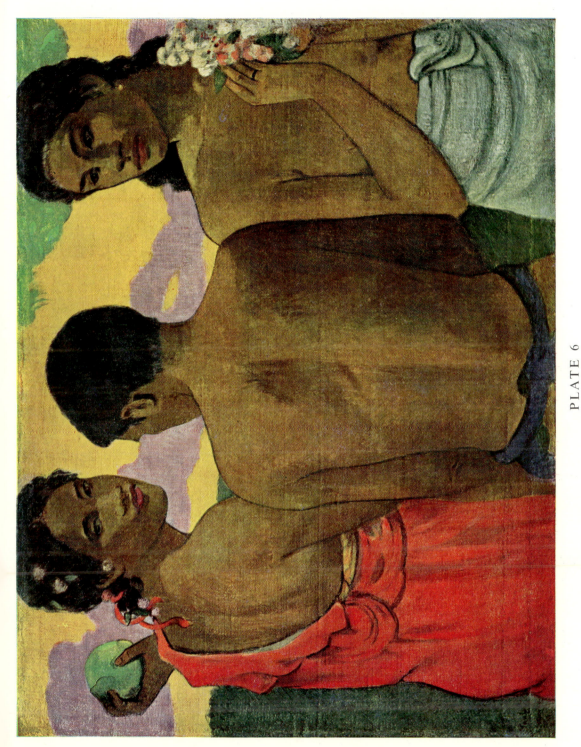

PLATE 6

NOBLE SAVAGE: Three Tahitians by Paul Gauguin (1843–1903).

'BACK TO THE LAND': The sentiment of the outmoded windmill.

'DECADENCE': 1. 'Oscar', Oscar Wilde (1856–1900). A *Vanity Fair* cartoon.

2. Aubrey Beardsley, by W. R. Sickert.

'DECADENCE': 1. *Messalina*. A pen drawing by Beardsley (1872–1898).

2. *The Apparition*, by Gustave Moreau (1826–1898).

THE DIVINE RIGHT OF KINGS: The German Emperor Otto III surrounded by ecclesiastical and secular dignitaries. From the *Reichenau Gospels,* c. 1000.

ROYAL PREROGATIVE: Title-page from the first edition of *Eikon Basiliké* (1649), by William Marshall.

DRAMATIC UNITIES: Euripides (c. 485–406 B.C.). One of the greatest Greek playwrights.

SOCRATIC METHOD: Socrates (469–399 B.C.)

175

ENTHUSIASM: Edward Irving (1792–1834) 'enthusiastic' preacher during the Romantic Movement. Portrait by Christopher Faithful Pack.

DEISM: Lord Herbert of Cherbury (1583–1648), probably by W. Larkin.

177

FREEDOM? Painting by Van Gogh (1853–1890) after a woodcut by Gustave Doré.

DON QUIXOTE: with Sancho Panza. Lithograph by Honoré Daumier (1808–1879).

COLOUR BAR: Special entrance for coloured people, in Miami Beach, Florida.

FREEDOM OF SPEECH: 1. Speakers at Hyde Park, London.

FREEDOM OF SPEECH: 2. Heckling a speaker, Hyde Park, London.

PLATE 7

ORIGINAL SIN: Adam and Eve by Hugo van der Goes (d.1482).

each new set of circumstances; and it is only by applying right reason to each problem as it arises that we can, from day to day, achieve the Golden Mean.

One step broken, the great scale's destroy'd

The **GREAT CHAIN OF BEING** stretched from the throne of God to the humblest item of creation – each link of it representing a level of being – plants above inanimates, animals above plants, men above animals and the angelic hierarchies above man. No link was missing: if any intermediate species could bridge the gap between two differing species, then such a link was to be found in nature. The universe was as rich in diversity as it conceivably could be, God's creative goodness being infinite.

The history of this profoundly influential idea may be traced back at least to Plato. Why, he asks in the *Timaeus* (c. 350 B.C.), did God create a world at all? Because he was good and could not 'begrudge' existence to any kind of creature. If any less than the full range of possible beings were in fact brought into being, God would reveal himself as less creative than he might have been, less than perfect.

The unbroken continuity of the Chain was memorably brought out by Aristotle's study of natural history. The divisions between species were not rigid or clear-cut. With some 'marine forms' it was even hard to tell whether they were animals or plants, so gradual were the transitions from one plane of existence to the next higher or next lower. To Aristotle, God alone possesses fullness of being. All else has a measure of 'privation'; only a little in the case of the angels, but to an increasing degree as the hierarchy is descended, 'lessening down', as James Thomson wrote in *The Seasons*, 'From Infinite Perfection to the brink of dreary nothing, desolate abyss!'

In the Middle Ages Abelard took the Great Chain of Being seriously enough to draw from it a plain, though unpopular, implication. The world could not have been different from what it is: in every respect it is the product, not of free or arbitrary choice on God's part, but of necessity:

I

God *could* leave nothing uncreated, no possibility unrealized. Abelard's view was rejected by Bernard of Clairvaux; and St Thomas Aquinas, though he shows definite sympathy for Abelard's position, allied himself with Bernard.

To say that the world could not have been better than it was, reduced God's wrath at Sin (and the whole drama of redemption) to a hopeless enigma. Therefore in the *Summa Theologica* St Thomas wrote, 'God *could* make other things than he has, or could add others to the things he had made'. To orthodoxy, creation and redemption alike are the outcome of God's absolutely free decision.

Platonists of the early Italian renaissance found in the Chain of Being a powerful weapon against non-Christian naturalisms. Any attempt to think of man as fundamentally an animal among animals could be parried by the insistence that man's position in the Chain brings him 'much nearer to the blessed angels than ... the brutes' (Marsilio Ficino: *Five Questions Concerning the Mind*, 1476). Pico della Mirandola (1463–1494) daringly claimed that man's place in the universe was even more remarkable: for although every other created being had its fixed rung in the Chain, man had no such fetters imposed upon him. He could be a beast or a seraph as he chose. The Chain of Being becomes a Jacob's Ladder which a man may climb or descend, and so determine his own destiny. 'According to thy longing ... thou mayst have what abode, what form, thou thyself shalt desire' (*On the Dignity of Man*, 1486).

Surprising as it may seem, it was the outworking of this same fertile idea (far more than the astronomical theories of Copernicus, Kepler or Galileo) which helped to overthrow the medieval world-picture in the sixteenth and seventeenth centuries. Was ours the only solar system? the only inhabited planet? Was the universe finite? Even without the telescope, a believer in the Chain of Being could say 'no' to each question: for if God imposed limits to the work of creation, then he would have begrudged being to worlds and systems *beyond* these limits. 'Why', asked Giordano Bruno (1548–1600) 'should we say that the divine goodness, which is capable of communicating itself to an infinity of things ... is niggardly?'

The eighteenth century witnessed by far the most widespread employment of the idea, not only among philosophers and theologians, but equally in imaginative literature. The optimists' slogan 'this is the best of all possible worlds' was a manifest corollary of the completeness and goodness of the original creation as the Chain of Being pictured it. The amount of evil in the world, they argued, could not have been greater or less: all degrees of perfection and imperfection must have their place in the Chain. The proportions cannot be altered, for, wrote Alexander Pope, 'one step broken, the great scale's destroy'd'.

But, as in the medieval debate, not everyone was consoled by the assurance that evil was inevitable. To Voltaire, for instance, such a deterministic explanation, if true, made evil not more endurable, but less so. It was to despair of being able to eradicate it in the least degree. Samuel Johnson (1709–1784) too boldly attacked the whole conception of the Great Chain. Taken rigorously, the idea implied that all possible intermediary species must be created (and this meant an *infinite* number of species, not a plausible claim); worse still, that there should be 'the greatest Number possible of every Sort of beings', which is simply (and mercifully) not the case.'

The greatest single transformation which the idea has undergone came gradually towards the end of the eighteenth century and was complete by the mid-nineteenth. Hitherto the Chain had been conceived as static in time, every link in place at the first creation. Biology in particular found it harder and harder to accept this picture of the world. The record of the rocks and the findings of comparative anatomy could be interpreted most intelligibly if it were granted that some species had ceased to exist in the remote past and new species had successively appeared. Surely the Chain had not been created complete in the beginning: perhaps its completion is the *goal*.of the cosmic process. In 1770 d'Holbach could speak of nature 'assembling in her vast laboratories' new, unknown types of being. The final and decisive demonstration that no doctrine of a static universe was tenable came in Darwin's account of evolution in *The Origin of Species* (1859).

If ceaseless creativity could be seen as the very life of God, philosophers and poets of the Ro-

mantic Revival saw it also as the true life of man. Previous periods, and earlier theories of art, had stressed the beauty of simplicity, of obedience to strict exacting forms: romanticism, reversing this, brought out as never before that great assumption which had always been contained in the Chain of Being but so long suppressed – that fecundity, diversity and richness of modes of being are *good in themselves*; for it was God's goodness that in the beginning spilled over and filled the pitcher of creation to the very brim.

At the present day, although forms of the Great Chain idea are living elements in religious traditions such as the Thomism of the Roman Catholic Church (the fourth of St Thomas's *Five Ways* to God argues from 'degrees of being'), the prevalent scientific outlook finds it uncongenial. The scientist (and the empirical philosopher) indeed recognize order, richness and degrees of development in the world, but they deny that any single, neat diagrammatic pattern like the Chain of Being can do justice to its complexity. The believer in the Chain assumes that if *in theory* he could conceive a type of existence, that by itself could entitle him to say, 'such a being exists': he assumes further that he can answer the question '*Why* does it exist?' Both assumptions clash with the empiricist's conviction that questions about matters of fact cannot be reliably answered simply by 'taking thought', but only by 'looking and seeing'.

Immortal dame

MRS GRUNDY personifies conventional social opinion on matters of conduct and morality and propriety.

The lady is first found in English literature in a romantic comedy called *Speed the Plough* by Thomas Morton (1764–1838), produced at the Theatre Royal, Covent Garden, in 1800. She does not appear as an actual character in the play; but constant allusion is made to her by the two principal comic figures, Dame Ashfield and her husband, the former of whom tests every incident by reference to what Mrs Grundy will think of it, while the latter is contemptuous of his wife's obsession with the opinions of their neighbour. Thus in Act I, Scene I, Farmer Ashfield says, 'What dant thee letten her aloane then – I do verily think when thee goest to t'other world, the vurst question thee't ax 'il be, if Mrs Grundy's there.'

To call a person a Mrs Grundy today would imply that he or she took too censorious and prudish a view of improper or scandalous conduct, and would carry with it an insinuation of cant and hypocrisy. But that is not its original meaning. As described by Morton, the Grundy family have much more in common with the Jones family in the modern phrase 'keeping up with the Joneses'. That is to say, they are the family next door, who are always a little richer, a little smarter, a little more advanced in their opinion than we are, and whose exploits and ideas we must constantly strive to emulate if we are to keep our place in the fashionable world.

Thus, Farmer Grundy's wheat commands a better price than that of his neighbour, Mrs Grundy's butter is 'quite the crack of the market', and the highest commendation which the Ashfields can bestow on a young man is to say that 'the Miss Grundys, genteel as they think themselves, would be glad to snap at him'.

Within the next half-century Mrs Grundy changed from the pattern of provincial and rustic fashion to a grim custodian of public morality. There is indeed a hint of this second meaning in Act II, Scene III, of *Speed the Plough*, where Dame Ashfield bemoans what Mrs Grundy will say if her daughter has a shameful love affair; but even here the character is conceived of rather as an exultant rival than as an impartial but ruthless judge. The explanation must be sought in the transformation which came over the manners and morals of English society in the first half of the nineteenth century. No contrast could be greater than that between the coarse and dissolute elegance which characterized the fashionable world in Regency times and the atmosphere of stern piety and solid family respectability which is connoted by the word 'Victorian'. This respectability was not a veneer, but a strong hard crust.

Many factors combined to bring about this change, the important point being that the revolution in manners was inspired by the personal ex-

ample of the Queen and Prince Albert, and radiated from Court circles downwards through every rank of society. Respectability became not only a moral virtue but also the hall-mark of fashion. And, although it was firmly based on genuine religious conviction and complete acceptance of a severe moral code, it went, as fashions usually do, to extreme lengths; it also led to hypocrisy.

Some of the manifestations of Victorian 'decency' seem to us absurd. Full-length skirts were invariably worn because it was considered improper for women to reveal any part of their legs, and, by a curious transference of thought, it became for a time fashionable for housewives to cover their tables with huge cloths falling to the ground, for fear the exposure of table-legs might raise suggestive thoughts in those who saw them. Again, in a book of etiquette published in 1863, ladies were exhorted not to allow books by female authors to be found on the same shelves as those written by men. A dispensation was permitted, however, in the case of books written by authors married to each other.

These and other excesses not unnaturally aroused opposition and ridicule, and it became common to apply the name of Mrs Grundy to those who, because they were so fashionably respectable themselves, were over-zealous in seeking out and condemning the lack of respectability in others. In 1845 Tennyson was writing of 'us poor devils whom the Grundyites would not only not remunerate but kick out of society as barely respectable', and within the next two decades the phrase had taken on its present meaning.

While the definition of the term has remained fixed for a hundred years, the kind of beliefs which would give rise to a charge of Grundyism must necessarily vary as varying social and economic pressures change ideas of what is or is not decent behaviour. What was merely the accepted standard of propriety for one generation may well be the Grundyism of the next. Few people today protest seriously against the wearing of slacks by women. Yet no fiercer – or more successful – campaign was waged by Mrs Grundy than that against the attempt of Amelia Bloomer to introduce 'trowsers' for women in 1851.

ILLUSTRATION: Page 229.

H

The idea of Hamlet?

HAMLET, for all the thoughts and ideas he inspires, cannot be separated from the tragedy in which he is portrayed; like a fly in amber he is embalmed in an Elizabethan melodrama, which for more than three centuries has stirred the minds and hearts of men and women.

More important than the scholar's labyrinthine search for consistency of character, for the key to Hamlet's troubled soul, for Shakespeare's intentions, is our own personal direct response to the substantial idea of this Prince of Denmark, this *man*.

> What is your substance, whereof are you made
> That millions of strange shadows on you tend?

Hazlitt said: 'Hamlet is a name; his speeches and sayings are but the coinage of the poet's brain. What then, are they not real? They are as real as our own thoughts. It is *we* who are Hamlet.'

Schlegel, who translated the play into German and whose conclusions about it were akin to Coleridge's, has defined this idea more clearly: 'Hamlet is single in its kind; a tragedy of thought inspired by continual and never satisfied meditation on human destiny and the dark perplexity of the events of this world, and calculated to call forth the very same meditation in the minds of the spectators.'

In Hamlet's soliloquies, his thinking aloud in his isolation – an individual soul set against the machinations of this world and the dread and uncertainty of the next – in the acute translation of his feelings into thoughts as he sounds the depths of doubt, self-examination and self-criticism, the perils of the human situation are borne in upon us. Overhearing Hamlet's thoughts as he discourses to himself, we enter his soul – and our own. This is an experience with no parallel of

similar intensity in literature. It is found later on in Mozart's operas, where the arias break away from the dramatic action to reveal the poignant vibrations of the human soul, and, again, in Beethoven's late quartets; and there is something of it in Leonardo da Vinci's Gioconda, who has exercised a similar spell on the beholder, her soul shadowed forth for all to wonder at, and still remaining a mystery.

It was Edward Dowden (1843–1913), one of the greatest of Shakespeare's critics (*Shakespeare: A Critical Study of his Mind and Art*, 1875), who maintained that Hamlet was a mystery which could not be reduced or analysed. To those who seek for an idea underlying the character he replied: 'The vital heart of the tragedy of Hamlet cannot be an idea; neither can it be a fragment of political philosophy. Out of Shakespeare's profound sympathy with an individual soul and a personal life, the wonderful creation came into being.'

This wonderful being, Hamlet the Prince, whom Ophelia describes before misfortune had overtaken him:

> The courtier's, soldier's, scholar's, eye, tongue, sword,
> The expectation and rose of the fair state,
> The glass of fashion, and the mould of form,
> The observ'd of all observers ...

appears in the play as one whose perfections are shattered and fragmented by misfortunes. It is as if Shakespeare had taken the ideal man of the Renaissance, set forth in Castiglione's *The Courtier*, and overwhelmed him with circumstances too great to bear, making him, not the arbiter but the instrument of fate, into 'a pipe for fortune's finger to sound what stop she please'.

This is what Goethe means when (in *Wilhelm Meister*, Book V) he says that Hamlet has no plan: 'The hero has no plan, but the piece is full of plan.' Goethe went on: 'It is events alone that push him on, and accordingly the piece has somewhat the amplification of a novel. But as it is Fate that draws the plan, as the piece proceeds from a deed of terror, and the hero is steadily driven on to a deed of terror, the work is tragic in the highest sense, and admits of no other than a tragic end.' Goethe describes this operation of Fate: 'Here is this play of ours, how strange! Purgatory sends its spirit and demands revenge;

in vain! All circumstances combine and hurry to revenge; in vain! Neither earthly nor infernal things may bring about what is reserved for Fate alone. The hour of judgment comes. The bad falls with the good. One race is mowed away, and another springs up.' Hamlet belongs to a doomed house.

Is Hamlet, then, not a tragedy of revenge, but a tragedy of inaction, as some have taken it to be? Or rather a long essay in suspense, bearing from scene to scene the doubt that the deed will ever be done? Is it the tragedy of a genius caught fast in the toils of circumstance, or, as Coleridge thought, the tragedy of a man who has become a creature of meditation, thereby losing his power to act?

Must we, after all, search for a key to the character and for the meaning of the tragedy? If not in an idea or a philosophy, against which Bradley has warned us, perhaps it is to be found in some pull of opposites or tension of contraries that informs the play. Read Goethe, Dr Johnson; read Coleridge, Dowden, Bradley, to name only a few; climb the many-sided mountain of Shakespeare criticism. Reaching the top we may decide, fretted by so many contrary winds, that the secret of Hamlet lies not in any consistency of character, but in a sustained dramatic and poetic tension between reason and emotion in a man in whom both are developed to the point of genius.

An unhappy occupation

The **PURSUIT OF HAPPINESS** first appears as a phrase in the American Declaration of Independence in 1776, and describes what many people think the basic activity of mankind. They believe, that is to say, that in the long run men aim at power, wealth or knowledge only to increase their happiness, and that all their activities can be referred to this aim.

Most thinkers have agreed that happiness is a good thing. Only perhaps certain Christian puritans, whether Catholic or Protestant, have argued that it is actually better for a man to be unhappy in this world. And even they have looked forward to the next world as a place (at least for them) of happiness, and regarded this as satisfactory. So there is no point in discussing whether happiness is desirable or no. The pertinent questions come when it is asked: Is happiness *the* goal in life, to which all others are subordinate, or is it one among a number each of which have equal or better claims to our attentions?

Then again, assuming that happiness is at least a very important thing, should it be *aimed* at, or should we aim at other things, and expect it to be added on as a by-product of our activities? These are the questions on which opinions differ, and which should be answered if we want to know where we stand.

Aristotle begins his *Ethics* with the assertion that all men agree that happiness is the ultimate goal of man, and only disagree about what it is. Most philosophers of the ancient world, whatever they thought happiness was, agreed with Aristotle on this. Even the Stoics, who preached devotion to duty and an emotional withdrawal from the world, justified their attitude by arguing that only in this way can a man preserve his equanimity, his private peace of mind; and this, to them, was as near as one could hope to get to happiness.

Plato alone, Aristotle's teacher, perhaps thought otherwise. In the *Republic* he tries to show that even if the just man were unhappy he would still be more admirable than the unjust man, and his lot would be more desirable. But it is a necessary part of his argument that the just man would in fact be happier than the unjust man, and if he really tried to separate happiness from what we may call integrity, so as to show that the just life is in itself desirable, he would destroy his whole previous analysis of justice. Since, therefore, the most desirable life, as he pictures it, is also the happiest life, it is arguable (though doubtful) that Plato also thought happiness to be the supreme good.

In the seventeenth century certain philosophers such as Hobbes thought that man was actuated ultimately by fear. Fear, however, is merely the reverse aspect of the desire for peace and comfort. So this doctrine is only another way of saying that the chief aim of man *is* the pursuit of happiness.

Although the phrase 'the pursuit of happiness'

was coined, as we have seen, in the eighteenth century, its best-known embodiment is in the nineteenth-century philosophy of Utilitarianism. This philosophy, as formulated by Jeremy Bentham (1748–1832) and James Mill (1773–1836), held that actions are good or bad according to whether they increase or decrease the pleasure of mankind; and, as a consequence, that one should always aim at actions which increase the pleasure of mankind. Mill's son, John Stuart Mill, believing the definition was too narrow, substituted the notion of happiness for the notion of pleasure. This revised view, that all actions, all laws, and all customs have as their ultimate justification the increase of human happiness, is today very widespread, and may be said to be the normal view of liberal men in Western countries.

But there is much to be said against the view that happiness is the chief good. The conundrum 'Would you rather be a pig happy or Socrates unhappy?' reminds us of the penalty we may pay for being human. In Karl Popper's words: 'For those who have eaten from the tree of knowledge, paradise is lost.' The virtues of truthfulness, good faith and loyalty may well conflict with the desire to preserve happiness, and who shall say that they shall always be sacrificed to it? Although much of the Christian ethic is designed to increase happiness, some of it is not. The churches themselves believe that many other things are more important, though not all would agree with Cardinal Newman when he said:

'She [the Catholic Church] holds that it were better for sun and moon to drop from heaven, for the earth to fail, and for the many millions who are upon it to die of starvation in extreme agony, as far as temporal affliction goes, than that one soul, I will not say, should be lost, but should commit one single venial sin, should tell one wilful untruth, ... or steal one poor farthing without excuse.'

We may now ask: Assuming that it is at any rate very important, can and should we *aim* at happiness? It is here that the true limitations of the utilitarian and similar beliefs begin to show. When much of the world is positively unhappy, then they are reasonable and laudable as an incentive to improvement. But when most people are not positively unhappy, then the increase of happiness becomes a matter of subsidiary importance. The truth is that the utilitarian slogan

is much better phrased in terms of the decrease of unhappiness than the increase of happiness. If it be limited in this way, then it can be seen for what it is, an essential intermediate goal for human effort. The world being what it is, this goal must bulk very large today. But once the major sources of misery are removed, the decrease of unhappiness takes its true place as no more than a necessary first step.

Aristotle has a phrase describing pleasure which might well be applied to happiness. It is, he says, like the bloom on youth. Happiness is something which comes when we are doing something else, and enjoying it, and we cannot by its very nature aim at it. Indeed, the very phrase 'the pursuit of happiness' has an unhappy connotation of failure. One pursues what one has not got, and the pursuit of happiness suggests a continual struggle after an unattainable goal. The fundamental goals of man are quite different. They are knowledge, power, the creation, achievement of all kinds. Happiness comes as an added prize when these are pursued satisfactorily, and all else is well. But to pursue happiness itself will always be a fruitless and *unhappy* occupation.

ILLUSTRATION: Page 222.

Living 'in his mild and magnificent eye'

HERO-WORSHIP is the passionate admiration of leaders of thought or action, dead or alive, but normally felt to have especial strength or courage. It is as common and necessary an ingredient of society as the religious impulse, for which it is sometimes an emotional substitute. It can range from the schoolboy adulation of a house-prefect or football captain, to a national and ecstatic identification with a popular demagogue. Its objects extend from games mistresses to Hitler, and can also embrace the saints.

Most primitive peoples worship heroes, who are often their ancestors – but their ancestors endowed with superhuman virtues which may also have become symbolic. This propensity existed in the ancient Greeks, from whom so many of our ideas derive. It was usually pre-Homeric cults which survived with them, and the heroes were demi-gods: sometimes real gods who had been degraded, but always (like Hercules) intermediate between true gods and historic human personalities. The reverence became attached, however, even to people of doubtful virtue, and in some stages of Greek thought almost all men who were remembered at all were remembered as heroes, until the term was loosely applied to outstanding figures even in their lifetime. It is said that at Teos incense was offered to a living flute-player, and in Thessaly even slaves were on their death described as heroes if they had memorable qualities. Heroism already, indeed, meant notoriety, and it became little more than that worship of the spectacular individual which we still see accorded to sportsmen or popular entertainers.

The real Greek 'Heroes', however, remain the mythical characters best known to non-classicists from the Victorian children's book *The Heroes*, written by Charles Kingsley in 1856. The psychologist can also study them as evidence of the normal human attitude to various recurrent situations. Heroes can be seen, in the jargon, as 'father substitutes'. The Jewish books of Kings and Judges embalm a similar reverence, with perhaps a higher ingredient of actual historic remembrance.

The Germans have always been highly susceptible to what is now known as the leader-principle, and Teutonic myth has known many heroes – some of them parallels with those of the ancient world, some from their own imagination. These heroes have superhuman qualities, and their legend has remained in northern Europe as strong, almost, as that of the Christian Saints. These superseded the ancient heroes in many parts of the Continent. Siegfried, Dietrich and Beowulf all have their cycles, and in England such popular figures as Robin Hood probably inherit many of the same characteristics. The Teutonic heroes were in the main, however, historical personages, even if they took on semi-divine attributes or were interpreted as symbolic forces. Siegfried (or Sigurd as he was known in the Scandinavian sagas), a hero of light overcome by the powers of darkness – the mist-people (Niebelungen) – is a chief figure, but there are many others. England adopted or adapted many of the heroic ideas, and applied them to such figures as the semi-mythical Arthur, Alfred the Great, Richard Coeur-de-Lion, Guy of Warwick or Hereward the Wake.

English hero-worship had another source in the rich legends of the Celts. Those connected with Arthur were perhaps the greatest. The Celtic legends of their heroes constitute a main source for our pre-history, literature, folklore (a word coined in the eighteen-forties) and romance. The medieval period also created its other romantic Christian heroes – Roland, Charlemagne and the Cid. Meanwhile the East, too, was weaving the histories of Saladin and Harun al-Raschid. All countries and ages have their folk heroes.

Clearly hero-worship is ineradicable in human beings. At its highest it can mean selfless identification with high ideals and a proper reverence for outstanding ability or character. The attitude of mind involved was perhaps best analysed and expressed by the Scots historian and sage Thomas Carlyle (1795–1881) in his book of essays *On Heroes, Hero-Worship and the Heroic in History*. He said, 'As I take it, Universal History, the history of what man has accomplished in this world, is at bottom the History of the Great Men who have worked here. They were leaders of men, these great ones; the modellers, patterns, and in a wide sense creators, of whatsoever the general mass of men contrived to do or attain: all things that we see standing accomplished in the world are properly the outer material result, the practical realization and embodiment of Thoughts that dwelt in the Great Men sent into the world: the soul of the whole world's history, it may justly be considered, were the history of these.' The economic theory of history has superseded Carlyle. Yet his picture combines a classical commonplace with a contemporary reality.

Writing of the hero as king, Carlyle also said that he 'is practically the summary for us of *all* the various figures of Heroism, Priest, Teacher; whatsoever of earthly or of spiritual dignity we can fancy to reside in a man, embodies itself, to *command* over us, to furnish us with constant practical teaching, to tell us for the day and hour what to do'. The Victorians loved and revered great men, and many accepted such words cheerfully. Their obvious loyalties were for Gladstone, Disraeli or the cricketer W. G. Grace. Yet reaction and the idealization of the Little Man were already apparent.

Meanwhile the philosophy involved was an invitation to dictatorship, which is Hero-worship at its worst – the hysterical acclamation of a political demi-god. 'No man is a hero to his valet' – in other words, familiarity with a character breeds contempt, and the prophet has no honour in his own country. Understandably enough, therefore, dictators are rarely of the nationalities over which they have sway. Napoleon was not a Frenchman, Hitler was not a German, Pilsudski was not a Pole, and Ataturk was not a Turk.

Hero-worship was regarded as an important character-builder in the English public school; it is implicit in Service discipline. It can also lead to mass emotion of the worst kind. Its political and social dangers today are obvious. In the British Isles it is normally sublimated into excited ('fan' from fanatical) admiration for entertainers, professional sportsmen and other press-inflated, or radio-inflated, or television-inflated characters. This does not diminish its importance.

ILLUSTRATION: Plate 11.

Folk-Soul to Master Race

HERRENVOLK (Master Race) expresses the claim to hegemony of one people over others. It came into current use with the National Socialist regime in Germany and described the pre-eminence in the world of the German people which was said to be due, not to any cultural and intellectual achievements, but to membership of a special, the Aryan, race.

The phrase was first used by Paul Lagarde (1827–1891) in his *Deutsche Schriften*. He was a muddle-headed but gifted and influential German visionary and conservative anti-semite who advocated a greater Germany whose racially pure inhabitants would embrace the Christian religion, shorn of its Jewish elements. Lagarde wrote that 'wherever the Germans arrived they brought inward aristocracy with them, for they were of a royal turn of mind'. This did not prevent him from discarding the eminently German name of Boetticher he had inherited from his father for the foreign, yet high-sounding de Lagarde of his mother. Lagarde himself merely adopted ideas

which had been popularized by the German romantics in the early nineteenth century.

Chief among these was Johann Gottfried Herder (1744–1803), who developed the concept of the organic folk-nation and opposed it to the politico-juridical concept of the state that was prevalent in the Age of Reason and Enlightenment of the eighteenth century. Every nation, according to Herder, was an organic personal whole – 'a plant of nature' which finds its expression in the 'national spirit', the 'folk-soul'. By *Volk* he understood more than an association of citizens, more than a people: a tribal and emotional community.

Herder felt that the Germans had failed to develop their own folk character sufficiently, and he deplored the foreign influences which then dominated German culture. He elevated German nationalism and patriotism into 'a great human virtue'. If Rousseau upheld the goodness of men, Herder glorified the goodness of the folknation, but at the same time he realized the dangerous extremes to which his theory tended. He did not subscribe to a rigid racial theory (although he regarded the Jews as aliens in Europe), and he did not single out the German nation as the chosen people of the earth. But these later doctrines could be traced back to his idealist utopia of 'perpetual peace' in which the folk-souls of all nations would unfold themselves and yet live peacefully side by side like differently coloured roses in a garden.

Herder's saving stipulations were forgotten by his successors. The romantic philosopher Karl Friedrich Schlegel (1772–1829) seized upon the idea of the *Volk* as the basis of the nation, and the concept found a wide response in the period of fervent German nationalism after the Napoleonic wars. The patriotic writer, Josef Goerres (1776–1848) introduced the idea of the ties of blood which bind the *Volk* together; these became subsequently one of the basic tenets of Nazi ideology.

The philosopher, Friedrich von Schelling (1775–1854), espoused the metaphysical totality of the folk-nation to which the individual must be sacrificed. In order to recapture their true spirit, he wrote, the Germans must cast out all decadent foreign elements and influences. Another writer, Adam Mueller, believed that the individual derived his significance from membership of the eternal *Volk*, a doctrine which was perfected by the philosopher Hegel (1770–1831), whose teachings had a very deep influence in Germany. In his *Philosophy of History* Hegel advanced the thesis that humanity had finally come to manhood in the German race, which was not, perhaps, a far cry from the Nazi verse

> Am deutschen Wesen
> Soll die Welt genesen.

(German character shall be the saving of the world.)

The doctrine of the *Volk* was supplemented by the ideas of Aryan supremacy, and the first to formulate the doctrine of the Master Race in these terms was a Frenchman, Comte Arthur de Gobineau (1816–1882), in his *Essay on the Inequality of the Human Races*. There he proclaimed the superiority of the white race over the coloured races, and the supremacy of the 'Aryan' among white men. The composer Richard Wagner (1813–1883) borrowed Gobineau's ideas and made them the basis of his own anti-semitism and Aryan cult, of which Bayreuth, the Wagner city, became later an effective expression. Richard Wagner's son-in-law was an Englishman who became a naturalized German, Houston Stewart Chamberlain (1855–1927). In his *Foundations of the Nineteenth Century*, Chamberlain proclaimed that the Germans were the supreme people within the Germanic races and the Germanic language the supreme vehicle of intellectual and cultural achievement. Again, this doctrine became the basis of later wilder fantasies such as that Shakespeare had been in fact a German. 'The higher development of mankind', Chamberlain wrote in 1901 to his friend, the Emperor Wilhelm II, 'is bound up with Germany, a mighty Germany spreading far across the earth the sacred heritage of her language, affirming herself everywhere and imposing herself on others ... God builds today upon the Germans alone.'

Another German writer who was one of many influenced by the anti-semitic campaign which Chamberlain had started was L. Woltmann (1871–1907), who went one better: 'The Germanic race is called to fetter the earth in its domination, to exploit the treasures of nature and the physical forces of men.'

Upon all these ideas, the National Socialists, and in particular their leading exponent, Alfred Rosenberg (1893–1946), were able to build. Had Herder been alive in the Third Reich, his pacifism and internationalism would probably have sent him to a concentration camp; yet the literary romantics may, with much justice, be regarded as the precursors of the *Herrenvolk* ideology. They were a group of literary snobs or life-starved professors who talked but did not act. But through them nationalism saturated German literature and the German universities, and took hold of the German middle classes in the nineteenth century.

Friedrich Nietzsche (1844–1900) must also be mentioned as a telling example of how the Nazis were able to exploit the thinkers of the past. Nietzsche's 'superman' and his famous phrase 'beyond good and evil' seem to have a superficial link with the catchword, *Herrenvolk*. In fact, Nietzsche himself had distinguished 'bad' from 'evil', and uttered the warning that he did not mean 'beyond good and bad'. Likewise, his *superman* was an individual, not the collectivized entity into which the Nazis had turned it. Indeed, Nietzsche's superman and 'beyond good and evil' were converted by the Nazis into something Nietzsche most hated: German nationalism. Yet, however loose the connexion, Hitler was justified in acknowledging a debt to Nietzsche when he wrote: 'the inequality of the races is the innermost will of nature. The Superman must rule the world to promote the victory of the better and stronger and the submission of the worse and weaker.'

Note his linking of 'better' with 'stronger', of 'worse' with 'weaker'. It was the logical conclusion of the old doctrine that might is right and that morality is not an absolute and universal, as Christianity claims, but a relative and national concept.

There is moreover no connexion at all between the *Herrenvolk* and the 'chosen people' of the Bible. That the Bible uses this term in no racial sense is clearly stated. It says, in fact, that Israel was chosen not because of any superior qualities, but precisely because the Jews had no such qualities: 'The Lord did not set his love upon you, nor choose you, because you were more in number than any people ... but because the Lord loved you' (*Deuteronomy*). Israel was chosen as a people because God's purpose was to unite all men in a single spiritual people to save them and lead them to communion with him.

The fact that the concept of a Master Race has had different expressions in different countries, should perhaps restrain one from dismissing it as rank nonsense. In Italy a line of similar ideas can be traced from Mazzini to Mussolini; in England, from Wordsworth to Kipling, and there are a number of eminent non-German authors who endorsed the German racial claim; the historians Guizot and Stubbs were prejudiced in favour of Teutonism; Disraeli thought that race was determined by blood, and not by language or religion; Carlyle showed unqualified admiration for things German, and the American sociologists, Madison Grant and L. Stoddard, borrowed certain basic ideas of German racialism.

It is not to accept the Nazi pretensions about the *Herrenvolk* to hold, as some ethnologists do, that the Germans are a noble racial type or possess a peculiarly ethnical magic of power. It was precisely because this doctrine had some foundation in fact that it became all the more dangerous and menacing. But it is not self-evident that these racial values, even if they exist, are the decisive values. The essential thing is always the one upon which spiritual emphasis is laid. Nazi Germany propounded the doctrine of racial superiority as a religion and a programme; the point is not the alleged absurdity or otherwise, from a scientific point of view, that the English should have ruled over Indians, the French over Arabs, the Dutch over Malayans or the Germans over Slavs, but the moral falsity and essential aggressiveness inherent in the creed of the master race. (See also *Anti-semitism, Superman*).

ILLUSTRATION: Pages 224, 225 and 226.

Highbrow and lowbrow

HIGHBROW AND LOWBROW are expressions which the Americans claim to have invented – a transference of Caliban's description in *The Tempest* of apes, 'foreheads villainously low', to the classification of human beings. But although Mencken in *The American Language* dates the words 1905, when Will Irwin first spoke of highbrows in the *New York Sun*, in his supplement he traced the adjective 'highbrowed' back to 1875, and its companion to 1855. Lowbrow was in current use in an American university (Stanford) round about 1895. The words reached England by 1908; and they were given an early currency by H. G. Wells.

The history of the words themselves, though, gives only a slight reflection of the ideas they signify. If Roget's *Thesaurus* now groups them under Scholar and Ignorance, in common usage very few people would think of applying them to degrees of knowledge. The ideas are almost entirely pejorative, the highbrow being, supposedly, a person conceited with his own intellectual or cultural tastes, and a lowbrow a person of vulgar tastes and interests. But the concealed snobbery is both negative and positive. While it would seem harmless for people to be, though pharisaically, proud of their attainments, it is an astonishing reflection on our society that many more are proud to proclaim themselves ignorant and vulgar, or to proclaim that they deliberately cultivate what the eighteenth-century writers would have called 'low pleasures'. 'Culture' is being almost obliged to become a private vice.

Johann Kaspar Lavater (1741–1801) tried to systematize physical characteristics as clues to personality – a wonderful instance of the adventures of the new materialism. He drew attention to types of faces which, in human beings, recall the facial structure of other animals – some of us are dogs, others sheep or lions. His illustrated work on human physiognomy makes amusing reading; copies can sometimes be found in second-hand shops.

It was an easy step from this to the invention, in 1808, by Franz-Josef Gall (1758–1828) and J. C. Spurzheim, of the pseudo-science of phrenology. Popular at first with the early nineteenth-century intellectuals and artists, the reading of bumps became a frightening indoor game with the Victorians, though it has now fallen into disrepute. Gall located beneath the frontal bumps all the higher intellectual operations (ideation, order, calculation, language, reasoning, perception) as well as such qualities as benevolence. It followed that those with a high brow were richly endowed, while those with villainously low foreheads were not.

Long before the American coining of 'highbrow' and 'lowbrow', novelists had, consciously or unconsciously, adopted the popular view of the highbrowed high-minded hero and his counterpart, the low-browed low-minded villain, that was latent in the myth-making of Lavater and Gall.

In 1925 *The Times Literary Supplement* suggested the fussy neologism *mezzo-brow* for its readers who have safe opinions and 'middlebrow' is now well established. Aldous Huxley in the late nineteen-twenties noted that 'Today "highbrow" is a term of contemptuous abuse. The fact is surely significant. In decent Anglo-Saxon society one may not be a highbrow.' Tracing the use of these notions to the spread of education since Forster's Act of 1870, Huxley was able to sigh with relief that 'there is as yet no actual persecution of highbrows', in *Music at Night*, 1950.

Two other quotations may be set side by side. Virginia Woolf (1882–1941), English novelist and daughter of the cream of Victorian intellectualism, wrote in a letter to the *New Statesman*: 'Now there can be no two opinions as to what a highbrow is. He is the man or woman of thoroughbred intelligence who rides his mind at a gallop across country in pursuit of an idea. That is why I have always been so proud to be called highbrow. That is why if I could be more of a highbrow I would. I honour and respect highbrows. Some of my relations have been highbrows; and some, but by no means all, of my friends.'

Contrariwise the middlebrow essayist Robert Lynd (1879–1949) in an essay called *No Intellectuals* wrote: 'In England the intellectual nowadays is usually called a highbrow, and seldom is the term highbrow used as a term of praise. The ordinary man, however, in attacking highbrows, is merely defending himself from his lower-browed tastes. He feels as superior for not liking Bach as he believes the highbrow feels for liking Bach. His resentment of highbrows is perhaps a mark of his love of equality, and he will not have it that a man who can read *Paradise Lost* or *Finnegan's Wake* with enjoyment is on that account a better man than he.'

ILLUSTRATION: Page 278.

Inevitable futures

HISTORICISM assumes that history reveals the operation of a law, that its course is an inevitable sequence of stages of evolution or change, and that when the law is correctly understood, the future, being inevitable, can be predicted.

A historicist theory is a generalization about the pattern of history which not only classifies its past, present and future stages, but asserts the principle which can explain the transition from one stage to the next. Among the most important thinkers who would now be regarded as historicist in outlook are Hegel, Marx, St-Simon, Comte, Spencer, Spengler and at the present day Arnold Toynbee. All these, however, differed about details of the principle which, they thought, determined the flow of events; they differed in their classification of stages and in their mood about the future–some were optimistic and some pessimistic.

To Karl Marx it was the relationships amongst the different classes of men in the system of production which shaped history and gave the stamp to particular epochs. Each period could be identified by the kind of property which the élite in the productive system owned. Because of the conflict which existed, in Marx's view, between the various classes, each period contained the seeds of its own dissolution. As a submerged class became ascendant, it would overthrow or simply replace the élite and establish its own hegemony. Thus slavery, feudalism and capitalism succeeded each other with inexorable logic. The end of this historical process would be reached with the victory of the last submerged class, the wage-earning proletariat, over the owners of capital, and the abolition of all private property-rights in the means of production.

This would bring to an end not only the inequality between classes (to which private property inevitably gave rise) but the very existence of classes at all. Mankind would then at last be free of the class conflict which had oppressed it from the beginning of its history.

St-Simon (1760–1825) and Auguste Comte (1798–1857), for whom human progress lay in the growth of science, saw history in a similar fashion as inevitable evolution through three ages. These were, in their terms, the theological, the metaphysical and finally the positive age, when social life would be completely reorganized on the basis of positive knowledge, *viz.* science.

Common to all historicist thinkers, then, was their belief that history had to pass through certain necessary states, and similarly was moving inevitably towards a certain destiny, irrespective of the intentions of mankind. Whether these phases are seen as cycles of decline and fall or as a progression of states culminating in a final and henceforth unchangeable state, is an accident of the essential historicist outlook.

Historicism is in essentials a fusion of a sense of historical continuity with the scientific spirit, but with a misunderstanding of each. Opposed to it is a view of history in which the past is certainly regarded as influencing the future, but in a wholly different frame of reference – that at any given moment mankind has before it choices of action which are limited by the circumstances of time. Such, for example, would be climatic factors and the existing level of industrial technique.

But, given these limitations upon what a person can do, the fact remains that in order for him to do anything at all he must more or less explicitly decide to do it. Even simply deciding to wait for what he thinks is inevitable, and not do anything to resist it, is a decision between possible choices. The choice he will make is not, of course, idiosyncratic, but is dependent on customs and tastes. These supply him with standards without which he could not reach a decision at all. But in using standards to decide upon a line of action, he is none the less using will.

The fact that these decisions can to a great degree be predicted, when we know the customs and tastes of the people, does not alter this. We know that most Frenchmen would prefer wine to water. They choose wine not because they have to, but because they want to. All this was effaced by the historicist theories, which explained behaviour as a necessary reaction to conditions. The contention which is central to Marxian theory that people would *have* to behave in a certain way because it was in their interest to do so, seems, on the surface, to supply a motive for action. But it overlooks the fact that in order for people to act in their self-interest, they must want do do so, and that this cannot automatically be assumed to follow from a knowledge of it.

What happens in any one age influences succeeding ages by shaping the circumstances, the choices which are presented to the actors in the historical drama, and the ideas and standards by which they will be made. A decisive event is one the outcome of which, had it been different, would have made a fundamental difference to the course of history. That is, it would have removed the possibility of a choice of profound significance. The defeat of Nazi Germany was such a decisive event for the maintenance of Western civilization.

A signal error of historicism is the notion of a necessary pattern of evolution in history. What takes place is, on the contrary, to be regarded as the outcome of a multiplicity of events, some of which were decisive in giving direction to what followed, some of which were not. Thus feudalism was followed by capitalism, where this did occur, only because the conditions of feudal society had in fact broken down. This was due to a variety of things, such as the centralization of the monarchy, which could not possibly be subsumed under a single law of evolution. On the other hand, capitalism could not simply evolve out of feudalism. A number of events, such as the Reformation and the geographical discoveries of the Renaissance explorers, were decisive in creating the conditions under which it emerged. If they had not all taken place at that time, the course of history would have been different.

Furthermore, the various stages of all the historicist theories reveal themselves to be grossly over-simplified classifications. They are treated as homogeneous epochs with nothing of importance in common. But such things as the pursuit of power and honour take place in all ages, and are, in fact, an intrinsic aspect of social life.

Finally, how can a science be audacious enough to predict a future state as inevitable? All that science can do is to establish that under certain conditions people can be expected to behave in a certain way. But can we possibly know all the conditions that will be present in future states, particularly when this involves the occurrence of two or more events in a specific time relation to each other? For example, could anyone have predicted at the beginning of the war when Hitler was going to die? Yet if he had been killed at the time of his attempted assassination, the course of present-day affairs would be different.

In fact, historicist theories are not theories at all. They do not make predictions along the lines of 'If A and B, then C will follow', but rather what have been described correctly as prophecies. They have abdicated from the task of trying to supply mankind with the answer to the question of what must be done in order to achieve the good life. They have done this by saying essentially that nothing can be done (except, perhaps, to adjust oneself to the inevitable future). Because of this they may be severely charged with moral bankruptcy.

The curious thing about these theories is that when repeated often enough they may be accepted as inevitable. Those who do so may then work to achieve the goal prophesied. Or else those who disapprove of the goal may be convinced even then that there is nothing that can be done to resist it. So the prophecy may seem to be fulfilled. It is this which makes such theories dangerous for liberal societies, particularly when the goal prophesied – the irresistible wave of the future – is a totalitarian state.

ILLUSTRATION: Page 219.

Touch wood

HUBRIS, says Euripides in a play produced in 429 B.C., consists in wanting to set oneself above the gods.

This would not have been news to his audience; for the idea that the gods keep a jealous eye on the activities of the human race had long been almost a commonplace of Greek thought. Already in Homer (whose poetry was put together in all probability before 800 B.C., and has been called the Bible of the Greeks), when one of the insolent young men who are hoping to marry Penelope strikes the ragged beggar who is really Odysseus, her husband, come home at last, one of his companions cries: 'You did ill to strike a helpless wanderer, you fool, if by any chance he is one of the gods of heaven. For the gods in many guises, like strangers from foreign lands, travel from city to city, observing the lawlessness [hubris] of men, and their respect for law.'

This watchfulness on the part of the gods, and the consequent punishment with which they were thought to visit those guilty of hubris, soon became personified in the goddess Nemesis, whose name means 'one who gives what is due'. Hesiod, writing later than Homer (who uses the word *nemesis* only of *human* retribution), makes her the daughter of Night. A most vivid description of this sinister power occurs at the beginning of a poem in praise of Virgil written (in Latin) by Angelo Poliziano (1454–1494), who was perhaps the most brilliant of all the scholars at the Court of Lorenzo de' Medici, and a fine poet.

High above us in thin air there hovers a goddess, wrapped in cloud. Her robe gleams white, and her hair streams behind her as she plies her strident wings. It is she who subdues unruly ambition, it is her anger that threatens the arrogant, and hers is the power that crushes the spirit of haughtiness in men, wrecking the prosperous and all their pomp. The Ancients named her Nemesis, child of silent Night and Ocean. She wears a crown of stars: her hands hold a bridle and a bowl. There is terror in her smile as she thwarts our crazy plans and breaks our wicked wills; for, like a wheel that turns, she reverses high and low, ruling our lives by the law of contraries, inconstant as the shifting winds.

It is no accident that this noble yet appalling vision haunts the city-states of the Renaissance no less than those of ancient Greece, for the overthrow of princely magnificence was as common in the one as in the other; and Dürer's engraving of the goddess, inspired by Politian's lines, provides a curious link between the two periods.

It was long believed that the sight of a man enjoying power and riches was of itself sufficient to arouse the jealousy and resentment of the gods. Solon the wise Athenian warned the fabulously wealthy Croesus of this; and the advent of Nemesis was not long delayed. Herodotus (c. 483 –c. 425 B.C.) gives the text of a letter written by Amasis, king of Egypt, to his friend the tyrant Polycrates, whose affairs were prospering exceedingly:

It is pleasant to learn of the well-being of a friend and guest. But I like not these great successes of yours; for I know how jealous are the gods; and I do in some sort desire for myself and my friends a mingling of prosperity and mishap, and a life of weal and woe thus chequered, rather than unbroken good fortune. For from all I have heard I know of no man whom continual good fortune did not bring in the end to evil, and utter destruction.

However, as we have seen, Homer contrasted *hubris* with obedience to law; and Hesiod in one place spoke of *nemesis* as our feeling of guilt when we have done wrong. This interpretation of the doctrine of divine retribution shows the gods punishing those who transgress the law of righteousness, which is the law of heaven. This finds its grandest expression in the dramas of Aeschylus (525–456 B.C.). It is no longer because of his wealth, power and victories that a man is punished: it is for yielding to the temptations which these bring with them. Agamemnon's fall is due not to his triumph, nor to the long years of bloodshed at Troy, but to his arrogance and pride on his return – to his making himself equal to the gods.

In one form or another, the doctrine of nemesis has proved fatally fascinating to historians (see *Historicism*). Herodotus, the father of history, sees its workings everywhere, and above all in the overthrow of Xerxes which forms the central and tragic theme of his great book. Likewise Thucydides (c. 460–c. 400 B.C.), in writing the history of the rise to greatness and the subsequent collapse of Athens as an imperial power, has imparted to his narrative the general structure of a tragedy in which success breeds *hubris*, and so leads to its own destruction. But the most remarkable application of the doctrine to the problems of history belongs to our own time. Professor Toynbee in *A Study of History* expresses his conviction that by some recurrent bias in the nature of things, those who create some new thing become fascinated by its charms, can see nothing beyond it, and eventually, like the ironclad Mesozoic monster-reptiles, fall victims to their own speciality. This recurrent pattern which he finds in history Toynbee calls the Nemesis of Creativity. In this, the latest stage of its development, the doctrine of nemesis has lost its old connexion with the gods. Yet even today many feel safer for the touch of wood when they boast, and they feel obscurely apprehensive if success is unusually prolonged.

Toynbee is not the first to rationalize the goddess. 'Nemesis or a sense of righteous indigna-

tion', wrote Aristotle in his *Ethics*, 'is a good quality halfway between the bad qualities of enviousness and maliciousness, all three being concerned with pleasure and pain occasioned by what happens to our neighbours. For the man who is righteously indignant is pained at the sight of unjust prosperity, whereas the envious man goes too far and is upset by prosperity of any sort, while the malicious man goes to the other extreme and actually rejoices at unjust prosperity.'

But the feeling that the matter goes deeper than this persists, and has never been better expressed than by William Blake, who wrote: 'The prophets Isiah and Ezekiel dined with me, and I asked them how they dared so roundly to attest that God spoke to them ...' Isaiah answered: 'I saw no God, nor heard any, in a finite organical perception; but my senses discovered the infinite in everything; and as I was then persuaded and remain confirmed, that the voice of honest indignation is the voice of God, I cared not for consequences, but wrote.'

ILLUSTRATION: Page 276.

Humanism and the humanities

HUMANISM is a word with a short history in its present meaning. It is mostly used to describe a system of thought or an attitude of mind concerned with human nature, or in which human nature is the standard by which all things are measured.

'Humanist' is an epithet frequently applied to people of good will who cannot readily be classed in any of the other unwieldy categories now current; in France in particular it is used as a *tertium quid* between 'Christian' and 'Communist'. In a narrower sense 'humanism' signifies familiarity with subjects taught in the arts faculties of universities.

In both senses, the words indicate a concern with what classical and silver Latin writers called '*humanitas*'. This word was used variously to describe mankind, the notion of humanity – 'for men will perish, but human nature, of which the individual is an image, survives' wrote Seneca in the first century A.D. – and various human attributes, especially mortality. Particularly it implied that which is worthy of the best in man. The Roman historian Tacitus wrote that 'among Britons the imitation of Roman refinement goes by the name of *humanitas*'. Cicero, however, used it in a most specific sense, to describe familiarity with Greek philosophy and literature, these being the highest achievements of the human spirit and intellect. Paradoxically enough, this most specific use of the word is ultimately responsible for its present meaning.

During the Dark Ages and Middle Ages the word gained a different currency: as an antinomy of '*deitas*', '*humanitas*' came to mean the nature of fallen man. More technically, certain of the fathers used the word to describe the human nature of Christ, and consequently, in a theological context, the heresies which deny the divine nature of Christ go by the name of humanism.

Ciceronian '*humanitas*' was forgotten until about the middle of the fourteenth century, when it was restored, largely through the agency of Francesco Petrarcha (1304–1374), the greatest Italian poet after Dante.

Petrarch has in fact always been regarded as the father of humanism. 'This man', wrote Leonardo Bruni, a Tuscan humanist, some thirty years after Petrarch's death, 'restored the study of humanities, which was then in abeyance'. In Petrarch were united the rhetorical and grammatical traditions which were native to Italy, and the classical scholarship based on a critical scrutiny of texts, which had developed in France. He was also connected with the political movements which, following Dante, sought the reunion of Italy through a revival of the prestige of Rome.

Petrarch's attitude to the material of history and his re-reading of the classics had an immediate application. A Roman notary, Cola di Rienzo (1313 or 1314–1354), who had been sent on a delegation to the Papal residence which was then in Avignon, met Petrarch there; and Cola's revolt in 1347 opened with an inflammatory speech, which was in fact a lecture explaining the inscription, kept in the church of St John Lateran, which recorded the decree of the senate conferring imperial power on Vespasian. Cola exhorted the people of Rome to reassert their sovereign power and restore their past glory. All exponents of '*humanitas*' were characterized by this association of textual criticism with political action, by a Petrarchan allegiance to French scholarship and Italian rhetoric, and a passionate striving to achieve the classical perfection of eloquence, art and manners.

At first the general movement was limited to the desire of rhetoricians and theorists of poetry to improve their style by a reading of the classics. This study soon extended to history and moral science – rhetoric, after all, is best taught by example. The method gained yet another application when the Florentine architect Brunelleschi, accompanied by the sculptor Donatello, travelled to Rome in 1401; the two artists measured and recorded as many classical ruins as were accessible and applied what they had learnt from this, much in the way of the rhetoricians and the poets. As the studies grew, the search for the lost sources became more enthusiastic. Much classical material was gathered, mostly manuscripts from Greek and northern European monasteries.

The study of Greek, too, was reviving. It had been very much stimulated by the awakening interest in Plato, which was to be one of the main intellectual forces in Italy in the fifteenth century. Manuel Chrysoloras, a Byzantine scholar, was lecturing in Florence from 1396; and Florence received a flood of Greek scholars at the time of the Council of Florence (1438–1443). But even before the time of Chrysoloras, Boccaccio (1313–1375) put up with a repulsive Calabrian monk, Barlaam, solely because this old man was a Greek scholar.

The notion of *humanita*, or *literae humaniores*, became defined. It was the study of grammar, rhetoric, poetry (meaning largely the theory of poetry), history and certain aspects of moral philosophy, on a philological basis, with a view to restoring the forgotten and 'correct' standards. It was this idea of a return to classical thought and manners, the search for ancient '*virtu*' which gave the period its name 'Renascence' (rebirth). The exponents of *humanità*, who were either attached to universities or the Papal court, or else were employed as secretaries of princes or of city-states, referred to their subjects as *humanità*, alluding to Cicero's use of *humanitas*, and to its definition by the third-century grammarian, Aulus Gellius, as 'That which the Greeks call παιδεία [paideia] and we call sound education in the liberal arts'.

While the humanities were at first limited to Latin, Greek was soon included in the humanists' equipment, and when the movement had spread beyond Italy into Germany and France, Hebrew was also included.

Because of the insistence on linguistic and textual studies, the discovery of new documents and the revelation of forgeries, many of the humanists found themselves in conflict with authority, especially authority resting on the unquestioning acceptance of oral traditions or shady documents. So Lorenzo Valla (1407–1457) passed through a difficult period after publishing his discovery that the *Donation of Constantine*, a document which was used to justify the existence of the Papal states, was a forgery.

When the Reformation came, there were humanists on both sides of the great divide: Catholics like Erasmus, Protestants like Melanchthon. The word 'humanism', and indeed many of the ideas which it evokes, did not occur until a later date. In fact, in the seventeenth century, as the humanist methods and scholarship became increasingly diffused, and were incorporated into the various subjects which border on the humanities, so the word *humanità* lost its emotional content and became stylized and rather obsolete.

It was revived again in the nineteenth century, when historians, and particularly German historians, began an intensive study of the Italian Renascence; it was then that 'humanism' came into being. Certain scholars saw it not only as the most important, but treated it as the sole intellectual movement of its time, and having given it this undue importance, bestowed on it virtues which its protagonists would never have claimed for it themselves. In the end humanism came to be considered as a fully fledged philosophical movement, and even as the creation of an entirely new attitude of mind. In this sense the word passed into common speech, and assumed a meaning parallel to that of 'liberalism', a word with a similar derivation; without, however, quite losing its original sense. 'We talk of knowing Greek and Roman antiquity, which is what people have called humanism', Matthew Arnold defined it in the eighties of the last century. But by that time the word had already taken the hazier sense.

In the eighteen-thirties a reviewer had written of an author whose opinions were 'more consonant to truth, as well as to an enlightened humanism'.

ILLUSTRATION: Page 227.

I

The I.Q.

I.Q. stands for 'Intelligence Quotient', which is a measure of a person's intelligence found by means of an intelligence test. Before marks gained in such a test can be useful as information about a person, they must be compared with some standard, or norm. It is not enough simply to know that a boy of thirteen has scored, say, ninety marks in a particular test. To know whether he is clever, average, or dull, his marks must be compared with the average achieved by boys of thirteen in that test.

In 1906 the psychologist, Alfred Binet (1857–1911), devised the standard in relation to which intelligence has since been assessed. Binet was asked to find a method of selecting all children in the schools of Paris who should be taken out of ordinary classes and put in special classes for defectives. The problem brought home to him the need for a standard of intelligence, and he hit upon the very simple concept of 'mental age'.

First of all, he invented a variety of tests and put large numbers of children of different ages through them. He then found at what age each test was passed by the average child. For instance, he found that the average child of seven could count backward from 20 to 1, and the average child of three could repeat the sentence: 'We are going to have a good time in the country.' Binet arranged the various tests in order of difficulty, and used them as a scale against which he could measure every individual. If, for example, a boy aged twelve could only do tests that were passed by the average boy of nine, Binet held that he was three years below average, and that he had a mental age of nine.

The concept of mental age provided Binet, and through him, other psychologists, with the required standard. It enabled him to state scores in intelligence tests in terms of a norm. At first, it was usual to express the result of a test by the difference between the 'mental' and the 'chronological' age. Then the boy in the example given would be 'three years retarded'. Soon, however, the 'mental ratio' was introduced; that is to say, the ratio of the mental age to the chronological age. Thus a boy of twelve with a mental age of nine has a mental ratio of 0·75.

The mental age was replaced by the 'intelligence quotient' or 'I.Q.'. The 'I.Q.' is the mental ratio multiplied by 100. For example, a boy of twelve with a mental age of nine has an 'I.Q.' of 75. Clearly, since the mental age of the average child is equal to the chronological age, the average I.Q. is 100.

Binet found that intelligence develops evenly throughout childhood until about the age of sixteen, and that from then onwards there is no appreciable growth. Thus the average adult has a mental age of sixteen. 'This form of statement is useful for individuals whose scores are not higher than those of the average child of sixteen. For higher levels of intelligence the method is of doubtful value,' says Professor E. L. Thorndike in *Intelligence Tests* (1950).

Alfred Binet and Sir Francis Galton (1822–1911) were the pioneers in the general field of intelligence testing. Galton, in 1885, set up in the South Kensington Museum, a laboratory where people could have their intelligences measured by a series of tests. Under the influence of the American psychologist James Cattell (1860–1944), many tests of special mental powers were devised and used widely in the United States from 1890 onwards. In France, Alfred Binet produced in 1906 what may be called a standardized interview consisting of thirty questions and tasks, many of which were chosen from Cattell's tests of special powers now familiar to all psychologists. In 1908, in collaboration with the psychologist T. Simon, Binet further improved this 'metric scale of intelligence', and he finally revised it in 1911. The intelligence tests developed by Binet and Simon are now used all over the world.

Today intelligence tests are used by school medical officers in Great Britain in the diagnosis of mental deficiency, in the initial grading of children in schools, in Child Guidance Clinics and in vocational guidance. In industry many firms are now employing such tests to assess aptitudes for various kinds of work, a practice also adopted by the Civil Service. Perhaps the most startling evidence of the spread of intelligence tests is their use in the Armed Forces of the principal nations in the Second World War.

In England, intelligence tests have many detractors. Those who advocate them say that this is because intelligence itself is not much admired in an age in which such words as 'highbrow' (q.v.), 'clever' and 'intellectual' are almost always used in a denigrating sense, and where the tendency is to admire character more than brains. Hostility to intelligence tests may also be due to the fact that they excite fear even in people of proved ability. A judge of the High Court was recently heard to remark that the thought of submitting to an intelligence test filled him with dismay.

Such tests have been distrusted because too much has often been claimed for them. Some enthusiasts, ignoring the fact that success in anything depends on special abilities and on temperamental qualities as well as on intelligence, have said that intelligence tests by themselves are adequate criteria for all kinds of activities and occupations, an extravagant claim which has naturally aroused opposition. Well-conducted tests, intelligently applied, and taking into account emotional and temperamental factors, are agreed by leading psychologists and educationists to be of value, especially in the testing of young children and in the diagnosis of mental deficiency.

The Immaculate Conception

The **IMMACULATE CONCEPTION** is a phrase in which 'Immaculate' means free from sin, and 'conception' refers not so much to the act of conception as to the being conceived.

It is applied to Mary, the mother of Jesus Christ, and is intended to convey that she was without sin from the first moment of her existence. The first moment of existence of a human being, possessing a rational soul, is not easy to determine, and no Christian body has made any definite statement on the matter. However, the being is now usually held to exist from the first moment of the union between the male seed and the female ovum. But in medieval times it was generally held that the human being only came into existence at the time of the quickening of the foetus, several months after the act of generation; the rational soul was supposed to be infused into the physical body at that time. It was this that led to controversy about the idea that Mary was 'immaculate' from the first moment of her 'conception'. In plain language she could not have been perfect before she existed.

But there was another issue which made it important to emphasize that Mary was not immaculate until the first moment of her own proper existence, that no perfection was inherent in her as a human being automatically, as a result, for instance, of some special grace given to her parents. Catholic theologians hold that human beings are subject to the disorder, the lack of perfection, which we call sin, and that their way of release from this state is solely through the redemption of the world by Jesus. They insist that Mary naturally received this heritage of disorder, original sin (q.v.), which is common to all human beings, but was freed from it from the first moment of her existence by the foreseen merits of her son Jesus's redemptive life. The collect for the Feast of the Immaculate Conception reads: 'O God who, by the immaculate conception of the virgin, didst make her a worthy habitation for thy son, and didst, by his foreseen death, preserve her from all stain of sin; grant, we beseech thee, that through her intercession we may be cleansed from sin and come with pure hearts to thee, through the same Jesus Christ, thy son, our Lord.'

The Immaculate Conception is, then, a rather technical analytical description of the idea that Mary the mother of Jesus was perfect. This idea can be seen clearly in Christian writers from the earliest times. 'The new Eve' is the commonest title given to Mary by the early Fathers of the Church; in this title was included the idea that to Mary was restored the perfection which Eve possessed in her innocence, together with a new spiritual perfection, implied in the words of the angel to Mary at the annunciation: 'Hail Mary, full of grace.' 'Full of grace' has been taken generally by theologians to indicate Mary's spiritual perfection, her sanctification. The tendency to trace this perfection back to its origin in her mother's womb has scriptural backing from the analogy of St John the Baptist, who is described as being filled with the Holy Spirit while still in his mother's womb (St Luke i. 15).

The celebration of the feast of the conception of the Virgin is of early medieval origin. It is possible that St Ildefonsus instituted such a feast in Spain sometime after 667, but the documentary evidence is not certain. The first certain evidence of such a feast comes from England. At Winchester in 1030, and under the Abbot Ælwin (1034–1057), the feast was kept on 8 December, nine months, that is, before the feast of Mary's birthday on 8 September. The feast seems also to have been kept at St Augustine's at Canterbury about 1050. There is evidence of the feast being kept much earlier, but it is inconclusive.

In the twelfth and thirteenth centuries the feast became a live issue in the Church, and celebration of it was actually forbidden in some places. This prohibition was based on the idea that Mary could not have been perfect as a mere physical existence in the womb of her mother, prior to the time of her 'conception' as a human being, at the time of the infusion of a human immortal soul into her body, as already explained. There was no calling in question her freedom from sin from her birth, and before her birth, till her death. St John the Baptist was universally held to have lived such a sinless life, and it was naturally supposed that the mother of Jesus must have been the most perfect of all human beings.

In time the issues were clarified and it became possible to put them into final form. This was done by Pius IX in the Bull *Ineffabilis Deus*, on 8 December 1854, which stated 'The doctrine which declares that the Most Blessed Virgin Mary, in the first instant of her conception, by a singular grace and privilege of Almighty God, in view of the merits of Jesus Christ, the Saviour of the human race, was preserved exempt from all stain of original sin, is a doctrine revealed by God, and therefore must be believed firmly and constantly by the faithful.' There were many protests at the time from non-Catholic bodies; on the grounds that the Catholic Church was 'adding' to the deposit of revealed truth left to mankind in scripture. On the other hand, the Catholic Church claims to have the divinely given power, and duty, to unfold and elucidate the full implications of revealed truth.

ILLUSTRATION: Plate 14 and Page 312.

'No word for scholars'

IMPERIALISM – in the sense of power exercised by a dominant community over subject communities – is an ancient idea; but the implication that the exercise, or extension, of such power is morally desirable is relatively modern.

The term could come into use only when the principle was no longer taken for granted. True, modern historians and sociologists have written studies of ancient Assyrian and Egyptian imperialism, Greek imperialism and Roman imperialism; but in doing so they have used a new concept to illuminate events and institutions of periods remote in time.

Assyrians, Egyptians, Greeks and Romans were not in the habit of arguing about the rights and wrongs of 'imperialism' – even though their leaders followed policies which can intelligibly be described as 'imperialist'; and even though one can find – in Thucydides' dramatized account of the discussion between the Athenian generals and the Melian embassy, for example – an exposition of 'imperialist' principles which has a strongly contemporary flavour.

The actual word 'imperialism', in its sense of 'seeking, or at least not refusing, an extension of the British Empire in directions where trading interests and investments require the protection of the flag', appears to have come into common use in the last quarter of the nineteenth century. Lord Carnarvon could say in 1878: 'I have heard of imperial policy and imperial interests, but imperialism, as such, is new to me.' By the eighteen-nineties the term had been adopted both by those

who approved, and by those who rejected, the doctrine; by the *Westminster Gazette*, which explained how the 'vivid realization of the British Empire as "a world-wide Venice with the sea for streets", gave a decisive impetus to what may be called, in the slang of the day, "the new Imperialism" ' (1895); and by the *Daily News*, which spoke of 'that odious system of bluster and swagger and might against right on which Lord Beaconsfield and his colleagues bestowed the tawdry nickname of Imperialism' (1898).

Why did the word – 'no word for scholars', according to Professor W. K. Hancock – only establish itself at this late date? Modern empire-building – the process whereby Europe thrust its frontiers, its traders, settlers, missionaries, administrators and policemen into the non-European world – had been going on at least since the end of the fifteenth century. If Burke could state his theory of empire adequately without using the term 'imperialism', why did Lord Rosebery feel the need for it?

The answer seems to lie in the special characteristics of this late nineteenth–early twentieth-century phase of colonial expansion. First, its scale and tempo: between 1880 and 1920 the greater part of the African continent, of the Arab world, of China and south-east Asia, with such oceanic islands as had hitherto been left unmolested, was brought directly or indirectly under the control of the chief colonial powers: Britain, France, Belgium, Germany, the Netherlands, Portugal, Italy, the U.S.A.

Second, the competing claims of these powers for colonies, protectorates, spheres of influence and – later – mandates, brought into being new zones of inter-European tension in the world outside Europe: Egypt, Morocco, the Nile Valley, the Congo basin, Persia, Manchuria. Europeans were compelled to think of their future as in some way linked with the outcome of crises in remote places with unfamiliar names – Agadir, Fashoda, Kiao-Chow.

Third, since the states involved in this struggle for empire were for the most part parliamentary democracies, operating systems of universal or manhood suffrage, their governments were faced with the problem – new, apart from Athenian experience – of conducting imperialist policies with the consent of the governed; and of presenting these policies – involving expenditure of blood and treasure, and a reversal of earlier liberal attitudes – in terms which would secure the approval of 'all or most men'.

Hence the need for an imperial ideology, which could be stated in suitable ethical language, and commend itself alike to British nonconformists, German Lutherans, Belgian Catholics and French *libres penseurs*. It was partly for this reason that the imperial idea affected all aspects of national life and thought – above all in Britain: found expression in imperial history, imperial sociology, imperial philosophy, imperial theories of government, imperial poetry, imperial romance and an imperial popular press.

One further characteristic of this phase of colonial expansion was the fact of controversy: imperialist orthodoxy was quickly challenged by an anti-imperialist heresy – or heresies. And, though Britain has been rightly regarded as the best laboratory specimen of the new imperialism, the debate itself was international: Joseph Chamberlain, Jules Ferry, Karl Peters, King Leopold II, on the one side; J. A. Hobson, Jean Jaurès, Rosa Luxemburg, Lenin, on the other.

The imperialist thesis – though, of course, it was stated in cruder and subtler forms – consisted in the main of an amalgam of doctrines, drawn from different sources: a pseudo-Darwinian conception of the inevitability of conflict in human, and particularly international, affairs, and the survival of the fittest, or the most aggressive, national types; a pseudo-Calvinist belief in one's own nation as a nation 'elect' – specially ordained by God (or 'Providence' or 'History') to increase the welfare and improve the manners of less-favoured peoples; a neo-Hegelian view of the nation-state as the embodiment of an ethical idea; a neo-mercantilist theory of the necessity for colonies as a market for manufactures, and an insurance against poverty, unemployment and class-war; and a neo-Malthusian theory of their usefulness as a dumping-ground for surplus population. As William Watson modestly put it, in *The Inexorable Law*:

> We have reigned
> Augustly; let our part be so sustained
> That Time, far hence, shall hold our memory dear!
> Let it be said: 'This Mistress of the sword
> And conquering now, this Empire swoln with spoils,

> Yet served the human cause, yet strove for Man;
> Hers was the purest greatness we record.'

The classic statement of the anti-imperialist heresy is to be found in J. A. Hobson's *Imperialism* (1902). His argument can be reduced to three main propositions:

First, the 'tap-root' of modern imperialism is economic. The drive for empire arises out of the chronic 'under-consumptionist' tendencies of advanced capitalist economies. Thus the main purpose of expansion (however justified in colonial apologetics) is to maintain a falling rate of profit. At this stage of history the governments of imperialist countries become little more than executive committees of merchants and investors, interested in the goldfields of the Rand, a Berlin–Baghdad railway, or Congo rubber.

Second, the effect of imperialism is not merely to disrupt the traditional social systems and values of the colonial peoples; but also to corrupt the colonizing nation: to stimulate a spirit of jingoism, racial arrogance, moral humbug, delight in violence; to strengthen the pressures for intellectual conformity (particularly in Oxford and Cambridge); to weaken the institutions of liberalism by re-exporting into the Home Counties retired proconsuls and nabobs, who introduce into British public life the authoritarian habits of mind which they have acquired in their dealings with Asians and Africans; and, above all, to increase the tensions leading to international war.

Third, the solution to the problems raised by imperialism is to be found in social reform, and a progressive raising of domestic standards of consumption – which will render unnecessary the drive for colonial markets and investment outlets.

Lenin, who in the preface to his *Imperialism* (1917) warmly acknowledged his debt to Hobson, accepted, in essentials, Hobson's first two propositions, and rejected his third. Drawing on a work of Rudolf Hilferding's, *Das Finanzkapital* (1910), Lenin placed greater emphasis upon the rôle of the banks, of monopolies, and of the export of capital, in the genesis of imperialism. He was more interested, too, in the effect of imperialism upon the Labour movement– particularly in the development of the attitude which he described as 'opportunism' among the Labour and

Trade Union leadership of the wealthier imperial countries, bought, as Lenin saw it, with the proceeds of colonial loot: and he quoted with approval Engels' remark that 'even Tom Mann ... is fond of mentioning that he will be lunching with the Lord Mayor'.

For Hobson's reformism Lenin, of course, had no use. Imperialism, in his view, could be abolished only by the combined attack of the revolutionary proletariat in the imperial countries and revolutionary nationalists in the colonies. While Hobson was the father of a generation of British radicals – from Brailsford to Brockway – Lenin's definition is still the point of departure for Communist thinking throughout the world:

> Imperialism is capitalism in that stage of development in which the domination of monopolies and finance capital has taken shape; in which the export of capital has acquired pronounced importance; in which the division of the world by the international trusts has begun, and in which the partition of all the territory of the earth by the greatest capitalist countries has been completed.

One consequence of this critique of empire was that 'imperialism' acquired a rhetorical – in addition to its original descriptive – meaning: it became a rude word. We are none of us imperialists now. Indeed, there are hardly any empires: only a Commonwealth of Nations, a French Union, an integral Belgian-Congolese State, etc. Yet the word still has its uses. Only it is necessary to distinguish between 'imperialism' in its traditional sense – referring to the ascendancy of European over non-European peoples (which still survives in Africa and parts of Asia); in its semi-technical sense – referring to the Hobson–Luxemburg–Lenin theory of the social causes and consequences of this ascendancy; and in an extended sense – referring to the new kind of ascendancy enjoyed by the H-Bomb powers.

ILLUSTRATION: Pages 268 and 269.

Hero and individual

The **CULT OF THE INDIVIDUAL** can be of two types, roughly divisible into the Classical, where the hero or leader is the man most perfectly embodying the ideals and aspirations of the group, and the Renaissance-Romantic, where society prides itself on producing a wide variety of highly-developed personalities and thus creates a tradition of individual liberty, which may later be exploited by minority groups – tycoons, gangsters or artists.

It is not easy to be an individual in a primitive tribe in which physical lives and attitudes are intensely regulated. Only when a tribe begins to develop, does the collective choral interest in ritual turn into the saga and the drama of heroes, of glorious deeds, with the chorus sinking back into 'doddering and pottering old men, moralizing on an action in which they are too feeble to join'.

Tribal ceremonies are collective and monotonous; primitive work-songs have as their aim the psychic and physical co-ordination of the group. The appearance of the hero suggests the leader of a people in motion, with new situations requiring new responses. Yet in drama the Greek hero retained his organic relation to his people, as instanced by the retention of the chorus and by the religious atmosphere of the whole scene; the danger of the Greek hero is that he will show *hubris* (q.v.) and over-pass the limits of his exceptional and individual nature.

Enlarging upon this point, the poet W. H. Auden has given an intricate formula for the description of individuals in ancient times. The hero of the Greek poets was exceptional by nature; he was lucky because he was endowed with virtue, and his danger lay in his attempting to turn his natural talents into spiritual ones, for *hubris* was pretending to become what you already were. On the other hand, the Platonic hero was spiritual, capable of freeing himself from body and passions and of knowing the divine ideas; his danger was that the *Eros* might undo him, that he might claim to be endowed by fortune with what he could only become. Auden then proceeds to say that it is the Jewish-Christian hero who alone does justice to both nature and spirit; Abraham and Job are neither exceptional by nature nor by philosophical intuition (it would be presumptuous to know the mind of God), but they are obedient to God when they can choose to be disobedient. Thus 'only the religious hero is an historical individual at every moment of his existence'.

The Middle Ages, dominated by religion and

by an hierarchical structure which discouraged social movement, would be generally considered deficient in individuals. It was the Renaissance which emphasized free expression and the development of the all-round man – humanists such as Aeneas Sylvius or Erasmus, artist-scientists such as Leonardo, artist-adventurers such as Benvenuto Cellini, patron-princes such as Lorenzo de' Medici; all these were alike concerned with the fullness of life, and alike presented human fallibility.

The New Monarchs, owing much to Machiavelli's *Prince* (1513), were a trifle too outwardly magnificent, and inwardly too contriving and cynical, to be heroes in the classical sense. Elizabethan tragedy was built upon this cult of individualism, exemplars of which are Faustus and Macbeth, Iago and Volpone, and above all Edmund in King Lear, a genuine Machiavel, entirely secular, to whom pity, love and fear are irrelevant. A new individualism of the Renaissance also stares out of portraits, for instance from the self-portrait in the National Gallery, in London, of the wild Salvator Rosa, 1615–1763. It persists in romantic portraits, *e.g.* of the poet in his dreamy rôle, like the portrait of Wordsworth by H. W. Pickersgill.

The deepening of the religious sense in the Reformation tended to strengthen that individualism which went so well with capitalist enterprise; Man's relations with God could be achieved without the mediation of priests or good works, and it was by the inner light of grace (the 'dark lanthorn of the spirit') that men like Cromwell acted. When the religious wars subsided and a stabler, more sophisticated society emerged, the individual resumed for a while his classical rôle of embodying the attitudes of his group – in the eighteenth century one survived like a Lord Chesterfield or a Gibbon, or else went mad like a Cowper or a Blake.

Nevertheless Puritanism had left an ineradicable mark, so that when the Romantics again discovered the delights of the Self they did so with a strong moral bias, emphasizing the importance and general acceptability of their own psychological processes (Wordsworth and Coleridge) or bitterly criticizing a society which disapproved of them (Byron and Shelley). Wordsworth's *Prelude* (1805) is an enormous attempt to make egotism respectable; Jean-Jacques Rousseau's *Confessions*, which he began in 1765, had been an even longer one to give egotism truth and charm. Goethe declared that all his works were 'fragments of one great confession', and thus arose the idea of the individual artist as prophet, law-giver and seer.

Temperamental peculiarities were now sharpened by social and economic facts; the new industrial middle class, described by Matthew Arnold as philistines (q.v.), had little use for the artist or the man who found no fulfilment in commercial success and a somewhat hypocritical respectability; it was thus that egotism became isolation and artists retired to ivory towers (q.v.).

Preoccupation with the individual now extends from American manuals on 'How to be a real person' and 'How to gain friends and influence people' through the whole fabric of psychology and psycho-analysis to the metaphysical anxiety of theologians and philosophers. Nowadays it is the loneliness of man which claims most attention. An aspect of this loneliness, and of the desire to escape from it, can be seen in the quite extraordinary degree to which artist-thinkers, including Yeats, Rilke and D. H. Lawrence have created their own autonomous systems. Sartre the existentialist believes that it is only through the anguished realization of our loneliness and freedom that we may finally achieve an authentic existence.

ILLUSTRATION: Plate 2 and Page 267.

The one among the many

The **INDIVIDUAL VERSUS THE STATE** as a relationship is one of the main problems of political thought. Aristotle remarked that man is a political animal: he is born into society, utterly dependent on this medium. The state should therefore reflect and foster the best in individuals rather than debase them. It should be ultimately responsible to society as a whole. This can be achieved only through the maximum personal freedom compatible with the order necessary for a harmonious commonwealth.

In primitive times the problem is not acute. The majority are illiterate, with little sense of individuality. What Bagehot called 'the cake of custom' makes for cohesion; religion and taboo are expressed in social rites, and the centralized state has not yet developed. With the rise of civilization, government and war, new leaders, priests and administrators emerge. The old hereditary chieftain or king often becomes a mere mascot. Predatory exploitation, as well as constructive government, comes about. Individuals change and disrupt the fabric of society. Yet a united front of government and religion persists, as, for example, in the cities of Mesopotamia and Egypt. It was in the Greek cities that the problem of the individual and the state was first extensively discussed. Even here the original tribal solidarity persisted, while the moral responsibility of individuals and the need for them to participate in decisions were recognized. Their organic relationship to their native city is assumed and emphasized by both Plato and Aristotle. Plato, indeed, in his *Republic* and *Laws* sacrifices the individual to society so completely that he has been termed an arch-enemy of liberty. Religion is still not regarded by Aristotle as a private, unworldly, concern, but as the worship of the civic Gods and ancestral traditions.

After the conquests of Alexander and of Rome, the city-states of antiquity were swamped in a universal Empire; at the same time, the élite of this civilization had become deeply self-conscious. The old civic loyalties were no longer adequate, and new universal philosophies – Stoic and Epicurean – related the individual to a cosmic order in which he could participate by way of reason and self-discipline. He could either play his part nobly in public affairs, or, like Diogenes, attempt to withdraw from society. Before the coming of Christianity, the individual is already asserting himself against the State.

With the Christian revolution, the traditional union of religion and state power was further broken down. If the most important things in life are outside the province of the state, it becomes a necessary evil rather than the culmination of human endeavour. While patristic thought generally enforced obedience to the Empire, and Constantine was regarded as head of the Church and State – a tradition which continued through the Byzantine Emperors to the Russian Tsars – the breakdown of the Western Empire and the rise of the Papacy promoted the medieval conflict of Church and State. This conflict was later intensified by the Protestant assertion of individual conscience. It encouraged the modern conception of liberty. While the Christian ideal of commonwealth, both in Christendom and within the medieval realm, discouraged individualism, the power of the state in relation to society was diminished both by the appeal to the Church and the appeal to conscience. The appeal to conscience shaded into an appeal to anarchy among the extreme Protestant sects. The criticism of the state by conscience was reinforced by intellectual scepticism.

With the emergence of rationalists in the seventeenth century, the relation of the individual to the state was defined in novel, utilitarian terms. The medieval notion of social contract was employed to present the individual as one who bargained to surrender an original, fictitious, liberty in return for protection. Thomas Hobbes in *Leviathan* (1651) regarded the state of nature as 'nasty, brutish and short': the ruler was simply a policeman. If he failed to create security, allegiance could be transferred to someone who could. The individual is loyal to the state not through instinct or religion, but through fear and interest. This contractual view was further developed by the utilitarian philosophers, Bentham and Austin, who held that the state should clear the ground for the free play of a beneficent economic competition, and act simply as a night-watchman to protect property. The pendulum had swung from the extreme of primitive social solidarity to an extreme individualism.

With the Romantic movement, this utilitarian individualism was modified by a psychologically more normal view; Burke depicted individuals as 'born into society', part of an organic community extending over generations past and to come. Hegel created a romantic cult of the world-historic folk nation, of which the state was the supreme expression. He coined the term *totalitarian* for the whole tradition and environment of a people. The French philosophers, Saint-Simon and Comte, advocated an authoritarian, managerial society, inspired by a new religion. Comte, in the manner of Plato, wished to restore

the ancient unity of Church and State characteristic of antiquity. Marx predicted the abolition of
the state, and its absorption in a free communist
society. But he desired to achieve this through the
existing state by the dictatorship of the proletariat. He was, therefore, strongly criticized by the
anarchists, who had inherited in rationalist form
the old sectarian tradition.

Proudhon and Bakunin, individualists who
wished to by-pass the state altogether, believed
that the Marxist revolution would get no further
than the phase of dictatorship. This fear has been
realized in the totalitarian Russian state. Both
the Fascist totalitarian state, and the Russian
dictatorship identify the state with society. Both
revive the cult of the state characteristic of antiquity. Both attack individual freedom.

The alternative to this solution is not anarchy.
It is rather the control of state power through a
constitution. This ultimately depends upon the
general way of life of a free society. The most
effective advocate of this view was the English
philosopher T. H. Green, whose *Principles of Political Obligation* (1872) combined a dynamic, an
ordered and a moral view of society. The individual, he argued, should be free, under the law,
to participate in churches, trade unions, universities and other organizations independent of the
state, in which the best sense of the society is expressed. This vigorous influence can change the
climate of opinion which the flexible constitutional state is geared to reflect.

Green was unwilling to allow state interference with personal property, but his social-
democratic heirs believed that social justice could
only be secured through a redistribution of property by the state. How far this policy should go
is one of the principal aspects of the problem of
the individual and the state today. Meanwhile,
they are unlikely to be reconciled by a return to a
primitive totalitarianism, or by an assertion of
individualist anarchy. Liberty is best secured by a
constitutional state responsive to the will of a
vigorous institutional and personal life within its
frame.

This freedom is precarious unless the establishment of the rule of law in the outer world prevents the constitutional state, forced to follow
the totalitarian example, from becoming the
garrison state and so stultifying itself by inter-

ference with the personal freedom on which its
vitality depends. The individual who desires personal liberty cannot be merely a member of a
nation-state: he must be a citizen of the world.

The inferiority complex

INFERIORITY COMPLEX, a term much
thrown about in common speech, was invented
by the psychologist Alfred Adler (1870–1937),
who began his career as a disciple of Freud, but
soon began to doubt whether Freud was right to
find in repressed sexual desire the paramount
cause of neurosis.

In 1912 he ceased to work with Freud, and
started a new school of what he called 'Individual
Psychology'. 'Individuals', he wrote, 'do not
form their unconscious memories all round the
same central motive – sexuality, for instance.'
Each individual, he believed, has a different need,
an inferiority for which he seeks compensation.
'The method of Individual Psychology begins and
ends with the problem of inferiority.'

In Adler's teaching there is a distinction between the *inferiority complex*, which is an abnormality and the principal element of neurosis, and
the *feeling of inferiority*, which is present in everyone and is a normal reaction of the individual to
the inevitable difficulties of life.

Adler defines the inferiority complex as follows: 'The inferiority complex appears before a
problem for which an individual is not properly
adapted, or equipped, and expresses his conviction that he is unable to solve it.' According to
this view every neurotic has an inferiority complex. But one neurotic is distinguished from another by the kind of situation in which he feels
unable to continue to cope with life, by the limits
he has put to his striving and activities. The essential difference between the neurotic and the
'healthy individual' is to be found in the differing
ways in which they face the problems of life.
Both may feel inferior when faced with a difficult
task; but the healthy person will react 'realistically'; he will learn the appropriate means by
which the task may be accomplished, and his

initial feeling of inferiority will act as a spur urging him on towards success.

The neurotic, on the other hand, while needing success as a compensation for a feeling of inferiority, fears failure so much that he will seek to avoid facing the testing difficulties that must be overcome before it can be achieved. By evading the initial difficulty he makes it harder for himself to cope with similar future difficulties. The idea becomes fixed in his mind that he is incapable of doing so, and thus he has converted the original and natural feeling of inferiority into an inferiority complex.

The neurotic will be unable to bear his inferiority complex. He will still struggle to get rid of it. 'His goal is still to be superior to difficulties, but instead of overcoming them, he will try to hypnotize himself, or auto-intoxicate himself into *feeling* superior. Meanwhile his complex will intensify because the situation that produces it remains unaltered, the provocation is still there. Every step he takes will lead him further into self-deception, and all his problems will press in upon him with greater and greater urgency.' (Adler, *What Life Should Mean to You*, 1923).

A person with an inferiority complex, while still struggling for a feeling of adequacy, has at heart given up hope of overcoming the difficulties that face him. If a situation makes him feel weak, he escapes, and tries to find one that he can dominate. If, for example, he cannot hold down a job, he may attempt to reassure himself by being a tyrant to his wife and children. If he feels inadequate socially, he may try to stifle the feeling by boasting. But the inferiority complex will remain, and be 'the lasting undercurrent of his psychic life'.

Inferiority feelings (in contrast to the inferiority complex) are not, Adler held, in themselves abnormal, but are in fact a sound and realistic appreciation of man's place in the universe. 'It is because the individual man is inferior and weak that we find him living in society. It is the aim of psychology to train people to live well with others in order to help decrease the effect of this natural weakness. The history of social progress tells the story of how men co-operated in order to overcome deficiencies. Therefore we must look at the whole social context of the facts we study. We must look at the environment to understand the particular goal of superiority an individual chooses in order to compensate for his feeling of inferiority.'

Adler held that these feelings of inferiority and the attempt to overcome them are 'the canon of all the improvements in the position of mankind. Science itself can arise only when people feel their ignorance: it is the result of the striving of human beings to improve their whole situation, to know more of the universe and to be able to control it better. Indeed it seems to me that all our human culture is based upon feelings of inferiority.'

Feelings of inferiority are only harmful, Adler found, when they develop into an inferiority complex. Organic inferiority, or being so dominated when a child as to be made to feel inferior through loss of independence, or being hated and judged to be of no use in the world, determines a definite pattern of behaviour. This pattern is the reaction against handicap. The sense of handicap results in dependence, and the consequent fear common in any environment in which a person has never learned to fend for himself. This sense of incompletion makes the patient seek compensation, a 'goal of superiority' which, since he cannot really believe in himself, he is unable to achieve. This is the state of affairs out of which the inferiority complex develops.

Personal inheritance

INHERITANCE gives man the power to direct the destination of his property after death, and although it is perhaps difficult to envisage a time when he had not this power, it is of comparatively modern origin, like the right of property itself which with it, jurists of the seventeenth century went so far as to say, was founded on Natural Law.

Among the primitive tribes all property was regarded as belonging, not to individuals, but to the family or group, though it was subject to the full control of the chieftain. No questions of succession therefore would arise except on the death of the head of the family, whose successor would acquire the right to administer the family property simply as incidental to his chieftainship. Isaac's mistaken blessing of Jacob, instead of his elder son Esau, amounted not so much to a will as to a nomination of Jacob as his successor.

The rules governing the devolution of the chieftainship seem to have had certain common characteristics in most tribes, which reappear in many later codes of intestate succession. Generally males were preferred to females, descent was traced through the male line, and the first-born son was preferred, though in some nomadic tribes, where the elders would have scattered, the youngest son succeeded. Patriarchs, however, probably had the right to exercise some choice in the matter. Jacob, for instance, disowned his eldest son, Reuben, and of his grandsons 'set Ephraim before Manasseh'.

When in the course of time recognition was given to some individual rights of property, various rough rules of intestate succession evolved and at least movable property descended to more than one person. But in no event would men have considered disinheriting their families. The solidarity of the group was regarded as all-important. For this reason under many systems land would descend intact to the first-born, and Moses commanded the daughters of Zelophehad to marry only into their fathers' tribe, 'so shall not the inheritance of the family remove from tribe to tribe'.

A community would sense the need for a right to dispose of property by will only when the rules governing intestate succession came to be regarded as unsatisfactory, because they did not ensure that all of a man's near kindred would be provided for adequately. The concept of the will as a weapon of disinherison was a far later development; and it is significant that the earliest form of Roman will and one of the earliest known to history, *testamentum calatis comitiis*, was a public process sanctioned by a legislative act of the assembled people.

During the succeeding centuries new forms of will were evolved; intestacy came to be dreaded by the Romans, who could wish no worse fate to their enemies than to die without a will. A problem soon presented itself, which confronts the framers of all systems allowing free testamentary disposition. The will-making power, which is designed to strengthen and preserve the family, comes to be misused, so that dependants are disinherited. Counter-measures then have to be taken. In Rome these took the form of intervention by the Praetor, who introduced the concept of *Legitima Portio*, a part of his estate which a testator has not power to alienate to the exclusion of persons entitled on his intestacy.

This concept finds its place in almost all codes which owe their origin to the Roman Law. In Scotland, for instance, a man who dies leaving a widow and children can dispose of only one third of his movable property ('the dead's part'), one third will go to his widow as '*jus relictae*' and another to his children as 'legitim'. Similar customs prevail in France and Germany and in many parts of the U.S.A. In New York, for example, a surviving spouse and certain other relatives may elect to take either under the will or as on intestacy.

English laws of inheritance have followed this general pattern, but, in spite of a recent reaction, there is still unusual freedom of testation. Until the sixteenth century the Englishman's right to make a will at law was limited to chattels, and even this was subject to a doctrine of 'legitim', which was rigidly applied by the Ecclesiastical Courts. Land devolved automatically on the eldest son as heir, though local customs prevailed in some districts under which land devolved on all the sons of the deceased in equal shares ('gavelkind'), or even on the youngest son ('borough English'). Such customs were exceptional, however, and the doctrine of heirship was one of obvious expediency in feudal times, since it made for strong local government in the absence of central authority, and facilitated the collection by the lord of feudal dues. It was finally abolished in England only in 1925, since when, on a man's intestacy, his land and chattels have devolved in exactly the same manner, and primogeniture has conferred no advantage whatsoever.

The Statute of Wills 1540 enabled Englishmen effectively to devise their land as well as their personality, and the gradual decay of 'legitim' left testators completely free to disregard family claims, save for a limited right of 'dower' in favour of the widow, which could be defeated by various conveyancing devices. This almost absolute power conformed with the individualism which has characterized the last four centuries, but some protection for dependants came to be thought necessary. Accordingly the Inheritance (Family Provision) Acts of 1938, amended by an Act of 1952, gives some remedy to dependants for whom testators have made inadequate provision. Such persons may apply to the Court for provision out of the estate up to certain specified limits, the Court being given a wide measure of discretion.

The position in England is still very different from that in countries where a doctrine of legitim appertains. Widows and children have no right whatever to be left any fixed ascertainable part of the testator's estate. The new statutes merely enable the Courts to intervene in extreme cases. There is no set limit to 'the dead's part'. Furthermore, the right, which still exists, to 'cut off with a penny' adult children who are under no disability, gives the elder generation a larger measure of power in the family than it enjoys in most Continental countries or in the United States.

The extent to which citizens of any state are to be given freedom of testation must depend largely on the prevailing ideas of property. Does man have an absolute right not only to enjoy his possessions as he chooses during his lifetime, but also to control their enjoyment from his grave? Is he by contrast to be regarded as a trustee for his family with a mere right of user during his life? Or does he hold his possessions as a mere trustee for the community at large?

No system can follow the first of these theories without some reservations in the interests of public policy. Even in preceding centuries English courts would never enforce conditions which offended against law or morality, and the so-called Perpetuity Rule further limits the periods of time for which testators may direct their property to be kept in settlement.

Complete adherence to the second of the three theories has proved equally unsatisfactory. Under Mohammedan law no wills were allowed and there was no primogeniture; wives took a seventh of the landed estates, sons took in equal shares and daughters took equal half shares. The ensuing endless partition of the land was to make it almost inalienable, with disastrous economic effects in countries such as Egypt, Iraq and the Sudan.

Somehow the law must find the happy mean among the three theories. The most striking recent development in ideas of inheritance has been the employment of Estate Duty not merely as a means of raising revenue but as a deliberate method of minimizing inherited wealth. Perhaps the present trend, at least in this country, may go back to those days when property automatically reverted to the community on death.

Systems which allow inheritance by individuals must always be open to criticism because they allow persons to reap where they have not sown. Yet even the Soviet Union allows individual inheritance, which is unlimited in amount, because it recognizes that widows and dependants must be provided for and incentives must be offered to men to sow for posterity. The critics of personal inheritance must seek comfort in the reflection that 'The fool inherits but the wise must get'.

The breath in the man

INSPIRATION is the possession of human intelligence by an external spirit or god whose breath uses it as a vehicle for authoritative speech or poetry.

As a religious notion it is of far greater antiquity than tongues of fire at Pentecost.

The Hebrew prophets from Moses onwards are represented as human beings in direct contact with the deity, who used them for the expression of his laws. Inspiration could also take the form of being chosen to perform certain acts: Noah to build his Ark, Solomon to build a temple, Joseph to flee into Egypt. But those who were so possessed did not always have authority invested in themselves, and one of the main functions of the priesthood in all primitive religions was to interpret, and either accept or condemn, the revelations of the inspired.

Not only Christianity, but also Jewry, Hinduism, Islam and Zoroastrianism lay claim to base their teachings on directly 'inspired' books. Of religions that are still active today, only Buddhism and Confucianism appear to be exceptions in this respect.

Greek and other mythologies give numerous instances of possession and inspiration – for instance the Delphic Oracle speaking by the Pythia, the priestess of Apollo, and the orgies by which worshippers made spiritual contact with Dionysos.

Properly speaking, 'inspired' religious works are books written by human beings at the dictation of a god, so that 'God is truly the author of the book produced'. This does not mean that the writer sees God or knows truly that God is dictating to him. The 'inner voices' of Joan of Arc, which in comparatively recent times show the old principle at work, were not recognized by the Church as being authentic until her canonization in the twentieth century.

Ever since the Reformation there has been a growing tendency in higher criticism (seen in Voltaire's *Philosophical Dictionary* and the work of Renan) for laymen to apply the apparatus of archaeological and historical methods to inspired works, with an increasing scepticism of their authenticity. Among other sections of the lay community this has been offset to some extent by the growth and popularity of 'Spiritualism' in which lay 'mediums' continue the pagan tradition of the Greek and Egyptian Oracles. However, there is a vast difference between superstition of this kind, and the claims to inspiration of such religions as Christianity and Jewry, which have not only a trained priesthood but also a high moral and spiritual teaching behind them.

It is only a step from the idea of inspired prophets and scriptures, to the notion that men may be vehicles of inspiration in other ways. Thus the *Ion* of Plato is concerned with the inspiration of a mere actor or rhapsodist who was a famous interpreter of the *Iliad*. Socrates, in this dialogue, carefully distinguished Inspiration from both knowledge and art, and he declared that 'the authors of those great poems which we admire, do not attain to excellence through the rules of any art, but they utter their beautiful melodies in a state of inspiration, and, as it were, possessed by a spirit not their own'.

This shows at the same time a degeneration of the concept of inspired religion and a tendency (which still persists) to identify poetry with religious ritual and beliefs.

This Platonic theory of poetic inspiration has, since the Middle Ages, been part of the stock-in-trade of poets in Western Europe. Chaucer's invocation in *The House of Fame* is addressed to Apollo and evokes the Muse Calliope. If Chaucer's address has the charm of ingenuousness, by the time we reach the Elizabethans and, worse still, the inflated pretensions of even the best Augustans, the imploration of the Muses has become a tedious convention. In the Christian society it could not be expected that the inspiration of the pagan Muses could be taken seriously either by poets or by their public.

Since then, there have been powerful attempts to reinstate poetry in terms of inspiration. Shelley insisted that 'poetry is indeed something divine. It is at once the centre and circumference of all knowledge; it is that which comprehends all science, and that to which all science must be referred.' But the disadvantage of the inspirational theory is, clearly, that it reduces the power of the artist over his own mind, his own skill; and though Shelley's wonderful description of the imagination as a fading coal and his view that when a poet begins to write 'inspiration has almost ceased' is echoed in Collingwood's theory that the true work of art is not the finished product, but the *idea* in the poet's mind before composition, this almost mystical view appears as an affront to intellect. Shelley and his followers (such as Yeats, or the Abbé Bremond in his *Prière et Poésie*) were fighting a losing battle in the minds of an enlightened public.

Coleridge was on better ground in attempting to give a rational account of imagination; so was Wordsworth in his attempt to create a clearly defined type of poetry by an act of will. The breaking-point of the inspirational theory, in literature, may be taken as Edgar Allan Poe's essay *The Philosophy of Composition*, in which he showed or pretended to show how his poem *The Raven* had been composed deliberately according to conscious principles. In our own time T. S. Eliot and Paul Valéry have opposed to Inspiration what might be called a theory of crystallization; and this seems to be borne out fully by Livingstone Lowes' remarkable analysis of the creative process in *The Road to Xanadu* (1930), his study of Coleridge.

The poetic process still remains to a great extent mysterious, and though the psychologies of

Freud and Jung have thrown light on the less conscious parts of it, the term Inspiration is still used to describe the elements which remain obscure. Yeats's poem *The Cap and Bells* was written as a result of a dream, and though its symbolism is patently sexual, its total strangeness is such that the most sceptical reader will not refuse Yeats's comment that 'the authors are in eternity'. Perhaps the most significant recent use of the term was that of the French poet, Paul Eluard: 'The poet is he who inspires others, rather than he who is inspired.'

ILLUSTRATION: Plate 4 and Page 263.

'*Instinctively*'

INSTINCT was used as a convenient umbrella to cover all forms of behaviour which were neither explicable responses nor the result of the conscious exercise of intelligence. For this reason the word is disliked and mistrusted by many biologists.

One large group of actions, commonly but incorrectly described as instinctive, is the result of simple reflex responses of the same general kind as the well-known reflex jerk of the knee. The essence of a reflex response is the sequence of (1) sensory perception (not necessarily unconscious), (2) nervous conduction from sensory to effector units, (3) effector responses. In the study of the lower animals it has been found convenient to divide reflex responses into two main groups. Does the response to the stimulus consist in an increase or decrease of activity? Or is it directional? Responses by increase or decrease of activity, described as *Kineses*, are exemplified by the behaviour of woodlice when placed in dry surroundings. The response of the woodlouse is to walk. The stimulus of dryness is removed if the woodlouse by this means enters moist surroundings, and it therefore ceases to walk. To describe this behaviour as the result of 'an instinctive liking for moisture' would not only convey less information, but would in fact be misleading. The common accompaniment of increased activity of movement by an increased frequency of changes

of direction does, however, produce a very good imitation of searching behaviour.

The directional group of responses are known as *taxes*, positive or negative according to whether the direction of movement is towards or away from the stimulus. Thus phototaxis denotes response to light, geotaxis to gravity (literally, to the earth), chemotaxis to a chemical stimulus and rheotaxis to a flowing medium, especially to a stream in the case of river-living fishes. In this way a very large proportion of the behavioural responses of the lower animals have been explained.

In man, 'instinctive' is used often as if synonymous with 'automatic' or 'unthinking', although the responses so described may be the result of movement patterns not natural to the species (for example, that of a 'smash' in tennis or taking a catch in the slips at cricket), or of complicated responses to stimuli which cannot even be recognized, though they are based clearly on past experience. A motorist, driving on a winding road between high stone walls, may assert, for example, that he knew 'by instinct' that a car was about to meet him round the next corner, and that in consequence he had applied his brakes and pulled in to the left. More probably his attention was attracted by some movement of reflected light, not consciously perceived, which first entered his consciousness as 'car approaching'.

In insects and birds especially there still remain a large group of complicated sequences of behaviour which show particular characteristics: that they cannot have been learnt; that having been once begun they are usually carried to completion; and that the function which they serve must be unknown to the animal, so that they cannot be explained as the result of conscious intelligence, even if this were otherwise plausible.

Such behaviour is correctly described as 'instinctive', although 'innate behaviour' is used in preference by an important school of workers. Many examples are connected with mating or reproductive behaviour. This is presumably because successful reproduction is of such predominant importance to the survival of the species that there is a strong and direct selection in favour of any adaptation making for it. But to say this affords no explanation of the physiological basis of the 'drive' which produces its full effects in the adult, without a prior opportunity for development or 'rehearsal'; in some cases (*e.g.* some nesting birds) it is known all the same that performance is improved by experience. It can be supposed only that, after the initial stimulus, almost certainly hormonal or external or a combination of both, each subsequent stage of conduct serves in some way to 'trigger' the next.

Some of the most convincing examples are afforded by solitary bees or wasps which deposit their eggs in elaborately constructed nests, which are stocked with food for the larvae, and finally sealed. The female which exhibits this behaviour cannot have learnt it from the previous generation, which is already dead. Neither can the requirements of the larvae be supposed to have been appreciated. Nor can differences between one species and another, for example in nest construction, be explained otherwise than by a behaviour-sequence the potentiality for which is inherited. On the other hand, the fact that fertilization precedes nest-building provides a fairly clear indication of the hormonal drive by which the sequence is initiated.

Why biologists so dislike the word 'instinct' will now be apparent. They apply it reluctantly, if at all, to a residue of complex sequences of behaviour not to be explained as reflex responses or as acts of conscious intelligence.

The veil of iron

IRON CURTAIN as a phrase was first used by Winston Churchill as Leader of the Opposition in the House of Commons speaking in a foreign affairs debate shortly after the Potsdam Conference in 1945.

He described the difficulty of obtaining any reliable information about what was happening in Eastern Europe because of the 'iron curtain' which had divided the Continent. He used the phrase again a few months later in 1946 in his speech at Fulton, Missouri, when, with the President of the United States in his audience, he urged Anglo-American solidarity against the new danger arising from Soviet domination of Eastern

Europe. Since that time the term has been in common use to indicate the separation of the states of the Soviet *bloc* from the rest of the world, and the phrase 'Iron Curtain countries' has become synonymous with territories under Communist rule.

The significance of the term lies not in the difference of social order distinguishing Communist-governed countries from others, but in the extreme secretiveness characteristic of Communist régimes. This, in turn, is primarily due to the enormous importance attributed to propaganda in Communist politics. The Bolsheviks came to power in Russia at a time when modern methods of mass propaganda were being developed in the wake of large-scale commercial advertising, and they believed that by use of the new techniques the masses of the Russian people could be led wherever the party-state wanted them to go.

For this purpose it was necessary not only that they should be convinced of the truth of the principles on which the régime was based, but also that they should accept whatever version of particular facts and current news the leaders thought it good for them to believe; it followed that nobody must be permitted to find out or report any information not in accord with the official handout. As far as internal publicity was concerned, this end could be attained by party control of press, radio, films and public meetings and by making it dangerous to contradict the government propaganda even in private conversation. But the propaganda was directed to other countries as well, and it was desired particularly to project for Western nations a picture of Russia under the new régime which would seem to be highly attractive in liberal or democratic socialist terms.

This aim clashed with the claims of international freedom of the press whereby foreign correspondents of newspapers were entitled to travel about freely and report without censorship from the countries to which they were appointed. To prevent reporting of facts which they did not wish to be known, the Communist authorities in Russia tended more and more to obstruct the gathering of information by foreign journalists, partly by restricting their freedom of travel and partly by a system of police observation which made Soviet citizens afraid to talk freely to them. Residence of other foreigners was also closely restricted, and tourist travel was virtually confined to trips of carefully conducted parties to selected show places.

It thus became extremely difficult to find out what was going on in the Soviet Union – the Ukraine famine of 1933 was at the time successfully concealed from the outside world – or what its people were thinking; it is this state of affairs which was extended from the Soviet Union itself to territories under Soviet military occupation and control in Eastern and Central Europe from 1944 onwards.

Apart from the purpose of sustaining the officially projected picture of society under the new régime, and preventing leakage of any information contrary to it, the Communist states have also habitually taken measures much more rigorous than those normally employed by governments to conceal facts which might be useful to an enemy power in time of war. The concept of espionage was extended to cover not only armaments, fortifications and military plans, but also the location and capacity of industries, the building of roads, railways and airfields and even detailed geographical features, all of which must be hidden from potential foes in case a tactical local advantage should be lost.

Thus during the last war, whereas the German army possessed the most minute survey maps of Britain which could be freely purchased from shops, they were hampered in their invasion of Russia by an almost complete lack of reliable maps. To this extent the Soviet secretiveness certainly brought advantage in time of war, but if other countries did not have such advantages, it was mainly because they were unwilling to restrict the movements of visiting foreigners to such an extent.

In addition to the aim of concealing from foreigners facts which might be used politically to the detriment of the government or strategically to the harm of the state in time of war, the policy of the Iron Curtain serves also to insulate a population under Communist control from the contaminating influence of the non-Communist world. Only persons specially screened and certified as reliable are permitted to go abroad or have close contacts with foreigners; the mass of the people must be carefully safeguarded from an infection which it might not be able to withstand. By reducing contact with foreigners to a minimum a government can ensure that there is very little check on its claim that those who live under its rule are better off in every way than the inhabitants of other countries. The trouble taken to prevent harmful foreign influences reaching Communist-ruled peoples – including strict censorship of literature and films and jamming of broadcasts – indicates an extreme lack of confidence in genuine popular support for these régimes, in spite of the assertions that they have their peoples solidly behind them.

On the other hand, the Communist states do not hesitate on their side to make full use of democratic political liberties to carry on propaganda in capitalist countries; thus advertisements in Britain for the Soviet English-language magazine *News* exhorted the public to read in it 'the other fellow's point of view'.

The 'Curtain' has indeed interposed a barrier to intercourse and cultural contact between two great sections of mankind in an age when air, sea, road and rail transport and radio telecommunications have technically brought human beings all over the world closer together than ever before in history. The curtain is one of 'iron' because it is kept in position by force. But historical experience suggests that curiosity – the desire in a secluded country to know what is going on in the world outside – may gradually become a political factor strong enough to compel rulers to raise the curtain, even if only slightly at first.

Another factor may be the world-wide pressure, of which the peoples behind the Curtain cannot be kept entirely ignorant, for a prohibition of atomic weapons combined with effective inspection to ensure observance of any agreement which is made. Inspection, involving the right of neutral inspectors to go anywhere, is incompatible with a system barring foreigners from large areas of a nation's territory or preventing them from having direct contact with the local population, unless under supervision.

The problem of 'the Bomb' is thus closely related to the problem of 'the Curtain', and if a solution can be found to either, it may be one which applies to both together.

ILLUSTRATION: Page 122.

The ivory tower

The **IVORY TOWER** is where an artist is supposed to live and work, and insulate himself against the problems of ordinary life.

To the Marxist critic, James Joyce inhabited an ivory tower, despite his realistic subject-matter, because he was concerned with style and language (formalism) and had little interest in politics. Others, who are not Marxists but simply robust and commonsensical in their outlook, apply the phrase to writers whose intellectual power expresses itself in subtle analysis and psychological penetration. H. G. Wells suggested that Henry James's magnificent but circuitous style resembled not an ivory tower, it is true, but a vast cathedral on whose altar reposed nothing more significant than a dead kitten and a piece of string; 'Ivory Tower' has been applied to the habitat of Marcel Proust, to the cork-lined room in which he embroidered his delicate reveries, through clouds of friar's balsam. But to do this is to forget Proust's intense moralism and the comic genius of his social satire. The phrase Ivory Tower is not one of serious critical evaluation. It can be used very loosely ... and, of course, is so used.

Tennyson was aware of the potential gap between artist and society in his poem, the *Palace of Art*. The result is romantic and confused. He constructs not merely an ivory tower but a whole ivory St Pancras Station. In a setting of mountain scenery, owing much to Wordsworth and Shelley, he imagines a vast edifice in which the poet's soul protected by clouds of incense flung from the peaks and by a rainbow formed from the mist of several waterfalls, rejoices in its separation from society as it wanders through halls decorated to suit its every mood. The heroes of Art and History are represented in paintings and in stained glass. Singing to itself, the poetic soul no longer cares whether the earth is at peace or war, or what theological conflicts may be afoot, for it is secure in its sense of moral superiority and can give itself up to a God-like contemplation of the varying creeds of men.

> O God-like isolation which art mine,
> I can but count thee perfect gain,

> What time I watch the darkening droves of swine
> That range on yonder plain.

However, after three years of this, there is an abrupt change, brought about by the Almighty Himself. God, who knows the 'abysmal deeps of Personality', assists the poet to a sharp but ultimately restorative nervous breakdown, first instanced by despair at his solitude, but continuing through a series of hallucinations worthy of Coleridge or de Quincey.

The soul finally deserts its ivory St Pancras for a simple 'cottage in the vale' where it may 'mourn and pray'.

This conclusion seems ambiguous, for the soul does not entirely reject the palace towers, which it admits to be lightly and beautifully built, but suggests that it will be able to inhabit them again only when it has purged its crime and can bring others with it.

From this point of view the ivory tower is an attitude of mind *distinct from* the successful art which it has created, and in which it has been embodied; the solution is to turn a privately owned palace into a community centre.

If Tennyson's allegory lacks exactness, his psychological picture of the modern artist is a good deal truer to life. No artist can produce an aesthetically satisfactory edifice in a state of real isolation, but he can *feel* isolated (often because of the isolation his contemporaries experience without being aware of it), he can reject the standards of those around him and then be guilty because he does so; his nervous excitability can lead to God-like pride or saintly humility, or simply acute depression.

The artist must have some isolation, he must be able to get far enough from his material to look at it, and he needs a certain practical screening-off in order to concentrate ... not for nothing did Rainer Maria Rilke have his Duino and Muzot, Yeats his tower of Thor Ballylee, Robinson Jeffers his Californian keep, Firbank his Eiffel Tower restaurant, and, one might add, James his mysterious backache; furthermore, the artist's temperament will estrange him from many of the superficial aspects of life; it is only when a later generation, capable of divining the main lines of development in a previous age, feels that an artist has ignored or misinterpreted all the challenges

Continued on p. 231

PLATE 8

SANCTITY: St Francis in Meditation by Zurbaran (1598–1664).

THE PHILOSOPHER'S STONE: The means of achieving it. The king (or gold, or conscious self);
the sun and moon look down slantwise at their opposites.

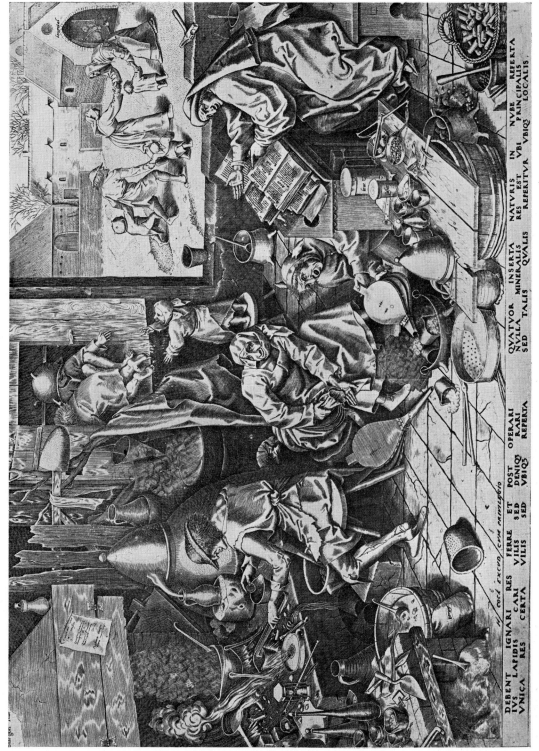

ELIXIR OF LIFE: *The Alchemist in his Laboratory.* Engraving after Pieter Bruegel (c. 1525–1569).

THE LAND OF COKAYGNE: Painting by Pieter Bruegel.

EXISTENTIALISM: Jean-Paul Sartre (b. 1905).

THE IDEA OF GOD: 1. Wayside Calvary in Switzerland.

2. Vågå Church, Norway.

'THE PURSUIT OF HAPPINESS': This phrase appears in The Declaration of Independence (4 July 1776).

AREOPAGITICA;

A

SPEECH

OF

Mr. JOHN MILTON

For the Liberty of UNLICENC'D PRINTING,

To the PARLAMENT of ENGLAND.

Τὸ λό θερον δ᾽ ἐκεῖνο, εἴ τις θέλει πόλι
Χρησόν τι βέλαμ᾽ εἰς μέσον φέρειν, ἔχων.
Καὶ ταῦθ᾽ ὁ χρῄζων, λαμπρὸς ἐσθ᾽, ὁ μὴ θέλων,
Σιγᾷ, τί τέτων ἐστιν ἰσαίτερον πόλι;

Euripid. Hicetid.

This is true Liberty when free born men
Having to advise the public may speak free,
Which he who can, and will, deserv's high praise,
Who neither can nor will, may hold his peace;
What can be juster in a State then this?

Euripid. Hicetid.

LONDON,
Printed in the Yeare, 1644.

FREEDOM OF THE PRESS: Title-page from the *Areopagitica* by John Milton, 1644.

THE HERRENVOLK: 1. Nazi soldiers in Germany.

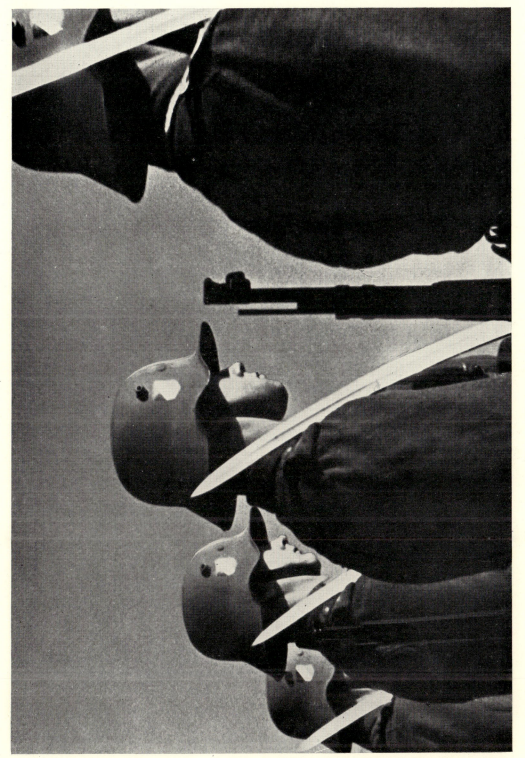

THE HERRENVOLK: 3. J. G. Herder (1744–1803) by Anton Gatt.

HUMANISM: Leone Baptista Alberti (1404–1473); architect, musician and painter.

FUNDAMENTALISM: Philip Henry Gosse (1810–1888), Fundamentalist and biologist, made famous in Edmund Gosse's *Father and Son*.

'MRS GRUNDY': *Portrait of a Londoner* by Gustave Doré (c. 1833–1883).

THE DEVIL: Painting by Andrea Orcagna (c. 1308–1368) from the Campo Santo, Pisa.

230

PLATE 9

NATURE: Cloudy Study by John Constable (1776–1837).

relevant to his sensibility, retreating when he could well have advanced, that the opprobrious phrase of Ivory Tower should perhaps be used.

ILLUSTRATION: Page 264.

L

The economic free-for-all

LAISSEZ-FAIRE, the doctrine that the state should not interfere with the natural workings of a nation's economy; that economic forces alone, working through private individuals, should shape economic welfare, died at the end of the nineteenth century and was buried in the twentieth.

Although old men may still speak of the funeral with regret, and we may admire the spirit which inspired the creed, it has ceased to have any meaning beyond the general one that one's economy should be as free from interference as possible. In our own day the freest economy would be judged an impossible tyranny by our laissez-faire ancestors. Indeed, we may now consider it remarkable that such a doctrine should ever have found a climate congenial enough in which to flourish; and we may regard the age of its triumph as an interlude between the long centuries of economic regulation.

The actual origin of the term is obscure; but it certainly may well go back to the story of the manufacturer and the French statesman Jean Baptiste Colbert (1619–1683) – that Colbert asked what the state might do to help industry, the merchant replying, 'Laissez-nous faire' – 'leave it to us'. The doctrine became widespread amongst writers on trade and economic theory in France (the Physiocrats) and in England in the eighteenth century, spreading from the mercantile community oppressed with close controls on overseas trading and domestic industry, to become in the nineteenth century a generally ac-

L

cepted creed. It began as part of a much wider and deep-rooted intellectual movement, the philosophical optimism of the Enlightenment. Men were rational beings; given adequate knowledge they would do the right thing, and by each individual trying to gain his own particular ends, through a 'natural harmony' in the nature of things, the good of all would result.

Although not the first, the greatest of the philosophers of natural harmony – which is the philosophy of laissez-faire, and of economic individualism – was Adam Smith (1723–1790). His book, *An Inquiry into the Nature and Causes of the Wealth of Nations* (1776) was written in the confidence that this natural harmony exists. In particular he wrote against the mercantile system whereby the state regulated the economy, believing that this control made matters worse:

The statesman who should attempt to direct private people in what manner they ought to employ their capital would not only load himself with a most unnecessary attention, but assume an authority which could safely be trusted not only to no single person but to no council or senate whatsoever.

Instead, the profit-seeking individual, by adding to the wealth of the community, would benefit all, the greater his freedom the greater the benefit – and here is the positive optimism of the laissez-faire doctrine: The individual

generally neither intends to promote the public interest nor knows how much he is promoting it. He intends only his own security, and by directing that industry in such a manner as its produce may be of the greatest value, he intends only his own gain, and he is in this, as in many other cases, led by an invisible hand to promote an end which was no part of his intention.

In exactly this spirit the London merchants petitioned to Parliament in 1820 and some London citizens in 1818, that both trade and industry should be free. Unrestricted competition, they claimed, would bring about the most efficient deployment of the national resources, the best distribution of rewards and consumer choice, with stable prices at the lowest efficient level. Upon the assumption of a stable currency linked to the gold standard, this doctrine became accepted as a creed by the 'Manchester School' of economists in the England of Huskisson, Peel and

Gladstone, Cobden and Bright, McCulloch and John Stuart Mill (who introduced the term laissez-faire to England, in 1848 in his *Principles of Political Economy*). In the great Victorian boom after 1850, 'free enterprise' was less restricted by the state and private interests than ever before.

In normal times the state was to do little but act as a referee at home and the protector of national interests abroad, by providing policemen, a judicature, and a navy. (Even Adam Smith in the eighteenth century had defended the Navigation Laws which regulated shipping, on the grounds that security was a need which came before opulence.) Above all, the state was to defend the freedom and the sanctity of contract, whereby freely-choosing individuals freely contracted obligations to one another. Such an attitude meant that the state should not try to change institutions, or control their development, implying at best that the results of naturally working economic forces were all for the best, or at worst that interference would only intensify the evils.

Above all, laissez-faire was the creed of merchants prospering from international trade – particularly the carrying and entrepôt trade; and just as it was becoming the faith amongst the merchants, the state began to assume some control. It was plain to all that economic forces, while creating vast wealth from which all classes were to benefit, were causing new social problems, above all the problems of work in factories and life in industrial towns. Where there was no equality of bargaining power, freedom of contract could be abused, so the state, under pressure, began to enforce action against these abuses. After the first Factory Act, in 1833, to control child labour, the nineteenth century saw the state slowly widening its claims to enforce minimum standards of safety, health and education upon the community, limiting hours of work and the exploitation of labour – fencing in that freedom of contract which was the citadel of laissez-faire.

Where natural forces did not produce them, the state was to legislate for these minimum standards of satisfaction; today in the Welfare State, the public watchdog stands on guard against want, fear, unemployment and exploitation; and to that degree the doctrine of laissez-faire has been abandoned.

At no time, of course, did laissez-faire provide a complete formula for state policy (if absolute, it would mean absence of government, or anarchy), but it expresses a conviction that the 'minimum' state, concerning itself only with security, was also the best for the wealth and happiness of its citizens. The demand came at a time when the growing giant of trade and capitalism was flexing his muscles against restriction; and without doubt the economic freedom and individual initiative inspired by laissez-faire greatly stimulated the national wealth, and despite the evils of industrial towns, laissez-faire did raise the standard of living for all, as travellers to England were quick to point out, and as countries not fortunate enough to have suffered an early industrial revolution now realize.

New domestic problems and external difficulties came in the twentieth century. The state had intervened extensively already in the social and economic relations of employers and workers, and was laying the foundations of national insurance schemes. Capitalism, when left to itself, now seemed to bring recurrent and deepening crises, when mass unemployment forced the state to try to curb fluctuations by giving work, regulating investment, the banking system, and public demand, and by helping some industries which could no longer help themselves entirely. Perfect competition, with its protection to the consumer if not to the worker, was also breaking down where individual concerns were getting large enough to dominate the market.

Much more important, two world wars broke in pieces that international equilibrium based on free trade and stable currencies, creating such disparities of wealth and wants amongst the nations that the paupers in the international community had to control their flows of goods and money. If this was the heritage of war and nationalism, wartime conditions themselves forced states to run their economies to direct all energies towards the national survival; such controls postwar conditions have tended to perpetuate. To return to the minimum state of 1850 in the conditions of 1950 would cause bankruptcy and disaster.

This means that laissez-faire is dead – the conditions which encouraged its birth and favoured its growth having passed away. Yet though the claims of laissez-faire have to be restricted, and though the minimum rôle of the state in the economy has of necessity to be much greater than before, that does not make either the corporative state or complete socialism the inevitable alternatives. Economic and social conditions have made us guide the invisible hand of Adam Smith fairly firmly. It is another decision entirely whether we want to give it all the freedom possible, control it more strictly than we do, or amputate it altogether.

Dies irae, dies illa

The **LAST DAY** is the end of the world, as foretold both in Christian and non-Christian theology; when every human soul will be judged by God, and saved or condemned.

Practically all peoples, whether civilized or savage, have assumed that the world is bound to end some day. Some of them (*e.g.* the Mayas of Central America) have supposed that when this happens the world will simply be reborn, and a fresh cycle of human history will take place; and so on indefinitely. But it has been much more commonly believed that the world will end with some colossal disaster – sometimes with a last desperate battle between the forces of Good and Evil (as in Norse mythology); that the souls of the dead will then be judged; and that Time will then pass away, and give place to Eternity.

The teaching of Christ, in the Gospels, is that the Last Day will be the time of His reappearance on earth, to judge all mankind. It will be heralded, first by calamities in the world itself, and then by the shattering of the world from outside. 'Nation will rise in arms against nation, and kingdom against kingdom; there will be great earthquakes in this region or that, and plagues and famines; and sights of terror, and great portents from heaven' (Luke xxi. 10, 11). Then 'The sun and the moon and the stars will give portents, and on earth the nations will be in distress, bewildered by the roaring of the sea and of its waves; men's hearts will be dried up with fear, as they await the troubles that are overtaking the whole world; the very powers of heaven will rock' (Luke xxi. 25, 26). 'They will see the Son of Man coming upon the clouds of heaven, with great power and glory; and he will send out his angels with a loud blast of the trumpet, to gather his elect from the four winds, from one end of Heaven to the other' (Matthew xxiv. 29).

With the Second Coming of Christ, the dead will rise again and be brought to judgment. 'God ... has fixed a day when he will pronounce just judgment on the whole world' (Acts xvii. 31). The judgment will be carried out by Christ Himself, with the Apostles enthroned beside Him: 'I promise you, in the new birth, when the Son of Man sits on the throne of his glory, you also shall sit there on twelve thrones, you who have followed me, and shall be judges over the twelve tribes of Israel' (Matthew xix. 28).

Here was a splendid and awful and instructive subject for the medieval painter, and the maker of stained glass; and, later on, for the superb poetic and pseudo-scientific prose of Thomas Burnet (c. 1635–1715) and for cosmic canvases by wild romantics including Francis Danby (1793–1861) and John Martin (1789–1854). 'Here,' wrote Burnet, in an apostrophe of magnificence,

here stood the Alps, a prodigious range of stone, the load of the earth, that covered many countries and reached their arms from the ocean to the Black Sea; this huge mass of stone is softened and dissolved, as a tender cloud, into rain. Here stood the African mountains, and Atlas with his top above the clouds. There was frozen Caucasus, and Taurus, and Imaus, and the mountains of Asia. And yonder, towards the north, stood the Riphaean Hills, clothed in ice and snow. All these are vanished, dropped away as the snow upon their heads, and swallowed up in a Red Sea of Fire, (Rev. xv. 3). *Great and marvellous are thy works, Lord God Almighty; just and true are thy ways, thou King of Saints.* Hallelujah.

Christ made it clear that all his followers were to live in constant readiness for the Day of Judgement, but that no one knew the time when it would come. However, certain of his prophecies seemed to suggest that the time might be close at hand. As a result, for centuries many Christians were certain that the Second Coming was imminent; and every natural disaster that seemed to threaten civilization was taken as heralding its approach.

The *Revelation of St John the Divine* provided material for many detailed forecasts of the end of the world. William Miller (1782–1849), a Baptist contemporary of the painter John Martin, after exhaustive study, fixed the probable date for it as 1843; his followers founded a sect called the Adventists, which survived the failure of 1843 to live up to expectations, and subsequently split into a number of sects, disagreeing with each other on the next choice of a date. A number of Adventist groups are still in existence, of which the Seventh-Day Adventists are the best known. Most of these sects believe, according to *Revelation*, that the Second Coming of Christ will not be the occasion of the Last Judgement, but will precede it by a thousand years. During this period, the 'Millennium', Satan will be chained up, and Christ will reign on earth with his Saints; Satan will be released for a short time just before the end.

Forecasts of the Last Day continue to be made. Believers in British Israel maintain that the date of the end of the world can be learned by examination of the Great Pyramid; while Jehovah's Witnesses, a sect founded in America by C.T. Russell in the eighteen-seventies, assigned 1914 as the beginning of the end – a prophecy, made some thirty years earlier, which had something to recommend it. In general, those who assign an approaching date for the Last Day are not noticeably downcast when the year passes and the prophecy is unfulfilled; they amend the time to a date still in the future. Their followers, however, are sometimes seriously inconvenienced. An African tribe in the nineteenth century, persuaded that the Last Day was only a few months off, killed and ate all their cattle. When the world failed to end on the appointed day, they found themselves faced with starvation.

The Catholic belief on the subject of the Last Day is that it will undoubtedly come, but that, as Christ himself told us that we could not foretell its arrival until it was imminent, there is no sense in trying to guess the date. Catholics believe that the world will end in a general conflagration, in which all humanity will perish (conceivably this might happen as the result of some new type of bomb). All the dead will then rise again, and each of us will receive the judgement of Christ on his throne; a judgement that will not be private, like the judgement we receive at the moment of death, but known to all mankind. The judgement will take place in time. When it is over, time will cease to exist, and we shall find ourselves, either blessed or damned, in eternity.

Protestant theologians, other than those of the Adventist and similar groups, are not given to much discussion of the Last Day. Protestant opinion on the subject, even within the Church of England, is divided. Anglicans believe in the Resurrection – some, however, maintaining that only those destined for Heaven will be resurrected; but there is a general tendency to regard the Last Judgement as purely symbolic.

Jewish opinion has been different at different times. In the time of Christ, some believed in the Resurrection; the Sadducees, however, did not, and they were inclined to laugh at those who did. Their belief was that God would certainly appear on earth, after a time of terror and disaster; but it would be to establish an earthly kingdom, in which the dead would not share. Present-day Jewish belief, and in particular that of Reformed Judaism, is disinclined to accept the Resurrection.

The Moslem idea of the Last Day, on the other hand, bears a strong likeness to the Christian belief from which it is derived. Gabriel will blow the Last Trump; the earth will dissolve in convulsions; all those living will die on the second blast of the trumpet, and all the dead will rise again on the third. There will then be a general judgement; after which the souls of the faithful will cross into Paradise over a bridge as wide as the cutting edge of a sword, while the damned will fall off it into Hell.

ILLUSTRATION: Pages 274 and 275.

The law of the land

The **RULE OF LAW** is a phrase which indicates that the law of the land is supreme and that certain fundamental obligations are binding upon citizens dealing with each other.

This supremacy of the law in England has its origin particularly in the struggle between the Crown and Parliament as to who was to have the supreme power; the ascendancy gained by Parliament in 1689 finally established the principle that the law of the land as laid down by the legislature was the binding force, and abolished the arbitrary power which the Crown had been trying to exercise by means of the Court of Star Chamber and other devices.

The 'Rule of Law' acquired a special significance when Professor Dicey, one of the greatest English law professors, delivered a series of lectures in 1885 in which he set out three meanings that may be attached to the phrase.

These were approved by the Committee on Ministers' Powers Report in 1932. In the first place Rule of Law means the absolute supremacy or predominance of regular law as opposed to the influence of arbitrary power, and excludes the existence of arbitrariness or prerogative or even of wide discretionary powers on the part of the Government. Englishmen are ruled by the law, and by the law alone: a man may be punished for a breach of law, but he can be punished for nothing else.

The Rule of Law, again, means equality before the law or the equal subjection of all classes to the ordinary law of the land administered by the ordinary law courts: the Rule of Law in this sense excludes the idea of any exemption of officials or others from the duty of obedience to the law.

Thirdly and lastly the Rule of Law means that the law of the constitution (the rules which in other countries naturally form part of a constitutional code) is not the source but the consequence of the rights of individuals, as defined and enforced by the courts; in short, that the principles of private law have with us been by the actions of the courts and Parliament so extended as to determine the position of the Crown and of its servants; thus the constitution is the result of the ordinary law of the land.

Absence of arbitrariness implies that the law is comparatively certain and can be easily ascertained, and that the citizen will be punished only for a breach of the law as laid down by the legislature and not at the whim of some official. Judges, of course, exercise a discretion in the penalty they inflict; but it is a discretion which must be judicially exercised. They have no power to create an offence not known to the law.

A recent development in the opposite direction has been the introduction of delegated legislation, whereby a minister is given wide powers under an Act to make regulations, so creating a very large number of new offences not properly subject to parliamentary review. A good example was the creation of a large number of regulations under the Defence Regulations 1939; under regulation 18b the Home Secretary was empowered to detain anyone whom he had reasonable cause to believe came within a certain class of suspect. It was held by the House of Lords in Liversidge *v.* Anderson 1942 A.C. 206 that the courts had no power to investigate the grounds of the Minister's belief provided he had a belief which in his mind was reasonable. Many regulations are today delegated to ministers, and in this sense the Rule of Law does not have quite the same force as in 1880.

Officials are in the same position as the ordinary citizens and all are equal before the law, with a few exceptions, which include foreign diplomats and their staff, who can obtain exemption from the legal process, though generally this immunity is waived. Treaties may give foreigners resident in Great Britain the right to be tried by their own courts and exemption from process in English courts, an example of this being the position of the American forces under the Visiting Forces Act. Trade unions have certain exemptions; so do public authorities, against whom an action has to be started in a shorter time than against an individual. Judges have protection against actions for libel or slander in the exercise of their judicial function, but can be sued in the ordinary courts in the ordinary way for any other breach of the law.

There are some who are subject not only to the ordinary courts of law but also to their own professional bodies, who keep a strict control over them; they can be and often are punished for breaches of professional etiquette and behaviour as well as for actual breach of law. Among those subject to a double law in this way are doctors, solicitors, barristers, the clergy and trade unionists.

As for the third meaning attached to the Rule of Law – that private rights depend not on some constitutional rules but on the ordinary law of the land – this finds its expression in Acts of

Parliament and in the decisions of the courts which have gradually set up a body of principles in individual cases. Great Britain has no formal written constitution setting out the rights of the citizen. His personal freedom is protected by a remedy in the courts for its infringement (*i.e.* a writ for Habeas Corpus or an action for false imprisonment); his freedom of speech is unlimited, subject to the law of slander, blasphemy or treason.

ILLUSTRATION: Pages 270 and 271.

'Canst thou draw out leviathan with an hook?'

LEVIATHAN (he might as well have used the word Behemoth, for both occur within a few lines of each other in the Book of Job) was the symbol given to the state, as he saw it, by the philosopher Thomas Hobbes (1588–1679). His conception influenced the thought of his own time and of most subsequent philosophical historians. When his great work appeared, in the middle of 1651, its frontispiece was a landscape above which towered the body, from the waist up, of a crowned giant, holding a sword and crozier, and composed, rather horribly, of the figures of tiny human beings. Its full title was '*Leviathan, or the Matter, Form and Power of a Commonwealth, Ecclesiastical and Civil*'. It remains, in many respects, highly topical, though *Leviathan* was a product of its time: the Civil War.

Thomas Hobbes was born just outside Malmesbury, in Wiltshire, and we learn much of him from his contemporary John Aubrey (1626–1697), the antiquarian, who was born a few miles down the road, nearer to Chippenham. Hobbes's father was a clergyman, described by Aubrey as 'one of the Clergie of Queen Elizabeth's time – a little Learning went a great way with him and many other ignorant Sir Johns in those days; could only read the prayers of the Church and the homilies; and disesteemed Learning ... as not knowing the Sweetnes of it'. The father was involved in a brawl, and had to fly the country. The young Thomas was brought up by an

uncle who was a glove-maker, and he afterwards went to Oxford. The Principal of Magdalen Hall (now Hertford College) recommended him to the Cavendish family, who wanted a tutor, and he remained closely attached to them for the whole of his long life of ninety years, living for eighteen of them as a member of the family. He taught, played music and tennis, which he kept up till he was over seventy, sang ('when he was abed, and the dores made fast, and was sure nobody heard him ... not that he had a good voice, but for his health's Sake') and studied geometry. Later he applied the laws of gravity to morals and politics, the absorbing preoccupation of his time. He enjoyed also the acquaintanceship of Descartes and Galileo, and was for a time secretary to Francis Bacon, Lord Verulam (1561–1626). 'His Lordship', wrote Aubrey 'would often say that he better liked Mr Hobbes's taking his thoughts than any of the other, because he understood what he wrote.' He understood, but he did not slavishly follow, and was all the time working out his own theories. He wrote of them privately for his friends, and then, in Latin, in the political pamphlet *De Cive*. Finally (by this time in exile in Paris, where he had become tutor to the young Prince of Wales, who was to become Charles II) he started *Leviathan*. Aubrey tells us how it was written. 'He walked much and contemplated, and he had in the head of his Staffe a pen and ink-horne, carried always a Note-book in his pocket, and as soon as a notion darted, he presently entered it into his Booke, or els he should perhaps have lost it. He had drawne the designe of the book into chapters, and knew whereabouts it would come in. Thus that booke was made.'

Leviathan ranges over the whole relationship between God, the state and the individual. It is often suggested that its analysis owes everything to the political requirements of the time, and that Hobbes was merely the apologist of a party. It is hard to see that this can be true, seeing that the book made him suspect both to Royalists and Republicans. Confessing himself to be a cowardly man, Hobbes nevertheless expressed a view which, right or wrong in itself, required courage.

Machiavelli (1469–1527) had introduced the secular idea of man's relation to the state, and to an extent Hobbes followed this, and his ideas were held to be 'atheistic' as a result. Whilst he believed in a God above all other sovereignty, he did certainly say that 'it is with the mysteries of our religion, as with wholesome pills for the sick, which swallowed whole have the virtue to cure, but chewed over are for the most part cast up again without effect'. His approach was, in an age of intense theological controversy, essentially rationalistic.

Hobbes felt that the first need of society was order, and therefore a power armed with absolute authority for the enforcement of order – the great artificial man or master, Leviathan. The Reformation had partially destroyed the medieval idea of the state: a pattern of people working for God through his appointed rulers. Current events in the seventeenth century had destroyed the extension of this into the doctrine of the Divine Right of Kings (q.v.). Hobbes felt that the ruler had behind him the authority of God, but if he issued orders which were against the will of God, as laid down by law, he was clearly not acting as ruler and could be disobeyed. For Hobbes did not see, as had most philosophers since Aristotle, Society as natural to man; to him it was an artificial condition, entered into by a Social Contract.

Hobbes did not literally suppose that such a contract had ever been made and signed. But by the process of purely mechanical reasoning he investigated the theory that the authority of a king resided in a contract made between him and his people, that they would obey, and he would perform the duties of his office. If either party broke the contract, the other was absolved from fulfilling his own share. Hobbes felt that to the government, whatever its form, absolute obedience was due. This belief cynically included another, obviously convenient at the time: that if one government had been overthrown by another, the absolute loyalty of the individual citizen was automatically transferred to the new power. It could be cheaply summarized as belief that, for the subject, might in the sovereign (or other head of state) was right. Yet this would be an oversimplification.

Hobbes's philosophical timidity – put forward with intellectual boldness – lay in his belief that the primary object of the ordinary person and his supreme duty is to preserve his own life by perfect obedience to the state. Morality, he attempted to show, rests on statute law. The laws of nature were binding only when they were also the commands of the sovereign. Without control of this kind he felt that the result would be, in the best-known quotation from his work 'no Arts, no Letters, no Society; and which is worst of all, continuall feare, and danger of violent death; and the life of man, solitary, poore, nasty, brutish, and short'.

In his own day Hobbes's doctrines were rejected by all parties, and he was involved in controversy and sometimes danger until his death – although Charles II himself regarded 'the old bear' with his characteristically amiable tolerance. The Cavaliers, although he claimed to be on their side, would have none of him because they wanted their king to rule by Divine Right. The opponents of the monarchy did not believe ultimately in sovereignty. Others still believed in theological and not secular rule. Yet Hobbes's influence on the following generation was immense, and his theories of qualified absolutism still form part of the background of political theory. They have been quarried in many causes.

ILLUSTRATION: Page 277.

Three rights of man

LIBERTY, EQUALITY, AND FRATERNITY was the rallying-cry of the French Revolution, and it has become a watchword of all who rebel against despotism. These three words epitomize the hopes of everyone who attacks autocratic governments or privileged classes. The arguments for a revolution, or its manifesto, may make long and complicated reading; Liberty, Equality and Fraternity is a phrase every man can understand.

The idea underlying these words is that men are born with certain rights; when a state refuses to grant these natural rights, the citizens may claim them by force. This doctrine lay behind the Declaration of the Rights of Man, the document drawn up by the National Assembly in France in 1789. It set out the principles on which France was to be reformed and was the manifesto of the French Revolution.

Among the many clauses of this famous Declaration, two above all were calculated to attract and inspire men. The first states that 'men are born and remain free and equal in rights', and the second that 'the aim of every political association is the preservation of the natural and imprescriptible rights of man. These are liberty, property, security and resistance to oppression'. Liberty, Equality and Fraternity is thus an excellent popularization of the highlights of the Declaration.

The ideas which the Declaration expressed were not at all new; many eighteenth-century thinkers had attacked despotism in similar terms (though always at the risk of the censor). Denis Diderot (1713–1784) the editor of the *Encyclopédie*, believed that man had an indestructible right to political liberty; Jean-Jacques Rousseau (1712–1778), the author of the *Social Contract*, believed in the right to self-government. There was a widespread belief that every man was born with certain rights with which his very humanity endowed him.

It was the American colonists' revolt against England in 1776 which provided the first public proclamation of the rights of man. The Declaration of Independence states that 'we hold these truths to be self-evident: that all men are created equal; that they are endowed by their creator with certain inalienable rights; that among these are Life, Liberty and the Pursuit of Happiness'. Here were the ideas of liberty and equality that were to inspire Frenchmen to revolt four times in a hundred years, and were to stimulate revolutions all over Europe.

Many Frenchmen fought in the American War of Independence, coming back to Europe filled with the new ideas, and there is a possibility that the phrase Liberty, Equality and Fraternity was current before 1789. The first recorded use of the words was in 1793, when the revolutionary Cordeliers Club passed a resolution calling on all landlords to paint on their walls: 'Unité, indivisibilité de la Republique. Liberté, Egalité, Fraternité ou la mort!'

During the revolution every act of liberation, and many of destruction also, was done with the justification of these three words, so that Madame Roland could cry as she went to the guillotine in 1793, 'O Liberty, what crimes are committed in thy name'.

From the very beginning it was clear that liberty meant one thing to one man, and something quite different to another. If contemporaries could interpret liberty differently, the differences between the meanings of the idea with the passage of time must be greater still. Every generation and every society thinks in terms of its own needs when interpreting any of the three words. A list of the rights of man drawn up in the twentieth century might read very differently from one made in 1789, each would reflect those values held to be essential at the time, especially those that were thought to be in danger.

When the phrase Liberty, Equality and Fraternity was first used, liberty was thought of as freedom from oppression. As the Declaration of Rights put it: 'Liberty consists in being allowed to do whatever does not injure other people.' This meant not only political and religious freedom, but also economic freedom, or *laissez-faire* (q.v.).

Although this negative view of liberty persisted, it became evident to some perceptive thinkers that it was not despotism, but majority rule that was the new threat to freedom. In his *Essay on Liberty* of 1859 John Stuart Mill saw that individualism and the views of minorities might be threatened in democracies where the attitude of the mass prevailed. This leads to a new conception of liberty, as a positive means to an end. This goal is the fullest development of every individual citizen, and to achieve it some of the old freedoms may have to be set aside.

In the West this positive interpretation of liberty has not endangered the fundamental liberties of the mind. When President Roosevelt drew up his Four Freedoms in 1941, the first two were freedom of speech and expression, and freedom for every man to worship God in his own way. These are rights which are considered so essential that men will die to preserve them, today as in 1789. Liberty is still a word with enormous power to inspire men's thoughts and actions.

It is the interpretation of equality which has changed most since 'Liberty, Equality and Fraternity' were first proclaimed. In 1789 equality was thought of only in social terms. It meant that all men were to have the same rights, and that all titles and remnants of feudalism were to be abolished; the noble and the beggar were to call each other 'citizen'. The Declaration of Rights makes it clear that equality was not to extend to economic affairs, and it emphasizes the sanctity of property rights.

Not until the 1848 revolution in France did men fight for equality in a different sense. St-Simon (1760–1825) and Louis Blanc (1811–1882) had preached state ownership of land and industry, and many rebelled in 1848 in order that the nation's wealth should be more equally distributed. The right of the property-owners to undisputed possession was being challenged; instead, the poor were beginning to claim that they had a right to a decent livelihood.

A few weeks before the revolution broke out in Paris in 1848, Karl Marx had published his *Communist Manifesto*, a document destined to have an even wider influence than the Declaration of the Rights of Man. He brought the doctrine of economic equality to every man's attention; henceforward equality could never again be thought of merely in political and social terms. Marx taught that liberty is useless to the starving; the state's first duty is to provide food and work for its citizens, and not intellectual luxuries. Capitalism must be abolished and economic equality established according to the doctrine 'from each according to his ability, to each according to his needs'. Only when these material conditions have been satisfied should the state turn its attention to securing its subjects' liberties.

Since Marx's day every state has abandoned *laissez-faire* to a greater or lesser degree. Nowhere has complete equality of income been established, but in the western democracies today there is a definite endeavour to remove gross inequalities. There is first the idea of equality of opportunity, through free education and benefits for children, and second the attempt to see that no one sinks below a minimum standard of living. This is what Roosevelt meant by the third of his freedoms, freedom from want.

While liberty and equality can be secured by laws and written constitutions, fraternity is a much more intangible value. Fraternity means comradeship, friendliness and willingness to help one another; it is the spirit of unselfishness and love for one's fellow men. Without fraternity, liberty and equality are empty, and if it existed everywhere there would be no need for formal guarantees of freedom from oppression and help for those in need. The French and Russian revolutionaries expressed it by calling each other 'citizen' and 'comrade', but it is an ideal which exists in every democracy.

When the French demanded Liberty, Equality and Fraternity, they never doubted that the three could all be realized simultaneously. Some thinkers, however, and notably the French politician Alexis de Tocqueville (1805–1859), author of the brilliant *Democracy in America* soon saw that there was a basic incompatibility between liberty and equality, because each presupposes an entirely different theory of the purpose of the state. In the state which considers the guarantee of liberty its prime duty, men will inevitably use this liberty to make themselves rich, while others will become destitute. Such a state will also hesitate to interfere with its citizens' freedom to educate and protect their children as they think fit. Where the state feels bound to obtain equality, it will have to wrest property from the rich, and to maintain this equality it will have to take over the direction of economic affairs itself. De Tocqueville saw that equality extended to education may lean towards mass thinking, and to contempt and finally persecution of minorities. Thus equality might abolish liberty, and liberty make equality impossible.

In the modern Welfare State there is an attempt to combine liberty and equality; and while neither is complete, it seems as good a compromise as can be hoped for. Perhaps liberty has been curtailed unduly, but it is to an infinitesimal degree compared with the curtailment in the Communist states, where freedom has been completely sacrificed to equality.

Facts and figures

LIES AND STATISTICS are coupled, since few people will admit to being 'good at figures': they will even boast of being 'hopeless' at them. This is so even when the figures should be easy, *e.g.* the number of twopenny-halfpenny stamps to be obtained for half-a-crown, or the change due from a florin after buying two five-penny-halfpenny bars of chocolate and a tube of peppermints costing threepence. But the citizen today is bombarded with many figures arrived at by very complicated mathematical processes indeed, requiring the use of slide-rules, logarithmic tables, and worse. More, they often seem to go against common sense, as when they inform him that the cost of living is stationary, whereas the evidence of his bank balance suggests quite the opposite. Since figures of this kind baffle the plain man, he is tempted to find truth in the saying 'There are three kinds of lies – lies, damned lies, and statistics'.

It is not certain who first made this remark. It has been attributed to Disraeli, Abraham Hewitt, Labouchere, Christopher Holloway, and Arthur Frost. It was known to Mark Twain, who, in his autobiography, gave it to Disraeli, so it seems likely that it first gained currency somewhere between fifty and a hundred years ago. The strongest tradition is that Disraeli first said it, and certainly it seems in keeping with the character of one who, on being told that he was to be Chancellor of the Exchequer, said that he knew nothing of finance and received the reply, 'You know as much as Canning knew ... They will give you the figures.'

In considering the justice of the sentiment, it is only fair to the statistician to recall the dictionary definition of statistics as 'numerical facts or data collected and classified', which limits the use of statistics to matters that can properly be expressed in numbers: that is, to tangible things that can be counted and to abstract quantities that can be measured or calculated.

This principle may seem to be obvious, but it is often neglected, and that is partly why statistics get a bad name. For although the limits of the use of statistics are wide, yet they rule out large fields of human activity and human experience. For instance, a manufacturer may quite easily get statistics that will tell him roughly how many people use his products, because both people and products can be counted, but he will find it far more difficult to discover from statistics why people like – or dislike – his product, because

likes and dislikes are matters of emotion, and emotion defies statistical computation. Again, it may be perfectly reasonable to use statistical methods to estimate how many people, on a given day, think they would vote against the Government if on that day there were an election, and expect to get a reliable answer – again, because people can be counted. It is far less reasonable, however, to expect a reliable answer if you use your estimate to forecast how many people will vote against the Government at some election in the future, even in the near future, because future action is not amenable to numerical measurement.

Moreover, since mathematics are the foundation of statistics, and the foundation of mathematics is clear thought, it is desirable that statistics should not be abused by muddled thinking; yet muddled thinking about statistics is very common. Consider averages, for instance. Probably no statistical conception is more familiar and in commoner use than the idea of a simple arithmetical average, yet few ideas are more commonly misunderstood and misapplied, and few are more misleading if misused. One example may be quoted from the figures of the 1951 Census. These figures show that over half the households in the country at the time of the Census had either two or three people in them.

On this basis it seems reasonable to think of the 'average household' as one with two or three people, and for some purposes that idea may be useful. But it may also be harmful, unless it is remembered that the census figures also show that more people live in households with four or more people in them than in households of any smaller size; therefore most people in the country do not live in an 'average household' as defined by the number of its members. If false conclusions are drawn from the definition, however, the lie will not be in the statistics, but in the users of them.

Honest but ill-advised application of statistical methods, and muddled thought about statistics derived by methods properly applied may, as suggested above, account for a good deal of what the bewildered citizen thinks of as statistical lying, but which might more charitably be described as statistical ineptitude. It does not account for all of it. Figures of all kinds lend themselves very readily to the purposes of clear-minded people, and if the clear minds are also dishonest, then figures can lend themselves to purposes that are far from respectable. Moreover, where the scientist has prestige, figures have power, and if they are produced with a sufficiently authoritative flourish there is no great fear that they will be examined very critically by an inexpert audience. Thus people may be swindled by financiers of their money or by politicians of their votes, and here there is no question of statistical ineptitude: 'damned lies' is all too accurate a description.

Between blundering on the one hand and deliberate falsification on the other there is, of course, a broad middle way of usefulness and truthfulness for statistics. Indeed, if they were important enough in Disraeli's day to provoke him so intemperately, they are many times more important now. Without the continuous 'collection and classification of numerical facts and data' the fabric of the modern state – especially the welfare state – would not hold up, for neither commerce nor public administration could continue. 'Lies and statistics' there certainly are in modern society; but if the statistics were all lies, modern society would collapse.

The 'verification principle'

'LOGICAL POSITIVISM' was first attached as a label to the ideas of a group of scientifically-minded philosophers and philosophically-minded scientists who called themselves the Vienna Circle.

This group formed round Moritz Schlick when he was appointed to the Chair of Philosophy at Vienna after the First World War; and it included the mathematician Hahn, the sociologist Neurath, the physicist Frank, the mathematically oriented Carnap, Friedrich Waismann and others. They were in contact with Ludwig Wittgenstein and were much influenced by his *Tractatus Logico-Philosophicus* (1922), though he was never a member of the Circle.

After 1929 the Circle initiated a loosely bound international movement to organize conferences and publish a journal *Erkenntnis* (Knowledge). The Nazis broke up the movement and drove its members before them into scattered exile. Carnap, Reichenbach and the others went to America, where they found ready help in their project of an International Encyclopaedia of Unified Science.

The most famous doctrine of the logical positivists was the Verification Principle: the thesis that the meaning of a sentence lies in its method of verification. It was by the use of this that various kinds of utterance which for one reason or another did not seem to be even in principle verifiable, could be dismissed as nonsense, literally meaningless, without factual content. The *bêtes noires* were metaphysics and theology: but ethics and lyrical expression were in danger with the alleged intellectual bath-water. All significant utterances must be, it was claimed, *either* analytic propositions, the truth of which depends wholly and entirely on the meaning of the words they comprise, *or* synthetic factual propositions the truth of which depends solely on what is, as a matter of fact, the case in the non-linguistic world. This contention was a modernized version of what has been helpfully nicknamed Hume's Fork: 'All the objects of human reason or enquiry may naturally be divided into two kinds, to wit, *Relations of Ideas*, and *Matters of Fact*'.

Propositions of the former (analytic) kind 'are discoverable by the mere operation of thought, without dependence on what is anywhere existent in the universe'; whereas the truth of the latter depends on what happens to be the case, although it might have been otherwise.

It is in terms of this dichotomy that David Hume (1711–1776) advocates a purge as drastic as anything sponsored by any member of the Vienna Circle. 'When we run over libraries, persuaded of these principles, what havoc must we make? If we take in our hand any volume; of divinity or school metaphysics, for instance, let us ask, *Does it contain any abstract reasoning concerning quantity or number?* No. *Does it contain any experimental reasoning concerning matter of fact and existence?* No. Commit it then to the flames: for it can contain nothing but sophistry and illusion.'

On the positive side the Vienna Circle were concerned with the advancement of science, in which they considered that their part was to 'be employed ... in clearing the ground a little, and removing some of the rubbish that lies in the way to knowledge' – taking these words of John Locke to apply to various anti-scientific doctrines; and to tackle the logical problems which arise within the sciences – problems of conceptual clarification, of tightening up the logical structure and of showing how the concepts, the language, of different sciences are related to one another. The emphasis on science as the sole source of knowledge justifies the use of the word *Positivism*: the emphasis on logical problems justifies the epithet *Logical*.

To these logical problems they brought the new quasi-mathematical apparatus of symbolic logic, to which Bertrand Russell has so greatly contributed. As an example of the possible importance of conceptual analysis they had Einstein's study of the notion of motion, which, although a piece of philosophy, was involved fundamentally in his theories of relativity. And they hoped to be able to establish the unity of science on the basis of the contention, called 'physicalism', that the concepts of all the other sciences could and should be reducible to physical ones; and that psychology and biology had no need for any irreducibly purposive or teleological ideas peculiar to themselves.

Logical Positivism made one brilliant convert in England, A. J. Ayer, whose devastating *Language, Truth and Logic* (1936) is what English amateurs of philosophy usually have in mind when they speak of Logical Positivism. But though no mature professional philosophers in England, with the doubtful exception of Professor Ayer himself, now maintain this kind of position, the term 'Logical Positivist' is almost universally misused as a label for the views of all those who present philosophy as a logical study of language.

These philosophers of language (abundant particularly in Oxford, the boom town of philosophy) are considerably unlike the members of the Vienna Circle. They would never think of signing manifestos, or formulating philosophical programmes; they reject all labels, preferring to think of themselves not as members of any party, school or faction, but simply as philosophers. They would argue that while the verification principle may be all very well in natural science, as the single universal criterion of meaningfulness it is quite preposterously restrictive (indeed,

members of the original Vienna Circle found this, and were forced to introduce a category of 'important' or 'deeply significant' nonsense for some of the utterances for which it left no room). They are generally not exclusively or even primarily interested in natural science. They are as reluctant as the Logical Positivists were willing to make general claims about the meaninglessness of metaphysics: preferring to attack problems singly and piecemeal.

Though generally but by no means always secular and scientific in outlook, they are not anti-religious crusaders, or crusaders of any other kind.

Logical Positivism in the accurate sense of the views of the Vienna Circle and of the movement they initiated is a closed incident in the history of thought, which, though influential, has now exercised its influence. Logical Positivism, in what must presumably be recognized as a second though vulgar and misleading sense, is very far from being dead. It is indeed one of the liveliest intellectual forces in England, one which is only just beginning to be felt outside the philosophical faculties of the universities and which will surely begin soon to make a deeper mark on many branches of thought – political, moral, religious and literary.

Loyalty, citizen and state

LOYALTY as a word has been in use in English since the fifteenth century, and has had a variety of different meanings in its time. The common denominator between all of them is the idea of constant devotion, whether to a person, a society or a pledge. It was once employed in a specialized sense to signify marital fidelity; in contemporary English it often means enthusiasm for the Royal Family, and in current political controversy on the other side of the Atlantic it has come to mean fidelity to the American constitution and, in particular, immunity from Communist influence or belief; the slightest communist contact can make one's loyalty suspect.

'Loyalty', however, has a special significance

in the history of thought. In medieval eyes it was the cardinal social virtue, the bond of social peace and the foundation of all the practical arrangements for defence, production and distribution on which society rested. Feudalism rested on a set of distinct ideas about men's relationship to God and each other, and the central theme of these ideas was the concept of personal loyalty. The 'tenant-in-chief' received his land from the king in return for performing certain services to the king, notably, for providing him with soldiers to defend him. In turn, the 'tenant-in-chief' let his land to knights who were sworn to defend him when in need and who made up the forces he supplied to the monarch when called upon to do so.

Land was also held by other forms of tenure. It might, for example, be held in return for the tenant's services as a farmer, whether performed by him personally on the landlord's estate or given in the shape of agricultural produce. Religious orders held their land in return for praying for their patrons or for the community at large. So there was created a vast hierarchy of mutual obligations, mostly personal in character, with the king at its head as the ultimate owner of all land and the ultimate protector of all people. The feudal relationship was sometimes expressed in an oath of fealty which the tenant took to his lord on receiving his tenure, an oath still taken in the Coronation service by the monarch's tenants-in-chief.

Yet these mutual rights and duties did not arise from what would today be called a contract. The essence of a contract is that those who take part in it are free agents: they come together voluntarily for their common advantage. The relationship of lords to their tenants was a relationship, not of contract, but of status; the parties were not free to decide whether they should enter into it or to bargain about its terms. Men inherited their rights and with them their duties, and these rights and duties were seen as belonging to a fixed universal order as inevitable as the motions of the heavenly bodies.

Medieval society was static. The fact that most people in the Middle Ages lived and died where they were born made it possible to found social relationships upon this concept of inherited personal rights and duties. The birth of a middle class which lived by commerce with the ends of the earth, and not by the cultivation of land, the alliance of this middle class with the Crown against the pretensions of the great feudal lords, and the beginning of an age of more or less quick communication combined to make the assumptions of feudal society out of date. In an age of individualism, the old idea of personal loyalty necessarily weakened. The infinitely complicated network of links by which men were bound together in one community under one head gave way before a new kind of society in which everything that stood between the individual at one extreme, and the monarch at the other, tended to be disparaged. Once the crown, with the aid of the new middle class, was able to subdue the old nobility, its authority could be asserted directly through paid officials, such as royal judges, and loyalty acquired a new character. Henceforth it was direct loyalty that was given to the person of the monarch.

When, in turn, royal power was surrendered first to the middle classes and then to the people at large – a process which went on with increasing rapidity throughout Europe after the French Revolution – loyalty assumed yet another form. It was no longer personal loyalty at all, but loyalty to an idea, the idea of the state or the idea of humanity at large. To liberals this has always seemed to be a process of liberation. To them personal loyalty, as distinct from loyalty to an idea or to the whole collectivity, seems to involve a denial both of liberty and equality. If one man is as good as the next and should be as free as the next, it is intolerable that any man should be under any authority save the authority of all men as expressed in the general will of the community.

To Conservatives this so-called general will of the community has always seemed to be a tyrannical thing, a fiction which simply conceals the power of a majority or of those who can manipulate the majority. Once the individual is freed from all special loyalties to his immediate neighbours, he is left, so the Conservative spokesmen like Edmund Burke (1729–1797) argue, defenceless before the organized power of majorities. It is the special loyalties on this view, a man's loyalty to his family, his village or parish, his profession or his trade union, which protect individual freedom, and all these loyalties imply accepting for some purposes an authority other than that of the state. Even these lesser loyalties are no longer purely personal, but, since they are loyalties to people who are seen and met every day, they have more of the feudal quality about them than the abstract loyalty of the democratic state.

Then, again, the modern or liberal view of loyalty seeks to found all loyalties on contract; that is to say, on the consent, explicit or implied, of the parties concerned. The individual cannot be bound except by his own will. Thus, the state itself is seen as arising from a contract, although in fact all kinds of sophistry have had to be used to prove why men who, after all, did not choose to be born into their particular states, can be assumed to have contracted to obey those states. The effect of these sophistries, according to conservative thought, has been simply to create the illusion that the individual in obeying the majority is obeying himself; also, to make the majority irresponsible by relieving it of all sense of obligation to the past and the future. Burke in his *Reflections on the French Revolution* (1790) states the conservative view in a passage which expresses the old idea of loyalty in its relationship to political thought:

It [the State] becomes a partnership in all science; a partnership in all art; a partnership in every virtue, and in all perfection. As the ends of such a partnership cannot be obtained in many generations, it becomes a partnership not only between those who are living, but between those who are living, those who are dead, and those who are to be born.

The chief ingredients in the old idea of loyalty, derived from the social theory underlying feudalism, were personal obligation and permanence. This old conception has been challenged by a new one of which the chief ingredients are the ideas of individual equality and personal freedom from all restraints save those imposed by the whole people through the state. The tendency has been for the objects of loyalty to become more and more abstract, but neither conception has won complete ascendancy, and traces of both are still visible in the political and social thinking of European countries.

M

The slave of a slave?

TYRANNY OF THE MACHINE – man's fear of being dominated by his scientific inventions – is by no means a result only of the Industrial Revolution. The legends of Icarus, Prometheus, Pygmalion and above all Frankenstein testify to man's age-old fear of his own powers of invention and of the consequences of too great a presumption in defying the powers of nature.

The idea underlying Greek tragedy, with its conception of nemesis, was that of mental or spiritual presumption. The tyrant, avid of power, was portrayed as responsible for his own downfall. Modern science has given man a new kind of power, that of technics. It is no longer the isolated individual upon whom the retribution of nemesis may fall. It is the entire human race. A collective defiance of 'the gods' has become a practical possibility. Instead of being tyrannized by a passion or a 'failing', man is in danger of being tyrannized by a gift or talent. He is the victim not of his weakness, but of his strength.

There is irony in this. For if the prophecies of disaster are finally realized, the result will not be tragedy in the old sense; but comedy. The clown who trips over a device of his own making excites laughter. If mankind blows itself to pieces with its own infernal devices, another race of beings (if such existed) could at best ridicule its foolishness and stupidity.

The development of mass-production between the two wars, especially in the United States, inspired a social philosophy which enjoyed for a time a considerable vogue. This was called Technocracy. According to the principles of Technocracy, the old idea of society ruled by statesmen, politicians and bureaucrats had become thoroughly outmoded. For thousands of years men had been ruled through their emotions by means of rhetoric. A dictator was a man who achieved supremacy over his fellows as much by words as actions – as much by *dicta* as *gesta*. Even in democratic regimes the chief engine of government was the parliament, or 'talking-shop'. With the development of applied science, the regulation of society could be achieved with greater economy, efficiency and freedom. Bureaucrats ought to be replaced by technicians; statesmen by far-seeing experts. Dictatorship would thus be exercised by Science itself, thereby ushering in the most benevolent and rational of social systems.

With the rise of the totalitarian régimes, Technocracy lost the influence it had enjoyed. The mirage of a scientific society, rationally and justly administered, faded before the storm-clouds of an irrationalism without parallel in history. One of the most terrible features of the new régimes was their exploitation of technics for wholly destructive ends. Technocracy had implied the benevolent domination of technics. Totalitarianism revealed, at great cost, a truth to which the practical scientist may remain obstinately blind, namely that technics are only a *means*.

The word 'tyrant', which derives from the Greek, signified in antiquity a ruler who had obtained supreme power not by legitimate means but by usurpation. And it is this aspect of tyranny that is implicit in the current use of the phrase, 'Tyranny of the Machine'. While relieving mankind of a great deal of sheer drudgery, the machine has imposed upon its creator a new form of drudgery, namely the increasingly exacting task of maintenance. The leisure which the machine-age was supposed to afford mankind has been mysteriously whittled away. Instead of enjoying more time for social intercourse with his fellows, man spends a great part of his leisure in listening to and looking at machines.

Even the time that he 'saves' is unproductive; we move heaven and earth, it has been said, to save five minutes and then have nothing to do with them when we have saved them. All this points to an inescapable conclusion: machines have imposed a new *rhythm*, if not a new tyranny, upon our lives. And as the psychologists tell us, the rhythm of a mechanistic civilization, with its stereotyped insistence, runs counter both to the seasoned rhythm of nature and to the more subtle rhythms of human life. This is the reason why advocates of the Simple Life almost always recommend as a first step to freedom the abolition of machinery.

An early protest against the application of machinery to industry was made by the so-called Luddites, who engaged in machine-breaking in and around the year 1811. To these bewildered people, led by the mysterious and perhaps fictitious character King Ludd, the machine was a threat: it would deprive them of their livelihood; but they also saw in it the symbol of a force obscurely hostile to mankind. Their action was futile; machinery had come to stay. But the feeling of uneasiness did not decrease. It was reflected in the more articulate protests of such nineteenth-century 'seers' as Ruskin, Morris, Samuel Butler and Carlyle. In every age man has dreamt of a perfect society. At one time it was felt that happiness would result from relieving man of the task of working by the sweat of his brow. The Utopias of the twentieth century, for example, Aldous Huxley's *Brave New World* (1932), represent a profound and bitter disillusionment with this notion. A new form of terror had arisen whereby human beings, subjected to systematic conditioning, had been reduced to the status of automata. This seemed to be the *reductio ad absurdum* of the mechanistic organization of society. Men were becoming objects of calculated reaction. The 'utopian' vision of a world wholly governed in this manner took the form of an anti-Utopia, George Orwell's *1984*.

The problem has been posed whether the future belongs to a race which not merely devises new and miraculous machines but somehow consists of super-machines. Such speculations have been encouraged by news of recent investigations into the human brain. The extent to which the brain, and indeed the entire nervous system, resemble a machine is a matter of vigorous controversy. To the Behaviourist, there is no doubt on the subject: man is an automaton, controllable by the conditioning of his reflexes. In support of this view, he cites the extraordinary functional resemblance between the human brain and the giant electronic devices sometimes called 'machines that think'. The study of these machines has grown so elaborate that the new science of Cybernetics (literally, the science of 'governors') has come into existence. Seizing upon its data, popular imagination has envisaged a world in which machines, acquiring a quasi-life and independence of their own, proceed to organize the world.

This notion seems plausible, yet is based upon a serious misapprehension. However complicated and 'clever' they may be, machines are still no more than the prolongation of our sense organs. Their cleverness, like that of the most elementary gadget, is ours. Detachment does not mean independence; a machine cannot employ itself. To think otherwise is to confuse consciousness with behaviour, choice with discrimination. A robot may perform the most extraordinary feats of skill, precision and calculation. It cannot know that it has done so, nor can it know when it has failed. This is because a robot, like a balance, can discriminate but not choose. It is we who, profiting from its discrimination, proceed to the act of choice, which is always a conscious act. The most cleverly constructed apparatus, like the 'animals' invented by Dr Grey Walter, forms a 'determinist' system; which requires a determiner; which must finally be a conscious agent.

Assuming that the development of Cybernetics produces apparatus of even more remarkable range and scope, man will still be master of his creations. But he will be a master increasingly burdened with technical responsibilities. It will be true of him, as of no tyrant of antiquity, that 'the master is the slave of the slave'. He will have to make up his mind whether a mechanistic civilization makes life tolerable, or whether it leaves room for life at all. Yet, the very fact that the problem perturbs him proves he is more than an automaton; just as the fact that he can construct machines of gigantic power proves, not that he is himself a machine, but that he is an expert mechanic.

ILLUSTRATION: Pages 440 and 441.

Three materialisms

MATERIALISM has three distinct meanings – it is a philosophical term, a scientific concept and a catch-phrase with moral implications.

In everyday speech the word carries with it a *nuance* of condemnation, although it does not necessarily convict a man of moral turpitude. In the popular mind Materialism signified a concentration upon 'things' and the acquisition of 'things' for the sake of personal advantage. It implies giving priority to the satisfaction of bodily instincts. Above all, it signified the inclination to amass as quickly as possible the means to such acquisition and such satisfaction, namely money. A materialist is a man who not merely neglects the 'things of the mind', but despises the higher virtues of self-sacrifice and unselfishness. Thus when preachers and publicists denounce the 'materialism of the age', they have in mind the popular worship of wealth, the pursuit of pleasure and the tendency to live for the moment.

While this popular use of the word may be criticized for its vagueness, it does provide some valuable clues to its meaning in science and philosophy. The academic thinker sometimes tends to assume that the ordinary man has no business to use certain words unless he knows their 'philosophical' meaning. To this it may be retorted that the philosopher has no business to use certain words unless he knows their ordinary or popular meaning; for it is from common experience and our talk about it that all speculation starts out. Philosophers who fail to realize this, forget that their own experience, at least in great part, is 'common experience'. When they become ill or fall in love they do not do so in a special philosophical manner; they behave much as other men do.

The scientific view of Materialism may be considered by concentrating upon the idea of matter. The 'things' the materialistic person is obsessed by are material things. Even if he pursues or covets objects which are non-material, such as things of beauty, he either values them in material terms or treats them as pieces of matter. One obvious characteristic of a piece of matter is that it can be measured. The thing is 'there'; it can be shown to have reality by its conformity to an agreed standard. (In the same way, the materialistic individual likes to have 'something to show for his money'.) A second characteristic of a piece of matter is that nothing happens to it without the impact of external forces. A third is that a piece of matter confronts every other piece of matter from the outside. However much it may be divided, a piece of matter never reveals or discloses an inside or centre.

These characteristics, which are experimentally verifiable, have become commonplaces of scientific textbooks. Without their acceptance, scientific investigation would be impossible. And the impressive achievements of science in modern times seem to justify the belief that the world investigated by science is the only world of which we need take account: that which is measurable becomes identified with reality itself. The scientific success in investigating and manipulating matter has led to the philosophical belief that reality is in essence material. Thus the scientific spirit has been accompanied by a new and revolutionary belief, Materialism.

This transition from a scientific criterion to a philosophical belief seems both logical and inevitable. That view of matter dates from the seventeenth century and the rise of modern science. Galileo and Descartes are the two figures most closely associated with this new impulse towards scientific enquiry. Galileo (1564–1642) was not merely an experimenter of genius; he had a remarkable grasp of the principles upon which his experiments and calculations were based. 'The Book of Nature', he said 'is written in the language of mathematics' – a revolutionary statement on account of the theoretical conclusions deducible from it. If the key to the secrets of nature was a mathematical key, the aspects of nature not susceptible to measurement were evidently less important and even less real than the measurable aspects.

This assessment of value was reflected in the description given by Galileo to the two orders of qualities. To the measurable aspect of nature he gave the word 'primary qualities'; to the non-measurable, 'secondary qualities'. Strictly speaking, only the secondary aspect was 'qualitative': for this aspect included not merely such characteristics as colour, but such aspects as value. This distinction, or rather separation, was in due course translated into more philosophical terms. The quantitative aspect of reality was labelled objective; the qualitative, subjective.

His contemporary, René Descartes (1596–1650), arrived at similar conclusions by a consistently philosophical approach. In addition to distinguishing primary from secondary qualities, he introduced a sharp division between the mind and the body. The body could be studied scientifically only by supposing it to work on the analogy of a machine. The chief difference between a man and an animal, however, was that man possessed a mind or soul which somehow inhabited the machine. Descartes extended or 'extrapolated' this mind-body distinction to the whole of nature. As an 'external world' susceptible of measurement, nature was 'objective' reality. The soul or spirit, embracing all qualities and values, formed 'subjective' reality.

The chief difficulty in Descartes' conception was the exact nature of the interrelation between soul and body. Whereas the body could be measured and its laws understood, the soul was an invisible 'sprite' whose activity remained inexplicable. Moreover, the scientist soon found that in pursuing his investigations he needed no hypothesis such as a soul or spirit. Such occult entities could be left to the theologians, the metaphysicians and the poets. Scientific reality was the world of matter. And if science was the highest – as it was certainly proving the most successful – form of thought, no other world could be said to enjoy any real existence.

The theory of Materialism was therefore as much encouraged by the Cartesian philosophy as by the laboratory experiments of the scientists. As a philosophy, it was the outcome of concentration upon one aspect of the mind–body dualism to the exclusion of the other. Materialism might be called the 'religion of quantity'. A. N. Whitehead pointed out in his *Science and the Modern World* (1925) that this religion gave birth to the ideas of the 'blind' operation of natural forces which tortured the finer minds of the nineteenth century. The first counter-attack against materialistic ideas, however, was launched by the poets of the Romantic Movement. With their emphasis upon feeling and sentiment, they afforded a solace to those who, like John Stuart Mill, had been brought up in an atmosphere of calculation and utilitarianism. For the belief in spiritual values did not die; it merely remained on the defensive. The very word Materialism suggests a battle-cry rather than a calmly accepted 'belief in matter'. And nineteenth-century Materialism was a revolutionary force, on account of its having issued from the laboratory and the study into everyday life. Materialism was colouring moral standards to such an extent that even a scientific materialist such as T. H. Huxley grew perturbed.

At the beginning of the twentieth century the view of matter entertained by scientists changed radically. For centuries matter had been represented as a hard, impenetrable substance composed of millions of atoms like billiard balls. Men talked of 'brute' matter. Developments in micro-physics soon exposed the unsoundness of this view. The material world seemed to dissolve into a series of 'waves' or undulations; and the laws governing them made allowance for notions of probability and even uncertainty. To some this new 'world-picture' seemed to anticipate, if not to involve, the death of materialism. There was talk of science having made room for spirit.

Such expectations have proved groundless. Matter is still matter (if not 'brute' matter), for all its being frayed out into waves and undulations. Nor is 'uncertainty' another term for the operation of spirit or mind. In so far as modern science continues to employ a technique of measurement, its conception of nature will be materialistic. And as long as modern philosophy accepts no other way of interpreting the world, its creed will be Materialism. If traditional Materialism fails to satisfy so many thinking people, the reason is not that science has abandoned the belief in matter, but that Materialism denies some of the deepest facts of experience.

No account of this subject would be complete without reference to a special form of Materialism which dominates the minds of hundreds of millions of men at the present day. This is Dialectical Materialism (q.v.), the official philosophy of the U.S.S.R. In Dialectical Materialism one of the main characteristics of matter of which we have spoken is repudiated. This is the idea that matter cannot act unless 'acted upon' from outside. According to the new view, matter is selfacting; it produces from within itself a series of states or forms from which everything, including social systems, develops. Matter is 'alive'. From being the 'religion of quantity', Materialism surreptitiously takes on some of the characteristics of a religion of quality. In so doing it ceases to be Materialism except in name. The creative impulsion present in matter is equivalent to the *entelechy* or energizing spark which the biological theory of Vitalism regards as animating the organism. It presupposes a miracle, a *deus in materia*. No doubt it is this element of mysticism, however disguised, which lends to Dialectical Materialism its potency as a gospel commanding passionate allegiance, stimulating social effort, and satisfying the profound religious instincts of the people whose creed it has become.

McCarthyism above McCarthy

MCCARTHYISM is a belief that essentially the danger of Communism lies in the subversion of lawful government by the infiltration into key positions of influence of Communists and fellow-travellers, that such infiltration caused Russia and China to become Communist, and that the counter to such influence is the ruthless persecution of all Communists, fellow-travellers, and sympathizers, both inside and outside the courts, by public accusation, merciless publicity and every other method, whether honourable or dishonourable, of discrediting their reputations.

Though named after and chiefly associated with Senator McCarthy, the Republican Senator from Wisconsin, McCarthyism is an older and greater force than McCarthy himself. It derives its nature partly from a tendency long apparent in American politics, partly from the international situation and partly from the methods McCarthy uses and the position he holds.

The first famous victim of anti-Communist persecution was tried in 1919, when America was swept by a frenzied fear of radicalism. A man called Gitlow had issued a Manifesto asserting that 'the Communist International calls the proletariat of the world to final struggle'. He was accused of 'inciting the overthrow of the government'. Although there was little public support for Communism, and although any agitator who read these pages to a mob would hardly have stirred them to violence except possibly against himself, so great was the public fear that the words were held to be an incitement, there was held to exist a clear and present danger to the Constitution, and Gitlow was gaoled.

Gitlow was at least tried in a court of law. McCarthyism as such first emerged with the House Committee on Un-American Activities, appointed in May 1938. The purpose of the Committee was 'to conduct an investigation of (1) the character and objects of un-American propaganda: (2) the diffusion ... of subversive and un-American propaganda ...' etc.

The use of vague words like 'subversive' and 'un-American' in its terms of reference enabled its members like medieval inquisitors to sit as judges to determine the existence of heresy.

The work of the Committee, which had its heyday from 1939 to 1949, was chiefly notable for three features: firstly it drew attention to a number of organizations carrying on the work of the Communist Party under false labels and a number of people holding Communist views, including Alger Hiss.

Secondly, it regarded its purpose, as stated in a House Report of 1940, as the 'task of protecting our constitutional democracy by ... pitiless publicity'.

Thirdly, not only those connected with Communism were attacked and discredited, but also those-connected-with-those-connected-with Communism. An extreme example was the Committee's report on the Southern Conference for Human Welfare in 1947, which was listed as subversive. One of the reasons given was the following: 'Entertainer at the Washington meeting', the report disclosed, 'was Susan Reed, employed by Cafe Society, a night club owned by Barry Josephson, brother of Leon Josephson, a leading Communist.'

At a time when ferocious attacks on disloyalty and a general fear of internal subversion were already major phenomena in American politics came the revolution in China. For fifty years or more China had received disinterested assistance from the U.S.A. America had sent missionaries to China, had sent help to Chinese Universities, had helped China against Japan and had in general regarded China as its special protégé in international affairs. Chiang Kai-shek was almost an American hero. Hence the American public could only regard the success of Communism in China as an international betrayal.

The success of the revolution, it was felt, must be due to a Communist conspiracy from within, helped from without by Communist sympathizers in the U.S. Government and elsewhere. Fear of Communism increased, and hysteria mounted.

Such was the feeling of the nation when on 19 February 1950, the hitherto little-known Senator from Wisconsin made a speech at Wheeling, Virginia, in which he said, 'I have here in my hand a list of 205 names that were made known to the Secretary of State as being members of the Communist Party and who nevertheless are still working and shaping the policy of the State Department.'

McCarthy was born on a Wisconsin farm in 1908. At twenty he was working in a chain grocery store in Manawa, Wisconsin; then he turned his attention to law. It is related that as a student of law McCarthy gained his lowest marks for legal ethics. By the age of thirty-one he had been elected a State Judge, known for the quantity rather than the quality of his judgments. In 1946 McCarthy was elected a senator, and had become in addition Vice Chairman of the Joint Committee on Housing, Senate Banking and Currency Committee, Senate Committee on Expenditure and Special Senate War Investigating Committee. His career up to date has shown him to be a man of enormous energy and tenacious memory.

Apart from a violent attack on the Army for 'torturing' Nazi soldiers accused of shooting American prisoners at Malmedy, McCarthy had made little impression on Washington. The Wheeling speech brought a change. He varied the original figure of 205 to eighty-one and then to fifty-seven and produced only four actual names. He never waived his senatorial immunity from libel action as promised. But information flowed in from thousands of well-wishers eager to help one so utterly opposed to Communism in the State Department, and the McCarthy investigating machine was born.

Another turning point in McCarthy's career is perhaps to be found in the attack on General Marshall, whom Truman and many other Americans regarded as the greatest living American. 'His every important act for years' said McCarthy in 1951, 'has contributed to the prosperity of the enemy.' Although this attack had little effect, it was symbolic. It showed that McCarthy was no respecter of persons. Not even popularity or eminence could give any immunity from his assaults. Later McCarthy showed he was as eager to attack Republicans as Democrats.

As a result of McCarthy's accusations only one member of the State Department has to date been actually suspended. But he has captured a great many other scalps. Senator Tydings called his original charges 'a fraud': against McCarthy's opposition he was not re-elected to the Senate. Senator Benson proposed that McCarthy be expelled from the Senate: he failed to be re-elected himself. To date, McCarthy has clashed several times with the Executive: on the whole he has had the upper hand. One of his outstanding triumphs was in March 1953, when he personally secured an arrangement with Greek owners of 242 ships not to trade with Iron Curtain countries. At once Stassen, the head of the Mutual Aid Programme, accused McCarthy of 'undermining' the work of the Executive; but later Stassen was forced to admit that he meant 'infringing' rather than 'undermining'.

McCarthy's enormous personal influence is partly the result of his personality, partly of his position. A senator is not an American Member of Parliament. He has far greater national prestige. He is independent of the Executive and of party discipline. He stands for re-election only once in six years. In addition, the Senate runs its own committees, which can hold public enquiries. Of one of these Senate committees, the Committee on Government Operations, McCarthy is chairman.

McCarthyism is an American problem. At present it is associated with McCarthy himself, and with his own fortunes it will probably prosper or decline. But essentially McCarthyism is more than the man. It has its hold on America because of American fear of Communism. Ever since the enormous casualties suffered by the U.S.A. in the Korean War, to America Communists have been not so much the holders of a dangerous theory, as fifth columnists and traitors. While such feeling persists it will be exploited.

Historians will probably pass lightly over McCarthy's career as one among the many symptoms of political emotion after the Second World War; he may perhaps occupy no more than a footnote in a history book. Nevertheless the browsing type of historian will find years of cynical research before him as he reads and checks the scorebooks of the mighty mudslinging match that has been going on between McCarthy and his various opponents. On both sides strong hits were made with investigatorial mud diligently raked up by research teams. Both sides may then appear in their true colours – i.e. not so black as painted.

ILLUSTRATION: Page 326.

Miracles and natural law

MIRACLES have been defined as direct interventions of God in the world of nature and history which defy those laws through which God usually orders and controls the created world. A presupposition of belief in miracles would therefore seem to be a belief in God, but in fact Christian apologists have traditionally used miracles as evidence for God's existence and activity. The universe is conceived as obedient to natural laws, and only by a deity could these laws be suspended. In miracles there is just such a suspension of natural law.

It is this definition of a miracle as 'a breach of natural law' which David Hume (1711–1776) criticized in a chapter of the *Enquiry concerning Human Understanding*. The essence of Hume's argument is that by a natural law we mean a set of events which have invariably been observed to occur in ordered sequence. Thus, to claim that an event is a breach of natural law is to claim that its occurrence runs contrary to the testimony of universal experience. But no other testimony could possibly prevail against the weight of universal experience, and hence no testimony as to the occurrence of a miracle could carry conviction.

This argument Hume reinforces with reference to various notorious fraudulent claims regarding miracles, but the sum of his conclusion is not just that we have no adequate evidence for the occurrence of miracles, but that we *could* have no such evidence. Cardinal Newman attempted to answer Hume by arguing that we cannot know *a priori* whether or no miracles are possible, but only by examining in detail the evidence for particular miracles. He might have added that Hume discusses only the validity of testimony by others to miracles and never considers the possibility of our being eye-witnesses.

None the less, if we define a miracle as 'a breach of natural law', then the notion of a miracle is self-contradictory. By a law of nature we mean a sequence of events which is observed to occur uniformly and without exception. Should we discover an exception to what we have hitherto held to be a natural law, we must either abandon the law or modify our formulation of it, so as to account for the exception. And as soon as we have noticed this, it is clear that there can be no breaches of natural law. Any event which seems to be such a breach must either prove on closer examination not to be so at all, or if it is an exception to what we took to be the rule, then the occurrence of the exception is sufficient proof that this particular sequence of events is not amongst those governed by invariable natural law.

Hence we can divide all alleged breaches of natural law into those which are not really breaches and those which prove that there was no natural law to be broken. If we define miracles thus, there are no miracles.

The New Testament, however, never envisages miracles in this way. They are referred to in the gospels as 'signs' and what they signify is the presence of the Kingdom of God. The miraculous quality of the events resides not in any alleged scientific inexplicability of the events, but in the way in which they show the power and the love of God. Thus the Feeding of the Five Thousand is a sign of God's power to feed, one that recalls the manna with which God fed his people in the wilderness. But did the Feeding of the Five Thousand (recorded in each of the four writers of the gospels) happen? Does not the claim that it did conflict with all our experience? Do miracles happen?

The miracle stories of the gospels are of two kinds. There are those, such as the accounts of healing, which are easily credible in the light of modern discoveries made by psychological medicine. But there are also those miracle stories which allege unique and extraordinary happenings, such as the Feeding of the Five Thousand, Christ's Walking upon the Waters and, above all, the Resurrection. That extraordinary happenings occur the findings of psychical research have perhaps made us readier to believe. But in order to establish the occurrence of such miracles we would have to establish both the occurrence of the extraordinary event in question and the fact that such occurrences are the work of divine grace. So many occurrences have been believed or disbelieved without any investigation.

The most convincing evidence for miracles is perhaps their recurrence in our own time. The life of the Curé d'Ars (St John Vianney) in the last century, in which great personal holiness was closely associated with supernormal happenings (he lived for years feeding only on the sacrament of Holy Communion), is the best retort to those who assert dogmatically that miracles do not happen. It is, of course, true that belief in miracles can easily degenerate into gross superstition and that such beliefs can be fostered by charlatans. One of the principal weapons of antireligious propaganda in the Soviet Union after the Revolution consisted in demonstrations of how bogus miracles, such as weeping statuettes, could be contrived. But in the record of the Curé d'Ars' self-sacrifice and devotion it is not the defiance of ordinary physical probability that impresses one so much as the context of love and service in which these signs of some extraordinary power were exercised.

Claims to miracles have marked the whole history of the Christian religion, and are of course also found in the other great world religions. The types of miracle could not be more various. St Francis, with his ability to love, subdue and transform the animal as well as the human creation, is perhaps the supreme example of the Saint who works miracles, not as an alternative to more ordinary exertions, but simply because the graces of holiness appear to overflow spontaneously from him.

To say this is not to preclude the possibility of psychological and physical explanations of miracles. It is simply to suggest that if these extraordinary events called miracles do happen, they must be explained rather than explained away.

ILLUSTRATION: Plate 3.

A clean sweep of the past

'MODERN ART' has acquired a meaning distinct from 'Contemporary Art'. It implies not solely what is produced in our time – or has been produced in recent times (irrespective of its character) – but that which in character specifically belongs to the modern age and has a vital connexion with new and changing elements in life and thought.

By 'modern age' we mean substantially the twentieth century, though it would not be easy to fix an exact date for the beginning of the 'modern' idea. In painting, for instance, the art which took the lead, there is a logical sequence and connexion of ideas that takes us far back into the nineteenth century. The urge to break free from the past and to find a new path is already to be seen in John Constable, and some might even date 'Modern' art from the famous Paris Salon of 1824, when his *Hay Wain* made so great an impression by its new outlook and treatment.

Or modern art and the opposition to it might be pushed back even further to the brilliant, sharp naturalism of Caravaggio (1565–1609) who broke with an established idealism.

A clean sweep of the past, in the sense of subject-matter and technical recipes that have become outworn, is essential to the idea. The ground is cleared by the gradual disappearance of mythological, historical and classical themes. Gustave Courbet (1819–1877) is modern in his 'Realism', that is, in painting his own world. Edouard Manet (1832–1883) emphasized his aim by using the word 'contemporanéité'. The quality of being 'contemporaneous' is further illustrated by the French Impressionists (some of whom were still living in the early years of this century), not only in painting the life around them, but also in the employment of a contemporary or novel method of interpreting light and colour.

The idea takes the still more definite form of a search for the absolute and primary essentials of art with the three great 'Modern' pioneers, Paul Cézanne (1839–1906), Paul Gauguin (1848–1903) and Vincent Van Gogh (1853–1890). Though all three were connected with the Impressionist movement to some extent, they were none of them satisfied with the imitative aspect of Impressionism, as a record of atmospheric and fortuitous effect. The thought of a new beginning and a still deeper research was in their minds. Their respective conclusions have been powerful in shaping the 'Modern' idea.

Cézanne looked for an essential principle of structure; it was his pregnant thought that 'everything is geometry', that underneath the accidents of nature lay a beautiful order in terms of sphere, cone and cylinder. This idea was carried to its logical conclusion in the Cubist movement of c. 1910, when the attempt was made to reveal an abstract geometric order.

Gauguin directed attention to a primitive purity in 'uncivilized' art. Europe, in his own phrase, might be 'rejuvenated by barbarism'. His work in the South Seas helped to stimulate interest in the natural and spontaneous operation of the instinct for art. The 'modern' trend in this sense became a process of discovery and a synthetic use of traditions previously despised or regarded as outlandish. Thus the essential plastic virtues of negro sculpture have been a 'Modern' influence on both sculpture and painting (*e.g.* in the painting, the *Demoiselles d'Avignon*, 1907, by Pablo Picasso, now in the Museum of Modern Art, in New York). The basic idea is operative in the discovery of the European 'primitive' (*e.g.* Henri Rousseau, the 'douanier', 1844–1910) and of 'Child Art' (not without its effect on so gifted a Modern master as Henri Matisse).

Van Gogh represented the primitivism of direct emotional expression. Colours and forms with him do not merely describe things objectively, they convey intense personal feeling in their brilliance and vigour. This is an aspect of the Modern idea that finds development in a particular form with the Norwegian Edvard Munch (1863–1944) and the German 'Expressionists'. With Paul Klee (1879–1940) the aim was 'not to render *the* visible, but to render visible'.

Up to about 1910 the Modern idea can be studied in the work of individuals more or less isolated from a swiftly changing world: in various subsequent stages the effort was made to integrate it with an age unparalleled in scientific discovery and invention, speed of transport and communications. It is a sign of this effort that 'Modern' art associated itself with 'progress' and the Machine, and that it became prolific in manifestos bearing on these matters. Thus the Italian Futurists, whose outlook was first formed by Cubism, led by Filippo Tommaso Marinetti (1876–1944), expressed positive contempt for the art of the past and a worship of machine forms. 'A racing motor-car ...' said Marinetti '... is more beautiful than the *Victory of Samothrace*.' The idea was expanded by Guillaume Apollinaire, a consistent apostle of novelty, in his *Futurist Anti-Tradition* manifesto (1913), which advocated 'machinism', 'Total Music and the art of noise', and 'Words at Liberty'. It was now part of the plan that every form of expression should contribute a dynamic element of its own to a dynamic civilization.

It is clear that (in spite of the somewhat fantastic note of these pronouncements) the clean sweep of the past had a quite rational application, apart from painting. In architecture, for instance – one can scarcely imagine a Gothic airport – new inventions demanded new and simplified forms, related to those to which painting had found its pioneering way. This was one tendency of the modern idea, in the first post-war period, expressed in the periodical started in 1920 by the architect Le Corbusier, *L'Esprit Nouveau*, and strikingly epitomized in his well-known saying that a house 'is a machine to live in'. The idea applied with equal appropriateness to industrial products in general and hence we had the pre-Hitler 'Bauhaus' in Germany, where the value of abstract form and essential qualities of colour and material in design for the machine were taught by 'Modern' painters such as Klee.

That the mind was another field of research in which the 'Modern' painter might operate was suggested by expressionism; and it gained, by analogy, a fresh stimulus from Freudian psychology, evidenced in the dream-and-nightmare-like pictures of the Surrealists in the nineteen-thirties, and in those evocations of the subconscious still found in the non-representational paintings of today.

The latter may be criticized as an aberration from the great traditional craft of picture painting. Yet, on the whole, it is evident that the 'Modern' idea has been and is a powerful and far-reaching force. There are contemporary buildings, paintings, sculptures and other forms of art that remain comparatively unaffected by it; yet it is astonishing to review the extent of its influence. It is manifested in every important country, constituting the international style of our time, as distinctly as 'Gothic' or 'Renaissance', which were the international styles of the past.

ILLUSTRATION: Plate 16 and Pages 315, 316 and 317.

The New World redressing its own balance

The **MONROE DOCTRINE** is the name that was later given to President Monroe's declaration of American policy on 2 December 1823, to the effect that America would not permit the colonization or control of the New World by European powers. It is also applied to the permanent principles of American policy founded on that declaration.

Americans have always disliked the idea that any part of the New World should be ruled from Europe. In 1812 they tried, without success, to conquer Canada; and they were enthusiastic about the revolt of the Spanish American colonies against the King of Spain, which began in 1810. When the colonists began to win, the King of Spain turned for sympathy to the rulers of the reactionary European powers, who had been in control of Europe ever since Waterloo. Canning, the British Foreign Secretary, was afraid that these powers might try to intervene in South America against the rebels. Knowing that he could rely on the United States to share his dislike for such a project, he suggested to the American Government that Britain and America should issue a joint warning against it.

Afterwards, Canning took the line that he had been personally responsible for the American declaration; 'I called the New World into existence', he said, 'to redress the balance of the old.' To this day it is widely believed that the Monroe Doctrine was a British idea in the first place. This is not true. What Canning wanted was a joint declaration. But the Americans felt that it was beneath the dignity of their country 'to come in as a cock-boat in the wake of the British man-of-war'. President Monroe decided to lay down

American policy for himself; and he did it in the form of a Presidential message to Congress.

The first part of the declaration was a warning to the nations of Europe to found no more colonies in the New World. 'The American Continents', said Monroe, 'are not to be considered as subjects for future colonization by any European power'. He went on to issue a warning against any attempt to bring the new republics within the sphere of European power politics. The United States, he said, had no intention of interfering with any colonies still dependent on their mother country; but 'we should consider any attempt on their part [the European powers] to extend their political system to any portion of this hemisphere, as dangerous to our peace and safety.'

This announcement was badly received in Europe, by Canning as much as anyone. It was regarded as outrageous that America should forbid other nations to found colonies in vast regions which had not yet been explored, much less settled. In America itself, however, it was welcomed with great pride and enthusiasm. Americans felt that it added to the dignity of their still weak and undeveloped nation. More important still, it gave expression to a feeling that has always lain at the root of American history: the passionate longing of Americans to build a new, fresh world of their own, away from the ridiculous wars and the tangled politics of Europe.

For many years the actual power that kept European politics out of the New World was not Monroe's declaration, but the British fleet, as Monroe himself admitted. Gradually, however, America grew strong enough to look after this policy for herself. It was proclaimed in 1845 as a cover for President Polk's impending attack on Mexico; not that it formed the pretext for the attack, but it was quoted as a warning to the European powers not to come to Mexico's assistance. In 1853 the expression 'Monroe Doctrine' was first used, and the words soon acquired an almost mystic significance. During the American Civil War, France seized the opportunity of sending troops to Mexico; but in 1865 the Civil War ended, and the triumphant Federal Government compelled the French to go home. Such a challenge to the Monroe Doctrine has never been offered since.

Surprisingly, in view of their declared hostility to further colonization, the Americans settled their boundary disputes with Canada in the light of moderation and common sense. With other nations they were not always so reasonable. Their continual expansion of the Doctrine to give them more and more right of interference throughout Latin America led to a violent quarrel with Great Britain in 1895, in a dispute over the borders of British Guiana. On this occasion, Olney, the Secretary of State, declared, 'Today the United States is practically sovereign on this Continent, and its fiat is law upon the subjects to which it confines its interposition'.

Naturally, talk of this stripe was very badly received both in Canada and in the Latin American countries. The latter had never been really grateful for the Monroe Doctrine. With the example of Mexico before them, they considered that the United States itself was a far greater danger than any of the nations from which it claimed to protect them. Even when it became obvious that America had no longer any aggressive intentions, the Monroe Doctrine remained unpopular in Latin America. It amounted to protection from the dangers of the outside world, and they felt quite capable of protecting themselves. Furthermore, it amounted to an assertion of the right of the United States to be the natural leader of Latin America; and this was resented – particularly by Argentina, who claimed this right for herself.

Later and wiser American statesmen realized this feeling; and for thirty years they have been working hard to get rid of it. Earlier extensions of the Doctrine, by which in the past America had claimed and exercised the right of armed interference in unsettled republics, have been explicitly renounced. The Doctrine itself is being transformed. It is no longer simply an expression of America's own attitude to the rest of the New World. It is coming more and more to be regarded as part of the defence structure of both continents, and so as the common possession of them all. The exclusion of European politics from the New World is considered – reasonably, in the light of the last twenty years – as being a benefit to all its nations; and it should be for all of them to enforce it, as their common policy.

In another important respect the Monroe Doctrine has been given an entirely new interpretation. It used to be believed in America that no international undertaking could be allowed to interfere with the right of the United States to handle policy in her hemisphere as she chose. America refused to join the League of Nations, and consequently helped to ruin it; and this was partly because of her anxiety to preserve the Monroe Doctrine intact, and not join a body that might claim a right to intervene in a quarrel between her and another American nation. There are no such reservations about America's adherence to the United Nations. Isolationism is still strong in America, but it is becoming less and less likely that it will be able to lead the whole country away from co-operation in the name of the Monroe Doctrine. Thoughtful Americans no longer believe that the Doctrine excludes the New World from the authority of an international body.

ILLUSTRATION: Page 311.

Above morality

MY COUNTRY, RIGHT OR WRONG, heedless loyalty to one nationalist state, is part of the language of political demagogy, the more dangerous because at first sight it would appear to be justifiable.

The doctrine finds its most succinct critic in Dr Johnson. Johnson often spoke of Edmund Burke as an astronomer might speak of a comet whose course alarmed him. 'I was present', he told Boswell, 'when he maintained that a Member of Parliament should go along with his party right or wrong. Now, Sir, this is so remote from native virtue, scholastick virtue, that a good man must have undergone a great change before he can reconcile himself to such a doctrine. It is maintaining that you may lie to the public, for you lie when you call that right which you think wrong.'

Others have found more to complain of in this doctrine, whether it concerns party or country. It is not merely lying to the public: it often involves telling the public the lie it wants to hear, so that its conscience anyway will be at ease. The technique can be most fully studied in pronouncements of dictators, who normally use only those ideas

which have long staled, dredging up the silt from the bottom of the public consciousness. But there is no country existing whose rulers have not at some time or other magnified an incident for the sake of prestige. Behind such incidents 'lie the interests, the passions, and the destiny of mighty races of men; and long antagonisms express themselves in trifles'.

In the recent past, ideas such as 'A place in the sun', 'Imperialism', 'Pan-Slavism', 'encirclement', and the like, were not so much nouns, names of things, as totem poles. They were raised on high in self-justificatory attitudes: they invited either the barbs of the intellectual critic or the boots of a foreign army, and they were prepared to defy both. Tallest of the totem poles was National Honour, loudest of all the cries of its worshippers. It was not, so Lloyd George stated in his Mansion House speech of 1911, 'a party question'.

Perhaps because this was so it was never appealed to save in the last resort. Palmerston said that British interests were eternal, and Gladstone had answered him that the concert of Europe had its interests too; and the shadows of this celebrated dispute had fallen far indeed. 'My country, right or wrong', was therefore, by the time of the twentieth century, not accepted as a correct counter in diplomatic usage. Beneath its bluff frankness experienced Europeans perceived a cynicism that dismayed them: after all, interests had to be balanced, if not for the sake of all, at least for the survival of some. Compromises had to be bought and advantages bargained. To take up too early a stand, on the wrong foot and on a badly-sited position, was bad diplomacy, bad politics, bad sense – better, then, to leave emotional concepts of right and wrong out of consideration altogether. The Austrian statesman Metternich had once remarked that 'politics are always unjust; but we must take care that they should not become poisonous as well', and European diplomats had tried always to follow the suggestion.

It was the Americans who put the phrase 'my country, right or wrong' into popular currency. Washington was not, in the nineteenth century, an international capital, and it therefore saw no reason to mince its words. Americans called Europe in question, criticized its policies, its polities, and congratulated themselves that the United

States was not involved in any 'Old Diplomacy'. America was, by definition, different from Europe, and morally right to be so. The United States were dedicated to life, liberty and the pursuit of happiness, no one of which (it appeared) Europe gave a pin for. An American, though he might quite properly act as the rescuer of the European, had no other tie with him. To be an American was to be right, the American way was the right way, the American dream was the dream of all mankind, Americanism was right and un-Americanism was wrong: un-American activities were activities that belonged to the Old World. (Imperialism was un-American from the start, therefore Communism, too.)

So it followed that, if the United States, repository of all the highest of human aspirations and ideals, went to war, the cause was *ipso facto* just; and if it was difficult to argue this in the case of Texas or Mexico, an appeal to manifest destiny might be made instead: it was right that the United States should be the sole sovereign authority in the New World. Thus common sense, common interest, natural piety and natural patriotism conjoined together to fashion the idea of 'My country, right or wrong' – 'when right,' said Carl Schurz (1829–1906) in the Senate, 'to be kept right, when wrong to be put right!'

It was an idea that informed and infused this great people with endless vitality and enterprise: Providence would guard the American way so long as Americans guarded it themselves. It gave to them a national self-confidence that baffled the European visitor, who, looking for culture, too often was presented with a cuspidor, and who was constantly being told how much he had to learn. 'Whether moral or material interests be considered,' remarked Secretary of State Olney in 1895, 'it cannot but be universally conceded that those of Europe are irreconcilably diverse from those of America.' There were plenty on both sides of the Atlantic to agree with him.

But although coined in America and given a distinct imprint there, this idea of a heedless patriotism also gained currency in Great Britain. Particularly was this so in the age of conscious imperialism. The Service class that ruled India, and intended to rule Africa once the company promoters had been bought out, did not make much use of slogans, or patriotic songs, or ap-peals to the Flag; but they held themselves commissioned to the Queen and the country, not to governments, and they regarded patriotism, therefore, as a simple duty. In Service circles 'theirs not to reason why' was a notion that continued to have its fascination. Duty was the Service code, as Americanism was the code of Americans. The Services insisted always that India and the colonies, and the Services themselves, should never be made 'party matters' – politicians might be suffered at home, but their interference abroad in matters that they did not understand, or wilfully chose to misunderstand, was to be tolerated as little as possible. The Service code was supplemented and strengthened by the public-school code of loyalty to tradition and to discipline.

In such atmospheres ideas easily became ideals; an irreverent earlier generation had poked fun at 'painting the map red', but surely it was a duty laid upon us? Civilizing the world was the White Man's Burden, and the British were generally the whitest men we knew. An Opposition could be labelled, not merely wrong-headed, but seditious, 'pro-Boer', in such an atmosphere; an armaments race could appear not lethal, but merely exciting. It was one's duty to be patriotic, and no more was to be said. Upper- and middle-class England, knowing next to nothing of European politics and conditions, volunteered cheerfully, enthusiastically, for the colours in 1914, because the issue was so plain and so simple: we had a duty to protect Belgium.

The temperature has dropped since then. One of Galsworthy's plays, *Loyalties*, set a problem to his audience that they would hardly have grasped before 1914: that ideas, even good ideas, and ideals, even high ideals, may sometimes conflict, and from the clash may spring a disaster as great as was ever plotted by evil intent. Politicians are now chary of bluff slogans: no one asks his audience to give him liberty or give him death, or states that ethics have nothing to do with his country's conduct. They subscribe to the sentiment that Patriotism is not Enough, but they do not say what is Enough, and they do not say that you can dispense with patriotism: they deal mainly in the negative; warn you from excess, advise you to trust them and honestly hope, the most of them, that your trust will be justified.

What remains, then, of 'My country, right or wrong'? Even if no one now defines it, does the sentiment still exist?

It does, still; and still as a last resort. Patriotism may not be enough, but an honest belief in its moral worth is none the less essential to national survival. (Whether national survival is itself a good is, of course, another matter, as one finds if one asks in Dublin about Ulster loyalism.) The limitations of nations, as of men, are in fact the frame within which they must work if they are to work at all. Patriotism is one such frame. An international patriotism is hard to live up to: if we have a duty to the community, as we are so often informed, perhaps we show our awareness of this better here than in China, better among our own fellows, families and fetishes; and perhaps we show it best of all when those fellows and families and fetishes are under direct attack, however convinced the other side may be of the justice of its cause.

The alone to the alone

MYSTICISM has still no better definition than that of Plotinus, the Neo-Platonist philosopher of Alexandria (A.D. 205–270), through whom so much of Greek thought passed into Christianity: he called it 'the flight of the alone to the alone'.

The word itself is derived from the Greek mystery cults; and as in them, the candidates (*mystae*) passed after a journey with many stages through darkness into the light of initiation; so the *mystic* hopes that by training he may pass by various stages into union with the divine. But, while the Greek mysteries were performed in common, the mystic's path is solitary. He is not independent of outside help (for indeed, the path is dangerous as well as difficult) but, in the end, he is alone. This is true whether he is Christian, Mohammedan, Buddhist or Hindu; for there are mystics in all religions, and they form a spiritual aristocracy closely united by temperament, method, language, and achievement.

Mystics (like skaters and ballet dancers) usually begin young if they are to be any good: William Blake saw visions at eight or ten; St Catharine of Siena wanted to go and imitate the desert hermits at six; John Woolman the Quaker 'began to be acquainted with the operations of Divine Love' before he was seven, and read the *Book of Revelation* coming home from school, 'while my companions went to play by the way'; and as for St Teresa of Avila, she had scarce learnt to lisp a name of martyr (as Crashaw tells us), when

> Farewell whatever dear may be –
> Mother's arms, or father's knee!
> Farewell house, and farewell home!
> She's for the Moors and Martyrdom.

Nor is this precocity a purely Christian phenomenon; Rabi'a of Basra was still a slave-girl when her master, overhearing her prayers, set her free. For even in Islam, that most masculine of religions, women mystics have an unchallenged position of equality with men. And because of their precocity, few mystics have had experience of the process known as 'conversion'; they are (in William James's phrase) 'once-born' and not 'twice-born'. 'Certainly Adam in Paradise had not more sweet and curious apprehensions of the world, than I when I was a child', says Thomas Traherne; 'the green trees when I saw them first through one of the gates transported and ravished me, their sweetness and unusual beauty made my heart to leap, and almost mad with ecstasy, they were such strange and wonderful things.'

A very large number of mystics, also, are self-educated or uneducated people. Traherne was a cobbler's son; Boehme was a cobbler; Kabir from northern India was a weaver; Blake never went to school; George Fox wrote and spelt atrociously, and never took pen in hand if he could find an amanuensis. In spite of this (or because of this?) most mystics, including George Fox, have had literary gifts and many of them have been poets, including Milarespa, whose songs are sung all over Tibet; Jallal'uddin Rūmī, a *Sufi* like Rabi'a, who wrote in Persian; St John of the Cross, who wrote in Spanish; William Langland from fourteenth-century Malvern, and Emily Dickinson from nineteenth-century Massachusetts.

Yet the mystics are inevitably faced by difficulties of language in conveying their experience.

The figures of the *journey*, the *marriage*, and of *darkness* and *light* are used again and again, but at last become banal and inadequate; *paradox* is invoked, but in the end ceases to startle; and a symbolic dialect appears, which from the outside is often as uninviting as a chestnut burr, although from the inside it is full of sweetness. It includes the *monads* and *triads* of Plotinus, Eckhardt's *Nameless Nothing* and *Immovable Rest*, Boehme's *Urgrund*, the Abyss or the Great Mystery, Blake's *Albion* and *Jerusalem*, his *Urizen, Los, Luvah, Tharmas*, and the rest, which are at once a means and a hindrance, a mechanism and a revelation, a thorny hedge behind which a Sleeping Beauty lies enchanted.

Many attempts have been made to describe and distinguish the stages of their journey, but this, too, is very difficult, for they are not separated or descried mathematically. Ruysbroeck names seven stages; Hugh of St Victor, four; Walter Hilton, three; Evelyn Underhill sees five. In the East there are similar categories, and a similar lack of unanimity. As in the Greek Eleusinia there was a division between Lesser and Greater, so some authorities make *meditation* and *contemplation* the Lesser and Greater Halves of the Mystic Way.

In *meditation*, which can be taught and practised like any other school subject (and even marked, if desired), the student uses Reason, Memory and Will. He chooses (or is set) a subject, let us say his own death, or the Crucifixion, or the Last Judgement. Then (if he uses the method of St Ignatius Loyola's *Spiritual Exercises* (1548), as many, both Protestant and Catholic, did) he begins with a preparatory prayer for Grace. Using the memory he makes two preludes, one (the *compositio loci*) to evoke the circumstances, the other (according to the subject matter) to evoke the mood of the theme. He proceeds to the meditation proper, in which, using the reason, he elaborates three or five points that arise; and finally, having raised his spiritual temperature to the point where it kindles, he launches into the *Colloquy*, a free outpouring of the devotion aroused.

But these things will carry the disciple only a certain way; there comes a point where system fails, and indeed many of the great mystics have never consciously or regularly been instructed in

it, although their lives partly show the pattern. *Contemplation* begins when reason ceases, when no conscious plan is followed, and all the aids are thrown away, whether they are of the nature just described, or whether they are the systems of breathing and body control practised in Yoga and other Eastern systems; the arts such as archery and flower-arrangement followed in Zen Buddhism; the ascetic practices by which the body is tamed and the self reduced to submission; the *kyilkhors* or diagrams used in Tibet, drawn on paper or with coloured powders on the floor; or any other ingenious disciplines.

The novice is now becoming an adept, and he must go alone, but the higher he goes, the greater the danger – the danger of hallucination, of madness, the danger of spiritual pride, especially if his advance manifests itself in supranormal powers; levitation, second sight, sitgmatization or trance, Alexandra David-Neel has good examples of these in her book *With Mystics and Magicians in Tibet*. One guru (teacher) on hearing that another had boasted of walking across the river without calling the ferryman, remarked caustically: 'Such a trick is not worth the penny to pay the ferry.' Another, whose disciple had succeeded in materializing a demon which became his familiar, listened unmoved to the disciple's agonized confession of his loss of faith: the demon was only a hallucination. 'Exactly,' says the master, 'Gods, demons, the whole universe, are but a mirage which exists in the mind, springs from it, and sinks into it. That is what it is necessary for you to realize.'

Across the other side of the world, the English Quaker Isaac Penington (1616–1679) said much the same: 'All Truth is a shadow except the last, except the utmost, yet every Truth is true in its kind. It is substance in its own place, though it be but a shadow in another place (for it is but a shadow from an intenser substance); and the shadow is a true shadow, as the substance is a true substance.'

To this True Substance, then, the mystic now turns himself. However, there remains a greater danger than all: the Dark Night of the Soul through which the soul must pass. In its negative aspect it presents itself as despair, abandonment, utter joylessness, because all previous achievements must be left behind. But then the darkness becomes 'a deep and dazzling darkness'. 'The soul feels as if placed in a vast and profound solitude, to which no created thing has access, in an immense and boundless desert, desert the more delicious the more solitary it is. There, in this abyss of wisdom, the soul grows by what it drinks in from the well-springs of the comprehension of love.'

So to the union that no words can express, but which brings unity with all things. 'Now was I come up in spirit through the flaming sword into the Paradise of God. All things were new, and all the creation gave another smell to me than before, beyond what words can utter.' So George Fox. And across the world, Rūmī ends his song:

O ask ye no more of me. Were I to tell you more words of his,
You would burst your bonds. No roof nor door could restrain you.

ILLUSTRATION: Page 314.

N

Ideas of Nature

NATURE is most familiar to the modern mind in a sense derived from the Romantic writers, in particular, from Rousseau, Wordsworth and Shelley.

According to this view, Nature is assigned at once an important and also an elusive place in the human scheme. In the first place, Nature is not co-extensive with the whole of natural phenomena, but more particularly with the parts of it that make up the countryside – although, even here, it is not certain that Nature might not be more in evidence on a bomb-site than in a well-tended park. Again, Nature is not to be identified with any natural phenomena, with birds, trees, rivers or bushes, but it is a force that lies behind them and of which they are the manifestation; which leaves room for a number of attitudes ranging from a more or less articulate paganism

to the most attenuated belief in immanent powers or pantheism.

Again, Nature is our tutor but a tutor who uses the most oblique forms of instruction, and whose lessons are as likely to be grasped by the simple unthinking peasant as by the attentive scholar. And finally, this attitude to Nature, so far from being a stimulus to scientific enquiry, has on the whole tended to be anti-scientific in its attitude and opposed to all attempts to analyse and classify the phenomena of Nature. This attitude has received its classic formulation in Wordsworth:

One impulse from a vernal wood
May teach you more of man,
Of moral evil and of good,
Than all the sages can.
(*The Tables Turned.*)

or

His daily teachers had been woods and rills,
The silence that is in the starry sky,
The sleep that is among the lonely hills.
(*Song at the Feast of Brougham Castle.*)

But this note, first sounded a hundred and fifty years ago, has been heard time and time again since then in English literature: in Shelley, in some of Tennyson's poetry, in George Eliot's provincial novels, in Thoreau, in the poems and novels of D. H. Lawrence, where it is deep and daemonic, and in the novels of E. M. Forster, where it is gentle and whimsical. The degree to which one responds to it must be a matter of temperament and conditioning, but there can be no doubt that it is one of the most valuable and enlivening modes of modern sensibility and is found by many to be the surest palliative against the pains of a mechanical civilization.

None the less Nature has meant many things at different times and to different people; and a glance beyond – and beside – Wordsworth or Rousseau is required.

To Plato and Aristotle a person or thing was rightly employed *only* when it was employed in a fashion true to its nature. To the Stoics, the whole of morality could be summed up in the precept 'Follow Nature'. The difference between these two conceptions is important for a just understanding of either of them. Plato and Aristotle were interested in the way in which each kind had its own nature; whereas for the Stoics what was important was the sense of an all-embracing World Order exhibiting certain simple rational laws for work of the Divine Reason, so that the nature of any animate or inanimate thing could be inferred from seeing its place in the whole.

But the similarities between the two views are more important. Neither makes the 'nature' of anything what it actually did or was. Its 'nature' was rather its purpose: that for which it was made. Accordingly the view that morality can be expressed entirely in such terms brings us immediately up against two difficulties which must be resolved if it is to have any validity: the first is whether human beings, animals, etc., have been made for a purpose in the same way as such human artifacts as spades or chairs; the second is whether we can discover what this purpose is, whether we can, as it were, gain knowledge of the blueprints of the universal artificer.

In previous times, this view was widely accepted. The medieval belief in Natural Law is in large measure a continuation of the ideas of some of the French Encyclopaedists, and their English descendants, the Utilitarians.

'Nature', begins Bentham's *Principles of Morals and Legislation* (1789), 'has placed mankind under the governance of two sovereign masters, *pain* and *pleasure*. It is for them alone to point out what we ought to do, as well as to determine what we shall do. On the one hand the standard of right and wrong, on the other the chain of causes and effects are fastened to their throne.' In the nineteenth century this form of Naturalism received another lease of life with the impact of Darwinism, and the idea of revolutionary morals. In Herbert Spencer (1820–1903) we find what is right identified with what conduces to survival; and the theory of biological values has found adherents ranging from philosophically minded scientists to pamphleteers in favour of violent political parties.

ILLUSTRATION: Plate 9 and Pages 318 and 319.

Pulling oneself together

NEUROSIS is a functional nervous disorder, that is to say a disorder in which there is no structural or organic change in the system 'Neuroses', says Freud, 'are not things that happen to a person as an infection or an accident may, they are rather expressions of the personality designed to meet certain situations, to cope with certain difficulties, to achieve certain aims.'

Neuroses really constitute varieties of social adjustments, so that a person who is well adjusted to his environment may be called 'normal', whereas a person whose emotional attitude to experience sets up a conflict in his mind that results in mental or physical distress, or both, may be called neurotic. Freud held that neurotic reactions can be demonstrated with almost everyone, and that they are little more than a particular way of responding to difficult stages in mental development. Apart from superficial considerations, the distinction between normal and abnormal is here quite arbitrary.

There have always been two contrasting views about neurosis, the popular and the medical. The popular view is that neurotic ailments are due to a morbid imagination and a weakness of will. Neurotics are popularly held to lack moral fibre, and their troubles are often dismissed as mere self-indulgence, a means of obtaining sympathy and avoiding the ordinary responsibilities of life with which they would be perfectly capable of coping if only they would exercise a little self-control and 'pull themselves together'.

The term 'neurosis' has become widely known and widely misunderstood owing to the popularization of the teachings of psychologists, and in particular to the teachings of Sigmund Freud (1856–1939). The result is that it is often used indiscriminately as a stick with which to beat those who are difficult to understand and who do not appear to conform to the accepted canons of social behaviour, or more precisely with the views and prejudices of whoever happens to be wielding the stick.

The medical attitude towards neurosis has been strongly influenced by the popular attitude. The treatment meted out to neurotics has often been drastic, and whipping was prescribed until the beginning of the nineteenth century. Only gradually did the more modern method called 'kind but firm' establish itself. The official medical view at the turn of the century was that neurotic disorders were proper diseases for which the victims were in no way responsible. 'The difficulty was to ascertain the nature of the "disease" which was so plainly out of ordinary medical experience. The fiction was invented that there must be some such disease, but that unfortunately its traces in the brain were invisible, and so the term "functional disease of the brain" was coined,' wrote Ernest Jones in his *Abnormal Psychology* (1950).

It was Freud who first gave a specific meaning to neurotic symptoms. He held that they arise from repressed impulses of which the patient is unconscious, and serve a purpose that is unknown to him. When an impulse arises in anyone that is shameful by his standards, he may struggle with it in the full light of consciousness and repudiate it. In such circumstances, Freud says, no harm is done because the 'charge of energy' associated with the impulse is withdrawn from it. If, however, the personality draws back, as it were, after the first shock of conflict with the impulse, and debars it from further access to consciousness, then the impulse becomes 'repressed' and remains active in the unconscious. Eventually the repressed impulse breaks its way through at some point or other and produces symptoms. The symptoms are thus results of a compromise, for although they are substitute gratifications, they are nevertheless distorted and deflected from their aim owing to the resistance of the ego. (Freud, *An Autobiographical Study*.)

Freud taught that the impulses which most often meet with repression arise in the sexual sphere and have their origin in infantile sexuality. He regarded 'the Oedipus complex' as the kernel of the neuroses. 'Now you will be impatiently waiting to hear what this terrible Oedipus complex comprises. The name tells you: you all know the Greek myth of King Oedipus whose destiny it was to slay his father and to wed his mother, who did all in his power to avoid the fate prophesied by the oracle, and who in self-punishment blinded himself when he discovered that in ignorance he had committed both these crimes.' (Freud, *Introductory Lectures on Psycho-Analysis*.)

Freud said that in essence this tragic drama is re-enacted in every male child's mind; and that things proceed in just the same way, with the necessary reversal, in little girls. Even as early as the age of three, the male child is passing, in his sexual development, into the phallic stage. 'Now what does direct observation of children show us in regard to the Oedipus complex? Well, it is easy to see that the little boy wants his mother all to himself, finds his father in the way, becomes restive when the latter takes upon himself to caress her, and shows his satisfaction when the father goes away, or is absent. He often expresses his feelings directly in words and promises his mother to marry her; this may not seem much in comparison with the deeds of Oedipus, but it is enough in fact; the kernel of each is the same.' (Freud, *Introductory Lectures on Pyscho-Analysis*.)

Freud held that from about the sixth year till the time of puberty a standstill is observed in the sexual development which may be called a latency period. At the time of puberty, however, a very intense flow of feeling towards the Oedipus complex, or in reaction to it, comes into force. Since at this stage of development the idea of incest has become intolerable, these feelings must remain for the most part repressed and outside consciousness. Freud holds that one of the most important sources of the sense of guilt and anxiety which so often torments neurotic people is to be found in the Oedipus complex, which continues to exist in the unconscious.

The more successful the individual is in freeing himself or herself from the parents, the less likely is the unconscious Oedipus complex to manifest itself in the form of neurotic symptoms. A son is faced with the task of releasing himself from dependence on his mother in order to employ his energies in the quest of 'an external love object in reality'. He must reconcile himself with his father, or free himself from the father's domination, if, in reaction to the infantile revolt, he has lapsed into subservience to him. These tasks are laid down for every man, and in the reversed relationship for every woman.

When this detachment from the parents is not achieved, the neurotic personality develops. The son remains all his life in subjection to his father, in a perpetual state of guilt and anxiety; and is incapable of transferring his love from his mother to another woman. In the reversed relationship, the daughter's fate may be similar. In this sense the Oedipus complex is justifiably regarded as the kernel of the neuroses.

Alternative views concerning neurosis were put forward by Adler and Jung, both of whom worked in close collaboration with Freud, before breaking away to found their own schools of 'Individual Psychology' and 'Analytical Psychology'. Adler suggests that neurosis is almost always due to a sense of inferiority, or 'inferiority complex' (q.v.). Jung's view is harder to present, for it avowedly passes beyond the canons of science and enters the realm of philosophy and mysticism (see *Modern Man in Search of a Soul*, 2nd ed., 1933). Essentially Jung's teachings re-interpret those of Freud in more abstract terms.

Clearing the site

NIHILISM is essentially a denial of the existing order, and in philosophical terms Nihilism comprises the following propositions: nothing exists; nothing is knowable; nothing has value. This is hardly a very fruitful point of departure for philosophical reflection or for a system of thought; and, in fact, the first exponent of Nihilism in philosophic theory was also the last.

Gorgias of Leontini, in Sicily (c. 483–376 B.C.), one of the leading Sophists in Plato's time, a master of rhetoric and a travelling professor, as it were, who earned fame and wealth by preparing the well-to-do youths of Greece for their part in city government, wrote a treatise on *Nature or the Non-Existent*, in which he taught that nothing exists, that if anything did exist it would be unknowable, and that if it did exist and were knowable it could not be communicated. Although, like most of the writings of the Sophists, the treatise has disappeared, a detailed account of this philosophic nihilism is to be found in the Aristotelian Corpus.

Nihilism on this level sowed no pregnant thought in later philosophical writing. But the religious nihilism inherent in the Buddhist faith which contained, in the extreme Buddhist's concept of absolute truth an unqualified negation of the world of appearances, has affected western thought.

Schopenhauer (1788–1860) was one of the first to introduce the nihilist aspect of the Buddhist faith to the West. In *The World as Will and Idea* (1818), his doctrine of the Denial of the Will stems directly from Buddhist mysticism. In discussing the 'good man' he writes: 'The life we know, the good man willingly abandons. What he receives in exchange is void in our eyes, just because our existence compared to that is nothing. This new state Buddhist faith calls Nirvana – that is to say, extinction.' And again, 'We must banish the dark impression of that nothingness which we discern behind all virtues and holiness, as their final goal, and which we fear as children fear the dark; we must not even evade it like the Indians, through myths and meaningless words, such as reabsorption in Brahma or the Nirvana of the Buddhists. Rather do we freely acknowledge that what remains after the entire abolition of will is for all those who are still full of will, certainly nothing; but conversely, to those in whom the will has turned and has denied itself, this, our world, which is so real, with all its suns and milky ways – is nothing' – which is surely a very definite exposition of religious nihilism.

In the nineteenth century Nihilism played a part socially and politically in the idea that social progress is to be looked for only in the abolition of existing social institutions. In its extreme form this is the doctrine of Anarchism (q.v.), but first it was proposed in utopian form by William Godwin (1756–1836), then in evolutionary terms by Proudhon (1809–1865); and later on it reappeared as a movement under the name of Nihilism in Russia of the eighteen-sixties and seventies.

The political idea expressed by Godwin, is to be found in his *Enquiry concerning Political Justice* (1795) a work which threw Shelley into a febrile enthusiasm. Godwin dreamed of a new-made world, inhabited by perfect beings, without government, without laws, without trade or marriage, with peace permanently secured by the vigilance of public opinion. He outlined the complete wrecking of existing institutions, and drew a picture of the ideal simple life to come, based on abstract reason as the rule for human conduct, and with abstract good for its goal.

This utopian scheme contained so little understanding of human nature that it provoked only a shortlived notoriety.

Continued on p. 279

PLATE 10

ROMANTIC LOVE: April Love by Arthur Hughes (1830–1915).

INSPIRATION: *The Poet and his Muse,* by Henri Rousseau (1844–1910).

'IVORY TOWER': A Chinese view. *The Philosopher*, by Tai Ch'in.

264

THE GOLDEN AGE: Painting by Giorgione (c. 1478–1510).

DULCE ET DECORUM EST PRO PATRIA MORI : Sir Henry Newbolt (1862–1938), by Meredith Frampton, A.R.A. (1930).

ROMANTIC INDIVIDUALISM: William Wordsworth (1832). Drawing by H. W. Pickersgill (1782–1875).

IMPERIALISM: 1. Cecil Rhodes (1853–1902).

2. Rudyard Kipling (1865–1936), painted by P. Burne-Jones.

THE RULE OF LAW: 1. A High Court Judge, Hyderabad, India.

2. Magistrates' Court in England.

THE POLICE STATE: 1. Himmler's Germany.

2. Franco's Spain.

LAST DAY: 1. Detail from *The Seven Deadly Sins*, by Hieronymus Bosch (c. 1460–1516).

2. *The Last Day*, by the chief master of the 'Heures
de Turin'. (The right wing of an altarpiece.)

NEMESIS: Woodcut by Albrecht Dürer (1471–1528).

276

LEVIATHAN: Title-page of the book by Thomas Hobbes, 1651.

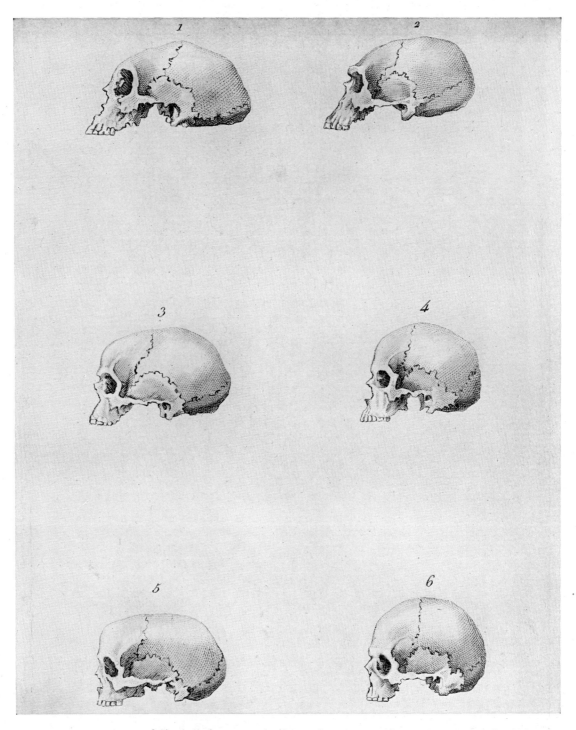

HIGHBROW OR LOWBROW? Six skulls from an early nineteenth century treatise on phrenology. 1 is Caribbean, 2 New Zealand, 3, 5 and 6 Scottish and 4 Chinese.

PLATE 11

HERO-WORSHIP: Detail from The Rape of the Sabines by Nicolas Poussin (1594–1665).

Proudhon in his *Qu'est-ce que la propriété?* (1840) maintained that property was theft, suggested an evolutionary method of dispensing with government, and had a far greater influence on nineteenth-century politics by reason of his more moderate approach.

The urge to abolish existing social institutions was of course grounded in the actual and overwhelming effects of the French Revolution, and in the early days of the Socialist movement it held its place, with the abolition of private property and the equality of individual men and women, as the socialist aim. It was only when the labour movement came to identify itself with State Socialism that the Anarchists broke away to form a separate party.

In Russia, the stream of socialist and liberal thought and ideas released by the French Revolution and the increasing scientific and materialist approach to social problems came into fierce conflict with despotic government, and produced the curious phenomenon of a whole generation of Nihilists, intent upon the affirmation of individual rights and the destruction of existing social forms.

Turgenev first gave the name of Nihilism to this revolutionary movement epitomizing it in the character of Bazarov, in his novel *Fathers and Sons* (1862) which was serialized in the *Russian Messenger*, the organ of the younger generation, only one year after the emancipation of the serfs. Looking back on this event in 1869, he said, 'I will not enlarge on the effect produced by this novel. I will only say that everywhere the word Nihilist was caught up by a thousand tongues, and that on the day of the conflagration of the Apraksinsky shops, when I arrived in St Petersburg, the first exclamation with which I was greeted was "Just see what your Nihilists are doing!".'

In *Fathers and Sons* Bazarov recognizes no authority of any kind and declares war on the conventional lies of mankind. He is a scientific materialist in revolt against tradition, sentiment, superstition, prejudices, against art and literature; and he believes himself to be governed by reason alone.

'Both I and Bazarov have told you', says Bazarov's friend Arkady to his uncle, 'that we recognize no authority of any sort.' Bazarov corrects him: 'Rather that we recognize no basis for action save the useful. At present the course most useful is denial. Therefore we deny.'

'Deny everything?' 'Deny everything.' 'What? Both poetry and art and – I find it hard to express it?' 'I repeat, everything,' said Bazarov with an ineffable expression of *insouciance*. 'Allow me,' interposed Nikolia Petrovitch [Arkady's father]. 'You say that you deny everything – rather, that you would consign everything to destruction. But also you ought to construct.' 'That is not our business,' said Bazarov. 'First must the site be cleared.'

The younger generation of Russians, finding themselves mirrored in the character of Bazarov, received the novel with loud protest. They described the hero as a caricature, and it was largely due to the furious reception of what he believed to be his best novel that Turgenev left Russia to live in Paris. Kropotkin tells us that he so identified himself with the Nihilist philosophy of his hero that he even kept a diary in his name, appreciating the current events of the day from Bazarov's point of view.

Looking back, perhaps Bakunin (1814–1876) was the chief source of inspiration for this Russian movement, which ended in smoke, because it had no real goal except the negative one of 'clearing the site'. This Russian aristocrat, revolting against the oppression of Poland and exiled for his dangerous opinions, developed as his revolutionary aims the destruction of the existing order of things in faith, words, economics and politics. He founded the International Social Democratic Alliance. In his own words: 'The Alliance professes atheism. It aims at the abolition of religious services, the replacement of belief by knowledge; Divine by human justice; the abolition of marriage as a political, religious, judicial and civic arrangement. Before all, it aims at the definite and complete abolition of all classes, and the political, economic and social equality of the individual of both sexes. And to attain this end, it demands, before all, the abolition of inheritance in order that for the future usufruct may depend on what each produces.'

Nihilism starts as a theoretical leveller, but in action it can only destroy.

ILLUSTRATION: Pages 320 and 321.

'When wild in woods the noble savage ran'

The **NOBLE SAVAGE** is a term which expresses belief in the moral superiority of primitive over civilized man. This doctrine became widespread and influential in the late seventeenth and eighteenth centuries, and the phrase dates in English from Dryden's play *The Conquest of Granada* (1670):

> I am as free as nature first made man,
> Ere the base laws of servitude began,
> When wild in woods the noble savage ran.

Those who used it believed that our slow progress from barbarism to civilization has corrupted the virtues of the natural man; while society has been enriched, the individual has lost his goodness and his liberty.

To the Greeks, such an idea would have been strange. Their whole life centred in cities which gave them protection against hostile neighbours, and there alone could they practise the arts of living freely. They were acutely conscious that they were civilized, and they were contemptuous of the 'barbarians' they came in contact with. Society, they believed, gave man the morality and the real freedom which the savage lacked in his unfettered ability to do his fellow harm. Man is a poor creature by himself; he needs the company and compulsion of others to make the most of his powers.

The Romans, admirers of good government *par excellence*, were hardly likely to admire the lawless savage. The historian Tacitus, on the other hand, writing in the first century A.D., saw merits in the behaviour of the primitive Germans of his day. He pointed out the contrast between their courage and chastity and the conduct of the decadent Romans of the time.

Christianity adds another idea. Man in solitude is not only barren by nature, he also has original sin (q.v.). Only by membership of the church and rigorous endeavour to keep her commandments can he lift himself up to nobility. It is the very 'laws of servitude' which make him noble, releasing man from his natural baseness.

With the coming of the Vandals and Goths and the fall of the Roman Empire, civilized man would be even more aware of the gulf which separated him from the barbarian invaders. The noble savage exercised his freedom in acts of destruction; and who would envy his liberty to kill and rape, loot and burn, knowing himself to be a probable victim? During the Middle Ages, Europeans scarcely came in contact with peoples less civilized than themselves. It was not until the voyages of exploration at the end of the fifteenth century that they were reminded of the existence of 'primitive' man once more.

The increasing horror of violence and the growing comfort of daily life made the free life of the savage even less enviable. The philosopher Thomas Hobbes, writing in his *Leviathan* (1651), gives a picture of man in his natural state living a life nasty, brutish and short. Few would have disagreed with him then. 'No arts; no letters; no society; and which is worst of all, continual fear and danger of violent death'.

For three reasons there was a great revolt in the eighteenth century against this view of man's nature. Men were beginning to doubt the existence of God, and the necessity and efficacy of Christianity. When the doctrine of original sin went out of fashion, so did the idea that man was evil by nature. At the same time reason began to replace faith as the guide to beliefs and behaviour. Although they now believed that men were naturally good, the philosophers could not deny that many people behaved extremely badly. They argued that this was because society was so irrational and artificial that the natural good in men became obscured and overlaid. The solution was to return to nature. Rational or natural morality would replace Christianity, and men would be freed from the obedience to false laws which had bowed them down with sin and bondage for so long.

The second reason for the revolt was the attack on despotism. This was especially true of France, where the philosophers found themselves hampered by the censorship. England had rid herself of a potential tyrant in 1688, but in France absolute monarchy remained unchallenged. If man was naturally good, it was asked, what need was there for the King or even the state itself? Their view of the state was a negative one; it prevented disorder rather than conferred tangible benefits. At the same time, in their inability to distinguish between state and society, men believed that the stateless savage lacked only the evils and not the benefits of community life. When early in the century Louis XV's reign added misrule to absolutism, the savage's liberty was even more enviable. Not all the French thinkers, however, wanted to do away with government; it was only a small band of extremists who went so far. Rousseau, a thinker and writer who had as passionate a love of liberty as anyone, says in his *Du Contrat Social* of 1762: 'The passage from the state of nature to the civil state produces a remarkable change in the individual. It substitutes justice for instinct in his behaviour, and gives to his actions a moral basis that was formerly lacking'. He saw that it was not the abolition of government that mankind needed, but self-government.

At the same time, interest in man in his natural state was becoming fashionable among thinkers. There was a far more confident attitude towards the whole of nature. As man's mastery over natural forces increased, he ceased to think of all nature as wholly chaotic and destructive, but instead ordered and reasonable. Instead of shutting their windows and barring their doors to keep nature out, they employed landscape gardeners to bring the 'natural landscape' right up to their windows. Fear of the untamed savage was replaced by rational thinking about him and his place in the world. Believing nature to be rational, they thought the savage must have his place in the ordered universe. In fact he was man as nature intended man to be; it was the artificial, social man who was base and evil, the savage who was noble. In some ways this doctrine of the Noble Savage was the belief in the Golden Age (q.v.) translated out of time into geography. In the Golden Age mankind had been simple and pure and natural. To go back to Dryden in his version of Juvenal's Sixth Satire

In Saturn's reign, at Nature's Early Birth,
There was that thing call'd Chastity on Earth;
When in a narrow cave, their common shade,
The sheep, the shepherds and their gods were laid:
When reeds and leaves, and hides of beasts were spread
By mountain huswifes for their homely bed,
And mossy pillows rais'd, for the rude husband's head.
Unlike the niceness of our modern dames,
(Affected nymphs with new affected names:)

The Cynthias and the Lesbias of our years,
Who for a sparrow's death dissolve in tears,
Those first unpolisht matrons, big and bold,
Gave suck to infants of gygantick mold;
Rough as their savage lords who rang'd the wood,
And fat with aƙorns belcht their windy food.
For when the world was bucksome, fresh, and young
Her sons were undebauch'd and therefore strong.

It is this belief in the moral purity of primitive man which was the most attractive aspect of the doctrine of the noble savage. Many who did not want to do away with Church and State were influenced by the ideal to look more critically at contemporary morals and institutions. While few believed the doctrine of a complete return to nature whole-heartedly, many found its moral challenge attractive.

How many thinkers who put forward this theory had had actual contact with primitive people? Many more Europeans were meeting backward races as they spread their dominion over more distant lands, but their tales do not seem to have affected the thought of the rationalists. Had they taken the trouble, the thinkers could have found out what primitive life was really like. They would have heard odd tales of kindness, of how the Red Indians took pity on the starving Pilgrim Fathers, for example. Yet for every story of mercy there must have been many of destruction, cruelty and perfidy. The European thinkers were not to be deflected; nothing shook their faith in the superiority of the uncivilized man, the man most in harmony with nature.

As what we name 'romanticism' became more definite at the end of the eighteenth century, there was a new reason for admiring the Natural Man. Men ceased to appeal to reason, and put all their faith in sensation instead; and the emotional attraction of the Noble Savage was very great. He obeyed his natural instincts, and his emotions were not trampled down by laws and conventions. Moreover, he lived amid the beauty of woods and plains. In every way his freedom was enviable.

While this aspect of the ideal of the Noble Savage became more powerful with the growth of towns and industry, the rest of it slowly faded away. Those who wanted to escape the towns did not wish to deny themselves the benefits of good government.

Now, in the twentieth century, the idea of the

Noble Savage is more than a hundred years out of date, leaving only its residues behind. With great advances in communications and literacy, not to mention anthropology (a science indebted to the stimulus of the idea of the Noble Savage), there is no one entirely ignorant of the way of life of remote peoples. It was to his remoteness that the appeal of the Noble Savage was partly due. His absolutely ideal quality has been shattered by more common and more frequent contact. The positive good a government can do is visible, and no one would wish to throw off the whole yoke of the state. Also we know that only the inculcation of the accumulated civilization of centuries turns the primitive infant into the civilized adult. Neither the European nor the Australian aborigine is 'good' by nature, but by training and example.

Nobody thinks that modern civilized society and the man it produces are perfect. But what is needed is reform not abolition. Few people want to return to nature and do away with society and the state altogether; that is not the road to greater nobility; and as a potent idea, the Noble Savage is dead.

ILLUSTRATION: Plate 6 and Page 313.

O

Ourselves and our destiny

ORIGINAL SIN is the explanation of human conduct and human destiny derived from the story of Creation and the Fall of Man contained in the first three chapters of Genesis. Adam and Eve broke God's command; and all their posterity are implicated in their transgression.

We begin with a desert; then from the dry ground a mist rises and waters it. God makes a man from the mud, and breathes life into his nostrils. God plants a garden 'eastward in Eden' and puts the man there; a river wells up and flows four ways through the garden. The garden is filled with trees, and in the middle are the Tree of Life and the Tree of Knowledge of Good and Evil. The man is ordered to take care of the garden, and he may eat of any tree, except the Tree of Knowledge of Good and Evil, 'for in the day that thou eatest thereof thou shalt surely die'. God decides that it is not good for man to be alone; and having made from the earth all beasts and birds, and brought them to Adam to be named, God then puts Adam to sleep.

From his side God takes a rib, and builds a woman. Adam names and describes her – bone of his bones and flesh of his flesh; and explains marriage: 'Therefore shall a man leave his father and mother and shall cleave unto his wife, and they shall be one flesh.' And both are naked and not ashamed.

The serpent is 'more subtil than any beast of the field', and tempts the woman to eat of the forbidden tree. 'Ye shall not surely die ... your eyes shall be opened, and ye shall be as gods, knowing good and evil.' The woman eats, and gives to her husband; now they know shame, and make aprons of fig leaves; this betrays their transgression to God, when he walks in the garden in the cool of the day. In vain they hide; in vain the man blames the woman, and the woman the serpent. The serpent has no one to blame, and is first sentenced: to be hated above all, to go on its belly, to be always at strife with man. Then the woman is sentenced: to the pains of childbirth, of need for man and subjection to him. And finally man is sentenced: 'In the sweat of thy face shalt thou eat bread, till thou return to the ground; for out of it wast thou taken: for dust thou art, and unto dust shall return.'

The ground brings forth weeds; the man and woman are clothed; and she has a new name, Eve, the mother of all living. Then God expels them from the garden, and sets Cherubims at the gate with 'a flaming sword which turned every way, to keep the way of the Tree of Life'. For now that man knows good and evil, and 'is become as one of us', he may take of the Tree of Life also, 'and eat, and live for ever.'

This story, beginning in the second chapter of *Genesis*, is one of many versions of the Creation myth current in the Semitic world. The two trees, the double name of God (Yahweh Elohim), the two names of Adam's helpmeet (Woman and Eve), suggest that it is already composite. It is preceded, however, in the first chapter of Genesis, by a quite different Creation story, with a God more tremendous, more remote, who from the void, in eight stages, creates and names Light and Darkness; the Firmament of Heaven and the waters; Earth and the Seas; Herbs and Trees; Stars, Sun and Moon; the creatures of the Seas; the beasts of the Earth; and Man, male and female, to whom God gives dominion over all. In six days the tasks are accomplished; 'and God saw everything that he had made, and behold, it was very good'. And the seventh day God rests from his labours, and blesses and sanctifies it. Here the story ends, on a note of triumph and not of disgust.

This first version, though close in some details to the Babylonian Gilgamesh epic, is very different in spirit both from the wrestling demons of Babylonian chaos, and from the muddled, endearing, homely creation of *Genesis II*. This God has no afterthoughts; he does not create with his fingers from the mud, but with his *fiat*; all is planned, and man is the last of creation: male and female man is created from the beginning. The only sign of confusion is the fitting of eight tasks into six days, which points to another version with a different time scheme.

Such arguments as these, however, belong to recent history. Before the Dutchman Jean le-Clerc in the late seventeenth century, and the Frenchman Jean Astruc in the early eighteenth, no one had thought of questioning the unity of *Genesis*; and the detective work which prised apart the original documents, as well as the parallels yielded from Sumerian tablets, belong to the nineteenth century. If we ask why these glaring contradictions were never noticed before, by the great minds of the Fathers and the Schoolmen and the Humanists, who knew the text almost by heart and criticized it with such subtlety, we must answer that they never thought in such terms. They interpreted by the weapon of allegory; but because of the latent contradictions, their allegory raised all manner of questions that demanded an answer.

Was creation good (as the first version concludes)? Or was it corrupted into thorns and thistles, curses and enmity, the pains of childbirth and the pains of death, and a Paradise from which man is kept by the flaming sword turned every way? Did God have to place temptation in man's way by putting the trees in the garden? What was the nature of Adam's transgression, and did its results affect him only, or all his posterity? If original sin is inherited how is this consistent with God's justice? Is the child spoilt at birth, or in what manner? Is death the primal punishment?

The Danish philosopher Kierkegaard, in the nineteenth century, pointed out the difficulty very clearly. Sin, he said, is an ethical and spiritual category; 'inheritance' is a natural (or we might say, legal) category. How then can we compound them? We are saying that something is inherited which by definition cannot be inherited. Kierkegaard answers: 'It must be believed. The paradox in Christian truth is due to the fact that it is truth as it exists for God. The standard of measure and the end is superhuman; and there is only one relationship possible: faith.'

Earlier, in the seventeenth century, Pascal had considered the same points and found them equally absurd and necessary. 'Certainly, nothing shakes us more roughly than this doctrine. Yet without this, the most incomprehensible of all mysteries, we are incomprehensible to ourselves. The knot of our destiny took its twists and turns from this abyss; and it is harder to conceive man without this mystery than for man to comprehend it.' And so we may drive the debate back to the Fathers, to Tertullian's attitude of *certum, quia impossibile* and to Augustine's *credo, quia absurdum*: 'It is certain, because it is impossible; I believe it, because it is absurd.'

This appeal beyond reason has, in fact, survived the appeal to reason. When nineteenth-century scholarship revealed the inconsistencies of *Genesis*, and destroyed its claim to represent an historical account of the Creation of the world, begun, as Archbishop Ussher claimed 'in the night preceding the 23rd day of October, being our sunday, in the year 4004 before Christ', it seemed as if the scheme of theology must fall to pieces. Either the world was not made in that way, or (in the memorable phrase of Charles Kingsley) 'God has written on the rocks one enormous and superfluous lie'.

Theology, however, survived. Until the

Renaissance, no one would have dreamed, like Archbishop Ussher, of endeavouring to pinpoint the day and hour of creation. The result of the crisis of faith has been to distinguish the truth of myth as a separate category, and to prove that it is essential.

If Original Sin appears, in some ways, a legalistic conception, it was in fact a lawyer, Tertullian, in the second century A.D., who first defined it; Cyprian, who took it up and gave it ecclesiastical sanction; and Augustine, who elaborated it as part of the whole scheme of Redemption. We are not bound to take literally the legalistic terms of the Fall and the Atonement, any more than we are bound to take literally Ussher's Biblical chronology. But we are bound to take seriously a conception which not only gives sense to many of the facts of history and experience, but which offers hope. For we can say, with Robert Barclay: 'Whatever literal signifaction this may have, we may safely ascribe to this Paradise a mystical signification, and truely account it that Spiritual communion and fellowship, which the Saints obtain with God, by Jesus Christ, to whom only these Cherubims give way, and unto as many as enter by him, who calls himself the door. So that, though we do not ascribe any whit of Adam's guilt to men, untill they make it theirs by the like acts of disobedience, yet we cannot suppose that men, who are come of Adam naturally, càn have any good thing in their nature, as belonging to it, which he from whom they derive their nature, had not himself to communicate unto them.'

ILLUSTRATION: Plate 7.

P

God as all, and in all

PANTHEISM is the name given to any doctrine or way of thought which tends to identify God with the universe; the belief that God is all, and all is God.

The name has never been appropriated to any particular body of doctrine: pantheism, rather, is a strain which has always tended to colour the thoughts and feelings of poets, philosophers and contemplatives, so that it is the pantheistic in human thought that is important rather than pantheism as such.

The earliest and in many ways the most thoroughgoing expression of the belief that the creation and the creator are one and the same is found in Brahmanism, the oldest religion of India. Composed in about 1000 B.C., the Vedas (the ancient Hindu scriptures) portray the world and everything in it as the manifold embodiment of God. Emerson's poem *Brahma* gives some idea of the spirit of these noble writings:

> If the red slayer think he slays,
>   Or if the slayer think he is slain,
> They know not well the subtle ways
>   I keep, and pass, and turn again.

But this extreme form of pantheism is more easily explicable by Andrew Lang's parody of Emerson:

> If the wild bowler thinks he bowls,
>   Or if the batsman thinks he's bowled,
> They know not, poor misguided souls,
>   They too shall perish unconsoled.
> *I* am the batsman and the bat,
>   *I* am the bowler and the ball,
> The umpire, the pavilion cat,
>   The roller, pitch and stumps, and all.

In Egypt, the deities Ra, Isis and Osiris were each at different periods identified with all that exists: Plutarch (c. A.D. 46–c. A.D. 120) records an inscription in a temple of Isis which read 'I am all that hath been, is, or shall be: and no mortal has lifted my veil'.

Among the Greeks, as one might expect, these beliefs assume a more intellectual character, and, in the speculations of Parmenides (born c. 510 B.C.), are the result of carrying to its logical conclusion the doctrine that the primary substance out of which the world is made is one. 'Parmenides' world', wrote Cyril Bailey, 'is thus a finite, eternal, indivisible, immovable, spherical, corporeal mass: motion, change, variety, birth and death, all that we know by the experience of our senses are mere delusions.' And Parmenides, at least according to tradition, was a pupil of Xenophanes of Colophon, who proclaimed that there was one god, the greatest among both gods and men, like unto mortals neither in form nor in thought – this 'one god' being in fact, as Aristotle tells us, 'the whole world'.

Though there is little of the pantheistic in Plato, his later followers, the so-called Neoplatonists, display a marked tendency to identify the material and the spiritual elements in the universe. Thus Plotinus (born c. A.D. 205) taught that the phenomenal world is a creation of the soul and has no real existence, matter being a mere receptacle for forms imposed upon it by the soul. And the Christian theologian Johannes Scotus Erigena (c. 815–877) reasoned that all things emanate from God and are re-absorbed into God:

He is said to be the cause of all things, seeing that from that Cause the whole circle of things which, after it, are created from it, diffuses itself into genera and species and numbers and differences, and whatever other distinctions there are in nature ... But seeing that all things which proceed from that same Cause will return to it when they shall come to their end, therefore it is called the end of all things and is said neither to create nor to be created; for after all things have returned into it, nothing further will proceed from it by generation in space and time, in kinds and forms, since all will be quiet in it, and will remain an unchanged and an undivided One.

In Europe, the philosopher Spinoza (1632–1677) was long regarded as the prince of pantheists. Samuel Johnson in his *Dictionary* (1755) defines *pantheist* as 'one who confounds God with the Universe: a name given to the followers of Spinoza'. Spinoza's system, universally detested as atheistic until the end of the eighteenth century, has received widely differing interpretations. Condemned by the free-thinking Bayle in his *Dictionary* (1701), he languished neglected until Goethe (1749–1832) first studied him sympathetically: since when his thought has been admired by poets, including Coleridge, as expressing in almost mystical terms the ideal unity of nature, and by Marxists and other materialists as being that of a thoroughgoing materialist and determinist. The fundamental thesis of Part 1 of Spinoza's posthumously published *Ethics* is that there can be only *one* substance which is self-

caused, and that this single substance must be identified with the universe conceived as a whole; this unique all-inclusive totality he therefore calls 'God or Nature' (*Deus sive Natura*). It is worth remarking that Spinoza was Jewish, and affords a further example of the tendency of monotheism and pantheism to converge and support one another.

The *word* pantheist ('all-is-God-ist') was coined in 1705 by the English deist John Toland (1670–1722), who in 1720 published his *Pantheisticon*, a work which gave much offence, and was called by the poet Pope, in a note to the *Dunciad*, 'the Atheist's Liturgy' – indeed, a future bishop of Cork declared that Toland 'meant to rival Mahomet'. But Pope himself incurred suspicion on account of the following remarkable (and exquisitely phrased) passage, in his *Essay on Man* (1733):

All are but parts of one stupendous whole,
Whose body Nature is, and God the soul;
That, chang'd thro' all, and yet in all the same,
Great in the earth, as in th'æthereal frame,
Warms in the sun, refreshes in the breeze,
Glows in the stars, and blossoms in the trees,
Lives thro' all life, extends thro' all extent
Spreads undivided operates unspent;
Breathes in our soul, informs our mortal part,
As full, as perfect, in a hair as heart;
As full, as perfect, in vile Man that mourns,
As the rapt Seraph that adores and burns;
To him no high, no low, no great, no small;
He fills, he bounds, connects, and equals all.

Many of the poets and philosophers of the Romantic Revival experienced pantheistic feelings towards nature – in Wordsworth's classic expression

... a sense sublime
Of something far more deeply interfused,
Whose dwelling is the light of setting suns,
And the round ocean and the living air,
And the blue sky, and in the mind of man

– lines incidentally remarkably similar in phraseology and perhaps even in feeling to those of the supposedly 'classical' Pope.

Thus pantheism is not and has never been a system: it is rather a vague intuition, an inarticulate mood which comes to men, and is variously expressed in terms of religion, of philosophy and of poetry.

Coleridge became highly suspicious of pantheism in Wordsworth; and wrote in later years, how he himself had been 'intoxicated with the vernal fragrance and effluvia from the flowers and first-fruits of Pantheism' – an admirable description – 'unaware of its bitter root'.

'The case is closed'

PAPAL INFALLIBILITY is a dogma of Roman Catholics which states that when the Pope speaks *ex cathedra* (*i.e.* 'from his throne', as head and teacher of the whole Church) on matters of faith or morals, he cannot err. This has been an article of faith of the Roman Catholic Church since 1870: to deny it is to incur excommunication.

Catholics do not, however, regard the Pope as infallible when he studies or speaks on other subjects; as a private theologian working on his own account he can err, and even more so should he pronounce on secular matters such as science, politics or history. Nor do Catholics consider that a Pope speaking *ex cathedra* is 'inspired' in the sense of the Pythian priestess who was thought merely an instrument of deity, a passive mouthpiece. A Pope, in contrast, must first make normal intellectual enquiries about a dogma; he can and does consult others. The peculiar prerogative claimed by the Pope is that when he makes *ex cathedra* pronouncements on faith or morals, these pronouncements are preserved from error. Personal wickedness in the Pope is not considered to nullify this.

The dogma of the Pope's infallibility has probably brought on the Roman Catholic Church more abuse than any of its measures. Opponents have regarded it as another proof of the fallibility of the Church and its arrogance. Many regard the decree of 1870 as a wily political move of Pope Pius IX both to gain a stronger spiritual hold on its followers as well as to recover his fading temporal and political powers. Perhaps the only sympathy of a sort the dogma has received from outside the Church was from George Bernard Shaw in the preface to his *Saint Joan*.

His much-quoted remarks on infallibility may be frowned upon by Catholic theologians but have some force:

Perhaps I had better inform my Protestant readers that the famous Dogma of Papal Infallibility is by far the most modest pretension of its kind in existence. Compared with our infallible democracies, our infallible medical councils, our infallible astronomers, our infallible judges, and our infallible parliaments, the Pope is on his knees in the dust confessing his ignorance before the throne of God, asking only that as to certain historical matters on which he has clearly more sources of information open to him than anyone else his decision shall be taken as final.

Catholics claim other kinds of infallibility within the Church. There is what is called the *passive* infallibility of the faithful. This can influence the formation and formulation of dogma. The doctrine of Papal Infallibility had been accepted implicitly or explicitly by most of the Church's members long before 1870. Similarly the doctrine of the Immaculate Conception grew inside the Church, sometimes against the judgements of theologians (St Thomas Aquinas and St Bernard both questioned the doctrine). Only after distortions, legends and doubts had scored the popular belief was the belief confirmed as a dogma in 1854.

Another infallibility is the infallibility of the whole Church considered as a teaching body, an *active* infallibility when compared with that of the faithful. In practice this infallibility centres on the bishops of the Church in council with the Pope at their head.

The proofs used by Catholics to justify their beliefs in Papal Infallibility are based on the New Testament and on tradition. Scriptural proof is based on three texts. In Matthew xvi. 18, Christ says to Peter, 'Thou art Peter and upon this rock I will build my church, and the gates of hell shall not prevail against it.' In Luke xxii. 31–32 and in John xxi. 15–17, Christ chooses out Peter for leadership, confirms his future pastoral duties and assures him of support. The interpretation of these texts and their implications are naturally disputed by opponents of Rome. One of the most important attacks is by George Salmon (1819–1904), the mathematician and theologian, in his *Infallibility of the Church* (1888), which did not receive a full Catholic reply in this country until 1954. Perhaps the Catholic views can be summarized as a belief that if God founded a church, he could not found one that would be left to flounder in uncertainty and without a sure final authority.

The proofs from tradition aim at showing not only the ascendancy of Peter (regarded as the first Pope) among the Apostles, but also the general primacy of the see of Rome from the time of Pope Clement in the first century and onwards. The authority of the Popes from the earliest times is claimed as one pertaining to doctrine as well as to jurisdiction. One famous instance is Augustine's acceptance of a letter from Pope Innocent: *causa finita est*, 'the case is closed'. That there were no early explicit definitions of Papal Infallibility is explained by the fact that there were not any really serious schisms until the eighth century. Only after the Reformation, and after the nationalism of the French 'Gallican' Church had raised strong doubts about the Pope's relation to the Church in different countries was the problem of the Pope's supremacy and infallibility openly discussed.

The Vatican Council of 1869–1870, the first since that of Trent (1545–1563), was convened by Pope Pius IX after he had conferred with many bishops. Many problems were to be thrashed out, points of discipline, teaching, liturgy and church government. But the issue of infallibility overshadowed everything. In the early stages of preparation there had hardly been a whisper about the doctrine. Quickly, however, requests were made to have the matter discussed. There were two parties. The so-called 'Gallicans' were loosely named after the school of thought, largely French in origin, that wished to limit the authority of the Pope and increase that of local bishops. Grouped with the Gallicans were certain German bishops. This 'Minority' had to cope with the 'Majority', the 'Ultramontanists' ('those beyond the mountains' a term used to describe those who held that the authority of the Church came from south of the Alps – Rome). Most Ultramontane of all was Pope Pius IX who did not favour the 'Minority'.

The Council was far from dull. Most of Europe was buzzing with interest and excitement. Politicians (including Gladstone) believed that inter-national issues were involved, and kept themselves fully informed. The deliberations of the Council were supposed to be secret, but enough rumours leaked out to enable newspapers, *The Times* included, to publish accounts. Most embassies were able to buy copies of the proceedings. The Council itself was not only exciting for the polychrome spectacle of almost 700 bishops in conclave, but for the rumbustiousness of debate. There was no lack of episcopal filibustering; roars of laughter and abuse were frequent; prolixity was almost the rule, so that when a Transylvanian bishop, and later a Peruvian bishop, waived the right to speak, there were cheers; an English bishop moved a motion on the alteration of a comma; a lively-minded Californian bishop continually popped up to make amendments – and all this in the nervous, stifling heat of Rome's summer. In the end the decree relating to Papal Infallibility was put to the vote. Some of the bishops left the Council rather than register a vote of *non placet* (it does not please). The final result was 533 *placets* to two *non placets*. The two dissentients, one an Italian bishop, the other the bishop of Little Rock in the United States, both gave their assent afterwards, as did all the bishops who were not present. The vote of *non placet* did not imply that these bishops disbelieved the dogma. It implied that they did not think the pronouncement timely. So ended the Vatican Council's deliberations: there was a thunderstorm which punctuated the discreet *placets* of the bishops.

The day after the Council finished France and Prussia were at war. A few weeks later the Italians captured Rome, which before had been garrisoned by the French, and all remaining shreds of temporal Papal power were blown away.

The results of the Council were not so devastating or momentous as feared. All the bishops had submitted. J. J. I. Döllinger, a leading German theologian, was a conspicuous rebel. He had been an Ultramontanist at first, but later attacked the dogma on historical grounds. He was excommunicated in 1871, and afterwards worked to join the various groups of Catholics who did not belong to Rome. These Old Catholics, as they are called, made a few gains after 1870. But there was no large-scale breaking away from Rome. The dogma of Infallibility had, however, closed the gates of compromise against other

Churches; there was a religious impasse. 'There is only one thing to be said in favour of the Roman system,' said Dean Inge (1860–1954), 'it works.'

Nature humanized

The **PATHETIC FALLACY** is now defined as that figure of speech by which Nature is supposed to feel human emotions and to share in human predicaments, in sorrow or in joy. As such it may be found in any manual of rhetoric (or even a school grammar), in the section labelled 'figures of speech', neatly illustrated with chloroformed specimens:

It is a figure peculiarly dear to the writers of the Victorian era, notably Tennyson and Browning:

> But the rose *was awake all night for your sake,*
> Knowing your promise to me;
> *The lilies and roses were all awake,*
> *They sighed for the dawn and thee.*
>
> (*Maud.*)

Treated in this way, the *pathetic fallacy* certainly becomes as peculiar as a piece of dead seaweed hanging on a wall. Even here, if replaced in context, it may be justified as a device for conveying states of mind, as George Crabbe consciously used it in *The Lover's Journey*:

> When minds are joyful, then we look around,
> And what is seen is all on fairy ground;
> Again they sicken, and on every view
> Cast their own dull and melancholy hue.

So, in Crabbe's poem, his lover riding out on a June morning finds that Nature's hand adorns even a rushy moor, where grow 'the sweet myrtle of the shaking ground' and 'the salt lavender that lacks perfume'. But after his Laura (christened Susan) has left him, Orlando (christened John) turns melancholy, and finds the scene melancholy too:

> And these vile beans with deleterious smell,
> Where is their beauty? Can a mortal tell?

But the pathetic fallacy, of course, is much more than a device of poetic chiaroscuro. It is a survival of older forms of thought, before Man and Nature were made antagonists; and the poet, in employing it, is performing his most important function of uniting the oldest with the latest.

One of the most overwhelming episodes of the *Iliad* is that of the fight between Achilles and Scamander in Book XXI. The river-god can no longer bear the Trojan losses, and the blood and corpses which defile his streams; he warns the Greek hero, Achilles, who defies him:

> Then rising in his Rage above the Shores,
> From all his Deeps the bellowing River roars,
> Huge heaps of Slain disgorges on the Coast,
> And round the Banks the ghastly Dead are tost.

Achilles, though first of men, is no match for a river in spate; he flees, but the flood catches him:

> Tir'd by the Tides, his Knees relax with Toil;
> Wash'd from beneath him, slides the slimy Soil –

and, desperate, Achilles prays to the Gods to save him from the fate of a peasant caught at a ford, and swept

> An unregarded Carcase to the Sea.

He is saved by the intervention of Poseidon and Pallas Athene.

The power of this passage lies in the fact that the poet is not employing a 'device' of poetic trickery, nor conveying a state of mind; he is recording factually an historic incident. Any river, as any man, or any God, hates defilement more than anything; it is certain to bring retribution. And any river loves the city which, time out of mind, has brought offerings and prayers to propitiate it.

Shall we regard this attitude of mind as primitive and superstitious? If it still prevailed, Londoners would still catch salmon in the Thames at Westminster; and if the American lumberjack still asked pardon of the tree as he cut it, and lamented as it fell, dust-bowls and soil-erosion would be unimagined horrors. It is perhaps no accident that the poem in our time which has had the most powerful influence is called *The Waste Land*, and is based on the pathetic fallacy that the health of a country is bound up with that of its king; and that his maiming will strike it into a desert.

Nor is it an accident that the greatest master of the *pathetic fallacy* in English is John Milton; for in him, more than any other man, the ancient world of myth, pagan and Christian, had come to terms with the questioning, analytical temper of Renaissance thought. Picture-thinking and logical process – Milton is a master of both; and for the health of humanity, both are needed. Here is Eve, with the apple in her hand:

> So saying, her rash hand in evil hour
> Forth reaching to the Fruit, she pluck'd, she eat:
> Earth felt the wound, and Nature from her seat
> Sighing through all her Works gave signs of woe,
> That all was lost ...

Mask and man

PERSONALITY derives from the Latin *persona*, the name given to the stylized masks worn by the principal characters in the theatre of the time. Thus it has come to mean the impression which a person gives of himself by his appearance, manner, way of talking, gestures and so on. Even the clothes he wears, or the kind of car he drives, may be considered part of his 'personality', an aspect made more forcibly apparent by the recurrent use of the word in advertisements. In such contexts, too, the word is often used synonymously with whole phrases such as 'elegant personality', 'impressive personality', so that by a natural transition of meaning we arrive at such expressions as 'The Pen with Personality', which on a strict usage would be meaningless.

More seriously, personality may be defined as the set of all those attributes which distinguish one individual from another. Personality is taken by psychologists as equivalent to the set of all characteristics of *behaviour* which distinguish one individual from another; the study of personality attempts to determine general principles of behaviour which are supposed to hold good for all individuals.

There are two main subdivisions of personality, temperament and character. Differences of temperament are held to be constitutionally determined, *i.e.* inherited, while character is supposed to be acquired by the individual as a result of his own personal experiences. Hippocrates (c. 460 B.C.–c. 370 B.C.), better known for the ethical code which governs medical practice to this day, was the first person to classify temperaments – for personality has always been of great interest to physicians, for its close relation to health and sickness. He named four types of temperament, the choleric, sanguine, melancholic and phlegmatic, which he supposed to be connected with particular bodily conditions. The choleric and sanguine types are alike in being quickly roused to interest, excitement or passion, while the phlegmatic and melancholic types are both slow and persistent by contrast. On the other hand, the choleric and melancholic resemble each other in that their interests are strong and intense, while those of the sanguine and phlegmatic are weak and feeble. This classification held good for most writers until a late period; and a knowledge of it illuminates much of the literature, *e.g.* of the Elizabethan age.

More recent classifications of temperament have been those of Jung, Kretschmer and Sheldon. Jung divided people into extroverts and introverts, both of which are then subdivided into four classes according to the 'psychic function' of which they make most use; Thought, Feeling, Intuition or Sensation.

The systems of Kretschmer and Sheldon are alike in being based on a supposed statistical correlation between certain traits of behaviour and certain types of physique. Thus Kretschmer believed that tendencies to excessive excitement and depression went with a stocky figure and rounded features, while a slender, lanky build was associated with emotional coldness and tendencies to withdraw from human contacts. Much research would still be needed to make classifications of this kind altogether valid.

Other modern ideas of personality and its classification are derived from theories of psychoanalysis. Neither Freud nor Adler were very deeply interested in classification. Adler, though, held that individual differences were largely determined by the ways in which the person attempted to compensate for feelings of inferiority occasioned by a relative physical inadequacy of some bodily organ or other (another form of the idea which has persisted from the earliest times, that differences of personality are caused in some way by physical differences).

Freud attached much importance to the relative strengths in the individual of various primitive instincts (again a 'physical' basis for personality differences.) This idea was taken much further by some of Freud's followers, notably Ernest Jones, who distinguished 'oral', 'anal', and 'genital' types of character, according to whether their main (unconscious) interest was in suckling, defecation or sexual intercourse. This classification, bizarre as it seems, has been very seriously taken by many psychiatrists.

On the whole, the study of personality now tends to shift to direct investigation of behaviour; by Erich Fromm the sociologist, for example, who carefully distinguishes between 'temperament' and 'character' as components of personality, and then divided a character into two main types, productive and non-productive. The non-productive type he divides into receptive, exploiting and 'marketing' groups.

Many of the terms which crop up in studying personality have an odd flavour of condemnation, as if the impulse to classify people came from an unfriendly attitude –

> I wish I loved the Human Race;
> I wish I loved its silly face;
> I wish I liked the way it walks;
> I wish I liked the way it talks;
> And when I'm introduced to one,
> I wish I thought *What Jolly Fun!*

The terms of original Hippocratic classification originally had no implication of praise or blame, but they are now used exclusively in a bad sense. A 'choleric' person is now one who is easily roused only to anger or peppery anger, a 'melancholic' person is now one who is persistently glum, instead of being merely persistent.

All these systems presume that an individual's personality endures, more or less unaltered, through life. This is true, unless the individual undergoes some very drastic experience, such as a brain injury, a very severe emotional or physical shock, or psycho-analysis, which may change all aspects of his personality, so that he 'doesn't seem like the same person' to his family and friends.

Such alterations of personality seem always to be associated with alterations in the memories available to the individual, a fact underlying the most recent theory of personality, the cybernetic view, according to which the behaviour, and hence the personality, of an individual are determined by two factors; the information at his disposal (of which his own memories are the largest part) and his inborn capacity to handle and organize this information. This hypothesis at least does justice to the extreme richness and diversity of personality.

O Philistia!

PHILISTINE, in today's vocabulary of contempt, signifies a complacently uncultured person with a mental horizon shut in by 'material' interests (see *Materialism*), with commonplace views, and with an inevitable bias (particularly in the arts) towards the trite, undisturbing and bathetic.

A Victorian critic might have insisted further on the Philistine's automatic resistance to new ideas and new developments in politics, religion, education, etc., but a flourishing contemporary form of Philistinism accepts enthusiastically what is apparently new in all these spheres if it can be accepted unthinkingly: the Philistine of the mid-twentieth century is as likely to be found at a 'progressive' conference as in a board-room or a vestry. Victorian and contemporary definitions have as common elements self-congratulation and an unerring instinct for the comfortably second-rate in ideas and expression (whether customary or new-fangled). The Philistine 'knows what he likes', and what he likes is shoddy.

As terms of abuse in this sense 'Philistine' and 'Philistinism' were first given wide currency in this country by Matthew Arnold, but other writers – notably Carlyle in *Sartor Resartus* (1833) and the *Life of Sterling* (1851) – had employed them before they came from Arnold's mouth in 1863 when he lectured at Oxford on Heine. (The essay was reprinted in his *Essays in Criticism, 1st Series,* in 1865.) 'A Philistine', Arnold wrote, 'must have originally meant, in the mind of those who invented the nickname, a strong, dogged, un-enlightened opponent of the chosen people, of the children of light.' (Carlyle in the *Life of Sterling* had described Philistines as 'bores, dullards, Children of Darkness'.) Disraeli once congratulated Arnold on his gift for launching catch-phrases, and 'Philistine' is probably Arnold's most notorious success in this kind. It is used with merciless reiteration in almost all his prose-works between 1865 and 1888.

Back beyond Carlyle the inventors of the nick-name were in fact German university students. 'The Philistines be upon thee, Samson' (*Judges* xvi. 9) was the text for a funeral sermon preached at Jena in 1693 on a student killed by townsfolk in a 'Town and Gown' squabble; whereupon 'Philister' became university slang for non-academic persons in the rôle of hostile outsiders. By 1800 the word had earned wider recognition in Germany with the meaning 'narrow-minded', and about 1820–1825 it was naturalized by English writers familiar with German culture, though its use in the plainer and different sense of 'enemy' of one kind or another goes back to seventeenth-century English.

Arnold's immediate source, it must also be said, was Heine himself – Heine in his *Englische Fragmente* having praised French accessibility to ideas and contrasted it with Teutonic wooden-ness: 'Paris is the new Jerusalem, and the Rhine is the Jordan which divides the consecrated land of freedom from the land of the Philistines.' Arnold seems not to have known, or to have for-gotten about this process of naturalization. '*Philistinism*', he wrote '– we have not the ex-pression in English. Perhaps we have not the word because we have so much of the thing ...'; and, after noting the French *épicier* and Carlyle's 'gigmanity' (those who can afford to drive about in gigs) as possible alternative terms, he decides in favour of 'Philistine', should 'we English ... one day come to want such a word'.

Nowhere does Arnold give an inclusive defini-tion of Philistinism. In *Essays in Criticism* the Philistine was already the lover of things as they are, as well as the opponent of the modern spirit of reasonable enquiry. (Macaulay is 'the great Apostle of the Philistines', the British Constitu-tion is a 'colossal machine' for their manu-facture.) In Arnold's *Celtic Literature* (1867)

Philistinism was identified with the Teutonic element in the English character. In *Culture and Anarchy* (1869) Arnold squarely described the Philistine as a member of the middle class: the 'Barbarian' aristocrat is now seen to be as 'in-accessible to ideas' and as resistant to change as any Philistine, but he is not regarded as intrin-sically hostile to culture.

In *Culture and Anarchy* Arnold discovers the tedium, narrowness and downright ugliness of middle-class life to be the most formidable enemies of enlightenment, and recognizes the hallmark of Philistinism in an over-emphasis on moral earnestness (Hebraism) at the expense of a free play of the intelligence (Hellenism). To him, this unbalance is the result of two hundred years of Puritanism, of which Dissent in its various forms is the living representative. But Philistin-ism is not restricted to middle-class Dissenters: all who too exclusively 'give their lives and thoughts to becoming rich' and believe national wealth and power to be synonymous with na-tional greatness are Philistines. Such people tend to oppose necessary state-action and are the victims of caprice in education, religious prac-tice, etc.

In *Irish Essays* (1882) the 'severe' and the 'jovial' Philistine are distinguished by Arnold in the persons of Mr Murdstone and Mr Quinion, characters out of *David Copperfield* (1849–1850). Whatever their differences, they share 'a defec-tive type of religion, a stunted sense of beauty, a low standard of manners'. These selected refer-ences fill out the Victorian idea of the Philistine, and Dickens's Mr Podsnap in *Our Mutual Friend* (1864–1865) may be regarded as the most com-plete embodiment of the idea in Victorian fiction.

Freed from a false but historically natural em-phasis on the Philistine's dislike of what is new and devotion to what is customary – an emphasis that, if insisted on, leads to the confusion of the Barbarian with the Philistine – the Victorian analysis of Philistinism is still valid. A Philistine is a self-satisfied lover of the second-rate. There is no reason to think that he is less numerous or less influential today than he was in the eighteen-sixties, though superficially he may appear to have changed. His manners are more genteel, if his morals are less robust. He is neither so re-ligious, nor so philoprogenitive, nor so insular, and he pays more lip-service to culture; but he remains as muddled and complacent, and he is still the prey of cliché-mongers, from the leader-writer to the popular preacher or politician. One may compare Victorian and contemporary Philistinism by setting the Bottles family of Arnold's *Friendship's Garland* (1871) beside the Dale family of the BBC's soap-opera, *Mrs Dale's Diary*. It is not very clear where the advantage lies.

ILLUSTRATION: Page 360.

All the secrets of Alkimy

The **PHILOSOPHER'S STONE** (*Lapis Philosophorum*) transmuted base metals into gold.

In most alchemical contexts, however, it is better to say that it transmuted base humanity into an 'incorruptible permanence', into the Centre of all things, the golden likeness of the Sun. As an eighteenth-century adept put it: 'Nay, but we wish that all men might seek and find not gold but God.'

Alchemists often used a double language which must be borne constantly in mind. Thus the material with which the Stone might be made lay all about, in earth, air, fire and water, the elements which were present both in nature and in man. All elements, not merely the base metals, contained within themselves the seed of gold, which with careful nurture might be allowed to grow until it filled the whole body with its radiance. This nurturing of the seed is the fundamental doctrine of alchemy.

The Great Work by which the Stone was accomplished was as beset with difficulties and dangers as much as any *via mystica*. The Primal Matter which contained the seed was hard to find, for all that it was immediately to hand. Some said, 'It is within you': it was thought they meant faeces. Some gave a clue in the acrostic: 'Visita interiora terrae, rectificando invenies occultum lapidem'. Others suggested other poisons, arsenic or mercury, and these became also chief ingredients of the Elixir of Life (q.v.). This was much to the point, for the path to the Stone led through death and resurrection. The Primal Matter must

be killed or, as some said, crucified, before perfection could be reached. For this reason, the Stone was often represented as a Phoenix, the symbol of rebirth: it was both the solution and the way to the solution.

The work was still not accomplished, however, when the seed of gold was extracted. Alone, the seed was powerless. Gold, being male, needed the female virtue of silver (or quicksilver) to complete it. The female seed must also be extracted from the 'metal' so that the marriage of seed with seed might bring fruit. Hence the all-embracing Stone was also styled a hermaphrodite, or a double-headed eagle, a conjunction of Sun and Moon or a union of Red and White – all symbols of duality in unity, for the Stone was a synthesis of all warring factions.

Yet this was not the end. From the nuptials of golden Bridegroom and silver Bride emerged their child in his 'red and white coat'. This 'golden boy' was the homunculus who, according to some alchemists, might actually be seen within the chemical vessels – for all these means of making the Stone were carried out practically, in the laboratory: they corresponded to outward as well as to inward investigations. The homunculus may also be thought of, however, in Sir Thomas Browne's phrase, as the 'man within'. Or he may be considered in the light of this passage from Paracelsus: 'Just as Mary received through the Holy Ghost, in a supernatural fashion, the Son of God, promised by the Father, so our pure Virgin the philosophic Mercury, in a miraculous way, has given birth again by the Holy Ghost, that is, in this case, by the Spirit of Mercury, to the high quintessence of all things.' The homunculus was, in fact, often referred to in terms of the quintessential Stone itself, although he might often be called only the embryonic form of it. The Stone was entirely present at all stages of the operation.

When at last the Stone was made, it was capable of transmuting all other metals into its own high quality. This it did by releasing the seed of gold which each contained and allowing it to prevail over the dross surrounding it. But – here lay the paradox which made all alchemical literature interminably confused – the Stone was the *only* means of thus releasing the seed. The process could not begin until the Stone had been found, and the Stone was its own First Matter, the Alpha and the Omega. This aspect of the Stone was commonly symbolized as the Ourobouros, or serpent curled round so as to devour its own tail. In this symbol, which can be found in Ancient Egypt, is contained not merely the self-annihilation implicit in the quest, but also its endlessness (for it is circular), its self-completeness and its duality in unity. In the Stone's beginning was its end, for the process never ended when perfection was reached. Once made, the Stone plunged back into the whole cycle of death and resurrection again.

Yet the Stone and the quest for it were not merely an endless repetition of pain and joy. Its perfection was everlastingly present: it was the Way and the Truth.

Many other associations have been made with the Stone. For many European alchemists from the Middle Ages onwards it was Christ, the immanent and transcendent God. For Chinese alchemists it was connected rather with the Tao. A tantalizingly corrupt medieval text seems to associate the Stone with the Holy Grail, which it calls *lapis exillix*. In the psychology of C. G. Jung, the Stone is equated rather with the kind of self that is said to reside beneath the level of normal consciousness. The possibilities of interpretation are as limitless as the Stone itself.

The quest for the Stone began, according to legend, in Egypt, and its originator was the Egyptian god Hermes (Thoth), Hermes Trismegistus, in whose Emerald Table the first principles of alchemy were laid down. Certainly alchemy – itself an Arabic word – was known to the Greeks living in Egypt in the early centuries of the Christian era, and it was at this time that symbolical interpretations were given to what before had probably been a purely practical concern.

From the Greeks, alchemy passed to the Arabs, and from them, with the invasion of Spain in the eleventh century, into Europe, where it was taken up with enthusiasm. By the thirteenth century it was firmly established, and written of by such men as Roger Bacon (c. 1214–c. 1294) and Albertus Magnus (d. 1280). At the Renaissance, alchemy was given a new direction by Paracelsus (c. 1493–1541), who not only made the symbolical aspects more explicit but also, bearing in mind

the aspect of the Stone as an Elixir of Life, declared that the true object of alchemy was the preparation of medicines.

A vast quantity of alchemical texts now began to be published, and charlatans ran riot. More serious contributions were made by the mystic Jakob Boehme (1575–1624), who described his religious experiences entirely in alchemical language. In the seventeenth century, however, the quest for the Stone began to yield to empirical science, although even Sir Isaac Newton was still concerned with both. In the eighteenth, alchemy ceased to interest serious scientists except as a historical phenomenon. On the other hand, poets have continued to be fascinated by the occult lore. Goethe studied alchemy as a young man and although he rejected its methods, retained a high regard for its symbolism. Both Rimbaud and Strindberg were enthusiastic students of alchemy. Yeats, an initiate, described all his poetry as an attempt to accomplish the Great Work, and James Joyce called himself the 'first till last alshemist'. His version of the Stone will be found on p. 293 of *Finnegan's Wake*, Rimbaud's in the sonnet, *Voyelles*.

ILLUSTRATION: Page 215.

Heed for the morrow

PLANNING is the science of taking thought for tomorrow. Forethought in itself is hardly a new concept, but it could be said that in the last fifty years forethought has been substantially transformed: it was mainly a private matter, and it has become mainly a public matter, emerging from the process with this new handle of 'planning'.

The credo is in essence the belief that engineering principles can be applied to every aspect of the community's physical environment and on any scale – that is, whether the community is tackled at the family or the global level. The technique of planning is one of assessing all the devious factors involved in establishing, say, a housing estate, or organizing a national economy to wage total war (q.v.), and then appropriately co-ordinating or subordinating or manipulating these factors to produce the most desirable result.

Such a procedure presupposes an accepted 'general good' as the criterion; this will sort out the jumble of 'musts' involved – the relative weight to be given to population density and to sunlight in housing, for instance, or to psychological and to material incentives in a production 'drive'. So planning tends to be equated with the political purposes for which it is used when, in reality, it is only a tool, only a means without a purpose of its own. Another fallacy has been to judge a government's planning only by its bad planning. This is sufficiently fair to the politicians, but is most unfair to planning, of which one may judge, as with good breeding, that the less one notices it the better it is.

Planning is not exclusive to our century. The Roman 'castra' was precisely planned; Washington, D.C., laid out after the American War of Independence, is the most celebrated example of the building up of a city as a great centre worked out in advance to its smallest detail (and, as it turned out, quite inadequately); Bath was replanned and rebuilt, as a unity during the eighteenth century – and has remained more or less within the limits which were foreseen; the London quarter of Soho, built by French immigrants, was a patch of the urban logic of France inserted into the haphazard building habits of the English. But the planning of earlier periods was mostly restricted to town planning, as these examples suggest. Nevertheless, Plato's *Republic* (and, much later, More's *Utopia* remain as early monuments of remarkable penetration in the theoretical planning of the state as a whole.

The necessity for practical planning on a broad scale arose as a result of the Industrial Revolution. The enormous acceleration of the community's expansion and of its activities, the great complexity of life under the new conditions and the conquest of distance that rapidly followed, made different countries and different parts of the same country inter-dependent as never before. A failure in the Irish potato harvest – to take a celebrated example – could now affect people in remote parts of the world. In such a context the abandonment of a pattern of haphazard development could only be a matter of time.

The First World War brought this time appreciably nearer. It gave an impetus to both national and international planning such as had never been experienced. The depression of the thirties drove this home. The Second World War provided Great Britain with a common purpose and a will sufficient to bear the extraordinary burden of controls which characterized the most intensive spell of planning the English have so far known.

Since the war the term 'planning' has become something of a red rag to John Bull. There seemed to be too many plans about during the Labour Party's post-war years in power, and these retained the war-time association between 'planning' and restrictions on the individual; moreover, several planned schemes (the plan for groundnuts, for example) were such failures as to throw suspicion on the rest. Yet planning is not a prerogative of any one party. It has become a necessity for individual countries in a world without balance. Centralized economic planning, also, need not always operate in the same way, nor does it have to rely upon direct controls.

Planning techniques, if the truth be told, are still tentative, and the possibilities of planning have not been all of them explored. As a discipline it is in its infancy. Some discredit has been earned by the association of planning with Communism and Moscow. The U.S.S.R. has certainly had more experience of planning at every level than any other country. It has certainly been ruthless with the Russian people in carrying out its plans. But two other things are equally certain – that by means of its famous Five-Year Plans the U.S.S.R. transformed in a few years a backward agricultural country into one of the leading industrial countries of the world; and that planning for a democratic state is not ineluctably (and mystically) compelled to share the bad features of planning in a totalitarian state.

Since the Second World War, planning, from the new planned cities of Great Britain to plans for international assistance or co-operation, reflects a wide belief in the humane and order-producing virtues of planning – even if planning is neither a panacea nor a means of reinstating the Garden of Eden.

ILLUSTRATION: Pages 322 and 323.

Spiritual love

PLATONIC LOVE as a philosophical notion may be found current at almost any period; but as a social cult it belongs to the Renaissance – beginning in fifteenth-century Florence, spreading through sixteenth-century Italy, and attaining its widest European currency in the early seventeenth century. As a notion, and as a cult, it has always been met with the same mixture of ecstatic devotion and ribald disbelief; and often from the same person.

Samuel Richardson's may seem the sensible reaction: 'I am convinced, and always was, that Platonic love is platonic nonsense' (*Pamela*, 1741); but it is more important to understand Platonic love than to mock it.

In the spreading of the cult the ladies deserve to stand first; for this was perhaps the first European movement in which they took the initiative – and some of them should be named: the Medici, at whose court in Florence the whole thing began, and who afterwards carried it to France; Elizabeth Gonzaga, Duchess of Urbino, who presides over Castiglione's discussions in *The Courtier* (1528); Vittoria Colonna, to whom at sixty-four Michelangelo devoted himself; Madame de Rambouillet and her daughter Julie (who kept the Marquis de Montausier in attendance for fourteen years); and Henrietta Maria, Queen of Charles I, who established Platonic love at the English court. In 1634 James Howell was writing to Philip Warwick in Paris:

... there is a Love called Platonick Love which much sways at court of late. It is a Love abstracted from all corporeal, gross impressions and sensual appetite, but consists in contemplations, and ideas of the mind, and not in any carnal fruition. This Love sets the wits of the Town on work, and they say there will be a Masque of it shortly, whereof her Majesty and her Maids of Honour will be a part.

The Masque was Davenant's *The Temple of Love*, in which the Queen, as Indamora, superintended the setting up of the Temple of Pure Love 'in a dull Northern Isle' and persuaded nine Persian youths, who arrived, to worship there. 'Certain young Lords dislik'd the Phylosophy, As most uncomfortable, sad, and new'; but soon they were all reading Honoré d'Urfés' *Astrée*, the manifesto of the movement (whose five volumes had appeared at intervals between 1607 and 1627), and arranging what liberties were, and what were not, allowed to a Platonick lover. It was clear, for instance, from Cardinal Bembo's arguments at the end of Castiglione's *Courtier*, that kissing was allowed:

The woman to please her good lover, beside the granting him merry countenances, familiar and secret talk, jesting, dallying, hand in hand, may also lawfully and without blame come to kissing ... for although the mouth be a parcell of the body, yet is it an issue for the words that be the interpreters of the soul, and for the inward breath, which is also called the soul ... Salomon saith in his heavenly book: O that he would kiss me with a kiss of his mouth, to express the desire he had, that his soul might be ravished through heavenly love to the beholding of heavenly beauty.

No wonder if, as Gibbon said in another connexion, 'insulted Nature sometimes vindicated her rights'. Davenant treated this situation in his play *The Platonick Lovers* (1636). Theander's friends arrange with a *chymist* to dose the Platonic lover with a preparation which aroused his baser desires, and the plot turned on the consequences. But the chymist was also knowledgeable about the Greeks, and complained:

My Lord, I still beseech you not to wrong
My good old friend Plato, with this court calumny;
They father on him a fantastic love
He never knew, poor gentleman.

That is true enough. In the discussion at Agathon's supper party in 416 B.C. (described by Plato in the *Symposium*) love between man and woman is indeed mentioned, but in a merely incidental way. Only Aristophanes (after getting over the hiccups) treats it with any respect, as he propounds the myth of love's origin. Men were once compound beings, with four legs, four arms, two faces and everything to correspond; they could walk, but when in a hurry turned cartwheels. They became so proud that they attacked the Gods; so Zeus split them in two, and the divided halves have gone seeking each other ever since. When they meet, they love; but the best, the overwhelming love, results when both halves are male.

Later in the evening Socrates explains that the wise woman Diotima (who was his instructress in the art of love) does not accept this theory of love's origin. Love, she says, is not the product of division. He is a spirit, conceived at a banquet of the Gods; his mother, Poverty, who had come to beg at the door; his father, Contrivance. So, like his mortal mother, Love lives always in want; and like his immortal father, he is always scheming and full of resource. He himself is neither mortal nor immortal; he belongs neither to the Gods (who have no need of him) nor to the base (who are quite satisfied with themselves), but to those in between. And these, beginning with the love of a single created being, may progress to the love of absolute beauty, which has no physical object.

'That violence wherewith a man doteth upon one creature, is but a little spark of that love, even towards all, which lurketh in his nature', as Thomas Traherne puts it; and Traherne (c. 1620–1674), besides being a Platonist, was perhaps also a Platonick, since his *Centuries of Meditations* were sent to an unknown lady 'as a mark of the wisest love'.

Plato's doctrines were, in fact, never quite lost sight of, even in the Middle Ages. They can be found among the Spanish Moors of the eleventh century, to whom European learning owes so much. Ibn Hazm of Andalusia, in *The Dove's Neck-Ring* (c. 1022), repeats the notion of the divided halves, of the passionate attachment of the soul to beauty and to 'perfect images', and sets chaste love above sensual. From Spain a strain of platonism passed into courtly love, but it had long been buried when the recovery of Greek enabled the dialogues to be studied at first hand in the fifteenth century.

Through the Academies of Florence and the other Italian cities, and through enthusiasts like Ficino, Pico della Mirandola and Bembo, Platonism was spread. In England its accent is heard intermittently in Sidney, Spenser and Shakespeare. Donne's poem *The Ecstasy* begins by stating, and ends by answering, the Platonick claim:

> Love's mysteries in souls do grow,
> And yet the body is his book.

But the first use of the *phrase* 'Platonick Love' in English belongs to Ben Jonson. In *The New Inne* (1631) he stages a formal Court of Love, in which Lovel pleads the new doctrine with the full weight of Jonsonian gravity:

> Love is a spirituall coupling of two soules,
> So much more excellent, as it least relates
> Unto the body; circular, eternall;
> Not fain'd, or made, but borne: and then, so pretious,
> As nought can value it, but it selfe ...

Lovel's prize was the orthodox platonic reward of a kiss.

After 1650 platonic love was crushed between the upper and nether millstones of libertinism and the puritan conscience, and had to endure the triumph of each in turn under the Commonwealth and at the Restoration. Its ardour declined into preciosity and the elaboration of artificial refinement which (in France) earned the mockery of Molière. Yet the universal appeal of preciosity shows that it answered a need of the time; and platonic love has undoubtedly added something permanent to the complexity of that ritual dance with which human beings seek each other's acquaintance. Perhaps Davenant was not wrong in his last word on the subject:

> There *are* Platonic-lovers, though but few
> The sect conceal'd, and still imagin'd new.

(See also *Romantic Love*.)

The boot on the face

A POLICE STATE is a country in which the security of the state is considered so much more important than the rights of individuals, that the political police are given practically unlimited powers, while the private citizens whose liberty is infringed has no redress in law. The term is generally applied to those states where the individual has no right to criticize the government, and few other rights of any kind; where the duty of being in full sympathy with the régime is held to be binding on all citizens, and is enforced by the political police.

The police state is an institution with a long and unpleasant history. Among the ancient Greeks, the Spartans had an organization called *Krypteia*, 'the Secret', whose function was to keep an eye on the large slave population and murder any slave who seemed to be dangerously gifted. Most of the Roman emperors maintained large numbers of spies, and used their evidence to dispose of prominent citizens thought to be guilty of dangerous thoughts. The Venetian Republic, even in the days of its decay, had a very efficient police system; dangerous individuals would suddenly disappear, and soon their bodies would be found hanging in public, with no explanation.

France under the first Republic and Napoleon I, and Russia under the last four Tsars, were both to some extent police states. But the most feared of all such organizations was the Spanish Inquisition, which for three centuries maintained a police state within a state. Suspects were arrested in secret, usually at night; they were tortured to make them confess, without always knowing what crime they were confessing to; they were not allowed to know the names of their accusers; and their families and friends could only guess what had happened to them, until they reappeared for acquittal or condemnation.

In many ways the Inquisition was the forerunner of the modern police state; but with a very important difference. It imprisoned, tortured and burned alive, not for the sake of the state, but for the sake of individual souls. Compared with a man's immortal soul, his liberty and his life counted for nothing. And if it was too late to save his soul, he could at least be prevented from corrupting others.

By the beginning of this century the Inquisition was an evil but distant memory. Even in Tsarist Russia the police system was beginning to give way before the pressure of public opinion; and throughout the Western world it seemed as if the march of inevitable progress was bound to go on increasing man's freedom and dignity year after year. Then came the shock of the First World War, and the Russian Revolution, which replaced an inefficient dictatorship, full of holes and limitations, by a monolithic totalitarian state. 'Progress' ceased to mean the development of individual freedom, and came, in the minds of many people, to mean the inevitable rise of the all-powerful state, in which the individual was simply a microscopic and expendable unit. Even those who still hoped and believed that individual freedom would increase, no longer believed that its increase was inevitable.

Police states rose up everywhere, even in countries that had a long and respected liberal tradition. Japan was essentially a police state; but Japan was a country that had never absorbed Western ideas of liberty and democracy in the first place. But Italy was in the centre of civilized Europe; and Italy (as well as Spain, where General Franco constructed a state on the Italian model) became a police state under the rule of 'Fascism', a political philosophy which seriously curtailed individual liberty and declared the individual to be nothing but the servant of the state.

Adolf Hitler, who became dictator of Germany in 1933, followed the example of Italy; but he went a great deal further, and achieved, in National-Socialist Germany, a police state of the worst type. The Gestapo, or secret police, were answerable only to Hitler; their victims could get no protection from the law courts; and they made free use of secret arrest, imprisonment without trial, anonymous denunciation, torture, indefinite imprisonment in conditions of degradation and starvation, and mass executions. The Germans had been used to the protection of the law. The list of things they might not do had always been very long, but they had known that if they did nothing illegal they were safe. Yet under the new régime they could be faced with torture and death for not having Nazi sympathies; for being of the wrong race; or for having anti-Nazi relatives (for the Hitler régime punished the family of the offender, if it could not catch the offender himself).

The vast majority of the German people accepted this state of affairs without protest. The individual no longer mattered; all that mattered was the German nation (see *Herrenvolk*). Germans were declared to be 'dedicated body and soul to the Leader', and the aim of every good German was 'Gleichschaltung' – bringing the whole of his life into conformity with Nazi principles. The police were the guardians of this process. In the words of an official declaration in

1937: 'Our political police is comprehensive because it is omnipotent.'

Even the German autocracy was limited compared with that of the Soviet Union. The belief that Russia under Lenin was a benevolent and idealistic state, and only developed into a tyranny under Stalin, is a myth. Lenin and his followers allowed no room for individual liberty at all, and regarded the concept as ridiculous. For Lenin, as for Stalin, the security of the Soviet state, and of himself as its ruler, was paramount; and he was prepared to defend it by getting rid not only of anyone who was a danger, but of anyone who might conceivably become a danger at any future time. There was only one real crime – hostility to the state – and whether that crime was expressed in deed, word or thought, or had not yet been expressed at all, was immaterial.

An early official statement said that when a man was accused of a crime there was no point in trying to find out whether he had actually committed it. 'You have to ask him what class he belongs to, what is his origin, his education and profession. It is those questions that should decide the fate of the defendant, and therein lies the meaning of the red terror.' In the words of Lenin himself: 'We must wipe off the face of the earth all traces ... of the policy of the Mensheviks and Social-Revolutionaries who speak about individual rights.' There could be no rights for the individual, as the individual was nothing; he was 'a multitude of one million divided by one million'. The whole existing generation was only 'manure for the future'. From such a standpoint, individual rights became meaningless.

At present the Soviet Union is the police state *par excellence*. The citizen has not only no right to leave the country; his movement from one town to another is restricted and may be prohibited altogether. The laws that he can break are innumerable, but he cannot be certain of avoiding disaster by not breaking them; for the essential crime is an incorrect attitude to the state, and that may be revealed by behaviour, or even by a manner, that is not punishable in itself. If he is tried, his counsel for the defence is expected to admit his guilt and demand punishment for it. If he is to make a public appearance at a trial, he may be broken down until he is ready to make any confession that is required; and if he makes his escape, his punishment will fall on his family. No amount of past service to the state will do him any good when he is accused; he will be made to confess that he was a spy and a saboteur all his life.

If he is lucky, he will be shot. Otherwise he will be sent to a penal settlement where he is fed only so long as he can work, and killed or allowed to starve when he can work no longer. This imprisonment is for a term of years, but is liable to be indefinitely extended; and if he finally survives, he returns to find himself an outcast, to whom it is not safe for anyone to speak.

Outside the Union all the countries in the Soviet bloc, including China, are police states. So is Yugoslavia, although there the pressure has been relaxed. Argentina and Spain are partial police states, in which the power of the state is to some extent limited by the force of public opinion.

The late George Orwell, in *1984*, drew a terrifying picture of a world entirely controlled by rival police states, all virtually indistinguishable. It was his belief that 'all the main currents of political thought were authoritarian', and that the tendency everywhere was towards the setting up of the all-powerful state. Whether the original purpose of this authoritarianism was to establish Communism or to fight against it, was immaterial; the end, in any case, was the destruction of freedom. He did not regard the destruction of freedom as inevitable, but he did consider it very likely, unless freedom was defended with more courage and intelligence than is being shown at present.

The danger is that many people will try to defend it by destroying it. The recent proposal of Governor Shivers of Texas, that membership of the Communist party should be punishable by death because of the harm it might bring to millions of people, is an example of this type of reasoning. If men are to be put to death not because they are guilty of crimes deserving death, but because their actions endanger the people (that is, the state), that state is already a police state; and whether it is Communist or anti-Communist is of minor importance; both are intolerable.

ILLUSTRATION: Pages 272 and 273.

The empirical conservative

POLITICS IS THE ART OF THE POS-SIBLE may be taken as the motto of an empirical conservatism which is best known through the writings of Edmund Burke (1729–1797), and which plays a particularly important part in the thought of all political parties in England.

The phrase suggests a series of distinct and familiar ideas. Here are some of them – that the first question to ask of any policy is 'Will it work?'; that the test of whether a policy or an institution will work is the test of actual experience – 'Has it or anything like it, ever worked in the past?'; that it is not enough to prove that a policy is just or even to show that it is physically possible to bring it into force. Will, it must also be asked, the amount of compulsion involved in bringing it into force be justified by the result? The state's business is not to create morality, so it must legislate on the basis of the moral convictions of the community, however imperfect they may be; justice is a luxury, stability and order are necessities; justice itself is not to be deduced by abstract reasoning from one or two dogmas, such as that all men are equal; it is to be arrived at by comparing and trying to reconcile opposing ideas, also by watching institutions at work in history and trying to infer from the way they function the way in which they ought to function; justice is a complex thing, since even when a body of principles has been set up, it remains to apply them at different times and in different places; accordingly, in every political judgement there will be an element of particularity as well as of generality, the principle finding its embodiment in some particular form which is adapted to historical and geographical circumstances.

The doctrine that man cannot escape from his environment, that his institutions and customs all bear the marks of particular conditions, geo-geographical and historical, climatic and cultural, is important in European Conservatism, and is especially associated with the writer Montesquieu (1689–1755), whose views, embodied in his famous *L'Esprit des lois* (1748), were mainly based on a study of English politics. This 'relativism' leads to a bias in favour of tradition over innovation; it is no use man's trying to start afresh and build Utopia from scratch; the institutions he inherits are the products of circumstances which he cannot overcome or live down.

It is such maxims as these that are implied in the saying that 'politics is the art of the possible'. It expresses one of the two main attitudes of mind towards the philosophy of the state. From the end of the eighteenth century onwards these two philosophies have struggled for ascendancy in Europe, the great debate between them beginning with Burke's famous attack on the French Revolution. Neither of them can be fully understood without reference to the other, so one must look at the utopian and rationalist theories which Burke attacked.

The great ambition of the eighteenth-century rationalist thinkers was to have a philosophy of politics which would be universal and which could be deduced by reason from a few simple, general principles. Starting with some such dogma as 'all men are born free', they tried to deduce a rational system of justice in which there would be no loose ends and no compromises, and which could apply at all times and in all places. The first problem then encountered was how to protect one man's freedom against the encroachments of another without curtailing freedom. They were optimists, however. They believed that, throughout a large sector of human affairs at any rate, peace, justice and order would result from simply allowing men to do as they chose.

The economic theory still known as *laissez-faire* (q.v.) was based on this belief. If producers were wholly free to compete with each other in serving the community, the community would get the best service; if all men started from scratch, hereditary privileges being abolished, and proceeded to compete with each other for eminence and distinction, they would find their natural levels in society. Justice and freedom, far from being opposed ideas, were complementary. It was the state, the government, with its prisons, its police and all its cramping restrictions on the individual, which had produced injustice. The larger and more sophisticated societies had become, the more unjust they had become; what was wanted was a return to primitive innocence and purity.

Above all, the mind must not be confused nor

the will paralysed by dependence upon tradition and custom which were the creatures of accident and self-interest: we must get back to essentials, not necessarily putting the clock back, but by trying to organize our more complicated modern lives on the basis of simple and universal principles.

This optimism gave way before hard facts. It became apparent that when men were free to compete with each other, chaos and tyranny, not peace and order, ensued. The leaders of enlightened thought began to appreciate the importance of power. Men, they decided, were not yet to be trusted with the exercise of freedom. It was true that their interests did not collide, but they were not aware of this; they must be purified from the effects of their history by a process of political education, and, in the meantime, power must be entrusted to the vanguard who were sufficiently in advance of their time to be given the leadership of society. Thus, the French Revolution, which began as a proclamation of liberty, ended in tyranny; but not before it had brought to birth some doctrines, like that of the transitional dictatorship, which were later to be extremely important in European political thinking.

To all this the classic reply of conservatism is – 'Politics is the art of the possible'.

As a comment on revolutionary and utopian thought, the statement has two chief meanings: in the first place, it criticizes the view that perfection in human institutions is ever to be expected, and it asserts the belief in Original Sin (q.v.). When perfection is sought, as during the Terror, it was sought by putting an unlimited power in the hands of men supposed to be in advance of their time; when justice is sought through a 'Rule of the Saints', it is ignored that the saints themselves are only men, and subject to all the imperfections of men. Tyranny is the price of the attempt to achieve perfection, a tyranny which begins with the noblest motives and ends in squalor and pettiness.

Secondly, the world as it is must not be arrogantly written off as the result of crime and accident in history; it is rather a guide to the world as it ought to be. All men, at all times, are imperfect; but also all of them contain some measure of good, and their very failings are misguided attempts to achieve good: only by studying the history of institutions can we discover the good that is inherent in them and the ways in which it can be fulfilled. By concentration on the *possible* we are led to a better understanding of the real nature of the ideal, for the ideal will not be a simple thing, but a highly complex harmony brought about through the reconciliation of differences.

Thus, the two approaches to politics stand out: those in the utopian tradition start with the principles and then set about applying them; those in the conservative tradition start with facts, look for the principles inherent in them, see that these principles must be modified in accordance with circumstance, and act in the knowledge that the permanent weaknesses of human nature set a limit to what they can ever hope to achieve.

ILLUSTRATION: Page 324.

A snowball on its way downhill

'ALL POWER CORRUPTS AND AB-SOLUTE POWER CORRUPTS AB-SOLUTELY.' The famous remark of Acton the historian (1834–1902), raises the central problem of political thought. It is perennial in all circumstances and in all societies. Its importance has been recognized by all the great political thinkers. Ordered government, and the enhancement of life which it can bring about, are impossible without sovereign power: yet liberty is constantly threatened by the abuse of sovereign power. It is therefore essential that power should be not only efficient, but also responsible. If power is captured by tyrants, it becomes destructive: if it is too much diffused, society breaks down.

Aristotle, like Acton, believed that unbridled power turned the heads of rulers and he cited lurid examples of tyranny in the Persian Empire. He insisted that the answer to tyranny was the rule of law; 'for man when perfected is the best of animals; but when separated from law and justice he is the worst of all'. This insistence on law or 'Constitutionalism' has an ancient pedigree – more ancient than that of arbitrary power. Primitive societies, which are highly conservative, are generally ruled by the tribal elders, rather than through the decisions of a single ruler. It is only with the rise of organized war that military dictatorship is likely to emerge.

Power, in fact, in primitive as well as in civilized societies, is inevitably conditioned by custom, ideas and ways of life. Even despotism has to reckon with the force of habit, with the loyalty or disaffection of soldiers and police, and to calculate how much the community as a whole will submit to. Otherwise it can only be tempered by assassination.

This form of despotism has been widely practised; and has, indeed, been compatible with elaborate civilization and art, but it demoralizes not only the rulers but also the ruled. It proceeds by a series of more or less veiled palace revolutions, dynastic murders and popular revolts. Although it may present an imposing façade, and even achieve peace over wide areas, it is liable to sudden collapse. The most notorious examples of the corruption of power have been provided by the Roman Emperors, whose misdeeds have echoed down the centuries. Nero and Caligula are still by-words. But they have been far surpassed by modern tyrants. Hitler achieved a range of devastation probably greater than that of Genghis Khan. He proved a classic example of the degeneration and madness which moralists have always declared are the tyrant's doom.

Yet power is necessary. Like a bucket of nitroglycerine, it is dangerous to handle, and elaborate precautions must be taken in its use. One must therefore define its nature and origins.

Some political thinkers have pronounced that power is in its nature absolute, since it can derive only from God through his representatives, ecclesiastical or lay. Sir Robert Filmer (d. 1653) and Joseph de Maistre (c. 1754–1821) believed this. Others have derived it from sheer conquest, and declared, with Hobbes and Hegel, that might makes right. Hegel stated that we 'are apt to forget the truth that lives in power'. This view implies a government of absolute power, and a resulting corruption which spreads throughout society. The ruler determines not only men's actions, but also their state of mind, and history is rewritten according to the demands of propaganda. In such a society, in the long run, technical incompetence is likely to develop.

Another justification of tyranny is for the tyrant to claim to be the embodied will of the society, as when Richard II declared that the laws of England were in his own breast, when Louis XIV said 'l'état c'est moi', or when Hitler, on the eve of the Röhm purge, propounded that he was the incarnate will of the German people.

All these theories of arbitrary power tend, as Acton and Aristotle observe, to corruption. What are the alternative theories of power? They are much more useful than the apparently realist theories already described. They derive power from the general life of the people as expressed through institutions to which government is ultimately responsible. The moral worth of individuals is recognized, and the sacredness of human life. These are safeguarded through institutions which differ in form, but which are, in principle, the same.

Such a commonwealth may be oligarchic, as was the British Constitution in 1688, and yet succeed in expressing the general interest of the society. It may also, as in Great Britain and the United States today, be based on universal suffrage; and it may, as in America, be safeguarded by an elaborate system of checks and balances. This may even tend to paralyse the executive or render the conduct of policy too slow at periods of economic and political crisis. In Great Britain, many authorities now believe that there is a danger of the constitution becoming unbalanced owing to the predominant power of the Cabinet and the House of Commons working through a great bureaucracy, unchecked by the Monarchy or the House of Lords. This danger may be real, but it is mild compared with that of a monolithic party, or a military dictatorship, since the machinery still exists whereby it can be remedied, if public opinion believes change is necessary.

Such flexibility – the power to find out where the shoe pinches, so that constitutional reforms can be made and governments removed through the will of the nation constitutionally expressed – makes compromise possible, and so avoids the disruption of the state by revolution and counter-revolution. The abuse of power, with its moral degradation and practical disadvantages, is therefore most effectively controlled through constitutional government in areas where the tradition and mentality of the people make it workable. It is likely that the problem of world-order, now so urgent, can only be lastingly solved through the development of the United Nations into a constitutional world government by consent.

The appeal of this kind of government is limited. That we have to recognize. Throughout history Acton's advice has been widely and consistently disregarded over great areas of the world. Karl Marx, for example, made the mistake of thinking political problems less important than economic laws; and while he made a profound economic diagnosis, he under-estimated the perennial and central importance of the problem of power. Thus Marx held that a free communist society would emerge from a period of dictatorship, miscalculating the corruption and lust for authority which dictatorship was bound to bring. Naturally, therefore, Marx's doctrines have been best carried out in areas where arbitrary power has been habitual.

The world is now divided, as Alexis de Tocqueville and Acton foresaw that it would be, into two camps. One is based on centralized and bureaucratic tyranny; the other upon the principle of constitutional government by consent. In one the corruption of power is rampant; in the other it is to a great extent controlled. Urgently, if civilization is to avoid an atomic World War – which would be the 'absolute' example of the abuse of power – the maintenance and further diffusion of the constitutional control of power are necessary. The central and perennial problem of political theory, defined by Acton, may well become the question of the survival of civilized mankind.

It should be mentioned that though the form of Acton's 'dictum' quoted above is the one in general use, the exact wording in a letter by him is: 'Power tends to corrupt and absolute power corrupts absolutely'.

ILLUSTRATION: Page 325.

Truth is what works

PRAGMATISM has been expounded by three American philosophers, C. S. Peirce (1839–1914), William James (1842–1910), and John Dewey (1859–1952), who have each developed quite different theories. The single most important view they have in common is a certain general attitude to the philosophical concept of 'truth'. Pragmatism rejects the idea that truth is absolute, objective and final, something independent of ourselves which we try, more or less successfully, to apprehend.

According to Pragmatism, what is true is 'what works': truth is not contemplated but achieved; it is the end-product of intellectual inquiry, much as a successful mechanical invention is the end-product of practical inquiry.

So Pragmatism has two elements, one negative or destructive, the other constructive. The negative element is not new, but at least as old as Protagoras, the Greek Sophist who put forward a thorough Relativism, both in ethics and in theory of knowledge: 'Man is the measure of all things; of what is, that it is; and of what is not, that it is not'. In Plato's dialogue *Theaetetus* this view of Protagoras is criticized as implying that each man's judgement is as true as any other's, which is a paradox. Socrates suggests that one man's judgement, even if it is not more 'true', might be 'better' than another's, rather as one doctor's prescription might be better than another's: but this is not pursued.

David Hume (1711–1776) professed a highly sceptical theory of knowledge: 'In all the incidents of life', he wrote, 'we ought still to preserve our scepticism. If we believe that fire warms, or water refreshes, 'tis only because it costs us too much pains to think otherwise.' Here Pragmatism emerges as the practical reconciliation of a paradoxical philosophy with the exigencies of common life. Judgement can be suspended, but not action. There is no truth, but we have to act as if there were. 'Acting as if' sums up this negative side of pragmatism.

There are good reasons why the constructive side of pragmatism had to await the Americans. The Greek philosophers were not merely unpractical men, they had a positive contempt for practical considerations. The Greek term *banaustikon* expressed the attitude of the 'gentleman' to the business of servants and slaves. Correspondingly, they had an exaggerated respect for the ideal of intellectual contemplation. To see – especially with the mind's eye – was nobler than to do; the very word 'theory' (*theoria*) means a spectacle. They favoured pure mathematics (for which Pythagoras had instituted a mystic cult) rather than natural science; geometry was untainted with sordid practical affairs. Plato in *The Republic* ridicules the idea that mathematics might be studied with a view to practical utility.

Christianity abolished the distinction between 'bond and free', slave and master; but for the intellectual world of the philosophers it substituted, not the practical world, but the spiritual world. In the Middle Ages, when intellectual as well as spiritual matters were the subject of clerical dogmas there was little scope for the idea of independent research. The Age of Reason saw a new rationalism with pointers to final and certain knowledge. Even in the reaction of the eighteenth century, leading philosophers still shared a cultural background not unlike that of the Greeks: they were, on the whole, men of leisure. In America, on the other hand, the absence of an aristocratic tradition, the complementary ideals of individualism and community, and the positive enthusiasm for science and scientific control, all combined (though in very different proportions) to favour the constructive side of Pragmatism in its three chief exponents.

William James borrowed the term 'Pragmatism' from Peirce, and being a more gifted writer gained currency for his own version of it at the expense of the original. James's pragmatism is well illustrated by his doctrine of religion. Truth is what works; belief in God is 'true' if it proves to be useful in practice; and religious belief does satisfy practical needs. This might be called Utilitarian Pragmatism.

Dewey calls his doctrine 'Instrumentalism'. What is fundamental is a process which he calls Inquiry; this is neither purely theoretical nor purely practical. 'Theory and practice' is itself a false antithesis perpetuated by the intellectualistic philosophy against which the Pragmatists protest. Inquiry is best described in biological terms: it is a process whereby a human organism tries to improve its relation with a temporarily unsatisfactory environment. Thoughts are 'instrumental' in this process, but thoughts are not purely mental events: we also think with our hands and tools. 'Truth' is the theoretical aspect of the

provisionally completed inquiry. This might be called Biological Pragmatism.

Both these types of pragmatism have been severely criticized. Even Marxist writers (who might have been expected to welcome a philosophy in terms of practical human activities) join forces with Bertrand Russell and common sense in attacking the pragmatist rejection of objectivity. According to such critics, truth is what corresponds with the facts as they are, not as we happen to investigate them. As against William James, for instance, people seeking religious instruction are interested in the question of whether God exists, not the question of whether it is useful to believe that he exists. As against Dewey, 'inquiry' presupposes some facts about which we inquire; an answer to our question is satisfactory because it is true, not true because it is satisfactory.

C. S. Peirce's pragmatism is less open to criticism. It is not primarily a theory of truth at all; it is a theory of definition, 'a method of ascertaining the meanings of hard words and abstract conceptions'. The method is summarized in the formula:

Consider what effects, that might conceivably have practical bearings, we conceive the object of our conception to have. Then, our conception of these effects is the whole of our conception of the object.

This is an attack on another traditional 'correspondence' theory: the 'correspondence' between a word and an 'idea' or mental content which is supposed to be what the word means. Pragmatism holds, on the contrary, that an expression gets its meaning from the practical experiences or procedures which its use suggests. Peirce's maxim expressed in the above-quoted formula has certain affinities with the Verification Principle of the modern Logical Positivists (q.v.), and indeed was used by him for a similar purpose, the 'elimination' of traditional metaphysics as 'meaningless'.

The theory of 'truth' is coloured by Peirce's familiarity with the methods of the physical sciences. What is it for a scientific hypothesis to be 'true'? Its truth cannot be tested by simply inspecting it and noting a 'correspondence' with a 'fact'. It has to be tested by its consequences. In certain cases – if, for instance, certain observations are obtained which would be predictable from the hypothesis – it is accepted; in others it is rejected. But who determines which consequences justify acceptance or rejection? Not the private investigator. Science is a co-operative activity, and questions of acceptance or rejection of scientific statements are decided by criteria which are public to the community of scientists. And so in general: 'truth' is what is accepted by public criteria; a true opinion is one 'in which the community settles down'. This might be called Methodological Pragmatism.

Within certain limits it is substantially correct: but the question remains, how far is it correct outside the domain of science – in history, for example, or theology, or philosophy itself? It is almost a commonplace among modern philosophers who would not call themselves pragmatists, that there are a number of philosophical questions (such as the problem of Determinism, of the foundations of ethics and politics), which can receive an ultimate answer only in pragmatic terms.

This represents, perhaps, a satisfactory compromise between the traditional contemplative philosophy with its associated concept of a static, independent reality, comprehended by a pure act of knowing – and the down-to-earth, shirt-sleeve philosophy of the workshops which the more extreme types of pragmatism have suggested. Human beings are not pure intelligences; and neither are they simply organisms. But thoughts, statements, theories, intellectual attitudes and philosophies are all functionally related to the particular problems a man has to deal with in his actual life in society.

God's foreknowledge

PREDESTINATION has relevance only in a context of Christian doctrine, in between the extremes of complete determinism and complete free will.

A dictionary definition for predestination is 'the belief that God has foreordained every action, and predestined every soul, therefore, to hell or salvation'. Apart from explicit statements by St Paul, the Gospel accounts of the relations of Jesus and Judas raise the issue in its sharpest form. The most circumstantial of the Passion narratives, that of John, makes it clear that Jesus had foreknowledge of even the most trivial of Judas's acts, the dipping of the morsel of bread, as well as the certainty that Judas would betray him. It is also clear that Judas was to be held accountable for what he did – 'Better for that man had he never been born' – and that he was not in any sense forced to do what he did. Some of Jesus's sayings in Judas's presence can only be construed as warnings, and in any case the final ruin of Judas was accomplished not by the betrayal, but by his suicide, his final refusal to acknowledge Jesus by asking forgiveness. So it is clear that Christians who take the Bible and biblical doctrine seriously, are forced to face vexing problems of divine foreknowledge and its consequences for freedom and responsibility.

One way out of the difficulty which has more to be said for it than appears at first sight was taken by the Anglican divine, William Beveridge (1637–1708), Bishop of St Asaph, when he wrote: 'God's predestination … must needs be infinitely above man's apprehension. So that a cockle-fish may as soon crowd the ocean into its narrow shell, as vain man ever comprehend the decrees of God.'

There are really two related but different problems in God's foreknowledge and his freedom. The first is by far the more important, because it gives rise to all the difficulties: it is only because we have to suppose that God foresees everything that we get into difficulties about his will, when we have to make him responsible for the terrible events of which we know him to have had foreknowledge. Yet it is on the problems created by God's will that the bitterest controversies have raged. At the time of the Reformation, for example, this was chiefly what was meant by predestination. Harking back to the dictionary definition, Calvin the French reformer (1509–1564) wrote:

By predestination we mean the eternal decree of God, by which he has decided in his own mind what he wishes to happen in the case of each individual. For all are not created on an equal footing, but for some eternal life is pre-ordained, and for others eternal damnation.

The sources of Calvin's concern are obvious: it is necessary to affirm the omnipotence and omniscience of God. Yet one can only feel that Calvin stressed these at the expense of God's mercy and his goodness. We *must* allow that God's freedom here is limited. Calvin seems to have missed the point made by St Augustine, who wrote:

It surely cannot be said that God himself has not freedom of choice because he is unable to sin.

The limitations are only apparent, they are only verbal, but they must be affirmed if we are not to caricature the Gospel teaching on God's mercy and his promise of salvation simply to free the notion of his omnipotence from all obscurity.

In his view on God's foreknowledge Calvin is unexceptionable:

When we attribute foreknowledge to God we mean that all things have ever been, and eternally remain, before his eyes; so that to his knowledge nothing is future or past, but all things are present.

He is in perfect accord with St Thomas Aquinas in his dictum that 'to God all time is eternally present'. This does not mean that God's foreknowledge is at all like that of a crystal-gazer; it means that to God there are no yesterdays, todays or tomorrows, that his foreknowledge is not advance knowledge, but present knowledge. It is only when we make statements about God's knowledge in human terms – and we have to express them in human language and thus force them into the inescapable partitions of past, present and future – that difficulty arises. But it is really an intellectual or imaginative difficulty, due to the linguistic impossibility of finding precise words to convey the relation between natural and supernatural. For some purposes, though obviously not for all, natural freedom and supernatural predestination can be related and treated as two distinct categories: ultimately they point to the same thing. If the supernatural contains the natural, whilst also spreading beyond the natural, it must seem as though supernatural predestination annihilates natural freedom. Yet it is also true that the natural has its rights and that its freedom is real. Actions which are determined freely must seem, as they did to Liebniz, faintly paradoxical; but without being irrational

this expresses obscurely a truth which it is not within reason's capacity to express in the round.

Predestination must mean that there are no ifs in history, no interesting possibilities, but the logical explanation that everything is for the best in the best of all possible worlds is not a tenable solution. That was Calvin's mistake. There are too many terrible events, too much evidence of an evil power at work to permit this. History is like an elaborate game. One player is supreme and is bound to win because he makes the rules. But he is perfectly fair, and once he has made a rule he will abide by it, and perfectly good, so that the rule itself will be the best possible rule. One of the rules is the free and responsible participation of all the players in the game; they must play the game, but how they play it is up to them.

The obligation may seem to contradict the freedom, but this is not so. Freedom is a word of power: to have power one must have existence first, to exist one must have a context; the context is the game, the freedom is the power to participate. It is only because one great player, the Devil (q.v.), has cheated that the game is in any way competitive at all, that it is a game, and that it is not a glorious ritual. Part of the contest is fought out in the world of men. Each man is not only a player in the game, but also a prize for which the evil player will go on cheating in order to win. He is clever, he has great powers which, once given to him, God will not take away. He will have triumphant successes, but they will always cost more than they are worth. When God became man, the Devil achieved his utter humiliation and his abject expulsion from the world by contriving his crucifixion, but only at the cost of expelling all those who choose to go with him from the Devil's world to God's heaven. Finally there will be no 'world', only heaven, and hell where the Devil is.

Predestination is an essential part of Christian doctrine, and must retain its force so long as that doctrine exists. But the contemporary concern, widespread outside the Christian Church, with attempts to unravel the 'laws of history', to explain the rise and fall of civilizations as something more than the collected histories of numerous individuals, suggests that the problems of predestination are real problems with a basis in human experience as well as biblical doctrine.

The idea of progress

PROGRESS, an essentially nineteenth-century concept, was unfamiliar in Antiquity, or in the massive and traditional societies of China, India and the Far East. The vast majority of mankind until recent times generally thought civilization more apt to degenerate than to advance. The Greeks and Romans saw history as a cyclic recurrence, and Hesiod depicted a Golden Age (q.v.), lapsing into an Age of Iron. A more hopeful view was expressed by Lucretius, who first used the term in something like a modern sense. He referred to primitive man as progressing step by step – *pedetentim progredientes*.

With the triumph of Christianity a more pessimistic view was again asserted. The world was regarded as merely the threshold of Eternity, a testing-ground where life was dominated by Original Sin (q.v.), which only Revelation could redeem. Further, the technological skill of Antiquity was never comparable to our own, partly because it was a slave-owning civilization where technology was despised. With the breakdown of this society into local and feudal provincialism, even confidence in the Roman achievement faded. The sparse and rudimentary thinkers who survived were in no condition to do more than transmit a garbled version of the conservative ideas of the past. And with the revival of speculation in the twelfth and thirteenth centuries interest centred on theological questions. There was still no conception of progress in the modern sense.

Even with the rise of Humanism in Italy and the development of more worldly interests, there was little idea of progress. Dante, Petrarch and Machiavelli all looked back to an idealized Roman Empire, and the scholars of the Renaissance were concerned to recover the great classical masterpieces rather than look to the future. Machiavelli regarded political affairs as being likely to degenerate and as largely determined by Fate. In the seventeenth century Hobbes's writings were still coloured by a static gloom, although he rejected medieval fatalism and thought that a fool-proof polity could be devised. John Locke, with his concern for property and business, and belief in toleration, held a more optimistic view, but it was not until the eighteenth century that the French rationalist thinkers postulated the modern idea of progress.

Voltaire (1694–1778) popularized the idea (if in a rather sceptical way), since he believed that Reason played a dominant part in affairs, in spite of the follies and crimes of mankind, and that its influence would increase with the destruction of religious dogma. A. R. J. Turgot (1727–1781) also held that the human race was destined to advance, not through Reason, but through 'instinct'. The tone of the influential French Encyclopaedists made for confidence in the improvement of society through knowledge. But Condorcet (1743–1794) was the most eloquent prophet of the idea of progress. His *Sketch of an Historical Picture of the Progress of the Human Mind* was published after his death, and in it he expressed the optimism of the American and French Revolutions. He was also passionately anti-clerical, and devised a secular 'map' of History in terms of successive advance. He believed that the history of civilization proved the fact of intellectual and political progress.

In England, Jeremy Bentham and Adam Smith both believed in improvement: Bentham endeavoured to achieve progress in law by applying utilitarian rather than traditional standards; Adam Smith held that if the economic system was understood and allowed to follow its natural course, great economic progress would come about.

These beliefs were encouraged by new philosophies of history. The Italian thinker, Giovanni Battista Vico (1668–1744), a pioneer in historical philosophy, had envisaged an Age of the Gods, giving place to an Heroic Age, in turn followed by a Human Age. Hegel also discovered a philosophy of history in which successive world-historic peoples dominated one another in a dialectical process – of which the culmination was the Prussian State. Similarly, Karl Marx held that a dialectic process, materialistically determined, was fated to produce a clash of world-historic classes, bound inevitably to give place to a dictatorship of the proletariat, which, in its turn, must progressively wither away into a classless society. Here poverty would be abolished by the release of the full powers of modern production, and social injustice would be rectified. Marx reflects both Hegel's dynamic view of history and the materialist optimism of the Industrial Revolution.

Liberal thinkers, meanwhile, increasingly propagated progressive views. Mazzini (1805–1872) was the most eloquent prophet of the idea. 'Progress', he wrote, 'is the Providential law.' He believed that the masses of humanity, now at last included in the benefits of civilization, would go forward in an idealistic fraternity in which national conflicts and class conflicts would be abolished. Comte (1798–1857) reinforced the idea of progress by a primitive sociology. He thought history had developed through three phases, the Theological, the Metaphysical and the Positivist. In the Positivist phase man would make himself. Inspired by an organized religion of Humanity, he would order the world aright. But where Mazzini was a democrat, Comte, following Saint-Simon, believed in the rule of bankers and industrialists.

The mid-nineteenth century saw the culmination of the belief in progress. Buckle and Lecky brilliantly depicted history in these terms; and although Winwood Reade's immensely popular *Martyrdom of Man* took a grim view of the past, it was inspired by brash optimism. Further, the scientific discoveries of the time – in particular, Darwin's theory of evolution – gave a new factual basis to the idea of progress, even if achieved through suffering and competition. Herbert Spencer, who advocated the survival of the fittest in society, supported the *laissez-faire* economists in the view that competition is bound to create progress.

This predominant nineteenth-century belief had never been accepted by the Catholic Church. Both Joseph de Maistre (c. 1754–1821), and even the liberal Popes, disbelieved in it. Their criticism was reinforced by the psychological discoveries which emphasized the importance of the irrational in human affairs. Georges Sorel (1847–1922) regarded progress as a typical 'bourgeois' myth. In our own day, Spengler and Toynbee have popularized pessimistic philosophies of history, and modern sociologists and anthropologists also, no longer believe in the universal linear patterns of development which earlier thinkers believed to be discernible.

Yet one cannot deny the fact of progress in the sense of the increased power of mankind over its environment. While there is no evidence of an inevitable law of progress, knowledge has achieved fantastic advances since prehistoric times. If political conduct can be adapted to the revolutionary conditions created by the discovery of nuclear power, the possibilities of further advance remain stupendous. Even if civilization were temporarily crippled by atomic war, it seems unlikely that modern knowledge would be lost. Progress in control of environment must be accepted, if not as a law, as a fact. On the evidence of the brief time-span of recorded history, this originally Western European idea is now increasingly acknowledged throughout the world. And increased power over the world and over himself gives man the promise, though not the guarantee, of the enhancement and enrichment of life.

ILLUSTRATION: Page 408.

Proletariat and working class

The **PROLETARIAT** in ancient Rome were those who served the state only by breeding. It was a derogatory term, *proletarius* (from the Latin *proles*, offspring) for the lowest class in the community, with the sense that 'riff-raff' has today.

In the social thought of the nineteenth century the word acquired a much more specific meaning. The proletariat came to denote the propertyless, wage-earning class created by the Industrial Revolution who had only their labour to sell. This conception of the proletariat was mainly due to the work of Karl Marx (1818–1883). To Marx the main feature of modern society was a conflict between the owners of the instruments of production – specifically industrial instruments – and the machine-tending proletariat. According to his theories this conflict would result in an inevitable revolution. As the proletariat became conscious of itself as a class, it would overthrow the bourgeoisie and establish a classless society.

Thus in the Marxian tradition the conception of the proletariat became romantically ennobled. In the first instance the proletarians were regarded as the victims of an unjust system of distribution of rewards brought about by capitalism. That is, they were not getting a proper share of the things which they produced with the sweat of their brows and the ache of their muscles.

Far from being the riff-raff of society, the proletariat had in its hands, according to Marx, the destiny not only of itself as a class but of all humanity. Because it was the 'last' submerged class, the revolution it would achieve would end class conflict. By contrast the riff-raff in Marxian sociology consisted of the *Lumpenproletariat*, those members of the propertyless stratum on the fringe of the industrial structure who could not be counted on to develop the sentiments of class loyalty and solidarity.

The esteem in which the proletariat came to be held in the radical socialist thought of the nineteenth century is analogous to the glorification of the Noble Savage (q.v.) in the eighteenth century. Both were regarded as possessing the highest virtues. The strength of the proletariat was held up in sharp contrast to bourgeois decadence and hypocrisy. Of course, this was not the first time in history that a movement of thought mobilized powerful sentiments on behalf of the underprivileged, nor was Marxism alone in the nineteenth century in doing so. Capitalism, with all the social freedom that it both created and presupposed, succeeded in generating great hostility to itself in the societies where it becomes established. This was felt particularly among aristocrats and bureaucrats and amongst the intelligentsia, who focused their contempt for the economic system upon its most representative type, the bourgeois or capitalist. This contempt involved a corresponding elevation of the working man.

Marxism in its literal text repudiates moral judgements about the actors in the historical drama it attempts to outline. Its alleged objectivity rested upon the premise that ideologies and other cultural elements are determined by material factors – what men think and how they behave are determined by the position which they have in the economic system. By this postulate the bourgeoisie behaved as they did, not because they wanted to, but because they had to, and were thus exonerated from moral turpitude. They oppressed the proletariat; but that was a necessary phase of historical evolution, in which the proletariat were being prepared for their part.

By the same token the virtues of the have-nots, the proletariat, must be less a manifestation of innate moral superiority than the result of *their* position in history and in society. If they were to rise and liberate mankind, that, too, was ordained by 'scientific' analysis. Marxism, though, could hardly remain cold analysis. Who could believe that a social class was destined to rise, revolt, and re-order human society without also developing the strongest moral and emotional enthusiasms in its behalf?

In consequence, Marxism became programmatic, concerned with implementing the revolution through the international organization of the proletariat and through the entry of the proletariat into political life. The First International Working Men's Association was founded in 1864. Marx himself played a leading part in drawing up its constitution; and declared in his inaugural address that the working class must achieve its own emancipation. On the face of things there was no need to take any steps to achieve what was inevitable; though Marx did maintain that effort would *help* the inevitable to come about less painfully and more efficiently.

Marx and his followers looked on themselves as the vanguard of the proletariat: in developing class consciousness among the workers, they, as intellectuals, were merely bringing them to a knowledge of their mission in history. Certainly the term proletariat came to mean much more than an occupational category. It became a symbol with which all (whatever their social position) who believed in the Marxian doctrines could identify. Engels, who was Marx's friend and collaborator, was a manufacturer; and Marx himself was certainly no member of the working class.

The looseness of the term was augmented by Marx's conclusion that world revolution, in the first, transitional stage, would be marked by a dictatorship of the proletariat. In Russia the dictatorship, in fact, had the only meaning which 'dictatorship of the proletariat' possibly could have, *i.e.* a dictatorship *in the name of* the proletariat. The ruling élite in the U.S.S.R. were no more members of the working class than Marx had been: they were professional revolutionaries who had theorized, agitated, and conspired to effect a change in power.

The theorists of the dictatorship of the proletariat can be charged either with conscious deception or with the greatest degree of self-deception conceivable in politics, since ruling and labouring are very different things, and they completely evaded the problem of political power.

The attempt to obliterate the distinction between the rulers and the ruled has long since been reversed. In this process the term proletariat has gone out of fashion in the vocabulary of Communist Russia. As a revolutionary symbol it is no longer really palatable to the ruling dictatorship – even though as part of their heritage it cannot be repudiated outright – since to them the revolution is now a thing of the past.

In the industrialized societies of the West, where Marx predicted a proletarian revolution which has never taken place, the term proletariat hardly counts any more as a symbol of politics, and is not applied by the workers to themselves.

In the United States, as an extreme example, even the term working-class, let alone proletariat, is neither a social nor a political reality. But American society is one in which over ninety per cent of the population regard themselves as middle class.

Double-talk

PROPAGANDA, the act of disseminating opinions, is an entirely normal activity not peculiar to any particular state of society or stage of history. With the advance of literacy and the extension of the political classes to embrace most of the community, it has acquired a new importance and, whether conducted by the state or by private persons who wish to influence the conduct of the state, it has become a regular feature of political life in most civilized countries.

In the last half-century a science of propaganda has developed. A new phenomenon called the 'mass mind' has begun to be an object of scientific enquiry, and the results of these enquiries have been turned to many practical uses. This new science was not invented by exponents of totalitarianism nor are the techniques which it has developed used solely to support political dictatorships. One of its pioneers, Graham Wallas (1858–1932) was, for example, an English Fabian and a professor at the London School of Economics.

The starting point of propaganda is the belief that pure reason is only one factor in determining people's opinions, and that, as the size of the audience which is being addressed increases, this factor becomes progressively less important. Men's likes and dislikes are determined by a complicated set of mental associations, many of which are purely arbitrary. These associations are largely produced by environment; people pick up preferences from each other; thus, particular classes develop common psychological reactions, and in this sense it is possible to speak of a 'class mind' or a 'national mind'.

The practical importance of these conclusions is obvious. If you wish to control the behaviour of large groups of people, it will be necessary to understand their 'social sub-conscious'. Advertising agents, for instance, have discovered by elaborate experiments that certain words like 'glamour', 'luxury', have a powerful appeal for certain types of consumer. The same technique is practised, usually in a far more rudimentary form, by politicians in the democracies. The choice of every party catchword depends on some judgement, however ill-informed, about mass psychology. Phrases like 'property-owning democracy' and 'fair shares for all', are obviously selected for what is supposed to be their emotional appeal – for the set of pictures they evoke in the mind – rather than for their rational content.

The science of public relations, which is only an extension of advertisement, uses the same methods and works on the same material. A public-relations officer may give elaborate consideration to the type of writing-paper which his employer uses and to the immediate effect which the sight of it is likely to produce upon those with whom he does business. So propaganda has come to mean the art of exploiting irrational impulses, tastes, prejudices, which may arise from purely accidental causes, but which are now seen as important in deciding human behaviour.

Naturally the word propaganda has acquired an unpleasant ring. It is humiliating to admit that so much of human behaviour arises from the irrational. The case for popular government rests on the belief that the 'average man' is capable of rational judgement; anything which undermines this faith, undermines democracy. Yet it would be wrong to suppose that belief in the necessity of propaganda in the running of modern life implies a complete repudiation of belief in the average man's rationality. Nineteenth-century thinkers exaggerated the importance of reason, and other factors do exist which have a legitimate place in shaping human judgement. It would be extremely unhealthy – as well as impossible – for men to think rationally about everything they did, and reason itself provides no motive for action; it fulfils its function partly by acting as a censor of motives. Men should be capable, for example, of reflecting on the reasons for which they go to war, but while they are actually fighting their morale will have to be sustained by symbols with an emotional appeal; this can be done without invalidating the reasons for which the war is being fought. Thus propaganda may be held to have a legitimate rôle, as well as an inevitable one, in the running of a free society. Nevertheless a free society must always be aware of the dangers in propaganda: it must try not to use propaganda in ways which impair the capacity for rational judgement, and it must try not to resort to deliberate lying. The question is where is the dividing line to be drawn.

Here a clue comes from the French syndicalist writer Albert Sorel (1842–1906). As a socialist Sorel was preoccupied with the problem of making the working classes aware of injustice and inducing them to rebel against capitalist tyranny. Sorel therefore elaborated the theory of the Myth. The habit of rational thought, the habit of analysis, of splitting ideas up into their component elements and meditating upon them, was, he believed, an example of decadent bourgeois civilization, and something of which the working classes must be cured. Common men would never learn all the arguments against capitalism and then rationally set about destroying it; what was needed was one simple, striking idea on which the working-class mind could be fed. The idea which Sorel proposed was that of the general strike. The working-class mind must be fed on the notion that one day there would be a general

strike, that all the workers would band together in a single dramatic act of resistance which would send capitalism tottering to the ground. The constant expectation of this day would play the same part in Socialism as the expectation of the Day of Judgement had played in early Christian history.

This idea of the general strike was simple, evocative and symbolically true. It might be that the general strike would never happen, it might be that the working class was really not a single entity, but a series of mutually jealous groups; these things belonged to the degrading realm of fact. Get people thinking about the general strike, and the latent division between the haves and have-nots, at present obscured, would become real; the myth would come true by dint of being believed, and, in the process, the working-class movement, instead of being bogged in endless analysis and discussion, would become a heroic religion. The function of the Myth was thus to express deep truths underlying and contradicting mere facts; its justification was the result which it produced.

Sorel's influence, alas, was not on Socialism: it was to him that Fascism and Nazism owed their conception of propaganda – totalitarian propaganda, the distinguishing characteristic of which is not simply the distortion of truth, but the substitution of an entirely new conception of truth: those who defend propaganda of this kind do so by arguments far more dangerous and sophisticated than the argument, advanced by Machiavelli, for example, that the end for which the lies are told justifies the means. They do not merely appeal from fact to absolute truth, for they usually have great contempt for abstractions. Their theory is that the great fundamental truths can be appreciated by the masses only when the mass mind is liberated from facts, and these truths must be expressed in simple concrete terms which themselves look like statements of fact.

The doctrine of racial supremacy, for example, may not 'come alive' until it is dressed up in the form of a series of mendacious statements about the activities of a particular race; these statements will be held to be true in the sense that they express a fundamental truth (in other words, agree with a preconceived theory) which could not otherwise be understood; and it will also be

Continued on p. 327

PLATE 12

CHIVALRY AND COURTLY LOVE: Flemish Parade Shield, late 15th century.

MONROE DOCTRINE: James Monroe (1758–1831), fifth President of the United States.

THE IMMACULATE CONCEPTION: Painting by Murillo (c. 1617–1682).
(*See* also Plate 14.)

NOBLE SAVAGE: *Omaih*, by Sir Joshua Reynolds (1723–1792).

MYSTICISM: St Theresa in ecstasy, by Bernini (1598–1680), in Santa Maria Della Vittoria, Rome.

'MODERN ART': Abused on its first appearance: *St Matthew and the Angel*, by Caravaggio (1565–1609).

315

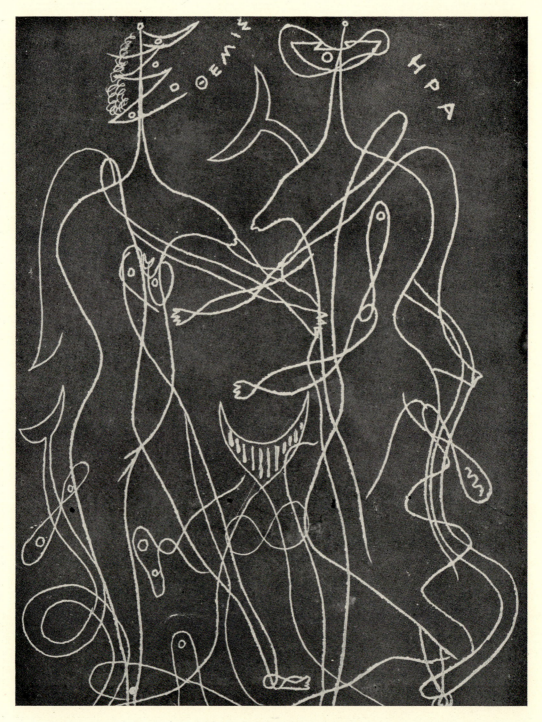

'MODERN ART': In our time. 1. *Themis and Hera*, by Georges Braque, 1934. Engraved plaster.

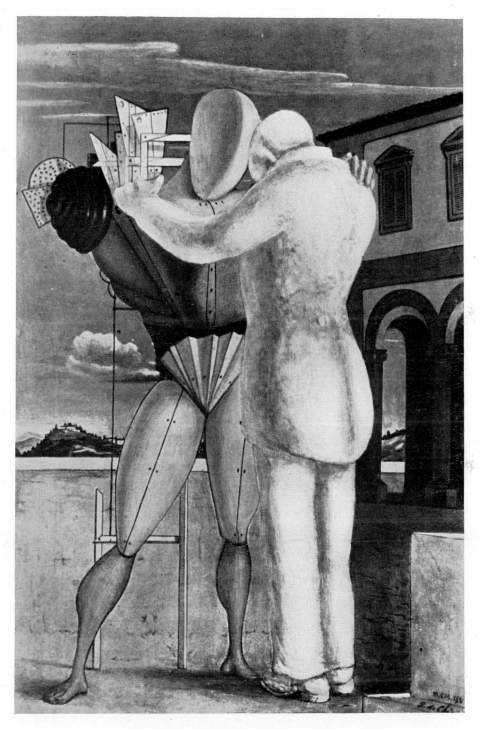

2. *The Return of the Prodigal,* by Giorgio de Chirico (b. 1888).

ROMANTIC NATURE: 1. *Valley with Winding streams.* Watercolour by J. R. Cozens (1752–1799).

2. *Skelwith Force, Westmorland*, by William Havell (1782–1857).

319

NIHILISM: 1. A. Schopenhauer (1788–1860).

2. Prince Kropotkin (1842–1921).

PLANNING : 1. The nineteenth-century town : Manchester.

322

2. The planned town : Harlow New Town, Essex.

'POLITICS IS THE ART OF THE POSSIBLE': Edmund Burke (1729–1797).
From the studio of Reynolds, 1771.

324

'ALL POWER CORRUPTS AND ABSOLUTE POWER CORRUPTS ABSOLUTELY': Lord Acton (1834–1902).

MCCARTHYISM: 'Jo' McCarthy, Republican Senator for Wisconsin, U.S.A.

PLATE 13

ASCETICISM: A group of Mughal Ascetics.

claimed for them that they are true, in a profound religious sense – in the sense that they evoke heroic behaviour, so that those who believe them testify to their truth by their noble deeds.

The insidiousness of this type of argument needs no emphasizing; its real object is to make the dictator, the party, or whatever the source of propaganda may be, an unfettered master of fact.

By these ideas Hitler's famous passages on propaganda in his book *Mein Kampf* must be judged. His preference for simple, striking, concrete statements, his contempt for the analytical mind and his belief that it is the source of profound weakness in any political movement, all bear the marks of Sorel, one of those nineteenth-century thinkers who have ruled the twentieth century from their graves.

The same influence is clearly present in the propaganda of the Communists with its central myth of Class Struggle. Between this deadly philosophy of 'Truth' and the empirical attitude towards propaganda maintained in the democracies, there is a profound difference, which must be perpetually recognized and understood. The more thorough the science of mass psychology becomes and the more expert its techniques become, the greater is the temptation to find a philosophy which will give its practitioners the grim chance of showing how clever they can be.

ILLUSTRATION: Pages 361 and 407.

Minorities, weakness and all?

PROPORTIONAL REPRESENTATION implies that members of any representative assembly should be elected in such a manner as to represent all sections of opinion in proportion to their voting strength in the electorate. Applied to the English House of Commons it would mean that the number of seats held by the various parties would be proportional to the total votes cast in their favour over the whole of the country, instead of corresponding to the number of constituencies gained by a majority vote.

One form or another of proportional representation is used in many democratic countries at the present time, but it has never been adopted in

P

the United Kingdom. At first sight, the case for proportional representation in any democratic country seems overwhelming. Its equitable basis is obvious: if the representative assembly is to be truly representative of the electorate – a fundamental of democratic government – then the assembly should undoubtedly reflect all the political opinions held by the electorate, in the same proportion. The case against proportional representation is that, equitable or no, it might bring certain disadvantages to offset the benefits.

In Great Britain, the country is divided into constituencies averaging 56,000 electors, each returning one M.P. – the candidate elected being the one who secures the most individual votes. This system of 'First-past-the-Post' is extremely simple. Yet, where there are more than two candidates standing in any constituency, the one who receives the most votes may well only represent a minority of the total voters in the constituency; and as certain areas are 'strongholds' of a particular party, that party's candidate may be elected with a very large majority, which from that party's standpoint consists of 'wasted' votes.

These two evils cancel themselves out in the case of two strong parties; but this system means that a party with a majority of votes tends to be returned with an even larger majority of seats, whereas a small party seldom gains seats in any degree proportionate to the votes cast for it. On the other hand, owing to the division of the country into constituencies, it is quite possible for a party to be returned with a working majority in the House, when it represents only a minority of the total electorate.

Of the many systems of obtaining proportional representation, the one most widely advocated in this country is that of the 'Single Transferable Vote', based on proposals originally put forward by Thomas Hare in 1859 and later strongly supported by John Stuart Mill. Under this system the country would be divided into a number of larger constituencies, each returning from three to seven members. When voting, the order of preference of candidates would be given and all majority or 'surplus' votes not required after the election of a candidate, together with all 'lost' votes for candidates who obviously cannot receive enough votes to be elected, would be distributed proportionately amongst the remaining candidates. A candidate who would not have been elected on 'first preference' votes only, may thus be elected after receiving a number of 'surplus' or 'lost' votes from other candidates.

Electors would not need to hesitate before voting for an unlikely candidate, since if that candidate is unlucky, his votes will be transferred according to their second preferences. Fewer votes, therefore, would be 'wasted', and the seats in parliament would be more nearly proportional to the total votes cast. This, it is claimed, would allow the election of more independent candidates and make for a more vigorous parliament, less accountable to the party machine.

Yet proportional representation might do little to prevent the election of a government representing only a minority of the total voters; and what is worse, it might encourage the election of a party that only had a minority in the House itself. Critics have calculated (in so far as such computations are valid) that under proportional representation, out of the last eight general elections in Great Britain, only two would have been likely to return a party with a clear working majority. This is no doubt a great weakness of proportional representation, since a government works best under a party with a clear majority and faced with a strong single party in opposition.

The chief objection to proportional representation therefore seems to be that it would make for weak government; strong majority governments would be infrequent; the elections would seldom give a clear mandate to any party to go ahead with a vigorous legislative programme, and the power of the ordinary voter to give his sanction to a definite policy would thus be seriously weakened.

Vox populi

PUBLIC OPINION, as the prevailing sentiment of a community, became an explicit conception at the end of the eighteenth century. Instances of expressions of popular feeling, of primitive systems of election, can be found for the earliest and least civilized of human societies; in

Greece, relatively advanced forms of democratic government had been established by the fifth century B.C. However, by 1800 three essential conditions for the creation and recognition of a public opinion in the countries of Europe and North America were in process of being fulfilled: first, recognition of the importance of the individual, irrespective of class or wealth, Secondly, grouping of individuals into clearly defined units – 'nations' to the politician, 'markets' to the businessman; and thirdly, development of the means to detect and communicate the state of mind of the individuals comprising each of these units.

'Public opinion' was recognized first by the politicians, only later – as the industrial Revolution was followed by the development of mass-production and 'mass-markets' – by the businessmen.

According to the political idealists of the time of the French Revolution and immediately after, public opinion was a force for the good – wise, judicious, still (despite the influence of the Romantics) rational after the pattern of the eighteenth century. This view had some coincidental support in the fact that at that time it was still only the more educated and intelligent members of society who could raise their voices and be heard. The spread of democracy however had its opponents not merely in those who resisted it in favour of other forms of government but in those who doubted whether, despite increased standards of education, the people as a whole could be trusted to exercise good judgement. Their doubts were reinforced, towards the end of the nineteenth century, by the evidence of social and individual psychology that man both as an individual and as a member of a group cannot be relied on to act solely in the light of reason. These contrasted views of public opinion – as a good or evil genius – are still current today.

The modern tendency is to attach equal importance to every individual's opinion, to count 'ayes' and 'noes', by means of a vote, a referendum, conducting a survey of opinion. The prime difficulty in this is to express the issue in a question to which a simple answer can be given, and at the same time to frame the question so that it does not suggest its own answer. (Consider as an extreme example the difference between 'Should the Monarchy be retained?' and 'Don't you agree that the Monarchy should be retained?') Collecting the votes of a whole nation is a lengthy and costly affair; the technique of the 'straw-vote', the 'poll' associated with the name of Dr George Horace Gallup (b. 1901), the American statistician, has therefore been developed to avoid some of the expense and waste of time involved. Statisticians and mathematicians decide what size and type of smaller group 'sample' can be taken as representative of the larger group whose opinion is wanted.

Even when the poll has been taken, public opinion may change, and the sample may cease to represent the majority view. (Indeed the publication of the results of a poll has itself on occasion been known to change the course of public opinion overnight.) Further, even if all controversial topics could be condensed into the form of simple questions, the reasons for the answers given to the questions may be relevant. The streamlined technique of the Gallup Poll still consumes time and money. It can also make a serious mistake. President Truman's defeat of Governor Dewey must have been a sharp surprise for those who had faith in statistical predictions. For these reasons it is impossible that the conventional organs of public opinion should be dispensed with.

This conclusion carries with it the corollary that the process of ascertaining public opinion is far from straightforward. If, for example, a politician wants to know the state of public opinion on a given topic, he may begin by reading the editorials and reports and letters published in his newspaper. He then has to compare these with what appears in other newspapers and periodicals. He listens to what is said in Parliament and at public meetings; he reads and hears views from his constituents (and in his turn may convey these to Parliament); he compares all this with what he originally anticipated public opinion would be, and with what he has known it to be in the past years.

To avoid being mistaken he requires experience, faculties of observation and deduction, and above all the means to collect fresh information from as wide a range of sources as possible. The Press carries immense responsibilities in providing this information, since it is organized to col-

lect and disseminate it rapidly over wide areas. Hence both the arguments for a free Press and the attacks on it by those who doubt whether it faces its responsibilities seriously and scrupulously. Whilst the businessman has only his own disadvantage to consider if he acts on false information, the Press carries the main burden of conveying public opinion to those who are elected to carry out its wishes.

To the Press, appeal via radio, television and cinema has been added. All these exercise a more direct, emotional effect than the written word. The danger of concentrating these powers of persuasion in the hands of a few has been frighteningly demonstrated in the record of the totalitarian states. A statement of Lord Beaverbrook also aroused comment when he told the Royal Commission on the Press in 1947 that he ran his *Daily Express* 'purely for the purpose of making propaganda, and with no other motive'. 'Propaganda' – a word of religious origin which literally means 'things which should be spread around' – has been described as an example of a 'good word gone wrong'.

In every society there are deeper influences which withstand as well as assist these consciously applied efforts to mould public opinion. The influences of religion and of political and social traditions developed in the course of generations are always present, though they have been undermined by the impact of two world wars, the great social upheavals of the century, and the astonishing progress of technology, which have thrown up many problems to which the old ways of political thought provide no ready answer.

In civilized states the principle is accepted that it is ultimately the opinions and sentiments of the common man that are paramount, the responsibility for both expressing and forming these opinions and sentiments lies primarily with a very much smaller number of groups and individuals who speak for the churches or propound new philosophies. It is to these people that we have to look if the growth of public opinion is to be sound and healthy. It was Abraham Lincoln who expressed this cardinal truth: 'He who moulds public sentiment goes deeper than he who enacts statutes or pronounces decisions.' (See also *Propaganda*.)

'No fit religion for a gentleman'

PURITANISM, 'that word of many shades', indicated in its original historical sense the extreme wing of Protestantism which believed that the Reformation had not gone far enough, and which set out to purify the English Church of Papist symbols and of the moral laxity evident in it towards the end of the Elizabethan age.

Puritanism embraced various dissenting bodies – Presbyterians, Anabaptists, and Brownists, for example – but the early growth of the movement was within the Church itself. In the seventeenth century the word took on a political significance, for as royalty allied itself increasingly with high Anglicanism, so the Puritans became identified with the struggle against the king for the political liberty of Parliament.

In a wider sense Puritanism has always signified an attitude of mind, a moral force confined within no system or historical period. The fundamental ideas are an individual approach to God through the Scriptures, severe morality, and simplicity of worship and life. The word derives its popular meaning from the extreme aspects of its development. 'Puritan' and 'puritanical' are used with the cry of Sabbatarian and kill-joy. A Puritan conjures the figure of a vain moralist, soberly dressed and abnormally preoccupied with sin, whose face is 'set like a flint', and whose head is full of scriptural texts. In their anger writers of the Restoration so ridiculed the absurdities of the movement as to obscure its true value. Yet Puritanism, during the best part of a century and particularly in its early stages, drew to itself some of the best brains and highest spirits of its time. It reflected generally the feelings of a majority of the nation and powerfully influenced the English way of life. Not for nothing did Macaulay describe Puritans as 'the most remarkable body of men, perhaps, which the word has ever seen'.

It is possible to find principles similar to Puritanism at work before the Reformation, in the doctrine of the Franciscans and in those followers of Wyclif, the Lollards, who based their life on a literal interpretation of the Bible. The word itself, however, appears first in 1564. The break with Rome had been accomplished, and most of the clergy accepted without question the doctrine laid down by the reformed Anglican Church. More ardent minds, fortified by the example of Calvinist Geneva, where some of them had found refuge during the Marian persecution, wished to remove all taint of Popery and to lead the Church back to a simple form of government and worship. In the past, interpretation of the Bible had been in the hands of the clergy, but the reformers wished to make it the literal guide to each individual life. In reaction against the laxity and self-indulgence which were the worst features of an uninhibited age, they preached the need for self-discipline, industry, and abstinence.

At first they asked no more than toleration to be allowed to preach their own sermons, to hold Bible study circles, and to discard the rites and vestments which were linked in their minds with Rome, and which could not be shown from the Scriptures to be necessary. Influential members of the Privy Council sympathized with these views, and the Puritans were adept at soliciting help in Parliament. Yet Elizabeth and Archbishop Whitgift remained adamant, and the campaign, which reached a climax in 1585, slowly died down. It was the respect in which the Queen was held and the threat of invasion that had prevented more violent steps. The scurrilous attacks against the bishops contained in the Marprelate tracts – Whitgift himself was nicknamed his Gracelessness of Cant – represented the extreme Presbyterian view. By the end of the reign the Puritans had been to some extent subdued, but they had taken root and already the idea of the 'English Sunday' was at war with the idea of 'Merrie England'.

Under Stuart kings the frustration of Puritanism expressed itself in anger as the danger of invasion receded and as the first James and then the first Charles joined hands with the Church on the doctrine of passive obedience. The Millenary Petition of 1604 reflected the claims of Puritanism to go its own way, and the Hampton Court conference made it clear that James meant to enforce conformity. Parliament grew more independent, and, with a Puritan majority, drew further apart from the king in its attempt to maintain its liberties. In Charles's reign Laud, the diligent disciplinarian of Anglicanism, further provoked the growing body of dissenting opinion by his rigid insistence on conformity. Petitions, culminating in the Root-and-Branch petition (1640), joined against the increasing irksomeness of episcopal rule.

When it came to standing against the king and abolishing the ecclesiastical courts and the episcopal hierarchy, moderate opinion hesitated. But with the Civil War extreme Puritanism and the Presbyterian system of Church government were sanctioned on the grounds of political necessity. It was urgent to rally the country against the king under the banner of 'No Popery', and also to come to some agreement with the Scots, whose army had crossed the border. The bishops were swept away, and the door was opened to the extremists.

Churches were defaced and stripped, and laws were enacted to enforce Sunday observance. Christmas Day was abolished, travel on Sunday was restricted, and soldiers were given the right of entry into private houses to see that the law was observed. It is not surprising that after the Restoration Puritanism should be discredited. The Puritan was sneered at for

> Hanging of his cat on Monday
> For killing of a mouse on Sunday.

Laws excluding dissenters from office and forbidding the holding of religious meetings were passed, and some 2,000 Puritan ministers gave up their livings. The movement survived, particularly among the working-class communities, and out of it grew the nonconformist movement. But for many years it was not only oppression that caused its decline: Men had been made to 'eat religion with their bread' until they were tired of it.

The Puritan may have been regarded as a pedant and an introvert, but his abstinence and abomination of idleness provided a counterbalance to the 'materialism' of the later Elizabethan age, and his zeal prevented the growth of absolute monarchy. That he was also a potent force is clearly illustrated in the history of New England. Some of those whom religious persecution drove abroad took with them Puritan principles. The effect of this influence is still felt today in the political and religious life of the United States.

In the army the qualities of Puritanism made Cromwell's Ironsides a formidable force, fed on texts and seeing the hand of God in every gain or loss. Charles II might say of Puritanism that it was no fit religion for a gentleman – and it is true that as the Elizabethan age receded the nobler spirits fell away – yet Puritanism was able to inspire Milton and Bunyan to write messages of invincible hope in prose that has not been surpassed. Puritan belief in honesty, thrift, and hard work gave England a leading place in industry and commerce. 'The principles', wrote Dr John Brown, 'of Puritanism – obedience and righteousness – are the binding forces without which society would go to pieces; but while recognizing the value of these it failed, at least many of its followers failed, to recognize also the value of the more graceful and genial elements of human life.'

Q

Inward prayer

QUIETISM was a movement which arose as a consequence of the Counter-Reformation.

It began with a loss of confidence in the Renaissance view of man. 'What a piece of worke is a man! how Noble in Reason? how infinite in faculty? in forme and moving how expresse and admirable? in Action, how like an Angel? in apprehension, how like a God? the beauty of the world, the Parragon of Animals; *and yet ...*' Hamlet's *and yet* was destined to sound through the century. With the dissatisfaction about man went doubt about the churches men had created, about religious institutions in general and about human reason and the whole world of nature: this was fed by the wars of religion and the disputes of the sects, it led on the one hand to scepticism, and on the other to Quietism.

All over Europe groups of men and women began to sit down together, without outward direction by priests or ministers, to practise silent,

interior prayer. In Italy they were called the Pela-
gini (from their leader, Giacomo di Santa Pela-
gia, a Milanese layman) in Germany, Behmenists
(from the mystic, Jakob Boehme) in Holland, Col-
legiants, in England, Seekers. Their importance
was not in their power or weight, but in their multiplicity and their anonymity; each local group
was usually unaware of the others; as William
Penn (1644–1718) said:

Many left all visible churches and societies, and wandered up and down, as sheep without a shepherd, and as
doves without their mates, seeking their beloved, but
could not find Him (as their souls desired to know Him)
whom their souls loved above their chiefest joy. As they
came to the knowledge of one another, they sometimes
met together, not formally to pray or preach, but waited
together in silence ...

These groups cut across the divisions of Catholic and Protestant, and there seemed at first little
that the fiercest Inquisitor or Zeal-of-the-land-
Busy could take exception to in the innocent
practice of meeting for prayer. If it was mystical,
what of that? Catholic Europe recognized that
mysticism had made Spain the very keep of the
castle during the Reformation siege; St Ignatius
Loyola in the *Spiritual Exercises* had laid down a
method of meditation that was used by Protestant and Catholic alike, and made it the motive power of the Jesuits; St Teresa of Avila had
done likewise for the Carmelites; and now in
their wake came Juan Falconi (1596–1638) of the
Order of Our Lady of Mercy.

Working, like St Teresa, through correspondence, Falconi wrote in 1628 a letter on silent
interior prayer. 'Dwell in silence. Think of nothing, however good, however sublime it may be.
Dwell only in pure faith in God and in utter
resignation to His Holy will.' Long after he was
dead his letter was printed: in Spain in 1657,
shortly afterwards in Italy, and then in France;
where, at the end of the century, Madame Guyon
was to reprint it with her own works again and
again. It was the first manifesto of Quietism. She
could never have guessed what difficulties and
heartburnings for herself and others would arise
through Quietist doctrines. At one time she was
herself imprisoned.

Then came Molinos. Miguel de Molinos, Doctor of Theology of Coimbra, was born in 1627,
and about 1665 left Spain for Italy, where his
success was rapid and overwhelming; Pope
Innocent XI gave him apartments in the Vatican;
from the highest to the lowest people sought his
spiritual counsel; and five theologians, of the
Franciscan, Trinitarian, Jesuit, Carmelite, and
Capuchin orders (four of them Censors of the
Inquisition) backed his *Spiritual Guide* which appeared in 1675. Ten years later Molinos was a
prisoner of the Holy Office, facing charges of
sixty-eight errors of doctrine, and others of gross
immorality; he was condemned in August 1687
and died in 1696. Molinos was the victim of his
own success (it was said that 20,000 letters of
consultation were found in his apartment when
he was arrested). There was no place for the
Church in the citadel of interior prayer.

The *Spiritual Guide* distinguishes between two
states of religious life: *meditation* and *contemplation*. Meditation uses reason, memory and will;
it endeavours to extirpate sin and doubt; it takes
as its material the mysteries of faith and the central truths of Christianity. Contemplation does
not begin until all this has been left behind, until
reason and even imagination are abandoned,
until sin is disregarded, and everything is still,
without word or thought or creaturely activity.
It is the Devil who tempts us to lament over sin:
'telling thee of thy misery and making a giant of
it. O blessed soul, open thine eyes; and shut the
gate against these diabolical suggestions, knowing
thy misery and trusting in the mercy divine.'

The soul must attain an annihilation of its own judgment ... willing as if it did not will, desiring as if it did not
desire, understanding as if it did not understand, thinking
as if it did not think, without inclining to anything, embracing equally contempts and honours, benefits and
corrections.

In the very moment that Quietism was condemned in Italy, a new chapter opened in France.
Its central episode was the contest between Bossuet and Fénelon, which went on from 1693 to
1699; a struggle in which, according to Bossuet,
the whole of religion was at stake, and in which
the antagonists were worthy of the issues. Like
Hannibal and Fabius, St Bernard and Abelard, or
Lincoln and Robert E. Lee, they were so perfectly
opposed in taste, temperament and talents, that
the story became larger than life, and seemed like

some vast allegory of mankind, in which even the most casual onlooker must choose his side. The colouring of the drama came from its paradox: Fénelon, the heresiarch, was the one who was well connected with Versailles and the Vatican, an ultramontane who acknowledged the supremacy of the Pope in spiritual, and the King in temporal, matters. Bossuet, on the other hand, had followed his election as Bishop of Meaux in 1681 by biting the hands that fed him. His was the voice behind the Declaration of the French clergy of 1682, which accepted the infallibility of the Church Universal, but denied that of the Pope (*all* bishops are direct successors of the Apostles). In temporal matters the Church must be independent of the King. Yet in the end both Pope and King had to back the gallican Bossuet against the submissive Fénelon.

The dispute arose over the writings and activities of Madame Guyon (1648–1717), author of *Spiritual Torrents* and *The Short and Easy Method of Prayer* (with other works which, in the end, filled a collected edition of forty volumes). The soul is separated from God by its selfhood, and even its desire for states of grace becomes infected with self; but once this can be destroyed and the soul made utterly indifferent to earthly things, it can be filled with 'pure love'; the divine life becomes its nature; it is then capable of 'spiritual fecundity'. 'I was a participator in all the divine mysteries, and I was associated in divine maternity with Jesus Christ.'

At this point, orthodoxy took alarm; Madame Guyon found herself barred from her stronghold of Saint-Cyr, estranged from her patroness Madame de Maintenon, and under correction from her Bishop. On the advice of Fénelon, she appealed to Bossuet to arbitrate. He agreed with great reluctance; he was not interested in mysticism or holy females; he was much more concerned to unite Protestants into the Church than to start any new heresy hunts. Nevertheless he was driven step by step into a condemnation listed under thirty-eight articles, and Fénelon (who was waiting to be installed as Archbishop of Cambrai) signed them.

Immediately Bossuet had consecrated him, Fénelon wrote his *Explanation of the Maxims of the Saints*, and re-established his Quietist position. Bossuet had now to deal with Fénelon, in an atmosphere of scandal, intrigue and a pamphlet war on a European scale. Bossuet's *Account of Quietism* (1698) made the most of the extravagances of the movement, and pointed out that while it insisted on the weakness of the creature, it deprived him of all the support of the Church; Quietism was a substitute religion, the hidden enemy of Christianity. Fénelon was condemned; he died in 1715.

So far as the Catholic world went, Quietism was finished, but in Protestantism it was just beginning. Bishop Burnet (1643–1715) had been one of the most interested witnesses of the work of Molinos. A section of the Church of England became impregnated with Quietist doctrines; its most influential mouthpiece was William Law, whose *Serious Call to a Devout and Holy Life* (1729) Samuel Johnson declared 'the first piece of hortatory theology in any language'. 'The Saviour of the World, the eternal Word of God lies hid in thee, as a spark of the Divine Nature', says Law. 'Seek for him in thy heart, and thou wilt never seek in vain, for there He dwells.' In the *Spirit of Prayer* (from which these words are taken) he calls on the sinner to hush his own powers and voices, so that the Spirit may have free course. 'The last State of the Spirit of Prayer is its highest Union with God in this life.'

But the finest fruits of the Quietest movement, after the scandals and disputes had died away, were reserved to its old age. Every reproach made against it is silenced by lives like those of the Quakers Thomas Shillitoe (1754–1836) or John Woolman (1720–1772). They knew Madame Guyon not as a frail and sometimes overpowering French lady, but as a prophetic voice. 'In pure silent Worship', wrote Woolman, 'we swell under the Holy Anointing, and feel Christ to be our Shepherd. Here the best of Teachers ministers to the several Conditions of his Flock, and the Soul receives immediately from the Divine Fountain, that with which it is nourished.'

In this Communion, with impeccable modesty, delicacy, strength and tact, John Woolman lived and died.

Quietism has been treated above as a completely European phenomenon. But under various names this idea of complete spiritual passivity before the diety has long existed in the East, in Hinduism and Buddhism.

R

Religion as opiate

RELIGION AS THE OPIATE OF THE PEOPLE, originates as a phrase in Karl Marx's *Introduction to a Critique of Hegel's Philosophy of Law*:

Religion is the sigh of the oppressed creature, the kindliness of a heartless world, the soul of soulless circumstance. Religion is the opiate of the people. The removal of religion as the illusory happiness of the people is the demand for its real happiness. The demand that it should give up illusions about its real conditions is the demand that it should give up the conditions which make illusions necessary ... Criticism has torn away the imaginary flowers with which his chains were bedecked, not in order that man should wear his chains without the comfort of illusions, but that he may throw off the chains and pluck the living flowers. Criticism of religion disillusions man so that he may think, act, and shape the world as one who is disillusioned and come to full understanding, so that he may move on his own axis and thus be his own sun. Religion is but the false sun which revolves round him while he is not yet fully self-aware.

These drastic generalizations simply take for granted that all religious ideas are on the same footing, and that they are one and all illusions; and they direct attention on to the only questions then remaining of what social and personal functions they fulfil, and how they are to be disposed of. In this Marx's approach is strikingly similar to that of Freud in *The Future of an Illusion* (1928); in which he states without argument or qualification that various major religious notions are 'patently infantile ... incongruous with reality'; and proceeds to develop a psycho-analytic explanation of the fact, which in consequence is otherwise mysterious, that these notions are sincerely held by so many able people.

Both Marx and Freud presupposed acceptance of earlier secular criticism. Both denied that there was any truth to be found which could not in principle be revealed by the methods of science: 'No', Freud wrote, 'science is no illusion. But it would be an illusion to think that we can get elsewhere what science cannot give'; and neither would have any truck with the idea that to face reality with open eyes without benefit of illusions must remain the prerogative of an intellectual and moral élite.

Marx, however, insisted that these alleged illusions had the important personal and social functions of consoling people in the hardness of their lot and discouraging them from revolting against it: whereas Freud's emphasis was on their supposed dependence on infantile wishful thinking without any utopian illusions that social change could ever remove all the personal griefs in which people have need to be consoled.

For all his sympathy for the sighs of the oppressed creature longing to find a heart in the heartless world, and in spite of the trappings of Hegelianism, Marx's notions about religion were often not different from those of the agitator jeering at 'pie in the sky when you die'. In the *Communist Manifesto* (1848), which he wrote in collaboration with Friedrich Engels, there occur such passages as 'Law, morality, religion, are to him [*i.e.* the Communist proletarian] so many bourgeois prejudices, behind which lurk in ambush just as many bourgeois interests', and 'the parson has ever gone hand in hand with the landlord'.

Elsewhere Friedrich Engels gave indications of somewhat greater sophistication, noting in his *Ludwig Feuerbach* that 'the Calvinist reformation served as a banner for the republicans in Geneva, in Holland, and in Scotland, freed Holland from Spain'. What could serve thus as a revolutionary banner cannot be always and everywhere merely an opiate.

Lenin was even more dogmatically, uncompromisingly and without qualification hostile to religion than Marx: stating in his pamphlet *Religion* 'the idea of God *always* dulled the social emotion; replacing the vital by the deadening; it has *always* been an idea of slavery – the worst inescapable slavery' (italics his); yet later in the same work Lenin concedes 'There was a time in history when ... the democratic and proletarian struggle took the form of a struggle of one religious idea against another'.

Although in practice the Soviet Government has now reached an accommodation with the churches in Russia – though not of course with the Vatican – and though no one in Russia any longer expects the immediate withering away of religion any more than they do that of the state, the crude Marxist dogmas have not yet been revised.

The idea that the religious beliefs of the masses are instruments for their control by their rulers goes back as far as fifth-century Athens. There is extant a fragment from a play by Critias, a disciple of Socrates and a relative of Plato, in which he expounds the theory that the notions of God and of a future life of rewards and punishments were invented by some shrewd man as devices to ensure obedience to the laws when the authorities were not looking.

In the fourth century Aristotle in his *Metaphysics* spoke of the beliefs in the anthropomorphic gods of Greece as 'myths that have been introduced to persuade the multitude, and on account of their utility in regard to social custom and the public good'. The historian Polybius, writing in the second century B.C., was also willing to 'venture the assertion that what the rest of mankind derides is the foundation of Roman greatness, namely superstition. This has been introduced into every aspect of their private and public life, with every artifice to awe the imagination ... my view is that it has been done to impress the masses ... All that can be done is to hold them in check by fears of the unseen and other shams of the same sort. It was not for nothing, but with deliberate design, that the men of old introduced to the masses notions about the gods and views on the after-life. The folly and heedlessness are ours, who seek to dispel such illusions.'

Of course the idea that religion was all a matter of deliberate scheming policy is naïve: that is not how things happen in history. Naïve again is the notion that all religious ideas are on the same level (instead of being, as they are, fantastically various); that there is absolutely no possibility of rational defence of their truth (as if say the *Summae* of St Thomas were simply and manifestly preposterous); and that for all men everywhere they have all fulfilled the same single function (though for many their religious beliefs are a source of labour and anxiety rather than of con-

solation). Yet that 'notions about the gods and views on the after life' have been successfully exploited for the purposes for which Critias and Aristotle and Polybius believed they had been invented, is also a plain matter of fact. And not merely of dead past fact, either. Those who in the 1948 elections in Italy issued the poster of a voter alone in a polling booth with the caption 'Stalin cannot see you: but God can' knew what they were doing.

ILLUSTRATION: Pages 366 and 367.

Freud and repression

REPRESSION is thought of as something highly undesirable which Victorian parents did to their children, but which now, due to the discoveries of Freud and other psychologists, no enlightened parent would dream of doing today. Educational reformers have often proceeded on the assumption that all training, discipline and correction of children are repressive and therefore harmful and to be abolished. Hence a great deal of puzzlement among everyday people who are trying their best to bring up their children on the right lines.

The confusion arose in the first place from a simple misunderstanding. According to the dictionaries, the word 'repression' has been in use since before Shakespeare's day to mean the action of checking, restraining, putting down or keeping under *something bad or objectionable*. Here is the first surprise: for it is obvious that, if repression is used in the sense of putting down something bad, then, whether that something is a riot or one's own or another's outburst of bad temper, its 'repression' will be highly desirable. It should also be noted that in this usage, repression is something which a person does consciously and deliberately. There is nothing 'psychological' about repressing a mutiny.

This is only half the story; for the word 'repression' is also a technical term belonging to the system of theory and practice which Sigmund Freud developed under the name of psychoanalysis, for the treatment and study of the human mind in sickness and health.

Freud distinguishes three kinds of mental processes. 'He uses the term "conscious" ', writes Dr Ernest Jones, Freud's greatest exponent in this country, 'to denote mental processes of which we are at a given time conscious, "preconscious" to denote mental processes of which we can spontaneously and voluntarily become conscious (*e.g.* a memory out of one's mind for the moment, but which can be readily recalled) and "unconscious" to denote mental processes which the subject cannot spontaneously recall to consciousness, but which can be reproduced by employing special devices (*e.g.* hypnosis, psycho-analysis etc.).'

The force which prevents an idea or a feeling from passing from unconsciousness to consciousness is what Freud calls the 'censor'. This term 'must not be taken to mean a sort of psychic entity placed on the boundary between the unconscious and the preconscious and hindering the passage of every impulse contrary to the person's conscious wishes. The word "censor" denotes the sum total of ideas, memories, feelings, etc., which exercise an inhibitory power over other groups of ideas.' (Freud himself writes: 'I hope you are not ... picturing to yourselves the censor as a stern little manikin or spirit who lives in a little chamber of the brain and there discharges the duties of his office.')

The action of the censor in preventing ideas and feelings from becoming conscious is called by Freud 'repression'. Thus *all* unconscious mental processes are, by definition, repressed. Moreover, the appropriateness of the term repression for the process whereby the contents of the unconscious are kept out of consciousness is immediately apparent when we realize that the repressed part of the mind (*i.e.* the unconscious) is, as Dr Jones explains, active, animal, infantile, non-logical and sexual.

It is obvious that if we are indeed born with powerful instincts of this nature, then their 'repression' in the old sense of keeping under something bad or objectionable is essential, if the child is to develop into a civilized human being instead of remaining a savage animal. Thus, according to Freud, repression of animal instincts is a fundamental necessity for the normal, healthy development of a human being.

There is, however, this very important difference between the ordinary and the Freudian use of the term 'repression'. According to Freud, repression is a process which occurs within the unconscious part of the mind; in other words, the censor is itself part of the unconscious, which is thus composed of two elements: the repressing unconscious (or censor), and the repressed unconscious, so it is a misuse of the term to speak of repression, as something which one person can do to another or (consciously) to his own desires. 'Repression' has to be distinguished from 'suppression', which means the deliberate keeping under of one's own or another's conscious thoughts or impulses – what is normally called self-control or discipline.

The small boy who controls his desire to fidget in school because he knows that he is supposed to sit still during lessons, is neither repressing himself nor being repressed by the teacher. He is being trained to *suppress* his unruly impulses for his own good, a procedure which Freud sees as normal and necessary.

So, correctly understood, the Freudian theory of repression does not support the view that children should be left to follow their instincts without correction or training. It is, of course, true that harsh and unfeeling treatment of a child may cause undue repression to occur within the child's mind, and that this may lead to mental ill-health; but there is nothing in the writings of Freud to suggest that the combination of firmness and love which everyone knows to be the best way to bring up a child is anything but beneficial.

The poor man's sins are glaring

ONE LAW FOR THE RICH AND ONE LAW FOR THE POOR typifies the traditional lament of the under-privileged that true justice can be had only by those who can pay for it.

The phrase itself may well have been first used by early nineteenth-century radicals, since there are references to it about 1830. The underlying sentiment, however, is traditional in most countries of western Europe and admirably sums up centuries of pessimistic social feeling. Typical of this is the old Spanish proverb 'The Rich break the laws and the Poor are punished for it'. As Thomas Love Peacock wrote:

The poor man's sins are glaring;
In the face of ghostly warning
  He is caught in the fact
  Of an overt act –
Buying greens on a Sunday morning.

The rich man's sins are hidden,
In the pomp of wealth and station;
  And escape the sight
  Of the children of light
Who are wise in their generation.

The rich man has a cellar
And a ready bottle by him;
  The poor must steer
  For a pint of beer
Where the saint can't choose but spy him.

The phrase of 'one law for the rich and one for the poor' at least implies the existence of law, and of the Rule of Law (q.v.); which meant little to the ordinary citizen before the fifteenth century, and would have meant nothing at all in the twelfth century. Under feudalism it would not have occurred to the villein that the Lord of his Manor should be treated in the same way as himself. Gradually, however, the Rule of Law and the idea of the 'King's Peace' were established. Any 'breach of the King's Peace' became punishable as a crime against the king himself, and the king's subjects, rich and poor alike, were treated, in theory, in the same way before the Royal Courts, under the 'Common Law' or law common to all. Here was undoubtedly 'One Law for the Poor'; the 'other law' was not exactly for the rich; it was for the educated.

This privilege of the educated came about in a curious way. Henry II, in order to conciliate the Pope after the murder of Thomas à Becket in 1170, abandoned all claims to punish clerics convicted of crimes by the ecclesiastical courts; this led to the most notorious privilege in the history of English criminal law – by which any 'criminous clerk' could plead 'Benefit of Clergy' and so escape punishment by the lay court. Even in the thirteenth century the trial of clergy themselves was becoming a farce; later, when the practice of allowing 'Benefit of Clergy' was extended to those only indirectly connected with the Church, the abuse was complete. Benefit of Clergy was claimed by so many persons that to decide whether an accused was entitled to it, the courts adopted the rule-of-thumb test of seeing whether he could read the first verse of the 51st Psalm:

'Have mercy upon me, O God, after thy great goodness: according to the multitude of thy mercies do away mine offences.'

A verse soon to be known as the 'Neck Verse', since by reading it the accused could escape the noose.

Statutes, however, were passed limiting the benefit; and by the middle of the sixteenth century it was virtually restricted to cases of theft.

Not until Tudor times was any real attempt to enforce a uniform system of royal justice for all the king's subjects without any substantial privileges for any section of the community. This universal justice was not always obtainable. In the seventeenth century scant ceremony was wasted on the poor and uneducated criminal, though the position of wealthy defendants who could afford to be legally represented was quite different.

In the seventeenth, eighteenth and nineteenth centuries the law in civil disputes developed so technically and esoterically that Sir Henry Maine remarked 'substantive law must be searched for in the interstices of procedure'. The effect of this was that none but the lawyers themselves could understand the law, let alone the means of invoking it. Litigation had become cumbersome, slow and costly to the litigant, whether he won his case or not: local courts had fallen into disuse, and inexpensive means of settling disputes over small matters did not exist.

Reform of both criminal law and civil procedure was long overdue by the eighteenth century. Ordinary disputes between members of the public could be heard only by the Court of Common Pleas at Westminster or under the 'nisi prius' system by the Assize Court of the County. The cost of taking a case to the Court of Common Pleas or the Assizes was hopelessly out of proportion to the sums in dispute, while the lengthy procedure of the Court of Chancery in matters of wills and estates became a byword, echoing the words of Milton, written over a hundred years before:

Litigious terms, fat contentions and flowing fees.

The early nineteenth century saw the beginning of a hundred years of reform, mitigating the fierceness of criminal law and simplifying the civil procedure. County Courts were introduced in 1846, giving the poor man once more comparatively cheap and speedy justice in disputes over small amounts.

Yet the cost of an action in the High Court was steadily increasing, and after the First World War law reformers agitated for some means of help. A person with a genuine case was often prevented from going to the High Court for a remedy, because he knew that success would still leave him out of pocket over his costs: 'The Courts, like the Ritz Hotel, are open to all.' A rich man or corporation could set the pace; they could threaten to take the case to the House of Lords, which often persuaded opponents to accept less than their due. Many appeals were little more than gambling on costs, and in one case Lord Justice Mackinnon referred to 'the costs game' and remarked that 'the spice of a gamble may now be added to the joys of litigation'. Poor Persons' procedure was introduced first of all, whereby those who had less than two pounds a week could be helped in the costs of their defence in criminal cases.

After the Second World War, free legal aid for those of limited means was brought in by statute. Thus, for the first time in the eight hundred years' history of the Royal Courts, their justice was, literally, free to those who could not afford to pay for it.

Critics of the Legal Aid system, however, say that owing to the upper income limit we now have 'One Law for the Rich and the *Officially* Poor', and point out that rich men are still able to indulge in lawsuits which their poorer brethren – if they are not poor enough to be entitled to legal aid – cannot afford. This is true: rich men are always privileged to some extent. But it is no longer true that 'Laws grind the Poor and Rich men rule the Law'.

Human rights

The **RIGHTS OF MAN** is a political doctrine which holds that whatever the laws of the country in which he lives, every man has a right to have certain things which it would be unjust to deprive him of; a right to do certain things which it would be unjust to prevent him doing; and a right not to suffer certain things which it would be unjust to inflict on him. This doctrine has had a profound influence in late eighteenth-century politics and has left a lasting impression on our social thinking today.

Although every civilization has seen a struggle by its subjects to assert and extend their rights against rulers, the real origin of the doctrine is to be found in the idea of a transcendent natural law. Notably in Roman Law and later in the teachings of medieval scholars there was apparent a glorification of a natural law, a law universal and ideally just for which human laws were but unsatisfactory and makeshift substitutes. Thus St Thomas Aquinas wrote: 'Every law framed by men bears the character of law to that extent to which it is derived from the law of nature. But if on any point it is in conflict with the law of nature it at once ceases to be law, it is a mere perversion of the law.'

To men like St Thomas Aquinas natural law was simply the will of God. But by the seventeenth century a new school of thought had developed. Natural law was the law which prevailed over men in the original state of nature. The rights men had then were their natural rights. 'Men living together according to reason, without a common superior on earth with authority to judge between them, is properly the state of nature', wrote John Locke. It should be pointed out that by 'reason' he meant natural law. Locke envisaged an early paradise of virtuous anarchy; no governments to tyrannize, no police, no lawyers, no administrators. An attractive picture. But unfortunately, since some men tend to be inconsiderate enough to disregard the dictates of reason and the voice of natural law, men were forced to enter into a Social Contract to protect their rights. Hence governments, lawyers and administrators.

The most famous exponent of the theory of the

Social Contract was Jean-Jacques Rousseau (1712–1778). Being a man who showed a certain contempt for the meretricious blandishments of civilization, he saw natural man in a rather more earthy but no less happy state. To him primitive man was a glorious Noble Savage, unburdened by government, laws or the complexities of organized society – in contrast to his civilized condition. 'Man is born free but everywhere he is in chains', said Rousseau. For rulers had abused the powers they had been given, and the natural rights of man were in abeyance everywhere.

To restore man to his original rights was the aim of most political reformers in the eighteenth century, among whom Thomas Paine (1737–1809) author of *The Rights of Man* (1791–1792), is the most celebrated. An eloquent exposition both of the rights of man and of the social contract he was believed to have made for their preservation is found in the American Declaration of Independence. In 1776 the leaders of the American Revolution drew up a statement to justify their break with the British Crown. This was their faith: 'We hold these truths to be self-evident, that all men are created equal, that they are endowed by their Creator with certain unalienable rights; that among these are life, liberty and the pursuit of happiness; that to secure these rights, governments are instituted among men, deriving their just powers from the consent of the governed ...'

The American Revolution was followed by the French Revolution, and the American Declaration of Independence by the Declaration of the Rights of Man and of Citizens by the French National Assembly in 1789. The list of human rights was added to, and property, security and resistance to oppression took their place beside life, liberty and the pursuit of happiness.

The days of Thomas Paine, the Republican revolts against arbitrary government that inspired the American and French Revolutions, were the heyday of the doctrine of the Rights of Man, though it has continued to exercise its influence. But the nineteenth century saw a competing philosophy arise, the school of the Utilitarians, who often showed a scant respect for their rival to the reformer's heart. Bentham called the Declaration of the French Assembly a metaphysical work. He divided its articles of faith into three classes: those that were unintelligible, those that were false, and those that were both. It had apparently escaped the notice of their champions that inalienable rights of man might irreconcilably conflict. Hence the Utilitarians advised men to look, not for the natural rights of man, but for what was most conducive to the greatest happiness of the greatest number.

Yet that the doctrine has survived is attested by the recent Declaration of Human Rights by the United Nations General Assembly in December 1948. It reveals a greatly expanded list: freedom from arbitrary interference with privacy; right to work and form Trade Unions, to rest, to enjoy the Arts and many others.

What merits does the doctrine have and what is its value today? Philosophical objections to it are many; and they are obvious. What happens if one man's right to property jeopardizes another's right to social security, or vice versa? No enumeration of rights can resolve the conflict. Some outside principle must be applied.

What are the rights of man, and how do we know what they are? It would hardly be feasible to discover them by historical or anthropological research into the habits of man in his early state. The discoveries would prove startling or embarrassing or both. Since Darwin, it would appear from applying this method that it was an inalienable and natural right of man to swing from trees.

Many, again like the authors of the Declaration of Independence, have held the Rights to be self-evident truths, presumably discernible by direct intuitive perception. Unfortunately self-evidence is an unreliable guide. Many widely different Rights have been self-evident to a great many different people. An extreme example is that of a correspondent of *The Times* who claimed for all men a natural right to walk across golf courses.

How choose one right rather than any other? Burke, who in his *Reflections on the French Revolution* admitted equal rights 'but not to equal things', used the doctrine to justify all manner of inequalities. Yet his views were no less logical (or more logical) than Thomas Paine's, which he attacked.

It might be useful to analyse what we do when we assert a right. Asserting a right is not stating a fact. From a failure to realize this stems much of the delusion about rights. If one says that a man has a right to social security, one is not saying that he has something like, say, a house. One only makes a recommendation. One is calling on the community to see that the man has social security. Declarations of Right are therefore essentially political recommendations, which explains why what may appear to one person to be the most obvious and self-evident right of man, may seem to another person to be a denial of all right. As society changes, ideas of justice change, political recommendations change and ideas of the rights of man change and develop accordingly.

But although the doctrine has philosophical weaknesses, that is far from saying that it has no political value. Its value lies not so much in the fact that it has advocated 'The Rights of Man', as in the particular rights which its champions have upheld. The Social Contract theory, with which it is intimately connected, places most emphasis on the duty of ruler to ruled, unlike the theory that the state is an organic whole, which emphasizes the duty of ruled to rulers. On the whole, the champions of the Rights of Man have opposed tyranny, favoured equality and extolled the universal brotherhood of man. They have been the instigators of democracy. They have laid the foundation for modern ideas of social justice.

'All men are born equal' is hardly a self-evident truth. It does not mean that men have equal talents or similar physiques. But it is a magnificent monument left by certain idealists who wanted no man, whatever his religion, race or colour, to be treated with discrimination by the law, and who wanted government to be modelled and shaped in such a way as to give all men as far as possible an equal opportunity to live life as they please.

ILLUSTRATION: Page 362.

The question of morality

RIGHT OR WRONG? This is the basic question of all morality, whether it be European or Oriental, whether it affects ideas concerning a divinity, behaviour with regard to the State or

one's neighbours, or the rules of a parlour game. As a concept it has no definable origin, for there was never a point in time when people were unaware of the difference between right and wrong – morality is a condition of human social existence, and the specific categorization of *this* is right or *this* is wrong has arisen from differing social conditions.

However, the stage at which it first becomes fully articulate and started the philosophical controversy which is as vigorous today as it was in Plato's time, occurred when people found themselves able to ask not only 'Is this or that right or wrong?', but 'What is there about this which *makes* it right, or about that which *makes* it wrong?' People have always known that certain actions are right and others wrong, but the question of the *essential* difference between them has no final answer – it remains a philosophical speculation.

Right and wrong can be given their meaning by the simple notion of conformity to rule. Moral right or wrong are definable in terms of moral rules or principles of conduct. What is morally right can be identified with what conforms to a moral rule, only if the rule itself is not called into question. But what if it is? This is the really crucial stage, and in Western philosophy it occurred in Greece in the fifth century B.C. Conventional morality based on a system of rules and customs was wearing thin under the impact of the Great War between the Athenian and Spartan coalitions. Thucydides wrote:

In times of peace and prosperity, as opposed to wartime, both public policy and private life are governed by higher moral principles. But war, by imposing hardships and controls on daily life, produces an aggressive mentality and degrades people's character according to their wretched conditions. The result in this case was a general state of public disorder in all countries. As time went on and the earlier atrocities became an accepted fact, the later ones were marked by refinements of technique and novel methods of retaliation. Even words lost their proper meanings and were changed to suit current propaganda ... Even family ties were broken for the sake of party loyalty ... Relations between people were governed not by the security of established law and custom, but by the prospect of selfish gain in defiance of the law.

In such conditions men were ready to listen to the Sophists who were already challenging the authority of traditional ideas about right and wrong, just as later Jesus Christ adopted a critical attitude to the moral rules of the Pharisees.

Can the rule according to which an action is right or wrong be itself right or wrong? We are inclined to say impatiently 'Of course': but it has not always been commonplace to be critical (and self-critical) about moral codes. We recognize that a wrong action may be performed in the belief that it is right (for example, an act of war, if we are pacifists); there is a rule according to which the action is right, but the rule itself is wrong; and finally, even if our own rules of action are right (as we must believe), at least it is *possible* to ask whether they are right or wrong. But this is highly sophisticated; primitive people regard their moral codes as beyond challenge.

The question 'Can a moral rule itself be right or wrong?' has been answered in three ways. (1) 'No, because it is always right': this is primitive absolutism. (2) 'Yes, because it can be tested by reference to some superior rule – which is itself unquestionable': this represents philosophical absolutism. (3) 'No, because it is neither right nor wrong; there is no superior rule by which it can be tested; the rules are just what they happen to be; change them and you change what is right or wrong': this represents extreme relativism.

Primitive absolutism comes first, historically. Then relativism was asserted by the Sophists (*e.g.* by Protagoras: 'Man is the measure of all things', and by Thrasymachus: 'Right means what is in the interest of the stronger'). They made clear for the first time the fundamental distinction between law and morality, between what is lawful or customary and what is right. But moral sceptics like Thrasymachus had distinguished the two elements only to discard the second. This drove Plato to retort with philosophical absolutism – his famous doctrine of the *Republic* that what is right or good depends on the Form of the Good which is the supreme object of philosophical knowledge.

Since then philosophical ethics has oscillated between the extremes of absolutism and relativism. On the whole, absolutism tends to find favour in two types of historical situation. One is the situation of peace, order, settled government and general agreement about what is right and wrong: for instance, the primitive closed society;

the Roman Empire; or the eighteenth century in England when Bishop Butler could say

There is in reality an universally acknowledged standard of virtue. It is that, which all ages and all countries have made profession of in public: it is that, which every man you meet puts on a show of: it is that, which the primary and fundamental laws of all civil constitutions over the face of the earth make it their business and endeavour to enforce the practice of upon mankind.

(*Dissertation on Virtue*, 1736.)

The other situation which favours Absolutism is the opposite extreme: when disorder or discontent are so intense that intelligent men react in one of three ways: either with ambitious plans for large-scale 'social engineering' based on a moral ideal (Plato); or with an 'ivory tower' type of morality such as Kantian Idealism (Kant wrote: 'Two things fill the mind with ever new and increasing admiration and awe ... the starry heavens above and the moral law *within*', and held that it was good to will what was right even if one was never able to do what was right – in the conditions of eighteenth-century Prussia). Or, thirdly, one may react with a conscious unworldliness (for instance, in early Christianity).

Between these two extreme types of situation, relativist views are found; for example, Epicureanism in the Hellenistic world, after the decay of the traditional social morality based on the city-state ideal, and before the establishment of the permanent world-empire of the Romans. Today the strongest influence making for relativism is the impact of anthropology, which finally refutes Butler's placid assumption that all people recognize a common morality.

The thesis of relativism should not be confused with subjectivism or even scepticism. Relativism does not hold that what is right or wrong is merely what I approve or disapprove of, still less that there is no such distinction as right or wrong at all. It is a negative thesis, denying what philosophical absolutism asserts, namely that there is a universal moral code, an absolute standard of right and wrong. Relativism does not imply, as is often said, that any moral code is as good as any other, for although there is no absolute standard of comparison, there is a relative standard, namely the one which we in fact adopt; and again relativism does not imply that there is no such thing as moral progress or decadence, for although there is no absolute progress or decline, there is certainly progress or decline relative to some standard. What is right or wrong is what is in accordance with, or contrary to, the moral principles which we adopt in answering the question 'Right or wrong?'; and although these principles are not universal, they are not merely private either.

Two alone ...

ROMANTIC LOVE was the dream of a universe peopled by two alone, where they and time stood still. It began at first sight; it was an instantaneous spell. It was something to be *desired*, and not something to be *lived*; a possession, rather than a relationship ('Get me the girl,' said Faust to Mephistopheles). It foresaw no development; it was complete in itself.

For its perfect expression, therefore, the lover should be an exile, cut off from the community of his birth, and so emancipated from the ties of society; the beloved, a girl of alien race, for whom the lover could feel an elemental passion, to be expressed in kisses rather than words; its setting, a desert island, a lonely tower, or a ship. Byron's *Don Juan* (1819) found it after shipwreck on a Greek island, with Haidee, the brigand's daughter:

> They fear'd no eyes nor ears on that lone beach;
>   They felt no terrors from the night; they were
> All in all to each other; though their speech
>   Was broken words, they *thought* a language there, –
> And all the burning tongues the passions teach
>   Found in one sigh the best interpreter
> Of Nature's oracle – first love – that all
> Which Eve has left her daughters since her fall.

Trelawney found it sailing the Indian Ocean in his schooner with her Arab crew, when he discovered that by the custom of her people he was wedded to the girl he had rescued from slavery and death, the shy, submissive, but intrepid and fearless Zela:

And love was thus ignited in my breast, pure, ardent, deep, and imperishable. Zela, from that day, was the star I was destined to worship; the deity at whose altar I was to offer up all the fragrant incense of my first virgin affections, feelings, and passions. Nor did ever saintly votary dedicate himself to his god with intenser devotion than I consecrated my heart to Zela.

And Shelley dreamed the same dream for Emilia Viviani, shut up in a Pisan convent:

> Say, my heart's sister, wilt thou sail with me?
> Our bark is like an albatross, whose nest
> Is a fair Eden of the purple East;
> It is an isle under Ionian skies
> Beautiful as a wreck of Paradise ...
> But the chief marvel of the wilderness
> Is a lone dwelling, built by whom or how
> None of the rustic island people know ...
> This isle and house are mine, and I have vowed
> Thee to be lady of the solitude.

That was in 1821; and one may find a shooting of the same line in 1931 (and in the context of Greek myth) by the characters of Eugene O'Neill's *Mourning Becomes Electra*. Orin, the Orestes son, rages against his mother, Christine (Clytemnestra) and her lover, Captain Adam Brant (Aegisthus), crying: 'And my islands I told her about – which was she and I – she wants to go there – with him!'

But islands, of course, are not obligatory; the essential conditions can be reproduced at home. Baudelaire found his odour of musk and havana, his sorceress with thighs of ebony, in Paris. To be an exile, one need only be at odds with society, and this can be achieved in many ways: by drink, drugs, politics, atheism, violence, or the act of love itself. But, though these and other failings are becoming to the man and irresistibly attractive to the woman, she herself is required to be innocent; physically innocent for preference, or at least spiritually innocent – intact though married, a white lily even if prostitution be her trade.

Whereas courtly love had been frankly adulterous, romantic love is a virgin passion; and whereas the courtly lover sought a dame of high degree, the romantic lover seeks a maid of humble station. For with the miller's daughter or the cottage girl all the objects of romantic love are secured at once. Social disapproval is automatic. The difference of class ensures that they will have no language in common but that of the heart and the petals of the daisy: 'He loves me, he loves me not.' By 'betraying her', the gentleman is at the same time able to provide the isolation which is the equivalent of the Ionian isle; to prove that his passion is stronger than social law; and to prepare for the remorse which will destroy him, when he stands in the churchyard over her lonely grave.

Romantic love is *irresistible*; it has absolute priority over any other claim whatsoever: family ties, duty to country or to a cause, friendship. (This was true in life as well as art: Dilke destroyed his career; Parnell 'betrayed his country' for Kitty O'Shea.) Other codes in the past have, of course, recognized the compulsive nature of infatuation – Paris driven mad by Aphrodite and bringing destruction on Troy for Helen's sake; or Tristran drinking (by accident) the *lovendrinc* which was intended to make certain the love of Iseut and King Mark. But romantic love is extravagant, and glories in it. Because the cult of the past, of distant places and times, is part of romanticism, the romantic lover remembers Helen and Iseut:

> I played a soft and doleful Air,
>   I sang an old and moving Story –
> An old rude Song that fitted well
>   The Ruin wild and hoary
>
> She listened with a flitting Blush,
>   With downcast eyes and modest Grace;
> For well she knew I could not choose
>   But gaze upon her face.
>
> I told her of the Knight, that wore
>   Upon his shield a burning Brand;
> And that for ten long years he wooed
>   The Lady of the Land.

In this song of Coleridge's (*Lyrical Ballads*, 1800) the significant thing is the way the lover watches the effect ('And so I won my Genevieve'). Romantic love is self-conscious. Zaida, the Arab lady in one of Landor's *Imaginary Conversations*, tells us how little she wants: 'A bath, a slave, a dish of pilau, one jonquil every morning, as usual; nothing more. But he must swear that he has kissed it first.' She was paralleled by young ladies who, in real life, received each morning (sometimes for years on end) a single flower. Such a gesture may begin by being spontaneous; it must end by being contrived.

Tieck's hero, Emilius, in *The Love Charm* (1812) cherished in secret his 'love for an unknown fair one, who dwelt in the opposite house, and who kept him all day long at home, and waking through many a night'. This 'ardent listlessness', as Keats called love in *Endymion*, was thought magnificent and not absurd, and was admired and emulated for a century to come. But because of the way it was born, because the fair one was unknown, because it was love 'at first sight', it carried with it an atmosphere of dread:

> I saw pale kings, and princes too,
>   Pale warriors, death-pale were they all;
> Who cry'd – 'La belle Dame sans merci
>   Hath thee in thrall!'
>
> I saw their starv'd lips in the gloam
>   With horrid warning gaped wide,
> And I awoke, and found me here
>   On the cold hill side.

The witch, the Lamia, the demon lover, the fairy lover are never far away from romantic mythology. But whether her magic was white or black, whether she redeemed by her purity or dragged her victim into the abyss, the beloved was always an enchantress and never a woman, except in her patience and her pity. Like Solveig in Ibsen's *Peer Gynt* (1867) or her equivalent in real life, the wife of George Romney the painter, she might wait a lifetime for the truant's return; what she could not do was to live with him in a ripening, changing, deepening relationship; to become mum and dad, grandpa and grandma; sharing tiffs and tensions, baby's diapers and the change of life.

Romantic love, therefore, was *sad*. It was sad even when it was happy; for the romantic lover remembered time and change, and sighed with Lamartine by the lake-side:

> Time, stay your course; and you, propitious hours
>   Suspend your flight.
> Leave us to savour these bright days of ours,
>   Their swift delight.
>
> In vain I plead; the moments will not stay;
>   Time darts and flies.
> I bid night pass more slowly; and the day
>   Is in the skies.

Therefore death becomes the companion of romantic love; for in death the loved object is halted in an attitude like the figures on Keats's Urn: 'For ever will he love, and she be fair.'

Sadder still, when it was thwarted. 'Only he who knows longing knows what I suffer ...' *Sehnsucht*, the German word, holds it all as nothing else does; but Alfred de Musset's heroine echoes the sentiment: 'Je veux aimer, mais je ne veux pas souffrir.' Impossible to agree with Shakespeare's Rosalind: 'Men have died from time to time, and wormes have eaten them; but not for love'. In the romantic period, many died for love, pining away, going into a 'decline', or shooting themselves. Society is cruel, fate unrelenting, life disappointing; and so the end of romanticism is Count Axel in Villiers de l'Isle-Adam's novel *Axel* (1890). He offers Sara a bowl of poison and they drink it together as the only fulfilment of their love. Had they been more intimate, the beauty of her body would have bound him captive to this life, which is never what one dreams. 'Live? Our servants will do that for us.'

The ties of ideas and the manner of men's living are never better illustrated than by romantic love. Schliemann walking hand in hand with Minna Meincke at eight years old, telling her of his resolve to dig up buried Troy; and forty years later as a rich millionaire, realizing his dream. Turgenev hurrying across Europe to the feet of Pauline Viardot; Chopin in Majorca with George Sand. But the most convincing tribute is that of someone as staid as the English actor Macready, in the mingled feelings of his tribute to *La Malibran*, that lovely gipsy whose death in Manchester at twenty-eight in 1838 left Europe in tears:

> I felt as if my mind was stunned; it was a shock that left me no power to think for some little time ... so rich in talent, once so lovely, with so much to enchant and fascinate, and so much to blame and regret – suddenly taken from a world so full of delight to her, and to which she was so frequently a minister of delight. I once could have loved her, and she has since said that she loved – 'was in love with' – me. Had I known it for certain, I might have been more miserable than I am.

Hector Berlioz, less stable than Macready, ran the gamut of it all. Watching Shakespeare in Paris, he fell in love with the Irish actress Harriet Smithson. She was indifferent; despair was his

portion. He sought solace with another, changed his sky and went to Rome; in vain. He came back to find Harriet and impose the dream on her; in the end she married him. The second hell of romanticism, ennui, waited for him. His boredom drove him into the arms of Madame Recio; but when Harriet died he was full of remorse. To complete the pattern, one more twist was needed; in middle age he sought out the little girl with pink shoes whom he had loved at fourteen; the lost innocence of childhood beckoned. But the lady was a grandmother, and was too wise to give him more encouragement than to be godfather to one of her grandchildren.

But, absurd as it seems, romantic love, this conspiracy of outlaws against the treason of society, this assertion of instinct, this liberating and vindicating force, this world of moonlight and forest, of nightingales and roses, can still cast its spell, even though it has now become a kitchen philosophy lurking behind the privet hedges and window-curtains of suburbia, and glorified in technicolor with stereophonic sound on the silver screen. Go back to the beginning:

> Si tu veux, faisons un rêve.
> Montons sur deux palefrois;
> Tu m'emmènes, je t'enlève.
> L'oiseau chante dans les bois.
>
> Je suis ton maître et ta proie;
> Partons, c'est la fin du jour;
> Mon cheval sera la joie,
> Ton cheval sera l'amour.

ILLUSTRATION: Plate 10 and Page 359.

The king's prerogative

The **ROYAL PREROGATIVE** developed from the medieval ideas about the divine right of kingship (q.v.). The king's function was to govern, to lead his people in war, to give them justice in time of peace and to maintain and preserve the law.

The king, however, although given chief place in the body politic was not absolute; he was 'under the law', but more important he must govern under advice. That is, he was expected to consult the great council of the magnates of his kingdom before making any great changes in the law or any important policy decision. Yet it was only slowly that any subject ventured to claim more than the right to give advice and the limitation of the prerogative became practical politics. In 1215 most of the English baronage rebelled against King John and forced him to assent to the long list of grievances for redress, known as Magna Carta. Although this Great Charter was in fact a treaty between John and his barons, it was cast in the form of a statute, a command of the king to his people. In it the king promised to renounce a number of prerogative practices for the future, but no fundamental restraints on the prerogative were attempted; the king was left in other matters to govern as before.

Just over forty years later a new and greater crisis arose, between Henry III and his barons. This time the rebels went further, and in addition to the redress of a host of grievances, they demanded the setting up of a permanent council of magnates, which would represent the 'common consent of the kingdom of England' and which would choose the king's chief ministers and hold them responsible. Had they been successful, the king would have been reduced to merely the first amongst equals and the prerogative would have hardly been royal in more than name.

These ideas were too advanced for the time, and the barons, frightened at what they had done, quarrelled amongst themselves, and in the end allowed Henry III to assume his former authority. Still, limitations on the prerogative had been attempted and were not forgotten.

Out of all this grew the instrument through which the prerogative was in the end successfully restricted – i.e. Parliament. The great barons were already part of the great council of the realm, from which the king took advice from time to time. But as government grew, it interfered more and more in matters of local politics, and its interference and its power were largely dependent on the willing co-operation of the local gentry, on the unpaid labours of the knights of the shire who eventually became the justices of the peace. It used them for preserving law and order, for assessing and collecting taxes and in all kinds of administrative tasks.

The government became increasingly depen-

dent on them, and from the thirteenth century onwards they play an increasing part in politics.

Of only slightly less importance were the principal burgesses of the growing towns of medieval England. In the great crisis of Henry III's reign both sides appealed for the support of these classes, and within fifty years their representatives were being summoned along with the great baronage to meetings, called in contemporary slang Parliaments, 'talking-shops', in order to treat with the king on matters of finance and such business as he chose to put before them.

After 1322 the representatives of the Commons, as they were called, although in fact they were all chosen from the local aristocracy, gained the statutory right of summons to every parliament.

Parliament was perhaps the greatest medieval contribution to the English constitution, but it would be a mistake to over-estimate the importance of the Commons in it, or to over-estimate its general effectiveness as a limitation on the royal prerogative. Yet by the advent of the Tudors, it had deposed kings, attacked archbishops, charged great men with treason and opposed the barrier of the English common law to some of the claims of the Pope. True, it had usually done all these things at the promptings of powerful men backed with armed force; but it alone could give the cachet of lawfulness to what had been achieved.

From the accession of Henry VII until the reign of Elizabeth, the Commons were apparently the willing and submissive agents of royal despotism. But throughout Elizabeth's reign, in spite of her great popularity and autocratic temper, the Commons were growing in power and confidence. Early in her reign they made their weight felt in a matter peculiarly close to the royal prerogative. Elizabeth, as 'supreme governor' of the English Church, required Parliament to enact a new English prayer-book; she was forced to accept a more Protestant version than she in fact desired, mainly through the opposition of the Commons. The Commons were decidedly puritan in temper and Calvinistic in religion and trouble began in earnest with the accession of the Stuarts.

James I held very strong traditional views on the strength of the royal prerogative and the divine right of kings. But the puritan Commons were not impressed by the claims of sacramental, anointed monarchs. For them such things were superstition; authority had to be justified by right use. James and his son, Charles I, roused the Commons' anger almost equally by their insistence that matters of taxation belonged to their prerogative powers, and by their High Church religious policy. When things came to a head, the more resolute of the Commons were prepared to deny the prerogative altogether. But the unhappy experience of Cromwell's dictatorship led to a certain reaction.

Nevertheless it was now clear that the royal prerogative had in practice been decisively limited and that the Commons shared in its exercise as well as the King, especially in matters of finance. Yet for more than a century to come the Crown still exercised considerable prerogative powers; the king still largely controlled the appointment of their chief ministers and had considerable influence on legislation. George III, for example, enjoyed authority in England very similar to that of the American president in the United States at the present time.

The final turn which denuded the Crown of all political authority was the rise of the party system in the nineteenth century. Earlier 'parties', such as the Whigs and Tories, had really been composed of the friends and connexions of great political personages. The new parties were the nationally organized and tightly controlled bodies which we know today. They were able to choose their own leader who by virtue of his disciplined following in the Commons must either be Prime Minister or Leader of the Opposition. The leader had to satisfy the party, not the Crown, by his choice of subordinates and his legislative programme. In this way the Crown has been virtually expelled from politics.

The measure of the distance travelled may be taken by the embarrassment of King George V when, on the retirement of Bonar Law, he was placed in the position of choosing a leader for the Conservative Party.

The royal prerogative has no longer a practical political existence, though Parliament has not succeeded in acquiring the whole of it. The party managers and their organization are important in the choice of the personnel of cabinets and the choice of political programmes: so that the limitation of this form of extra-parliamentary prerogative may still become a live political issue.

ILLUSTRATION: Page 173.

S

Saints and sanctity

SANCTITY, or holiness, is a quality that the writers of the Old Testament see as supremely belonging to God himself. In the great moments of religious experience men may become aware of that holiness, of the sacred, overpowering and majestic quality of the divine.

Holiness as a quality of God becomes also a quality of those places where God dwells – in the earlier days of the Old Testament, the Ark of the Covenant and, later on, in the Temple at Jerusalem. So to touch the Ark was to court immediate death. We can see here the link with primitive notions of *taboo*. The *taboos* of early society are those rules which must not at any cost be transgressed. We have no certain account of their origin. What is certain is that a distinction between the sacred and the profane is vital to most primitive societies and that a general experience of the sacred in early man underlies the profound beliefs about the holiness of the divine nature in the Old Testament.

The New Testament sees the divine holiness as made available to men through grace, so that in the life of the Church sanctity is a distinguishing mark. St Paul can refer to a local church quite simply in 'the Saints that are at Ephesus' and so on. But from the earliest days it was obvious that sanctity was the goal of the Christian life for all, but was attained in this life only by a few. Some, renowned for their sanctity, were revered in life by the Christian community to which they belonged and after their death this reverence would grow into a cult. So the first canonizations were effected. In time the Church developed legal forms for canonization and set out certain criteria which can be applied to test whether or no we may rightly refer to a man as 'Saint so and so'.

Those who have been canonized have varied immensely in type of character. There have been administrators and social reformers like St Vincent de Paul, contemplatives like St John of the Cross, founders of religious orders like St Benedict. What the Church never denied, but many Christians insufficiently recognized, is the large number of uncanonized Saints there have been and are in the world, and above all how much of sanctity is to be found in other religions. For many people in the modern world the saintly figure *par excellence* was Gandhi, and the saints of modern Hinduism have been a powerful force in Indian life.

Sanctity means more than goodness. It is a quality with a peculiar grace and one that arouses awe. It may be cultivated apart from specific religious beliefs, and within religion the extent to which it is valued has varied at different times and places. There is no doubt that the Buddhist striving after the extinction of selfhood in Nirvana often produces in Buddhist monks qualities of character akin to sanctity. Poverty and charity seem the inevitable concomitants of sanctity, and the lives of the Saints associate it with the power to work miracles (q.v.). A single-minded devotion to his cause also marks the Saint.

The psychologist would explain sanctity in terms of sublimation. The Saint withdraws from the external world those energies which the ordinary man devotes to its affairs. Some of the Saints, for example, have broken all family ties. Similarly the desires which manifest themselves in sexuality are transformed by the Saint. These energies he sublimates and puts at the service of his search for holiness. Hence the Saint has a unified character, but one that may do less than justice to certain aspects of human life.

Saintliness to the modern mind has become largely associated with the more debased aspects of popular religious art, the plaster statuette and the tinsel halo. So it tends to be confused with pious religiosity and priggish self-righteousness. The way in which lives of the Saints tend to be written has encouraged this.

The question arises whether sanctity is to be found only within the confines of religion, or whether it might not survive as a characteristic of certain individuals within a society that had entirely lost its religious beliefs. This problem has preoccupied the contemporary French novelist and thinker Albert Camus, whose novel *La Peste* (1947) contrasts the heroic virtue of the Christian with that of the atheist in the conditions of plague.

Camus sees the atheist who sets no limits to moral attainment as the essential Saint of our time.

ILLUSTRATION: Plate 8.

Dubito, ergo sum

SCEPTICISM derives from the Greek verb meaning to enquire critically and hesitantly and as a doctrine signifies that the human mind is incapable of knowing reality. So by scepticism one may understand either a general doubt concerning accepted beliefs and ideas of reality, or a positive doctrine that there is no belief whatever of whose truth we may be certain. The two great sceptics of the Ancient World were Pyrrho of Elis (c. 360–270 B.C.) and Sextus Empiricus (c. A.D. 200). Both were concerned to promote scepticism for ethical reasons, in the belief that man can find peace and tranquillity only within himself, and that any search for truth in the world of external reality is bound to be frustrated.

The ancient arguments for scepticism are in the main twofold. First, the sceptics point to the fact that sense experience is private. 'How can I know that the colour I see and call *red* is the same colour as that which you see and call *red*? For if what I see as red and call *red* you see as green and call *red* and vice versa, how could we ever know that our actual experience of colour is in fact different?' And if sense experiences may differ, is there any certainty that in experience there exists a trustworthy guide to the nature of reality?

Secondly, experience of the senses may be delusory on some occasions. In hallucinations, for example, imagination allows a city in a desert, an advance towards it and the discovery that it is not there. But if sometimes what we think we see is the product of imagination, can we ever be sure that the whole world around us is real and not imaginary? In dreams we are persuaded that what we see is real. Is our persuasion of the reality of the external world not just another dream? Hence the conclusion that we can be certain of nothing, we can know nothing. But as early as Pyrrho the paradox of scepticism was perceived – if we know that we can know nothing then we do know something. So Pyrrho argues that we must doubt even scepticism.

The real weakness of the Pyrrhonian case, however, lies elsewhere. We can only argue that sense experiences differ if two can be compared and found to differ. The only possible comparison that we can have is one that enquires in what situations we should each use the word 'red'. If we agree completely as to the situations in which the word is applicable, then we have all the agreement that we either need or desire. There *are* those who see colours differently, the colourblind. We learn that a man is colour-blind because he fails to distinguish colours that the majority are able to distinguish, and so we can discriminate between those who share our experience of colour and those who do not. Hence the fallacy of calling sense experience 'private'.

Secondly, we are aware of hallucinations because they are exceptional. When one sees a city in a mirage, one discovers that the city is not really there by the test of sense experience, by trying to touch the walls, walk through the gates and so on. We test sense experience by other sense experience. So the whole notion of particular hallucinatory experiences is dependent on accepting sense experience as in general trustworthy, and cannot be used to argue its deceptive power. To call an experience 'a dream' is to predict that in time we shall wake up. An indefinite failure to wake up is enough to justify us in refusing to call reality 'a dream'. The fundamental positions of scepticism are fallacious.

The term 'scepticism' is sometimes extended to cover specific doubts in the sphere of religion over and above general doubts concerning the nature of reality, and to inculcate the habit of doubt would seem to attack the foundations of any system of dogmatic beliefs. Yet it is curious to note that both in philosophy and in religion

doubt may be made the coping-stone for belief. For Descartes a process of systematic doubt enables us to discover just what it is that we cannot doubt. What we cannot doubt is our own thought of doubt – 'I think, therefore I am'. On this basis, Descartes constructed a detailed metaphysical system. The fallacy of Descartes is to suppose that if one can doubt everything, one cannot doubt that there is someone to do the doubting. For we might be, as Tweedle-dum and Tweedledee suggest in *Alice through the Looking Glass*, characters in someone else's dream, who will disappear when they awake. And even if one cannot doubt 'I think, therefore I am' perhaps the *I* can doubt whether the *I* cannot doubt it. But, as we have already seen, a general doubt as to experience, of the kind Descartes proposes, is unnecessary.

In religion also doubt has been proposed as the starting point of belief. Blaise Pascal (1623–1662) saw in doubt the failure of human reason to solve the problems of man's nature and destiny. 'The Pyrrhonian Philosophy', he wrote, 'is the correct one', but what Pyrrho has proved is that one must find a solution for one's problems outside philosophy. Reason must give way to faith: 'The heart has its reasons of which the reason knows nothing.'

In David Hume's *Dialogues on Natural Religion* (written about the year 1751) the philosophical sceptic and the defender of faith are made allies against the theologian who would found his belief on rational arguments for God's existence. Hume's defence of faith is largely ironical, but he can approach Pascal's position in saying that, 'to be a philosophical sceptic is, in a man of letters, the first and most essential step towards being a sound believing Christian ...'.

Historically, scepticism has made its contribution to philosophy rather by the refutation of dogmatic positions than by its own doctrines. The part of scepticism in contemporary philosophy is played by those philosophers who have emphasized the importance of language. Ludwig Wittgenstein, Professor of Philosophy at Cambridge both before and after the last war, was largely responsible for the suspicion of all speculative systems of thought which dominates contemporary philosophy. 'Philosophy', in Wittgenstein's words, 'is not a theory, but an activity', the activity of clarifying and analysing the logic of our language. So the philosopher would no longer enquire as to the nature of reality or as to how far it is knowable, but would ask what kind of an assertion we make when we say either that reality is knowable or that it is not.

Is it empirical? verifiable by sense experience? Obviously not, for what is being put in question is the trustworthiness of the senses.

Do we then make a statement about anything when we assert that reality is or is not knowable, for surely all statements must be verifiable by looking at the world?

So scepticism and anti-scepticism would both be viewed as illegitimate attempts to make general statements about reality and how far we know it.

ILLUSTRATION: Page 409.

Knowledge for what?

SCIENCE IS THE NEW RELIGION is a formula which neatly sums up an important belief in modern European social thought, the belief that science and religion are always at war. On one side, religion, a set of irrational beliefs about the nature of the world; on the other side, science, truth, at last, established by observation and experience.

Obstructing free enquiry was the Church, which sought to imprison the mind with its superstitions and magic and lull men into accepting their lot: only by deceit and the most obstinate hostility to any free intellectual progress could the Church maintain its power, its natural allies being thus the enemies of any social or political progress which might give more freedom to the human spirit.

Stemming from the anti-clericalism of the Renaissance, this belief was newly energized during the Enlightenment in the writings of such men as Voltaire, Condorcet and Tom Paine. It was carried further in the nineteenth century in the agnostic radicalism of Marx, summed up in his phrase discussing religion as 'the opiate of the people'.

At the heart of the idea of science as a religion is the assumption that there is a single kind of truth to be established either on scientific or on religious grounds. Reason was thus seen to be in competition with revelation and faith as criteria for the *same* truths. It is one of the major contributions of modern sociology and anthropology to have shown how religion and science are two human activities. The conflict which may exist between them, particularly between philosophers and theologians, can thus be seen as an historical accident, not as the result of an intrinsic opposition.

Science, on the one hand, deals with the explanation of phenomena which can be observed. It grows when a theory which was confirmed by observation no longer fits with new observations. The theory must then be recast in order to explain these new observations. The achievement of this is a scientific advance. For a proposition to be a scientific one, it must be formulated in such a way that it is capable of being *disproved* by new observations. In the light of this, such a statement as 'there is a life after death' can never be judged to be either true *or* false on the basis of science. There are no observations that can be made either to confirm or disprove the statement. So it is not a scientific proposition; but a statement about a phenomenon outside science altogether – *i.e.* there is no *scientific* proposition which could ever possibly replace this statement as being more accurate.

Religion, on the other hand, so far as it is concerned with observable phenomena, deals really not with their explanation but with their interpretation. It gives them a meaning, it places them in a context in which human beings are brought into a relation with the supernatural. For example, why should a young man be stricken with an incurable disease in the prime of life? Science may be able to say why he caught it. It cannot say 'why' it is right or just that such a thing should happen to him. This is the province of religious belief such as 'it is the will of God'. Religion satisfies spiritual needs, and it reduces the pain of the inevitable frustrations of human life. It does this, not by providing individuals with demonstrable knowledge, but by inspiring them with its beliefs.

Religion, then, deals with the sacred, science makes a rational approach towards the profane. One does not conflict with the other, or need not conflict with the other.

However, in Western Europe, religion has been the object of elaborate intellectual speculation leading to complex theological systems. These have attempted to link together ideas about God with ideas about nature, such as, for example, the movements of the planets. So theological systems have thus collided with science precisely about those things which could be submitted to observation. The conflict has been exacerbated only where the theologians believed that their views about nature under-pinned their views about God. Thus they succeeded in making ideas about nature sacred. In their view at one time for a person to *disbelieve* in any item of the Biblical revelation was morally iniquitous. Where the Church claimed a monopoly of truth, there was very real conflict between it and those who stood for free enquiry. The most famous case is that of Galileo, who was forced by the Church to abjure his belief that the earth moved. Yet this does not prove a conflict between religion and science – only between the ceremonies themselves and scientific activity. It is rather the result of special historical conditions which gave the Church such a monopoly of power in the spiritual as well as in the intellectual realm and which fostered the rise of its particular theology.

On the other hand, for science to be proclaimed as a new religion is as pernicious in its consequences as the theological invasion of the realm of science. This claim for science is illustrated most explicitly and in a very extreme way in the writings of Saint-Simon (1760–1825) and his followers. Instead of positing a conflict between religion and science and, then rejecting religion altogether, they claimed that there was no conflict, because the two were identical in scope. To Saint-Simon religion was a body of ideas. For the educated, these would be scientific ideas; for the uneducated, they would be rites and beliefs accepted on faith. Here, too, experience that is intrinsically religious – *e.g.* mysticism – is conceived of as an inferior form of intellectual experience. Saint-Simon was not prepared to grant that religious experience was intrinsically different from rational speculation about the nature of the world.

Where a body of ideas about nature is raised to the status of a religion, either explicitly as in the work of Saint-Simon or implicitly as in Communism, the result is to corrupt ethical standards of behaviour. In giving the veneration to scientific propositions that should only be given to the Gods, these propositions are being made into criteria of justice. That is, one is saying that if a thing works, it must be ethically right. Also the door is opened, unwittingly or not, to using knowledge to control the ignorant, without the check of ethical criteria. Saint-Simon's view that 'religion is the sum of the applications by which enlightened men govern the ignorant' would legitimize the activities of a tyrant who would manipulate men for his own ends by propaganda (q.v.). The Nazi hypothesis that if you tell a big lie often enough, it may soon be believed is, after all, true under certain conditions. It works. Instrumental knowledge of this type in human behaviour must be subordinated to moral principles, or there can be no ethically guided social relations between individuals.

There is another dangerous consequence of the careless, naïve deification of science – that scientific progress may be confused and identified with moral progress or, simply, progress in general. The main question must always be, knowledge for what?

Scientific method

SCIENTIFIC METHOD developed gradually during long periods of time. To take an early statement, Newton in 1672 wrote:

> The best and safest method of philosophizing seems to be, first to enquire diligently into the properties of things, and of establishing those properties by experiments, and then to proceed more slowly to hypotheses for the explanation of them. For hypotheses should be subservient only in explaining the properties of things, but not assumed in determining them; unless so far as they may furnish experiments.

To 'enquire diligently into the properties of things' was not a novel procedure. Between them, the civilizations of Egypt, Mesopotamia and the Indus Valley initiated the arts of irrigation, brickmaking, the use of stone for building and the rudiments of sanitation. They invented the weighing balance, developed measurement to the point of discovering rules for dealing approximately with right-angled triangles, and invented the calendar. They knew enough about the human body to guess that the heart might be a centre of its working. Clearly they had enquired diligently; they may in some sense have established properties by experiments. But it is doubtful if the Egyptians, who contributed most, 'proceeded to hypotheses'.

The Greeks, on the other hand, proceeded to hypotheses with enthusiasm. If the fitness of living forms to the functions which they fulfil is accepted for this purpose as a hypothesis, then it can be said that Aristotle's idea of zoology included the making of observations, and the putting forward of a hypothesis, but not its testing by experiment. In general, the contributions of ancient Greece were rather the tools used later in science than scientific method itself. These contributions included the rational approach, logic, and deductive geometry.

Roger Bacon is usually credited with the earliest emphasis on experiment. In his *Opus Maius* (1268), he wrote:

There are two modes in which we acquire knowledge, argument and experiment. Argument shuts up the question, and makes us shut it up too; but it gives no proof, nor does it remove doubt and cause the mind to rest in the conscious possession of truth, unless the truth is discovered by way of experience.

The practice of experiment developed more slowly. Bacon's contemporary, Peter Peregrinus, experimented on magnetism, and anticipated many of the conclusions reached by Gilbert of Colchester in his book *De Magnete* (1600). As the Renaissance approached, there was in Italy a growing interest in experimental enquiry which paralleled the interest in the Greek language. But there is little tangible before Leonardo da Vinci; and, even his known achievements appear rather as a mixture of intuition, curiosity and practical skill than as illustrations of procedure. He was his own law. With Galileo, anticipated in part by Stevinus of Bruges, there was a greater concentration of effort and a more systematic procedure, recognizable as science in action.

Francis Bacon, Lord Verulam, contemporary with Galileo, would be described now as a philosopher of science. He realized the importance of experiments made for the special purpose of discovery, and the difficulties, but not fully the limitations, of the inductive method. On the one hand, he saw that an effort was required to look for 'contrary instances', placed great stress on the method of 'exclusion', and reached the concept of the 'crucial experiment'. On the other, he limited his method by omitting from it the use of hypotheses which involved unobservable properties, but which might yet lead to testable predictions, and he overrated it in concluding that 'after the rejection and exclusion have been duly made, there will remain at the bottom, all light of opinion vanishing into smoke, a Form affirmative, solid and true and well defined'. No one would now claim that such final certainty was attainable. Bacon left as perhaps his most valuable statement that 'all true and faithful natural philosophy hath a double scale or ladder, ascendent and descendent; ascending from experiments to the invention of causes; and descending from causes to the invention of new experiments'.

With the addition of hypotheses (as above), this is the scientific method.

Newton's statement already quoted goes on:

For if the possibility of hypotheses is to be the test of truth and reality of things, I see not how certainty is to be obtained in any science; since numerous hypotheses may be devised which shall seem to overcome new difficulties. Hence it has been thought necessary to lay aside all hypotheses, as foreign to the purpose.

Again, in the often-quoted General Scholium at the end of the *Principia*, he wrote:

Hitherto I have not been able to discover the cause of those properties of gravity from phenomena, and I frame no hypotheses, *hypotheses non fingo*; and hypotheses, whether metaphysical or physical, whether of occult qualities or mechanical, have no place in experimental philosophy. In this philosophy particular propositions are inferred from the phenomena, and afterwards rendered general by induction.

Newton's words, 'unless so far as they may furnish experiments', show at least that he saw the positive contribution which could be made by hypotheses. It is perhaps a reasonable interpretation that their use was not therefore excluded from his own mental processes; that, like

Bacon before him, he felt the need in his time to avoid purely speculative explanations; that, unlike Bacon, he saw the impossibility of arriving at final certainty; and that his well-known dislike of controversy was connected both with his austere manner of presentation and the extreme statement in the General Scholium last quoted. In short, 'so far as they furnish experiments' represented his real view of the rôle of hypotheses in scientific method. A hypothesis is good and useful if it can be tested; if this condition is not fulfilled, it is more likely to limit thinking than to encourage it.

The same comment applies with equal force to the construction of theories, which, logically, are best regarded as hypotheses that are more fully worked out and cover wider areas of knowledge than do the simpler kinds of hypothesis. It is not an essential element in a theory that it should be intellectually satisfying in all respects. Neither can it be assumed that a theory, however successful and however satisfying, can in any circumstances attain to finality. The results of any one experiment, if reproducible by others, may in principle necessitate the replacement of even an apparently well-established theory. In these circumstances, it is necessary that the new theory should reproduce the results of the old one within that area in which it was satisfactory, and should lead to further results which are not deducible from the old theory. This cannot, in general, be achieved merely by a process of addition and modification; the foundations of the new theory may be different from that of the old one, as different as Einstein's system of dynamics is from Newton's.

There has been an increasing trend in physical science towards a separation between the theoretical and experimental workers in the different sciences in the sense that it is unusual for the same individual to work in both capacities. Largely for this reason, complete developments of theory are now quite often undertaken in anticipation of the evidence which will confirm or refute them. The change of timing which this involves is the result rather of personal considerations than of a change in method, though it is potentially dangerous.

One useful observation can be made about scientific method: scientists when carrying out research and making discoveries do not consciously apply scientific method; nor do they sit down, as it were, before a collection of facts and deliberately try to start the process of Induction.

Most discoveries and advances have been made in ways which can only be described as unscientific; intuition and chance combined with the in-intellectual preparedness of discoverers seem to have been the main components of scientific progress. Darwin's idea of the survival of the fittest came to him suddenly after he had been reading (for relaxation) the *Essay on the Principle of Population* of Malthus. 'I can remember the very spot in the road, whilst in my carriage, when to my joy the solution occurred to me.' Strangely enough, A. R. Wallace who independently reached the same conclusions as Darwin, was also reading the *Essay* of Malthus, 'then', he wrote, 'it suddenly flashed upon me that this self-acting process would improve the race'. Many discoveries seem to have been made in almost frivolous circumstances and with unlikely stimuli, not by any rigid logical method.

It should be mentioned too that working scientists avoid being drawn into discussions about scientific method. As a result most of the discussion has been at the hands of philosophers and, especially, logicians who themselves would be incapable of organizing or carrying out scientific research. Today the 'Philosophy of Science' is as much the concern of philosophers as scientists; the latter admit they often flounder helplessly when invading Philosophy. In any case scientists feel that their career of enquiry uses a practical art and not a science and thus avoid introspection concerning method. Even in the more theoretical parts of science where mathematics is the main tool we find that inspired guessing is a common process, which has to be proved afterwards by 'rigid' proof.

Fluttering palpitations

SENTIMENTALITY is sentiment projected to embarrassment, feeling expressed in a facile or affected way. Sentiment ('true feeling') was, in the eighteenth century, the pulse by which a man's mental health was judged; sentimentality was his heart in a fluttering palpitation.

From 1740, which saw the publication of *Pamela, or Virtue Rewarded* by Samuel Richardson (1689–1761), sentiment and its attendant sentimentality occupy a central position in the development of art and literature. Before 1740 'sentiment' signified a satisfactory blending of thought and feeling, an opinion and a manner of expressing it, a felt idea, so that we find critics examining Milton's or Spenser's or Chaucer's 'sentiments' as if they were considering something as precise as syntax. After *Pamela* the emotional element in the blend predominates over the rational. Artists are in danger of becoming excessively tender, refined, soft. This is seen in the paintings of Greuze, Morland, Wheatley, and occasionally in Romney and Reynolds. But it is through the literature of the second half of the eighteenth century, and particularly through its lesser prose, that the sentimental tide flows in full flood.

In the poetry of such men as Young, Collins, Gray, Cowper and Burns the expression of a personal mood – generally a conventional 'poetic' mood, such as melancholy, benevolence or 'pathetic sublimity' – is more important than the clear objective announcement of universal truths. The emphasis shifts from the imitation of Nature through classical models to the production of 'originals'; an artist who would previously have been praised for his wit and for the correctness of his 'sentiment', is now praised for his personal genius. One curious by-product of this change from public attitude to private mood was that the English began to win an international reputation for suicide – 'These are the dark November days when the English hang themselves!' commented Voltaire, while Edward Young brooded darkly on:

The knell, the shroud, the mattock and the grave;
The deep damp vault, the darkness, and the worm.

The liberation of sentiment produced no great poetry, but prepared the ground for the Romantics who were to follow.

In the astonishingly rapid and full growth of the novel after *Pamela*, sentimentality was always present. Richardson's novels, unlike Defoe's, are impelled by emotional situations, and not by plot. They are long, they are manifestly sentimental, yet saved from the weaknesses of mere sentimentality by an accuracy of psychological detail, and by a certain grandeur in the design and proportion. They require prodigious acts of faith and patience, amply rewarded, in the reading of them.

'Why, Sir,' said Dr Johnson, 'if you were to read Richardson for the story, your impatience would be so much fretted that you would hang yourself. But you must read him for the sentiment.' Walpole was one reader who found himself fretted by the sentimentality of the third novel, *Sir Charles Grandison*. He reached hanging-point at the fourth volume of six: 'I was so tired of sets of people getting together and saying, "Pray, Miss, with whom are you in love?"' This, of course, is the germinal situation of sentimentality: young ladies in love, involved in the eternal triangles and geometrical entanglements of passion.

Richardson gave the novel emotional appeal. In Henry Fielding's opinion he gave it too much, and *Pamela* produced his counterblast against sentimentality, *Shamela*, a year later. But Fielding (1707–1754) was shouted down by the concerted voices of a large choir of lady novelists, under the influence (as was Richardson himself) of the French tradition of *grands sentiments*. Variations on the major theme of sentimentality were made in the tender novels and so-called 'scandal chronicles' of such writers as Mary Delarivière Manley, Eliza Haywood (*Fortunate Foundlings, Betsy Thoughtless, Jemmy and Jenny Jessamy*), Charlotte Lennox, Sarah Scott, Mrs Sheridan (the dramatist's mother), Frances Brooke, Elizabeth Griffith and Mrs Inchbald. Their books were extravagantly popular, especially with the young lady readers who formed the bulk of the novel-reading public, devouring sentimental French, German and English fiction with a voracious impartiality, their appetites fed by the newly-fashionable circulating library – called by Colman in his *Polly Honeycombe*, 'that evergreen tree of diabolical knowledge'.

These novels were marked by a palpitating fervour, a cloying sweetness of expression, a striving after sublimity and an earnest desire to bring about moral reform in the hearts of the bounders who move so decoratively through them. In *Humphry Clinker* (1771) Smollett ruefully remarked that novel-writing was then 'engrossed by female authors, who publish merely for the propagation of virtue, with so much ... knowledge of the human heart ... that the reader is not only enchanted by their genius, but reformed by their morality'. In the last two decades of the century, Fanny Burney gave some check to excessive tenderness with *Evelina* (1778), in which she shows herself as much interested in structure as in emotion. Her subsequent novels, *Cecilia* (1782), *Camilla* (1796), and *The Wanderer, or Female Difficulties* (1814) are less palatable, although a moral passage in the last chapter of *Cecilia* gave Jane Austen (a decidedly unsentimental novelist) the theme and title of her *Pride and Prejudice*.

When Sterne's *A Sentimental Journey through France and Italy* first appeared in 1768, the word 'sentimental' puzzled both English and Continental readers. He explained his meaning in a letter to a friend: 'I told you my design in it was to teach us to love the world and our fellow creatures better than we do – so it runs most upon those gentler passions and affections.' Yorick makes 'a quiet journey of the heart in pursuit of NATURE, and those affections which arise out of her', savouring the situation of the moment 'with sweet emotion'. Sterne's example was followed by Henry Mackenzie and Henry Brooke. Harley, the hero of Mackenzie's *The Man of Feeling* (1771), faces situations with a touchingly sentimental incompetence, paralysed into inactivity by the poignancy of life – the solitary state of the delicate soul, the hardness of life for a private soldier or the victim of a business fraud. Mackenzie's principle, laid down in 1777 in his *Julia de Roubigné* (an echo of Rousseau), is that 'memoirs of sentiment and suffering may be found in every condition'. Brooke, whose *Fool of Quality* (1765–1770) also follows Rousseau's *Emile*, states a similar case for the sentimentalist: 'The truth is that people live incomparably more by impulse and inclination than by reason and precept'. And 'even the wild Indians feel the sweet compunctions and emotions of the human heart'.

Sentimentality is part of the sub-plot of that history of the eighteenth century novel, which is usually represented in terms of the 'social realism' and 'biting satire' of Smollett and Fielding. But it is Smollett and Fielding who survive. The works of Mrs Inchbald and her companions, weakened by softness in the very texture of the words, require a sheaf of sentimental lavender to preserve them.

In the theatre a similar conflict between sentimentality and true feeling was in progress. The choice lay between 'laughing' and 'weeping' comedies, 'the truth of laughter' and 'the luxury of tears'. On the one hand, dramatists like Arthur Murphy and George Colman produced farce and satire, and opposing them were the weepers, led by Hugh Kelly and Richard Cumberland (satirized by Sheridan as Sir Fretful Plagiary in *The Critic*). The highly sentimental and moral plays of the weepers – *False Delicacy*, *The Romance of an Hour*, *The Wheel of Fortune*, *The Widow's Only Son*, and many more – were extremely popular, and had it not been for the genius of two men, Goldsmith and Sheridan, sentimentality would probably have held the stage unchallenged. Goldsmith set his face against 'flattering every man in his foible'. In his *Good Natur'd Man* (1768) he mocks at the moody sentimentalist, prone to melancholy. 'Ah! my dear friend,' remarks Croaker, 'it is a perfect satisfaction to be miserable with you.' Sheridan similarly scourges the falsities of sentiment. 'Well, there is nothing in the world so noble as a man of sentiment!' says Sir Peter Teazle of Joseph Surface in Sheridan's *School for Scandal* (1777), just before the screen is removed to reveal that he has been deceived, possibly cuckolded, by the noble man of sentiment.

However, sentimentality in the theatre survived. The end of the century saw melodramas and plays of humanitarian purpose, like Holcroft's *The Road to Ruin*, Morton's *The Slave* and Mrs Inchbald's *Such Things Are*, plucking as earnestly as ever at the heart-strings of the public.

In the nineteenth century sentimentality in art and literature continued undiminished, laying a new stress on patriotic emotions, and on those which play with tender fondness round children and the sanctity of the hearth. 'Bubbles' by the erstwhile pre-Raphaelite, Sir John Everett Millais, is a direct descendant of Greuze's *Espieglerie*, but Tiny Tim, Little Lord Fauntleroy and Eric are new arrivals, giving the ground to the Peter Pantheism of Sir James Barrie. In the drawing-room sentimentality was as solemn a fixture as the potted palm. Drawing-room ballads were melodious outpourings of molten and melting emotion ('Come into the Garden, Maud'), although sometimes they contrived artfully to combine tenderness with moral indignation. Drawing-room sentimentality was, if anything, exceeded by that of the music-hall, whose sentimental songs are impossible to render without a catch in the voice and a constricted throat.

In our own time we have seen sentimentality, always at a premium in time of stress or actual war, commercialized and organized more ruthlessly than ever before. The cinema, the Press, the popular song widely disseminated by the radio, the women's magazine – all combine to offer us sentiments not our own, more glamorous and attractive than those shoddy and humdrum feelings which – advertisements tell us – flicker dully in the untended human heart. The sentimental portrait-painter of the last two centuries has largely been replaced by the commercial artist. The sentimental novelist, catering for an audience of women, continues as popular as ever, with his equally sentimental counterpart, the 'tough' writer of sadistic and mildly pornographic thrillers which bear most of the artistic symptoms of sentimentality.

In art, sentimentality rarely survives in any real sense, except as a curiosity, because it is self-destructive: an over-softness and deliberate 'working-up' of feeling produce corresponding vices in execution. In life, it will survive as long as the heart survives, beats and, under unusual stimulation, palpitates.

ILLUSTRATION: Pages 370, 371, 372 and 373.

The Seven Sins

The **SEVEN DEADLY SINS**, of course, do not appear in the Bible. The list, as the Middle Ages knew it, ran as follows: *Superbia*, Pride (always the first); *Invidia*, Envy; *Ira*, translated Anger, Wrath or Hate; *Luxuria*, Lechery; *Avaritia*, Covetise or Covetousness; *Gula*, Gluttony; and *Accidia*, Accidie, Sloth or, as the *Ayenbite of Inwit* (a fourteenth-century treatise on the Nagging of Conscience) calls it, 'Slacnesse'.

Characteristically, their opposites, the Seven Cardinal Virtues, are much less known, and are more rarely and less vividly portrayed. They are *Humilitas*, *Caritas*, *Patientia*, *Castitas*, *Eleemosyna* (largesse or bounty), *Abstinentia* (abstinence or sobriety) and *Vigilantia*. Note, also, that the two 'remedies' about which the authorities differ most are those for Sloth and Avarice. The *Ancren Riwle* (a Handbook for Anchoresses written about A.D. 1200) answers Sloth with *gostlich gledscipe*, Holy Joy; Langland's *Piers Plowman* (c. 1370) chooses *Pees* (which our jargon might call The Undivided Mind); while Chaucer's Parson, in his grave, wise and lovely sermon, calls for '*Fortitudo* or Strengthe; that is, an affeccioun thurgh which a man despyseth anoyous thinges'.

Moreover, as the Parson reminds us: 'Everich of thise chief sinnes hath hise braunches and hise twigges', and through these twigs the medieval theologians, moralists, preachers and artists were able to lay out a veritable Linnaean scheme of moral turpitude and redemption, with its genera and species. Thus the Parson, 'among many another twig that I can nat declare', gives the species of Pride as Disobedience, Boasting, Hypocrisy, Disdain, Arrogance, Impudence, Swelling of Heart, Insolence, Elation, Impatience, Strife, Contumacy, Presumption, Irreverence, Pertinacity ('when man defendeth his folly, and trusteth too much in his own wit') and Vain Glory.

Many resources were available to bring such lists alive. There were striking and singular names, witty and pithy definitions; Surquidrie ('when a man undertaketh an enterprise that he ought not to do, or that he may not do') or Wanhope ('despair of the mercy of God, that cometh sometimes of too much outrageous sorrow, and sometimes of too much dread'). There were illustrations such as the Penitent Thief on the Cross, to show the folly of Despair. Each sin came in human shape, identified and described: Wrath with the whites of his eyes showing, snivelling with his nose, and biting his lips; Avarice beetle-browed and bleary; Gluttony with his rumbling guts, drinking a gallon and a gill, until he coughs up a caudle in Clement's lap; Accidie lying in bed in Lent with his leman in his arms till matins and Mass be done. These examples are from *Piers Plowman*, but others as vivid might be taken from Dunbar, from Stephen Hawes, from Marlowe or from Dekker. Not merely the writers, but the preachers gave their imaginations rein: 'Lust consumes the body ... It destroys the tongue of confession, the eyes of intelligence, the ears of obedience, the nose of discretion, the hair of good thoughts, the beard of fortitude, the eyebrows of holy religion.' The *Ancren Riwle* gives each Sin its attendant beast: the Lion of Pride, the Adder of Envy, the Unicorn of Wrath, the Scorpion of Lechery, the Fox of Avarice, the Sow of Gluttony, and the Bear of Sloth. Nearly four hundred years later, the Sins are still riding their beasts through Spenser's *Faerie Queene*; but Avarice has now a Camel, Lechery a Goat; and Envy, riding a Wolf, carries the Serpent in his bosom.

Inevitably the Sins formed one of the chief themes of medieval drama. In fact, the earliest Morality play known, the *Paternoster Play* of York, was concerned with 'all manner of Vices held up to scorn, and the Virtues held up to praise', and among them was a *Ludus Accidie*, a Play of Sloth. The text has disappeared, but presumably each of the seven petitions of the Lord's Prayer was matched against a Vice and a Virtue. And this raises the issue of the mystic significance of numbers, and pre-eminently of seven. From the seven days of the week to the seven stars in the sky, from the seven years of apprenticeship to the seven lamps in the Apocalypse which are the seven spirits of God, from the Seven Sleepers of Ephesus to the Seven Sages and the Seven Champions, from the seven hills of Rome to the Seven Seas and the Seven Wonders of the World, the Middle Ages never grew tired of making these bundles or setting them off against each other. But the primacy of seven (though challenged by three, thrice three, and five) was justified by the fact that God made it the basis of creation. We might say, more prosaically, that it goes back to the point where mathematics, astronomy and magic meet in the calculations of the first magi, of Sumeria or earlier, who framed the calendar.

But the first place we know in which Virtues and Vices are tied into sevens is the *Psychomathia*, an epic poem of the Christian poet Prudentius, written about A.D. 400. The soul as a battle-ground (the theme of the poem) was, of course, already a commonplace for Stoic and Christian thinkers alike, and some of the antagonists had been named much earlier: Ovid, for instance, provided in the *Metamorphoses* the stock description of Envy, pale of face and lean of body, which the Middle Ages used again and again. Prudentius went further, though his list only partly corresponds to the later standard; he included Paganism, Sodomy and Discord (in the shape of Heresy), which represented the pressing moral problems of his time, as well as Wrath, Pride, Avarice and *Luxuria* (who stands for Greed rather than Lust). Each Sin already has its attendants: *Amor*, *Jocus* and *Petulantia* are the sutlers of *Luxuria*.

Through the Dark Ages preachers and theologians carried on a kind of unending General Election to the Seven Places. There was no lack of candidates; *Accidia* already appeared in a fourth-century list drawn up for monks by Cassianus, a contemporary of Prudentius. But through the whole process, from first to last, moral discrimination and poetic image were never far apart. The results might be presented in a form as straightforward as the Homilies of Ælfric (c. A.D. 1000), but were just as likely to take shape in a visionary poem, a Doomsday or a Descent to Hell, or an allegory like the *Sawles Warde*, in which Wit is Lord of the Castle, Will his capricious wife, the Virtues his daughters, and the Senses his servants (c. A.D. 1200). The visionary poem may even be translated into the cool prose of a Chronicle, as Matthew Paris tells the dream of Thurkhill, snatched up by St Julian from his Essex home, and shown the Infernal Pageants of Hell. It is just this mythological quality that prevents the Seven Deadly Sins from being desiccated into moral precept or warning, and keeps them lively even for posterity. The Seven Sins have even made the entrancing topics of a recent French film with a Certificate A for adults.

ILLUSTRATION: Page 368.

What does it signify?

SIGNIFICANT FORM as a term was coined by the art critic, and English champion of Post-Impressionism, Clive Bell. It first appears in print in his book *Art*, published in 1913, written while the Second Post-Impressionist Exhibition was open at the Grafton Galleries in London. This exhibition and its forerunner in 1909 were arranged by Bell's friend and partner in argument, Roger Fry, who by these exhibitions and by his writings did as much as anyone to introduce to England the new art of France and the Continent and to set the tone of English thought on the arts up to the present day. The doctrine of Significant Form must be considered as much in the context of this revolution in taste as in the history of theories of art.

Significant Form as a criterion of a work of art is introduced in the first chapter of the book, the *Aesthetic Hypothesis*: 'There must be some quality without which a work of art cannot exist ... what quality is shared by all objects that provoke our aesthetic emotions? Only one answer seems possible – Significant Form. In each, lines and colours combined in a particular way, certain forms and relations of forms stir our aesthetic emotion. These ... I call Significant Form and Significant Form is the one quality common to all works of visual art.' Clive Bell went on to extract from works of art everything that is not form: narrative, the beauty of beautiful women, all that concerns human needs and all that is a mirror of man's conception of man and the world; finally he is left with – Significant Form. In the same way one might put a red, a yellow and a blue ball into a bag, and having removed the red and the yellow, declare that the remaining one – believe it or not – is blue; and – believe it or not again – is a ball. It is to say that the property in common between things which exist in space and which provoke an emotion is – that they exist in space (have form) and provoke an emotion (are significant). Yet there are certain hypotheses which are implicit in Clive Bell's argument.

He stated that all works of art must have some quality in common without which 'when we speak of "works of art" we gibber'. He stated his belief that there is a particular 'aesthetic emotion' aroused by works of art. This is not argued; Clive Bell merely says that 'all sensitive people agree' to it, and in this way he simply makes an appeal to the need of his readers to feel themselves 'sensitive'. This idea itself is based on the allied but not identical assumption that shapes, colours and their relationships are capable of conveying emotions.

This idea has a long history and is at the root of much nineteenth-century art theory, and even practice, but experiments show it to be quite insufficient to account for ordinary feelings about art. However, it is possible to train people to react to works of art solely in respect of the amount of gold on them or the number of candles burning in front of them, and it is all too easy to make people read them according to a fashion, or according to the words of a critic.

Clive Bell, however, does not elaborate this idea in the way that, for example, it was elaborated by the French artist Georges Seurat (1859–1891) (rising lines indicating gaiety, falling lines indicating sadness, etc.). He uses it only as a way of distinguishing works of art from beautiful things in nature, on the ground that in the first the forms signify emotions, while in the latter they are only finely proportioned. Seurat wanted the intellect to be in firm control of the subject matter. A deliberate form and pattern was therefore imposed on the subjects painted.

Significant form is more fully expressed by Roger Fry (1886–1934) in his book *Vision and Design*. Fry, unlike Bell, realized that the emotion peculiar to art is aroused in us simply because we have learned to look at works of art in a special way. The doctrine of Significant Form was more useful as a means of popularizing modern art in England than as a general theory. It set a vague embrace around French art from the impressionists onwards, and also around the latest historical discoveries, the painting of El Greco, Byzantine mosaic, negro sculpture, Bushman rock drawings, etc.

The remains of significant Form are still recognizable in much English discussion of art and art journalism, though the doctrine is mated with a theory of truth to materials, with psychoanalysis, with theories of art as the expression of the spirit of the age (Zeitgeist), and art as the reflection of the condition of society (Marxism). An undercurrent of Significant Form can be detected whenever a picture is discussed in terms of shapes, whenever a group of people is referred to as 'the great triangular mass in the middle of the picture'.

Individual, Society and Ruler

The **SOCIAL CONTRACT** is a picturesque fable disguised as an historical fact. It appears to be a piece of antiquarian speculation in which it is asserted that once upon a time there was no such thing as society, only an anarchic state of nature full of self-assertive individuals, which proved so inconvenient that the individuals banded together and subscribed to a contract, by which they consented to surrender some freedom of action in return for mutual protection and greater security.

Perhaps no important political thinker took the idea of an actual, historical, contract seriously, but there is no doubt that the idea was made to perform a serious intellectual and imaginative function in political systems of thought. Its main purpose is to make plausible the belief that the individual precedes society both historically – hence the contract – and in terms of obligations and rights. The individual matters more than society: social authority is only to be respected on condition that it behaves.

To many it will seem that these notions about the individual and society are self-evident and in no way dependent on the dubious historical fact of an original contract. Yet this is not so. These notions and the contract with them are essentially modern, post-Renaissance ideas. For the ancient world, and the medieval world too, Aristotle's famous dictum 'Man is a political animal' was taken for granted – man, that is to say, is not basically an 'individual'; he is a citizen; it is as natural to have social obligations, rights and relationships, as it is to have arms and legs. In other words, society is itself a state of nature and no notion of a contractual relationship between them can arise.

An excellent demonstration of the irrelevance of a theoretical original contract to this kind of political thought may be discerned in medieval political thinking. In the earlier Middle Ages, at any rate, something which could be called a Social Contract did exist. Military service and the payment of taxes were provided for by a series of bargains between ruler and subject, in which the subject received so much land and security of tenure in return for a promise to discharge cer-

tain specified obligations. This is feudalism, yet feudal political thought had no trace of anything like a theory of Social Contract. Men accepted the view that society was natural, however its obligations were, in fact, apportioned out; their political thinking was concerned to enquire how society could be made good; what obligations were incumbent upon particular stations in life; what was the duty of a prince, a subject, a churchman? How far could anyone, princes included, do what they liked and how far was their power limited?

The change came after the Renaissance and it may be explained, not so much by intellectual and moral ferment, as by the rise of despotic monarchies, which, enlightened or not, claimed absolute obedience by divine right. The Social Contract in its most popular form was thought of as a contract between king and people, and was a natural reaction to this kind of claim.

Yet however valuable the idea may have been as a basis for a reasonable resistance to tyranny, it was a defective and also a double-edged intellectual weapon. The classic case of the use of the Social Contract to justify political freedom and the right of resistance is that of John Locke (1632–1704). Locke was concerned to justify the Glorious Revolution; at the same time he set prudent limits to the duty of resistance and rebellion. He modified the idea of a contract between king and people and replaced it by the notion of the king as trustee: 'all power given with trust for the attaining of an end being limited by that end, whenever that end is manifestly neglected or opposed, the trust must necessarily be forfeited, and the power devolve into the hands of those who gave it.'

Locke's justified rebellion is very mild; it is much more like an angry shareholders' meeting voting no confidence in the board than a real revolt, and his contract is not genuinely original because the state of nature which he posits as preceding society is about as violent as the smoking or sleeping room of a London club.

Locke indeed states that 'man is born free as he is born rational' and he will have nothing to do with the idea that freedom is the right to indulge one's uninhibited will. His theory is really traditional Aristotelian social thought with a dash of contractual individualism. But whatever his

Continued on p. 375

PLATE 14

IMMACULATE CONCEPTION: Birth of the Virgin. Dutch School, 15th century.

ROMANTIC LOVE: *Venus and Adonis*, by Pierre-Paul Prud'hon (1758–1823).

'PHILISTINE': Matthew Arnold (1822–1888), who attacked 'Philistine' taste.

PROPAGANDA: Josef Goebbels (1897–1945).

361

THE RIGHTS OF MAN: From *La Révolution Française*, by J. F. Dayot.

ROMANTICISM: 1. *Adonis, George III's Charger*: Lithograph by James Ward (1769–1859).

ROMANTICISM: 2. *Slate Quarries*, by J. Crome.

3. *Vesuvius in Eruption*, by Samuel Palmer (1805–1881).

365

RELIGION AS THE OPIATE OF THE PEOPLE: the Communist notion: 1. The Tyrolese peasant tells his beads.

2. The peasant woman prays by the relics.

THE SEVEN DEADLY SINS: Detail from a painting by Hieronymus Bosch (c. 1460–1516).

SUPERSTITION: The dog pulls up a mandrake root.

SENTIMENTALITY: I. Gravestone in the Pet Cemetery, Los Angeles.

2. A larger view of the cemetery (note the flowers on the graves).

SENTIMENTALITY: 3. *The Inconsolable Widow*, by Jean-Baptiste Greuze (1725–1805).

4. *The Broken Mirror*, by Greuze.

373

GENEZO

UNUA LIBRO DE MOSEO

---

1 EN la komenco Dio kreis la ĉielon kaj la teron. 2 Kaj la tero estis senforma kaj dezerta, kaj mallumo estis super la abismo; kaj la spirito de Dio ŝvebis super la akvo. 3 Kaj Dio diris: Estu lumo; kaj fariĝis lumo. 4 Kaj Dio vidis la lumon, ke ĝi estas bona; kaj Dio apartigis la lumon de la mallumo. 5 Kaj Dio nomis la lumon Tago, kaj la mallumon Li nomis Nokto. Kaj estis vespero, kaj estis mateno, unu tago.

6 Kaj Dio diris: Estu firmaĵo inter la akvo, kaj ĝi apartigu akvon de akvo. 7 Kaj Dio kreis la firmaĵon, kaj apartigis la akvon, kiu estas sub la firmaĵo, de la akvo, kiu estas super la firmaĵo; kaj fariĝis tiel. 8 Kaj Dio nomis la firmaĵon Ĉielo. Kaj estis vespero, kaj estis mateno, la dua tago.

9 Kaj Dio diris: Kolektiĝu la akvo de sub la ĉielo en unu lokon, kaj aperu la sekaĵo; kaj fariĝis tiel. 10 Kaj Dio nomis la sekaĵon Tero, kaj la kolektiĝojn de la akvo Li nomis Maroj. Kaj Dio vidis, ke ĝi estas bona. 11 Kaj Dio diris: Kreskigu la tero verdaĵon, herbon, kiu naskas semon, fruktarbon, kiu donas laŭ sia speco frukton, kies semo estas en ĝi mem, sur la tero; kaj fariĝis tiel. 12 Kaj la tero elkreskigis verdaĵon, herbon, kiu naskas semon laŭ sia speco, kaj arbon, kiu donas frukton, kies semo estas en ĝi mem laŭ sia speco. Kaj Dio vidis, ke ĝi estas bona. 13 Kaj estis vespero, kaj estis mateno, la tria tago.

14 Kaj Dio diris: Estu lumaĵoj en la ĉiela firmaĵo, por apartigi la tagon de la nokto, kaj ili prezentu signojn, tempojn, tagojn, kaj jarojn; 15 kaj ili estu lumaĵoj en la ĉiela firmaĵo, por lumi super la tero; kaj fariĝis tiel. 16 Kaj Dio faris la du grandajn lumaĵojn: la pli grandan lumaĵon, por regi la tagon, kaj la malpli grandan lumaĵon, por regi la nokton, kaj la stelojn. 17 Kaj Dio starigis ilin sur la ĉiela firmaĵo, por ke ili lumu sur la teron, 18 kaj por ke ili regu la tagon kaj la nokton kaj faru diferencon inter la lumo kaj la mallumo. Kaj Dio vidis, ke ĝi estas bona. 19 Kaj estis vespero, kaj estis mateno, la kvara tago.

20 Kaj Dio diris: La akvo aperigu moviĝantaĵojn, vivajn estaĵojn, kaj birdoj ekflugu super la tero, sub la ĉiela firmaĵo. 21 Kaj Dio kreis la grandajn balenojn, kaj ĉiujn vivajn estaĵojn moviĝantajn, kiujn aperigis la akvo, laŭ ilia speco, kaj ĉiujn flugilhavajn birdojn laŭ ilia speco. Kaj Dio vidis, ke ĝi estas bona. 22 Kaj Dio ilin benis, dirante: Fruktu kaj multiĝu, kaj plenigu la akvon en la maroj, kaj la birdoj multiĝu sur la tero. 23 Kaj estis vespero, kaj estis mateno, la kvina tago.

24 Kaj Dio diris: La tero aperigu vivajn estaĵojn, laŭ ilia speco, brutojn kaj rampaĵojn kaj surterajn bestojn, laŭ ilia speco; kaj fariĝis tiel. 25 Kaj Dio kreis la bestojn de la tero, laŭ ilia speco, kaj la brutojn, laŭ ilia speco, kaj ĉiujn rampaĵojn de la tero, laŭ ilia speco. Kaj Dio vidis, ke ĝi estas bona. 26 Kaj Dio diris: Ni kreu homon laŭ Nia bildo, similan al Ni; kaj ili regu super la fiŝoj de la maro kaj super la birdoj de la ĉielo kaj super la brutoj, kaj super ĉiuj rampaĵoj, kiuj rampas sur la tero. 27 Kaj Dio kreis la homon laŭ Sia bildo, laŭ la bildo de Dio Li kreis lin; en formo de viro kaj virino Li kreis ilin. 28 Kaj Dio benis ilin, kaj Dio diris al ili: Fruktu kaj multiĝu, kaj plenigu la teron kaj submetu ĝin al vi, kaj regu super la

PLATE 15

ART FOR ART'S SAKE: Old Battersea Bridge by J.M.Whistler (1834–1903).

limitations, Locke gave English politicians a working basis for their political thinking which did duty for generations.

It was Thomas Hobbes (1588–1679), the one English political thinker of the stature of Aristotle and Rousseau, who made the most thorough use of the Social Contract, at the same time doing more to kill the idea than any other single man. Hobbes's system is simple enough. He attempts to construct a completely analytical theory of politics – that is, to make politics like geometry, deducible from a few simple and self-evident axioms. Certainly his axioms are basic; 'That when a thing lies still, unless somewhat else stir it, it will lie still for ever, is a truth no man doubts of'. Taken together the axioms give Hobbes's system a deceptive cogency because it is so difficult to find out where it goes wrong. What they add up to is that in the original state of nature, man's life was 'nasty, brutish and short'.

Unlike Locke, Hobbes was unmoved by the myth of the Noble Savage (q.v.); for him unsocial nature is simply horrible. The Contract can be deduced from this state of nature, which is so unpleasant that men *must* combine to end it. Any form of society is better than 'nature', even the worst tyranny, therefore rebellion is never justifiable and is indeed the greatest sin. Thus the Social Contract is turned on its head and used to justify a tyranny more compelling than any theory of the divine right of kings (q.v.).

Hobbes has been more reviled than followed; but the clarity of his thought and the excellence of his style made the Social Contract a much less attractive proposition for later libertarian thinkers. The last great thinker to take the idea as an important one was Jean-Jacques Rousseau (1712–1778), who called his most famous work simply, *Du Contrat Social*. Yet an original contract has no real place in Rousseau's system. For Rousseau, society is based on the general will, which is not created by any contract; and if examined closely is in fact a sophisticated form of natural reason. Rousseau, like Hobbes, insisted on the total surrender of individual liberty to society and the impossibility of contracting-out.

The notion is now quite dead. Our age is too historically minded to accept pseudo-history of

R

the kind demanded by the Social Contract. Yet it did great service to mankind, it pointed out the need for limited authority and limited obligation and it did serve as an intellectual basis for resisting despotism.

Monetary reform

SOCIAL CREDIT is the name given to an experiment in monetary reform, devised by Major C. H. Douglas (1879–1952), and involving the control of credit with the object of adjusting the supply of money to the output of goods.

The first of several books he wrote on the subject, *Economic Democracy*, appeared in 1919, and it was believed to be his experience in costing accountancy during the First World War, when he was sent by the Air Ministry to reorganize production and costing at Farnborough, that first turned his interests to the working of the credit system. Although the movement attracted some supporters, it did not make much headway in Great Britain, though it drew world-wide attention when the party bearing its name won provincial elections in Alberta, in Canada. That party has been in power ever since, but constitutional difficulties prevented the theories of Major Douglas from being put into practice.

His theory was that in spite of a vast actual and potential reservoir of goods for which mankind has a use – a reservoir swollen by the products of new labour-saving machinery – a large part of the population was unable to get at these goods. This industrial output he attributed as much to technological improvement as to labour and management, and he argued from this that the public had a right to the fruits of this production. Of all the money paid out by industry, only a very small percentage ever came into the hands of consumers and was offered in exchange for goods. Not only was all money saved lost to the fund of purchasing power, and also all those items (such as interest and depreciation allowances) that were not paid directly to consumers. This led Douglas to advocate the establishment of some form of national credit control with the power to balance every issue of goods with an equivalent issue of purchasing power. The manufacturer would sell below cost, the difference being made up to him by grants of credit, or the consumer would receive tax-free dividends from the government. This would be accompanied by a drastic reduction in taxation, and would involve the rigid control of the banking system.

The natural objection that this would flood the country with paper money was met with the argument that the credits would not be in respect of goods already existing, but would balance the expense of the intermediary products, which were themselves the basis of industry in the future, and which were included in the price of the existing article. While it is generally agreed by economists that purchasing power may sometimes with advantage be stimulated, the main objection to the system is that there are more natural ways of achieving this. One critic has described it 'as a very roundabout method', arguing that the distribution of money to consumers might cause only a spurt in purchases of current goods and have little perceptible influence on the volume of investment. It is also objected that in the long run all costs normally emerge as personal incomes.

The years of economic instability between the wars was good ground for fostering new remedies. Douglas maintained that tariffs and capital levies and other economic devices of the political parties were a failure. He saw in Socialist plans for public ownership another step on the road to Communism, and he was a firm believer in private enterprise. Support for his campaign came more from the Dominions than from Great Britain. New Zealand and Western Australia had their adherents, and then in 1935 the Social Credit Party that had been formed a few years before by William Aberhart (1878–1943) in Alberta, came to power.

Douglas had been appointed Chief Reconstruction Adviser to this Government, but he remained in England and became increasingly dissatisfied that the fundamental steps of reducing taxation and of creating credit were not taken at once by the new Government. Within a year he had resigned, believing that William Aberhart and his colleagues should have dealt more strongly with the banks. Later, attempts were made to put the scheme into effect; and legal and constitutional objections were successfully raised in the Supreme Court of Canada.

Yet the Social Credit Party continued to flourish in Alberta. They had come to power at a time when the state was heavily in debt and at a time of severe depression. Since then prosperity has returned, thanks in part to good harvests and to new discoveries of oil in 1947. The same party has been returned to power at every election since, but it cannot be said that the plans envisaged by the founder have been carried out. It is true in a sense that Social Credit cannot be said to have failed in Alberta because it has not been tried, but it is equally true that the restoration of sound economic conditions seems to have rendered it superfluous. The greatest value of the scheme so far has been the stimulus it has provided to new economic thought.

Socratic explorations

The **SOCRATIC METHOD** of conducting a discussion or argument is basically the method of question and answer. Whoever is conducting an argument according to this method will pose a series of questions whose purpose is to draw out the opinions of the person interrogated so that they may be submitted to scrutiny. Since the participants speak by turns, the one asking a question and the other answering, the whole conversation will be in the form of a *dialogue* (a word which in Greek means simply a conversation); and the Socratic method is accordingly sometimes called *Socratic dialectic* or just *dialectic* (which in Greek means the art or method of conversation).

The method takes its name from Socrates (469–399 B.C.), the Athenian philosopher who first practised it. As is well known, we possess nothing actually written by Socrates – in this our knowledge of his teaching resembles our knowledge of the teaching of Christ. It is from the writings of his followers Plato (c. 429–347 B.C.) and Xenophon that we learn of his characteristic method of argument. But in order to appreciate its novelty, it is necessary to have some idea of the character and aims of Socrates.

In the first place, Socrates lived in the period when Athens was at her greatest. His contemporaries included, beside Plato, the dramatists Aeschylus (c. 525–456 B.C.), Sophocles (496–406 B.C.) and Euripides (485–c. 406 B.C.), Pheidias (d. 417 B.C.), the sculptor of the Elgin marbles, and the great statesman Pericles (d. 429 B.C.), as well as the historians Herodotus (485–425 B.C.) and Thucydides (c. 460–c. 400 B.C.). For Athens it was an age of expansion and self-confidence: and the city was full of able men in every walk of life, including many who professed to teach the arts of clever reasoning and persuasive speaking to young men on the threshold of public life.

It is probable that Socrates at first interested himself in the speculations of physical philosophers like Heraclitus and Anaxagoras, who sought to discover the underlying causes of natural phenomena. But he found their doctrines mutually contradictory and of no practical application, and so turned his attention to what was to occupy him for the rest of his life – the study of human thought and, above all, human conduct.

Socrates' method of investigating these topics consisted in going about the city of Athens, where life was lived largely out of doors, and engaging one person after another in conversation. He would, for example, buttonhole a well-known general in order to ask him what he meant when he spoke of *courage*, or enquire of a man whom he knew to hold sincere religious beliefs what exactly he meant by *piety*. His reason for doing this, we are told, was that, in reply to a questioner, the priestess of the Delphic oracle had asserted that no man was wiser than Socrates. Convinced of his own ignorance, Socrates set himself to test the truth of this statement by examining the leading men of his day with a view to discovering how wise each really was. Not altogether surprisingly, he found that however skilful or experienced a man might be at his own calling, he would nevertheless be unable to give a satisfactory verbal definition of the key ideas connected with that calling; from which Socrates concluded that he was indeed wiser than all other men, at least to this extent, that they knew nothing, and thought they knew everything, whereas he both knew nothing and realized that he knew nothing.

A Socratic discussion, as represented in the dialogues of Plato, regularly begins with Socrates asking someone for a definition of an abstract idea such as *justice* (as in *The Republic*), *piety*, *democracy* or *government*. The person thus questioned is usually ready with some more or less plausible formula, which he trots out in answer to the question. Socrates will now ask one or two questions about the reply he has received – ostensibly to make sure that he has understood it, actually in order that the speaker may depart to some extent from generalities and commit himself to a definite statement.

As soon as his victim has arrived at a definition which seems to himself to be entirely satisfactory, Socrates proceeds to put to him (in the form of a question) a set of circumstances in which the proposed definition obviously breaks down. (A simple example occurs when Cephalus affirms that *justice* means telling the truth and paying back what one has received. 'But if a friend who had lent us a weapon were subsequently to go mad, would it be acting justly to return it to him in these circumstances – or for that matter to speak only the truth to a man in that state?' asks Socrates. The first book of *The Republic* contains many instances besides this one.)

Accepting this criticism of his first attempt, the speaker will now qualify his original definition – only to be met once again with an example before which the new formulation breaks down. And so the dialogue proceeds, with each new attempt at a definition improving on the previous one, yet in its turn proving unsatisfactory.

It is clear that in real life a man would begin to feel foolish at an early stage of a cross-examination on these lines: but even in the dialogues of Plato, where Socrates is often shown conversing with young men whose aim is to learn to think clearly about the topic under discussion, it is rare for him to arrive at a definition which satisfies him. This is not surprising. It was Socrates, as Aristotle tells us, who first attempted to give definitions of general terms: he was, in fact, the inventor of definition as such. So it is natural that he should have expected his remarkable logical discovery to prove to be the key to all human knowledge. In fact, there is only a limited range of words which are susceptible of concise verbal definition; and abstract words such as beauty, truth and justice, each of which has a whole range of uses of which each single one is subtly different from those nearest to it, are of all words in the language the least suitable for this kind of definition.

Indeed, that this is so is the most striking fact that emerges from the Socratic dialogues; for the further Socrates pushes his exploration of the manifold nuances of meaning which a particular word is capable of, the less likely does it seem that these many aspects of the word's character can be expressed within the narrow confines of a concise verbal definition.

It is as an instrument for *analysing* familiar yet complicated concepts that the Socratic method is of supreme importance and value. It is a central method of working in philosophy, where, as always, to travel hopefully is more important than to arrive.

ILLUSTRATION: Page 175.

The rod

SPARE THE ROD AND SPOIL THE CHILD appears first as 'He that spareth his rod hateth his son' in the thirteenth chapter of *Proverbs* and continues, in numerous variant forms, down the ages. Authority has been least intermittent where children are concerned.

Even the libertarian Milton, defender of free speech and free divorce, and open to all the progressive influences of the Renaissance, is said to have driven his first wife away partly through the violence with which he beat the nephews he was coaching, and the dismal screams which resulted. As a Christian he was well aware of the doctrine of Original Sin (q.v.); in the light of the Fall of Man, children and women were equally suspect as 'weaker vessels', closer to Nature, perhaps, but closer to a Nature which had been flawed by the loss of Eden; and only discipline could correct the frailty of Eve and the 'animal spirits' of her offspring.

Furthermore, a classical scholar could find support in the vigours of Spartan training. According to W. B. Yeats, the great Aristotle himself had 'played the taws Upon the bottom of a king

of kings'. If Milton's idea of education was repressive for theological reasons, more secular periods did not necessarily mean an improvement. At home the child was a little adult, who must be forced to put away childish things, while at school he was flogged because a very few masters were often faced with a near-mutinous gang of hooligans, themselves adept at torturing each other.

In his *Father and Son* (1907) Edmund Gosse tells how he was caned for some trivial misdeed as early as his sixth birthday, with a result very different from the tearful repentance demanded by the Victorian father: 'I have to confess with shame that I went about the house for some days with a murderous hatred of my Father locked within my bosom.' Nevertheless even voices out of the Age of Enlightenment would have justified the action. Dr Johnson commended one of the Headmasters of Westminster School, the redoubtable Dr Busby (1606–1695), for his savage discipline. Busby claimed that his rod was a sieve through which his pupils had to pass. Johnson held that 'Children being not reasonable, can only be governed by fear', and consequently revered his own tutor, Mr Hunter, precisely because of his severity: 'My master whipt me very well. Without that, Sir, I should have done nothing.'

Such views were popular, no matter what philosophy might be in force, long after the Renaissance had introduced the more generous views of a Vittorino da Feltre (1378–1446) or a Colet, long after Rousseau and the English Romantic poets had asserted the natural goodness of the child, watching with delight the reactions of little Hartley Coleridge to a waterfall or a mountain. Although the young Pico della Mirandola learned piety and wisdom unmolested, the young Robert Browning browsed peacefully through his father's library, the young John Stuart Mill performed prodigies of infantile memory for Wisdom's sake alone, the average boy was well beaten, on every possible occasion.

And not only the boy, for the cruel Nathaniel Eaton of Harvard College (1609–1674) is said to have laid about his usher with a 'Walnut-tree plant big enough to have killed a horse'. Gifted men have put on record their unhappy memories of school: John Dryden declared of his seventeenth-century boyhood that he would remember his stern master until his dying day, the poet

Southey was expelled from Westminster in 1792 for contributing an article to the school magazine against the prevalent beatings, while Lord Lawrence (1811–1879), the famous Governor-General of India, remembered that he was flogged every day of his school life except one; on which he was flogged twice. Numerous rebellions occurred as a result of the lack of understanding between masters and pupils. John Keate (1773–1852), who once flogged more than eighty in a day, faced such a mutiny when he was headmaster of Eton. The longest occurred at Harrow, lasted three weeks, and was only subdued by the militia.

And yet, years before, a very different view had been expressed by the sceptical Montaigne (1533–1592) in his twenty-fifth essay. Montaigne believed in a liberal education which would develop an all-round personality, capable of moving easily through the various strata of the social world, appreciative of its delights and inured to its hardships. He argued for a 'sweet-severe mild-nesse' to replace the savagery which 'doth more bastardize and dizzie a wel-borne and gentle nature'.

He was evidently familiar with schools which were no more than 'prisons of captivated youth', where there was nothing to be heard but 'whipping and bawling', the children terrified and the masters perpetually in a rage (like Keate, who believed ill-humour was the only expression a teacher could legitimately wear). How, Montaigne asked, can you expect to attract an immature and timid mind to its book by a frowning countenance and 'handsfull of rods'? Thus he sees his education for life taking place in schoolhouses strewn with flowers rather than with 'bloudy burchen-twigs' ... a charming picture which has come literally true in these days of Nature Study tables and cresses grown in blotting paper.

Despite the reforms of Dr Thomas Arnold (1795–1842) at Rugby, educational theory remained unprogressive throughout the nineteenth century. What really happened was that schools in which the boys, left entirely to themselves for long periods, had organized themselves into robber bands, were changed into formally-organized, games-conscious and pompously ethical little worlds, busily preparing their middle-class inhabitants for the task of ruling a colonial empire.

E. M. Forster's Sawston School was no doubt a less dissolute place than the schools attacked by Locke or by Cowper, but it was essentially philistine. Although Arnold had been little interested in caning, preferring to burden his charges with that intense moral earnestness which did so much to damage their future lives, the rod was not abolished – it was rationalized and integrated into the prefect system. Masters were no longer expected to strike boys in a fit of anger; they must administer punishment in cold blood, as a moral duty. Bullying still existed, but in the bureaucratic context of fag-masters and fags. Only recently have schools begun to look upon the child as an interesting and valuable person in himself, who has every right to be happy during the days of his childhood and who is quite capable of disciplining himself if he is provided with stimulating work.

Even now, despite the success of project-work and co-operative group activities, British disciplinary methods are possessed, at least in the Public and Grammar Schools, by a deep conservatism, in which they lag far behind the United States and much of the Continent. And even though the cane is disappearing from hundreds of Junior and Secondary Modern Schools, the corporal punishment enthusiasts are still active, demanding the re-introduction of the birch for juvenile delinquency.

> In longer letters to *The Times*
> Good men pontificate on crimes
> They were not tempted to commit:
> 'Flogged we were, and proud of it.'

The Zeitgeist

The **SPIRIT OF THE AGE** first appears in the historical philosophy of the German Romantics, Herder and Hamann in the second half of the eighteenth century, in the guise of the 'Zeitgeist'. Hard to define, it is used by them in the sense of an objective spirit working in every facet of life in a particular period of history, producing a similarity of ideas, of style and forms of social life.

Herder, writing soon after the appearance of Kant's revolutionary *Critique of Pure Reason* in 1781, made use of the concept to emphasize the unity of human life, to show that reason and feeling were *not* distinct sources of knowledge, but stages in a single harmonious activity in which the individual shares in the life of the whole community. Herder and his contemporaries, by means of historical and sociological studies, were concerned to overthrow in Germany the dominion of outworn French classical ideas, and they returned to the inspiration of the Middle Ages to lead the Germans back into their own cultural path of development.

Goethe (1749–1832), who in youth was fired by Herder's ideas (which embraced nature, history, philology, customs; art, thought, religion and poetry, imbued with the spirit of humanity and harmony) makes Faust re-define the 'Zeitgeist':

> Was ihr den Geist der Zeiten heisst
> Das ist im Grund der Herren eigner Geist.

– in effect 'What you call the Spirit of the Age is fundamentally the spirit of individual men', and this interpretation has been used by many writers ever since, in seeking to discover the currents of an epoch in the thoughts and activities of great men. Thus, Leonardo da Vinci as the epitome of 'universal man' in the Renaissance, Brunel as the embodied spirit of mechanical invention in the industrial revolution, T. S. Eliot the dry poet characterizing the spiritual deserts of our time.

The expression was first used to grasp the elusive spirit of humanity which had been freed from the medieval hold of the Church and to direct it into new channels of independence. Ernst Moritz Arndt (1769–1860), German poet and political writer used *Geist der Zeit* as the title of his political work, begun in 1802, which contained a violent attack on Napoleon, and a call to the German people to unite. The spirit of the age is used as a weapon in the armoury of freedom.

Heinrich Heine (1797–1856) the poet, himself one of Liberty's most ardent champions, gives an account in *Religion and Philosophy* of the rôle played by the Romantic Philosophers in freeing the Germans from the tyranny of foreign ideas and restoring them to an awareness of their own inheritance, at a time when the French were actually bringing their tyrants to the guillotine. The ferment of thought and action at the turn of the eighteenth century was evidence of the spirit of the age at work, a revolutionary spirit in the development of history.

In England the phrase, keeping some of its revolutionary implications, was used as the title for a gallery of portraits of English poets and philosophers by William Hazlitt in 1828. His *Spirit of the Age* contains critical assessments of Wordsworth, Coleridge, Byron, Bentham, Godwin, etc., seen as it were through the lens of liberty. Wordsworth's genius is described as 'the pure emanation of the Spirit of the Age'. He takes the 'simplest elements of nature and the human mind to compound a new system of poetry', breaking with the past, and beginning anew with the bare board of poetry.

If we examine our own time for traces of the 'spirit of the age', what do we find? Siegfried Giedion, the Swiss scholar, in his *Space, Time and Architecture*, first delivered in the U.S.A. as lectures in 1938–1939, believes that the spirit of our age is hard to characterize owing to the breakdown between thought and feeling in the modern world. This breakdown was caused by the *laissez-faire* attitude of the nineteenth century, and by the enormous advances in science and technology which leave men unable to keep up emotionally with these developments. This has produced a state of unbalance. Giedion compares this state of things to an orchestra with all its instruments ready, but with each instrumentalist separated by a soundproof wall from his fellow players.

Yet the spirit of the age can be more clearly seen in retrospect, when time has allowed for its effects to develop in action or in works of art. Looking back to the early nineteenth century, it is now possible to discern the same spirit at work in poets, in scientists preoccupied with the theory of light, in the light-invaded canvases of Turner, where form is almost dissolved in light reflections (Thomas Young, whose researches into light and colour vision he may have known, wrote in 1801 'a luminiferous Ether pervades the universe, rare and elastic in a high degree', which might do as a text for Turner's later pictures) and eventually in the Crystal Palace, that combination of wood, glass and iron, erected in 1851, in which, according to a contemporary observer, 'All materiality blended into the atmosphere', and evoked 'a new kind of imagination which sprang directly from the spirit of the age'.

Gentlemen v. Players

SPORT AS A CHARACTER-BUILDER is a peculiarly English concept, developed during the ninteenth century. It is quite different from admiration for athletic or sporting prowess, which has been common to most nations at all times. It had a great impact on a few generations, more particularly the powerful middle classes whose sons went to the major English and Scottish public schools. It is now on the wane: sport may be held to be a means of demonstrating national character, but not so much now an ingredient for developing personal character.

Sport meant originally training for war or for the chase: it was severely practical. Because for primitive peoples war and the chase were all-important parts of life, sport was also a part of religion. Even dancing round the maypole had at first a religious significance, and the earliest football – a dangerous mêlée between contiguous villages – represented a substitute for what had earlier been tribal warfare. Gradually hunting ceased to be mainly for food, and physical perfection no longer had a necessary outlet in war. What had been functional became merely a social attribute and, later, an industry.

The English idea derived particularly, however, from a special interpretation of the Greek attitude towards sport, and especially athletics. The Greeks saw the exercising of the human body as an important part of the integrated life – the ideal expressed by their Roman successors as 'mens sana in corpore sano'. To be athletic was part of the duty of a good man, and so an expression of character. As early as the sixth century B.C. the Greeks were perfecting sculpture to illustrate the ideal body – the proportioned figure of the young athlete. Male Athenians exercised naked in public, and in Sparta the women did the same.

All this natural manifestation of the Greek spirit was not consciously connected with amusement or health, but an outflow of natural energy and the love of life. A good carriage, well-turned limbs and physical courage were the attributes of the good man, a complement to self-control and intelligence. Gymnastics were for the body, and music for the soul. The emphasis of physical training was on military drill, competitive team games and athletic sports. Participation was all-important, not observation, and style, not results. Once at least every day a young man would go to the gymnasium strip, oil, sprinkle dust upon himself and scrape it off with a strigil. Then he would exercise, bath and re-oil his body. He was dedicated to grace and rhythm. An awkward athlete would be hissed like a bad actor, and exercises were often performed to the sound of the lute.

The climax of the Olympic Games saw a pilgrimage from all over the Greek world, and for the winners there was the highest prize in their civilization – a crown of leaves. It was an amateur sport, and the specialist was deplored, with the Pentathlon – a five-fold contest exercising all parts of the body – the supreme event. There must be moderation in all things, and just as no part of the body should be developed at the expense of the rest, so the body itself must not be developed at the cost of mind or spirit. Socrates deplored runners with over-developed legs and boxers with over-muscled torsos.

Inevitably the Greek ideal concept of sport became muddied in practice. Specialization and professionalism appeared early. There was 'pot-hunting': national and other sectional interests became more important than the gracious expression of physical perfection. The games themselves fell into disrepute. The Romans vulgarized sport, and as the classical world declined, sport had all the vices, and worse, that critics find in professional sport today.

The ideal was, however, recognized and respected by those who sought to find the best habit of life for boys (first, and later for girls) in nineteenth-century England. Dr Arnold of Rugby (1795–1842) founded a system which was to combine Christianity and knowledge, extending the idea of the 'scholar and gentleman' to the new middle classes. But there were no compulsory games in the Rugby he created. Boys still came mainly from the country, and accepted field sports as a normal part of their background. Sport still meant poaching for the pot to the agricultural labourer, and was part of the uncontroversial habit of life of the upper classes.

By the end of the nineteenth century this had changed, and compulsory games were the rule in most 'good' schools. It was felt that 'playing for the side' in a team-game, and doing so with unselfishness, was an important part of the discipline of life. Boxing, which had been the rowdy if vigorous pursuit of Regency rakehells and mobsters, became 'the noble art of self-defence'. It was pointed out again that self-control was all-important, and that style was better than brawn. 'Professional' as an adjective in sport was felt, as it had been in the high days of Greek culture, to be the ultimate and damning criticism (cf. all that remains implicit in the annual cricket match of *Gentleman v. Players*).

As had happened in Greece, the idea became debased. Boys played not for the side but to get into the side. Professional sport was increasing and becoming an industry and a vast social phenomenon. Amateurism, which had been regarded as essential for true sport, became tinged with compromise ('expenses' were paid), and finally was regarded as something vaguely patronizing. Sport became international, and other standards than English ones, and still less Greek ones, prevailed. Results, and so specialization, became more important than style.

The conception of sport as a character-builder was sometimes priggish. It was often forced too far, and was clearly a handicap to the boy who was physically clumsy. Yet the basic concepts, of playing for a team and not for oneself, of balanced self-control and regard for style rather than for results, were a permanent and perhaps a very valuable ingredient in the British character. Rebels built their characters in other ways; but for a few generations the blend of Greek idealism and eighteenth-century heartiness had a powerful influence on English people, and the world in which Britain was then the most powerful nation.

ILLUSTRATION: Pages 410 and 411.

How do you live?

STANDARD OF LIVING is a phrase used synoptically to describe how people live, and especially to indicate whether their lives are, in a material sense, rich or poor.

Thus the standard of living of the people of Great Britain is said to be high because over many centuries they have so increased their wealth and so distributed it amongst themselves that their lives today are in general much safer, easier and more comfortable than the lives of most of mankind.

By contrast, the standard of living of the people of India is said to be low, because so little wealth (in proportion to the population) has been created in that country and distributed among its inhabitants that the lives of most of them remain 'poor, nasty, brutish and short'. 'Standard of living', as the phrase is commonly used, does not comprehend the spiritual, emotional or intellectual content of people's lives: it is an economist's term, and is usually confined, quite properly, to the things that are an economist's business.

Many more or less technical terms of economics circulate in the discussion of public affairs today. Among them, in a democracy, 'standard of living' must be one of the most highly charged with political potency, for where politicians depend for power on the freely cast votes of the masses, the standard of living of the masses must become (except in moments of acute external danger) the chief issue of politics, and whatever touches that issue, or can be made to touch it, is potentially a very powerful political weapon. Thus in Great Britain today both great parties must hope for office only as they are thought to show zeal for improving – or at least maintaining – the economic welfare of the working classes; and matters are the stuff of politics today which seventy years ago (before the general grant of manhood suffrage) would scarcely have entered a statesman's head, and which, if they had done so, would certainly not have seemed to him proper or even possible subjects for government action. 'Standard of living', indeed, by its acceptance as a catchword of party controversy, symbolizes the penetration of politics by economics which has accompanied the spread of democracy in Great Britain.

Nor is standard of living an idea of power only in domestic politics, whether of Great Britain or of any other country. Among the many emotions that go to make up Asian and African anti-colonial nationalism, discontent with a standard of living much lower than that of the former colonizing peoples is not the weakest. It is the explanation, in part at least, of economic policies set on foot by newly independent nations (and by some others, too) which, by interfering with traditional patterns of trade and encouraging the development of manufacturing industry at the expense of primary production, influence and sometimes embitter international relations.

Moreover, the concern of the white man to preserve his standard of living, and the opposed determination of the black man to improve his, do more perhaps than anything else to screw up the tensions of the present conflict in Africa.

As the idea of a standard of living is playing its part in a struggle almost over (the assault on Asian empires) and in a struggle scarcely begun (between the races in Africa), so also it is at work in the struggle that principally torments the world today – between Communism and the liberal states of the West. Communism has generally been most successful where standards of living are low, and it is most fiercely repudiated in the United States, where 'the American way of life' has among its principal ingredients the highest standard of living in the world. The defence of existing high standards and the raising of low ones are therefore recognized as cardinal principles of the strategy of 'cold war' (q.v.): hence the fabulous outpouring of American wealth in foreign aid and the concern of both America and Great Britain for the welfare of 'under-developed countries', as expressed most authoritatively in 'Point Four' and the Colombo Plan.

Unfortunately for the practical politician, standard of living, like many other ideas that inspire and divide nations, is no more than an airy generalization. For purposes of action – for legislation, say, or for negotiating wages – it needs to be defined. But efforts at definition lead only too often to barren argument – about spending power, perhaps, or about calory-intake, or about the number of motor vehicles per head of the population. Or they can produce equally barren quasi-metaphysical disputes on the difference between a luxury and a necessity – which is tobacco, which is lipstick, which is a holiday? Even if a definition can be devised which will serve at a particular moment of time, it is almost immediately pushed into obsolescence by the progress of economic change, as the history of the British Index of Retail Prices demonstrates.

Also the effort to raise or maintain a country's standards by the grant of aid from outside may generate as much jealousy as gratitude, and any attempt to apply the standards of one country to the tastes of another is liable to be no less prolific of misunderstanding: the truth of both these observations is attested by American experience in Europe since the Second World War. So the difficulties which the idea of a standard of living raise for the politician are at least as great as the opportunities for rewarding action which it suggests.

The interior monologue

The **STREAM OF CONSCIOUSNESS** or internal monologue is a device by which the novelist attempts to get inside his characters' heads in order to represent, with more or less realism, the rapid, various and seemingly inconsequential flow of ideas and feelings.

James Joyce (1882–1941) is the acknowledged master of this technique, and it was only after the success of *Ulysses* that renewed interest was shown in its originator, Edouard Dujardin, whose *Les lauriers sont coupés* was first published in 1887. Dujardin was called upon for a definition of what he had tried to do years before in his story of a young man taking an actress out to dinner – significantly described by Remy de Gourmont as 'a transposed anticipation of the cinema' – and he explained that 'the internal monologue, in its nature on the order of poetry, is that unheard and unspoken speech by which a character expresses his inmost thoughts ... lying nearest the unconscious ... without regard to logical organization ...'

Critics were not slow to point out that this was

scarcely as revolutionary as had first appeared. The Elizabethan soliloquy was one example. Not only is Hamlet able to acquaint the audience with his uncertainty on the question of suicide, but in other plays, where a less intellectual hero is involved, the poetry leaps illogically from one idea to another and compresses attitudes into metaphors and symbols. When Macbeth sees 'pity as a naked new-born babe', he is taking such a leap and unconsciously revealing his moral imagination through his use of apocalyptic material. The same thing is true of dramatic poetry from Browning's *My Last Duchess* to T. S. Eliot's *Gerontion*. André Gide has found similar instances in Dostoyevsky's *House of the Dead*; Wyndham Lewis has pointed out Mr Jingle in *Pickwick Papers*; while Mr Harry Levin offers the following example from the diary of Fanny Burney: 'Well; I am going to bed – Sweet dreams attend me – and may you sympathize with me. Heigh ho! I wonder when I shall return to London – Not that we are very dull here ...' and so on.

However, the relevance of stream of consciousness to the problem of the novel, and indeed to the modern crisis which the novel reflects, goes deeper than these ancestors. Stream of consciousness has been a weapon with which the isolated and self-conscious artist, concerned since Flaubert with form and style, has attempted to find a more personal meaning to life than was provided by the naturalists, without altogether sacrificing a scientific objectivity. The sociology of Zola became the psychology of the novelist Virginia Woolf (1882–1941), and a materialistic concept of environment and heredity was succeeded by a vitalist conception of the individual existing in a state of flux. The 'slice of life' thus surrendered to a 'luminous halo'.

The point was made by Virginia Woolf in her criticism of the realism of Bennett, Wells and Galsworthy: feeling that the 'essential thing' had slipped away in novels devoted to exterior appearance, and that what matters is the 'myriad impressions – trivial, fantastic, evanescent' which the mind receives in an 'incessant shower of innumerable atoms', she turned from life as a 'series of giglamps symmetrically arranged' to the' semitransparent envelope' around consciousness. This connects with E. M. Forster's belief that the 'tapeworm of Time' is less important than some essential reality close to music, and has its bearing on Marcel Proust's pages of artistic reverie, with Walter Pater's hard gem-like flame glowing somewhere in the background. Lacking both a generally accepted pattern of belief and a secure status in society, Joyce and Mrs Woolf drew upon the *montage* of the cinema, impressionism in painting, Wagnerian *leit-motif* and the discoveries of psycho-analysis, to grapple with the problem of Time and existence itself, since lesser more secular considerations (of politics, class relations, science and war) were relatively uninteresting.

Thus Maynard Keynes, friend of Woolf and Forster, declared 'nothing mattered except states of mind, our own and other people's, of course, but chiefly our own. These ... were not associated with action or with achievement or with consequences.'

Such states of mind were explored in 'silence, exile and cunning' by Joyce and in upper-middle-class Bloomsbury by Virginia Woolf, who was something of a disciple. However, there are vast differences between their two methods. Joyce has by far the richer apparatus. The two chief protagonists of *Ulysses* are very different people (as compared with, say, Mrs Dalloway and Septimus Warren Smith), and Joyce is able to show them thinking and feeling in very different ways, while it has often been said of Virginia Woolf that her own highly cultured sensibility engulfs her characters, almost all of whom are from the same class anyway. Bloom's earthiness (the kidneys he devours for breakfast, the girls he meets on the beach) can thus be contrasted with the Hamlet-obsessed intellectualism of Stephen far more vividly than Virginia Woolf's differentiation of characters in her novel *The Waves*.

Also Joyce's interior monologue is much freer, much more realistically staccato, and is capable, like the verse of the Jacobean dramatists, of drawing in an immense range of meanings and associations, many of which are derived from his habit of showing language raw in the mind, without syntax, but rife with sound linkages and puns.

Virginia Woolf is a gentler monologist, helping the reader out with such phrases as 'She thought' and 'One remembered', emphasizing relatively few themes and building up a consciously beautiful 'poetic' atmosphere, whose glitter is nevertheless full of danger as each ecstatic impressionistic wave is sucked back into the trough of non-existence. But what is perhaps most significant is that both Virginia Woolf and Joyce were not satisfied with the stream of consciousness alone; they experimented restlessly with the resources of language, literary illusion, more formal patternings; and both (Joyce to an alarming, if not pedantic degree) relied on a substructure of symbols.

This practice has been followed by their successors; and it seems that the deployment of brilliantly observed fragments and atoms still demands a deeper coherence, that the autonomous creator is not quite satisfied with his art alone, and that the ultimate direction of the stream of consciousness is bound up with the moral dilemma of the individual.

Storm and stress

STURM UND DRANG, meaning storm and stress, derives from a play by a young German dramatist F. M. Klinger (1752–1831), or rather from the name of his play *Wirrwarr; oder Sturm und Drang* (1776).

It was applied to the generation of writers to which Klinger belonged and it well describes their hectic dramas and unbalanced lives. Up to the seventeen-seventies Germany had been deeply under the influence of the Age of Reason (*die Aufklärung*) and what German writing there was followed French fashions. But a reaction was beginning; the philosopher J. G. Hamann thundered against the prevailing rationalism; the theologian and literary critic J. G. von Herder explored the ballads and popular poetry of many countries and translated them into German, thus laying the foundations for a new style of German writing, and from France itself came the voice of Rousseau proclaiming the superiority of the feelings over the intellect.

The writing of these young men is largely unread today. The most brilliant of them, J. M. R. Lenz, ended his days in a lunatic asylum; an-other, G. A. Bürger, is remembered for one ballad only, *Lenore*, which was inspired by our own Border Ballads and had the distinction of being translated both by Walter Scott and D. G. Rossetti. But for a while both the great German writers of that epoch were members of the group. Schiller's first great dramatic success *Die Raüber* (1781) is a play in the *Sturm und Drang* vein, so is Goethe's *Götz von Berlichingen* (1773). Schiller, however, submitted himself to the discipline of serious study, and Goethe, by a supreme effort, overcame his own violent emotionalism and found a middle course between this fervid Romanticism and the formal classicism of the poetry he had written before he met this movement.

It is chiefly for its impact on Goethe that *Sturm und Drang* now seems important. As a student at Strassburg he met Herder, was introduced by him to Shakespeare and other English writers, came to admire Gothic architecture, came to write lyrical poetry of true feeling, and embarked upon a love affair with the country pastor's daughter Friederike, which he violently broke off for no clear reason. The Strassburg days were the climax of his association with the *Sturm und Drang* group. 'With that decision to grant my personality its inner and peculiar freedom,' he wrote, many years later in his autobiography, when looking back on the year after he left Strassburg and Friederike, 'I drifted into the queer condition in which "Werther" was thought out and written'.

'Wertherism', the psychological malady of the next decade, was the logical outcome of *Sturm und Drang*, with its encouragement of the unbridled feelings. Goethe took a legal post in the town of Wetzlar and there fell in love with a simple young lady called Charlotte Buff, who was already engaged to an acquaintance of his. It was a position which permitted neither advance nor retreat; in his 'peculiar condition', Goethe luxuriated in his sentimental feelings, and was on the point of 'letting outward circumstances take their course', when suddenly he felt once again impelled to make a sudden and theatrical departure. After returning home to Frankfurt, he was beginning yet another affair when the news reached him of the suicide of an acquaintance, the outcome of an unhappy love affair.

Goethe was recalled to his senses, and in four weeks wrote the novel which revealed the weakness of himself and all his generation.

Werther (1774) tells the tale of his love for Charlotte Buff, but instead of ending with its hero's precipitate departure it leads to the suicide of the man whom Goethe had put in his place. Thus at the outset of the Romantic Age, this young man of twenty-five had both expressed its violence and uttered a warning of its dangers. If his friend Lenz, 'a shooting-star over the literary horizon', as he called him, could have taken that sermon to heart, he might not have burnt out in madness, and Germany would have had another major poet. But the lesson of *Werther* was lost on that generation, and the book was actually blamed for the wave of romantic suicides in the next years.

Both *Sturm und Drang* and *Wertherism* seem to have responded to something in the German spirit. For in the Romantic era that followed the age of Goethe both the violence of the former and the sentimentality of the latter broke out again. The plays of Heinrich von Kleist (1777–1811), a far better dramatist than any of Lenz's generation, are full of storm and stress, while the disorderly work of Georg Büchner – now chiefly known for his play *Wozzeck* (1879), on which Alban Berg wrote his opera – seems to be the product of both tendencies. Again, after the First World War, the movement in the theatre known as Expressionism whose leaders were Georg Kaiser, Ernst Toller, and Franz Werfel, reverted to the same pattern.

Both *Sturm und Drang* and *Wertherism* are in essence anti-rational movements, which seek to justify emotional violence and call it poetry. In the first case the violence is directed outwards, and the writing is aggressive, sometimes nationalistic, and usually shrill; in the second it takes the form of self-pity, or sentimental pity for its characters. At its worst, in the case of the late nineteenth century dramatist Franz Wedekind (1864–1918) it is preoccupied with suicide and morbid sexuality. Against it stands the supreme sanity of Goethe, who saw through it and warned the world of its dangers almost before it had begun to take a hold.

ILLUSTRATION: Pages 412, 413, 414 and 415.

'I teach you the Superman'

The **SUPERMAN** is an ideal fashioned by the philosopher Friedrich Nietzsche (1844–1900).

Nietzsche went beyond Carlyle in seeking heroic virtue. He was insufficiently impressed by any living or past great man to find in them, as Carlyle found in Cromwell and Frederick the Great, fit candidates for idealization. 'Naked have I seen both of them, the greatest and the smallest man: all-too-similar are they still to each other. Verily even the greatest found I all-too-human!' (*Thus Spake Zarathustra*, 1885). From 1873, Nietzsche's most important work was devoted to his ideal of a coming humanity. 'I teach you the Superman. Man is something that is to be surpassed ... What is the ape to man? A laughing stock, a thing of shame. And likewise shall man be to the Superman ... Let your will say: the Superman shall be the meaning of the earth.' (*Thus Spake Zarathustra*.)

Nietzsche set himself the task of 'rearing the Superman'. For him this meant the destruction of all values that prevented man from surpassing himself. In particular Nietzsche attacked Christ's teaching, which was fit, he believed, only for slaves; and he set up against it a 'master-morality' for those men who were by nature noble, courageous, strong, proud and of 'great healthiness'. The leading principle of his new system of valuing was: 'All that proceeds from power is good, all that springs from weakness is bad.'

Nietzsche's teaching, and especially his masterpiece *Thus Spake Zarathustra*, was addressed to the so-called 'higher men' – that is to say, to those most filled with disgust for the degenerate nineteenth century, which, according to Nietzsche, had finally let loose all the slavish Christian virtues. 'Ye higher men, learn this from me: on the market-place no one believeth in higher men. The populace blinketh: "We are all equal".' The Superman was to spring from the antithesis of the botched modern social man whom Nietzsche despised. 'Whatever is of the effeminate type, whatever originateth from the servile type, and especially the populace-mishmash: – *that* wisheth now to be master of all human destiny – O disgust! Disgust! Disgust! These masters of today – surpass them, o my brethren – these petty people: *they* are the Superman's greatest danger!' Nietzsche's contempt for the mean and weak arose, he said, out of his love for the ideal of the Superman.

Much of *Thus Spake Zarathustra* is written in answer to an imagined cry of distress from the 'higher men'. Nietzsche loved, but refused to pity, those 'higher men', who had failed in an age at variance with them. Such failure, he held, was far nobler than the mean success of the complacent, virtuous little people who wished only to maintain themselves 'best, longest, most pleasantly'. 'What is great in man is that he is a bridge and not a goal: what is lovable in man is that he is an over-going and a down-going ... the higher the type, always the seldomer doth a thing succeed. Ye higher men, ye steps to the Superman, have ye not all as yet been failures? Be of good cheer; what doth it matter? How much is still possible! Learn to laugh at yourselves, as ye ought to laugh! What wonder even that you have failed and only half-succeeded, ye half-shattered ones. Doth not man's *future* strive and struggle in you? Man's furthest, profoundest, star-highest issues, his prodigious powers – do not all these foam through one another in your vessel?'

Nietzsche foresaw the dangers threatening the twentieth century, and he welcomed the coming wars and revolutions as a means for the masculinization of the world. ' "Man is evil" – so said to me for consolation, all the wisest ones. Ah, if only it be still true today! For the evil is man's best force.' By evil Nietzsche meant all that is accounted evil in the 'slave-morality', namely in particular pride and power. 'Man must become better and eviler – so do *I* teach. The evilest is necessary for the Superman's best. It may have been well for the preacher of the petty people to suffer and be burdened by man's sin. I, however, rejoice in great sin as my great consolation. Such things, however, are not said for long ears. Every word, also, is not suited for every mouth. These are fine, far-away things: at them sheep's claws shall not grasp!'

The gospel of the Superman met with silence, then contempt and finally with rejection. Nietzsche was rejected in Germany, branded as a madman, infidel and corrupter of morals. The conservatives condemned him as a revolutionary, and the socialists detested his aristocratic contempt for the mob. Nietzsche died in 1900 in utter obscurity, having been first, according to his sister, made mad by isolation and loneliness. During the First World War Nietzsche became widely known and infamous owing to the activities of the Allies' war propaganda. His name, variously mispronounced, was bandied about by a patriotic populace, and the ideal of the Superman became a symbol for all that was most vile in the 'Hunnish' spirit.

Hitler did not mention Nietzsche in *Mein Kampf*, but the internal organization of the Nazi Party was based upon the Führerprinzip, a doctrine elaborated by the intellectuals of the party, such as Rosenberg, in whose *Der Mythus des 20 Jahrhunderts* (1930) are to be found distortions of Nietzsche's teaching.

The gospel of the Superman was allied with the spirit of militarism and the worship of force. When Nietzsche talked of getting 'beyond good and evil', he wanted to lay the foundation of what he conceived as a higher kind of good. It is none the less true that at the level of actual experience Nietzsche's 'beyond' tends to become a 'beneath'; and the way up, in practice, a way down.

Yet it should not be forgotten that all Nietzsche's teaching was activated by a love of what he found noble and hopeful in man. 'Out of love alone', he says, 'shall my contempt and my warning bird take wing; but not out of the swamp!' And Nietzsche makes Zarathustra say to the 'ape of Zarathustra': ' "This precept, however, I give unto thee in parting, thou foaming fool: Where one can no longer love, there should one – pass by!" ' (See also *Herrenvolk, Hero-Worship*.)

ILLUSTRATION: **Page 445.**

'Cowardice about the supernatural'

SUPERSTITION comprehends a whole catalogue of mental attitudes and behaviour. 'It is difficult to mark the limits of superstition', wrote Voltaire in his *Philosophical Dictionary;* even so, it is a disposition to see an occult hand in events and propitiate that occult power.

Historically, there has been a constant battle between old superstitious beliefs and practices and new interpretations of natural phenomena based on scientific observation, producing revolutionary effects, *e.g.* Copernicus's proof that the world was a revolving globe and Darwin's evolutionary theory. Superstition has come more and more to mean irrationalism, as the scientific approach to life has gained ground.

Theophrastus (370–287 B.C.) in his *Characters* attempted a definition: 'Superstition seems to be simply cowardice about the supernatural ...'

The superstitious man is one who will wash his hands at the fountain, sprinkle himself at the temple font, put a bit of laurel leaf into his mouth and go about for the day. If a weasel run across his path, he will not pursue his walk until someone else has traversed the road, or until he has thrown three stones across it. When he sees a serpent in his house, if it be a red snake, he will invoke Sabazius; if the sacred snake, he will straightway place a shrine on the spot. He will pour oil from his flask on the smooth stones at the crossroads as he goes by, and will fall on his knees and worship them before he depart. He will not tread upon a tombstone or come near a dead body or a woman defiled by childbirth, saying that it is expedient for him not to be polluted. Also on the fourth and seventh days of each month he will order his servants to mull wine, and will go out and buy myrtle wreaths, frankincense, convolvulus.

Both Greeks and Romans manifested this 'cowardice about the supernatural', founding their public and private enterprises upon auguries and prognostics calculated from the anatomy of beasts at sacrifices, the scraping of poultry and the flight of birds. The Greek word for superstition, *deisidaimonia*, meant fear of the deity; it was not necessarily a word of contempt, for it could mean the same as our 'God-fearing'. The Latin word *superstitio* has, more or less, the meaning of the English word; the word is said to come from *super*, above, and *sto*, stand, expressing the feeling of having some being standing over us. It is probably a fanciful etymology. The Romans, though more superstitious than the Greeks, were not completely credulous. Cicero went to the trouble of writing his *de Fato* and *de Divinatione* to see if there was anything rational in superstitions.

Christianity is supposed to have swept away the superstitions adhering to the pantheistic view of life, but in fact it took many of them over, transforming them and overlaying them with Christian meaning, while developing its own. The Middle Ages are regarded as a period when superstition ruled men's minds. The Church enforced her doctrines by terrifying means. Minds innocent of the written word were more open to visual suggestion and mental images, and the Church revealed not only the heavenly aspect of Divine Grace but the hideous promises of Hell, in 'doom' paintings, for example. Medieval man lived in fear of the Judgement Day, the Devil, Hell, the 'everlasting bonfire'. This can well be envisaged by comparing the spirit of blessed peace and innocence which informs the mosaics of the churches in Ravenna, one of the earliest cradles of Christian religion and art, with the much later Byzantine frescoes in the little churches of Moldavia at the foot of the Carpathian Mountains, which contain the most appalling factual details of the machinery of Hell; and mark a change of emphasis from the contemplation of the Divine Compassion to the exploitations of human fears as a deterrent against sin.

Superstition throve in the dawn of the Renaissance in Italy, and in fact gained in strength from the revival of ancient Greek and Roman literature. At this time the belief in an after-life began to waver, and many people found support in the prophecies and calculations of events made by astrologers, who were attached to the courts of ruling princes. The practice of magic and necromancy was much in vogue. Benvenuto Cellini (1500–1571), in his *Life*, describes a fantastic night spent in the Colosseum at Rome, an ordeal by magic, which, even though magnified by exaggeration and boasting, does show the susceptibility to occult influences then ruling.

But if there is any doubt about this, Shakespeare can bear witness in a thousand passages to the wellspring of superstition in the Elizabethan mind. In *Venus and Adonis*:

Look how the world's poor people are amazed
At apparitions, signs, and prodigies,
Whereon with fearful eyes they long have gazed
Infusing them with dreadful prophecies.

Shakespeare uses the superstitious idiom because he knows that it will awake a sympathetic echo in his audience, and make the flesh creep. In places, he actively chides the superstitious for their folly, as in the passage in *King John* (Act III, Sc. 4):

No natural exhalation in the sky,
No scope of nature, no distemper'd day,
No common wind, no customed event,
But they will pluck away his natural cause,
And call them meteors, prodigies, and signs,
Abortives, presages, and tongues of heaven,

which is Theophrastus over again.

In 1608 the Puritan Bishop Hall (1574–1656), perhaps in imitation of Theophrastus, published his *Characters of Vices and Vertues*, in which he describes the superstitious man: 'Old wives and starres are his counsellors, his night spell is his guard, and charms his physicians. He wears paracelsian characters for the tooth ache; and a little hollowed wax is his antidote for all evils.'

The *Spectator* in 1710 gives an exact account of a very ridiculous and superstitious lady, concerned for 'the stranger in the candle', 'a dream portending misfortune', the disaster of the spilt salt, the crossed knife and fork, etc., etc. Addison, in another passage in the *Spectator*, reflects upon the causes of the decline in superstition, and attributes it to 'enlightenment by learning and philosophy'.

Voltaire did not hold such an optimistic view of its decline, since he associated superstition with brands of religion. He says in his article on the subject in the *Dictionnaire Philosophique*: 'Today [in the seventeen-fifties] one half of Europe thinks that the other half has long been and still is superstitious. The Protestants regard the relics, the indulgences, the mortifications, the prayers for the dead, the holy water, and almost all the rites of the Roman church as a superstitious dementia ...' He comes finally to the conclusion that the fundamentals of one sect of Christians are considered superstitions by the rest, and that superstition and fanaticism go hand in hand.

We still obey old superstitions – throwing spilt salt over the shoulder, not walking under ladders, etc., and we still invent new ones, for instance in the Royal Air Force, where danger and the unfamiliar element of the air produced a new range of superstitions and propitiatory behaviour – notably the half-serious belief in gremlins. This may well apply to other dangerous occupations, cave-exploring, submarine navigation, and so on.

ILLUSTRATION: Page 369.

T

Matters of taste

TASTE or **GOOD TASTE** among human beings arises because their social life is intrinsically founded upon mutual respect for conventions. It is thus impossible to imagine any group in an organized social existence whose members do not have occasions to pass judgements about each other and about their standards which are, in fact, judgements of taste. Even men with a romantic quest for freedom from what they regard as the artificial restraints of civilization, who flee from such society, find it difficult, if not impossible, to abandon all its standards. This is so because these standards have been built into the deepest layers of their personalities.

Standards then are rooted in the very structure of human behaviour, and judgements of taste, with respect to these standards, are social. However, these standards concern the decencies on one hand and the proprieties on the other which not merely can be confused with each other but very often conflict.

The decencies refer to the sentiments that a person expresses in his treatment of another – whether, for example, he is kind, cruel, generous, selfish. The proprieties, on the other hand, are much more concerned with conformity to specified forms of behaviour. In part they overlap with the decencies – that is, are intrinsically matters of morals. Such, for example, would be the case with the simple courtesies like acknowledging thanks, for which standardized social patterns exist in most societies. A person who fails to thank another to whom thanks are due commits a mistake which is a reflection, not upon his knowledge, but upon his character. Of course, the more intensely the relations between human beings are regulated by conventions and rituals – imperial China is a classic example – the more do the decencies become intertwined with the proprieties. In China, an immoral person was one who did not respect the ceremonial etiquette, particularly when it was concerned with filial piety.

But the proprieties are also concerned with things that are purely conventional and intrinsically have very little to do with morals at all. Such, for example, would be the intricacies of table manners. Is a person any the less good because he doesn't know which fork to use? Further away yet from morals are those standards concerned purely with aesthetic tastes.

Certainly the existence of both the decencies and the proprieties presupposes some degree of stable social organization of a group whose members have a minimum of psychological security. Where men are reduced to a brute struggle for survival, they are not inclined to respect anything except, perhaps, superior force. The 'artificial' aspect of the proprieties in particular presupposes a considerable distance from the pressure of the struggle for existence. Peasant and primitive societies have conceptions of 'good form' and have elaborate ceremonies, even more ritualized than civilized ones.

But when one thinks of the most characteristic things with which these rules and rituals are concerned, they are of two kinds. First come the simple decencies that are expected of all who partake of the solidarity of the village, such as hospitality and helping neighbours in times of trouble. Second come those rituals in which man seeks to bring himself into harmony with nature, particularly the mysteries of its cyclical changes, such as in the rites of spring and harvest festivals. Here, too, belong those great biological changes in men themselves – birth, puberty and death – which are the occasions of ceremonial celebration.

Primitive societies are too traditionalized for a conscious preoccupation with 'good taste'. Where the standards by which men act are so stereotyped by tradition that they are regarded as sacred, men cannot, as it were, get outside these standards. Art under these conditions is not typically pursued for its own sake or evaluated by purely artistic criteria, but remains an instrument of religion and magic. This is not to say that very beautiful things cannot be produced in these circumstances; but only that they are not likely to foster reflection about the standards of judgement. In order for this to happen, they must be de-sanctified.

For all these reasons the home of the most intense preoccupation with taste and fashion is the urban community and was until the nineteenth century to be found particularly intensified in the Court. Here, in the first instance, is a leisure class whose members are part of a self-enclosed world which has and makes its own rules.

For the most part these rules of Courts had nothing to do with nature at all. The Court in France during the *ancien régime* periodically moved from Versailles to Fontainebleau for no other reason than the fact that it was 'done'. So intricate and elaborate was the etiquette of Versailles that Louis XV, before bringing Madame Pompadour to live at Court, thought it prudent for her to have a period of instruction with one of the experienced courtiers. Without a knowledge of the etiquette, to which the king himself was bound, she would have been ridiculed.

With their leisure courtiers are likely to develop a sensitivity to beauty; with their wealth they are in a position to become patrons of individual artists. Where they are cut off from the rest of the society, as they were at Versailles, and dedicated to a life of pleasure, they are in a social situation in which to view their behaviour itself as a 'work of art'. They develop a style in which all their tastes, sensibilities and standards are fused into a pattern. It is not necessarily a pattern with internal *logical* consistency. For instance, there is no logical reason why those who hunt have to have hunt balls. They are simply 'done' as part of a round of activities.

Some of the problems involved in the analysis of taste can be seen more clearly in the relations between established social élites and the newly rich. From the viewpoint of the élite they are distinguished from the typical *parvenu* by their family background and their superior standards for treating other persons – in other words, the decencies. They may feel that they treat social inferiors with more respect than the newly rich do. In their view, the newly-rich are generally contemptuous of the poor and obsequious towards the great.

But there is also the belief in the superior propriety of their patterns of consumption – that they 'know' how to spend their money. To the established, the typical *parvenu* is ostentatious, anxious to show his possession of luxuries. In this image one of the *parvenu's* most characteristic violations of the canons of good taste is thus 'overdressing' – wearing luxuries in situations where they are inappropriate. The image is thus a criticism not merely of what he does but of what his motives for doing this are – what kind of a man he is in a moral sense. So basically it asserts that there is a disproportion between the status which the *parvenu* claims and that which he is entitled to by virtue of his inner qualities.

This image is in part correct, but there is something of fundamental importance missing from it: the perception that individuals who are rising in the social scale are engaged in a quest for the 'right' style of life. If they are anxious to show anything, it is not merely that they have certain possessions but that they have the 'right' tastes in having the 'right' possessions as contrasted with the 'wrong' ones. This results in an excessive preoccupation with having 'good taste'; where their family background does not have high prestige, the importance of taste itself as an index of their qualities rises.

It is perhaps for this reason that in urban communities the individual who can set fashions has such an important part to play; for it is he who decides what is in good taste for people who have very little confidence in their own standards of judgement. At the extreme is the individual who has no aesthetic sense at all (at least to begin with) and who places himself completely in the hands of a guide. The art dealer plays such a rôle. His client may have no other standard than that if a thing is expensive (that is, desired by others), it must be intrinsically worth having. This is the most complete abnegation of taste.

Short of this extreme the combination of the groping beginner, anxious to develop aesthetic sensibilities, and the aesthete may be an extremely happy one for the growth of art. It is certainly a situation in which the latter can exert influence. It has been suggested that Holbein was able to paint the portraits of *parvenu* magnates with such depth and accuracy because his subjects were not socially secure enough to reprove him for painting them as they really were.

Yet it is with the extreme noted above in mind that intellectuals and aesthetes may denigrate conventionalized good taste as something weak and petty, even though it be explicitly distin-

guished from vulgarity. Their admiration of an object rests, in their beliefs, not simply on the fact that it is fashionable to like it, but upon their appreciation of its beauty. This, too, can degenerate into an extreme – Bohemianism – where knowledge of the mere fact that something is conventionally approved inhibits one's appreciation of it. But, at any rate, they are the innovators who dare to revalue and to combine elements of what had appeared to be discordant styles, into new ones according to the criterion of beauty. Because of its unfamiliarity the new taste will hardly be assimilated by those who are most fearful of being out of fashion. On the contrary, it will penetrate the worlds of those who pride themselves on being above the crowd. Even in such circles, the new taste will soon become conventionalized or disappear – as something erratic and random and not likely to be seen again. If the former, it becomes fashionable amongst those who think they have 'really good' taste.

To what extent this 'good taste', then, is spread throughout the rest of the society depends upon the network of communications and the degree to which individuals think it proper to imitate those in superior social groups or classes.

Stone, bronze, iron ...

The **THREE AGES SYSTEM** is more familiar in rather loose descriptions of prehistoric times, as when we say 'a Bronze Age barrow', or 'an Iron Age hill-fort', or a 'Stone Age axe'.

The system and the idea that man had gone through three stages of technological development was worked out in Scandinavia in the early nineteenth century as a scientific concept, though there had been suggestions of the scheme before. The Greeks had speculated on the stages of man's early past and Lucretius (98–55 B.C.) in his *De Rerum Natura* argued that man first used his nails and teeth and stones and wood, then copper and, still later, iron. This was a very shrewd guess at the way man had developed technologically in Europe; but it was only a guess like the other early ages postulated by the Greeks, for example the Heroic Age and the Golden and Silver Ages.

As antiquarians in the post-Renaissance world of European scholarship began to concern themselves with the remains of prehistoric man, and particularly with stone and bronze tools which were found by chance or in excavations, they began to speculate whether these tools did not belong to a time before man knew the use of iron. The opening up of the world in the eighteenth and early nineteenth centuries and the first travellers' tales and ethnographical descriptions of stone-using savages provided examples of technologies comparable with those vaguely postulated for man's early past in Europe.

In 1813 the Danish historian Vedel-Simonsen wrote: 'The weapons and implements of the earliest inhabitants of Scandinavia were at first of stone and wood. These folk later learnt the use of copper . . . and only latterly, iron . . . Therefore, from this point of view, the history of their civilization can be divided into an age of stone, an age of copper and an age of iron.' In 1816 C. J. Thomsen became the first curator of the Danish National Museum. He arranged the collections from prehistoric Denmark according to Vedel-Simonsen's scheme, and when the Museum was first opened to the public, there were rooms for the Stone Age, the Age of 'Brass' or Bronze, and the Age of Iron.

This was still a notion – a notion of how to arrange archaeological objects, and of how man's tools had developed; and this notion was soon shown to be a fact by excavations in the Danish bogs and the Swiss lake-dwellings, where the succession of the Three Ages was proved stratigraphically. Though there was opposition for a considerable while to classifying antiquities according to ages of stone, bronze and iron – and the old Museum labels 'Ancient British' and 'Gothic' died hard – very gradually the Danish scheme won acceptance.

As it did so, it became elaborated. The Stone Age was divided into two, an Older Stone Age characterized by chipped tools, and a Newer Stone Age characterized by polished tools, and the names Palaeolithic and Neolithic were suggested for these. Later a third Stone Age intermediate between these two was distinguished, and called the Mesolithic. And as, technically

speaking, modern man might be said to be still living in the Iron Age, the prehistoric Iron Age was re-labelled the Early Iron Age. Thus the earlier Danish formulation of the three ages has become the modern five-age scheme of Palaeolithic, Mesolithic, Neolithic, Bronze Age and Early Iron Age.

This five-fold framework is that mainly used at present in the description and classification of prehistoric remains, and the whole scheme has often been described as the foundation stone of modern archaeology. To a certain extent this is true; before the Danes used it, there was no way of describing different periods of time or different cultures in the prehistoric past. Everything was known to be prehistoric, but there was no way of separating different levels of time. The stratigraphical evidence of geology and the legitimate inferences from the idea of successive technologies gave depth to the ideas of the prehistoric past and enabled a succession of cultures, industries and peoples to be built up.

The system is now outliving its usefulness. In many areas it is not applicable. It was devised for northern Europe. In much of the Near East a long age of copper preceded the use of bronze, and many of the prehistoric cultures of the Near East and the Mediterranean are technologically so evenly balanced between the use of stone and copper for tools and weapons that archaeologists have invented the terms Chalcolithic and Eneolithic to describe them. Yet even with these limitations – even if we are now prepared to see in the Mediterranean a succession of Palaeolithic, Mesolithic, Neolithic, Chalcolithic, Bronze Age and Early Iron Age – the system is still unsatisfactory, because it is based on a preconceived evolutionary view, and because it has been forced to describe archaeological, cultural and chronological categories at the same time.

The nineteenth-century acceptance of the doctrine of organic evolution predisposed men to think naturally of cultural evolution, and the Three Age System in its development seemed to show a simple example of technological progress. In the twentieth century we have begun to understand the diffusion of culture in prehistoric Europe, and we have become acquainted with the realities of the loss of useful arts. Groups of people lost, for example, the art of metal-working as they spread through Europe; the collective tomb-builders of southern Spain used copper; but their descendants who built tombs of the same type in Brittany and Britain did not use metal, and must formally be classified as 'Neolithic'. Once the idea was accepted that Neolithic communities could be derived from copper- and bronze-using communities the Three Age System began to look slightly absurd.

Detailed studies of prehistoric chronology in Europe have shown that there is a zoning across Europe of prehistoric technology. When the Hittites were making iron tools in Anatolia, the people of Greece and Crete were using bronze, those of many parts of Denmark and Ireland were in the Neolithic Age, and those in northern Scandinavia in the Mesolithic Age. So these are not strictly 'ages', but 'stages' of technology. Modern archaeology has developed separate terminologies for points of time in the prehistoric past which are described by exact years or by geological events (such as phases of the Ice Age or of post-glacial vegetation).

The Three Age System now survives, then, only as a generalization about the technical development of prehistoric man. It is still perfectly true that in central and northern Europe man used stone tools for countless millennia before he learnt metal-working, and that the first metal used was copper and the copper-tin alloy which is bronze, and that iron was only used late in man's prehistoric career as a metallurgist. The sociological implications of these successive ages are still important. Any metal-working is a complicated craft demanding specialized labour. Bronze tools were made and used all over Europe – not only in those areas where copper and tin were to be found. So it is a prerequisite of a Bronze Age that there should be extensive trade connexions, that a society should be so developed as to use for its basic tools and weapons materials unobtainable locally, and that there should be specialization of labour. Iron is much more plentiful than copper and tin; and iron tools are more effective than those of copper and bronze. The advent of the Early Iron Age did mean more metal tools and the possibilities of more intensive agriculture, forest-clearing and the cultivation of the heavier soils.

Thus the idea of the Three Ages has been a tool of great value; like other tools, it wears thin or wears out.

Total war, total victory

TOTAL WAR is war waged by whole nations rather than by their armed forces alone, using every means at their disposal. Nowadays it is characterized by large-scale air attacks directed against civilians, and by conscription of wealth and manpower. Its aim is unconditional surrender of the enemy or annihilation.

Though the expression 'total war' is comparatively new, the practice is not, for it was the rule until the eighteenth century. Not every conqueror massacred or enslaved the whole population of a vanquished territory, but it was not thought particularly reprehensible if he did. Cato the Elder at Rome, in the second century before Christ, used to hold up every debate in the Senate by refusing to speak to the motion and proposing instead 'that Carthage should be destroyed'. He meant it, and Carthage was finally destroyed – utterly – even the site was ploughed up. On the whole the Romans owed their success as empire builders to their ability to act with restraint towards conquered peoples, but sometimes the words which Tacitus, one of their great historians particularly interested in their military exploits, put into the mouth of a British chieftain were true: 'They make a solitude and call it peace.'

In the Middle Ages the code of chivalry, which evolved amongst the aristocracy of western Europe and which was emulated by the Muslim Saladin, had a mildly civilizing effect on war as seen from behind the vizor of a well-armoured knight on a strong well-armoured horse. But to the peasant over whose country the war was fought – the Hundred Years War between England and France, for instance – it was 'total'. There was no mercy for him or his family or their few possessions.

The savageries of Europe, however, were kid-gloved when compared with the holocaust wrought by Jenghis Khan (1162–1227) and his successors in their conquest of Asia.

Neither the Renaissance with its emphasis on the dignity of man nor the Reformation with its insistence on the importance of individual worth brought with them any new effective views about the need for warfare to become more humane. On the contrary, the rivalry of Catholics and Protestants in the ensuing 'religious wars' plunged Central Europe into the uniquely horrible Thirty Years War (1618–1648), which resulted in the death of perhaps as much as half the civilian population.

The Thirty Years War was the last 'total' war in Europe before the Second World War. While it was still in progress the Dutch jurist Grotius was at work on a system of international jurisprudence to distinguish between just and unjust wars. He also believed in trying to mitigate the horror of war by imposing moral obligations on the combatants – respect for neutrality, keeping faith, sparing women and children and old people. These ideas had their influence at the time and a hundred and fifty years later bore fruit in the shape of the International Court at The Hague and the Geneva Conventions on prisoners of war.

The warfare of Europeans in the eighteenth century was widely spread over the world. This afforded relief to the peoples of Europe, but they also benefited from the changed nature of warware. Small professional armies manœuvred and fought, and a decision was reached with less suffering to civilians. War had become more formal. It was no longer a struggle between religious faiths which could be used as an excuse for wholesale pillage and massacre. In the words of the Swiss jurist Vattel (1714–1767) 'The troops alone carry on war, while the rest of the nation remain in peace'.

The Napoleonic wars at least began with a faith behind them – the defence of the ideals of the French Revolution; but in spite of this and of the huge armies engaged, these wars did not lead to a return to the barbarities of the seventeenth century. To take only one instance, treatment of prisoners on both sides compared very favourably with modern practice under the Geneva Convention. Half a century later, in the Crimea, it was still possible to regard war as a spectacle rather than an affair in which the whole nation was involved. Civilian tourists could visit the army and ladies picnicked in a position from which they could see the firing.

When did the tide turn? When did standards begin to move back towards those of the Thirty Years War and Jenghis Khan? Perhaps ten years after the Crimea, when the Prussians struck at Austria (1866) and then at France (1870). These were not in themselves exceptionally terrible wars, but they were the first testing ground for the ideas of Carl von Clausewitz (1780–1831), whose book *On War* has become a classic, indeed *the* classic, on the subject.

Much of what Clausewitz wrote is advice about tactics and strategy based on the careful analysis of many campaigns. He explained, for instance, the importance of keeping enough troops in reserve and how to make the best use of terrain. He pointed out the important part played by surprise in the victories of, among others, Napoleon, Gustavus Adolphus and Hannibal. After weighing up the respective merits of audacity and caution, he concluded that 'no military leader has ever become great without audacity'. And of course he discussed how cavalry might be used to the best advantage.

None of this was revolutionary. It was when he stressed the importance of civilian morale ('Public opinion is won through great victories and the occupation of the enemy's capital') that he diverged from the eighteenth century, with its concentration on the balance of material forces in war, and helped to prepare the way for modern war propaganda.

Clausewitz also provided justification for a policy of ruthlessness. 'Any moderation shown would leave us short of our aim. We should be unwise not to make the greatest effort in order to render the result absolutely certain. If the country suffers greatly from this, no lasting disadvantage will arise; for the greater the effort the sooner the suffering will cease.' Finally he justifies war, in his most famous phrase, as 'a mere continuation of policy by other means'.

The First World War bore the marks of 'total war', though the phrase was not yet current. There was disregard for civilian lives in the invasion of Belgium and in unrestricted submarine warfare. There was, as the war dragged on, a realization that only the assumption by the government of unprecedented powers over men and material at home, could lead to victory in the field. But it was only after the war, in Germany, and particularly after the Nazis came to power in 1933, that twentieth-century total war was meticulously planned. The expression 'total war' perhaps dates from this time.

Ludendorff, the famous German general of the First World War, published a book in 1935 called *Der totale Krieg* in which he expressed the view that war was an aim in itself and not simply the instrument by which a policy was pursued, as Clausewitz had suggested: 'all the theories of Clausewitz have been turned upside down,' he wrote. 'War is the highest expression of national life. Therefore politics must be subordinate to the prosecution of war.' 'Total war', wrote a German army publication, 'will end in total victory. Total victory means the utter destruction of the vanquished nation, and its complete and final disappearance from the historical arena.'

ILLUSTRATION: Pages 420, 421 and 422.

The voice of the past

TRADITION as a powerful idea goes back to the language of Roman Law; and, like so many Roman ideas which have retained their validity, it is connected with notions of property.

Trans-dare, to hand across, to hand over; from simple rules about gift and barter the word was transferred to the more complex law of inheritance. In course of time it came to be applied not only to the inheritance of objects, but also of ideas, customs and laws, especially if they were handed on by word of mouth. Also, at the time of the early empire, the historian and naturalist Pliny the Elder spoke of 'a custom which has been handed down to us', *'traditus mos est'*.

In fact it is religious and family customs, and particularly the first, which in most societies form the residue of 'that which is handed over'. Secular community customs are less enduring, and do not have such importance attached to them. The religious character of tradition and the importance of the idea of 'handing over' from person to person by word of mouth is underlined by the frequent prohibition against the recording of the doctrines or the rules of practice observed by religious groups. Such prohibitions operated among the Buddhists, for instance, among many of the mystery religions of the Near East and the Mediterranean basin, and in many pagan groups all over the world.

To a limited extent the prohibition operated even in those religions which possessed codified laws and doctrines. Besides the body of laws which God gave to Moses on Mount Sinai, Jewish authorities said that he also conveyed to Moses a number of unwritten precepts. These 'halakot' multiplied both in number and authority as more questions regarding the interpretation of the written law arose, until it was claimed for them that they were all received by Moses from God directly, while, at the same time, it became obvious that some sort of editing was necessary to make them coherent. But the prohibition was so strong that as late as the second century A.D. one of the great Rabbis maintained that 'the man who records oral traditions is like one who burns the written law'.

Besides this 'normative' tradition of the 'halakah' – meaning tradition in the sense of the 'trend of things' – there was another body of Jewish traditions, that of the 'kabbalah', meaning 'that which is received'; the kabbalah approximates much more closely to the oral teaching of mystery religions and of modern freemasons and to the commonly accepted idea of tradition. This body of neo-Platonic speculations on the written revelations and the law illustrate the rather particular sense which 'tradition' may assume in such a closed group as a religious sect or a 'closed-shop' society.

The whole body of traditional teaching among the Jews was known by the name of the 'precepts of the ancients'. Its definition in a clear form and at an early date is due to the existence of written documents of an absolute authority, which were often incomprehensible without some comment or illustration. This idea of tradition was taken over, almost bodily, into Christian thought. As among the Jews the rabbinic succession was transmitted from master to pupil by the 'laying on of hands', so in the Christian Church sacramental and teaching power was conferred on a bishop by the 'laying on of hands' of some one or more brother bishops, while minor powers, such as that of priesthood or deaconate, were conferred by another kind of 'tradition', the handing over of the instruments of power to its operator – 'In that a priest is made by the tradition of the chalice, patten and host into his hands', as a recusant writer has put it.

The Christian doctrine of tradition is first stated clearly by St Paul in the first Epistle to the Corinthians xi. 1. 'Be ye followers also of me, even as I am of Christ.'

'Appeal to tradition', then, was one of the most important factors of theological speculation and argument. The strength and importance of oral teaching may be demonstrated by the absence of a universally accepted formula of Christian doctrine until early in the fourth century. Many heretical writers and preachers appealed against the growing body of received opinions and customs to scripture as against tradition. John Wyclif rebuked his enemies because they were, he says, 'i-bounden only by a positive lawe or a tradycion that thai han hemsilfe made'. Until the Reformation made a precept of their protests, Wyclif and his predecessors ran against the main current; and although outside the Catholic and orthodox camp there remained even then a few defenders of tradition – '... We have tradition; namely, that we so believe, because both we from our predecessors and they from theirs have so received', writes Richard Hooker (c. 1554–1600), one of the first apologists of the Church of England – the appeal away from the situation sanctioned by a continuity of belief and custom to a text of scripture and later also to private revelation became increasingly important.

This pattern of appeal either to a known archaic precept of belief on the one hand, or the complete rejection of the received ideas as against some real innovation on the other, are repeating patterns of violent change. For violent change either forces people to look for assurance to a lost and golden age, or else imposes on them the necessity to consider every choice from first principles. Tradition becomes a particularly important idea at times of such tension and rapid development. For this reason the Romans found it so much more important, while establishing their empire, to appeal to their past for precedent than the Greeks had ever done; for this reason also,

medieval epic poems about the Roman, Trojan, or simply the fabulous, antiquity of Britain were translated into the prose of chronicles and quasi-chronicle romances.

As the idea of progress and unlimited benefits from the growth of production grew to unprecedented importance about the middle of the eighteenth century, so the idea of tradition, associated as it was with ecclesiastical usage, grew extremely unpopular. 'The more ancient the abuse, the more sacred it is', remarks one of the characters in Voltaire's play *Les Guèmes*. Throughout the nineteenth century recourse was had to appeals away from tradition. It would be enough to quote the fashion for 'pure' style in architecture, whether 'gothic' or 'renaissance' for single buildings; while at the same time no precedent was quoted for the erection of whole towns. In England great tracts of by-law planned districts defied any tradition of urban building that might have existed. But after the disenchantment with progress which occurred about the beginning of the present century, a new interest in tradition may be remarked. This is true of the religious, philosophical and sociological spheres. And the appeal away from tradition is again increasingly made to some archaic factor rather than to *a priori* reasoning or private judgement exclusively. Faith in tradition has produced some grotesque results; the science of genealogy shows the immense trouble people have taken to obtain a view of the sequence of their ancestors. Grubby origins do not matter – so long as they go back far enough. It is not always vanity, it is a desperate wish to join hands and not feel cast off. It is oddly like the behaviour of the little last duckling trying urgently to catch up with the convoy of its brothers. He *must* join up with them. It is unthinkable that he might explore on his own for a while.

A 'link with the past' gives a feeling of strength. Small nations, in fear of losing their personality and individuality in the presence of powerful neighbours, have invented all kinds of pageantry and nonsense to regain ancient greatness. Their attempts to revive semi-obsolete languages are often misguided self-determination. Will these ersatz roots pushed into the past suck up nourishment and strength? Or have we a situation where shorn Samson has a wig made of the hair

Delilah had cut from him? He puts on the wig and hopes to be his old self.

Great Britain is notorious for its 'maintenance of hallowed traditions', though most other countries are as prone to this probably harmless vice. The existence of such survivals as Beefeaters and the probably useful custom of Beating the Bounds, the narrow escape of the aristocracy from fossilization because of their commercial convenience, all do not necessarily imply any primitive urge for tradition and continuity. What is implied is a fondness for the picturesque coupled with a shrewd idea of its value for prestige and tourist attraction. To read any deeper meaning into the survival of Town Criers is silly.

But, however much we may try to brush away tradition by common sense, it will always re-emerge from its exiles (brief ones usually) to train the future the way it wants to go.

ILLUSTRATION: Pages 416 and 417.

'I am born from age to age'

TRANSMIGRATION OF SOULS, sometimes called Reincarnation, is common as a doctrine to both Hinduism and Buddhism.

Like all religious doctrines, it can be understood on two planes. There is first the plane of popular understanding. To millions of Hindus and Buddhists the idea that life is but one of a series of lives, each following the other in consequence of good or bad conduct, is an intelligible, if awe-inspiring, doctrine. The striking and baffling inequalities between one man and another, whether due to fortune or temperament, require explanation. The human mind cannot reconcile itself to the fact that such differences result from mere chance. Why should they not be due, in some obscure fashion, to merit or desert?

Secondly, if the soul is immortal, as the sages have taught, it must have enjoyed existence from eternity. Why should it not have passed through other existences, and be able to look forward to future existences? Given the inherent failings of human nature, and the need to strive towards perfection, men require opportunities for improvement for which one brief life-span is in-

sufficient. In order to attain immortality, they need a greater measure of mortality.

Finally, human beings are surrounded by millions of other living things. Why should experience be restricted to the plane of humanity? Is it not possible that 'our' other existences have been lived in different forms, some higher and some inferior? Such ideas have naturally occurred to the ordinary man in the course of puzzling over life and its meaning.

The doctrine of transmigration has been interpreted on a higher and more philosophical plane. According to the great metaphysical thinkers in the Hindu and Buddhist tradition, this *literal* interpretation of Reincarnation is a crude, if understandable, error. Transmigration is not a change in either time or place. The human soul does not enter one living form after another. It passes through a series of 'states'. Of these states only one is realized in bodily form. There are others which may be termed disembodied. To picture the soul as re-entering a body different from that which it vacated, or as inhabiting a lower animal, is fanciful superstition. Having passed through a cycle of existences, some 'gross' and some 'subtle', the soul finally achieves emancipation or deliverance (*Moksha*). Except by analogy, this process cannot be said to take 'time'. Time is a feature of the bodily or material condition. Since release from this condition is the most difficult of all to achieve, however, the whole process has come to be 'materialized'. This is particularly true of modern theosophic doctrines, with their emphasis upon a series of 'carnal' transformations.

Between these two interpretations there is obviously a wide gulf. But it is a gulf no wider than that between the doctrine of hell, as expounded by Christian theology, and the popular idea of hell as a *place*, with the lurid imagery associated with it. Hindu thought has always observed a distinction between *Smirti*, or 'inner' doctrine, and *Sruti*, or 'outer' doctrine. And this distinction between the 'esoteric' and the 'exoteric' is found equally in other faiths. No religion can dispense with mythology, and Hindu mythology is the most elaborate in existence.

Behind the doctrine of transmigration is a view of the universe at once majestic and sombre. Hindu thought has no equivalent to the Christian idea of the Creation of the World. The world may not have been created at all. One of the Vedic hymns says:

Who verily knows and who can here declare it,
Whence it was born and whence comes this creation?
The gods are later than this world's production,
Who knows then whence it came into being?

Instead of a beginning there is merely an endless repetition or beginning again. The history of the universe consists of a series of cosmic cycles. Each cycle or *Kalpa* is formed of a thousand great ages or 'great years' called *Mahayugas*, and each of these 'great years' is divided into four epochs or *Yugas*. As the successive epochs of the *Mahayuga* pass, the righteousness of mankind diminishes. The final epoch, the *Kaliyuga*, is that in which evil, now the dominant force, causes mankind to sink into an abyss of disorder and wickedness.

The *Kaliyuga* is the epoch in which we are living. Its characteristic philosophy is materialism and a worship of the things of the body. Ignorance of the truth was never more extreme. For, as the great Hindu philosopher Śaṁkara said, 'all that belongs to the body is ignorance. It is visible and perishable as bubbles of air.'

Hindu and Buddhist mythology represent nature and life – indeed the whole cosmos, which is itself alive – as moved by a kind of blind and unappeased desire. Desire and pain are synonymous. The cycles of the world, like the cycle of human life, are compared to wheels of suffering. Desire is like a wheel, because the satisfaction of desire gives birth to another desire. So the wheel turns. The individual soul becomes involved with cycle after cycle of existence (for the great cosmic cycles are paralleled by smaller or microcosmic cycles), and thus assumes endless shapes and forms. But this 'migration' is not haphazard. It conforms to a law. The law of *Karma* is the thread of meaning and logic which informs an otherwise unintelligible universe.

Karma, a word around which much fanciful mythology has been woven, means 'work' or 'action'. With the development of Hindu and especially of Buddhist thought, this general meaning acquired a particular significance. *Karma* was that which everybody carried about with him, as he might carry a burden, until by

righteous living and the attainment of true knowledge he was able to shed its encumbrance. Just as his fortune in this life depended upon his conduct in the sum of his previous lives, so his exertions here and now determined his future existences. The law of *Karma* is not necessarily fatalistic. On the contrary, it encourages human exertion. But it is the kind of belief which, misunderstood or distorted, may easily lead to fatalism. In India the system of Caste, though probably originating from conquest and subjection, seemed to derive its sanction from the law of *Karma*. To be born into a particularly low caste might be a misfortune, but it was a deserved misfortune. Society could not intervene in a matter of inscrutable divine disposition.

Although the law of *Karma* might seem cold and pitiless, its operation lent meaning to the lives of many who would otherwise have fallen into despair. Being but one of a number of states of existence, terrestrial life could be endured as the possible gateway to something better; and there was no harm in the rich and powerful knowing that tyranny and extravagance might be visited elsewhere by appropriate punishment. As opposed to its seven heavens, Hinduism preaches the existence of three times as many hells. Moreover, even the most macabre descriptions of the Christian hell compare favourably with the revolting horror of the Hindu underworlds. In spite of this emphasis upon divine retribution, the Hindu conception of transmigration excludes an eternity of punishment. The soul might visit a series of 'purgatories'; it might turn for epoch after epoch on the wheel of rebirth; but finally, having purged itself of the last vestige of desire, it would attain to salvation and *Moksha*. Paradoxically, many a Western critic who expresses horror at the idea of *Nirvana* as total oblivion, has subscribed to a view of eternal damnation scarcely less terrifying.

Although the Buddha (sixth century B.C.) repudiated much of the Hindu tradition in which he was born, he seems to have accepted without question the doctrine of transmigration and *Karma*. Indeed, his followers regarded him as himself the eighth reincarnation of the god Vishnu. The title Buddha means 'Enlightened One'. Sakyamuni, as the Buddha was called after the name of his clan, believed that he would be succeeded in due time by another Buddha, Maitreya. The idea of a succession of Saviours or Liberators, born in human form to rescue humanity from spiritual ignorance and to hasten their release from the chain of births, is deep-rooted in oriental tradition.

In the great poem called *Baghavad-Gita* (The Lord's Song), Sri Krishna is made to say: 'Whenever there is decay of righteousness, and exaltation of evil, I make myself a body: for the protection of good, for the destruction of what is evil, for the sake of maintaining virtue, I am born from age to age.' In due course, the tradition of Buddhism called *Mahayana* (the 'Great Wheel', referring to the body of orthodox doctrine) elaborated the idea of *Bodhisattvas*. There were Buddhas who voluntarily abstained from entering eternal bliss for the sake of directing sinful humanity along the path of righteousness. Even the Buddhas had their burden of *Karma* to carry – an idea not unknown to Christian doctrine. At the hour of his death the Buddha is said to have had a vision, realized in a single instant, of the whole of cosmic history with its chain of births.

Forming a kind of confirmation of his Buddhahood, this revelation caused his final message to mankind to be one of encouragement and hope: 'Work out your salvation with diligence.'

ILLUSTRATION: Pages 418 and 419.

The Bread and Wine

TRANSUBSTANTIATION is the scholastic idea that the substance, the inner nature of a thing, may be changed whilst its accidents, its outer appearance, remains unchanged. Based on the Aristotelian notion of matter, this idea was used as a philosophical explanation or description of what happened to the unleavened bread and the wine at Mass. They remained in appearance bread and wine, but their substance was changed into the body and blood of Christ.

Roland Bandinelli, the future Pope Alexander IV, was probably the first man to use the word, when he was a professor at Bologna University in 1140. In the second half of the twelfth century the word becomes increasingly common in sermons as well as in dissertations. Its use was canonized at the Lateran Council in 1215, which declared that transubstantiation brought about the presence of the body and blood under the species of bread and wine. St Thomas Aquinas says: 'The change is entirely supernatural, produced simply by the divine power, like the virginal conception.'

Theologically, and indeed historically, the idea is based on words in the gospel, primarily on the sixth chapter of St John's gospel, where Jesus says: 'My flesh is real food, my blood is real drink. He who eats my flesh and drinks my blood lives continually in me, and I in him'. The words are repeated several times, and are emphatic. They were the cause, so St John says, of many disciples leaving Jesus because they could not believe what he had said. This statement of Jesus is confirmed in his words and actions at the Last Supper, where he offers the Jewish Pasch, and then goes on to offer a new Christian sacrifice, clearly and deliberately instituting a new ritual: 'Take, eat, this is my body ... Drink ye all of it; for this is my blood.' These words are from St Matthew's Gospel. In St Mark's and St Luke's Gospel, although the wording is slightly different, there occurs the same unequivocal statement about his body and blood.

The early Church believed that the bread and wine were transformed in some way into Jesus's body and blood at Christian sacrifice and worship, although the words 'Mass' and 'Transubstantiation' had not been formulated.

Today, belief in the transubstantiation of the bread and wine at Mass into the body and blood of Christ is a distinguishing belief of Catholics. It is *de fide*, part of the Church's belief. Catholics actually believe that this 'miracle' happens. The priest is held to be ordained for the principal purpose of offering the sacrifice of the Mass.

The priest's task is to offer in sacrifice the body and blood of Christ and to feed the people with it. By him alone, using the ritual of the Mass, can the bread and wine be changed. It is generally held that this change is effected by the 'words of consecration', the words, that is, of Jesus at the Last Supper: 'This is my body', etc. These words, as they occur in the Mass, are actually part of a description of what Jesus did; they are 'reported speech'. And there are considerable difficulties of a historical and theological sort for supposing that these words are the exclusive means of effecting the change of transubstantiation.

Belief in transubstantiation was crystallized, and its popularity enshrined in the Festival of *Corpus Christi*, and the office for it written by St Thomas Aquinas.

A true definition of the traitor

TREASON as generally understood today, means a criminal act done by someone owing allegiance to a sovereign state calculated to endanger or overthrow the foundations of that state. In the Middle Ages (indeed until 1828) it was 'treason' (in law) for a wife to kill her husband, a servant his master, or a priest his bishop – these crimes being termed 'petit' treason to distinguish them from breaches of duty owed to the king, of which 'high' treason was, and still is, the proper description. So there was an element of personal treachery in treason, which made the word 'traitor' evoke strong feelings of hatred and contempt. Dante, writing in the fourteenth century, placed the traitors in the lowest circle of the Inferno and with them Judas Iscariot, as the worst traitor of all.

This same element has persisted as part of the English law of treason throughout its history, though today it is reflected in the wording rather than in the application. In 1769, Sir William Blackstone wrote in his *Commentaries* (Book IV, Ch. 6):

Treason, *proditio*, in its very name (which is borrowed from the French) imports a betraying, treachery, or breach of faith. It therefore only happens between allies ... ; for treason is indeed a general appellation made use of by the law to denote not only offences against the King and Government, but also that accumulation of guilt which arises whenever a superior reposes a confidence in a subject or inferior, between whom and himself there subsists a natural, a civil, or even a spiritual relation; and the inferior so abuses that confidence, so forgets the obligation of duty, subjection, and allegiance as to destroy the life of any such lord or superior.

Blackstone also called treason 'the highest civil crime'. The law of England on the matter depends upon the Treason Act of 1351. Of the treasons declared by it, five are still treasons today: (1) Compassing or imagining the King's death, or that of the Queen, or of their eldest son and heir (the Regicides were tried under this head after the Restoration). (2) Violating the King's Consort, the wife of his eldest son and heir, or his eldest daughter unmarried (under this head Anne Boleyn was convicted as being a party to her own violation). (3) Levying war against the King in his realm (the Jacobite supporters of the '45 were held to be traitors under this head). (4) Adhering to the King's enemies (both Sir Roger Casement in 1916 and William Joyce in 1946 were convicted under this head for aiding the Germans in time of war). (5) Slaying the Chancellor, Treasurer or the King's Justices while in their places doing their offices – a head of no practical importance though it is still the law.

Forgery of the Royal seals or coinage was also declared to be treason, but since 1832 such offences have been reduced to mere felonies.

Under this Act (and, indeed, at Common Law before it) only those who owed personal allegiance to the King could commit high treason. Thus when, in 1305, William Wallace was charged with treason in opposing Edward I by force of arms, he was alleged to have done so 'being unmindful of his fealty and allegiance', and replied that whatever he had done 'he had never been a traitor to the King of England' because he had never sworn any oath of allegiance.

The same principle applies today, but it is allegiance to an impersonal state rather than to a personal sovereign that is regarded as the prerequisite of treason. In effect this means that a subject can and an alien cannot commit treason – unless by residence within its boundaries he seeks the state's protection. Invasion by a foreign army is no treason; espionage (however brave and patriotic the spy) is.

After the Wars of the Roses the legal conception of treason was changed and broadened. With the growth of the 'national' state, opposition to the current government, particularly if it involved a risk of public disorder, came to be viewed with increasing alarm, and until the eighteenth century the Act of 1351 (together with many statutory additions) was a weapon in the hands of those in power to enforce compliance with their policies – in particular the dynastic and ecclesiastical policies of the Tudor and later Stuart sovereigns. 'Compassing the King's death' was held to include any plot to restrain his freedom of person or of action (which often meant no more than any movement for constitutional or religious reform); 'levying war' was extended to cover any concerted attempt to overawe Parliament or Ministers so as to secure the passing of any particular measure, or to achieve any general object by force – such as the destruction of all dissenters' meeting-houses, although in reality such attempts were often no more than serious riots.

Two new forms of treason created by statute in the reign of Queen Anne are still law: (a) to hinder the succession to the Crown of the person entitled thereto under the Act of Settlement and (b) to maintain in writing the invalidity of the line of that succession.

At the end of the eighteenth century the use of the law of treason to enforce particular policies or to keep public order fell into disfavour. An attempt to convict Lord George Gordon of treason for his part in the Gordon Riots of 1780 failed. Since then the extreme barbarities of the punishment have been mitigated (today it is death by hanging), and forfeiture of property has been abolished. Crimes which are not really directed against the state are dealt with under less drastic enactments, though they may still be, in strict law, treason. Even attempts to endanger the Sovereign's personal safety are usually punished under milder statutes expressly enacted for that purpose.

The consequence is that only acts which are really directed against the safety of the state are dealt with as treasonable, and in practice this means that in Great Britain no prosecution for treason is likely except in time of civil or international war. This is not true everywhere; in countries where the régime identifies itself closely with the state any active opposition to that régime is liable to be declared treason, in much the same way as opposition to the policies of Henry VIII or Elizabeth I was said to be treason. The grounds put forward for this are that to oppose such a régime is in fact to endanger the foundations of the state, a proposition which may well be true where the constitution is authoritarian rather than democratic.

'Trotskyist deviation'

TROTSKYISM is a 'deviationist' view of Marxism stemming directly from Leon Trotsky himself. In 1906 Trotsky was confined in the Peter-Paul fortress at St Petersburg charged with insurrection, and was waiting trial for the leading part he had played in the unsuccessful Revolution of 1905. He was then President of the St Petersburg Soviet. He passed the time in writing essays and pamphlets one of which, called *The Balance and the Prospects – the Moving Forces of Revolution* was of the greatest importance as a fundamental statement of his point of view. In this pamphlet Trotsky reviewed the abortive Revolution of 1905 in the perspective of Russian history; and then, turning to the international scene, he defined the place of the Russian Revolution in modern European history. This work was the most important and radical restatement of the conception of Socialist revolution since Marx's *Communist Manifesto* of 1848, and for decades it was the object of fierce controversy.

Trotsky questioned the assumptions of the Marxists of his time. The Marxists held that before revolutionary socialism could rise to power in Russia, there must first be a 'bourgeois' revolution that would transform semi-feudal Tsardom into a modern industrial capitalist society. According to the Marxists the old capitalist countries of the West were ready for a socialist revolution that would succeed while Russia was still engaged in its bourgeois revolution.

Trotsky believed that the working class would be obliged to carry the Russian Revolution from the bourgeois to the socialist phase, even before the socialist upheaval had begun in the West. The Russian bourgeoisie, he held, was incapable of revolutionary leadership because it had been unable to acquire confidence in itself and independence. 'So prodigious has been the rulers' initiative and so sluggish and torpid has been

Russian society that in Russia even capitalism appeared as the child of the state.'

The state and not private enterprise had laid the foundations of modern industry. Russia had entered the twentieth century with a weak urban middle class who formed only 13 per cent. of the total population. Russia had no social class comparable to the concentrated mass of urban craftsmen who had formed the backbone of the French middle class, and had made the French Revolution. The Russian Revolution of 1905 had shown that the bourgeoisie was too weak and too frightened to direct the uprising against autocracy, and so the initiative had passed to the industrial workers.

It followed from this, Trotsky argued, that the Revolution, if it succeeded, would end in the seizure of power by the proletariat. The Marxists held that in backward Russia, unripe for socialism, the workers must help the bourgeoisie to seize power. Trotsky countered by declaring: 'In a country economically backward, the proletariat can take power earlier than in countries where capitalism is advanced ... The Russian revolution produces conditions in which power may pass into the hands of the proletariat before the politicians of bourgeois liberalism have had the chance to show their statesmanlike genius to the full.'

Trotsky was blamed by his critics for wanting Russia to 'jump over' the bourgeois stage of development, foretold by Marx, and for advocating a policy that would oppose the industrial workers, a small minority, to the rest of the nation. Was he advocating, his critics asked, the dictatorship of a minority?

Trotsky believed that the Revolution itself would be carried through by the industrial proletariat alone. The old order would be overthrown in the towns, and there the industrial proletariat would be master. The Revolution would be achieved by this minority, acting as a spearhead; but for its consolidation and continued success it would depend upon the support of the majority of the people, that is to say upon the peasants. 'The proletariat in power will appear before the peasantry as its liberator.' The proletarian government would sanction the seizure of the large estates by the peasants and would guarantee their holdings against the landlords, and in this way the government would win the peasants' support. The proletarian government would keep the initiative, but it would rule in the interest of the overwhelming majority.

The crux of 'Trotskyism', in its domestic aspect, consists in this conception of the peasantry's place in the Russian Revolution. Trotsky believed that the international and domestic aspects of the Revolution were closely interwoven. He expected that eventually there would be conflict between the peasantry and the proletarian minority. The peasants would support the Revolution only while it was breaking the power of the landlords; and then, because of their narrow local and proprietory interests, they would oppose the two main features of proletarian policy – 'collectivism' (q.v.) and 'internationalism'. Thus the new régime would, after its initial success, discover its essential weakness, and would be obliged to look for help in international revolution.

Without the direct state support of the European proletariat, the working class of Russia will not be able to remain in power and transform its temporary rule into a stable and prolonged socialist dictatorship ... This will from the very outset impart an international character to the development of the events ... If the Russian proletariat, having temporarily gained power, does not carry the resolution of its own initiative on to the ground of Europe, then the feudal and bourgeois reaction will force it to do so ... Nothing will be left to the workers but to link the fate of their own political rule, and consequently the fate of the whole Russian Revolution with that of the socialist revolution in Europe.

The illusion inherent in Trotsky's argument was that European economy and society were already ripe for socialist revolution. Trotsky when he wrote in 1906 did not imagine that the Russian Revolution would be able to survive without international aid. He underrated the internal resources and vitality of revolutionary Russia. His views, however, were accepted by all Bolshevik leaders, including Stalin, in the years between 1917 and 1924. The clue to Trotsky's error is to be found in his appraisal of the Russian peasantry. He did not foresee that the peasantry would be unable, because of its political helplessness and lack of independence, to resist collectivism. It did not occur to him that a proletarian party would be able to govern and rule a huge country against the majority of the people. He did not realize that the Revolution would seek to escape from its isolation and weakness into totalitarianism.

For the rest of Trotsky's life, as a leader of the Revolution of 1917, as founder and head of the Red Army, as protagonist of a new International, and then in exile, he was to abide by his ideas of 1906, his early and brief statement of doctrine.

By 1927 Trotsky's doctrine of international revolution had been rejected by the Communist Party, and the accepted policy was that socialism must be built within the frontiers of a Soviet State set within an alien and hostile world. In 1927 Stalin sponsored a policy of industrialization combined with the enforcement of collectivism upon the peasants, and he became the chief protagonist of the 'five-year plans' of economic reconstruction.

In 1927 Trotsky was expelled from the Party, and presently deported to Turkey. At the Moscow trials (1936–1938) he was accused of being an arch-traitor who had collaborated with Nazi Germany to overthrow the U.S.S.R.; and he was assassinated in Mexico on 12 August 1940.

ILLUSTRATION: Page 443.

Is it true?

'TRUTH IN ADVERTISING' as a working slogan, is less than half a century old. 'In an advertisement it is allowed to every man to speak well of himself,' wrote Dr Samuel Johnson in *The Idler* in 1759. 'Promise, large promise, is the soul of an advertisement ...' Though he was critical of the advertisers of his day, Dr Johnson did not call for 'truth in advertising' – a notion which might well have seemed to him as unreasonable as 'truth in poetry'. It was adopted, in a fervent mood, by the Associated Advertising Clubs of the World, at their conference in America in 1911. At this time advertising was not yet spelled Advertising. It still suffered under the odium created by dishonest vendors, notably of patent medicines. Reputable manufacturers declined to advertise their wares in the mendacious company of quacks. Both in order to inspire public confidence and to attract lucrative new business, advertising had to reform itself. Already certain advertising agents had proved that a policy of honest advertising was not necessarily suicidal; but the example of others showed that dishonest advertising could still produce spectacular, if short-lived, profits.

It was obvious from the start that 'truth in advertising' could never be construed as 'the truth, the whole truth and nothing but the truth'. No one could reasonably expect an advertiser to balance the advantages of his product with a catalogue of its disadvantages (the manufacturer of a steam car who admitted that 'a slight puffing occurs when climbing a grade' was being a good deal franker than his successors would deem necessary). Nor was it sensible to expect an advertiser to abstain from what lawyers called 'a reasonable flourish' – like the slogan 'Worth a guinea a box', or 'Pure as the tear that falls upon a sister's grave' (a port wine slogan).

The flourish had to be one which could not be misinterpreted by men of common sense, one which involved playful or poetical exaggeration, one which lawyers would be unlikely to challenge. In 1891 the British courts had ruled that 'promise, large promise', if couched in sufficiently specific terms, could not be dismissed as a mere flourish. A manufacturer who had offered to pay £100 to anyone who contracted influenza while protected by his 'carbolic smoke ball' was called upon to pay that sum to a Mrs Carlill. Mr Justice Hawkins ruled that a vendor making a promise 'must not be surprised if occasionally he is held to his promise'.

But, short of promising money, there remained a wide field in which an advertiser's fancy could exercise without incurring legal risks. Where did untruth in advertising begin? Was it a lie to call an infant food 'Doctor So-and-so's Food' when it was invented by a team of chemists? How dishonest was it to pretend that the secret of a drug had been whispered by a dying nun to a Himalayan explorer? The advertiser was prepared to justify this kind of fancy on many grounds. It was necessary, he might say, to arrest public attention. If the product was a good one and the lie was an innocuous one, what harm was done? In any event, he would argue, faith in a product, however built up, was necessary to help the sufferer towards a cure.

The policy of 'truth in advertising' was re-affirmed from time to time by the advertising interests. In 1924 the advertising clubs promised 'to seek the truth and to live it', and expressed the belief that 'truthful advertising builds both character and good business'. This was the period when, egged on by the psychologists, advertisers had begun to stress, not the physical facts of their products, but the possibilities of joy, ease, adventure or social superiority to be derived from using them. This face-powder would bring a girl lovers; that hair-cream would bring a man promotion.

Advertisers appealed to the buyer's instincts and emotions. In the 'promise, large promise' of this kind of advertising, truth was a quantity difficult to isolate. But if fancy could not be curbed, direct misrepresentation could. The advertisers' own professional bodies were able to impose 'codes of ethics' on some, but not all, of the offenders, prohibiting certain kinds of false claim and misstatement. The law also helped to root out misrepresentation when voluntary action proved inadequate. One effect of all this was a tendency by the less scrupulous to observe only the letter of the law. Thus, when the use of the word 'cure' was banned, 'remedy' began to creep in. There was always someone ready to argue that 'woollen' did not mean made wholly of wool, but only partly of wool. Advertising was in danger of becoming a battle of wits between seller and consumer – and the wits of the seller, who had more to lose, were usually the sharper.

Nevertheless, from one cause or another, the proportion of truth in advertising has increased conspicuously since the slogan was first introduced. The modern public, subjected to high-pressure advertising from infancy, has an increasingly shrewd idea of how much to believe in any one advertisement. It knows how to discount Hollywood superlatives; it knows that testimonials by public figures are unlikely to be inspired by a disinterested passion for truth in advertising. The public would be unhappy, however, if its advertisements were not leavened by a certain infusion of whimsy. Francis Bacon recognized that 'a mixture of a lie doth ever add pleasure'. So long as the flourish is not deceptive, so long as the promise is not fraudulent, so long as

there is no direct misdescription, the public is unlikely to demand a more stringent standard of 'truth in advertising'. As a pure ethical concept, truth in advertising can never be realized. There can only be a workaday compromise.

U

Deep in the unconscious

The **UNCONSCIOUS** is a technical term used by Sigmund Freud (1856–1939) in his theory of psycho-analysis to denote collectively those of a person's mental processes which the person cannot spontaneously recall to consciousness, but which can be reproduced by employing special techniques such as hypnotism or psycho-analysis.

Freud distinguishes these *unconscious* mental processes from both *preconscious* and *conscious* mental processes, a terminology which he himself introduced. He expounded these concepts in his *Introductory Lectures on Psycho-analysis*, delivered at the University of Vienna between 1915 and 1917:

The crudest conception [he wrote] of these systems is the one we shall find the most convenient, a spatial one. The unconscious system may therefore be compared to a large ante-room, in which the various mental excitations are crowding upon one another, like individual beings. Adjoining this is a second, smaller apartment, a sort of reception-room, in which consciousness resides. But on the threshold between the two there stands a personage with the office of door-keeper, who examines the various mental excitations, censors them, and denies them admittance to the reception-room when he disapproves of them ...

Now this metaphor may be employed to widen our terminology. The excitations in the unconscious, in the ante-chamber, are not visible to consciousness, which is of course in the other room, so to begin with they remain unconscious. When they have pressed forward to the threshold and been turned back by the door-keeper, they are *incapable of becoming conscious*; we call them then *repressed*. But even those excitations which are allowed over the threshold do not necessarily become conscious, they can only become so if they succeed in attracting the eye of consciousness. This second chamber may be suitably called *the preconscious system*.

(An example of a preconscious excitation would be the reader's recollection of how his breakfast table looked this morning – as this existed in his mind *before* this sentence attracted the 'eye of consciousness' to it.)

Now I know very well [Freud went on] that you will say that these conceptions are as crude as they are fantastic … I know they are crude … Still, I should like to assure you that these crude hypotheses, the two chambers, the door-keeper on the threshold between the two, and consciousness as a spectator at the end of the second room, must indicate an extensive approximation to the actual reality. I should also like to hear you admit that our designations, *unconscious*, *preconscious* and *conscious*, are less prejudicial and more easily defensible than some others which have been suggested or have come into use, *e.g.* sub-conscious, inter-conscious, co-conscious etc.

The action of the *censor* (the technical name for the forces represented in the illustration by the door-keeper) in keeping the contents of the unconscious out of the pre-conscious (and so a portion out of consciousness) is termed repression.

According to Crichton-Miller, among the chief characteristics of the unconscious as described by Freud are that it is infantile and largely sexual, entirely a-moral, ruthlessly egocentric, illogical and dominated by the principle of obtaining pleasure and avoiding pain.

The Unconscious represents within each of us the infant, the primitive man and also the animal. The whole work of racial culture and individual education only serves to reclaim the [zone of the preconscious system]. Below that there is a chaotic activity of which [consciousness] knows nothing and cares less. Now and again [it] hurls an unworthy idea down into the obscure depths, never to see it again.

According to Freud, all our conscious mental processes have their origin in the unconscious. It follows that in order to understand the origin of apparently pointless or inexplicable conscious mental occurrences, such as dreams, the inability to recall a familiar name, or such phenomena as

the hearing of 'voices', it is necessary to bring to light the unconscious material which is the cause of them. This view was already being put forward before Freud first published his findings. Pierre Janet's *L'Automatisme Psychologique* – in which (in the words of Dalbiez) he 'developed the concept of the dependence of certain hysterical symptoms on unconscious representations in a really masterly manner' – appeared in 1889, four years before the publication by Freud and his collaborator, the Viennese physician Joseph Breuer, of their first article on *The Psychic Mechanism of Hysterical Phenomena* (1893).

This article contains the earliest statement of the view that symptoms can be cured by the single process of bringing into consciousness their unconscious causes.

Breuer's discovery [wrote Freud in 1915–17] still remains the foundation of psycho-analytic therapy. The proposition that symptoms vanish when their unconscious antecedents have been made conscious has been borne out by all subsequent research; although the most extraordinary and unexpected complications are met with in attempting to carry this proposition out in practice. Our therapy does its work by transforming something unconscious into something conscious, and only succeeds in its work in so far as it is able to effect this transformation.

Freud's own uniquely original contribution was the development of an entirely new method of 'transforming something unconscious into something conscious'. This was the celebrated associative method, which consists in asking the patient to suspend all criticism and all voluntary direction of his thought, and to let the stream of consciousness flow, describing its progress to the analyst. Finding that this was successful in enabling unconscious material to be brought into consciousness, Freud abandoned the use of hypnosis and suggestion, which till then had been the mainstays of psychiatrical treatment; and psycho-analysis was launched on its remarkable career.

The psycho-analytical concept of the unconscious came into being as the result of the work of Freud and Breuer among patients who were suffering from various forms of mental illness. As the theory developed, its scope was extended, first by Freud himself and then by his followers, to a variety of mental phenomena outside the field of mental illness. McDougall (who prefers the term *sub*conscious) classifies these as follows:

(1) subconscious operations producing results similar to those of normal thinking;
(2) supernormal manifestations in the domain of intellect and character, including the production of works of genius, religious conversion and mystical experiences;
(3) supernormal influence of the mind over the body;
(4) supernormal processes of communication between mind and mind.

There is no doubt that these excursions have often gone a long way beyond the limits of the plausible, not to say the rational. There has recently appeared, for example, a full-scale psychoanalytical interpretation of the philosopher Berkeley's writings which entirely neglects the actual arguments on which Berkeley's fame rests, regarding them merely as further 'symptoms' for study. Again, psycho-analytical methods have been professedly applied to the elucidation of characters in fiction – Hamlet is a favourite 'patient' for this 'treatment' – in spite of the fact that neither the characters nor their authors have (for obvious reasons) been through the arduous and lengthy process of self-revelation which is necessary before any Freudian analysis can be effected.

Writing in 1912, McDougall found it necessary to protest against the loose and totally unscientific way in which people were already speaking of the 'subconscious mind', the 'sublimate self', etc. His words are equally relevant to much subsequent talk about the 'unconscious':

It cannot be too strongly laid down, in view of the popularity of these catchwords, that, as commonly used, they are little or nothing more than words that serve to cloak our ignorance and to disguise from ourselves the need for further investigation. For the ordinary procedure is to postulate a 'subconscious mind', and then merely to assign to its agency all the various phenomena of a supernatural character, its nature remaining completely undefined and its capacities for the production of marvels being regarded as without limit i n any direction.

Finally, remember that Freud's views were changing continuously over the forty years or so during which he worked on his theory: thus in

The Ego and the Id (1923) he announced that he had found in practice that the division into *conscious*, *preconscious* and *unconscious* was not satisfactory, and proceeded to replace it by a new division into *ego*, *superego*, and *id* – the id being by no means synonymous with the unconscious, though the two concepts overlap to a considerable extent. So when reading Freud one must bear in mind the criticisms, not only of other schools of psychiatry, but also of Freud himself.

The underdog

The **UNDERDOG** referred originally to the losing dog in a dog-fight (the winner being the 'top dog'). Hence it meant anyone who was downtrodden, oppressed or socially inferior. The phrase was current in America before 1880.

Concern with the underdog is a comparatively recent development. For thousands of years the civilizations of the ancient world flourished on his labour, without taking any notice of him, except to see that he had just enough food to work on and was instantly disposed of if he became rebellious. It is said that the building of the Great Wall of China cost a million lives; and the tradition that it was built with the blood of the Chinese people has been handed down for nearly four thousand years.

All the ancient world took slavery for granted. A defeated people were enslaved, and were expected to be grateful that they had not been massacred. They and their children became the property of their owners, and could be sold or killed off if they ceased to be useful. It showed a great advance in humanity when the Emperor Trajan, in the second century A.D., punished a wealthy Roman who had thrown a clumsy slave into a pond full of man-eating fish. The Greeks were kinder to their slaves than the Romans, because they were naturally more humane; but they too, almost without exception, regarded slavery as part of the natural order of things. The philosopher Aristotle, in the fourth century B.C., argued that it was impossible for a man to be truly civilized unless all the really unpleasant work was

Continued on p. 423

PLATE 16

MODERN ART: Christ in the House of His Parents by J.E.Millais (1829–1896).

PROPAGANDA: A painting of Stalin in the *Hotel Moscow*.

VOLTAIRE.

Il vit le dernier siecle expirer chez Ninon
De Virgile à trente ans il ceignit la couronne,
Des lauriers de Sophocle il orna son automne
Et sema son hyver des fleurs d'Anacreon.

Borit

PROGRESS AND REASON: F. M. A. de Voltaire (1694–1778).

408

SCEPTICISM: René Descartes (1596–1650).

'SPORT AS A CHARACTER BUILDER': 1. *The Young Spartans*, by Edgar Dégas (1831–1917).

2. Amateur Boxers.

STURM UND DRANG : 1. The young Goethe (1749–1832), watercolour by H. W. Tischbein, 1787.

2. The old Goethe dictating to his secretary. Painting by Johann Joseph Schmeller, 1831.

STURM UND DRANG: In Art. 1. Dante addressed by Ugolino frozen into the ice. Drawing by J. H. Fuseli (1741–1825).

2. *Odin calls to the Prophetess on the edge of Hell,* by J. H. Fuseli.

415

TRADITION: 1. The Norroy and Ulster King of Arms proclaims a new Sovereign, London.

2. Arriving at the Paris Opera.

TRANSMIGRATION OF SOULS: 1. Standing Buddha guarding the reclining Buddha at the Galvahara, Ceylon.

418

2. Seated Buddha, Ceylon.

TOTAL WAR: 1. Warfare as single combat. Medieval painting c. 1200.

420

2. From *The Disasters of War*, by Goya (1796–1828).

TOTAL WAR: '*What odd mirrors they make nowadays*'. Lithograph by Honoré Daumier (1808–1879).

done for him, partly by slaves and partly by free men lower down in the social scale than himself.

For Greeks and Romans, as for the rest of the ancient world, civilization could exist only if it was borne on the shoulders of a vast army of have-nots.

The rise of Christianity brought a change, since it taught men to realize that other men possessed immortal souls which had to be respected; and since, in addition, it taught all Christians that their own souls would be imperilled if they neglected the poor. But the habit of regarding the majority of mankind as much less important than a privileged few, persisted. The fighting class at the top of society, the kings and nobles, were important; and so were the priests, though it was to their advantage if they were also nobles. The rest of the population hardly mattered. They might become rich, but they and their descendants would always carry the stigma of being 'base-born' – that is to say, descended from people who had worked.

There were protests, from time to time, against this state of affairs. In every country the peasants and the townspeople periodically rebelled; and in one of the most famous of these rebellions – the English Peasants' Revolt in 1381 – the leader, a priest named John Ball, led his followers with the famous slogan:

> When Adam delved and Eve span,
> Who was then the gentleman?

But the idea that most men and women should be content to remain in a condition of hopeless inferiority was not seriously attacked until the eighteenth century.

The attack was led by the 'philosophers'; a number of witty and cultivated Frenchmen who were not of noble birth themselves, and were dissatisfied with a state of society that prevented them from rising to the top. They advanced the revolutionary idea that all men were endowed with equal rights at birth, and that the differences in status that had arisen between them were artificial and ridiculous. 'Man is born free', said Rousseau, 'and everywhere he is in chains.' Sympathizers in other countries responded in increasing numbers. The American Revolution was inspired by the new egalitarian doctrines. The Declaration of Independence, issued in 1776, begins with the

T

words: 'We hold these truths to be self-evident, that all men are created equal, that they are endowed by their creator with certain inalienable rights, that among these are life, liberty, and the pursuit of happiness' – although many of the signers of this Declaration owned negro slaves, whom they had no intention of regarding as equals.

The result of all this was the French Revolution, which began as the dream of the prosperous middle class, but soon developed into the seizure of power by the real underdogs. They called themselves the 'sans-culottes', because they wore the trousers of the poor, instead of the knee-breeches that were the mark of the well-to-do. They went cheerfully to war with practically the whole of Europe at once, proclaiming that they brought 'war to the noble's castle, peace to the peasant's hut'. In the end they were defeated, but the world as it had been before the Revolution could never be brought back. In the end, the liberty and equality of all citizens came to be accepted over most of Western Europe and much of the rest of the world.

The French Revolution had concerned itself with the underdog politically, but not economically. Political inferiority was regarded as an unreasonable barrier, to be got rid of; but if a man had less money than he needed, that was his own business, and his own fault. It was not until the nineteenth century that a man's right to become as rich as he could manage was seriously challenged by a series of revolutionaries. The most famous of these, Karl Marx, believed that only another and a far more fundamental revolution would do the proletarians any good. But enormous progress in improving the lot of the poor was made in the nineteenth century and at intervals in the twentieth; and it was usually those countries that went about things most peaceably, instead of using up their energies in class hatred, that achieved the most. The progress was so great and so continuous that many people complacently took it for granted that it would go on indefinitely, until a state of all-round perfection was reached. This optimistic belief failed to survive the First World War.

Much of the progress since that time has been made in the opposite direction. Hitler's New Order – aptly described as 'the oldest order in the world, that of master and slave' – was only one of a number of attempts to create more and more underdogs, and to push them down into a condition of partial or total slavery. The Russian slave labour camps, and Dr Malan's plans for depriving the South African negro of such advance as he has been able to make, are part of the same picture; for the underdog is a useful animal. If everyone has a fair share of whatever is available, whether of wealth or of political power, nobody will get very much; but if a country can be run by a small minority living on the work of the rest, every member of the ruling class can be rich. Aldous Huxley, in *Brave New World*, prophesied a society where the riches would be enjoyed by a select few, while lower and lower classes of hereditary skilled and unskilled workers were artificially conditioned not to want the privileges they could not have. George Orwell, in *1984*, told of an even more horrible state of affairs; a development of Communism to the point where the Inner Party run the country, the Outer Party carry out their orders, and a horde of uneducated 'Proles', living in slum conditions, do the manual work. In many countries the condition of the underdog is still improving, and it is possible that in some of them there may some day be no underdogs; but it would be a mistake to believe that this will come about automatically, as the result of 'Progress'.

Efforts at world peace

The **UNITED NATIONS** is an international organization for the preservation of world peace. It was set up on 24 October 1945 by the fifty states that had been fighting against Germany, Italy and Japan in the Second World War. Twenty-six of those states had previously signed the United Nations Declaration of common war aims on 1 January 1942, and it was there that the phrase 'United Nations' was first used.

Though the United Nations is a new body, the idea of an international organization to preserve peace is derived from several different lines of thought that go back for many years. As Lowes Dickinson said in 1916 in *The European Anarchy* 'In the great and tragic history of Europe there is a turning point that marks the defeat of the ideal of a world-order and the definite acceptance of international anarchy. That turning-point is the emergence of the sovereign state at the end of the fifteenth century.' Ever since then there have been men who have argued, with Lowes Dickinson, that 'it is as true of an aggregation of States as of an aggregation of individuals, that if there is no common law and no common force, the best intentions will be defeated by lack of confidence and security ... and there will be a chronic state of war.'

A common law and a common force for all states imply a world government and the first proposal for such a government was put forward by the Duc de Sully (1560–1641), chief Minister to King Henri IV of France. In his *Grand Design* Sully envisaged Europe being governed by six national councils and one international council: the latter, which was to be composed of delegates from all participating states and be in permanent session, was to decide all questions of common interest and to control a composite army to which each state would contribute. After Sully, many other plans for a world government were put forward at different times, including ones by the philosophers Kant and Bentham, but none was ever adopted because states were too jealous of their sovereignty and ordinary people too unwilling to be governed, even indirectly, by foreigners.

The second line of thought is of more recent origin. States have in the past often formed alliances with each other, some offensive and some defensive, but they were mostly short-lived and directed against particular enemies. After the Napoleonic Wars, however, the victorious states agreed by the Treaty of Chaumont in 1814 to act together for twenty years to suppress any attempt by force to alter the status quo established by the Peace Treaties. Their attempt, the 'Concert of Europe', broke down because of the refusal of Great Britain to help Russia, Austria and Prussia suppress movements for constitutional reform that began to shake some of the ruling dynasties of Europe in the subsequent decade. The idea, however, that states should deter each other from resorting to violence by agreeing in advance to combine against any state that did so was revived in the early part of the twentieth century under the name of 'collective security' and soon became generally accepted.

The third line of thought was the development of the idea that if only there were some impartial tribunal to resolve disputes between states when they arose, states would not need to go to war. For example, in 1623, Emeric de Crucé had been emboldened to propose in his book, *Le Nouveau Cynée*, that a council of ambassadors representing the more important states should be established, and that this council should have the right to require all international disputes to be referred to its arbitration, whilst all the various states should agree in advance to be bound by its decisions. His scheme was not adopted, but the development of public international law after Grotius, the Dutch jurist who lived from 1583 to 1645, greatly strengthened the case for such a tribunal. In 1920, therefore, the Permanent Court of International Justice was set up at The Hague prepared to adjudicate upon any disputes between states where both parties agreed to accept its jurisdiction.

The fourth and last line of thought is the oldest of all. From very early times men have realized that states would be less likely to fight if their representatives had the opportunity to get to know each other and to discuss their differences. The nineteenth century saw a whole series of congresses between that of Vienna in 1815 and that of Berlin in 1878, each called to deal with an urgent specific international problem. In 1899 and 1907, however, international conferences were convened at The Hague to discuss the general possibility of reducing armaments; and though those conferences failed, the value of a permanent conference, where differences could be discussed as soon as they arose and before they had grown too great, was clearly seen.

The effect of the First World War, with its unprecedented horror and carnage, was to persuade millions of people to accept this idea of an international organization to preserve peace: and on 8 January 1918 President Wilson, in addressing the Congress of the U.S.A. and laying down fourteen points which constituted his country's war aims, gave as the last and chief of these 'a general association of nations must be formed under specific covenants for the purpose of affording mutual guarantees of political independence and territorial integrity to great and small states alike'.

In response to that initiative, the League of Nations was set up in 1920. However, because any state could veto any decision at any meeting, and because the U.S.A. never belonged to the League at all, whilst the U.S.S.R. belonged only from 1933 to 1939, the League was very far from being a world government, and was virtually powerless as an instrument of collective security. Moreover, only trifling disputes were submitted to the Permanent Court, and the opportunity for meetings and discussions which the League provided was not, alone, enough to prevent the outbreak of a Second World War in 1939.

As a result of the League's failure the United Nations was set up, as President Truman said in 1948, for three basic purposes: 'The first was to prevent future wars by creating a kind of economic condition throughout the world which is necessary for peace. The second was to provide the kind of organization which would help countries to settle their differences peacefully without shooting each other. The third purpose was to provide an organization by which the peace-loving countries could act collectively against threats to peace by an aggressive country.'

It was hoped that the United Nations would be more effective than the League because the U.S.A. and the U.S.S.R. belonged to it and because the power to take action to prevent breaches of the peace was given to a small body of eleven states in permanent session, the Security Council. However, for this body to be able to reach any decision, China, France, the United Kingdom, the U.S.A. and the U.S.S.R. have all to be in agreement, and since they rarely are, the United Nations has been, in the words of Professor Gilbert Murray, writing in 1953, 'in its political aspect, a disappointment just as the League of Nations was'. However, Sir Gladwyn Jebb, thinking of the bloodshed stopped in Palestine, Indonesia and Kashmir after United Nations intervention, said in the same year that though 'the record of the U.N. has been disappointing in some respects it has not been bad when it comes to pacific settlement'. Moreover, though the new International Court of Justice has so far only had minor disputes to deal with, the fact that the United Nations does serve as a permanent meeting-ground and conference certainly helped to resolve the Berlin crisis in 1948, though some might agree with Mr Clement Davies, who said in 1953 that 'instead of harmonizing the interests of different states by open negotiation, the United Nations serves as a sounding-board and megaphone for emphasizing their differences'.

On the other hand, in fulfilment of what President Truman called its first purpose, the United Nations by its Economic and Social Council has done a great deal to improve economic and social conditions in the world. Through its affiliated organizations, the World Health Organization and the United Nations International Children's Emergency Fund in particular, it sent for example thirty tons of vaccine and plasma to Egypt in 1947, and so halted a vast cholera epidemic; it reduced the number of malaria cases in Greece from two million to fifty thousand by spraying the mosquitoes' haunts with insecticide; it has vaccinated over ten million children against tuberculosis; and it has cured nearly one million people in Asia of yaws by injecting them with penicillin. The importance of their work was pointed out by Mr Malik of the Lebanon, who said in 1948 'the need for the Security Council is in inverse proportion to the success of the Economic and Social Council'. Indeed, 'the hopeful fact about the United Nations is that with the full consent of the great powers, some machinery is in process of being built through which they can, if they will, make a world society work'.

ILLUSTRATION: Page 454.

Reversing Babel

'UNIVERSAL LANGUAGE' means a language which could be learned for the express purpose of international communication between people whose mother tongues were different. It could be a language already in existence, or one specially created for the purpose. It would be an auxiliary language, not aiming to replace any existing languages, though it might eventually have that effect.

No such language exists at present; but the need for one has long been evident, and the attempt to supply the need by the creation of an artificial language goes back more than three hundred years. Europe, in particular, is in a linguistic confusion that cries out for a common language. The people of Europe speak and write forty different languages. Five languages are in use within two hundred miles of London. In Yugoslavia the Croat and Serb languages are practically the same, but they are written in different alphabets. Switzerland has four official languages; Belgium has two. By comparison, North and South America, which have only four official languages between them, are exceptionally fortunate. In Western Europe the idea of unity is making slow headway; but it is still difficult to see how countries are going to come together in a lasting union so long as their peoples do not understand each other.

There have been international languages in the past. The conquests of Alexander the Great in the fourth century B.C. spread Greek, the language of his army and Empire, from Greece to the borders of India; and for centuries thereafter Greek was the international language of Eastern Europe and the Middle East. The expansion of Rome, which began shortly after Alexander's time, made Latin, in the same way, the universal language of Western Europe. At the time of the arrival of Christianity every educated man in the Roman Empire, or in the semi-civilized countries to the east of it, knew Greek or Latin, and many knew both. Wherever the Apostles went they could make themselves understood; and the result was that Christianity spread across the Empire in a generation.

When the Roman Empire broke up in western Europe (in the fifth century A.D.), Latin remained as the international language. Priests and monks spoke it; laws were written in it; travellers relied on it; wandering scholars sang songs in it. When, from the fifteenth century onwards, the Renaissance brought back the study of classical Greece and Rome, the homely, easy Latin of the Middle Ages was replaced by the complicated classical Latin of Cicero's time; and for several centuries scientific works, histories, treatises on law or philosophy, etc., were mostly written in this refined Latin.

Unfortunately, classical Latin, unlike medieval Latin, is a very difficult language. A fluent command of it required a very good education, and it could then only be understood by those whose education had been equally good. From the seventeenth century, Latin, as an international language, rapidly declined. During the eighteenth century the language of polite society, even in Russia, was French; but it lost this position with the French Revolution, although it is still to some extent the official language of diplomacy to this day.

It has frequently been suggested that the best way to have a universal language would be to take a language that is already widely spoken, and persuade the world – or at least Europe, for a start – to learn it as a secondary language. English, French, Spanish, Russian and German have all been suggested for this purpose. Unfortunately, they, and all other 'natural' languages, contain great difficulties of grammar, syntax, spelling or pronunciation; and they all contain a great wealth of difficult idiom. They were not, after all, designed so as to be easy for foreigners; they simply grew. An even more serious objection is that the world-wide spread of any one language involves the world-wide spread of its literature and culture; and this would be violently resented by all those who disapproved of that culture, or who thought that their own language and culture should have been chosen instead.

Latin or Greek, being 'dead' languages, would be free from this objection. But classical Greek would be much too rich and difficult a language for more than a few scholars; and classical Latin, though simpler than Greek, is still very complicated and difficult. However, Professor Peano, of Turin, was attracted by the idea of a simplified Latin – on the lines of the popular Latin of the Middle Ages, but even easier. His language, which was brought out in 1903 and is now called *Interlingua*, was constructed on his principle: 'The best grammar is no grammar'; and in effect is Latin modernized, and with all the grammar cut out. Interlingua, and a rival on the same lines called *Romanal*, are both easy, logically constructed, and euphonious; and each has a number of supporters.

Attempts to construct a new, 'artificial' language go back to the early seventeenth century; but at first they were made up out of the inventor's head, on 'philosophical' principles, with no reference to any existing languages; and consequently no one, not even the inventor, could memorize them. The first important step forward was the invention of *Volapük*, by Father Schleyer, an Austrian priest, in 1880. Volapük was such an immediate success that Renan, the French writer, predicted that it would shortly replace the vernacular languages. However, Schleyer had made it impossibly complicated, with a more involved grammar than most 'natural' languages; and as he refused to allow the slightest change, it soon collapsed.

The most popular of all 'artificial' languages, *Esperanto*, was invented in 1887 by Dr Zamenhof, of Warsaw. It was built on the Latin roots found in Western European languages, with the addition of a number of words from German and a few from English. The grammar was simple, logical and easy to memorize; it could be learned in an hour. The language was described by G. K. Chesterton as 'a journalistic gibberish with plurals in -oj', but others have found it sensible and attractive. To this day, Esperanto has the largest following of any international language; its supporters hold periodical congresses, publish a number of magazines, broadcast radio programmes, and have their own anthem and their own flag – white, with a green star.

Of the large number of rival languages that preceded and followed Esperanto, the one with the largest following is *Ido*, which was launched in 1907. The word 'Ido' is Esperanto for 'offspring', and at first Ido was designed simply as a reformed version of Esperanto. When the majority of the Esperantists refused to alter their language, the supporters of Ido seceded. Ido omits a good deal that its founders thought superfluous in Esperanto, including the plurals in -oj.

In recent years there have been attempts to create an international language on rather different lines. R. J. G. Dutton's *Speedwords*, brought out in 1943, is founded on existing European words; but his aim is to make them as short as possible, and the commonest words consist of only a single letter, all twenty-six letters of the alphabet being used for this purpose. Professor Lancelot Hogben's *Interglossa* is founded on the international vocabulary of the scientist, who uses some words derived from Latin and considerably more from Greek. Compound words are built up on a logical formula, so that 'ergo-pe' means 'work-person', and 'patho-do ergo-pe' means 'nurse'.

Another attempt at a universal language is *Basic English*, which was brought out by C. K. Ogden in 1930. This is not a new language, but an attempt to make English easier to learn by reducing its vocabulary, and in particular by cutting down the number of verbs to eighteen. Ogden made no changes in grammar or spelling; there is no word used in Basic that is not already familiar in standard English. Unfortunately the result is a little bare.

No single universal language has yet captured the field. Esperanto has the largest number of supporters; but the student of Esperanto can hardly feel, as yet, that the language is going to be much use to him on his travels. Unfortunately, the field is disputed between several dozen rival languages, each with its own point of superiority over its rivals; and the champions of each language spend much of their energy quarrelling with each other. If they would all rally round one language and press for its adoption, they would have a much better chance of success. As it is, the layman is inclined, unfairly and unwisely, to write off the believers in an international language as cranks.

Here are the first ten words of the Lord's Prayer in the principal international languages:

Volapük: O Fat obas, kel bino in süls, paisaludomöz nem ola.

Interlingua: Patre nostro, qui es in celos, que tuo nomine fi sanctificato.

Romanal: Patro nostri, qui est in cieles, sanctificat estas nomine tui.

Esperanto: Patro nia, kiu estas en la chielo, sankta estu via nomo.

Ido: Patro nia, qua esas en la cielo, tua nomo santigesez.

Speedwords: Wi per qu e i celp, sak pi e vi nam.

Interglossa: Na Parenta in Urani, tu Nomino gene revero.

ILLUSTRATION: Page 374.

Votes for all

UNIVERSAL SUFFRAGE is a system of election in which every adult citizen has the right to vote. Its purpose is to give every member of the state a share in the choice of who is to govern, and it is an essential part of the machinery of democratic government. In the smallest communities the vote may give the citizen a personal part in choosing the chief officials, and even a direct share in deciding the daily questions of government; but in the great states of today, it can only give him a part in the election of others to carry out this task. As a modern concept, therefore, universal suffrage means voting for candidates to a legislative assembly (and in some countries also for certain officials).

Some think of the right to vote as a natural right, some regard it as a privilege conferred by the state, some think of it as one of the citizen's obligations. A democratic state may regard the vote in any of these ways; yet the second view may exclude many citizens from the franchise. The U.S.S.R., for instance, by its 1925 Constitution, gives the vote only to 'All persons living by productive labour and of a general utility'. In fact many so-called democracies, now and in the past, have not considered universal suffrage essential or even desirable.

While the idea of democracy goes back at least to the sixth century B.C., universal suffrage in its fullest sense is a very modern concept. Many communities have given the vote to all their citizens, but this might exclude slaves and the poorest men; some have reserved the vote for those of a certain race or religion; many have had a (high) property qualification; others again have demanded literacy. All, until within the last seventy years, have excluded women from the franchise.

While all these disqualifications have had to be abolished before a country can be said to be a true democracy, the mere institution of universal suffrage does not make a state democratic. It is the nature of the choice laid before the voter which is the true test of free institutions. In countries which allow no opposition party, there may be universal suffrage, but in practice little freedom in voting. The voter chooses at most between different candidates put forward by the ruling party. Other countries may allow free elections to a legislative assembly, but keep this assembly virtually powerless; this again is not democracy.

Even where there is real freedom of choice this freedom may be undone by other means. Unscrupulous, wealthy and powerful men can force the citizen to vote against his will, however much the government intends free choice. Only by secret ballot (first introduced in Australia in 1856) can one prevent bribery and threats at election time. There must also be careful safeguards against miscounting of the votes. Universal suffrage may be an empty formula unless these abuses are guarded against.

The history of the extension of the right to vote has closely followed the growth of democracy. The first important democracy was founded at Athens at the end of the sixth century B.C. Every adult Athenian male who had not been expressly disenfranchised for some grave offence was a member of the assembly. Not only did he choose directly those who were to rule (and he might well be chosen himself) he also voted on the questions of day-to-day administration, legislation and justice. Yet though this may seem the perfect example of universal suffrage, a system which gives every citizen a large share in the government of the country, in fact the suffrage was not universal. Women, resident aliens and slaves had no voice whatever in the conduct of affairs. On the other hand, the full manhood suffrage that the Athenians achieved was not given again until the nineteenth century.

One only finds traces of the idea of manhood suffrage in the Middle Ages. The host of warriors who signified their acceptance of a new king were only representatives of the people in the most general sense, and there was no formal voting.

When, as in England in the thirteenth century, a parliament was summoned for the first time, there had to be some system of electing members. It was thought at that time, and for many centuries to come, that the only people worthy of having a share in the government of the country were those who had a share of the country itself. This excluded everyone who did not own land from the right to vote. With the coming of the

Reformation, however, there was a step backwards. Only members of the Established Church were allowed to vote.

It was only with the violent upheavals and experiments of major revolutions that the idea of manhood suffrage was put forward again. The first of these to produce the idea was the Civil War between Charles I and Parliament. In 1649 a group of Cromwell's soldiers, calling themselves the Levellers, put forward a plan to extend the rights of the individual. One of the chief points in their programme was manhood suffrage. No one at that time thought of giving women equal rights with men: the proposal that all men should vote was revolutionary enough, and little notice was taken of it.

During the eighteenth century many thinkers were concerned with the idea that men are born with certain rights, and when manhood suffrage was again proposed it was as a natural right. In 1776 the American colonies drew up their Declaration of Independence against Britain: 'We hold these truths to be self evident: that all men are created equal; that they are endowed by their creator with certain inalienable rights.' It affirms that all government derives its powers from the consent of the governed, and that the object of government is to guarantee the rights of man. 'The consent of the governed' might lead, one would think, to universal suffrage. But the men who drew up the American Constitution would not take this step. They feared that propertyless citizens, having nothing to lose, would let themselves be tempted by extreme experiments, and would be at the mercy of demagogues. They were also afraid that the poor might use their power to expropriate the rich.

The same motives prevented the framers of the 1791 Constitution in France from granting universal suffrage. In many respects the French Declaration of the Rights of Man of 1789, the manifesto of the Revolution, echoes the American Declaration of Independence. It also bases sovereignty on the people's consent and declares all men to be born equal with inalienable rights. One clause in it is interesting: 'Law is the expression of the general will. All citizens have the right to take part personally or through their representatives in its formation.' Yet when it came to putting this doctrine of Liberty, Equality and

Fraternity (q.v.) into practice, the French were as fearful for their property as the Americans. The franchise was limited by a property qualification which excluded from the vote the great majority of the artisans of the towns. The Jacobins, when they came to power in 1793, drew up a new constitution giving manhood suffrage, but pleaded the war emergency as an excuse for not putting it into operation.

It is the nineteenth century which is the great era of progress towards universal suffrage. It was a time in which the unenfranchised were fighting for general emancipation, and the vote was one among the many rights they acquired.

Poverty and unemployment urged the propertyless on to fight for a share in the government. Dissenters claimed equal rights with Churchmen. The humanitarian movement worked to free the slaves, and women worked to free themselves.

In England occupiers of leasehold property swelled the number of voters further after the 1832 Reform Act; and by successive Acts in 1867 and 1884 the suffrage was extended to all male householders.

Meanwhile in the United States two major disqualifications were removed. After the Civil War slavery was abolished, and by the Fourteenth Amendment to the U.S. Constitution negroes were enfranchised (1866).

Still women were deprived of the vote. New Zealand was the first country to give it to them, in 1893. It was not until after the First World War that Britain and the United States followed suit. The U.S.A. gave votes to women in 1920, and England gave it in 1918 to ratepayers and wives of ratepayers over thirty, withholding total enfranchisement of women until 1928.

Nevertheless, universal suffrage is still not a world-wide practice. Several countries, including Switzerland, still refuse to enfranchise women. In much of Africa the negro's liberty to vote is still extremely limited. Certain countries, including Brazil and Chile, demand that voters should be able to read. Most Western countries however only admit disqualification through incapabilities such as minority, lunacy, or imprisonment.

While the process of emancipation which has brought extensions of the franchise is still going on, in the great western democracies universal suffrage has been achieved; it seems that it will only be a question of time before all countries claiming to be democracies follow their example.

The Ideal Nowheres

UTOPIA means in common usage an imaginary, ideal state. It means also the *Utopia* of Thomas (not yet Sir Thomas) More, written in Latin, and first published in Louvain in 1516.

It is not difficult to see why it became the prototype of all later utopias, although it was not itself the first. There had been Plato's *Republic*; there had been St Augustine's *De Civitate Dei*. The approach to the first was philosophical, not primarily imaginative. The origin of the second was cataclysmic, the sacking of Rome. Moreover, the title and concept of the City of God not only marked St Augustine's ideal order as unique, but also implied a sanction for the ideal which is inconsistent with the total lack of reality expected of a utopia.

From internal evidence, and as a classical scholar and philosopher respected by the greatest of his contemporaries, More must have read the *Republic*; he had lectured on the *De Civitate*. But although he drew on both, he imparted qualities to the *Utopia* which made it different in kind from its predecessors. He gave it the setting of a story; he began its writing as a diversion; and, above all, the state which he described was not only an ideal state, it was specifically nonexistent. His Utopia was not a εὖ (good) place, but an οὐ (not) place. The meaning since acquired by the adjective 'utopian' is thus etymologically and historically correct.

At the time when More wrote the *Utopia* he was approaching a turning point in his career. In the nineteen years since coming down from Oxford he had been called to the Bar, become the friend of Colet and Erasmus, been diverted from monastic aspirations to marriage, had four children and married again, and attained to an income three times the then salary of the Lord Chancellor. During the four years which followed the publication of the *Utopia* he was appointed Master of

Requests and sworn of the Privy Council, attended his king to the Field of the Cloth of Gold, and was knighted and made Under-Treasurer.

The turning point was his acceptance in 1515, 'at the suit and instaunce of the English Merchauntes', of membership of a difficult trade legation to the Low Countries. It was 'to while away time' during a period of waiting while on this mission that he wrote with careful polish the second book of the *Utopia* – the part which contains the main account of his imaginary country. The positive part of the book can thus be regarded as a return to the youthful interest of the young humanist who had lectured on the *De Civitate*, and between whose seriousness and *jeux d'esprit* his friends found it difficult to distinguish.

The first book of the *Utopia* was more quickly written on his return to London. It provided the fictional setting for the account already written, and an opportunity for the topical comments of the lawyer on the use of the death penalty for theft, and the social evils of enclosure and dispossession which drove men to steal. According to Erasmus, his reason for publishing the *Utopia* was to point out 'what was amiss in the state, especially in his own England'.

Politically and economically, Utopia was a form of oligarchical communism. There was a distinction between 'handicraftes men', whose six hours' work was enough to produce plenty, and an 'ordre of the learned' from which were chosen ambassadors, priests, rulers and finally the prince himself; although, by the commendation of the priests and secret election by the lowest level of rulers, the manual worker might be transferred from one group to the other in recognition of earnest and diligent study in spare hours. The lowest level of rulers, who alone were directly elected, were responsible chiefly for seeing that no one, not so exempted, was idle.

It was by these that the real rulers were elected, and 'lightly they chaunge them not'. Houses were rotated by lot at ten-year intervals, and necessary equipment taken by the head of the household without payment or authority from common stores. Gold was despised; priests were of exceeding holiness, 'and therefore very few'; and there were few laws and no lawyers. Bondmen were conveniently obtained from wrong-doers, not only in their own country, but from other countries which for the most part were glad to be rid of them.

For the fighting of wars there was available an unpleasing race of mercenaries, who fought 'hardeley, fyerslye, and faythefullye', and the more of them were killed, the better the Utopians thought it. They had also the advantage of a neighbouring land, with empty space in which new towns could be built, usually with the agreement of the inhabitants, but if necessary making war. There were 'dyvers kyndes of religion', and a decree of toleration, the case for which is argued solidly and at some length. It may be noted, however, that atheists were considered to have been kindly treated in being deprived merely of civil rights; they were counted 'not in the numbre of men', and were despised by all.

The interest of many later utopias is concentrated on particular aspects of organized existence on which their authors held strong views. Thus Campanella's *Civitas Solis* (1623) is notable for original views on education. The mechanical arts and physical sciences received a new emphasis, and no value was placed on 'consideration of the dead signs of things', and little on knowledge of languages, for which interpreters provided a working substitute. Bacon's *New Atlantis* (published posthumously in 1629) consists only of that part of his envisaged ideal commonwealth which most appealed to him: his design for a model college 'instituted for the interpreting of nature', and operating both through the conduct of experiments and the collection of information from other countries'. It is of some current interest that the conclusions drawn from research were to be disclosed to the state only if the college thought this desirable.

Samuel Butler's *Erewhon, or Over the Range* (1872) is, in effect, rather a satire of contemporary manners than a true utopia. With William Morris's *News from Nowhere* (1891), the stage is reached when the 'nowhere' quality belongs rather to the title than to the intention; its first publication having been in the monthly organ, *Commonweal*, of the Socialist League. Up to this period the imagining of ideal commonwealths had been an intellectual exercise, divorced from the world of reality, influential rather in ideas than as a contribution to practical statecraft. When, however, the attempt is made to realize the ideal, a possible new rôle is opened for the imaginative writer, that of the satirizing critic. Thus we find in George Orwell's *Animal Farm*, the story of a utopia that went wrong.

ILLUSTRATION: Page 73.

Every picture tells a story

UT PICTURA POESIS – 'A poem is a speaking picture; a picture is a silent poem.' According to Plutarch, the Greek poet Simonides (c. 556–468 B.C.) was responsible for this aphorism.

None of the early writers on the theory of art would have put on this remark the weight which it was later to carry. Plato, in the tenth book of *The Republic*, points out the relationship between the two arts in that both poetry and painting, being one degree further removed from reality than carpentry or other crafts (poetry making use of fiction and painting of illusion), are also in some ways inferior to them. Aristotle makes use of the analogy, accepting it as a commonplace of criticism. The Roman poet Horace, writing in the first century A.D., echoes Simonides' remark almost casually in his 'Epistle on the Art of Poetry':

> Ut pictura poesis: erit quae, si propitius stes
> Te capiat magis ...

A poem is like a picture; one will charm you more the nearer you stand; another if you stand away from it; this will prefer to remain in the shade, the other would rather be seen in the light, and does not fear the judge's critical scrutiny. This will please once only; the other, though seen ten times, will continue to delight you.

These views were, however, expressed before separation of the 'fine' from the 'useful' arts; before even the more ancient and deeply rooted division between the 'liberal' and 'manual' arts had achieved any definition.

On the old view poetry and painting had much the same status. They were both 'a method of making something', and here, in spite of other differences, they were equal with carpentry or shoemaking.

Music and rhetoric and the other liberal arts existed on a more abstract level. And although the 'liberal' arts had a kind of 'manual' incarnation – singing or instrumental playing in the case of music – they dealt with a larger field; Hugh of St Victor (1096–1141), a hymnologist and theologian, gives some idea of its scope in his summary of the teaching of Boethius (c. A.D. 480–524):

> The parts of music are first, the music of the universe, second the music of human beings, and third, instrumental music. Of the parts of the music of the universe, one is in the elements, one in the heavenly bodies, one in the changes of time. Of those which are in the elements, one consists in weight, the second in number, the third in measure ... Human music is partly in the soul and partly in the body, partly in the connection between the two ... Instrumental music is partly in striking – as in timbrels and strings; partly in wind, as in pipes and organs; partly in the voice, as in songs and chants.

The idea of the universal harmony stated in such precise terms made up the 'theory' of music, to which its 'practice' was related as the sunken part of the iceberg is related to the visible part. Guido of Arezzo (c. 990), a Benedictine monk and the reputed inventor of five-stave notation, asserted that the musician's competence depended on his acquaintance with theories such as that of Boethius: 'It is not skill (*ars*) which makes the true singer, but learning (*doctrina*); he who sings what he does not understand must be called a brute (*bestia*).' The hierarchical arrangement of the arts meant both that it was possible to establish a working relation between them, and that it was difficult to confuse their function. When the great Florentine architect, Leone Baptista Alberti, wrote to his collaborator, Matteo dei' Pasti in 1454 protesting against the latter's modification of his design: 'You see how the dimensions and proportions of the pilasters are generated; if you change them, you will make a discord in all this music', he was clearly referring to what Boethius would have classified as 'music of the universe'. It was Madame de Staël (1766–1817), the French novelist and *mondaine*, who first hinted at the changed relation between the two arts, when she remarked that 'space was, as it were, a frozen music'. Goethe also said 'architecture is petrified music'. The hierarchical relation has been replaced by the idea that these two arts, both being 'methods of making something', are parallel both technically and in their emotional impact.

Later in the nineteenth century the idea that all arts aspire to the condition of music became popular; in fact, the German architect Erich Mendelssohn (1887–1952) gave drawings of his architectural phantasies such names as 'Bach's Toccata and fugue in D Minor', while the terminology used by many apologists for 'abstract' art approaches dangerously near the language of musical criticism.

The tag that every picture tells a story has, since the beginning of the century, been the object of ridicule. This tag is in fact a rather distant relative of Horace's remark. The practice of drawing up literary programmes for plastic works of art had become common early in the Middle Ages; the notion that ecclesiastical authorities had a right to direct, control or inspire the literary 'content' of a picture or supervise the decoration of a building was given the status of a canon law at the second council of Nicaea (787), was usually interpreted generously. Clerics drew up the programme for the images which a building was to carry, and were often called to decide matters of symbolic colour, or the mathematical symbolism which should underlie a system of proportion.

This method of working was very much taken for granted, and was carried through beyond the fifteenth century. Botticelli (1444–1510) was an artist who made use of such literary collaboration in secular pictures such as the 'Primavera'. But the most important examples are the 'Stanze', the series of rooms in the Vatican palace, frescoed by Raphael (1483–1520) and his pupils, which obey a most elaborate and involved scheme, involving not only the separate paintings in detail, but also the relation between them. The indication of symbolic schemes was unfortunately boiled down to a literal and sometimes rather slavish copying of narrative accounts in painting.

It was at this time, in the seventeenth century, that Horace's remark was so frequently used by writers on art. One of the most important theorists, the French painter Charles du Fresnoy (1611–1668), opened his *De Arte Graphica*, a dissertation on painting in Latin verse, with the Horatian quotation; the book was widely read and discussed; Dryden had translated it within thirty years of publication, and two further translations in English verse followed in the course of the eighteenth century.

As against the theoreticians of the academies in the seventeenth and eighteenth centuries, the writers of the romantic movement first sought to define the limits of literature and poetry. Gotthold Ephraim Lessing (1729–1781), in his *Laokoon*, pointed out that painting described the relation between objects, while poetry dealt with events; and whereas the two arts overlapped slightly, their aims were very different. This reasonable distinction was taken to its extreme too soon; many painters deliberately sloughed off the preoccupation with content. Landscape and the 'still life' study absorbed an increasing amount of artistic output; and whereas these subjects had some literary motive in the sixteenth and seventeenth centuries, they had lost any such connotation by the beginning of the eighteenth. With the departure of the 'intelligible' subject the artist devoted an increasing proportion of his energy to the development of his technique as the only means of expression, and in fact a large proportion of the literary discussion of art during the nineteenth century is concerned with questions of technique.

The Impressionists particularly, although they had very much personal contact with writers and poets, were rarely influenced by them in choice of subject or the treatment; in England the pre-Raphaelite Brotherhood alone had very strong literary connexions. A new vitality was given to the link between literature and painting through the cubist and futurist movements at the beginning of this century; some cubist painters, notably Picasso and Juan Gris (1887–1927), used words from popular songs as patterns in their pictures, as lettering had been used in classical, Byzantine, and medieval painting. The leading poet of the movement, Guillaume Apollinaire (1880–1918), revived the device of the Calligramme, a poem written or printed into a shape connected with its subject-matter; a device which had been particularly popular in late Hellenistic times, and in the eleventh, sixteenth, and seventeenth centuries.

Although European art never achieved the close link between literature and painting which characterizes Chinese and Japanese art, where calligraphy and painting share the common technique of waterpoof ink laid with a brush, their development, certainly until the seventeenth century, shows many parallels. Although few modern writers or painters would give their allegiance to such a slogan as 'Every picture tells a story', yet the preoccupation with content has lately become a much more important issue than at any time in the last three hundred years.

V

No entrails entombed in entrails

VEGETARIANISM began, apparently, in the Golden Age. Many of its devotees have looked forward to a return of this period; all of them have consciously pursued the Good Life. The vegetarian ethic has constantly been associated with a religious or at any rate an idealistic outlook, whether sung by Ovid or by General Booth. Its exponents have ably argued the incompatibility of the slaughterhouse with any kind of Utopia – and Utopianism, whether romantic (Rousseau) or transcendental (Buddha), is their common ground.

The definition of a vegetarian is simple: he is 'one who on principle abstains from any form of animal food, or at least such as is obtained by the direct destruction of life'. The words 'on principle' eliminate the many millions who go without meat from circumstance rather than choice. These appear in Vegetarian propaganda as arguments to refute the charge of crankiness and to answer doubts about nutriment (the stamina of the Chinese coolies is most often quoted) – but their vegetarianism has no capital letter. It is not an Idea.

As to 'direct destruction of life' – this splits vegetarians into two groups: the ordinary ones, and the Vegans (sometimes called Fruitarians), who shrink from complicity in the destruction, or even use, of any animal life at all. They have been described by one eminent Vegetarian as the spearhead of the movement. They advocate a diet of fruit, nuts, vegetables and grains, and encourage the use of alternatives to all products of animal origin; this means that they exclude dairy produce and even honey. The Vegan Society issues lists of products, including cosmetics and polishes, which can safely be bought by Vegans.

But the majority of Vegetarians abstain only from fish, flesh and fowl – though in the Order of the Golden Age, founded at Paignton in 1904, Associate Members, as distinct from Companions of the Order, were allowed to eat net-caught fish.

The Vegetarian Idea has always been based on three major causes: health, economy and morals. The first is the simplest. Vegetarians point out that animals sometimes have communicable diseases, such as parasites or T.B., and that the flesh of artificially fed animals is full of excretory substances. A vegetarian diet is said to produce superior stamina and resistance to disease. Meat-eating is regarded as the source of most physical impurities, and Shelley went so far as to say that it was because Prometheus stole fire to cook meat that the vulture (disease) fastened eternally upon his liver.

The belief in Vegetarian longevity may be traced back to tales of the mythical Hyperboreans, who lived to be a thousand. But they dwelt 'beyond the reach of cold and storms'. More acceptable is Shelley's note on Old Parr, who, 'healthy as the wild animals, attained to the age of 152 years'. An Italian, Luigi Cornaro, having ruined his stomach by youthful gourmandizing, was forced to go on so spare a vegetarian diet that doctors thought he would never see the end of the fifteenth century. He died in his 101st year – 1566.

Physical fitness is also testified by the records of many Vegetarian athletes.

Economy: this includes both the social and the personal. It is asserted that the assimilable nutriment from a given weight of vegetable foods will cost less than the same nutriment in flesh foods; also that one acre of cultivable land under fruit and vegetables will produce from two to twenty times as much food as if the same land were used for cattle. Seneca pointed out that the vast quantity of lives one stomach absorbs represents the 'devastation of land and sea'. Modern Vegetarians agree.

There is perhaps an aura of complacent Good Works about some of the pamphlets published in the eighteen-eighties and eighteen-nineties – 'The Advantages of a Vegetarian Diet in Workhouses and Prisons'; 'Cheap Dinners for School Children'; 'The Dietary of the Troops'; 'The Best Diet for a Working Man', etc. But they did practise what they preached: even in 1884, 'How to Live on 1/- a Week' must have entailed frugality.

The economy of plain living leads naturally to the morality of high thinking. The moral reasons for Vegetarianism are strong: 'Thou shalt not kill', says the Bible. The Vegetarian contends that to murder an animal is sin, and that to eat meat is to have, however indirectly, what Emerson called 'complicity' in murder. Compassion and meat-eating are contradictory – ironically so when, with 'entrails entombed in entrails', the meat-eater calls himself an animal lover. To condone pain is bad for the character; to kill is warlike. Vegetarianism is a prerequisite of the peaceful state. Rousseau asserted that meat-eaters were more cruel and ferocious people than Vegetarians, and Shelley blamed meat-eating for the irritabilities 'that make a hell of domestic life', as well as for the more sombre and sensational vices of tyrants from Nero to Napoleon (But Hitler was a Vegetarian.)

The morality of Vegetarianism insists on temperance as well as compassion. Over-eating, says Pythagoras, makes the fiery particle earth-bound; Musonius, some 500 years later, declares that the vapour engendered by meat-eating 'is turbid and darkens the soul'. Physical disgust at bloodshed goes with moral or intellectual disgust at gluttony, whether of the elaborate Roman or of the Yahoo kind. Every period of gastronomical excess has produced its converts to Vegetarianism. Self-control is an essential condition of the Good Life. But this need not be bleak: the early Christians abstained from flesh on the principle of self-mortification, but the Vegetarian today has a good stock of recipe books.

This moral, economic and health-conscious idea may have begun simply as a revulsion against sacerdotal practices. There were Orphic Societies, probably vegetarian, in Greece in the seventh or eighth centuries B.C. The first recorded anti-flesh association in the Western world was founded by Pythagoras at Croton, before 500 B.C. This association, consisting basically of 300 carefully chosen young men, was ridiculed in a play by Alexis, which is said to have caused inextinguishable laughter. Later, the laughter turned nasty, and the society's headquarters were set on fire by an exasperated mob. Pythagoras escaped, and lived to tame a bear by introducing it to a vegetarian diet.

Plato, some one hundred years later, got the nickname 'fig-lover', and introduced the Vegetarian idea into his Republic. The workers are presented in a circle of songs and garlands, eating loaves of barley and wheat with salt, olives, cheese, boiled onions, cabbage, figs, peas, beans and nuts.

Hippocrates, Seneca and Plutarch were Vegetarians. Plutarch wrote a passionate essay on Flesh-Eating, in which he defied meat-eaters to kill their own food, spoke of the table 'spread with the mangled forms of dead bodies', and likened the preparation of meat with vinegar and spice to the embalming of a human corpse. Philostratus condemned clothing derived from butchery, and Porphyrius maintained that a vegetarian diet was the key to freedom of the soul.

To come nearer home, Sir Thomas More advocated Vegetarianism, also John Evelyn, James Thomson, Lord Chesterfield, Oliver Goldsmith and, of course, Shelley. On the Continent there were, among others, Rousseau, Voltaire, St Pierre (of the Vegetarian romance 'Paul et Virginie'), Lamartine, Schopenhauer.

The growth of the humanitarian outlook in the eighteenth century seems to have encouraged Vegetarianism; in the nineteenth century it had advanced in England so far as to be able to form itself into a society, at Ramsgate in 1847. This was the first British organization of its kind; in 1888 the London Vegetarian Society became an independent body. In the same year one of the most distinguished scientific exponents, Anna Kingsford, died, and the first issue of *The Vegetarian* was published, price one penny. There are now four Vegetarian periodicals in Britain, and a Ministry of Food census of ration books in 1952 established that there were over 89,000 registered Vegetarians in this country. The

International Vegetarian Union incorporates societies all over the world.

All Buddhists are Vegetarians; so are many members of Indian sects, some Roman Catholics and the Seventh-Day Adventists. Among famous adherents to the principle are Leonardo da Vinci, Socrates, Wesley, Wagner (in theory), Tolstoy, Gandhi, Shaw, Albert Einstein and Albert Schweitzer.

Some of the strictest Vegetarians have condemned not only meat and all animal products, but also stimulants such as alcohol, tea and coffee; condiments, sedatives, tobacco, medicine and minerals. But the movement has room for more convivial spirits, as long as they agree that human teeth, not generally long, conical, sharp and uneven, are not meant for the tearing of flesh.

Some Vegetarians do tear flesh for the sake of social etiquette – but the true adherent must be able to rest in peace under Pope's line:

> No murder clothed him, and no murder fed.

The Virgin Birth

The **VIRGIN BIRTH** is one of the *de fide* beliefs of the Roman Catholic Church concerning the miraculous conception of Jesus Christ. Parthenogenesis, parturition without previous fertilization of the female by the male, though in some creatures theoretically possible, is held by scientists not to be possible in man.

Many Christians, however, believe that virgin birth did in fact occur once in the history of the human race; they believe it happened miraculously when Jesus Christ was born. Their belief is based on various gospel statements; the first being part of the words which St Matthew says were spoken to St Joseph by an angel when St Joseph had first realized that his betrothed, Mary, was pregnant, and was thinking that he must somehow hide her shame. The second 'God sent the Angel Gabriel to a city of Galilee called Nazareth, where a virgin dwelt' is from St Luke's version of the Annunciation when an angel told Mary that she was to have a child.

Although the intention of the writers of these gospels is clear from these and other statements, yet it is not easy to build up an entirely irresistible case for the Virgin Birth, as a historical fact. Still, the historical witness to the Virgin Birth is in fact stronger than the historical witness to many other incidents which are universally held to have occurred. In the first Christian centuries no doubt was ever raised as to Mary's virginity. It was clearly held to be proven beyond any shadow of doubt.

St Ignatius of Antioch (A.D. 107) wrote: 'Jesus Christ was born of Mary, in truth according to descent from David, but by the Holy Spirit.' St Justin, not long after, also spoke of the 'virgin birth'. Innumerable other witnesses confirm the belief which was in fact enshrined in the two best known creeds, the Apostles' Creed and the Nicene Creed. The latter says that Jesus 'was incarnate by the Holy Ghost of the Virgin Mary, and was made man'. Reverence for Mary reached its climax at the Council of Ephesus in the fourth century where she was called 'the mother of God'.

Historically this might be seen as the conclusion of a generally held supposition, not really a statement of certainty so much as a witness to popular belief. Theologically from the Christian point of view it is seen as a recognition of a truth always implicit in the revelation left by Jesus Christ and his apostles. The Church, acting infallibly, guided by the Holy Ghost, declared that Mary was truly the mother of God. Virginity was essential to this definition. Jesus was truly God, and, in being Mary's child, he was not a child of her husband but her child through the power of the Holy Spirit. 'The Holy Spirit will come upon thee, and the power of the most high will overshadow thee' are the words reported by St Luke to have been said by the angel to Mary. The doctrine clearly has an integral place in the central Christian doctrine of the incarnation, of the word made flesh.

The doctrine filled a complex psychological need in man, and had its forerunners, or shadows, or 'types', in the various myths of virgin births, earth goddesses and so forth. The early Fathers of the Church called Mary 'The Second Eve', thus giving her a place of primacy over the whole human race; they looked back to the description of Eve in *Genesis* as 'The Mother of all living'. Mary became theologically and popularly 'the mother of men'. The idea was enshrined in the words of Jesus Christ from the cross by which he gave Mary as a mother to St John, and he as a son to her, perhaps the most moving words in the whole Bible.

When Jesus therefore saw his mother, and the disciple standing by, whom he loved, he saith unto his mother, Woman behold thy son! Then saith he to the disciple, Behold thy mother! And from that hour that disciple took her unto his own home.

In the West the idea of Mary's virginity has tended towards a rather narrow conception of 'purity'. But the essence of the idea has been retained in the consecration of virgins to God in the religious life.

Theologically the virgin birth is also related to the idea of Mary's perfection, not essentially but symbolically. Virginity is a sign of man's complete offering of himself to God, of his perfectibility, although it is not an essential part of such an offering or such perfectibility. Mary is held to be perfect through her immaculate conception (q.v.) which is sometimes popularly confused with the virgin birth, but which refers in fact to Mary's freedom from sin from the moment of her conception in the ordinary fashion in the womb of her mother. Virginity became a symbol of Mary's perfection, whilst her nominal marriage to St Joseph prevented it from casting a slur on marriage.

Nevertheless the virgin birth has in fact led to a general lack of theological attention to the sacrament of marriage, and to a long tradition of scorn and contempt amongst theologians generally for the specifically sexual relationship. Popularly it has led to a mixture of inhuman and essentially unchristian puritanism and debased sentimental adulation of Mary.

Today theologians are at pains to move a step forward to integrate the idea of virginity at a deeper level into Christian thought and practice, to develop its implications for the doctrine of the incarnation as applied to man, to promote conversely a deeper and more religious respect for the sacrament of marriage.

What is Life?

VITALISM, no less than its opposite theory, Mechanism, is an attempt to explain the nature of Life.

The question 'What is life?' has been asked in every age. It is a question distinct from 'What is existence?' or 'What is human destiny?', though these larger questions obviously include the biological one. The enquiry into the nature of *vital phenomena* received a particular stimulus from the publication of the evolutionary theory by Darwin in 1859. And although the mechanist–vitalist controversy dates at least from the time of Plato and Aristotle, it was bound to assume a new urgency with the development of the modern science of genetics. Finally, since the theory of evolution involved a wholesale readjustment of man's outlook on the world, the scientists tended to have recourse to philosophical terminology to give respectability and plausibility to their conclusions. So Vitalism and Mechanism are theories propounded by biologists in language borrowed, perhaps somewhat hastily, from philosophy.

The assumptions of Mechanism are that the phenomena of life are explicable wholly in physico-chemical terms – an explanation which has the merit of simplicity. Yet in spite of the popularity of materialist philosophies today, few scientists have embraced Mechanism without reservation. Most scientists proceed on the assumption, cautiously advanced, that Mechanism is merely the most *likely* hypothesis to explain life. Such hesitancy is understandable. For a study of organic life reveals certain processes for which a physico-chemical explanation seems inadequate, reproduction, for example. There is another powerful reason for calling the mechanistic theory in doubt. If the phenomena of life prove to have a wholly materialist origin, then all belief in 'spiritual values' collapses. To accept a spiritual explanation of the universe is to refuse to admit that life can be a mere cloak for the play of chance material forces.

So the quarrel between Vitalism and Mechanism centred chiefly round the problem of values. In order to allow a 'place' for spirit, certain biologists of the late nineteenth century, particularly H. Driesch (1867–1941), advanced a theory which was neither wholly mechanistic nor wholly 'spiritualistic'. To this theory Driesch gave the name of Vitalism. The Vitalist admitted that the laws of physics and chemistry explained much of the working of the organism. But not everything. Above all, they could not account for that aspect of the organism which distinguished it most strikingly from inorganic process – its dynamism. In addition to physico-chemical factors, therefore, Dreisch maintained that another force must be at work. Given the remarkable capacity of organisms and even embryos to regain their form after suffering material damage, it appeared that this force must be non-material in character. To find a suitable name for it was not easy. At first Driesch ventured to call it a 'soul'. Later, he spoke of a 'psychoid'. Finally, he revived the Aristotelian term of *entelechy*. The *entelechy* was the power whereby organisms developed and maintained their form. Being spiritual or at least psychological in character, such a power could not be directly observed. Although operating from outside space, it somehow 'worked itself into space', where its results became visible in a coherent structure. In other words, the *entelechy* was a metaphysical or metabiological concept. Vitalism was the doctrine whereby life was conceived as a spiritual force.

Driesch's theory, which created a stir in the field of science and philosophy alike, was developed, and it was also bitterly attacked. In 1911, the German-American physiologist Jacques Loeb declared that the artificial production of life was only a matter of time. To such scientists, Vitalism represented the abandonment of the experimental and descriptive (*i.e.* the empirical) method of investigation in favour of mere word-spinning. If Mechanism could not be proved, at least it was the theory most commendable to common sense.

The history of thought has repeatedly shown that when one scientific theory remains irreconcilably opposed to another, the reason is that both theories stem from a more fundamental 'dualism'. The dualism is a philosophical one. Many scientists would declare that their work is pursued independently of all philosophical considerations. This is an illusion. While their experiments are no doubt conducted with purely practical ends in view, the *explanation* of what

they are doing is made in terms of current philosophical ideas. Descartes is regarded as one of the founders of the modern scientific spirit because his theory of the relation between the soul and the body – between 'spirit' and 'matter' – has become the framework within which scientists, whether physicists, biologists, or psychologists, do their 'thinking'. The central feature of Descartes's theory is that while the soul lives 'in' the body, its spiritual nature is different in kind from the material which it animates. To use the expression made popular in Gilbert Ryle's book *The Concept of Mind*, Descartes originated the myth of 'the ghost in the machine'. With this in mind, it can be seen how the vitalist–mechanist controversy has been played out in Cartesian terms. In respect of its physico-chemical composition the organism *is* a mechanism. But something must set the machine going and ensure its maintenance. This is the *entelechy*. The *entelechy* is the spiritual 'ghost' whose activity, though unobservable, is deducible from its effects. The soul influences the body and interacts with it.

Just as Descartes provides no satisfactory explanation of how the mind–body interaction took place, so the Vitalists never provided a satisfactory explanation of how the *entelechy*, inhabiting the organism, causes it to act 'organically'. To meet this otherwise intractable difficulty, certain biologists abandoned Vitalism in favour of a theory less imbued with mysticism. This theory was Holism or Organicism, Holism, a term derived from the Greek, signifying the science of the 'Whole'. In order to combine the experimental approach with a non-materialist explanation of life, men such as J. B. Haldane, J. A. Thompson, J. G. Woodger, Von Bertalanffy, and J. C. Smuts (the statesman) have sought to show that the organism, though explicable in terms of physics and chemistry, derives its significance from being a unity or 'whole'. Such unities or wholes, progressively articulated, characterize Nature at every level. There is no 'vital spark', no occult *entelechy*. At any one moment Nature is nothing but a material assemblage. Viewed from another and more comprehensive point of view, however, the processes of organic development can be seen to 'work together' to promote a state of unity or 'wholeness' inexplicable in physico-chemical terms. Science describes the organism in

Continued on p. 455

WIDE OPEN SPACES: J. Fenimore Cooper (1789–1851).

TYRANNY OF THE MACHINE: Swedish calculating machine of 1853.

ANTITHESIS OF THE MACHINE: Milanese Bobbin lace, late seventeenth century.

VITALISM: Henri Bergson (1859–1941).

442

TROTSKYISM: Leon Trotsky (1879–1940).

THE WELFARE STATE: Lord Beveridge.

'SUPERMAN': Friedrich Nietzsche (1844–1900).

445

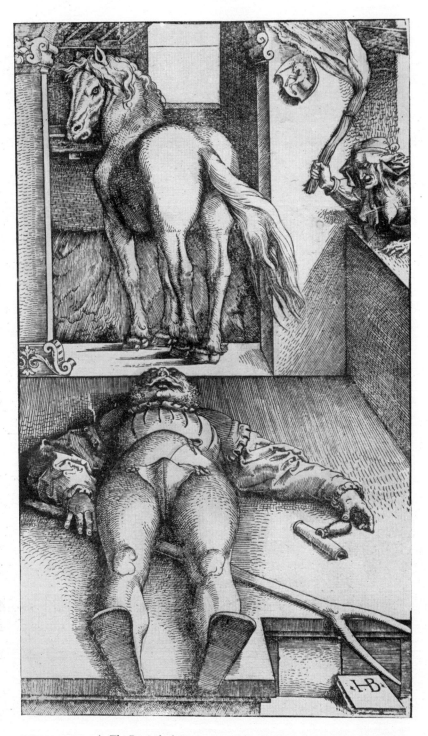

WITCH HUNT: 1. *The Bewitched Groom*, engraving by Hans Baldung (c. 1480–1545).

2. Witches. Etching by Goya (1746–1828).

WORKERS OF THE WORLD, UNITE: 1. A Labour demonstration on May Day, in London.

2. A May Day demonstration in Mexico City.

THE RIGHT TO WORK: detail from *Work*, by Ford Madox Brown (1821–1893).

The Thinkers contemplate the Workers. Carlyle and F. D. Maurice – another detail from
Ford Madox Brown's *Work*.

THE RIGHT TO WORK: and the Dignity of Labour. *The Stonebreakers*, by Gustave Courbet (1819–1877).

The Dignity of Labour Sentimentalized: *The Angelus*, by J.-F. Millet.

453

THE UNITED NATIONS: the new headquarters building in New York.

one language; philosophy in another. That which science describes in terms of material fact, philosophy can speak of in terms of spirit. 'The world of biology is the same as the world of physics and chemistry,' says J. S. Haldane, 'but this does not prevent it being differently interpreted.'

The holistic theory seems to resolve itself into a particular way of talking about facts otherwise admitting of material explanation. Instead of using plain language, Holism merely introduces an elaborate metaphysical vocabulary. Nor is such a vocabulary necessarily more 'spiritual' than any other. There is nothing particularly spiritual about a 'pattern'. It would seem that Holism has succeeded neither in refuting Vitalism nor in replacing it.

So the problem facing the modern biologist is to salvage the truth in Vitalism while purging it of its occult characteristics. Its value lies in its insistence that the physico-chemical explanation of life is incomplete. Some biologists and philosophers, acknowledging the evidence for a non-mechanistic hypothesis, are moving towards a psycho-biology, which would see the organic process to be unintelligible save as the manifestation of forces which are ultimately psychic in character, 'psychic' being understood not in a 'spiritualistic' sense, but in the sense of consciousness at a primary level, informing and underlying the consciousness associated with the brain and the nervous system.

ILLUSTRATION: Page 442.

Secure at home

The **WELFARE STATE** accepts responsibility for ensuring that the standard of living of none of its citizens falls below a certain predetermined level.

X

The idea of a welfare state seems to have been first specifically advocated as a practical possibility by Sidney and Beatrice Webb in their *Policy of the National Minimum* by which the state would 'guarantee to every worker, in all the contingencies of life, an unbroken sufficiency of the means of healthful existence'. Its origin as a phrase, however, is obscure. The words 'welfare state' were probably first used as a polemical epitome either of the Beveridge Report or of the objectives of the British Labour Party. Since 1948 Great Britain has been commonly described as the, or a, Welfare State.

Until the latter part of the nineteenth century, people had believed that the state's only duty to its citizens was to protect them from external attack and internal disorder. So Thomas Hobbes, the political philosopher, wrote in 1651 that 'The final cause, end, and design of men who ... live in commonwealths, is the foresight of their own preservation ...: that is to say, of getting themselves out from that miserable condition of war which is necessarily consequent ... to the natural passions of men when there is no visible person to keep them in awe'.

Consequently it was left to private charity to relieve the destitute. But there was one exception. Because the country had been for some time gravely disturbed by violent roaming bands of vagabonds, the Poor Relief Act of 1601 required every parish to provide food and shelter for any of its own inhabitants who were destitute, and so took the first small step towards establishing a welfare state in England.

In the nineteenth century the doctrine of *laissez-faire* (q.v.) had become widely accepted, and destitution was regarded simply as a sign of idleness or vice.

The rich man is invisible
In the crowd of his gay society;
  But the poor man's delight
  Is a sore in the sight
And a stench in the nose of piety.

The rich man goes out yachting,
Where sanctity can't pursue him;
  The poor goes afloat
  In a fourpenny boat
Where the bishop groans to view him.

By the Poor Law Amendment Act of 1834 parishes were virtually forbidden to provide relief, except in a workhouse, for anyone who was not actually incapable, physically, of earning his living, and workhouses were made as unpleasant as possible. Nevertheless, even one of the leading advocates of *laissez-faire*, Jeremy Bentham, the great proponent of Utilitarianism, wrote that 'the greatest happiness of all those whose interest is in question is the right and proper and only right and proper and universally desirable end of human action', and it was that statement of principle which formed the basis of most subsequent arguments for the establishment of a welfare state.

As the nineteenth century wore on, people's attitude to the poor and to poverty began to change. As a result of the Industrial Revolution, the disparity between the standards of living of the rich and the poor became steadily greater and more obvious, whilst the standard of living of the poor in the big new towns was seen to be not merely lower, but even less secure, than that of the poor in the slowly emptying countryside. At the same time the poor were becoming politically important, economically more powerful and increasingly articulate. By the three great Reform Acts of 1832, 1867 and 1884 the franchise was extended until all adult males possessed it; the number and membership of trade unions steadily increased; and the employers' need for workmen who were at least literate led to the two Education Acts of 1870 and 1891, which established compulsory universal free primary education.

By 1906 people's attitudes had changed sufficiently for the Liberal Party to be elected to office pledged to carry out a big programme of social reform. The Liberals' attitude was summed up by Winston Churchill, then a Liberal and President of the Board of Trade: at Dundee on 10 October 1908 he said: 'I do not agree with those who say that every man must look after himself, and that the intervention by the state in such matters [the relief of distress, the regulation of the general level of employment] will be fatal to his self-reliance, his foresight and his thrift.'

In 1908 the Liberal Government passed an Act providing non-contributory pensions of five shillings per week for those over seventy who could prove that their means came to less than £31 10s.

a year and who were of good character. In 1911, following the example of the German Sickness Insurance Law of 1883, the Liberals passed the first National Insurance Act. By that Act the whole working population were compulsorily insured against sickness and part of it against unemployment: employers and the state shared the burden of the premiums with the worker.

The philosophical foundation for the Liberal programme had been laid, not by Karl Marx, but by T. H. Green, Professor of Moral Philosophy at Oxford from 1878 to 1882, who had said:

The individual depends on the community for all that makes life worth living: the community must therefore secure for the individual all the conditions necessary for his full spiritual development ... The State exists to secure a 'good life' for its members, not merely to prevent their suffering concrete injuries.

Later on in its policy report *Labour and the New Social Order*, published in 1918, the Labour Party adopted almost the very words of T. H. Green:

The first principle of the Labour Party ... is the securing to every member of the community in good times and bad alike (and not only to the strong and able, the well-born or the fortunate), of all the requisites of healthy life and worthy citizenship.

During the next twenty-five years, that principle came gradually to be adopted by all political parties in Britain. The National Insurance Act was extended to cover more people and more eventualities. Administration of the Poor Law, however, remained in the hands of local authorities, and though a destitute person could get assistance from them outside the workhouse, it was necessary for his whole household to undergo a rigorous 'means test' to prove he needed it. The vast increase in destitution caused by the great depression of 1929–1933, moreover, showed that the task of ensuring that no one's standard of living fell below a certain level was almost impossible if there was large-scale unemployment.

Soon after the war broke out in 1939, plans began to be made for the reconstruction of the country when the fighting was over, and on 10 June 1941, the Coalition Government asked Sir William Beveridge (as he then was) to consider the problems of Social Insurance and Allied

Services and make recommendations about them. His report (December 1942) contained a plan, in effect, for a welfare state. The plan assumed 'comprehensive health services and the maintenance of employment':

The main feature of the plan [said Beveridge in the report] is a scheme of social insurance against interruption and destruction of earning power and for special expenditure arising at birth, marriage, or death ... In combination with national assistance and voluntary insurance as subsidiary methods, the aim of the plan is to make want under any circumstances unnecessary.

When the war was over the Beveridge Plan was by and large adopted by the Government, and was brought into being on 5 July 1948. It received this greeting from *The Economist*:

Next week there comes into force in this country the most comprehensive social security scheme that the world has yet seen ... By national insurance virtually the whole population is covered against the normal hazards of life ...; by national assistance ... a minimum income is guaranteed by the State to every person who can prove his need; by the National Health Service all medical, hospital, dental and ancillary services are to be available free to every man, woman and child in the land ... The Beveridge Report captured the imagination of the country by the simplicity of its aim – the abolition of want. The Social Security scheme, which is based on the report, is launched in far less auspicious circumstances; yet the very difficulties of the time make it a test of the people's will to work and ability to practice self-denial. If these are forthcoming, the scheme is large enough and bold enough to arouse the admiration and envy of other democracies.

ILLUSTRATION: Page 444.

Go west, young man

WIDE OPEN SPACES were once equated with wide-open opportunities.

Those days have gone – though not long gone: Hitler when he ranted on *Lebensraum* had his eye accurately fixed upon the Ukraine, a wide space indeed, if hardly an open one; Mussolini must have considered there would be something in Ethiopia worth having besides prestige and the names of the villages inscribed on the Italian Army's battle-honours, for he had already de-clared he was not 'a collector of deserts'. Goebbels's propaganda about the 'Have' Powers, who sat on unexploited emptinesses, denying them to the 'Have-not' Powers who alone had the skill and the will to exploit to capacity, was based on an emotional conviction: the Japanese interpretation of the same theme was based also on rational conviction.

These political catch-phrases have vanished, but it may be only for the present. Clearly Russia still thinks that a resurgent Germany will again turn eastwards for her field of adventure; and Australia and New Zealand, to name no others, await the day when Japan once more begins to speak of a 'Co-Prosperity Sphere' in Eastern Asia.

Yet politicians will hardly be able to restore to the idea of the 'wide open space', the emotional drive it once had. There is unlikely to be any involuntary trek to the Arctic or the Antarctic, to the steppe, to the Saharas of Africa and Australia, or to the basin of the Amazon. In the modern world an open space is of little value until a city block has been reared upon it. Space, now, has become the stock-in-trade of the merchants in fantasy, as a glance at the children's reading-matter will show: it is a non-terrestrial commodity, and until a pioneer generation of daring captains in plastic suits have finally settled accounts with the moon-devils and the agents of Saturn, ordinary travellers are unlikely to take single tickets on an inter-planetary service.

It was far otherwise in the nineteenth century. Journeys, often made under dangerous and always made under difficult conditions, were then worth one's while. In the century spanning from the eighteen-forties, eighteen million people left Great Britain. They went all over the world, but their Mecca was the West, in the Americas. Beyond that Atlantic frontier lay God's own country, where the winds from heaven blew unobstructed, where Nature had her cornucopia forever upturned, where one had only to seek in order to find.

Why starve in County Mayo when one could be off to Philadelphia in the morning? Why have new industrial ideas turned down by English employers when you could make your own fortune on them in Pittsburgh? Why beat your head against the class-barrier, bemoan your fate as the younger son? The American dream was first a dream made in Europe, troubling the sleep of the Italian peasant, the Czech official, the German shopkeeper, the political prisoner of all nations. Urban civilization as Europe knew it had betrayed too many of its inhabitants for the very idea of space, room to move, to breathe, room to live, not to become synonymous with the name of America. And Americans had even before the French Revolution taken out their patent on liberty. By the eighteen-thirties they were applying it to the world they themselves had made. American democracy was born not in the tide-water, Atlantic country, but in the American forest and along a successive wave of American frontiers in the hinterland, where all men were in fact – at least till the forest was cleared, the frontier staked, and the land laid ready for the incomer – what they were held to be in theory in the charter of American Independence: *equal*.

This was the great hope, the great prize, that the wide open spaces of the New World held out, to Americans themselves as well as to the European million. This was the ideal that made Fenimore Cooper's Mohicans (masters of the forest), Daniel Boone and Kit Carson (masters of the trail) the heroes not of one generation only but of five, that has made the 'Western' the single authentically and exclusively American product of the cinema. Go west, young man: the world is your oyster: gold is where you find it. The log-cabin become not an Irish shanty transposed, but a national shrine – and not Lincoln only, but John D. Rockefeller and Marshall Field had the good luck to be born on the farm.

Any man proves his worth in a place where the air is free and the land is cheap – and so in America, under the feet of the advancing westerner, range becomes ranch and ranch becomes homestead, until 20,000 men lined up in 1889 at the starting-point in Oklahoma to make the best of the last land-lottery while they may. As the century died, the horizon diminished; but the idea retained its essence, as ideal and as myth.

'Wide open spaces' had never needed much propaganda from intellectuals. Emigrant literature made space, land, and independence the commonplaces of its appeal; serious writers could only echo this, and few of them troubled. Anthony Trollope, who saw the United States in the days before the European deluge, and the Australian colonies both before and after the gold rush, allows himself only a few paragraphs on the boundless possibilities of both continents. Another kind of writer, with Coleridge and Chateaubriand as exemplars, continued to mould various Utopias beneath the heavens of the West, until this itself became a commonplace: there was no western American territory that did not boast its 'peculiar people', and Canaan might be found by the earnest anywhere along the Oregon trail, or by the Great Salt Lake, or in the San Fernando Valley before the orange-groves concealed it.

Too much wide open space induced too great a degree of intellectual and emotional licence; and only the American poet Walt Whitman (1819–1892), reporter and Utopian in one, was able to encompass the whole scene, significantly seeing it as one of struggle as great as any that had ever racked the Old, the narrow World. But he felt himself possessed of the spaces, the night, the stars of America, speaking with the voices of the oppressed and the voice of the liberation of American (and universal) man:

Through me many long dumb voices,
Voices of the interminable generation of prisoners and
    slaves,
Voices of the diseas'd and despairing and of thieves and
    dwarfs,
Voices of cycles of preparation and accretion,
And of the threads that connect the stars and of wombs
    and of the father-stuff,
And of the rights of them the others are down upon ...

The myth had still a stronger impact than the fact, even while the railroads contracted the open spaces and the progress of industrialism began to demand – to depend upon – concentration and urbanization. Irish and Italian peasants were pouring themselves not on to their own freeholds but into someone else's city slums, and the American East thus became at first the outpost, and in our own day the capital, of the urban world. This was true of the whole length of the Atlantic frontier, western section: in fifty years Buenos Aires, poised on the edge of one of the widest of the world's open spaces, has swelled to contain one-third of the population of the Argentine. To the immediate north, the story has been the same.

'The very vastness of the apparent resources of Brazil', observes a modern commentator, 'is the Brazilians' worst enemy.'

The myth of the wide open spaces has been contradicted by the fact as strongly elsewhere. The Dutch of Cape Colony went to look in their interior for that 6,000-acre farm, from which they might see their neighbour's chimney-smoke, though not the neighbour himself; but their Great Trek, by one of history's sharper ironies, wound at the last into the heart of modern Johannesburg, which bears sufficient witness to the trick that was played. The very vastness of Australia challenges every Australian economist and sociologist, who must start from the fact that Australians live in four great cities, and show every wish to continue to do so. Heirs of the industrial revolution, wherever they may be found, live to a pattern, of which wide open space is no part. Only eight million Americans are farmers: not men alone, but industrial techniques, must support the agricultural economy of great countries. The 'plow that broke the plains' is a museum piece – something else is required to sow and to harvest the great mid-West corn-belt. Soviet Russia, with all the space and all the men she can ever want, has never (apparently) been able to obtain all the techniques she could do with. One migrant movement which perhaps found space alone sufficient for its needs was that of the Chinese into Mongolia and Manchuria; but China has yet to enjoy her industrial revolution, and meanwhile there is no doubt that the Chinese farmer would exchange an intangible like the horizon for a higher standard of life.

Yet in western countries the idea of the wide open spaces has lingered. There is attraction, and social significance, in it: the English aristocracy developed interests in sports that required much elbow room, like the shooting of Scottish wild-life; and the American business-man, turned hunter at the week-end, still takes himself out of Denver or Detroit to his modern shack or cabin, set by some still lakeside – though never too far from the turnpike. But you can't do anything with fresh air, so Mr Dooley used to say, except breathe it; it is not, as once it was, part of the heritage, and real estate, of man.

ILLUSTRATION: Page 439.

Democracy and the 'priesthood of all believers'

The **WILL OF THE PEOPLE**, interpreted as the will which must be expressed by the people's government, is taken by some to be equivalent to democracy. Historically it is a fusion of two distinct ideas. Democracy is one of them, the other is 'Voluntarism'.

Voluntarism is the theory that moral distinctions rest ultimately on the will; that they are the results of choice and decision – a view that becomes clearer when it is contrasted with its opposite, the view that moral distinctions, like natural distinctions, inhere in objects or actions and can be discovered by enquiry and observation. As with most influential ideas, the origins of Voluntarism cannot be firmly fixed. It seems to be one of the component elements in the contention of the Sophists in Greece that distinctions of right and wrong are based not on Nature (*Physis*), but on Convention (*Nomos*).

In the Middle Ages the view is explicitly stated, though applied only in a very limited fashion in the controversy between Realists and Nominalists over the link between God and morality. Realists such as Aquinas maintained that God wills what is right because it is right, whereas Nominalists, such as Duns Scotus, and more certainly William of Ockham and Pierre D'Ailly, maintained that what is right is right because God wills it.

In the seventeenth century we find another explicit but again limited version of Voluntarism in Hobbes in his *Leviathan* (1651), where it is assumed that what is right is right because the sovereign wills it. Both these two expressions are limited, since according to them it is only for God or the sovereign, as the case may be, that what-is-willed is what-is-right; for everyone else, to discover what is right is a matter of discovering what is willed by the arbiter.

It is only in Rousseau, in the *Social Contract* (1762), then in Kant, that we find the view unashamedly expressed; though both maintain it is not just whatever one wills that is right; but only whatever one wills under certain conditions. For Rousseau the *volonté générale* is to be distinguished from the mere *volonté de tous*; and in

Kant the Rational Will is to be distinguished from the mere Empirical Will. Distinctions of this kind, though possibly required if this theory is to retain plausibility, have had certain disastrous practical consequences. The view that the path of social justice is determined by what the people wills, but that it is impossible simply by *asking* people to find out what they *really will*, has led straight to 'totalitarian democracy'. Rousseau said of the criminal's punishment, in a famous phrase, that he was 'forced to be free'; this recalls the various attempts in recent times to deceive, persecute and enthral the people in the name of the people. When Robespierre, the French revolutionary leader, spoke for the Jacobins and said, 'The general will is our will', he was anticipating the methods of demagogic dictatorship.

By Democracy is meant the view that the government should be *by* and *for* the people; as such it is a moral view, not, like Voluntarism, a view about how moral views are justified.

It is arguable that no political philosopher has ever denied that government should be in the interests of the people, or at any rate of the citizens (if we exclude those who, like Spinoza, denied the significance of any proposition about what government should do or should be like as opposed to what it is or what it is like). But though this is true, such views were generally held only at the expense of interpreting the interests of the people in the most attenuated fashion. So Plato thought government in the interests of the governed consistent with the advocacy of a rigid hierarchical system because he thought that real happiness consisted in performing the task, however humble, for which one is fitted; and some of the Fathers of the Church even thought that the rule of a wicked king could be similarly justified because it offered the means of atonement for Original Sin.

Accordingly the view that government should be for the people appears in a recognizable form only when criteria for assessing the interest or happiness of the people become reasonably precise and plausible. This occurs largely under the influence of the sensationalist psychology of the seventeenth and eighteenth centuries (Hobbes, Locke, the French Encyclopaedists, Hume, Condillac, and the Utilitarians) whereby man is con-

ceived as a mechanism acting entirely on the principles of the avoidance of pain and the pursuit of happiness. The high-water mark is Bentham's 'Felicitic Calculus'; an appalling term, but a method of measuring the social value of an action by calculating the four 'dimensions' of the pleasure that attends it, *i.e.* its intensity, its duration, its uncertainty or certainty and its propinquity or remoteness in time.

Belief that the real interests or happiness of the people is in some way assessable is one of the cornerstones of modern democratic thought. But the claims of Benthamism to provide such a method have been criticized on a number of counts, not all of which are equally important. It has been said that it ignores the *quality* as opposed to the *quantity* of pleasure that an action involves, that it takes into account only the satisfaction of existing needs and overlooks the creation of fresh needs; that it was formulated in ignorance of the existence of unconscious needs; that it ignores the value of *voluntary* action as such, irrespective of its 'felicitic' consequences.

The view that government should be *for* the people does not entail the view that government should be *by* the people; indeed, some of the more passionate crusaders of the former view, such as the French Encylopaedists, have been violently opposed to the latter view on the grounds of the stupidity, ignorance and prejudice of the mass of the people.

The history of political ideas shows that there are three main arguments.

(1) The argument that all men always act in their own interests (known as Psychological Hedonism): therefore if government is to be in the interests of the people, it ought to be government by the people.

This was the argument ably presented by James Mill, which converted Bentham from the benevolent despotism of his early years to the democratic attitude expressed in his later writings; and many democrats have trodden the same path. The argument is a poor one, since it takes as its premise an indubitably false psychological hypothesis.

(2) The argument that even if men can act other than in their own interests, it is still they who are best judges of their own interests: therefore if government is going to be in the interests

of the people, only the people have the know-ledge to run it.

This argument is sometimes known pictur-esquely as 'only the wearer knows where the shoe pinches'. It seems to have no more than a limited application in a complex modern society.

(3) The argument that even if men can act other than in their own interests and even if they are not always the right judges of what their own interests may be, to have a share in government is *in itself* one of the most important of human in-terests. This belief in the value of government *by* the people as merely a means to government for the people but also as an end in itself, is in a large measure the lay descendant of the Protestant belief in 'the priesthood of all believers'.

It is upon this argument that the real case for government by the people must ultimately rest.

The wish is father to ...

'**WISHFUL THINKING**' is thinking a thing to be true because one wants it to be so, without any basis of fact. It is a psycho-analytical term made popular which now describes the un-conscious expression of one's desires in accor-dance with one's opinion. It is the 'wish being father to the thought', an adage which goes back to Shakespeare's second part of *Henry IV*, and no doubt further still.

The recognition of the fact of wishful thinking by psychologists came some time before the actual coining of that phrase. Freud laid the foundations of it with his conception of neuroses and of dreams as being 'wish-fulfilling'. Later, in the nineteen-twenties, H. A. Overstreet uses the term 'wish-thinking'. Since he describes this process as one in which the thinking is based on a wish rather than on the facts of the situation, he is clearly talking of what we now call wishful thinking. He explains how a strong emotion or wish – (if it is fear, it is a wish to escape; if pride, a wish to appear great; if sex, a wish for gratification, and so on) – is behind most of our thinking; and he mentions several types of this wish-thinking.

There is the kind that makes us hide less credit-able motives and parade only those that do us credit; there is the kind that refuses to entertain ideas that may make us uncomfortable or dis-turb our enjoyment; there is the kind that can-not admit defeat and has to turn it into pretended victory; and there is the defence-mechanism type of thinking in all its forms.

Overstreet points out that 'our social and poli-tical life is so full of these pseudo-systems built up out of our strong wishes – fear, suspicion, hatred, ambition – that it seems as if only the most shadowy line can be drawn between the de-lusions of insanity and the biased and opinion-ated wish-thoughts of sanity'.

So wishful thinking is not only a widespread process of mind, but an insidious, harmful one. The answer to it is 'fact-thinking', as defined by Overstreet in his book *About Ourselves: Psycho-logy for Normal People*, which interprets civiliza-tion as an extension of 'fact-thinking'.

Its past triumph was the making of tools which 'cannot be dreamed or prayed or wished into existence'. Mathematics was a second triumph, logic a third. Logic is knowing precisely what one is talking about, it is ability to define, 'with single-ness of meaning, free of ambiguity'. So Socrates, who died for logic, died for fact-thinking. Fact-thinking, 'hard, rigorous, honest-minded', the human triumph, is represented as the passport to man's continued triumph, though over against it 'there is wish-thinking – the thinking which, in its mild form, is self-deception and evasion; in its extreme form, insanity.'

Wishful thinking is, perhaps, a species of emotional revenge for the rigours and honesties of fact-thinking. Overstreet considers that one of the next great conquests to be made in our human enterprise is the extension of fact-thinking into our emotional life. If we now allow emotion to swing our reason into line, we must somehow find a means of training our reason to swing our emotions into line. He thinks this can be done by teaching – just as mathematics, logic, the tech-nique of science have been taught.

That we can be taught to avoid wishful think-ing appears possible. It is certainly desirable. But to think that so drastic a reform of human nature could be effected other than slowly and painfully would in itself be mere wishful thinking.

KEY TO THE ENDPAPERS

The *School of Athens* was painted in 1509–1511 by Rafael in the Stanza della Segnatura in the Vatican. It is not possible to identify all the figures in the picture, and for some of the philosophers, Rafael portrayed some of his famous contemporaries.

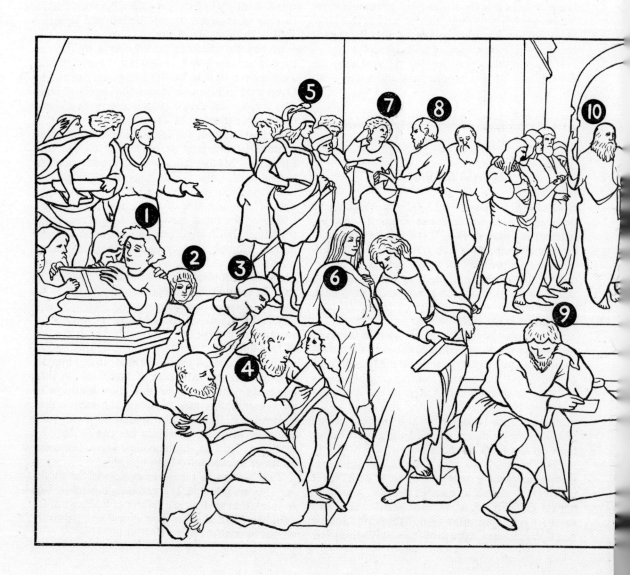

1. Epicurus
2. The young Federigo Gonzaga (?)
3. Averroes (?)
4. Pythagoras
5. Alexander of Macedon
6. Francesco Maria della Rovere, Duke of Urbino
7. Alcibiades
8. Socrates
9. Heraclitus (Michaelangelo)
10. Plato (Leonardo)
11. Aristotle
12. Diogenes
13. Euclid or Archimedes (Bramante)
14. Bessarion or Heliodorus
15. Zoroaster (Castiglione)
16. Rafael himself
17. Ptolemy
18. Sodoma (?)

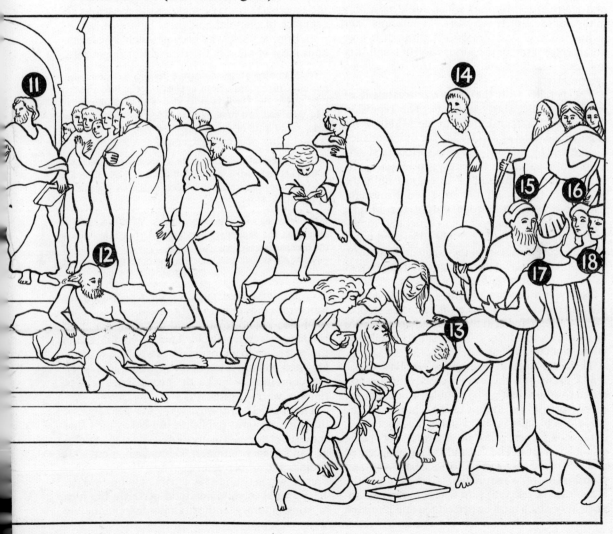

A burning question

WITCH-HUNT is a more or less new phrase for the detection and persecution of political or other opponents. It was perhaps introduced with two images in mind. The first was the image of that ritual proceeding in primitive societies leading to the exposure of one who has by poisoning, sympathetic magic, or other 'supernatural' means, harmed a member of the tribe. The second image is one, not entirely sentimental or hypothetical, of innocent, ignorant or merely unsympathetic characters being ducked, hounded, blackguarded and maltreated for crimes which could exist only in the minds of their attackers. 'Witch-hunt' was at first a savage and violent metaphor. It is now an accepted term for the persecution of a minority and the 'smelling out' of its true or alleged sympathizers.

The parallel with the historical treatment of witches is distressingly accurate. The repulsion felt for witchcraft in Europe in the Middle Ages is much the same as that feeling for opinions they dislike held by contemporary authoritarian states. Opposition is held to be heresy; to be suspect is to be guilty. In the cult of witchcraft both the Roman Catholic and the reformed Protestant Churches were, in Europe during the Middle Ages and later, equally fervent, cruel and undiscriminating. With the rise of liberalism and tolerance as accepted ideals in the nineteenth century, this battle against witchcraft was often thought of as an inexplicable outbreak of sadism.

Today, in a new age of faith – political, economic and racial – we can see a similar battle in progress. 'Objectivity' is in this atmosphere regarded as an intellectual luxury. There is only black and white, right and wrong.

There are trials in East and West. East of the Iron Curtain only those are accused who are prepared to admit their guilt in public. For the crime of witchcraft the authoritarian church in the Middle Ages also insisted upon, and obtained, confession. There was no question of being ashamed of this. The faithful majority accepted and approved any means to the discovery and punishment of abnormality. Criticism of the State (race or religion) is to witch-hunters an abnormality which must be persecuted and hounded

as animals attack one of their own kind which is deformed.

Witchcraft existed. There are physical evidences of it – charms, voluntary confessions, documents. It still exists, and is said to be on the increase in some parts of the world, notably Africa. The machinery of sympathetic magic, the covens of thirteen persons, and many of the practices and beliefs, are common to many ages and exist all over the globe. Witchcraft may have been an organized world movement, but this is at least doubtful. It may represent folk practices of former religions. It may represent recurrent psychological reactions to stock situations. To the theologian it may appear as the conscious acceptance of diabolic guidance: Satanism.

In Europe those who became witches were perhaps most of them in the three following groups.

(1) Members of pre-Christian fertility religions who put up a rear-guard action against the Church, and felt they served the Devil because that was what they were told their god had now become. They had perhaps vestigial racial gifts of second-sight or hypnosis: they had poisons. They were mainly ignorant and scattered.

(2) Intellectual rebels, affected by the mystery religions of the East and particularly that of dualism. They parodied the faith they had rejected in such conscious blasphemy as the Black Mass.

(3) Women, whose position in the Middle Ages was dependent and unhappy. If lonely and despised they would the more probably react to the tradition of matriarchal power and sexual freedom presented to them by cult subscribers.

Granting the existence of such people, there were thousands of innocent men, women and children also put to torture and death (although in England never legally by burning at the stake) for adherence to a movement of which they probably had no idea. Church law, civil law and lynch law combined to make the accusation itself, at times, a warrant of death.

The *Malleus Malleficarum* – the 'Hammer of the Witches' – was published in 1490 by the Chief Inquisitors for Germany, Fathers James Sprenger and Henry Kramer, Dominican monks. It codifies the whole campaign for the extermination of witches, and it is terrifyingly up to date. They would have understood perfectly the idea of contemporary authoritarians for eliminating 'heretics in society'. It was better that the innocent should suffer than that the guilty should escape. They were sober and sincere men, with the highest regard for truth, as they saw it. They had no desire to send their fellow-creatures to a screaming death. They were merely righteous, and fanatically sincere. It was years after the Inquisition had completed its main task, and when scepticism had crept in, that we find the admittedly manufactured evidence of travelling witchfinders, and prickers with collapsible needles.

Yet the *Malleus Malleficarum* is a hideous document. It defied all that we mean by the laws of evidence. It presumed guilt and advocated torture. It allowed virtually no defence, yet it made suggestions for ways to confuse the prisoner. 'Common defamation' (as in parts of the world today) was enough to merit arrest. But actual witnesses were an asset. Children were encouraged to betray their parents, and the evidence of criminals was admitted. The accused were not told who had accused them of what. As a great French lawyer of the seventeenth century said, 'The trial of this offence must not be conducted like other crimes. Whoever adheres to the ordinary course of justice prevents the spirit of the law, both divine and human. He who is accused of sorcery should never be acquitted ...' He rarely was. And confession, when necessary, was extraction by torture.

If the ordinary processes of law were so stretched against those accused of witchcraft, so the more was ordinary ill-will. Thousands must have died from mob violence.

There were real witches, self-persuaded witches, crooks and innocent cranks. Yet witch-hunting, many will think, was always cruel, and always wrong. The terror of a majority should never be allowed to harry a man because of a label. Lord Macaulay, now an unfashionable writer, perhaps summed it up when he wrote:

To punish a man because he has committed a crime, or because he is believed, though unjustly, to have committed a crime, is not persecution. To punish a man, because we infer from the nature of some doctrine that he holds, or from the conduct of other persons who hold the same doctrines with him, that he *will* commit a crime is persecution, and is, in any case, foolish and wicked.

ILLUSTRATION: Pages 446 and 447.

'He that will not live by toil
Has no right on English soil.'

The **RIGHT TO WORK** was a principle proclaimed by the French Government on 25 February, 1848, and moved by the historian and politician Louis Blanc (1811–1882). As a catch-phrase the sentiments it evokes merge with such others as 'the dignity of labour' to become tissue-paper brickbats in 'the class war'. But it also meant something very real.

Blanc was born in Madrid, when Spain was ruled by Joseph Bonaparte. He studied law, lived in Paris and in poverty, and thought all the evils of mankind stemmed from the pressure of competition; he therefore advocated the equalization of wages and the merging of personal interests in the common good: 'from each according to his ability, to each according to his needs'. Blanc's fervour and drive continued to exercise great influence on the development of socialism, in France and elsewhere. He married an Englishwoman and received, one may add, a state funeral in Cannes.

Man's attitude to work involves all philosophy, economics and history. It ranges between the extremes of the 'Slaves, obey your masters' and 'Workers of the World, unite!' (q.v.). Somewhere in between, representing the responsibility of undemocratic authority, is the remark of a Roman Caesar 'an Emperor must die standing'.

Primitive and undisturbed societies still often assume (to the irritation of European and American immigrants) that work is a tiresome necessity, if a necessity at all. Nature provides, man takes, and the rest is the good or bad employment of leisure.

This easy habit of life, although remembered in myth, was already impossible in the classical world, in which society was based upon slavery. Slavery, according, for instance, to Aristotle, was a natural state. Slaves had certain rights, but they were less than human ones. The good citizen was concerned with other responsibilities – the right to leisure, and the right way to employ such leisure. Christianity accepted the sociological position of this: it merely substituted the belief that service, in slavery or in freedom, was equally to be carried out for the glory of God.

Labour in the Middle Ages, the ages of faith, was therefore felt to be for the upholding of a society which was under the direction of the Almighty, through his appointed servants. The labourer must accept, cheerfully or not, the feudal economic conditions. Labour, philosophically, was the working out of man's duty of service to God – in the fields, the cloister or the battle against the infidel. There were periods of famine, there were peasant uprisings against intolerable conditions: but there was work for each, according to his station in life. If there was dignity in living, labour was part of it. Even after the Renaissance it was accepted that hard manual work was the proper lot of most men. 'But as no one is to live in his employment according to his own humour, or for such ends as please his own fancy, but is to do all his business in such a manner as to make it a service unto God', wrote William Law (1686–1761), 'so those who have no particular employment are so far from being left at greater liberty to live to themselves, to pursue their own humours, and spend their time and fortunes as they please, that they are under greater obligations of living wholly unto God in all their actions.' The leisured classes should employ their leisure; there was no general question of enforced leisure without means.

The ideal of a leisured upper class was challenged by the French Revolution at the end of the nineteenth century. The conditions which led to Louis Blanc's declaration, however, had arisen a hundred years before, in England, with the Industrial Revolution and the introduction of machines. At first the new processes, immensely profitable with world markets untouched, meant more and more work for those involved. Hours were intolerable. Pay was pitifully small. Both orthodox humanitarians and the new socialists tried to combat these conditions, and the worst of them were corrected. But another factor now appeared. Industry and agriculture rarely prospered at the same time. Worse, industry itself had its ups and downs: there were slumps, and unemployment. Huge bodies of men could not work if they wanted to, and most of them desperately did want to; no work meaning no food. 'A man willing to work', wrote Carlyle (1795–1881), 'and unable to find work, is perhaps the saddest sight that Fortune's inequality exhibits under this sun.' There were still people who could talk of 'the heaven-born employment of the hind', and wonder why the hind complained. By 1848 there were Chartists riots in England, and revolutions abroad. It was in these circumstances that Blanc moved his famous resolution.

The 'right to work' and the 'dignity of labour' were both accepted ideals long before the English Labour Party was founded in 1893. They had appealed to Ruskin, to Morris; they had found expression in paintings of a pre-Raphaelite and Christian Socialist tinge – instanced in *Work* by Ford Madox Brown (in the Birmingham City Art Gallery) depicting the strong navvy at work on the roads, contemplated by Carlyle and the Christian Socialist F. D. Maurice; and the 'right to work' is still implicit in the prevention of unemployment, a first principle by political parties in Great Britain.

The 'right to work' is now in harness with 'the right to leisure', most parties claiming to have systems which provide both work and leisure for everybody. Only a few sigh openly for the honest 'right to idle'.

ILLUSTRATION: Pages 450, 451, 452 and 453.

From the Communist Manifesto

'WORKERS OF THE WORLD, UNITE!' is a phrase taken from the last sentences of the *Communist Manifesto* written by Karl Marx and Friedrich Engels and published in London in February 1848. The full passage runs, 'The Communists disdain to conceal their views and aims. They openly declare that their ends can be attained only by the forcible overthrow of all existing social conditions. Let the ruling classes tremble at a communist revolution. The proletarians have nothing to lose but their chains. They have a world to win. Working men of all countries, unite: you have nothing to lose but your chains'.

This passage can only be rendered intelligible in the context of the Marxist analysis. All history is conceived of as a struggle between different economic classes, and just as, in Western Europe, feudal society was replaced by a capitalist system controlled by the bourgeoisie, so it is asserted that capitalism will by its very nature destroy itself and pave the way for a proletarian revolution, in which supreme power will vest in the 'dictatorship of the proletariat', and the competing claims of individual human desires will be regulated, not by the price mechanism, but according to social utility which is to be declared by the will of the people.

This historical process is 'inevitable'; yet it is incumbent on all Communists everywhere to join together to work for the coming revolution. Working men in all countries, it is assumed, have far more in common with each other than they have with their fellow-nationals, because they suffer a common exploitation by the bourgeoisie. Hence they ought to give their allegiance, not to their country, but to their class; they should refuse to join in 'capitalistic' or 'imperialist' wars, which are only the means of subjugating the proletariat more completely. All action must be oriented towards the consummation of the class struggle.

At the time when Marx and Engels issued the Manifesto as the programme of the Communist League, the working-class movement in Europe was weak and confused. No political party dedicated to the interests of the working man stood any chance of attaining power by constitutional means in any country of Europe. Indeed, until the working classes safeguarded their economic interests by the formation and development of trade unions, there was no secure basis on which any national political party could be organized. Dissatisfaction with the existing order of things could be expressed only through isolated and sporadic protests against repression. Examples were the July Revolution of 1830 in France, all the disturbances of the *Annus Mirabilis* of revolutions – 1848 and the long-drawn-out Chartist movement in England.

But little groups of discontented intellectuals made contact with each other in all the capitals of Europe, and the links between them were strengthened by the failure of the 1848 risings, which drove many of the Continental revolutionaries, including Marx, into exile in England. Indeed, until the Russian Revolution of 1917, the Communist movement existed largely through international societies and congresses of intellectuals and working-class leaders. These had few practical results, but they produced a clear and consistent body of revolutionary doctrine and achieved a solidarity.

Of the organizations, the most important were the International Working Men's Association (the First International), which was undermined by the outbreak of the Franco-Prussian War of 1870, and the International Socialist Bureau of 1889 – the Second International, that is, which lasted till the First World War showed that 'above the consolidated labour masses there stood labour parties which converted themselves into servile organs of the bourgeois state'. In other words, nationalism in Europe was still stronger by far than international class solidarity. It is still so today.

As a matter of revolutionary tactics, Marx himself had clearly realized in the Manifesto that, although the historical processes of feudalism, capitalism and communism were applicable to all countries, yet, in view of the different levels of development attained by different countries, the initial break with capitalism would have to be made nationally. The more advanced capitalism was in one country, the more it contained within itself seeds of its own destruction and the nearer it was to the inevitable revolution. Thus the first task of the proletariat in each country was to settle matters with its own bourgeoisie. After that the struggle would inevitably become international – 'to labour everywhere for the union and agreement of the democratic parties of all nations'.

The successful overthrow of the Tsarist regime in Russia by the Bolshevik Revolution of 1917 acutely posed the problem of international communism. The new rulers of Russia had to decide whether to ensure the success of the Revolution at home or carry the torch of Communism abroad. After the death of Lenin in 1924, the issue resolved itself into a struggle for power between Stalin and Trotsky, Stalin supporting the policy of 'Socialism in one country', Trotsky denying that a socialist state could survive alone in a capitalist world and pressing for an international communist crusade.

This conflict ended with the exile of Trotsky in 1929. Thereafter Soviet policy was mainly directed to the industrialization and economic rehabilitation of the U.S.S.R., through the series of Five-

Year Plans. At the same time, the functions of
international Marxism were performed by the
Third International, which was both the foreign
propaganda agency of the Russian Government
and the missionary centre of the gospel of world
revolution. In 1937 Trotsky founded in Mexico
a Fourth International. The ice-axe that killed
him in 1940 also ended this International.

The activities of this Third International were
often conducted with alarming candour, and
were apt, therefore, to embarrass the Soviet
Government in its efforts to seal Russia off from
Western interference until she was ready to take
her place as a great industrial power. During the
thirties the International concentrated mostly on
the support of the European communist parties
and on combating the rise of Germany and Italy
by means of the Popular Front against Fascism.
During the Second World War the existence of
the International was thought to threaten the
Russian alliance with Britain and the U.S.A.,
and accordingly it was dissolved in 1943, to rise
again after the war in the shape of the Comin-
form. This, however, seems to be an organization
more concerned with strengthening the economic
and political ties between the U.S.S.R. and her
satellites than with preaching the cause of world
revolution.

Yet it would be wrong to assume that the appeal to the workers of the world to unite is nowadays no more than an empty rhetorical gesture,
or a catch-phrase. The war-time policy of the
U.S.S.R. in furthering the cause of Communism
by the support of small groups of guerrilla fighters
or 'partisans', whose aims were at least as nationalistic as they were Marxist, has been continued
into the post-war era and has set the pattern of
Communist revolution in China and South-East
Asia. Nor, to the Communist, is there anything
inconsistent in encouraging national aspirations
in this way, since the formation of separate and
self-contained Communist states is only the prelude to a world-wide Communist régime in which
independent nation-states will wither away and
die and be replaced by the millennium of planned
Socialism on a global scale. (See also *Communism, Trotskyism, Dialectical Materialism* and
Capitalism).

ILLUSTRATION: Pages 448 and 449.

Yoga and Yogi

YOGA is one of those oriental beliefs which
have always fascinated the European and particularly the English mind. The Orient is 'mysterious', the oriental is 'inscrutable' and often credited with occult powers; and of all orientals the
most 'mysterious' and 'inscrutable' and 'picturesque' is the Yogi who practises Yoga.

The popular idea pictures him as a magician
or even sorcerer. He can stand on his head, bury
himself, anaesthetize himself and raise himself to
float in the air. He is known to sit for long periods
cross-legged, gazing at his navel and immersed in
meditation. What is the truth about him?

The practice of Yoga, first of all, is intelligible
only when related to its traditional system of
beliefs – the doctrine of *Vedanta*, the theological
basis of the Hindu religion.

Literally interpreted, Vedanta means 'the completion of the *Vedas*', which are religious hymns
of great antiquity, described by the orientalist
Max Müller as 'songs of spiritual knowledge',
and concerned with the worship and understanding of Brahman. To define Brahman as God is
misleading; in Hindu theology it represents a
kind of spiritual Source, a reservoir of divinity,
the ground of all creation or 'manifestation'.

This divine power informing the universe is
beyond the grasp of human reason. It is not so
much impersonal as superpersonal. The greatest of
Hindu philosophers, Śaṁkara (perhaps known
better in the West as Shankara), who lived in
about the eighth century A.D., maintained that
human knowledge or reason was confined to the
plane of illusion or 'Maya'. This did not mean
that the human mind was sunk in total ignorance; it meant that the human conception of
God, being limited, fell infinitely short of a true
apprehension of God's nature. Knowledge of
Brahman was attainable only by an intuitive

grasp of reality resulting from extreme mental concentration.

The idea of absorption in the Godhead as expounded in the Vedanta scriptures (particularly in the remarkable *Upanishads*) is difficult for the Western mind to grasp. All religions preach the final union of the creature with God, but the approach of Vedanta is not so much emotional as intellectual. In order to raise the mind to the highest level of consciousness, the bodily senses must be subjected to severe discipline. The key to this bodily and mental discipline is Yoga. The word in Sanskrit means literally 'yoke' (cf. the Latin *jungere*), but its true meaning is 'union'; and the primary purpose of Yoga is to free the mind from all distractions or 'hindrances'. Far from being an end in itself, its physical aspect is a means to an end. The Westerner who 'takes up' Yoga for the purpose of increasing his physical well-being is like an atheist who attends High Mass for the aesthetic satisfaction he gets from it.

Not merely is the discipline imposed upon the Yogi extremely severe, involving eight separate stages of control, but there are several systems of Yoga, each with its individual technique. The two most important are Hatha-Yoga and Raja-Yoga. The first is a preparatory discipline, which induces in the initiate a control of breathing or *prana*. Sometimes translated 'breath', this word means properly the 'vital force' or spirit. The control of *prana* is equivalent to the control of the mind itself. The complicated postures (*asanas*) adopted by the Yogi, such as the famous squatting position called the 'Lotus Seat', are merely aids to the attainment of such control. The feats for which Yogis are celebrated are due, when authentic, to the practice of a science of rhythm, which includes the suspension of breath as well as its regulation. Hence the more remarkable of their achievements, such as the prolonged arrest of the heart-beats. Even if the metaphysical basis of Yoga were proved to be false, the teaching of Hatha-Yoga would still contain much psychological truth; and it is to this aspect that the western enthusiast has been most keenly attracted.

Once mastered, the discipline of Hatha-Yoga makes the practitioner fit to take the next step towards *ekagrya* or 'one-pointedness'. The transition is from action to meditation, or contemplation. Despite a life-time of constant practice, most aspirants fail to progress beyond the first stage. The treatise of Swatmaram Swami called the *Hatha Yoga Pradipika* (literally 'a lamp' or 'enlightened commentary'), says 'there are many who are merely Hatha-Yogis without the knowledge of Raja-Yoga; I think them to be simple practicers who do not get the fruit of their pains'.

The reason is not difficult to understand: having the direct attainment of divine knowledge for its aim, Raja-Yoga forms a spiritual adventure which few see through to the end.

Hatha-Yoga is concerned with action, even though the activity is designed only to remove distracting influences. Action is always separated from its results. Meditation or contemplation, on the other hand, forms an end in itself. So Raja-Yoga is not a means to anything; the essence of it is the intuitive knowledge of Brahman or the Universal Spirit (Paramatman). A Yogi who succeeds in attaining this supreme knowledge passes into the condition known as *Samadhi*, or divine absorption. Owing to difficulties of translation, this final condition is sometimes represented in western languages to be a state of nescience or nothingness. The opposite is true. The attainment of Samadhi is equivalent to total emancipation or release from limitation of every kind.

Nirvana, the Hindu heaven, is a state not of emptiness but of plenitude. 'The Yogi in highest meditation', says Swatmaram Swami, 'is void within and without like a pot in the world space. He is also, like a pot in the ocean, full within and without.'

Teachers of the wisdom of Vedanta stress the absolute distinction between the 'academic' student of Yoga, however diligent, and the holy man for whom Yoga is a profound experience. According to the Vedanta teaching, men arrive at wisdom, if at all, by laborious and painful stages. One life is not sufficient for self-realization. Hence the doctrine of the 'transmigration of souls' (q.v.). The genuine Yogi is he who achieves in a single life-time that which others must learn in a succession of 'lives'.

The first and most authoritative exponent of Yoga was Patanjali, who lived according to some in the third century B.C., according to others in the fourth century A.D. He is reputed to be the author of a treatise entitled the *Yoga Sutras* (a series of rules or aphorisms). That he invented Yoga is most unlikely. The principles and practice of this technique are far too complex to have been the work of a single man. In stating at the opening of his treatise that he is undertaking a 'revision' of the doctrine, Patanjali confirms this impression. The *Yoga Sutras* contain much abstruse metaphysical teaching. This becomes intelligible, or at least easier to fathom, by studying the six *darshanas* which make up the Vedanta theology. The darshanas are neither philosophies nor systems; they are rather 'points of view' from which the supreme Principle of the universe may be apprehended. Yoga is a practical application of the third darshana called *Sankhya* (a word signifying 'number'). While Sankhya studies the universal Principle under the aspect of Nature and its various degrees of manifestation, Yoga consider man as a microcosm of Nature.

The metaphysics of Vedanta surpass in subtlety anything that has been evolved by Western philosophers. One aspect of the teaching, however, is of fundamental importance for a true understanding of Yoga. This is the identification, at the highest (or deepest) level of experience, between Brahman and Atman. Atman is the true Self as opposed to the individual ego. The purpose of existence, according to Vedanta, is to 'realize' this identification. 'Realize' is to be understood in two senses. Man must first learn to 'know himself', to discover the divine spark within him. Secondly, having discovered the secret of his nature, he must strive to throw off the veils of illusion and ignorance (*avidya*) with which he is encumbered, and so 'realize' himself as an element of the divine creative power.

It is to such self-realization or deliverance, undertaken with heroic determination, that the Yogi is called upon to dedicate his physical, psychical and spiritual energies. 'The Yogi who possesses perfect discernment', declares Śaṁkara, 'contemplates all things as subsisting in himself, and thus by the eye of knowledge discovers that all is One Spirit.'

ACKNOWLEDGEMENTS

Acknowledgements and thanks for the right to reproduce illustrations listed in the contents page are also due to the persons and institutions shown below. The following abbreviations have been used: – P.P.L. Picture Post Library; N.G. National Gallery.

COLOUR PLATES. *Plates* 1, 4 and 11 Louvre, Paris and Vizzavona, Paris. 2 and 8 N.G., London and Studio 51, London. 3 and 14 N.G., London and Fama Ltd., London. 6 Alexander Maitland Esq. and Fama Ltd, London. 7 Kunsthistorisches Museum, Vienna and Photo Meyer, Vienna. 9 Victoria & Albert Museum, London and Studio 51, London. 10, 15 and 16 Tate Gallery, London and Studio 51, London. 12 and 13 British Museum, London and Studio 51, London.

BLACK AND WHITE PLATES. *Pages* 24 and 25 By courtesy of the Trustees of the Tate Gallery. 28 and 71 Gerald Hammond, London. 33 From Vanity Fair, reproduced by kind permission of the National Magazine Co. Ltd. 72 Reproduced from *The Antediluvian World* by Ignatius Donnelly (Sampson Low Marston & Co. Ltd). 73 Reproduced from Sir Thomas More's *Utopia* (Routledge & Kegan Paul Ltd). 82 By courtesy of the Trustees of the Tate Gallery. 133 Victoria & Albert Museum. Crown copyright. 134 Reproduced by permission of the Trustees of the Wallace Collection. 168 From Vanity Fair, reproduced by kind permission of the National Magazine Co. Ltd. 170 By courtesy of the Trustees of the Tate Gallery. 171 and 174 Roger Viollet, Paris. 176 Arts Council of Great Britain. 178 Vizzavona Paris. 215 By courtesy of the Trustees of the British Museum. Print Room. 226 Professor A. Gillies. 230 Anderson-Viollet. 266 Reproduced from *The Life and Letters of Sir Henry Newbolt* (Faber and Faber Ltd). 317 Alfred Carlebach Studio, London. 318 Victoria & Albert Museum. Crown copyright. 359 Reproduced by permission of the Trustees of the Wallace Collection. 362 R. B. Fleming, London. 363 By courtesy of the Trustees of the British Museum. Print Room. 364 Victoria & Albert Museum. Crown copyright. 365 By courtesy of the Trustees of the Tate Gallery. 372 and 373 Reproduced by permission of the Trustees of the Wallace Collection. 412 P.P.L. 414 and 415 By courtesy of the Trustees of the British Museum. Print Room. 440 Victoria & Albert Museum. Crown copyright. 441 Crown copyright. From an exhibit in the Science Museum, South Kensington. 452 Roger Viollet, Paris. 453 Vizzavona, Paris.

For permission to include copyright material we are indebted to the following: P. 236 *Aubrey's Brief Lives* ed. Olive Lawson Dick (Martin Secker & Warburg Ltd). P. 404 *Freud's Introductory Lectures* (George Allen & Unwin Ltd).